Other Books by Bill James:

THE BASEBALL BOOK
1990

THE BASEBALL BOOK 1990

BILL JAMES

VILLARD BOOKS | NEW YORK | 1990

Library of Congress Cataloging-in-Publication Data
James, Bill.
The baseball book 1990.
1. Baseball—United States—History.
2. Baseball—United States—Records.
I. Title.
GV863.A1J37   1990   796.357'0973
89-43464   ISBN 0-679-72411-7 (pbk.)

9 8 7 6 5 4 3 2
First Edition
Designed by Robert Bull Design

DEDICATION

This book is for the little girl who asks me every day have I finished my book yet, and for the baby boy who presses his nose against the door and reaches up his little fat arms and lights up his face as if the sun had just returned from deepest outer space, at such a simple sight as me.

GHOSTS

I will probably never learn to see a baseball game the way that I want to be able to see one.

Some years ago, it occurred to me that there must be dozens of ballplayers in each generation who leave a mark on the game in one way or another, and that when you go to a game you can therefore see the tracks of hundreds of players. When you see the flap hanging down beneath a catcher's mask, who are you seeing? Steve Yeager, of course; Yeager developed that flap to protect his neck after he was nearly killed by a flying bat handle in the mid-seventies. When you see the coach's box, ignored as it is, who are you seeing? Arlie Latham, of course, the nineteenth-century player who, while coaching at third base, used to run down the base line screaming obscenities at the pitcher to try to throw him off his game; the box was put in to restrict Latham's movements.

When you see the weighted doughnut in the on-deck circle, who are you seeing? Elston Howard.

When you see the first baseman playing in front of the base runner, in his line of sight rather than behind him, who are you seeing? Willie Stargell.

When a hitter stands at the plate in a pigeon-toed crouch, who are you seeing? Rod Carew, of course; nobody did that before Carew.

In the course of any inning of a ball game, you should be able to identify at least forty players, forty "ghosts" on the field; you can see Roger Bresnahan and Candy Cummings and Babe Ruth and a dozen others at any moment. Bob Addy. Jimmy Archer. I didn't know about Bob Addy and Jimmy Archer until I started working on this book.

After stewing on this idea for about five years, I've become convinced that every player who plays the game at the major league level for any length of time leaves an image lingering behind him, that if you *really* understood the history of baseball, that if one could see baseball, so to speak, with the eyes of God, one could see in each and every baseball game the image of every good and great player who has ever played.

Of course, we don't have the eyes of God, and the things that we don't know (and therefore don't see) vastly outnumber the things that we do see. Although it happened just a few years ago, I don't know whose idea it was to put a concave end on the bat, rather than the convex end which had been used for the previous hundred years. I don't know who the first player was to use sliding gloves or who the first player was to change his shoes when he reached base nor the first player to wear sweat bands on the field, although this is all very recent. I know that somebody got hurt by tripping over a glove about 1950, which is why the fielders don't leave gloves in the field anymore, but I can never remember who it was.

But in any baseball game, I can identify ten or fifteen Kansas City players, just because I do know Kansas City baseball. Take, for example, Hal McRae, a very good player whose career almost certainly falls short of the Hall of Fame standard—yet who left probably a dozen marks on the game. Remember the McRae Rule? Do they still call it that, I wonder?

The rule was something of a misnomer, anyway. In the 1977 playoff, as I recall, McRae slid over second base to take out Willie Randolph before Randolph could make a return throw to first, and then simply lay on top of Randolph like a dead weight so that Willie could not get up in time to throw home while a crucial run came home. The next year they made a rule that said that the umpire should call the runner out at first if the baserunner from first slid into second in such a way that he couldn't touch the bag, which really wasn't what McRae had done, but it was Mac (and Billy Martin's bitching about Mac) who got them to thinking about the rule.

There is another rule in the books for which McRae is even more clearly responsible: the alternating DH in the World Series. Remember that from 1976 through 1985, the designated hitter was used either in every game of the World Series or in no games, alternating years. This meant that in the 1985 World Series, a non-DH series, McRae had no role to play although he had very substantially helped the Royals get into the series. Whitey Herzog, who has great respect for McRae, felt that this was wrong (as of course did Royals fans), and Herzog spoke out on the rule, saying "Why don't they just use the American League rule in the American League parks and the National League rule in the National League parks?" With both championship managers on the same side of the soapbox, the rule was passed the next year—and Hal McRae was again immortalized in the rule book.

Although I can't remember what it is, I am almost certain that there is a third rule for which McRae is responsible. It is not only in the rules that McRae lives on. McRae is also in the records of the game—indeed, all over the records of the game. McRae hit more doubles in a season than any other player since 1950, 54 in '77. He holds a huge number of career records for designated hitters, and, since there are no other career DHs young or old, seems likely to hold them for some time.

The record of Kansas City's division championships in '76, '77, '78, '80, '84, and '85—would all those flags be flying in Royals Stadium without McRae? Not likely, I think, so there's another place where he shows up, visible in the park. He didn't win a batting championship—but the story of the three-men-on-a-dime battle and ensuing controversy in '76 is still retold regularly, a part of the game's lore.

He is very alive in more transient ways, in our memories and in the impact that he had on the men that he played with; George Brett will tell you that whenever you see George Brett go for an extra base on a lazy outfielder, you are seeing Hal McRae in George Brett. Perhaps ten years from now we will still be seeing that in Kevin Seitzer. In our mind's eye we can still see McRae as clearly as today, on deck with his batting helmet cocked on the side of his head or driving a ball into the gap in right-center. My most vivid image of Hal McRae is of a play in the last week of the 1979 season, when he ran into second base standing up, taking the relay throw to first square in his forehead to prevent a double play. I always thought that that required phenomenal courage.

So Hal McRae, working on his third year of retirement, remains in many ways alive in baseball—and you know, you can say the same about several other Royals that I can think of. You can see Amos Otis every game, you know. Amos legitimized the one-handed catch. For a hundred years, outfielders had been taught to "catch the ball with both hands," never mind that nobody ever did; what they really did was catch the ball in the glove and quickly slap their bare hand on it. This was of questionable value, in that crossing your right hand over your body at the moment of a catch is an unnatural physical motion, and I've seen a good many outfielders knock the ball out of their glove while attempting to secure it. Anyway, outfielders of course had caught the ball one-handed before Amos in emergency situations, and Willie Mays had made famous the basket catch, but those were exceptions which had no lasting impact. Amos, more than anyone else, changed the habits of outfielders by his unique combination of grace, confidence, and stubbornness; this was how he caught the ball, and nobody was going to tell him otherwise. Eventually it caught on.

When you see the second baseman setting up on artificial turf in short right field, who are you seeing? Maybe somebody else would have figured that out soon enough, but it was Frank White who did; Frank was the first second baseman to set up fifty feet from second base on a routine basis. When you see a batter come to the plate with a line across his bat where the pine tar stops, who are you seeing? Of course.

When you see a pitcher fake a throw to third and then throw to first, you are seeing two old Royals pitchers, Al Fitzmorris and Steve Busby. Although this move had been used in the thirties and forties, Al Fitzmorris rediscovered it and picked off three or four runners with the move in 1974. Steve Busby, then a rookie, picked up the move and perfected it, and over a period of two or three years must have picked off a dozen runners with it, which brought it back into vogue. Now, of course, it never works; I haven't seen two runners picked off with that move in the last five years, but you still see people try it every week, so you're still seeing Fitzmorris and Busbby.

Do you see what I'm saying? If you *really* understood the game, don't you think you could see everybody out there? A player can leave his mark in the rules, in the records, in the equipment, in the lore of the game, or just in the way the game is played—but if he is a significant player, he will change the game. Every significant player adds something to the game.

We will never learn to see the game that well. But in a very real sense that is what this book is about—the attempt to learn to see everybody out there. *We are trying to identify the unique contribution that every player has made to the game.*

Now, not to be misunderstood; Jack Etkin has written an article on Hal McRae which appears in these pages, and that article isn't basically concerned with dredging up this kind of material. The "contribution" of each player can be understood in a broader sense. What I most fundamentally want is for a reader who reads about Hal McRae to have two things: an image of Hal McRae as a human being and an understanding of the role that McRae has played in baseball. I want the reader who looks up Luke Appling in this book to know what he is getting—a solid, fundamental account of Luke Appling and what he has meant to baseball.

To run at this from another angle . . .

I've spent an awful lot of time in the last twenty years with baseball record books. They're wonderful things, baseball records. Through illiterate numbers, baseball records convey multidimensional images, images of speed, power, durability, and a dozen other traits grafted onto a name and stretched across a period of time.

But when you go over those records often enough, you want more. You run through the records of Babe Adams often enough—194 wins, phenomenal control, pitched almost twenty years—you begin to wonder what his story was, how and why he pitched twenty years, how his life was changed by being a World Series hero. There are notes about him here and there, anecdotes. His 1909 World Series is often enough recalled, but who *was* he, and where can you go if you want to know?

Nowhere, before now. The Hall of Famers, they get four books a year written about them—but the life story of Joe Adcock, let alone Harry Ables, has never before been considered important enough to rate a serious, substantial review.

I did this book for precisely the same reason that I did the first *Abstract* in 1977: that I wanted to know these things, and nobody else was going to do the research. In 1977 I wanted a book that would tell me what each player hit against right-handed and left-handed pitching, and there was no such book, so I created one; I wrote to all of the teams to get the information, and I printed it myself. In 1977 I wanted to know what catchers were *really* the best at throwing out base runners, so I took the box scores for a season and counted how many stolen bases had occurred against each catcher.

By 1987, mostly because of the computer revolution, we had that kind of information rolling out the kazoo. I've never been much of one for opinions; I've always felt that information is the lifeblood of a book, that when people read a book they basically want to know something that they didn't know a minute ago. By 1987, my ability to surprise the reader with new information had almost evaporated—yet there were still a million things that I wanted to know about baseball, but couldn't find out. In 1987, I wanted to know who Spencer Abbott was.

So I decided to get serious about finding out those things. This book is the result of that decision. All my life, I've heard the story about Cap Anson, taking some heat in the papers about his age, playing first base one day in a white wig and false beard—but did it really happen? If so, when did it happen? What kind of person does something like that? All my life I've heard the story about Ed Abbaticchio losing a game-winning grand slam home run on a blown call by the umpire, but when exactly did that happen—when, and where, and how? Who was the lady fan who sued the Pirates when she was struck by the foul ball, and caused it to be revealed that she was sitting in fair territory? What was her name? Where, exactly, was she sitting?

These stories are recycled endlessly and that's good, because they're fun and that's part of the game. But doesn't anybody but me ever wonder what actually happened, what the original facts were?

I've always used my own interests as a touchstone. I've always figured that I'm not unique, that if I am curious about something, there are probably twenty other people who are curious about it, too.

So that's something I decided to do in this book—trace the facts. Again, it's exactly the same thing I was doing in the *Abstract,* but in a different way. I used to hear a hundred times a year about how this pitcher or that pitcher drew big crowds and paid off his salary several times over by the extra fans he brought in, so I checked the facts; from 1977 to 1984 I figured the average attendance per start at the games started by each major league pitcher. (I found that only one pitcher in that period, Fernando Valenzuela, had any real impact on game attendance.) It wasn't important, but I wanted to know, so I looked. In 1982 I got kind of curious about whether players tended to have good days on their birthdays—so I looked. This is the same thing; it doesn't really *matter* whether the stories that old Yankees tell Peter Golenbock are true or not, but I'm curious.

In the *Abstracts,* I tried to go beyond facts, and figure out how to assemble mere facts. I tried to develop a theory of offense and a more comprehensive theory of the game. I got criticized for that, because my beliefs would put me at odds with baseball insiders, but it didn't really matter; I was trying to understand the universe in which facts live. No, I misstated the case; I drew criticism for that because baseball people felt that I had overstepped my assigned role. A statistician doesn't argue with a major league manager about how an offense works; he is supposed to assume that his knowledge is inferior to the manager's.

In these books, I'll try to develop the same things in a different arena of facts. Rather than asking "What is it that makes an offense work?" I may ask "How is it that baseball got to be what it is today?" I may spend time trying to develop a theory of history, sometimes dealing with that question explicitly, usually implicitly.

In a sense, I know that it will be three or four years before I know what I am doing well enough to succeed. I mean, I may succeed in producing an entertaining book. I may succeed in getting on the best-seller's list—but it will be some time before I am able to push the underlying questions that I am trying to get at out into the open. But *if* I succeed, then I will be fired upon as a historian precisely as I was when I was seen as a statistician, because I have overstepped the role assigned to me.

I'm not making sense. . . .

Laying aside such things as humor, common sense and the ability to write a clear sentence, which some people will grant to me in excess and others will deny me completely, there were four things which defined me as a baseball writer in my previous career, and which I believe will continue to do so. Those four things were:

1. The habit of focusing on small, specific questions rather than large, general ones,
2. The willingness to pursue the facts on those small, specific questions to an uncommon length,
3. The fact that I make the attempt to build what I learn into a comprehensive framework of understanding, rather than placing the knowledge into an established framework, and
4. The fact that I have the whatever you call it, the courage, the arrogance, the foolishness, to occasionally tell professional baseball men that they are full of shit, that the things they believe are simply not right.

None of those things is really very different if one approaches baseball through its history or through its statistics.

Rather than focusing on a small fact which is represented in statistics, such as "How many players actually hit better when they have the platoon advantage than when they don't?" I will focus on a small historical question, like "When did catchers start squatting behind home plate?" Where I used to write a great deal about the systematic distortions of baseball statistics—in fact, that's basically what the *Abstracts* were about, the attempt to keep statistics from distorting baseball—now I'll write a certain amount about the systematic ways in which *the memory* distorts our perception of what happens.

I'm looking for ghosts, spectres on field. As, for ten years, I tried to teach people to look at statistics in context, I will try now to teach us to look at historical events in context, and by so doing to see in the baseball that is played today the living remnant of the game that was played yesterday. I pollute simple discussions with complex and difficult ideas that aren't a part of a traditional baseball discussion, and this irritates the hell out of a lot of people who just want to sit back and enjoy the game. I'm sorry, but that's my job as I see it.

ACKNOWLEDGMENTS

This book is primarily the work of four people—myself, Rob Neyer, Mike Kopf, and Jack Etkin. Rob works with me in an office in Oskaloosa, Kansas, and I'll give you an example of how things work at their best. I was trying to write an article about Spencer Abbott, who managed in the minor leagues for almost half a century. I had all of his records and some "information" about him—when he was born and died, etc.—but when I tried to write it up I knew it was wrong; it read like the *Baseball Register* in paragraph form. I asked Rob to go to the library and try to find some humanizing information about him, something that would tell the reader who he *was*, what was unique about him that made him able to manage in the minor leagues for forty-plus years.

When I opened the file again a month later, there were anecdotes about him, profiles of him, stories that he told and stories in which he was a member of the supporting cast. Rob had checked the index of who-knows-how-many books, eventually finding an old Tom Meany book in which there were several stories about Abbott. Abbott managed a year in Kansas City (1926), so Rob guessed there would be articles about him in the Kansas City papers in early 1926, which sure enough there were. Rob does other things here—writes drafts of articles, handles business.

Jack Etkin is a reporter for the *Kansas City Times*, a baseball beat reporter and feature writer. I have admired his work for several years. What he does well, I have always thought, is to take a name and face and stat line that you are probably familiar with, and put a human being behind it. He doesn't write about stars, generally speaking, nor about ordinary players at the moments when their faces flash across the screen because of crisis or transition, but about surviving in the business, about how people got to where they are and how they stay there.

That is also a pretty good description of what I want to do in the second section of this book—write about people, take familiar names and give them an identity, and since I knew that Jack could do it better than I could, I asked him to become involved in producing this, the first edition of *The Baseball Book*. In retrospect, I'm awfully glad that I did, not only because of the quality of his articles but also because we got so tied up in working on the "Biographic Encyclopedia" that several other projects which were intended for the second section of this book have not been finished. His profiles of Matt Winters, Bill Clarke, and others in the second section here can be read, in a sense, to help define what it is that I hope to do with this book over a period of years.

Mike Kopf also worked on his own, wrote his own articles about the 1989 baseball season as it was in progress, and then sent them in. While Jack wrote about people, Mike wrote about events, about the process of defining a champion through chance and controversy.

Mike wrote several articles for the *Abstracts*; some of you will remember him from there, and he's done a few things for *The Village Voice*. I wanted him involved with this book, I guess, because he is so different from a traditional baseball writer—colorful rather than cautious, at one time erudite and vulgar. Mike knows more about baseball history than almost any reporter, but he also knows more than I do about history, war, literature, and music, and he brings that knowledge to the baseball field as a generation of sportswriters once did, in a primitive time when misguided academics thought it was more important for a young journalist to know Sophocles than to practice his interviewing technique on a sophomore point guard. Late in the process Mike also came to the office and worked with us on finishing the "Biographic Encyclopedia"; some of his articles are also signed in that section.

The cover of this book is based on a detail from a painting of my wife, Susie McCarthy. With two small children to watch Susie has had perhaps the most difficult role to play of any of us in trying to get the book out—to bear the weight of the effort, without being able to be directly involved in day-in, day-out details, without being able to do anything really to speed it up. It was her task this time to endure the crunch.

The baseball season ends in mid-October and this book is supposed to be to New York in mid-November (it wasn't), so you can imagine what an effort it takes to produce a thousand-page manuscript in that interim. It isn't ever going to be easy, and I'm not ever going to be an easy person to live with, but Susie has gone through it with me for more than a dozen books now without shooting me or even divorcing me, for which I am deeply grateful.

The editor for this book, as it was for the nationally distributed *Abstracts*, was Peter Gethers; my agent remains Liz Dahransoff. Other people who were helpful in getting the book done include A. D. Suehsdorf, Craig Wright, Lloyd Johnson, Phil Dixon, Jim Carothers, Mark Alvarez, Bill Deane, Tom Heitz, Dan Okrent, Steven and Cathy Copley, Jason Dorfman, Kevin Harlan, Steve Grad, Miles McMillan, and Peter Sprengelmeyer. Some of these people know what specific contribution they made, and some of them probably don't. If I'm trying to write about somebody and I can't find a corner on them, I call up somebody I know and just talk about them; I couldn't find anything much to say about Tom Alston, so I called up Jim

Carothers, who was a Cardinals' fan in the fifties, and talked to Jim a minute. Problem solved.

We owe our gratitude to the library of the Baseball Hall of Fame in Cooperstown, to Watson Library of the University of Kansas, to the Ellis Library of the University of Missouri in Columbia, and to the Kansas State Historical Society as well as many others, some credited where there contributions were made.

This book is dedicated to my two small children, Rachel (age three) and Isaac (nineteen months), who don't understand why Daddy spends so much time at the office but aren't yet old enough to hold it against him when he comes home. This book is like Isaac, a baby, but by next spring something more than a baby, something which has real flaws which we'll have to work to remedy, and real possibilities that we will have to work to develop.

CONTENTS

INTRODUCTION

From here on, this book is divided into three parts.

The three sections represent, in a loose way, present, past, and future, or looked at in another way the three sections are about teams, people, and players.

The first section of the book is, in yet another manner of speaking, about the Making of the World Champions, 1989. Remember those Theodore White books, *The Making of the President?* This is different because sports are different than politics, but this section is essentially a review of the season just past, with a look at it not only as it appears in retrospect, but as it appeared internally.

A good bit of the work of reviewing the season just past has been done by Mike Kopf. The articles that Mike wrote are identified in three ways. First, of course, his name or initials are at the end. Second, I've asked the designer to give Mike his own identifiable style of heading, different from mine. And third, we left the right margin of Mike's articles ragged, unjustified right, so that a reader in reading this section will always be aware of whose article he is reading.

The second section of the book is, depending on how you look at it, about baseball history or about baseball personalities. This section of the book is intended to be, and will be over the years, pretty much free form; anything we do which doesn't exactly fit anywhere else in the book, we'll stick it in Section II.

The basic idea of this section was to write about baseball people in as many different forms as possible—profiles, interviews, biographies, straight history, subject histories, lists, fiction, autobiography, oral history, essay, drama, poetry, question and answer, humor, parody, anecdote, argument, whatever.

What there is most of this year is player profiles, and most of those were done by Jack Etkin of the *Kansas City Times.* His contributions should also be identified as his in several ways.

A subsection of Section II is the "Biographic Encyclopedia of Baseball," beginning here with the letter A. Once we got started on the "Biographic Encyclopedia," we spent so much time and energy on that that we didn't really get much else done that wound up in Section II, but over a period of years that is still the idea for this section—in fact, I'm not even certain we're going to do the Bio Encyclopedia next year, just because if we do it's hard to get anything else done. And the letter B is scary; we start writing ten pages mss. about all the stars whose names begin with B, and we've got three hundred pages right there.

(Late note: Due to the pressures of time and the desire of the editor to have the book available before the All-Star break, we were unable to finish the Biographic Encyclopedia, Letter A; what we have ends with Cap Anson. You may occasionally see comments in the book reading "see entry on Bobby Avila, Biographic Encyclopedia" or "see article on Luke Appling, Section II." These articles are written, but are *not* in this book. We'll pick up next season with Johnny Antonelli, or whoever comes after Cap Anson. Sorry.)

The third section of the book is "The Draft Adviser," the material which can be loosely described as being about the future, or as being about *players* as distinct from *people.* "People" are born, grow up, get married, have jobs, and die. "Players" run, hit, field, and throw. If you still don't see the difference, look up the three articles about Jim Abbott in this book; there is one in each section. The first article is about Jim Abbott as a news story, and focuses on the general topic of handicapped players. The second article is about Jim Abbott as a person. The third is about Jim Abbott as a player, about where he is and where he may be going.

"The Draft Adviser" tries to tie this book into your other interests as a fan, whatever those are. If you're a rotisserie player, it's a rotisserie Adviser. If you buy baseball cards, you can look at it to get a second opinion before buying a card. If you play Strat-O-Matic, it's a Strat-O-Matic draft crib sheet. If you're a Phillies fan, you see where I think your Phillies players may be going. That's what it's trying to be, anyway.

I'm going to close this explanation with a brief apology. This book desperately needs an index, but apparently we're not going to be able to get one done. The nature of this book is that a good portion of the book—half, at least—has to be written after the baseball season is over, but the book has to be in the bookstores by the end of March, and we're shooting for the middle of February. That leaves us about two months in between, so the production schedule for this book is stretched tighter than the hooks on Dolly Parton's Maidenform, and it just is not possible, in that time frame, to prepare and include an index. If you have a solution to this problem, speak up.

ONE

•

TEAMS

_____

CACTUS

A rizona in the springtime.
The sun overpowers the eyes. *Almost nothing is left of my Uncle Ivan's eyes.*

I have come to Arizona this spring because of the Oakland A's, not that Arizona isn't attractive on its own. The 1989 Oakland A's have just a chance, it seems to me, to be the best major league team since the mid-seventies.

Circle K convenience stores line the sides of the road, a city with no center. The young buildings fight for your attention with neon and color. Thirty years ago this was hardly a city. The first time I was here I asked another reporter where the old part of the city was. He laughed.

Many of the greatest teams in baseball history, like the 1927 and 1961 Yankees, were outstanding teams which lost a World Series that they should have won, and came back the next year determined to prove a point. The law of competitive balance: Teams which win tend to slack off. They don't work as hard; they don't take risks to make themselves better. They think defensively. But when a team combines the *talent* of a championship outfit with the *attitude* of a runner-up, the combination can produce—historically, often has produced—a team of exceptional quality.

The 1926 Series—that was the one where Alexander struck out Lazzeri. Nineteen sixty—that was the year of Mazeroski's home run. Add 1988, the year of Kirk Gibson's home run, and you have three of the most dramatic World Series—dramatic, in part, because the lesser team won. Fate has challenged the Oakland A's this year, left them with something to prove. And I'm here in Arizona because, if there is a great team in 1989, I want to feel the pulse of that team. I want to be able to say that I saw them play—that I saw them in the spring, and in the summer, and in the fall, that I walked on the field

with them and looked in their eyes, and that yes, they were a great team.

I have come to Arizona to see the Oakland A's play in spring training, and I had absolutely forgotten until I was here and driving down the road on which my father's brother lives that he was here, living a few miles down the road. I am stunned at my own callousness, shocked to discover how easy it is to forget someone that you love and respect if you don't see them or talk to them regularly.

And so on this last day of my Arizona trip, I drive to Apache Junction to visit Ivan and Doris, living cheerfully enough despite . . .

I probably shouldn't mention that I sort of knew the '89 A's would be a great team; you'll have to forgive me for that. It's an assigned part of my job to try to figure out what will happen next, and even though I'm not very good at it I am right once in awhile. Any other explanation of what I'm doing here would be a lie.

The A's today are playing the Giants in Scottsdale, spring training home of the black and gold. I wrote ahead to the Giants, and they assured me that they would have press credentials at the park. When I got to the park they had never heard of me, but I was here three hours early, and three hours early you can talk your way into the park because the guard figures nobody but a sportswriter is going to come to a spring training game three hours early with a laptop, and then the press box is easy.

A black man about my age leads the A's through morning calisthenics. He is a trim bodybuilder who makes the baseball players look soft. Another reporter tells me that the man is a karate champion with a reconstructed hip joint from

a serious injury in Vietnam. You'd never know; he bounces to the music, disco roaring from a boom box, and barks at the A's players to put more into the moves. You can see that they respect him, and they all respond except Dave Parker, who lies on his back and wiggles his arms like an overturned turtle.

Circle K stores line the road; I think Arizona has more K stores than cactus. I have forgotten my uncle's address, but I've been there before. You drive west of Phoenix five or ten miles on a road as flat as a shelf, and there's a K store on the right and the entrance to his village is on the left. This sounds easier than it is; most of the ten miles are broken up into spaces about the length of city blocks, and there is a K store so help me God every three blocks, and the entrance to a mobile home park is across the street as often as not. At last I find the right one.

The press box at Scottsdale Stadium has gotten too small. The "press box" is a long lunchroom table at the back of the concrete stands with folding chairs and plug-ins that don't seem to work today. There aren't enough chairs, and there isn't enough room to put the chairs that would be needed. The last time I was here there was plenty of room.

Next to me in the press box are two very attractive young people, trying to find something to say to one another. They nod a couple of times, and finally the man says, "So, what are you doin?" The girl says, "Fine." Long pause. "Hangin' out. Doin' the Mom thing, you know." I talked to him earlier; he is a reporter for a small city TV station near the Arizona-California border.

It is a shock to see Ivan—so much older than he was just yesterday, old and blind. An aching hip has made it difficult for him to leave his chair. Heart bypass surgery ten years ago, a bad back . . . still, just a couple of years ago he could swim, walk around and visit his neighbors, still had maybe twenty percent of his vision. Maybe it's five percent now; he doesn't see well enough to read or watch television or play cards.

So what do you do, when you are blind and barely able to leave your chair? He listens to the radio, and remembers the past. He always enjoyed life, unlike his brother who was my father. Ivan got out and did things—went to movies, went to good restaurants, would go to a ballgame now and then. Growing up I admired that about him, and hoped that I would be like him in that way.

In fact, one can hardly get into the damn park; people are pushed together like the fingers of a fist. Outside the park a half hour before the game there is a line from the ticket window all the way down the street, around the corner. They run out of tickets a few minutes later. Children cry; fathers grouch. People are actually scalping tickets to a spring training game, and that is a little bit of a shock, too.

My favorite thing to do at a ball park is to stand around the batting cage and watch the hitters take BP; I could do that for hours, and often I find I'm the only reporter there. Dave Parker chatters constantly, calling the pitch. "Hit and run," and he swings as if there was a hit and run. Canseco is hitting. "You lookin' good," Parker tells him, "Lookin' good." He looks like hell. He hasn't been able to swing a bat because of a wrist injury, and he looks nothing like Jose Canseco except in the face. Fifteen, twenty swings; he never hits the ball hard. I check the number, half convinced that Jose has run off the field and been replaced by Ozzie. "Lookin' good," says Parker again. "You handsome."

Parker and McGwire have some harsh words. . . . I can't tell whether they're kidding or serious. Something about picking up the scattered baseballs and putting them back in the grocery cart for the batting practice pitcher. "I do it every day," says McGwire. "What

do you do?" Stepping into the cage, McGwire says aloud "Runner on third, one out," then drives the first pitch to deep right-center, nodding in satisfaction as the imaginary runner trots home. (In the ninth inning of the game that very day, McGwire came to the plate with the A's one run behind, runners on first and third and one out. He drove the first pitch on the exact trajectory that he had hit the pitch in practice, not as far but far enough to send the game into extra innings.)

Even now, with almost everything taken away from him, Ivan gives you the sense that he is enjoying life a little bit. People come down to see him; he tells me who all. He must have had twenty visitors from the family or the home town since Christmas three months ago. People remember to go see him because he was always fun, always had time for you. I wish I was more like him that way.

From the right side he is a completely different hitter, but from the left side Felix Jose reminds me strongly of some hitter from the past . . . who is it? There is no sense, to be honest, that the ballplayers enjoy being young and strong and able to play baseball so well. Oh, maybe a few of them—Craig Lefferts seems to enjoy his part, and Felix Jose. Oscar Gamble, that's who he reminds me of. There's a difference, though. Oscar wouldn't chase that pitch a foot outside.

Unfair, unfair; this isn't for them to enjoy, it's for us to enjoy. This is their job, their profession. Ten, fifteen core players have the team made—but everybody else down here is under pressure.

Tony LaRussa scours each question carefully, trying to make sure it contains no implicit challenge to his strategy. I think again how strange it is to be working in a profession where a man is regarded as if he was some towering fucking intellect because he has a law degree from Florida State.

Mike LaCoss gave up six runs in the ninth inning, didn't get anybody out. "He threw the ball good," says Roger Craig, looking a trifle embarrassed to be saying this but determined to say it anyway. "That ball back through the middle, that could have been a double play. Would have turned the whole inning around."

Back in the A's clubhouse, LaRussa is playing the same game with Rick Honeycutt. " . . . but I want you to understand that I have it in perspective," he says, making exaggerated eye contact in the cacophonous locker room and pointing to himself as he says "I." In a 13–12 game there is a lot to be kept in perspective.

Ivan asks about my children, how Rachel has adjusted to having a baby brother. I tell him that she tries very hard to be good, but there is some jealousy, learning to share Mommy.

Yes, says Ivan, I remember that. I remember when my nieces and nephews came along, I was about ten. My mother didn't have too much time anyway, and I liked those babies awful good but I would have liked them more if they hadn't gotten quite so much of my mom's attention.

Youth is about the fight for attention; old age is about the fight for dignity.

The A's have my pass. The A's press box is as crowded as the Giants' was yesterday, but the facilities are better. This game is being broadcast; one can't imagine doing a broadcast from Scottsdale, with the facilities they have there.

It is good to be here; the park seems full of familiar faces. There's Roger Angell, interviewing Lasorda; after his interview is done other reporters surround Roger, and I can't get close enough to say hello. I see a familiar face . . . who is that? Ed Oiseth, it is; roomed with him at the SABR convention four or five years ago. He wrote Where Were You in '62. A young man I don't recognize comes up and introduces himself, says I spoke to his class when he was in college.

Canseco, who has batted only a couple of times all spring because of the wrist, is in the lineup today. On his first at bat he checks his swing. He shakes his hand, looks back to the dugout. He signals that the wrist is hurting; he is taken out of the game. The crowd boos. Before the game is over Canseco will be on a plane, heading to Children's Hospital in San Francisco, where they will look again at the wrist.

The press box buzzes with the news that Pete Rose, known to be a heavy gambler, is under investigation for betting on baseball games. What will happen, what will happen? The consensus is that the commissioner's office will have to clear the air before the season starts in a couple of weeks. We're guessing that they'll wait about eight or ten days, and announce that Rose has been warned to be careful about who he associates with. A couple of reporters leave in mid-game to go to Florida; they will spend the rest of the spring with the Cincinnati Reds.

He is remembering an emotion from sixty-five years ago, a little more. The memory jars me. Twenty-five years ago I saw a picture of Ivan as a three-year-old, blond hair curling over his shoulders. I asked my father why his hair was so long. Dad said he was Grandma's baby; she just couldn't stand to get him past that stage. The answer was gibberish to me; it called upon an emotion that I couldn't comprehend.

It puzzled me for a month, and then I forgot about it until now, and now, with a baby of my own, the words suddenly jump into focus. My memory converges with his, giving me for just a second a three-dimensional image of an old man as a small child. He is quiet now, smiling softly as if enjoying his life.

A TV reporter asks Dave Parker what he thinks of the mess his old boss is in. Parker expresses his confidence that Rose never bet on baseball, that his name will be cleared soon. The camera light goes off, and Parker, with the smile still frozen on his face, switches 180 degrees in mid-sentence. . . .

" . . . but I don't respect the man because he shitted all over me. He shitted on me and he shitted on Dave Concepcion. I don't like him or respect him, but I don't think he bet on baseball games." He says this last as a concession to honesty, as if "I didn't really lie to you *when* the camera was on."

Mark McGwire chases a pop-up near the dugout. He could have gone into the dugout after the ball and probably would have if it was a regular season game, but in the spring he watches it drop. The crowd boos again.

Todd Burns is throwing mostly changeups, effective ones. His motion is very deceptive, looks like he's throwing hard but the ball just floats in there. Uribe lunges at a pitch outside.

An inning later Burns is throwing Kevin Mitchell changeups inside, and Mitchell is popping them up. Finally Burns gets one out over the plate. Mitchell rips it off the wall, and scores the lead run. McGwire ties it up in the ninth.

Given an extra inning or two, Mitchell hits for the cycle. The fourth hit is a double to left; if he hadn't had a chance for the cycle I wonder if he would have tried for the two. If Luis Polonia could throw, he wouldn't have made it. The Giants win the game, 6–4 in eleven.

Reggie Jackson is at the game as a spectator, strolling through the crowd in a shirt the color of the sun. A throng forms around him; he acts simultaneously gracious and annoyed. Reportedly the real estate he has purchased in this area over the years is now worth twenty to thirty million.

A couple of years ago when I was down here I went to a minor league game, had a crowd of about fifty people.

There was an old man sitting in a chair near the dugout; somebody told me that was Carl Hubbell. Carl Hubbell?! Susie told me I should go say hello to him, but I couldn't.

Carl Hubbell died a few weeks ago.

Ivan and I talk about Carl Hubbell. Newspaper reports had him living his last years in poverty, but it doesn't ring true. He was a successful man, spent many years in baseball after his playing career. He died in Scottsdale. How many poor people live in Scottsdale?

We talk about old pitchers. As a young man Ivan saw Pete Alexander, when he was with the House of David team, playing an exhibition in a small Kansas town. Old age . . .

After the game LaRussa has nothing to say about Canseco's hand; he is waiting for news like everybody else. It's been a long day—spring training games run long even when they end in nine innings—and the players are anxious to get home. Leaving the park, I walk past Mark McGwire, Robby Thompson, and Earnest Riles signing autographs. There is a side entrance, but the people who want to know find out where and when the players will be leaving, and pack the gate with a wall of faces.

Walking ahead of me, Bill Rigney is leaving the park alone.

UNDER THE VOLCANOES

A trip to Royals Stadium for the opening day matchup of the Royals and Blue Jays was an opportunity to observe the updated editions of two of 1988's most active baseball volcanoes, temporarily off the volcanic disabled list, but eligible to come off at a moment's notice and turn the clubhouses into the equivalent of Pompeii, circa 79 A.D.

The eruptions in Kansas City were as unexpected as they were irrelevant to the outcome of the 1988 season—nothing the Royals could have done would have kept them within range of the Athletics. And yet, perhaps because of their unfamiliarity with volcanic proclivities, management's major priority in the off-season was not to pump up an inadequate offense, but rather to build a Maginot Line against further lava incursion. George Brett and Frank White were named co-captains in charge of team spirit, and John Mayberry, unforgivably forgiven for his 1977 post-season "toothache," was made coach in charge of preventing racial conflict. As spring training concluded, all seemed tranquil in the Royals clubhouse, yet the opening day result made it clear to those with sensitive ears that the rumblings had already resumed. With a runner on third and one out in the bottom of the ninth, and the Royals down a run, Frank White stepped to the plate. John Wathan called for the squeeze, White bunted foul, and eventually struck out. The game was lost, and quickly the question was raised: Why not pinch hit for White? The answer, of course, is that if you want to squeeze, Frank White is the batter to have.

Unfortunately the question goes deeper than that. The controversy over White being robbed of the '88 Gold Glove obscured the fact that offensively his season was wretched. Until he proves that he can turn it around, there is every reason to pinch hit for him in non-squeeze situations. But naturally, White does not see it that way. "Judging from what I've done in the past, it's too early in the year for that," was his comment when the subject was raised. Well, a fair follow-up question might have been, when won't it be too early? The middle of May? The Fourth of July? It seems obvious that no matter when Wathan decides that White needs to be pinch hit for, Frank is going to be furious. At that point steam may again be noticed in the clubhouse. And soon after that, Wathan may at long last lose patience with Willie Wilson's unacceptable on-base percentage and bump him from the leadoff spot. By then the sparks will almost surely be flying.

The situation in Toronto is similar, and yet different. While the Royals eruptions were mostly player versus player, the Blue Jays were a caldron of player versus manager animosity. George Bell and Jimy Williams seemed intent upon a reprise of the Reggie-Billy follies, and Dave Stieb, with a clause in his contract guaranteeing automatic extension if he pitched a specified number of innings, raged at what he perceived to be quick hooks. Every off-season morning I opened my newspaper confidently expecting to read that Williams had been fired, or Bell traded—I thought them as irreconcilable as Babe Ruth and Miller Huggins must have seemed after their starring roles in *Throw Miller from the Train*. But in a remarkable display of nerve—or folly—Pat Gillick and company not only retained their warring manager and left fielder, they held the entire team together, chose to stand . . . well, pat. And while this seemed absurd policy on the part of the third-place, nineteen-games-out Royals, there are arguments in its favor with regard to the Jays. For in spite of unrelenting turmoil from the first day of spring training, in spite of arguably the finest outfield in memory going collectively into the tank, in spite of a Key injury to the pitching staff; in spite, in sum, of the absolute and total enforcement of Murphy's Law, the Blue Jays finished only two games out. With age and injuries threatening to eliminate the Tigers and Yankees early, with the Bosox minus Hurst and embroiled in Margogate, and with the Brewers holding to the status quo and praying for good health, it does not take a cockeyed optimist to conclude that 1989 may well belong to Gillickan's Islanders, as is. The players, if their pre-season sound bites are to be believed, recognize that all their '88 bitching and moaning accomplished was to keep them from cashing post-season paychecks. That realization may prove enough to prevent eruption this year.

On the other hand, counting on volcanoes to subside of their own volition is always a risky business. Ruth and Huggins did eventually bury the hatchet, but in the era before free agency and the Players Association, it was easier for ownership to bring errant players, even superstars, to heel. Reggie and Billy are probably the relevant analogy, and they never ceased trying to bury the hatchet—in each other's skulls. Ancient civilizations, we are told, appeased their volcanoes with human sacrifices. Pat Gillick had the chance to lay down an easy sacrifice in the off-season, but chose not to. Jimy Williams was no doubt pleasantly surprised, but I'll wager he remembers all too well the recent fates of Pat Corrales, Buck Rodgers, and Dick Williams, successfully sacrificed at the last moment, their teams marching into the playoffs without them. I can't help but feel that this time, however, the pressure may be on Gillick and company; they've wagered a very great deal that their volcano will remain dormant through '89. I happen to think they're right, but if they're not, I wonder if the next sacrifice required will be that of someone higher up the ladder than Jimy Williams?

—Mike Kopf
April 3, 1988

VOLCANIC ADDENDUM

No sooner had the above been written, than events conspired to alter my perspective. Wathan did pinch hit for Frank White, not once but twice, and Frank seemed to accept it with equanimity. As for the Blue Jays, they lost to the Royals early on when, with runners on first and second, Ernie Whitt threw ball four into left field, chasing home the winning run.

Why do such things seem to happen only to managers who are skating on thin artificial turf? The turf may have gotten thinner two nights later, when Tony Fernandez's cheekbone was broken on an 0–2 pitch from Cecilio Guante, immediately following Kelly Gruber's tie-breaking home run. Just a coincidence, a frightening accident? The Blue Jays, publicly, went out of their way to absolve Guante of intent; indeed the general feeling seemed to be that one Dominican would never throw at another, which explains, I assume, the nonexistent crime rate in Santo Domingo.

—Mike Kopf
April 10, 1988

LIFE AFTER DEATH?

Two weeks into the '89 season, it seems apparent that the Yankees will win nothing, but there remains a larger question: has George Steinbrenner totally forgotten what it takes to win, or has he somehow lost the all-consuming desire to win? Granted, he was forced to lie low for a few years during construction of the super-collider, but he inevitably abandoned such nonsense, and with the signing of Jack Clark seemed once again the same old Steinbrenner. Or was he? First Clark, miffed at staying off the DL for the first time in the memory of even doddering graybeards, requests a trade back to the National League, and Steinbrenner, ever the kindly paterfamilias, accommodates him, and in exchange for a passel of mediocrities yet. Then, with free agent signings all the rage in the winter of '88–'89 and in a market that includes Bruce Hurst, the best he can do for pitching is to sign Andy Hawkins and Dave LaPoint. Sure, Hurst is a straitlaced Mormon who probably felt that switching to the Yanks would be akin to joining the Sodom and Gomorrah Twins. But the old Steinbrenner, the man who seduced Reggie and Goose and Winfield, would have proselytized Hurst with the fervor of a Joseph Smith; would have himself converted to Mormonism—even polygamy—if necessary. That Steinbrenner, a consistent target of our fear and loathing in an ever-changing world, cared not a fig for our disapprobation. All he wanted to do was win—in the worst way.

Now, he seems determined to lose in the worst way. Yes, I know the farm

FAIR GAME

In 1988 there were a couple of scuffles in the Royals' sanctuary, and one of the players—I don't even remember which one—was indiscreet enough to point out that each tussle involved a white player and a black player. Sportswriters are always aching to write about racial disharmony inside the clubhouse, but unfortunately the subject is taboo; even if you know that a player has the political sensitivity of the early David Duke, you can't write about it.

Unless they bring it up. Then, once it's out in the open, you can write whatever you want. It's like Jose Canseco's steroid use or Pete Rose's gambling or Cliff Johnson's being ugly; once the subject has been broached, the writer no longer bears the onus of being the one who violated the shibboleth. The ethical process, not to be indelicate or farfetched, is not unlike the ethical evolution of the rape at Big Dan's tavern (OK, so it is indelicate and farfetched, so sue me.) Once the violation has occurred no individual feels that he bears a responsibility for it anymore; it's just something that's being done. It's fair game. Gary Hart's sex life is fair game. Anybody can write about it, whether he knows anything about it or not—but try writing about Bob Dole's sex life, and you'd better be up to your ass in affidavits. Jim Wright's finances are fair game. At one point in the early seventies, Richard Nixon suffered an illness that was potentially life-threatening, and it was a big joke; comedians would say "phlebitis," and people would laugh. Nixon by this time was the ultimate fair game, so anything that distressed the miserable SOB was something to laugh about.

Gary Hart invited the press into his sex life by trying to stifle the rumors that he was a womanizer; "Follow me around," he said, "see what I do and who I'm with." Famous last words, the political equivalent of "Are the Dodgers still in the league?" Whether or not there really was racial tension in the Royals' clubhouse in '88 is unclear to me. Whenever there is a rain delay in Kansas City, and I must have gone to ten games last year which were delayed by rain, the Royals' black players would congregate in the dugout and tell jokes. You can always see them there—Willie Wilson holding court, with Tartabull and Thurman and Bo and a couple of others laughing as if they were near to split a stitch. But does it mean anything, that there is never a white player in the dugout during the rain?

Who knows, but it's fair game.

system has been gutted, making it difficult to once again mortgage the future to the present. But Steinbrenner did have one hole card remaining that he could have played as late as the day of the first home game, and unaccountably did not—Death Valley.

Does anyone even remember the glory that was once Death Valley? Four hundred sixty feet to deepest left-center, a monument of defiance to even the most powerful right-handed batters. The reconstructive surgery of the seventies converted it to essentially Life Support Valley, and then, inevitably, Steinbrenner began to diddle with the fences so that for all intents and purposes it's now Right to Life Valley. And where, pray tell, were all the pro-choice preservationists while this diddling was going on? Just mention adjusting the Green Monster and you'll incite a Massachusetts rebellion to make Lexington and Concord look like Rotisserie Revolution; suggest that ivy is perhaps not the ideal padding for a brick wall and you're liable to find yourself facing the same brick wall as Bugs Moran's minions on that fateful Valentine's Day; express the opinion that the ghosts of the Georgia Peach and Wahoo Sam might still find repose in a stadium with skyboxes, and you have every chance of being dispatched to confer with them (Incidentally, why has no one labeled the fear that if Tiger Stadium goes, Wrigley and Fenway must inevitably follow, the Domino's theory?); but plead the sanctity of Death Valley and you'll find that most fans do indeed have a strong belief in life after Death. I wonder, is all the sanctimony regarding the preservation of Wrigley, Fenway, and Tiger related to their reputations as great hitter's parks, with special emphasis on the long ball? Was the preservationists' reluctance to lay their lives on the line for Death simply due to the fact that there were no dingers in it for them?

The last step in the resurrection of Death Valley came prior to the '88 season, when Steinbrenner, with Jack Clark and Dave Winfield in the heart of the order, decided that all vestiges of mortality must be erased, and eternal life for right-handed power hitters became the order of the day with a left-center power alley of 399 feet, I thought it a shame, but I'll concede that I saw the logic of it. The extra homers the shortened fence gave Clark and Winfield probably did win the Yanks a few extra games. (On the other hand, the extra gopher balls coughed up by the pitching staff may have lost an equal number.) Steinbrenner wanted to win, and after all, the sainted Bill Veeck used to manipulate his fences in Cleveland on an almost daily basis, so who was to say the Boss was wrong?

But if "winning isn't everything, it's the only thing" still applies to Steinbrenner, will someone please explain why he didn't reinstate the Death penalty for the '89 season? He'd already dispatched Jack Clark, and he knew before Opening Day that Winfield would be sidelined for much, if not all, of the season. So who is he going to have taking shots at Right to Life Valley? Don Slaught? Steve Sax? Roberto Kelly? They rather pale by comparison with the visiting Jose Canseco, Bo Jackson, and Gary Gaetti, to name just three who shed no tears for the dearth of Death. Okay, so they recycled Steve Balboni to take advantage—should we throw away a chance to restore sixty years of noble tradition for the likes of Bye-Bye? Would the Cubs remake Wrigley if it turned out Mitch Webster was allergic to ivy?

Longtime Yankee fans must be seething, because at last George Steinbrenner has outdone himself—he's given them the worst of both worlds. He's always been a disgrace and an affront to the Yankee tradition, even if he retired numbers as frequently as Steve Garvey retired sex partners, but at least he put winning, star-studded teams on the field. Now, having depleted his portfolio of trade prospects, and surely mindful that the last man to attempt to rebuild strictly through free agency was Edward Bennett Williams, he reminds me of nothing so much as an aging Latin-American dictator whose power is slowly slipping away, and I wonder how long before the fans rise in open revolt? These are not long-suffering Cubs fans we're talking about, willing to accept defeat in exchange for a pleasant afternoon in the sun; these are fans bred, born, and raised in the expectation of victory. Now that expectation has apparently been snatched away, and is it possible that we live in an age where the fans' revolt could escalate into a successful coup that topples Steinbrenner from power? I know this: it is far too late in the day for a dictator to benignly preside, in the manner of Connie Mack or Clark Griffith, over a fiefdom of institutionalized mediocrity. And yet that seems inescapably the direction in which the Yankees are heading. I may be entirely misreading the situation, but if I were "Baby Doc" Steinbrenner I'd keep a suitcase packed, and a plane on call, at all times.

—Mike Kopf
April 17, 1989

OVERNIGHT RECON- STRUCTION

Surely I'm not the only one to notice that general manager watching has in recent years become as interesting as manager watching. The man in the dugout has always had the option of bunting or hitting away, staying with the starter or going to the 'pen, walking the opposition's slugger or pitching to him. Today's general managers, however, are the first generation to have equivalent choices: Re-sign your veteran players or let them go free agent; if they leave, sign other people's free agents, or rebuild gradually through the farm system, with perhaps some quick fixes via trade, or any and all combinations of the above. See John Schuerholz import another battle-scarred veteran; is he the next Jim Sundberg or the next Vida Blue? Watch Al Rosen, Dick Wagner, and Bill Bergesch duke it out for the rights to Rick Reuschel's late-season victories. Take in this season's revival of *Waiting for Godot* with Pat Gillick in the title role. And who'll win the battle (ongoing as I write) for the future of Mark Langston?

By contrast, good old days general managers were operating with hands tied behind their backs. This was of course due to the reserve clause, and although GM's of that era were only too pleased to be so stymied, it's interesting to speculate on how they would have dealt with a semblance of a free market. Branch Rickey has a reputation as big as all outdoors, and deservedly, but what if he'd had to negotiate in good faith with the likes of Dizzy Dean? Would he have squeezed him mercilessly until he was eligible for salary arbitration? As his free-agency year approached, would Rickey have rewarded Dean with a long-term contract, only to see him break his toe and diminish drastically in effectiveness? What about free agents from other teams? What if, lusting after Hack Wilson's power, Rickey had signed him away from the Cubs after his monster 1930 season, only to see him drink himself into mediocrity almost immediately?

All right, irrelevant supposition, and Rickey did after all expand the range of GM options by creating the farm system and pioneering the signing of black players. But in some measure today's fan judges a GM by his success in retaining quality players eligible for free agency, and on occasion obtaining one from the open market. A modern GM who tenders millions to his Dizzy Dean equivalent, then watches helplessly as an injury destroys his career, or who ponies up a fortune to bring in a Hack Wilson prototype, whose career is immediately compromised by drugs, is a strong candidate to become a free agent general manager.

But if GM's of the past were happily hamstrung by the reserve clause, they must have felt at least occasional frustration at the restrictions on their ability to make trades. Has everyone forgotten that just over thirty years ago inter-league trading as we know it today did not exist? Yes, late-season waiver deals of the type that are a minor scandal even today, and transactions for cash, but no out-and-out, one for one straight trades—*verboten*. And yet no one seems any longer to acknowledge the fact: On any list of baseball's momentous events since 1950—expansion, franchise shifts, free agency, domes, and artificial turf—the advent of an inter-league trading period has somehow gotten lost in the shuffle. I remember it was major news in Cleveland, where I grew up. Not surprisingly, Indians GM Frank "Trader" Lane immediately pulled off a blockbuster; nineteen-game winner Cal McLish, *et al.*, for All-Star Cincy second baseman Johnny Temple. Does inter-league trading's fast fold as a news story have anything to do with the fact that neither 1960 pennant winner obtained a vital part via the new window of opportunity, so its significance was easy to shrug off? Such was certainly not the case in 1961, when the Reds' unexpected triumph was fueled in no small measure by Tribe refugee Gordy Coleman, part of the *"et al."* in the Temple-McLish deal. In any case, inter-league trading quickly became another tool, this time eagerly conspired in (Maybe that explains why its significance was so quickly forgotten: Everyone accepted it, as opposed to the massive resistance that met free agency. Would anyone remember *Brown* v. *Board of Education of Topeka, Kansas* if the South had acquiesced quietly?), that GM's could use to build their ball clubs.

All of which is rambling preamble for an evaluation of why the Texas Rangers broke from the gate in stride. This was no slumbering giant awaiting its wake-up call; on the contrary, only Tom Grieve's calculated use of every possible GM's option could have achieved an overnight perestroika such as Gorbachev can only dream of. Grieve's first move, and his smartest, was the re-signing of much-desired free agent Scott Fletcher. That accomplished, there was no hesitation in packaging Curtis Wilkerson in the deal that netted Rafael Palmeiro and Jamie Moyer. With Palmeiro in the fold, and not needed in the outfield, Pete O'Brien became available for the Julio Franco deal. Then came the free-agent signing that shook the Lone Star State; forty-two-year-old Nolan Ryan in the Rangers' fold. Later Buddy Bell and Rick Leach would arrive as spare parts. By the time Spring Training began, this was a different Texas Rangers team.

Okay, so he made all the moves; what was the logic behind them, and can they work for the entire season? There's no arguing with the retention of Fletcher, but what about giving up a potentially brilliant reliever (Mitch Williams), a moderately talented left-handed starter (Paul Kilgus), and a useful utility infielder (Wilkerson), for Moyer and Palmeiro? Well, Moyer, with his 3.48 ERA in unforgiving Wrigley, certainly appears an improvement over Kilgus, but what about Palmeiro? If Moyer's ERA was excellent considering his home park, wasn't Palmeiro's powerless .307 average suspect for the same reason? Frankly, I would not have thought him the ideal replacement for Pete O'Brien. The deal with the Cubs also assumed that, *sans* Williams, another relief ace was in hand. Newspaper reports indicate that a HELP WANTED—BULLPEN sign was posted in Florida, and that Jeff Russell, fairly successful in the rotation in '88, answered it. Had I been Grieve or Valentine, I'd have hoped for someone with a more prepossessing resume.

The Julio Franco deal had two basic assumptions, aside from the acquisition of an excellent second sacker. The first was the Palmeiro for O'Brien switch, the second that Oddibe McDowell was never going to become the standout he seemed on first appearance. This was, I regret to say, a not unreasonable assumption.

Its corollary, however, that Cecil Espy (20 walks in 347 '88 at bats) was ready to replace him in center, and as the leadoff man, seemed a very dubious assumption indeed.

Two other pieces to the puzzle should be mentioned briefly. What if the nay-sayers who opine that Nolan Ryan is just another pitcher outside the Astrodome, that now he'll wilt in Texas heat, are correct? As the season started, I wouldn't have bet against them. And when Jose Guzman was sidelined, 1986 number one draft choice Kevin Brown was thrust into the starting rotation—is he ready? In the aggregate, all the aforementioned questions, coupled with the holdover doubts regarding Bobby Witt and Pete Incaviglia, to mention just two, would seem to add up to another year of eating Oakland's and Minnesota's dust.

And they may end up eating plenty of it, but three weeks into the season, it has to be admitted, Tom Grieve is looking like a genius. All of the pieces have fallen into place: Palmeiro is hitting, Espy is reaching base and stealing, Ryan is flirting with no-hitters on a regular basis, Russell has been excellent out of the pen, and Kevin Brown is getting quality starts. With the exception of Incaviglia and Charlie Hough, they're hitting on all cylinders. Can they keep it up indefinitely? Impossible to say; even if they can it might not be enough to repulse Oakland, awesome despite the absence of the Bash Brothers. I still think the questions about this team are valid, but it has yet to be proven that Tom Grieve doesn't have the answers. And if indeed he does, there's not much doubt who will be the American League Executive of the Year.

—Mike Kopf
April 24, 1989

In the end, the Texas Rangers roared and stumbled to 83 wins, which was their best record since the last time they had a better record. Bobby Valentine has been with the Rangers for almost five full seasons now, during which he has clearly established that he has considerable ability as a manager, and that he was hired at least three years before he was ready. In many ways Valentine is an irritating manager, farting around forever with pitchers who don't throw strikes, playing Pete Incaviglia in center field, carrying on and on with Tom House and his nitwit theories about pitching. He only started Incaviglia in center field for a few games and I'm sure would tell you that Incaviglia is a better outfielder than you think he is and he didn't have any better options, but I figure starting Incaviglia in center is tantamount to posting a sign in the clubhouse saying "We're not serious about winning here. Maybe we'll get serious next year."

The hot topic last spring was the Texas summer; did I think, people would ask me remembering my former career, that the brutal Arlington sun would bleach out the new Rangers as it had so many teams in the past? The Rangers do have a history of folding in July—about the time, Craig Wright notes, when the Arlington grass turns brown. Every baseball fan in Texas seemed to be worrying about this last May except Bobby Valentine, who picked his regular men and played them until they dropped. By July, the first six Rangers, more than for any other team in the division, had already batted 250 times. Julio Franco, hitting .339 through June, hit .290 after that, not that there is anything wrong with .290. Ruben Sierra dropped from .335 through June to .278 the rest of the way, not that he didn't have a Hall of Famer's year. Rafael Palmeiro dropped from .315 to .230.

I've tried to explain the principle involved for years with no particular success, but the question of whether the Texas heat prevents the Rangers from competing is a silly question; of course it does not. *The heat* is just a fact of life, a condition of the park like the dead air in Busch Stadium or the large foul ground in Oakland. What counts is whether the team makes the heat an ally or an enemy. Of course the Rangers can win in Texas—but I doubt that they can win if they don't get their regulars some rest.

That's not all that Valentine does that will drive you crazy if you are rooting for him to succeed. The Rangers defense was a little better last year, but it seems like it has taken him an awful long time to turn good defensive talent into an average defensive ball club. The Rangers as always led the league in walks, wild pitches and hit batsmen, so expecting their defense to play well may be a bit unrealistic.

But is was a *good* year in Texas; I knew I forgot to say something. The Rangers finished thirteen games better than they had in '88, and a thirteen-game improvement is nothing to sneer at—but was there any *real* improvement, beyond the fact that a forty-two-year-old free agent pitcher turned in a remarkable season?

Probably a little, but if you look that close at a woman she'll break your jaw. The Rangers *are* a young team on balance. This is a negative article, I suppose, but I'm not negative about Bobby Valentine or even Tom House (I have a few nitwit theories of my own); I'm just frustrated that they're not making more progress. The Rangers could vault forward next year if a couple of young players develop; let's nominate Bobby Witt and Mike Stanley. A strike could create an opening for the Rangers; a shortened season could work to their advantage. The signing of Gary Pettis should help the team. Pettis is an excellent player, and a player who fills two needs on the team—center fielder, and leadoff man.

One can make up a scenario by which anybody can win. What I see as most likely is that the Rangers will slip back a game or two, and Bobby Valentine will be House hunting by Halloween. By any standards—the standards of the nineties, seventies, fifties, or thirties—five years is a long, long time for a manager not to win. It reflects well on Tom Grieve that he has kept his patience, that he has kept the focus on improving the team rather than on stirring the waters. If he stretches his patience to more than six years, than the odds are that he himself will be, as Mike would have to say, Grieving.

REGARDING HAL "9,000" MORRIS

Just before the '89 season began, shock waves rolled through the Yankee organization when Dave Winfield elected to undergo back surgery that would sideline him indefinitely. How do you replace Dave Winfield? The Yankees' answer was to immediately trade for Mel Hall. Bob Brower was already on the scene, and after losing a pre-season battle with Roberto Kelly for the center field job, ended up sharing time in right with Hall. Then on Tuesday, April 25, Hall pulled a hamstring and went on the DL. Stan Jefferson was recalled from Columbus that very night, but after a protracted trial of two days, in which he batted five times, was found wanting and returned to Triple-A in favor of another outfielder named Hal Morris. On Sunday, April 30, Morris got his chance. He started in right field for the New York Yankees. Alas, early that same day the Yankees traded for Jesse Barfield.

I don't know if Hal Morris is considered much of a prospect; they say the Yankees system has been pretty much strip-mined of first rate talent. In '86 he batted .378 in rookie league competition, and in '87 a substantial .326 in Double-A. Moved up to Columbus in '88, he hit .296, followed by a cup of coffee with the parent club in September, where he went two for twenty, with nine strikeouts and no walks. He apparently has very little power, and if he was a serious threat to make the Yankees in '89, I never heard about it. And yet for one brief moment he must have thought himself blessed: Winfield was

gone, Hall was out two weeks minimum, Jefferson was back in Columbus; right field was between he and Brower, and since he was the lefty swinger, he figured to get his share of at bats; a legitimate ten day shot at showing the brass he belonged in the majors. He seemed that most fortunate of men—in the right place at the right time. Many long and illustrious careers have commenced similarly.

Then, the Barfield trade. I heard it announced at about noon in Kansas City, so I assume that when the day's action began at Yankee Stadium, Morris knew that his ten day courtship of the right fielder's job had been reduced to a one day stand. I wonder what went through his mind when he heard the news? Did he wonder exactly how Lou Gehrig fared on that long ago afternoon when he replaced an indisposed Wally Pipp? Did he still harbor a faint wisp of hope that a stellar performance on this day would keep him in the lineup occasionally, or at least still with the team?

In the first inning, with three runs already in and Don Slaught at second base and two out, Hal Morris came to bat. He singled to right (line drive? broken bat blooper?) and drove in the fourth run of the inning, his first as a major leaguer. Did he stand at first moments later and say to himself, "That'll show them; couple more like that today and they'll have to keep me around." Was he in fact so busy saying it that he didn't notice the catcher throw down to first and pick him off to end the inning?

There's not much else to say. Morris got one more at bat before an opposition pitching change brought on Bob Brower, and made out. Perhaps he hit a frozen rope at someone; *USA Today* remains silent. Tomorrow Jesse Barfield will be in the lineup, and unless right field is an injury-jinxed position for the Yankees this year, Hal Morris's '89 tenure in the show is probably at an end; indeed, his major league career may very well be over. Fifty years from now he'll likely be just another brief entry in the *Baseball Encyclopedia*, with no 1.000 batting average, or obstreperous nickname, to warrant a passing glance. That's the way it goes. But it might be nice if, as we agonize over pennant races yet to come, and reminisce fondly about great games and players of the distant past, it might be nice if our minds are occasionally joggled and we recall, however fleetingly, Hal Morris—and others of his tribe—who held out futile hope, even after the trade was announced, even after the pick-off throw that caught them by surprise and nailed them, dead to rights.

—Mike Kopf
May 1, 1989

BRIGHT LIGHTS, SMALL CITY

I saw Andy Benes pitch in the minor leagues. He lost, came into the game with a string of thirty-some scoreless innings, but lost.

They spent a million dollars refurbishing Lawrence-Dumont Stadium in 1978, and you'd never have known it. Wichita is three, three and a half hours from my home in Northeast Kansas; it's not a place you'd go every day. The stadium remained an old, dry, dirty, lifeless place with cockroaches in the men's rooms. A couple of hundred people a game came out. It was not absolutely without charm, in the way any quiet, rundown old stadium has a degree of charm, but it also wasn't worth driving three hours to see.

In October, 1988, the Wichita Pilots were purchased by Bob Rich, president of the company that makes Coffee Rich and Rich Frozen Foods, and also the man who got baseball moving again in Buffalo. Rich talked and arm-twisted the City of Wichita into spending $5 million over three years to renovate the Stadium again. It's all different now; they've only spent a third of the money, and you wonder how they have accomplished so much. Clean, shining restrooms. Sterile stands where you can put mustard on your hot dog. A modern PA system which plays music and makes announcements a trifle too loud but with a minimum of distortion. The bare cement under your feet has been covered with something to keep it from shining and give you traction while you walk.

The public relations man seems happy to have us here, gets us on the field and introduces me to Pat Kelly, the Wranglers manager (not the old out-fielder; a catcher of the same name, played three games for Toronto in 1980.) He could be Crash Davis—same career, same position, same engaging, no-bullshit-but-I-enjoy-being-here type personality. I asked him about a game I saw a couple of weeks ago, when he emptied the bat rack on the field after being kicked out of a game. Has he heard from the league president?

No, but he expects to shortly. We stand around the batting cage for forty-five minutes and talk about the players in the league—Brian Traxler, a square power hitter for San Antonio, fleet Ramon Sambo of El Paso. Kelly has several pitchers that he thinks could move up—Ricky Bones, Omar Olivares, Rich Holsman. His second baseman and third baseman are prospects, will probably get at least a look by San Diego sooner or later.

Benes . . . you can see that he's going to be good, despite the loss. Commercialization has run rampant. They sold the on-deck circles to an advertiser. They sold the roofs of the dugouts. Constant promotions, lights everywhere. I don't endorse this particularly, but it is wonderful to be here. The place is packed, and it crackles with every pitch. There is a great deal to be said for baseball on a human scale, where the parks *aren't* so big that the players seem small, where the players *don't* get paid a million a year, where the crush of the media *doesn't* leave the players fighting for their quiet souls. If I was an hour from Wichita, I think I'd be here twice a week.

SAY NO TO RUGS

I wonder if the death knell of artificial turf wasn't sounded on May 9,

when George Brett publicly blamed the Royals Stadium carpet for his latest injury, and swore he would never again play on it. It's hardly news that players have never had a high opinion of the synthetic stuff; when after the '84 season the Royals contemplated switching to grass, an informal poll of the team showed a twenty-four-to-one margin in favor of making the change. The turf was retained. Brett's outburst, however, even if vented in pure frustration and soon to be repudiated, looks like a giant step forward in the fight for grass. Play-me-or-trade-me demands are commonplace, but George's don't-play-me-on-the-carpet ultimatum is surely the first of its kind, and since he remains the franchise player in the eyes of the public, he cannot be ignored as easily as an informal twenty-four-to-one poll.

The reaction of the Kansas City Poo-Bahs to Brett's anti-rug tirade will be interesting. They can attempt instant appeasement with a full-time move to designated hitter, but that would negate the value—such as it is—of Pat Tabler and Bill Buckner, make it more difficult to work Jim Eisenreich into the lineup, and interfere with what may be a long-term plan to make Danny Tartabull—no asset in the field—the next full-time DH. And even as the DH, Brett would still have to run on artificial turf. I wonder if the brass could possibly be contemplating a compromise: Brett comes back and finishes the year at first, next year they switch to grass. Probably not, the present carpet isn't worn out yet, only Brett's body is. Management has always insisted that its preference for the unnatural is based strictly on fear of rain-outs, which are especially damaging to a team that draws many of its fans from hundreds of miles away. But groundskeeper George Toma promised them in '84 that a grass field could be implanted with no increased danger of rain-outs; they chose not to believe him. Is it possible that the Brett crisis will give sudden added weight to Toma's arguments?

Even if Brett is somehow mollified, and the controversy swept—literally—under the carpet, I think we've seen a genie turned loose, and as with most genies, it will prove difficult to get this one back in the bottle. Surely Brett will not be the last player injured on artificial turf to speak out—in this, as in many other things, he is likely to prove a role model. What if a much younger National League player, say Eric Davis, decides his frequent injuries are due to rug-related violence, and goes public *a la* Brett? What are the Reds to do—DH him? Let him grow a beard after all? Brett's complaints carry weight because he is Mr. Kansas City baseball, but younger players like Davis, lacking his stature, may have an even stronger bargaining chip—the threat of free agency. Who wants to be the next GM to bid farewell to an Andre Dawson, only to see him reborn in a grass environment?

I think we're still in for a long war, but May 9, 1989, may be to baseball history as the Battle of Stalingrad was to World War II—the inevitable turning point. Artificial turf will fight strictly defensively from here on out, a rear-guard action that can only delay the inevitable. When even the domes finally begin to abandon their carpets, we'll know that the end is near.

What's too bad is that when artificial turf finally runs up the white flag of surrender, George Brett will no longer be around to accept its sword. It's ironic that of all the great moments he's given us, the gargantuan blast off Gossage in the '80 playoffs, the measured and reasonable response to being called out for pine tar, the last great run at .400, it's ironic that the removal and destruction of the last shred of artificial turf from a major league ball park may stand as his monument.

—Mike Kopf
May 11, 1989

ALL THOSE DAMNED INJURIES

For the last two or three years, there has been an ongoing media story about the large number of injuries in baseball today. There are three or four theories often put forward about why the players of today get hurt so much, which you know as well as I do but I recap them quickly:

1. "Managers and coaches for the most part blame the weight craze," says Stan Isle in *The Sporting News.* Training with weights develops strength rather than flexibility.
2. Artificial turf. Hurts knees, hard on the ankles. "Turf's part of it," says Jim Leyland. "I don't think there's any question about that."
3. High salaries. Mega-buck contracts lead to injuries either because (a) the players don't care about playing once they've got the big money, or (b) players are afraid of risking their careers by trying to play hurt.
4. A general lack of toughness in today's athletes, if not in society as a whole.

Again in 1989, writer after manager after coach after veteran player after general manager after league president told us that he had never seen a season (or a team) with so many injuries, and that he did or didn't know what the reason for it was.

Well, let me tell you what I think. I think there are two basic causes:

1. Older players, and
2. Selective memory.

The minor factor is older players. In 1966 there was only one major league regular, not counting pitchers, older than age thirty-five. That was Elston Howard, who was thirty-seven. In 1989 there must have been—what, fifteen, twenty players over thirty-five still playing regularly? I don't know how many there were but my team had three of them playing every day and I didn't hear anything about it being an old team. There are many, many more players now playing regularly into their mid-thirties.

That's the minor factor. The big factor is selective memory: People simply don't remember how many injuries there have always been.

There's a very interesting article to be written some day about what baseball people remember and why they remember it. This isn't that article, but clearly, people simply don't remember injuries when they are remembering a season. The clearest example I can give you is the 1949 Yankees. Do you have any idea how many injuries the Yankees had in 1949? Seventy-one. The Yankees did an official list of them, seventy-one injuries—almost three per roster spot—which had caused Yankee players to miss at least a few days of playing time. These injuries were of the most serious nature imaginable—Joe DiMaggio, out for half a season, Tommy Henrich, a "transverse fracture of the second and third lumbar vertebrae," Johnny Mize, lost for more than a month shortly after his acquisition after his arm was pulled out of its socket, Charlie Keller, lost for most of the season with a back problem, Yogi Berra, out several weeks with a broken finger, Bob Porterfield, counted on a starting pitcher, as good as lost for the season with a torn muscle in the arm.

The image of the gritty heroes of the past spitting tobacco juice on a broken knuckle sits uneasily next to the hard fact that only one member of the 1949 Yankee team batted as many as 450 times. For all that we heard about injuries in 1989, could any major league team match the 1949 Yankees? Casey Stengel's battle against these injuries was, at the time, the central story of the 1949 season.

And yet, when people remember the 1949 season, do they remember this? The big baseball book of the last year was David Halberstam's *Summer of '49,* a recollection of the 1949 pennant race between the Red Sox and the Yankees. He says very little about the injuries; they are covered in one two-page essay. In time, the injuries have been washed from the memory.

If you look carefully at any season from that era, you can find frequent, serious injuries. Take the 1954 season. The Cleveland Indians won 111 games. Were they just exceptionally healthy all year? Hardly. All four regular infielders had serious injuries during the year, three of them suffering broken bones. *The Sporting News Baseball Guide* for 1955 reported that "injuries put a severe crimp in the White Sox cause," that "the Red Sox were especially hard hit by the injury jinx," that 1952 MVP Bobby Shantz was the "victim of arm trouble," that Brooklyn had fallen short primarily due to "a mysterious hand ailment suffered by Catcher Roy Campanella," that "the loss of Johnny Podres . . . also was a blow to Alston's pitching plans," that "the injury jinx also struck the Braves." Just a few of those who suffered very serious injuries in that one season, in addition to those mentioned before: Ferris Fain, Billy Pierce, George Kell, and Cass Michaels of the White Sox, Ted Williams and Mel Parnell of Boston, Henry Aaron, Eddie Mathews, Bobby Thomson, and Joe Adcock of the Braves, Alex Kellner and Gus Zernial of the A's, Gene Woodling and Enos Slaughter of the Yankees, Joe Black of the Dodgers.

A number of stars were hurt in

1989—but can the 1989 list of aching superstars match Ted Williams, Henry Aaron, Eddie Mathews, Enos Slaughter, and Roy Campanella? Can we match the list of the serious injuries of 1962: Mickey Mantle, Sandy Koufax, Al Kaline, Luis Arroyo, Frank Lary, Sherm Lollar, Gus Triandos, Dick Howser, Vern Law, and Minnie Minoso? What about the list of 1967: Jim Palmer, Frank Robinson, Bob Gibson, Juan Marichal, Tony Conigliaro, Al Kaline, Bill White, Chris Short.

Another way to look at it is to look through the careers of major stars. Everybody knows about Mickey Mantle, but did you ever look at the year-by-year log of Ted Williams? Bone chips in elbow after crashing into the fence in the All-Star game . . . broken collarbone requiring a steel pin in the shoulder . . . a bad back, pneumonia, lumbago, an injury to the arch of the foot when he slipped in the shower, a pinched nerve in his back. Or how about Ty Cobb—a spike wound that became infected, a cracked rib when hit by a pitch, a separated shoulder in a fall, another the same year while sliding, out two weeks with a boil on his leg, out two weeks with a wrenched knee, out almost a month after he spiked himself while sliding, a broken thumb suffered in a fight at a butcher shop, a wrenched ankle when he caught his spikes while sliding, surgery on his eyes. You know about the injuries suffered by DiMaggio and Hornsby, by Koufax and Jim Palmer.

Sure, there are a few players who suffer no more than two or three serious injuries in a career, like Musial and Aaron, Gehrig and Mays—but how about Willie McCovey, who had only four healthy seasons in his career, or Roger Maris, who had the same, or Willie Stargell, who never in his career played 150 games in a season and rarely got close, or Frank Robinson, who had

seven major injuries in his career, or Tony Oliva, who lost at least half of his career? Look at Hank Greenberg, for heaven's sake, or Dizzy Dean. Roberto Clemente was hurt so often in his early years that he was constantly accused of malingering.

What a walk through the careers of a few major stars will surely show you is that they suffer serious injuries, on the average, at least one season in four—and always have. Now, I ask you, *do superstars get hurt more often than ordinary players?* Of course they do not; on the contrary, they get hurt *less* often. That's one of the biggest reasons they become stars. There are many players who lose eighty percent of their careers to injuries, like Herb Score, Tony Conigliaro, Wayne Garland, Mark Fidrych, John Castino, Curt Blefray, Ken Hubbs, Bill DeLancey. . . . For every Stan Musial, there are a hundred players who *might* have become Stan Musial had it not been for their injuries, like Fred Lynn, Pete Reiser, Austin McHenry, and Tommy Davis. For every Johnny Bench, there are a dozen Ray Fosses (not even counting those who get hurt playing college ball or minor league ball, and never reach the majors).

Selective memories. "I see more injuries than I've ever seen in my life," said Don Zimmer last summer—a remarkable statement when you consider that Zimmer's own career was completely shaped by his repeated injuries. My estimate is, and I'm not doing a statistical study here, that a team going into a season has got to anticipate that 35 to 50 percent of its players are going to suffer serious injuries during the course of a season, and that this figure is probably not any different now than it ever has been. That means that if you're not lucky, if you have an injury year, you can lose seventy percent of your roster at one point of the year or another.

It's part of my job to be a skeptic, I

guess, I know that over the years I have started out to investigate the causes of some supposed change in the game many times, only to learn that the change had not really occurred. This doesn't mean that I completely discount the other explanations. Players probably *do* cause themselves some problems by doing excessive weight training—but do the injuries that weight training creates outnumber the injuries it prevents? I seriously doubt it. Artificial turf no doubt does create some injuries—but does the wear and tear of the hard surface cancel out the injuries that result from bad hops (Tony Kubek, 1960 World Series), poorly constructed drains (Mickey Mantle, 1951 World Series), twisted ankles from soft spots in the ground and torn up knees and ankles from spikes caught in the mud?

You can sort players into those who play most of their career on artificial turf, and those who play on grass fields, and then you can look at the career length of the players in each group. If the turf shortened careers, there should be a separation in the data. There is no separation of the data.

If artificial turf shortened careers, we would have expected careers to have become shorter in the seventies and eighties, when artificial turf came in. In fact, careers have gotten longer.

Maybe the high salaries of today do change attitudes—but I don't think human nature changes very much from generation to generation. The rules change; the people don't.

I know that some time this year, I will hear some manager say that he's never seen a team have so many injuries in a season as his team has had this year. I know I'll hear that this year, because I've heard it every year since I was ten years old.

But there's a difference.

When I was ten years old I believed it.

THE BEST

I t is very difficult, to begin with, to say exactly what is a "handicap." It was a season in which not all of the news was bad, but a good deal of it was absolutely awful. Even the stories which seemed headed for the heartwarming pages of *The Reader's Digest* in 1989 as often as not took a left turn and arrived as a punch to the gut, like the Dave Dravecky story. But there was one story in there that everybody had to love, and that of course was the Jim Abbott story.

From the Jim Abbott story as reported in the press, there was one thing that was conspicuously missing: historical perspective. There have been over the course of baseball's century a good many players who have overcome disabilities of different kinds to play major league baseball, and since it is the place of this book, as we see it, to bring historical perspective to the ongoing baseball discussions, we thought you should know about them.

When you start drawing up a list of handicapped players, you quickly realize that you don't really know how to define a handicap. Blindness, surely, would be a handicap—but what about extreme near-sightedness? Players who weren't considered handicapped in their own era, like Rube Waddell, might well be regarded differently today—while players who were regarded as handicapped in their own time, like everybody with bad eyesight before 1925, would never be considered handicapped today.

The dictionary is no help; it says that a handicap is "any encumbrance or disadvantage that makes success more difficult," a definition which includes everything. In any case, while we might be a little fuzzy around the edges, in general we recognize a handicap when we see one.

The first handicapped player to make a big name for himself in the major leagues was *Hugh "One Arm" Daily*, a pitcher. While working in a theater as a teenager, Daily lost the lower portion of his right arm when a fireworks display triggered accidently. According to Thorn and Holway in *The Pitcher*, Daily "rigged up a pad on the stump so he could knock batted or thrown balls into the air with it and catch them as they came down."

Daily was not quite a great pitcher, but his career definitely had its moments. In September, 1883, Daily pitched a no-hitter in the National League. Pitching for three teams in the Union Association in 1884 (a marginal major league), Daily compiled a list of sensational accomplishments, including:

> 483 strikeouts for the season
> (in 501 innings),
> Four one-hitters, including
> two consecutive, and
> Twenty strikeouts in a game.

On July 7, 1884, Daily officially struck out nineteen men in a nine-inning game. Actually, Daily struck out twenty men that day, but one man reached first base on a missed third strike. Scorers of that time did not credit the pitcher with a strikeout when that happened. That game was one of his one-hitters.

In the heyday of the railroads, America was teeming with people who had lost arms or legs in railroad accidents. Inspired by Daily's courage and determination, at least two teams of handicapped players formed in 1883, the "Hoppers," a group of employees of the Reading Railroad who had lost legs, and the "Snorkies," a team of people who were missing a hand or an arm. On May 23, 1883, according to Craig Wright's *The Man Who Stole First Base*, the Snorkies beat the Hoppers 34–11.

• The year after Daily left the majors (1888), the Washington Senators came up with a young man named *William Ellsworth "Dummy" Hoy*, who was to enjoy an excellent fourteen-year major league career despite being completely deaf.

Hoy was the class valedictorian when he graduated from the School for the Deaf in Columbus, Ohio. According to Harold Seymour's *Baseball: The Early Days*, "Hoy was a well-read gentleman with polished manners," and also "Hoy [accumulated a] substantial nest egg and acquired considerable property." He was a fine outfielder, a fine leadoff man, and set a record by throwing out three runners at home plate in one game.

• Coeval with Hoy was another deaf player, *Luther "Dummy" Taylor*, who pitched for the New York Giants from 1900 to 1908. He was the third starter on that team, with Mathewson and McGinnity the big two.

Taylor is believed to have been responsible for umpires calling strikes with their right arm; since he couldn't hear, he asked umpires to give a visual signal, and the fans liked it so it caught on. Taylor was born and raised in Oskaloosa, Kansas, a small town where our office is, for which reason he will probably be the subject of a more substantial biography later on. Like Hoy, Taylor was a well-liked and well-respected gentleman, who later in life had a good career working with the deaf.

• *Mordecai "Three Finger" Brown* was born in 1876, as a consequence of which his full name was Mordecai Peter Centennial Brown. He was one year younger than Luther Taylor, against whom he pitched many times. At age seven, Brown's right hand was severely injured when his hand was caught in a corn grinder operated by his older brother. The index finger of the right hand was amputated above the knuckle, and the little finger, a nerve severed, curled into a stiff, useless digit.

Just a few weeks later, Brown again injured the same hand when he fell while chasing a hog, breaking the third and fourth fingers. The hand was left a mess.

Brown, however, made a silk purse out of a sow's ear. The mangled hand gave him a unique grip on the baseball, and he learned to throw an extremely effective sinking fastball. Brown always claimed that the hand gave him a better "dip," which if true probably makes him the only major league player to turn what might otherwise be regarded as a handicap into a positive advantage, as the football kicker Tom Dempsey later did.

• Six days older than Brown was another Hall of Fame pitcher, *Rube Waddell*. Though not considered handicapped in his own era, Waddell was so emotionally and intellectually immature that he can reasonably be considered to have been handicapped by today's standards.

• *Pete Alexander*, one of the great pitchers in the history of the National League, was an epileptic in a time in which epilepsy was not reliably controlled by medicine. Alexander's epilepsy, like Waddell's problems, was aggravated by excessive drinking.

• In 1915 an amateur player named *Hugh McDonald* attracted considerable attention while pitching with *two* wooden legs. He pitched for the Beulah M. E. Church team in Kearney, New Jersey; they played a tough schedule of amateur and semipro teams, and McDonald apparently won all of his games. He hit for himself and was a good hitter, but by agreement other players were allowed to run for him.

• *Chick Hafey*, a Hall of Fame outfielder of the twenties and thirties, was extremely near-sighted, and wore thick glasses, in spite of which he was a tremendous hitter. Andy High, Hafey's teammate in St. Louis, once told me that Hafey was so near-sighted he couldn't read the signs in the train station; he'd have to ask a teammate which train to find.

• *Walter "Lefty" Stewart*, a pitcher who won one hundred games between 1927 and 1935, and won twenty games in 1930, was originally a right-hander, but began pitching left-handed after he lost a finger on his right hand.

• *Floyd Newkirk* pitched one game with the Yankees in 1934. From Ron Mayer's *The 1937 Newark Bears*, Newkirk was

> . . . following in the footsteps of the famous Mordecai Brown of another age. He had only three fingers on his pitching hand, having lost two in a childhood accident. The courageous Newkirk, gifted with an exceptional fastball and a sharp breaking curve, believed that his condition was more of a help than a hindrance.

• *Tom Sunkel*, a left-handed pitcher, lost the sight in his left eye as a result of a childhood accident with a pop gun. Despite this, Sunkel reached the majors in 1937, and stayed in the major leagues off and on through 1944. Sunkel also wasn't a bad hitter, hitting .321 in 1939.

• In late 1937, the same year Sunkel debuted, the Indians brought up a young player named *Hugh Alexander*. Alexander's hand was crushed in an oil-field accident that winter, in spite of which he is still employed in baseball to this day, and will eventually wind up in the Hall of Fame (See "Biographical Encyclopedia," Section II).

• The 1937 era seems to have been something of a hot period for disabled players. A man named *Bill White*, for many years baseball coach at the University of Georgia, organized a team of one-armed players in 1937. They used a two-armed catcher named Pete Morris, who was in the Yankees system, but otherwise they were all short an arm, as was White himself.

Despite the lack of a left arm, White had been an excellent amateur player, hitting .340 for a semipro team in Anniston (Alabama) in 1911. Later, he managed the Columbus (Georgia) team in the Southeastern League, as well as coaching Georgia. When he announced his intention to form the team, he had applications from sixty players. Several of his one-armed players had professional or semi-professional experience— by name, *Eddie Hartley*, *Seil Hicks*, and *Bertis Humphrey*.

White's team played exhibitions against minor league teams, and apparently did all right. White was an outspoken advocate for the ability of disabled players, and also developed special gloves and equipment for one-handed players. "Does a ball player really need two hands?" he asked. "Not necessarily. Eighty-five percent of the plays are executed with one hand. As for pitching, I would say a pitcher really needs to put two hands on the ball in only one pitch out of one thousand." (Thanks to A. D. Suehsdorf for information on Mr. White.)

• In November of 1938, *Monty Stratton*, a sensational young pitcher with the Chicago White Sox, lost his right leg in a hunting accident (his own rifle accidently discharged, and fired a bullet into his leg at close range.) Stratton resumed his career pitching on a wooden leg, and although he was not able to pitch in the major league due to an extreme lack of mobility, he did pitch for several more years in the minor leagues. His story was told in a movie starring Jimmy Stewart—one of three players on this list who went celluloid.

• The coming of World War II, of course, brought to the major leagues a large number of clearly handicapped players, who were left available to the major league teams when the healthy players were drafted. The best known of the war-time handicapped—indeed, the dominant symbol of World War II baseball—was *Pete Gray*, a one-armed outfielder. When Gray was six years old his right arm was caught in the spokes of a wheel, was mangled and had to be amputated. His story from then on is well-known. To amuse himself he learned to toss rocks in the air and swat them as they came down, became so proficient at this that he was accepted as a ballplayer, and became a good enough ballplayer to play a season in the major leagues during World War II.

• After his moment of fame, Gray earned offseason income by barnstorming against a one-armed Negro outfielder named *Jess Alexander*.

Among the other men who played in the majors during World War II were:

• *Jack Franklin*, who pitched one game for Brooklyn in 1944, Franklin was blind in one eye. Incredibly enough Franklin and Tom Sunkel, so far as I know the only two one-eyed players in major league history, were both from Paris, Illinois, and both pitched for the Dodgers in 1944.

• *Charley Schanz*, who won thirteen games for the Phillies in 1944, was ineligible for the draft because his eyesight was extraordinarily poor.

• *Barney Mussill*, also a pitcher with the Phillies in 1944, had been discharged from the army after an accident with a defective mustard gas container. He was hospitalized for three months as a result of the accident, was temporarily blinded and had serious vision problems afterward.

• *Dick Sipek*, an outfielder with Cincinnati in 1945, was deaf. Sipek had known Luther Taylor as a boy, when Taylor worked at the Illinois School of the Deaf, and Taylor had taught him some baseball.

• *George Binks*, an outfielder with the Senators in 1945 who was good enough to stick around until 1948, was deaf in one ear.

• Leading into the next class of players was *Bert Shepard*, a left-handed pitcher in the White Sox system in the early forties, who lost a leg in a plane crash in World War II (May, 1944). Fitted with an artificial leg, Shepard fought back to play in the major leagues.

Lieutenant Shepard pitched only one major league game, despite which he is an important figure in the history of World War II baseball. In a time in which young men were making extraordinary sacrifices on behalf of the country, Shepard was a symbol of baseball's concern for those young men. Wearing his baseball uniform in the hospitals and his army uniform in the clubhouse, Shepard was a goodwill ambassador for baseball.

• While Shepard didn't really make it as a major league pitcher after his injuries, two other players did. One of the heroes of the Indians 1948 World Championship was *Gene Bearden*, a twenty-seven-year-old rookie who won twenty games, led the league in ERA, pitched a shutout in the third game of the World Series and came in to save the sixth and final game.

During World War II Bearden was on the cruiser *Helena* when it was blasted by a torpedo. Scrambling onto a life raft, Bearden lost consciousness and floated twenty-one hours, unconscious, on the raft, bleeding from wounds in the head and knee. He was hospitalized for two years, and had aluminum plates placed in his head and knee. Bearden came back to star in the major leagues despite these injuries.

• A very similar story was that of *Lew Brissie*. Before World War II, Brissie was a standout first baseman and basketball player at a small college in South Carolina. In the early days of World War II,

playing with service teams, Brissie switched to pitching.

With the infantry in Italy in 1943, Brissie took twenty-one shell fragments in his leg. Doctors decided not to amputate the leg, but Brissie underwent many operations and spent months in the hospital. Discharged from the army in March, 1946, Brissie was signed by the Athletics despite a heavy, awkward brace on his left leg.

In 1947, just a year out of the hospital and despite the brace, Brissie had a sensational year in the Sally League, going 23–5 with 278 strikeouts. With the Athletics in 1948, the same year Bearden won twenty for the Indians, Brissie won fourteen games.

The stories of Bearden and Brissie are unusually similar. Both were excellent hitters. Both were big men, left-handed hitters and left-handed pitchers. And although Brissie did win sixteen games in 1949—still wearing the heavy leg brace—both pitchers faded quickly after a promising beginning.

• *Eddie Gaedel*, a midget, was used as a pinch hitter as a stunt by Bill Veeck in 1952.

I'm sure that to many of you it seems offensive to Jim Abbott to put Abbott, a great athlete, in a class with Eddie Gaedel, who was in the majors as a gimmick, and to be frank a rather distasteful one. But why is it offensive? Gaedel didn't ask to be made a joke, did he? Gaedel didn't ask to be born with his handicap, anymore than Jim Abbott did.

• Another gentleman who made a name for himself in baseball despite a handicap was *Donald Davidson*. Davidson stopped growing at the age of six due to a form of sleeping sickness; he was—and is—four feet tall. Despite this, Davidson had a long and successful career as a baseball executive with the Boston, Milwaukee and Atlanta Braves. "For a person of abnormal size," wrote Davidson in his autobiography *Caught*

Short, "I have been fortunate to live almost a normal life."

• *Don Zimmer,* of course, had a long major league career despite the famous steel plate in his head.

• *Bud Daley,* a pitcher with Kansas City in the fifties and the Yankees in the early sixties, had, as a result of a birth defect, a right arm that was shorter than the left and slightly malformed. Daley could use the arm and was a good athlete, although teams did attempt to take advantage of him by forcing him to field bunts.

• *Ryne Duren,* a pitcher with Kansas City and the Yankees in the fifties, and some other teams, was so near-sighted that it made doing ordinary things difficult for him.

Unless I am missing somebody, there appears to be after Daley almost a thirty-year gap before handicapped players began to reappear. I'm probably missing somebody obvious, somebody that we took for granted. There are several diabetics in there—Catfish Hunter, Santo, Hal Lanier—but one doesn't think of diabetes as a disability in our time. John Hiller fought back from a heart attack; I guess I could have listed him. I guess I don't feel the need to recount stories that will be familiar to my readers. In any case, in our own time we have several players other than Abbott who should be mentioned:

• The Montreal Expos have a young pitcher in their system named *Antonio Alfonseca,* who has six fingers on each hand.

• Another contemporary player who has battled a serious illness is *Jim Eisenreich,* Kansas City outfielder. In many ways, Eisenreich's story seems more remarkable than Abbott's, but unlike Abbott, Eisenreich's personality does not lend itself to journalistic development of his battle.

• *Curtis Pride,* a pitcher with the Pittsfield Mets in 1989, is 95 percent deaf.

The attitudes of society toward the handicapped have changed greatly and for the better in the last twenty years, and perhaps the reemergence of a few handicapped players is because of that. I can't help but notice that in the early days of the game, in post-Civil-War America, disabilities were fastened upon and discussed in a way that now seems insensitive. Hugh Daily was "One-Arm" Daily. William Hoy was "Dummy" Hoy and Luther Taylor was "Dummy" Taylor. Mordecai Brown was "Three-Finger" Brown. George Waddell was "Rube" Waddell.

But you know, those guys *were* in the major leagues. Why aren't there any deaf players in the majors today? Don't tell me it's because of their handicap; I don't buy it. See the ball, hit the ball, see the ball, catch the ball; you don't have to hear it. I wonder why, if we are now more sensitive to the handicapped, we haven't had more of them in the major leagues? Did we agree to stop calling them names—and at the same time, in some subtle way, agree to exclude them? You've got to wonder.

I don't want to nickname Jim Abbott "One-Arm" Abbott; in fact, I think that from now on we owe it to him to forget about the "disability," to stop talking about it. But don't you ever wonder if our sensitivity is well-considered? We're hypersensitive in this country about "cruel and unusual punishment," but the unspoken corollary is that sharp, intense pain inflicted upon a man to teach him not to do something is cruel, but to lock him away from his family for fifteen or twenty years is not. Old guides used to have frank comments about players' "Nationality." "Nationality—" they would say for Larry Doby, "American Negro." "Nationality—" they would say for Sandy Koufax, "Jewish." For some reason, that offends our ear today—but then, we don't really have any Jewish players anymore, do we?

What have we really gained by excluding this information from contemporary publications?

We have "handicapped" license plates now, granting special parking privileges to those who can't get around well. I've seen these plates issued to people whose "handicap" was obesity; they were so fat they couldn't get around. I don't quarrel with that; I figure if a guy can't get around, he can't get around, no matter why. But still you have to ask—does this sensitivity do us any good, as a people?

Well, good luck to Jim Abbott, and good luck to Jim Eisenreich and Curtis Pride, too. Nobody wins when people are not allowed to give to society whatever it is they have to give, and we have to admire those who remind us of that.

LOVULLO-BROWN SYNDROME STRIKES AGAIN

It shouldn't come as a shock that Sparky Anderson went on the disabled list on May 19, suffering from exhaustion. What's surprising is the root cause of the exhaustion, which I don't think is the Tigers' abysmal record, but rather his foolishly laying every bit of his considerable managerial prestige on the line in a hysterical attempt to turn this team around. "Experience don't mean nothing," said Sparky after dispatching Tom Brookens to make way for hard-nosed Chris Brown, and apparently it didn't, at least not his extensive managerial experience. Because experience should have told Sparky that you can't turn a fading team around overnight, and moreover, in a division that seems to be fading just as fast as any team in it, that a sudden turnaround is not even necessary.

Part of the problem may be that in the last two years Sparky critics have become an endangered species. It seems difficult to recall, but in the glory days of the Big Red Machine, Sparky had more than his share of detractors, and I do not exclude myself from that company. Who couldn't win if all they had to do was write Bench, Rose, Morgan, Perez, and Foster into the lineup every day, was the argument, and Dick Wagner seemed to lend it some credence when he dumped Sparky after writing in those hallowed names was suddenly no longer a guarantee. Of course he landed on his feet in Detroit, and after winning all the marbles in '84, his reputation was established—first manager to win the World Series in both leagues. Yet still there were rumblings. Like the Reds, the '84 Tigers didn't have to scratch and claw—and what else are Tigers supposed to do, after all?—their way through the pennant race. No, they won handily—handily enough that nattering negativists could be heard muttering, albeit with diminished conviction, if all you have to do is write in Trammell, Whitaker, Gibson, Parrish . . .

It was the 1987 come-from-nowhere division title, won in dramatic fashion on the last day of the season, that buried, once and for all, Sparky's critics. At last he'd taken a team to the top that was not highly touted, that did indeed scratch and claw like starving Tigers for every ounce of opposition flesh. Making out the lineup card was a cut and paste job worthy of Earl Weaver, and like Weaver, Sparky was now a certified genius, and his reputation was not diminished an iota when his overachieving Bengals seemed to run out of claws down the stretch in '88, finishing a well-beaten one game behind the Bosox.

But I wonder now if the universal acclaim heaped upon Sparky sowed the seeds of his eventual exhaustion. Because if everyone says you're a genius, isn't it incumbent upon you to find a way to win, even with a superannuated bunch of Tigers? Is the problem at base that Sparky was caught in life's oldest trap, that of living up to other people's expectations, rather than his own? How else explain the trade for Chris (Lou Gehrig's Antithesis) Brown? Do you think it a coincidence that Sparky's brother was one of Brown's high school teachers? It seems apparent that Sparky scouted Brown (or at least his attitude) through his brother, received a favorable report, and OKed the deal. It's the kind of move you make if you're one step ahead of the pack, if you're a genius. Unfortunately, it appears that more conventional baseball minds—like Sparky's old pal Roger Craig—had a more up-to-date scouting report. Then there was Torey Lovullo. Did anyone other than Sparky think he was ready? And did even Sparky have to be so implacable in his insistence that he was? I doubt if even Ted Williams was promised 600 at bats his rookie year. But then, isn't it the job of a genius to perceive a reality not apparent to traditional thinkers? It's what Earl Weaver did when, almost alone, he saw Cal Ripken as his shortstop. If Brown and Lovullo had come through, conventional wisdom would have received its justified comeuppance. But the conventional wisdom was correct this time, and is it stretching credulity to suggest that, having invested his entire managerial capital in Brown and Lovullo, the collapse was inevitable once he saw that there could be no return?

The sad thing is that it was all so unnecessary. The Tigers, playing in the AL Least, are not in a mortal situation. There was no reason to bet the house on Brown; they'd won titles with Brookens at third. Why sell your soul to Lovullo; Bergman and Moreland are far from the weakest links on this team. In spite of their current standing, the Tigers are entirely capable of rising up and playing above .500 ball, and if those slumbering giants, the Blue Jays, do not awaken, slightly over .500 could easily win the division. I think with a little rest and rehab, Sparky will realize that, come back with his batteries recharged, and possibly lead the Clemenceaus back into the race. Race or no, I'll wager he returns with his talent and desire intact—let's hope he allows his genius to remain at home.

—M.K.
May 21, 1989

DUEL

O n Friday, May 26, I should have invested in the stock market. I decided to take a day off, and wandered into a movie. The movie was *Winter People*, and I went into it cold, no Kopfism intended; I knew nothing about it. I thought it was a wonderful movie, probably the best movie I saw during the year, and then I went to a ball game, and it was the best ball game I saw during the year.

The Tigers have come to town hot, having won six of seven games since Sparky went on the DL with Lovullo-Brown Syndrome; after a slow start they have twitched to within three games of the division lead. With two out in the first Lou Whitaker singles and steals second, then scores on a single by Alan Trammell. Bo Jackson, fielding the ball back on his heels, makes a perfect flat-footed throw home, but the ball hits Whitaker on the arm and goes free, allowing the run to score and the inning to continue. Keith Moreland dumps a double up the right field line, scoring Trammell, and Detroit grabs a quick 2–0 lead. An inch to the right and Jackson's throw curls around Whitaker, and the inning ends without a score.

Floyd Bannister has nothing. In the second Mike Heath hits a four hundred-foot fly to center field before Bannister gives up two-out singles to Rick Schu and Gary Pettis. The inning ends when a line drive settles into the webbing of Frank White's glove.

Starting for the Tigers is a left-hander named Paul Gibson, a hard pitcher to figure. What is hard to figure at first is how he gets anybody out. He doesn't throw very hard or have a big breaking pitch or anything, and at least on this particular day he is working behind the hitters.

Gibson's stock in trade, I eventually

figure with the help of a videotape, is to play on the hitter's impatience. Changing speeds between slow, slower and slowest, he works constantly on the outside part of the plate, tugging on the hitter's inability to resist trying to pull a mediocre fastball. Bo drives the ball almost to the track in right, but the first time through the order most of the other hitters wind up hitting the ball weakly to the first base side. Gibson also throws the ball up in the batter's eyes, out of the strike zone; again, they can't resist trying to murder what looks like a fat pitch, and pop the ball up off their fists. The Royals don't score in the first or second.

In the third Bannister walks Trammell but picks him off first. Moreland singles. Ward rips a single into *shallow* left-center; Moreland, one of the slowest runners in the league, takes third on Wilson's arm. Kenny Williams singles; Moreland scores. Bannister has given up eight hits in three innings, all of them with two out, and the Tigers lead by three.

In the bottom of the third Bob Boone, going with the pitch, accepts a single to right field. Frank White, apparently trying to pull the ball, hits a fly to right. Willie Wilson takes a called third strike, inexplicably failing to trigger on a fat pitch. Stillwell drives the ball to left-center, deep, deep; the run will surely score.

I will never understand how Ken Williams caught that ball. There's not even anything you can say about the play—no impossible body control, no sudden weight shift, no quick movement to get rid of the ball a second later. It was all routine, except it was impossible. Williams, playing Stillwell in medium left, ran down a screaming line drive near the wall in left-center, threw his body on the turf and caught the ball.

When the Royals come out in the top of the fourth Gary Thurman goes to center field. I wonder if I have just seen the end of Willie Wilson's eleven-plus years as a regular. Has Wilson's failure to make an effort to throw out Keith Moreland going first-to-third on a single to shallow left-center, combined with his .192 batting average, finally taken the measure of Wathan's patience? I learn later that it was announced in the press box that Wilson came out of the game with a sore shoulder (*now* you tell us). He went on the disabled list the next day.

Rick Schu leads off the fourth with a double. Jackson, cutting the ball off down the line, guns down Schu at second, his second awesome throw of the game, but Frank White drops the ball, and for the second time the runner is safe. Nine hits.

This is point number one in Wathan's favor. Bannister, who came into the game 4–0, had given up only three runs. It would be easy for Wathan to stay just a little bit longer with Bannister— just one, two, three more hitters. A starting pitcher rarely is lifted in the first five innings unless he has given up four runs. Wathan brings in Luis Aquino.

Immediately the Tigers' luck turns. Bob Boone throws behind Schu at second. The ball gets away from the shortstop, and Schu heads for third—not seeing the ball strike the umpire's foot and land only inches away from Stillwell's glove. He is dead meat at third base. A ball is popped foul down the first base line; de los Santos races down the line and allows the ball to settle into his glove. I circle outstanding defensive plays on my scorecard; normally I circle one or two plays a game. This is the fifth play I have circled today. The fourth inning ends without a score.

Seitzer strikes out on a fastball in his eyes.

Jackson takes a high fastball and hits it a mile into the sky above center field.

Tartabull strikes out on an outside changeup.

A double play . . . should I circle this one? . . . keeps the Tigers off the scoreboard in the fifth.

Luis de los Santos almost always hits the ball to right field; if he played against Paul Gibson every day he would surely hit .600. An inside-out swing by Luis nets him a double. The ball gets away at second, but Kenny Williams, hustling in from left, keeps him at second. Frank White's ground ball to the opposite side, in this context, seems purposeful, and gets the Royals a base. Bob Boone again pops the ball into short right field, scoring the run.

No! Chet Lemon races in, dives for the ball and has it. The sixth circle, the best play of the game other than Williams's in left. De los Santos, thinking the ball would fall, is halfway down the line, and has to retreat to third.

Luis, the MVP in the American Association a year ago, is trying to establish himself in the major leagues, and not having much luck. He's locked behind George Brett to begin with, but as a line-drive singles hitter he could get some work in the majors and maybe develop, if it wasn't for the roster space being wasted on Bill Buckner. And why did we trade for Pat Tabler, anyway, do you know?

Anyway, this play will haunt de los Santos. Watching a tape of the game, I doubt that he could have scored. Chet Lemon, who has a good arm, caught the ball in very shallow right field, dived, rolled over, and popped up. If de los Santos had been coming I think he'd have been out—but for some reason, his failure to tag becomes something people talk about. In the press box the next day I hear it mentioned a couple of times; it shows up in the paper—not his double, not his fine running catch in the fourth, not the remarkable double play he would start a couple of days later, but

this, the failure to tag. He is sent back to Omaha a few days later.

The hitters begin to lay off the high pitches. Thurman walks. Stillwell walks, loading the bases (Luis is still on third). Seitzer drives the ball past Whitaker into center; the Royals trail by only one. A walk to Bo reloads the bases, bringing Pat Tabler up. His career average with the bases loaded: .559. He grounds to short, leaving it still 3–2.

A quick sixth for the Tigers, and the Royals threaten again . . . a walk to Frank White, a single by Bob Boone. Randy Bockus is up throwing in the bullpen; Al Kaline on the Tiger broadcast says "I think Tracewski is very serious about making a change. Gibson has not pitched through the sixth inning too many times." Gibson stays in, and the threat ends when Thurman takes strike three at the letters. Aquino rolls through the seventh.

In the bottom of the seventh Mike Henneman replaces Bockus in the bullpen. In the last two innings Gibson has walked four men. He walks the lead-off man—yet he stays in the game. The Royals lineup at the moment is eight right-handed batters and a switch-hitter; Gibson is a left-hander. The three, four, five hitters are up, in the late innings, with a lead, with a pitcher living on the edge of disaster—yet he stays in the game.

Kevin Seitzer bunts foul, forty feet down the line. Rick Schu races in, dives and catches the ball for yet another sensational defensive play. I circle this one, too—number seven.

To this point the game has been just a close game, merely a defensive spectacular, with a few freak plays thrown in, perhaps a career turning point, a bonehead play or two and three or four tiny little incidents on which the game has pivoted. Now it becomes something else, a managerial chess mismatch of the highest order. The game could have turned on one very simple thing—that one throwaway sentence, "In the bottom of the seventh, Mike Henneman replaces Bockus in the bullpen." Bockus had been up for several innings; he was ready to come in. Henneman and Bockus are both right-handers. Henneman is the late-inning reliever who sets up Hernandez, Bockus is the long man. When the seventh inning arrives, Tracewski naturally starts Henneman throwing—but not until the inning is under way. Bockus was ready to come in; Henneman isn't, so there is just an instant here when the Tigers, with their starter obviously staggering, don't have a reliever ready. Seitzer bunts, Schu makes the wonderful catch, and the dangerous moment passes.

Henneman comes in. He retires the four and five hitters quickly; the Tigers carry the lead to the eighth. There is a sense that the Royals may have missed their moment, that they may not get another shot.

In the top of the eighth Lou Whitaker takes a leadoff walk. Two options: Try to move Whitaker to second base, or play for a big inning and try to put it away. Frank Funk, the Royals pitching coach, visits the mound. This accomplishes two things:

1. It gives Montgomery a minute to get loose, and
2. Funk apparently tells Aquino to throw the first pitch to Trammell high and tight, just to find out if he is bunting.

Trammell does square to bunt, and the ball burrows in on him. I think everyone in the park thought the ball had hit Trammell, but it hadn't; it hit the bat. Tracewski has elected to play for an insurance run. A second bunt try rolls foul, and Trammell flies out.

Again, Wathan acts quickly; Montgomery enters for Aquino. On the second pitch to Keith Moreland, Whitaker

lights out for second; Boone throws him out easily. Moreland, hitting .336 in the early season, pops a single into right field. Gary Ward drives a single into center, Moreland pulling up at second. Sheridan runs for Moreland at second, a small thing which, like everything in this game, will grow larger later on. The inning ends on a strikeout, and Dave Bergman comes in to play first base, Moreland's spot.

Now, the critical eighth inning. Tartabull starts the inning with a single into right field. Brad Wellman pinch hits for de los Santos, an obvious giveaway that Wathan also intends to bunt. Bill Buckner appears in the on-deck circle instead of Frank White. The inning as Wathan sees it is clear: Wellman will bunt and stay in to play second, Buckner will pinch hit and stay in to play first, the offensive and defensive moves coming as a package. Wathan is playing to tie it in the eighth, and the heart of the order will be up in the ninth:

> de los Santos, 1b
> White, 2b

Those two are going out, and these two coming in:

> Wellman, 2b
> Buckner, 1b

The Tigers charge the plate; a bunt try rolls foul. Henneman fires up and in, as Aquino had at Trammell; Wellman pulls back. Ball two comes in high. At last Wellman gets it down, bunted to the third base side of the mound.

Schu, however, makes another phenomenal play. Charging from the time the pitch is thrown, Schu picks up the ball on the second soft hop, whirls and fires it immediately to second, where Trammell returns it to first—a double play.

The game appears over; the Royals have fired their bullet, and they missed. Wathan, however, doesn't give up; call-

ing back Buckner, he sends Eisenreich to pinch hit for Frank White.

The differences between Eisenreich and Buckner are subtle, subtle enough that I believe most managers would regard them as offensively interchangeable (remember, this is early in the season). Eisenreich is, like Buckner, a left-handed line-drive hitter, but with two crucial differences: Eisenreich is fast and will take a walk. Buckner can't run and doesn't walk, so his offensive value is not in his ability to *score* runs, like Eisenreich, but in his ability to drive them in. As much a critic of Bill Buckner as I've always been, and as much as I hate having him on *my* ball club, if he hits .280 he will drive in runs. Eisenreich, playing his role to perfection, works the count to full, and then fouls off four pitches, finally taking the walk on a pitch outside.

When a pitcher throws more than twenty pitches in an inning, his effectiveness usually drops dramatically. I've never seen a stat workup on it, but I'll bet you that when the pitcher on the mound has thrown twenty-five pitches in the inning, a .250 hitter becomes a .350 hitter. Eisenreich not only got on base, he made Henneman throw ten pitches, making nineteen in the inning.

Now, however, the defense is messed up; the complementary offensive and defensive adjustments have been thrown out of kilter. Sitting in the stands, I wonder what Wathan will do with his defense; his first baseman is out of the game, and he is left with four outfielders in the lineup, none of whom can play first base. Bill Buckner pinch hits for Bob Boone, leaving us with four outfielders and no catcher, but a tie game when Buckner rips the ball into right-center. Eisenreich scores from first on the single, Buckner taking second on the throw.

> de los Santos, 1b
> White, 2b
> Boone, c

are out. The following are in:

Wellman, 2b
Eisenreich, of
Buckner, 1b

Palacios runs for Buckner, and Macfarlane pinch hits for Thurman. Palacios, whom you probably don't know from Adam, is an odd type of player—an infielder-catcher who doesn't hit much or play very good defense at catcher but runs very well, is a good infielder and has an excellent arm. Of course! Why didn't I think of it. Look:

Second baseman pinch hits for first baseman

Outfielder pinch hits for second baseman

First baseman pinch hits for catcher

Other first baseman pinch runs for first baseman

Catcher pinch hits for outfielder
The defense is back together. Macfarlane rips the pitch into left-center, scoring Palacios with the lead run. It was Henneman's twenty-seventh pitch of the inning.

Stillwell bats now, drawing a walk on five pitches. At last Tracewski comes to the mound, bringing in his left-handed relief ace (Guillermo Hernandez) to face the right-handed Seitzer. He doesn't want to, of course, but by this time he has no choice. Seitzer walks to load the bases; Bo Jackson is the fifth hitter in the last six to have the platoon advantage. Jackson singles to center; two runs scores.

It's an incredible inning for Wathan. When he needed a bunt, he had one of his best bunters at the plate, even though it didn't work out. When he needed a man on, he had his best lead-off-type pinch hitter at the plate with the platoon advantage. When he needed an RBI, he had his top RBI-type pinch hitter hitting with the platoon advantage and a fast man on base. When he got the

single that could give him the lead, he had a fast man on second base to carry the mail. And when he got done with it, he had his defense set up—a decent catcher (Macfarlane), a good first baseman (Palacios), an outstanding second baseman (Wellman), and an outstanding center fielder (Eisenreich) already back in the game. He had reconstructed his defense *twice* during the inning, while filling every offensive need in an almost optimal fashion.

When the team was down, he didn't give up. When his offensive plan didn't work out, he immediately switched to a backup—and scored four runs with two men out.

The game, however, is not over; Steve Farr, the Royals last reliever, comes in for the save. Mike Heath is scheduled to lead off the ninth. Mike Heath is probably the worst hitter you can imagine to lead off an inning against a right-handed pitcher. To begin with he is, like Bill Buckner, a *late-in-the-inning* type hitter. His on-base percentage is poor. He doesn't hit for average, and he doesn't walk. He strikes out. He can't run. Plus he's a platoon guy. In 1989 he hit .321 against left-handers, .222 against right-handers, and that's a typical performance for him.

Incredibly, Tracewski allows him to hit. The Tigers' inning is set up exactly backwards—one of the poorest leadoff men in the league leading off, with Gary Pettis, one of the poorest RBI men in the league, due up third in case anybody should happen to get on.

Heath grounds to short.

Rick Schu, another right-handed hitter, grounds to third.

Pettis strikes out.

The Royals win.

Tracewski is one of those guys who's been coaching in the league for twenty years, and you always wonder why he never got a chance to manage. If this is a sample, I think I understand.

Tracewski screwed up the game twenty-eight ways from Sunday. He forgot to pinch run for Keith Moreland until after the single that should have given him a first-and-third situation, and when he did pinch run he used one of his top left-handed pinch hitters to run for Moreland, and then replaced him in the field with another one of his top left-handed pinch hitters. What's most annoying here is that *he had a good left-handed bench*—Bergman, Sheridan, Fred Lynn, and Matt Nokes. Two of them he burned in the eighth without getting them to the plate, and the other two he forgot about.

He let his starting pitcher stay in the game too long.

He let his first reliever throw more than thirty pitches in the decisive eighth inning.

He let Wathan have the platoon advantage uncontested at all of the critical moments of the game.

He wasted a brilliant defensive performance by his team.

He wasted an awful performance by the opposition's starting pitcher.

He decided to go all-out for one run in the eighth inning, first putting his cleanup hitter in the hole 0–2 by ordering him to bunt twice, then losing his runner on a stolen base try. The Tigers parlayed two hits and a walk into nothing.

And what's worse than any of that, *he gave up.* He had bullets left in the gun at the end of the game, and he didn't fire them.

There was no way to know it at the time, but this game was the end of the season for the Tigers. On May 26, their season turned for the final time. Three games out of first before this game, they would lose all three games of the series. A week later they would be nine games out. Their momentum would never shift again.

A CUBS FAN COPES WITH REALITY

Honestly, Doctor, I know better than to get my hopes up, really I do. They've pulled this trick a thousand times, and I'm not going to be taken in again. Here it is early June and the Cubs are in first place—I swear you could set your watch by it. But am I optimistic? Absolutely not. I can already see the fold at the end of the tunnel, just as it's happened so many times before. Why am I consulting you then, if indeed I am in complete touch with reality? Well, you see Doctor, there's this small voice that whispers to me; I ignore it most of the time, or tell it to go away, but every once in a while—not often—I find myself listening, and once I start listening I'm bound to admit that I hear some interesting statements. Like the fact that the Cubs have surged to the top with people named Gary Varsho, Dwight Smith, Lloyd McClendon, Darrin Jackson, and Doug DeCinces patrolling the outfield. What in God's name is DeCinces doing in the outfield, Doctor? Last I heard he was a washed-up Japanese third baseman. Pardon me? Doug Dascenzo you say, not Doug DeCinces? Well, Dascenzo, DeCinces, it's all the same. Anyway, and then the voice whispers about how the left side of the infield is an offensive dung heap, with Shawon Dunston giving off a particularly malodorous air. Try as I might, I find it hard to convince myself that previous early season Cubs ascendancies were fueled by substitute outfielders and hitless wonder infielders.

So then what about the pitching, Doctor? Here's where I tell the whispering voice either it's insane, or I am. I mean, Don Zimmer and Jim Frey build a quality pitching staff? Sure, and Laurel and Hardy can build a nuclear reactor. And yet, who can gainsay Rick Sutcliffe and Greg Maddux? Maddux even got off to a rocky start; is that insurance against second half doldrums? There was never anything wrong with Scott Sanderson that good health wouldn't cure. And imagine Frey prying loose Mike Bielecki from miracle man Syd Thrift and seeing him become a quality starter. That's when it becomes intolerable, Doctor, when the voice starts carrying on about the achievements of Jim Frey. The Bielecki steal is bad enough, but then there's Calvin Schiraldi setting the table for Mitch Williams, while Lee Smith and Jamie Moyer struggle. Thank God Palmeiro is hitting, and Gossage has found a home. Then there's this Pat Perry creature, with his under-two ERA that they got for Leon Durham. Is it possible that—no, I won't entertain the thought even for an instant, no matter how many voices I hear—that Jim Frey is really competent?

On my better days, Doctor, when the voice neglects to torment me, I survey the situation realistically. No way will the pitching hold up once the wind starts blowing out at Wrigley—they'll take 12–8 shellackings same as always. Sanderson's back will go spinal cord up and Schiraldi will have flashbacks to October '86, and feed his gopher accordingly. Dawson will come back, but his surgical knee will hamper him more than ever, and the other generic outfielders just aren't experienced enough to deal with a pennant race. Besides, the Mets will eventually kick into high gear, just like in '88. When the going gets tough, the Cubs will get choking.

But Doctor, what if they don't? What if for once in its life the voice is right? Just look around the majors; the Angels and Orioles in first place. If I'd heard a voice whispering that, I'd have had myself committed. What if, after all, Frey really has built a pitching staff that can stay the course? What if pennant race veterans like Sandberg, Dawson, and Law can provide the necessary reassurance to keep budding stars like Grace and Berryhill and the young outfielders from swallowing their Adam's apples? What if Frey has one more great trade in him, like Dallas Green in '84? What if it's just going to be one injury after another for the Mets? The voice keeps whispering those kind of questions, Doctor. It happens every year, and I thought I was inured to it. But I guess that deep down I'm just like every other Cubs fan—I can only deal with so much reality.

—M.K.
June 8, 1989

MIRACLE WEEK IN HOUSTON

I think if anyone deserved this, it was Houston Astros fans. I'm referring, of course, to the seven games the Astros played at home between June second and eighth, quite possibly the most exciting week's worth of baseball ever played in a single city, although you'd never know it to examine the national publications, which focused on only two of the games. Suffice to say that had this miraculous seven days of baseball been played in New York, or at Wrigley Field, it would already be immortalized in prose, poetry, song, and the producers of *Field of Dreams* would surely own the movie rights. But Houston baseball, like Rodney Dangerfield, gets no respect, so please bear with me as I try to make reparation for that immutable fact.

It all began, you may recall, with Mike Scott's one-to-nothing victory over the Dodgers on Friday night. This was a mere warm-up exercise, as it turned out, for the twenty-two inning Saturday-night-Sunday-morning marathon that finally ended when Mike Scioscia, who had already blocked two would-be winning runs off the plate like Pete Rose's attorney blocking a hearing, was unable to control yet another throw from the outfield as Bill Doran staggered past him. (Not to change metaphors in mid-stream, but why isn't Scioscia's nickname "Stonewall"? Has anyone ever done a better job of blocking the plate?) The throw, it should be noted, was made necessary by the base hit that went just over the glove of the leaping first baseman Fernando Valenzuela. Regular first baseman Eddie Murray, who had taken over third so that Jeff Hamilton could pitch, is three inches taller than Fernando. It would be interesting to compare their vertical leaps.

(A subsidiary point: Afterwards, predictably, Tommy Lasorda whined about the lack of a curfew: "What good is it for teams to be playing baseball at two in the morning? That's ridiculous. It's a terrible rule. How many fans are going to stick around at two in the morning? How many guys can you go through?" Well, Tommy, how many chances for a marathon classic do we get? Sure, most fans melt away after twelve innings or thereabouts, but doesn't it occur to you that the hard-core faithful who willingly stick it out into the wee hours are entitled to some reward for their perseverance, like a completed game? What do they get if play *is* stopped by curfew, a free ticket to the next day's continuation? And anyway, isn't that what we have the American League for, to confine all the chickenshit, like curfews and designated hitters, to one venue?)

Lasorda's anger could hardly have been assuaged later that day by the thirteen-inning quickie—made possible by Craig Biggio's two-out, ninth-inning homer—that terminated on Mike Scott's sacrifice fly. (And no, he was not a desperation pinch hitter; he was pitching relief, just as Orel Hershiser had for seven innings earlier that morning.) Then, after a night of somnambulance and a 10–2 pasting from the Padres (pity the unlucky fans who chose only this game out of the seven to attend), on Tuesday came the rally of the season—and I am aware that both the Blue Jays and Phillies battled back from ten-run deficits. The victory emerged when, down three runs with two out and nobody on, the Astros managed to load the bases; when Mark Davis, seventeen for seventeen in save opportunities, entered the game and promptly walked in two runs; when defensive catcher extraordinaire Benito Santiago failed to hold the game-ending third strike, failed to step on home plate for the game-ending force once he'd recovered it, and failed to hold on for the game-ending tag after Ken Caminiti rammed him, sending it into extra innings, when a mere outfield error resulted in a Houston victory.

After a three–two laugher on Wednesday, the Astros decided to revert to their miraculous comeback mode on Thursday. This time four runs were needed in the ninth to tie, but the overeager home team insisted on starting this rally with no one out. Two singles, a ground out, and another single produced one run and Mark Davis, but this time with the tying run at the plate. No matter, Craig Biggio doubles in the second run, and Davis wild pitches in the third. Alex Trevino, still heady from his game-tying strikeout of two nights previous, responds with a sacrifice fly, and it's extra innings again. Only this time the Padres do not fold; they pick up a run in the top of the tenth. Once again Davis can preserve victory, but a one out walk to weak-hitting Gerald Young allows Glenn Davis to bat with two out and the game on the line. And of course he cranks it—two-run homer, still another one run (yawn) triumph for the Astros and a share of the NL West lead. And for the fans, a week packed with more baseball excitement than a fiction writer would dare to contemplate.

I don't pretend to understand any of it. This still looks to me like a mediocre team: an indifferent starting rotation once past Scott and Jim Deshaies (although a strong bullpen), and an offense that begins with Bill Doran and ends with Glenn Davis. Before the miracle week, *Houston Chronicle* columnist Ed Fowler echoed the sentiments of many when he wrote: ". . . the current club is a crazy-quilt affair, the product of a stray idea here, cross-pollinated with a misguided notion there." But was Fowler unknowingly flirting with prophecy when he continued: "That's not to say it's without talent, only that talent without concept is like sex without protection. Sure it can be fun, but you never know what might happen."

Truer words were never spoken. June two to eight in Houston was the week in which everything that you never knew could happen, did indeed happen, and it couldn't have happened to more deserving fans. I mean the dyed-in-the-wool cranks, the ones who've endured the—numerous—dry years, as well as the heartbreaking denouements of 1980 and '86. I still contend that the '80 NLCS was the most exciting post-season series of my lifetime; where were VCR's when we really needed them? The '86 NLCS was no slouch either; there's a worthwhile book on the climactic sixth game, called *The Greatest Game Ever Played.* That might be stretching it, since even Jerry Izenberg would probably admit it would have been a tough sell to a publisher had the Astros come out on top, but never mind. The point is, Astros fans have seen more great baseball, with nothing to show for it in the end, than any other fans in baseball. Don't talk to me about the Bosox, at least they make it to the Series before everything goes wrong; at least die-hard Cubs fans

have the Friendly Confines and memories of Tinker to Evers to Chance; even supporters of the lowly Tribe can point to Series victories, a pantheon of Hall of Famers, and record-setting attendance. Tell me, what can Houston Astros fans point to? Jose Cruz was a great player, but few outside of Houston noticed, and he'll never make the Hall of Fame. Joe Morgan will end up in Cooperstown, but not for anything he did in an Astros uniform. Nolan Ryan left in a huff, and wouldn't it be ironic if he pitched the other Texas team into the post-season for the first time. Even their once-wondrous dome is behind the times; it lacks a retractable top. Only the Toronto Blue Jays, losers in the '85 ALCS after taking a three-games-to-one lead, and victims of a nightmarish final week that saw them cough up a seemingly secure '87 division title, and the Montreal Expos, last-second losers three years in a row to the Eventual World Champions, have tested the mettle of their fans similarly. The Kansas City Royals of the late seventies, gut-wrenching losers to the Yankees in three fiercely fought playoff series, left their fans despondent, but redemption, in the form of George Brett's monster home run in the 1980 ALCS, turned out to be close at hand. Houston fans have yet to achieve such a catharsis, and in spite of a decade's worth of miracles compressed into one brief, shining moment in June, it's doubtful that they will this year. That's why if any group of fans deserved a wholly unexpected seven-day tour of the Elysian Fields, I think these were the ones. For all you've suffered through, Houston fans, this glimpse of paradise was for you.

—M.K.
June 12, 1989

ON A DOWNHILL ROLL

O f all the teams to make an early exit from pennant contention in '89, the San Diego Padres are probably the most surprising. It was hardly shocking when the combination of old age and a mismanaged youth movement buried the Tigers early, nor was it astonishing that injuries left the overesteemed Pirates at the post, but San Diego has no similar alibi. Indeed, Jack McKeon seems to have fallen on his face with the players he wanted. Where did he miscalculate?

We can start with the pitching staff, and Messrs. Walt Terrell and Dennis Rasmussen. It's easy to imagine McKeon looking at Terrell's 1988 mark of 7–16 and thinking, "It was just an off year; he's a better pitcher than that." Maybe so, but it would be just as easy to look at his '87 mark of 17–10 with an over 4 ERA and conclude that it was just an on year, he's a worse pitcher than that. McKeon ended up finding out what he was the hard way. The situation with Rasmussen, who burned up the league for the Padres in the second half of '88, was more complicated. I'm sure McKeon was all too aware of his history, but it became a case of what are you supposed to believe, history or your own eyes? I can't blame McKeon for going with his eyes, but he certainly can't like what he's seeing from Rasmussen now. On the other hand, his confidence in Ed Whitson has been more than amply rewarded, as Whitson is on a course for his best ever season, a surprising turn of events that compensates for the failure of either Terrell or

Rasmussen, but not both. In the bullpen, McKeon's judgement has proved sound. First string set-up man Lance McCullers departed as part of a package, but Greg Harris and Mark Grant seem to have more than filled his shoes, while Mark Davis remains in the upper echelon of closers.

But it is his assessments of the rest of the team that now—with flawless twenty-twenty hindsight—appear to have been woefully inaccurate. The Jack Clark deal seemed a steal at the time: excess baggage pitching in exchange for desperately needed power. The excess baggage pitchers have struggled in New York, but no more so than Clark has in San Diego—is this destined to be one of the classic trades that hurts both teams? Don't be fooled by Clark's high OBP—he simply has not done the job. Did a season of designated hitting ill-equip him for full-time play back in the National League? There's been considerable comment as to how much production can be expected with people like Carmelo Martinez and Marvell Wynne batting behind him, but the success of Kevin Mitchell with perennial All-Stars Candy Maldonado and Ernest Riles in the on-deck circle tends to demolish that argument.

And anyway, there are plenty of players to blame for the team's offensive doldrums. Benito Santiago gets nothing but adulatory ink for his catching prowess, but McKeon might have noticed coming into '89 that his offensive game was already in serious decline. It happens when pitchers realize you'll swing at anything. John Kruk had gone into a similar offensive slide in '88, and to complicate matters for '89 was asked to take over right field, hardly his ideal position. On the other hand, Roberto Alomar's late '88 on-base percentage of .389,

coinciding with his switch to the leadoff spot, could have pulled the wool over Casey Stengel's eyes. But would the Old Professor have thought he could win with Garry Templeton at short?

All right, maybe this is unfair Monday morning quarterbacking, but surely McKeon must have suspected that, for all his machinations, this team was still capable of struggling offensively. And unlike some managers, he was in a position to do something about it. Because waiting in the wings as trade bait was highly touted young catcher Sandy Alomar, Jr., seemingly leading the majors in stimulating opposing GM's salivary glands. Not a day went by in spring training without mention of the innumerable blue chip commodities about to be traded for Alomar. But somehow, Trader Jack never got the deal done, in spite of the fact that everyone is crying for catching. Did he really expect to plug all his holes, garner a third baseman, shortstop, and outfielder, in exchange for one inexperienced player? Right now he would probably kill for another shot at Howard Johnson alone. It seems that McKeon is now in the position of the big game hunter who had the kill of his life in his sights, but hitched when it came time to pull the trigger, and never got a second chance. A deal can probably still be worked to plug one offensive hole, but water seems to be pouring in on too many fronts for the Padres to regroup for a pennant charge. McKeon, it seems to me, received an inordinate share of the credit for last year's impressive turnabout. I hope he's prepared to assume a concomitant portion of the responsibility for this year's impending fiasco.

—M.K.
June 26, 1989

The reason for doing research is that you pay a price for everything you believe which is not true. On the trip to Wichita to see Andy Benes pitch, I asked Pat Kelly how long he thought Benes might be with his team. He said that Benes had a lot to learn yet, which struck me as an odd thing to say, since Benes had about fifty times as many strikeouts as hits allowed at the moment. So I said, naturally enough, "What does he need to work on, in particular?"

Of course I realized before the words were gone that I had asked a question that Kelly really couldn't answer. A good manager doesn't criticize his players to the media. It's his job to tell Benes what Benes needs to work on, not to tell me.

But without realizing it, I had rubbed shoulders with what was to become a major story of the Padres' season. Benes did get to the majors in early August, and won six of ten starts. The Padres, with half a pitching staff, had dropped twelve games behind the Giants by late July, apparently dead. They called up Benes and began too late a sustained charge which would bring them within three games of the division's lead. Jack McKeon said at the end that the Padres had lost the pennant because people in his organization kept telling him that Benes wasn't ready to pitch in the majors, when he was.

On one level, McKeon is probably correct. If they had called up Benes in May, they probably would have won the pennant. To have called up Benes even a month earlier *might* have made the difference, figuring that one good game against the Giants can create a two-game swing in the standings. On another level, it is important not to forget that in a close race, there is not one thing which separates victory from defeat, but many things. The reason the Padres didn't win is that they didn't make the Sandy-Alomar-for-Howard-Johnson trade. The reason the Padres didn't win is that they didn't have anybody to hit fifth or sixth.

I hope it doesn't work out this way, because he's a good man, but it's obvious that Pat Kelly *could* get burned real bad on this. When McKeon says that the Padres didn't win because "people in his organization" told him Benes wasn't ready, it's obvious that among those people is Pat Kelly, perhaps at the top of the list. To be blamed for losing the pennant by the head man in the organization, even if your name isn't mentioned, doesn't do your career any good.

But what I want to know is, why in heaven's name did McKeon believe him? I don't mean to be rude, but anybody with the brains of a three-year-old knew that Benes was ready for the majors, didn't they? Benes in late May was 6–1 with an 0.78 ERA, averaging eleven strikeouts per nine innings. What else do you want to know?

Skepticism about minor league performance statistics is a pillar of old-school dogma; the fact that a pitcher has gone 17–6 in AAA ball is not to be taken as proof that he can win in the majors. In some cases, I can agree with that. In this case, it was silly, and Jack McKeon *should* have known that.

Look, I'm not saying that I'm smarter than baseball men. I'm saying that it is reasonable to expect them to know what *I* know. A caller on *Baseball Sunday* asked me in May who I thought would be the NL's Rookie of the Year. I said, of course, that it was too early to know, but that with Jefferies struggling and nobody really playing well, somebody still in the minors could wind up winning it, somebody like Andy Benes. I just assumed that the Padres would call Benes up by June; it was an obvious decision. I told the radio audience a half a dozen times that Benes had to be called up very soon.

Why wasn't he? Because I was wrong? No—because McKeon was wrong. McKeon gave away the NL West in 1989 to display his fealty to an element of old-school bullshit: that minor league stats don't prove anything. He can't blame that on the people in his organization. You pay a price for anything you believe that isn't true—and in 1989, the price was the NL West.

I will pick the Padres to win this division in 1990, with some misgivings. If they could play the 1989 season over again, and do the things they should have done, I'd bet on them for sure. They didn't have to do anything smart; they just had to do the obvious. Two obvious moves: Trade Alomar for whatever you can get, and call up Benes.

It's hard to get excited in November about a team with Garry Templeton at short and Ed Whitson as their top returning starter and Davis gone to $13 million worth of greener pastures.

But Whitson, Hurst, Benes, and Rasmussen compares fairly well to any other starting rotation in the division. Greg W. Harris could be an excellent starter. The bullpen is still excellent, still one of the best in the league. Gwynn is amazing and I love Roberto Alomar. Joe Carter isn't a great player, but he isn't Chris James, either; Alomar enabled them to turn Chris James into Joe Carter. The Padres were the best team in the league at the end of the 1989 season, and should be the best from the start in 1990.

GIANT STEPS

Yes, Steve Bedrosian is a fine reliever, but what do the Giants need him for? Last time I looked Craig Lefferts and Goose Gossage seemed to have short relief well under control. On the other hand, betting that Roger Craig and Al Rosen don't know what they're about has become a sure ticket to the poor farm. Look at what they accomplished in '87, restructuring the entire pitching staff in mid-season on the way to a division title. In '88 injuries to the restructured pitching staff and a power outage among outfielders led to a decline, so not surprisingly Craig and Rosen set out to restructure the outfield. Brett Butler had already arrived *via* free agency, and when Jeffrey Leonard's home run stroke deserted him, he was quickly dispatched to make room for Mike Aldrete, who was also found wanting and subsequently shipped to Montreal. This cleared a spot for an erstwhile third baseman named Kevin Mitchell, who seems to have blossomed since abandoning the infield.

But that's not the only way in which the Giants have been restructured. Since the original '87 revamping of the pitching staff there has been a major restructuring within the original restructuring. Mike LaCoss, for three years a starter in Frisco, suddenly begins the '89 season as the bullpen ace. Scott Garrelts, almost exclusively a reliever in his major league career, is moved to the rotation. Atlee Hammaker, always a starter until '88, becomes a swing man. Don Robinson, a reliever since his early years with the Pirates, returns to the rotation for '89. What other team, I'd like to know, would have the courage, the *chutzpah* if you will, to so totally rearrange their incumbent pitchers? Who else would be willing to put up with the second guessing if it didn't work? The Yankees made one move of this sort five years ago, shifting Righetti to the bullpen, and they're still taking flak over it. But maybe part of the genius of Craig and Rosen's approach is that they make so many unconventional moves that no one has the time to second guess any particular one.

I must confess that I'm no Giants fan, but it is impossible not to admire the way this organization operates. They don't just address their problems, they attack them the way Pete Rose attacked the game of baseball. If an organization can be like a player you'd have to call this one "Charley Hustle." Remember the famous home plate collision where Rose obliterated Ray Fosse? Al Rosen in '87 did the same in a more genteel way to Bill Bergesch and Dick Wagner, and threatens to do the same this year to Murray Cook.

A week ago it appeared that the Giants might be ready to draw clear and make a shambles of the NL West. San Diego has already succumbed, and the punchless Dodgers appear to be on the ropes. So far Houston and Cincinnati have managed to keep things interesting, but a sudden downward slide by either or both would not be a surprise. Not that this Giants team is without problems: The pitching staff is again injury-racked, the offense drops off considerably once you get past Kevin Mitchell, and right field especially remains a gaping hole that I don't think newly-acquired Pat Sheridan can fill, even in a platoon role.

But there I go again, second-guessing my own nominee for

the smartest organization in baseball. If Sheridan indeed doesn't work out, they won't hesitate; they'll get rid of him and find someone who can do the job. Count on it: By September they'll have a competent major league right fielder. And if the ship springs a leak somewhere else, they'll do more than stick a cork in it. This organization means business. My hat is off to them.

By way of contrast, The Kansas City Royals are in a desperate battle to stay in contention in the AL West. In the off-season, in spite of finishing miles behind the Athletics, they made only one major move—the signing of free agent Bob Boone. I thought this overall lack of activity a mistake, and said so, but it now appears they were correct in believing that the tools to contend were already within the organization. Since the season began, they have made an important acquisition in Terry Leach, now in the starting rotation. Given good health in the second half (Bo Jackson, Danny Tartabull, and George Brett seem never to appear in the same lineup) the Royals may very well have a shot at the division title. There can be no doubt that this organization wants to win. But they don't want to win as badly as the Giants do. Why do I think that? Because Willie Wilson remains on the team, and Wilson is obviously, incontrovertibly washed-up. He is no asset at bat and has even become (shockingly) a butcher in the field. There is no excuse for his continuation on a major league roster. Why then does he remain? Because of the contract Royals co-owner Avron Fogelman irrationally tendered him eons ago, which is paying him two million dollars this year. The Royals have already suffered the embarrassment of having to pay Dan Quisenberry huge sums to toil

(successfully) for the St. Louis Cardinals, and cannot bring themselves to admit that they've come up a cropper again. I can understand their feeling, but this is a pennant race, there's an outside chance they can win all the marbles. Do they really want to jeopardize that just because they're embarrassed to concede they're pissing money away on Willie Wilson? Everyone who pays attention to baseball knows it already anyway. As long as it's money pissed away, what difference does it make whether he receives it at Royals Stadium, or in his mailbox at home? I know Bob Lurie and Al Rosen wouldn't hesitate, they'd waive their own grandmothers if it would give them an edge in a pennant race. That's why the Giants are much more likely to be seen in the post-season than the Royals. The Giants want to win, period; the Royals want to win, but . . .

M.K.
June 28, 1989

THE PARITY PARTY

In the 1970's there were twenty divisional championship teams which successfully defended their titles. In the 1980's there were only three.

In the 1970's half of the division titles were won by the same team which had won the year before. In the 1980's less than one tenth of the titles were won by the defending champs.

The human mind searches ceaselessly for cause and effect relationships, so when championship teams stopped repeating in the 1980's there was a causal connection drawn between this fact and the other most obvious change in the game, that being the advent of free agency in the late seventies. It is human nature to make such a connection; in fact, it is *animal* nature, since it seems to have been shown that animals, even birds, do the same thing—search constantly for cause and effect relationships. That was what the *Abstract* was about, in a sense—the search for cause and effect relationships in contemporary baseball, while this book is more about the search for cause and effect relationships operating across time.

It is a part of my job to be a skeptic, and so throughout much of the decade I wondered if there *was* any real cause for the declining number of repeating champions, if it wasn't perhaps just a random fluctuation. The decade is over now, and we can now see clearly that it *wasn't* just a random fluctuation; there had to be a reason for it. If it is given that in two decades there will be twenty-three repeating division champions, the random chance that twenty of them will be in one decade and three in the other is about the same as the chance that the Republican party in '92 will replace Dan Quayle with Jesse Jackson.

In a sense, we are no longer faced with a phenomenon, but with a fact of life. So why *don't* championship teams repeat anymore? No answer, but a few thoughts:

1) To paraphrase Martin Luther King, Jr., the arc of history is long, but it bends toward parity. Throughout the twelve decades of professional baseball, the difference between the best teams and the worst teams has gotten constantly smaller.

I mean "constantly" in the most literal sense; if you measure the difference between the best and worst teams, you'll find that it was less in the 1880's than it had been in the 1870's, was less in the 1890's than it was in the 1880's, was less in the 1900's than it had been in the 1890's, and on and on in this manner until today. In the 1880's the best teams won 75 to 80 percent of their games, although one or two teams won more. In the 1900's, the best teams won 70 to 75 percent of their games. In the 1920's, the best teams won 65 to 70 percent of their games. Today, the best teams win 59 to 64 percent of their games, although one or two teams won more. In the next decade, it is extremely likely that the range will be more like 58 to 63 percent, although one or two teams may win more.

2) Very often, although random chance may not *create* a change, random chance may greatly *emphasize* a change which has some other cause. *Both* figures, in all likelihood, were random fluctuations—the twenty repeating champions of the 1970's abnormally high in the context of history, and the three repeating champions of the 1980's abnormally low. It is certain that there will not be twenty repeating champions during the 1990's, absolutely certain—but it is also extremely likely that there will be *more* than three.

3) Even historical trends which last for more than a century may eventually

reach maturity. We probably have not reached absolute maturity of this trend; forty years from now, there probably will be even greater balance among teams than there is now. But we probably are, in historical terms, *near* maturity. For several reasons which I will spare you, I don't think it is possible to get a great deal more balance among teams than we have now.

4) One measure of competitive balance is what is called the standard deviation of team wins. The standard deviation of team wins has reduced steadily over history, although not as constantly as some other measures.

The expansions of 1961, 1969, and 1977, of course, brought into the league very poor teams, and thus temporarily increased the standard deviation of team wins. This effect requires about ten years to completely wash out for each expansion, perhaps a little bit longer. In this way, the 1970's were somewhat protected from the normal contraction of the league over time, for as the league was being pushed together by the forces operating over time, it was being spread apart by the expansions.

In the 1980's we had not only the normal contraction over time, but also the evaporation of the "expansion effect" from the three expansions. Thus it *may have been* pre-ordained that there would be an unusually forceful contraction toward league-wide parity.

5) Baseball instituted a draft of young ballplayers in 1965, allowing the worst teams the first shot at the best young players.

My research has shown that the benefit of having the first draft pick or the high draft picks definitely *is* enough to contribute significantly toward competitive balance. In the thirties and forties there were teams that would finish in a *typical* year about 50–104, and in a bad year worse than that. My research has shown that with the advantage of drafting first, it would be almost impossible to sustain that level of performance over time; you'd just have to do an awful job of drafting.

Of course, the effects of this wouldn't be completely registered until the late 1970's, about twelve years after the first draft. So the 1980's were also the first decade in which the leveling effect of the June draft has been fully realized.

6) In the history of the game there are many brief periods when a league had no dominant team, and so the championship banner danced from team to team. If you look at some of those periods in retrospect, it's apparent that what happened is that the team which *should* have been the dominant team for some reason didn't do it. The classic example is the National League from 1958 through 1965, which was won by Milwaukee, Los Angeles, Pittsburgh, Cincinnati, San Francisco, Los Angeles, St. Louis, and Los Angeles.

Several of those teams were exceptionally weak for championship teams. If you set out to find the worst team ever to win a league title, two of the teams that you inevitably wind up with are the 1959 Dodgers and the 1961 Reds, and the 1960 Pirates weren't a whole lot better.

Looking backward, the reason for this is obvious: The Milwaukee Braves, who *should* have been the dominant team of the time, couldn't get their act together (see comments on Henry Aaron, "Biographic Encyclopedia"). A team with a formidable talent nucleus allowed five other teams to scrape and claw past them.

An almost equally good example is the Tigers of the mid-sixties. The American League champions, beginning in 1964, were the Yankees (1964), Twins (1965), Orioles (1966), Red Sox (1967), Tigers (1968), and Orioles again (1969). If you look at the talent on the rosters,

it's apparent now that the Tigers, with Bill Freehan, Norm Cash, Dick McAuliffe, Don Wert, Willie Horton, and Al Kaline, *should* have been able to win that league. In 1967 Mickey Lolich was the Tigers fourth starter—fourth in terms of games, starts, innings, and wins. Lee Strange was the Red Sox *second* starter—yet somehow, the Red Sox were able to beat them.

Now, back to the eighties. I think that *one* of the things that happened in the 1980's was that three teams which should have been kicking ass and taking names, as they say in the army, instead were picking grass and acting tame. Two of those teams are obvious: the Mets, of course, and the Toronto Blue Jays in the same time frame. The third team seems equally obvious to me, but you never hear it said: the Detroit Tigers, who from 1979 to 1983, failed to win the American League East despite by far the best talent base not only in the division, but in all of baseball. Unfortunately, Sparky Anderson spent most of the decade diddling around with Enos Cabell and Chris Pittaro. That Anderson was somehow able to escape responsibility for this, and get himself portrayed as a genius when the team finally did win, is one of the most remarkable public relations accomplishments of our time.

7) In the last fifteen years there has been a dramatic increase in the number of "bail-out" trades, August trades in which a team which is out of the pennant race trades a veteran in the last years of his career for a younger player or players to be named after the season. I believe that the first team to make these trades regularly was the Oakland A's in the early seventies. Now, these trades are so much a part of the game that fans anticipate them, speculate about them, criticize general managers of contending teams when they can't make them and criticize general managers of losing teams when they don't

make them. You didn't have that even ten years ago.

One of the large forces which shapes baseball over time is the evolution of the game to accomodate strategies. What many or most of these strategies involve is *learning to make appropriate changes*—learning how and when to use a relief pitcher (a process than began in the 1890's and appears to have matured in the late seventies), learning to use pinch hitters, pinch runners, defensive substitutes, switching from one pitcher carrying the team to two starters to three starters to four to five, switching from a regular to platoon combinations. This is a "roster strategy" rather than a "game strategy," but it's the same thing—someone figures out how to reallocate talent at a key moment to help them win, and other people, attempting to keep up, adopt the strategy.

But the effect of this roster strategy is to put a team into a pattern of contending in some years, and not in others. More teams now are in a position to contend; four teams in a division may be in a position to contend, rather than two. If a contending team can make a trade for a Steve Bedrosian or a Mookie Wilson, not to mention a goddamn Rickey Henderson, it may vault that team up to a level that it is impossible for any team to match year after year. The top teams begin asking themselves early in the year "Is this our year? Is this a year we can win? Or should *we* be the ones to bail out this year?"

The effect is that a team may wind up winning every second year or every third year over a longer period of time, rather than winning consistently for a shorter period of time. And, if you look at the eighties, that is part of what you see—very few teams winning repeatedly, but *many* teams winning twice in three years or twice in four years.

Al Rosen has become, in a sense, the model general manager of our time—not the best at evaluating talent, not the best at negotiating a deal, but the best at making that timely little trade that makes the difference in a close race. Better than anyone else, Rosen manipulates the roster through the season as a manager manipulates it through a game.

8) Well, what about free agency?

Free agency probably does play some role here. The role that I see free agency playing is rather different, almost opposite, from the role that is often suggested by journalists, which is that free agency tears apart championship teams.

Well, I don't see that free agency has torn apart very many championship teams. Is it the loss of free agents that has prevented the Mets from repeating? Is it the loss of free agents which has prevented the Blue Jays from dominating their division? I don't think so.

There is a lot of talk, of course, about the players of today jumping from team to team, but that's just talk; players of today do not, in fact, change teams more often than players of other generations. What *I* see is that there may be *too much* stability in personnel for teams to repeat.

Remember what was written about Casey Stengel, that his genius was knowing when to say hello to his players and when to say good-bye? Stengel would trade for a player, get a good year or two out of him, and then get rid of him.

Well, it's hard to do that today. When a player has a few big years now, he gets a big contract, usually a three-year contract. And that means that when he has a bad year, you're stuck with him. You can cover for him to some degree, but unless you want to eat his contract, you can't really trade him. Willie Wilson, as Mike correctly cited in "Giant Steps," is the classic example. The long-term contract has interfered with the Royals' ability to dominate not because it has created instability, but because it has created stability.

To a degree, this effect mitigates the potentially noncompetitive aspects of point seven, the bail-out trades. The bail-out trades *could* cause the league to pull apart, good teams from bad—except that there are all of those players who *can't* be moved. The effect: competitive balance.

9) Is parity good for baseball?

It is more good than bad. What parity means is that more teams are in contention. That's good.

Parity means that more teams go into the year thinking they can win. That's good.

There is a point. If parity reaches the point at which the teams seem indistinguishable, that's not good; that takes something away from baseball. But that hasn't happened, and I don't really think it will.

10) I suppose I should say something about what the historical forces are which create parity. What they are, in essence, is the push toward excellence—a movement of the bottom of the league toward the top, always pushing upwards, at one time pushing the quality of play higher and the margin of tolerance lower. Stephen Jay Gould's explanation of the process is excellent, and I endorse it completely.

Almost ten years ago, I wrote the first version of an essay entitled "The Law of Competitive Balance." The Law of Competitive Balance, as stated in the 1983 *Baseball Abstract,* is this:

> There develop over time separate and unequal strategies adopted by winners and losers; the balance of those strategies favors the losers, and thus serves constantly to narrow the difference between the two.

There's a long essay on the subject, which was reprinted a year ago in *This Time Let's Not Eat the Bones.*

What happened in the 1980's was simply that the law of competitive bal-ance asserted itself with unusual force. This has happened in every major spectator sport with the exception of college football, and it will continue to happen.

11) Could anything cause parity to go backward? Will we ever see a .700 baseball team again?

Nothing can stop the *process* of increasing parity, but there is something which is not unlikely which would throw it backward thirty or forty years. A new league. If a new league forms you could have a few years of absolute chaos in baseball—salaries going haywire, good teams suddenly being ripped apart and bad teams suddenly winning, teams jumping around the continent like bugs on a skillet, competitive major league teams in different leagues in cities which five years ago didn't have teams, teams folding in mid-season, the government stepping in to regulate the industry . . . who knows what all.

But the one certain consequence of a new league is that there would be a temporary interruption of league parity. The new league would have .750 teams and .250 teams, and the competitive balance of the existing leagues would also be dramatically reduced.

OMAHA

It would be nice to report that the College World Series was wonderful, that it was baseball as it was supposed to be, by which we mean of course that it was baseball much like it was before we remember it. I had called ahead for press credentials, planning to go up on Monday. Susie took ill with a stomach virus for a couple of days, so it was Wednesday before I could get up there. This is amateur ball, and the PR office brings new dimensions to the term "amateur." Despite fifteen phone calls, despite showing up at the park three hours early, despite repeated messages and repeated assurances that my credentials will be here later today or if not then tomorrow, they never are. I buy a ticket from a scalper and go in, and will do the same again tomorrow.

You've heard people say that good college ball today is comparable to AA ball. It would be nice to report that this is true. It isn't. Maybe half of the players on the best college programs are legitimate pro prospects. Everybody in double-A ball, by definition, is a pro prospect. Wichita last year had both a AA team, a pretty good team but nothing special, and a college team, the NCAA champion. I saw both play several times. If the two had met, the Wranglers (the AA team) would obviously beat the Shockers—not a hundred percent of the time, but whenever Benes was pitching and seven out of ten when he wasn't. The college athletes are just as good, or nearly as good. The best players are just as good. If you took two good college teams and made one team out of them, they could win the Texas League. But the back end of the roster is much stronger in AA ball than college ball, and the execution of fundamentals is just miles apart.

I probably shouldn't say this, but at times the quality of the coaching in college baseball is just appalling. There are a couple of conspicuous exceptions— the University of Texas team under Cliff Gustafson, not a particularly talented team in 1989, and Gene Stephenson's Wichita State team. But in both of the areas by which one evaluates a coach (reasonable strategy, and execution of fundamentals), the play in the CWS is just amazing—far, far below professional standards. I'm not talking about marginal decisions that you disagree with, like Don Zimmer moves when they don't work, or about one coach out-maneuvering another one. I'm talking about brainless stuff, slow runners lighting out for second base on a 3–0 count, the infield playing deep with a man on third in a critical situation.

On bunt plays there are bases left uncovered, wild throws, poor decisions, and pitchers who pick up the ball and look at all three bases trying to figure out where to make a play. If a ball is bunted along the third base line the pitcher will try to make the play three times in four, even though it is the third baseman's play; the pitcher, running hard to the line, has no chance to make the throw to first even though he can get to the ball quicker.

One time a ball was popped up about four foot in front of home plate, a mile high. The pitcher pointed for a long time, but nobody reacted, so finally the pitcher decided to take the ball himself. At which point the third baseman clotheslined him.

Major leaguers can make baseball look easy. From years of watching the pros, I guess I had begun to take things for granted. I expected more of college players than they could deliver. I expected them to have some idea about hitting the cut-off man, which a few of them do. In AA ball, ground balls scoot under the glove of diving infielders, and you know in the major leagues they would make that play. The same ball in the NCAA, and the shortstop as likely as not is nowhere near.

Between innings someone in a piece of lime green and orange bathroom carpet comes out and does little comedy-and-dance routines. One time he came out dressed in stripes, which I eventually realized were supposed to be prison stripes, and a curly black wig, and did a routine to the tune of James Brown's "I Feel Good." It would be nice to report that this didn't happen, but since it did it is at least satisfying to report that nobody thought it was at all funny, and a number of people looked at him as if he was a stupid racist jerk.

It would be nice to report that there was no dot run, but unfortunately there is, a one-dimensional dot run along a narrow scoreboard. The winner is "Red," although all of the Dots are the same color. The dot run is inane when you have a scoreboard on which to conduct it, and this imitation of a dot run, without the proper equipment, is embarrassing. It would be nice to report that the games were crisply and competitively played, that there were no interminable meetings and that games did not last three and a half hours because pitchers could not throw strikes. There are runners on base almost all of the time, and pitches frequently bounce in the dirt—but only the two teams which meet in the championship game, Wichita and Texas, show any ability to take advantage of this.

I've heard about the aluminum bats for years, but until I watched about six games in a row I didn't really appreciate the impact that the aluminum bats have had on the college game. What I had always assumed would happen with aluminum bats is that the hitters would develop an "artificial bat speed" by whipping around the light aluminum bat. What really happens is just the opposite. Because the ball will jump off an aluminum bat even if it is not well hit, the hitters develop lazy bats, driving the ball to the opposite field with late swings. This is a tremendous advantage for the hitter, who can wait on a pitch and still hit it hard—but almost no one in the College World Series shows a quick bat. Maybe Eric Wedge.

Very few people in the event seem to know when they should do anything. In one game the field gets wet, and it is still raining pretty hard. Wichita State starts bunting down the third base line. The pitcher comes over and tries to field the bunt, but slips and falls down. This happens four times before the umpires decide to suspend play.

Skip Bertman, the LSU Coach, allows his star pitcher to stay on the mound with a blister and no control for an outrageously long time, costing his team a game.

The scoreboard operator seems to have the count wrong or the score wrong or something wrong most of the time.

The Wichita Shockers will win the tournament; despite being seeded low they seem to me to be obviously the best team. The Shockers win, in large part, because they don't chase bad pitches (during the season they drew 522 walks in 626 offensive innings). They run the bases aggressively and well, stealing five times as many bases as they allow. Their athletes are no better than the other teams, but they are just as good and much better coached. The Shockers generate a huge percentage of their runs from a combination of walks and opponents' errors, while themselves playing defense far better than anyone else here. If the Shockers had a dominant pitcher, like Ben McDonald or Alex Fernandez of Miami, there would be no contest.

I can't stay for the last day of the tournament; I buy a Wichita State T-shirt on the way out. When I get back from Omaha, about three A.M. I click on the TV while getting ready for bed. When the picture comes up the first thing I see is my own face. ESPN is re-broadcasting the game from earlier in the evening, and I occupy the center of a crowd shot.

I'm glad I was there. I'm a professional baseball fan, and while you can definitely beat the hours in some other line of work, what it's hard to complain about is the work itself. Wichita has an amateur World Series, too, the NBC (National Baseball Congress).

Maybe next year, I'll try the NBC.

FOUR MEN OUT

On September 4, 1908, the Pittsburgh Pirates defeated the Chicago Cubs 1–0 when, in the bottom of the tenth, with two out and the bases loaded, Owen Wilson singled to short-center to end the game, and start a controversy. It seems the runner on first, a recent minor league call-up named Warren Gill, headed for the bench without touching second. Cub second sacker Johnny Evers, seeing this, called for the ball and stepped on the bag, completing the force and ending the inning with the game still tied. Except that umpire Hank O'Day had watched the runner from third cross the plate, and taking it for granted that the game was over, walked off the field. When Evers caught up with him and made his claim, O'Day stated that "Clarke was over the plate, so his run counted anyway."

But a subsequent—and futile—Chicago appeal to the league president, plus some excited newspaper commentary, must have planted a seed of doubt in O'Day's mind, because on September 24, in almost identical circumstances, O'Day agreed with Evers' appeal that Fred Merkle had not touched second, and thus was forced out, negating an apparent Giants victory, and setting in motion the still-debated "Merkle Boner" controversy.

I bring this up simply because people who were paying attention to the happenings in Pittsburgh on September 4 could not have been surprised at what transpired in New York less than three weeks later. By the same token, today's fans who bear in mind the events of July 1, 1989, in a run-of-the-mill game between the Brewers and Yankees, will not be astounded when another monster brouhaha breaks out that could make the Merkle Boner look like a dispute in a Sunday slow-pitch softball league.

The circumstances, you may remember, were much-bandied about in the press: Yankees with runners on first and third in the bottom of the eighth, one out. Dallas Green calls for the squeeze, but Wayne Tolleson's bunt is caught in the air by the pitcher, who casually tosses to first for the inning-ending double play. In the meantime, however, Mike Pagliarulo had broken from third, and seeing that he had no chance—or reason—to get back, simply crossed the plate and headed for the dugout to pick up his glove. And unbeknownst to everyone except plate umpire Larry Barnett, Pagliarulo's run counted. As Barnett later pointed out, citing Rule 7.10 of the Official Baseball Rules, since Pagliarulo had crossed the plate before the third out was registered, it was up to the Brewers to appeal at third, claiming Pagliarulo had neglected to tag up. Since they failed to do this, the run counted, and Barnett so indicated to the press box. The requisite portion of Rule 7.10 reads:

> Appeal plays may require an umpire to recognize an apparent 'fourth out'. If the third out is made during a play in which an appeal play is sustained on another runner, the appeal play decision takes precedence in determining the out. If there is more than one appeal during a play that ends a half-inning, the defense may elect to take the out that gives it the advantage.

As it turned out, Barnett's call was moot, since the extra Yankees run proved to be unnecessary insurance, and controversy was thus avoided. All very well, but that does not change the potential for serious turmoil in

another ball game, on another day. For no matter how well managers, coaches, and players know the rule book, I doubt that it will ever occur to any of them that, in the situation just described, an appeal must be made to nullify the run. Obviously, no one in the press box understood the implications, since Barnett's gesticulations to count the run went completely unnoticed. It's simply that the situation that produced the mystery run in New York is so rare that no one can be expected to know what to do about it on the spur of the moment; I think it's a miracle, and a tribute to Larry Barnett, that he did know what to do; I wonder how many other umpires can say in good conscience that they would have known to count the run?

And yet ironically, to make the indisputably correct decision in that situation is to court fearsome controversy. Because an unavoidable concomitant of the correct decision is the distinct possibility that no one will know what you've ruled, as was, in a different way, the case when O'Day declared Merkle out for not touching second. Most controversies, after all, are fueled by umpire's snap judgements on close plays, and are argued immediately. Even the less frequent disputes over rule interpretation, such as interference by a runner attempting to break up a double play, are haggled over instantaneously. But if a failure to appeal for the "fourth out" as mandated by Rule 7.10 results in an extra run, and no one in the dugouts or press box notices, there can be no argument—until the game is over. And then there is no cause for complaint unless the outcome has been inexplicably (to the team that neglected to appeal), shockingly altered. Barnett later stated that if he

had it to do over, he would have gestured more emphatically to the press box. But Rule 7.10 mandates that he take no action until the defensive team has left the field, and after that who is likely to be paying any attention to the plate umpire, no matter how fiercely he gesticulates?

Let's alter the scenario of the July 1 Brewers-Yankees game a bit. Suppose they're in the bottom of the eighth inning of a playoff to decide the AL East Championship. Score is tied, runners on first and third, one out, just as described earlier. Again Tolleson squeezes, the pop-up is caught and turned into an inning-ending double play. The plate umpire signals that the runner from third has scored, but again no one in the press box notices. Only this time the Brewers come to bat in the top of the ninth thinking the score still tied, and after three quick outs grab their gloves to play the bottom of the inning, only to find the umpires walking off the field. A national TV audience would sit stunned, the broadcasters at a loss to explain what happened, and the Brewers . . .

Do you think this would be enough of a controversy? Well, if planet Earth is fortunate enough to avoid nuclear holocaust or the total depletion of the ozone layer, then surely major league baseball will last long enough for an approximation of the above to some day come true. For just as Murphy's Law stipulates that anything that can go wrong will go wrong, so the rules of baseball stipulate that anything that can happen will happen. Anyway, now that the seed has been planted, as it was on that long ago day in Pittsburgh, take the time to explain to your children and grandchildren exactly what transpired in Yankee Stadium on July 1 of the year 1989. You may not live to see it, but you will at least have prepared them for a coming controversy of possibly cosmic proportions.

—M.K.
July 4, 1989

THE PAGLIA-RULO RULE

R ule 7.10 can be found in the rule book, one suspects, under the heading "Idiotic Rules," perhaps the sub-heading "Idiotic Rules—prob'ly never happen anyway." There is a good chance that some other way out of this potential quagmire may be established by the rules committee in January, and so this may be old news by the time our book hits the streets. Although Barnett apparently found the path out which is ordained by the league, it is something less than a clear path. The principle that the inning ends with the third out is, in almost all other respects, a holy principle, one of the foundations of the rule book—so why is it dispensed with here? You can't *score* a run after the third out, so why can you be required to erase one?

It seems to me that a proper set of instructions for the umpires, rather than stating that "Appeal plays may require an umpire to recognize an apparent 'fourth out,'" would begin with something like "There isn't any such thing as a fourth out," and build from that some way to avoid things like this happening. This isn't exactly difficult; all you need is a statement that says something like "a player who loses the right to occupy a base due to the end of the inning may be presumed to have been put out, even if no appeal is made." Am I missing something, or wouldn't an interpretation like that make a lot more sense than the one we have?

Speaking of which, where the hell does this appeal nonsense come from, anyway? Why don't the umpires just call you out if you leave the base too early? I assume there is a reason for it, somewhere in the early history of the game

something happened which caused it to be done this way, but what was it? This is anything but a rhetorical question, because I figure it is my responsibility to know stuff like this, and if nobody writes to tell me, I'll have to go back to the nineteenth century and try to figure it out myself, which might take a week.

Almost every screwy rule has a logical explanation. I know why you're out if you bunt foul on the third strike. I know why you're automatically out on a pop-up to the infield when a double play is in order. I may forget these things when somebody asks me on the radio, but I know what the explanation is and will remember it the next day. I have no idea why you have to appeal to get a guy called out for violating the rules.

It's an obviously unsound principle, the same one which caused the Pine Tar Flap; it doesn't add anything to the game except confusion. Think about what would happen if you enforced other rules this way . . . a basketball referee doesn't call three-second violations unless the defensive team appeals. A football referee doesn't call holding unless the defensive team complains about it. Or other baseball situations . . . a player who goes out of the baseline isn't called out unless the defensive team asks for it, let's say. How would any of this improve the game? Why don't we just change the rules to say that a player isn't entitled to tag up and advance if he leaves the base too soon, and if he does the umpire's going to call him out?

INTER-MEZZO

I'm always glad when the All-Star break arrives; it gives me the opportunity to take a step back from the game, to detoxify briefly, so to speak. You see, sometimes I fear that I've begun to take baseball too seriously. I have friends who say I've gone way over the line; can it be possible? After all, the true addict is always the last to know. Ask Wade Boggs.

Ah, but this year, to prove once and for all that said friends were grievously mistaken, I had made plans for the All-Star break that did not even include the All-Star game. You see, when an attractive, intelligent woman of my acquaintance informed me of her interest in attending a concert of the visiting Denver Symphony Orchestra, and asked would I like to make it a twosome, I accepted with alacrity, even though the performance fell on the very evening of the mid-season classic. I've always considered myself a man of taste and refinement, and it was long past time to renew my acquaintance with the finer things of life: music, profundity, aesthetics; it came as a shock to realize that I had attended no serious cultural event since last year's Three Stooges Film Festival.

So the next day I approached the box office to purchase tickets. To the smiling cashier I said, "I'd like two tickets to the Denver Symphony, upper deck, please."

She stared at me for just a moment. "Do you mean balcony, sir?"

"Yeah, sure, balcony, that's what I mean. You got two on the third base side?"

The stare lasted a trifle longer this time. "Do you mean left or right side, sir?"

By then I wasn't sure what I meant, but eventually I departed with two tickets, and a resolve to be more careful in the future. You'll be all right, I told myself; an evening of serious music will do you a world of good.

Came the night of the concert and the attractive, intelligent woman and I entered the hall, resplendent in our finest apparel. (In my case, Royals sweatshirt, Cubs jacket, Pirates hat.) Baseball seemed a million light years removed from my mind. "What a great composer Mozart was," said my beaming companion, as we made our way to the upper deck, "and what a tragedy that he died at thirty-five."

"You're right," I responded. "He could have lasted at least five more years as a DH."

"And to think," she continued, "that he died in poverty."

"Well, they didn't have free agency then; nobody made much money." Did I imagine the odd look that seemed suddenly to come over her face?

As we reached the upper deck and maneuvered toward our aisle, I restrained myself from crowing "I must be in the front row." But once seated, try as I might I could not resist the temptation to turn to the elderly gentleman seated on my right and observe, "Good seats, eh buddy?" He favored me with a grimace and I glanced about for some time before realizing that no beer or peanut vendors were going to appear.

Meanwhile, my companion was examining her scorecard and exclaimed, "All right, they're playing Schubert's *Unfinished.*"

"Unfinished, why is it unfinished? Was there a rain delay?"

"He only wrote half of it, two of the four movements; no one knows why."

"He must have been ahead going to the bottom of the fifth, and it started raining," I mused. "That's the only explanation. But then it would go into the record book as a complete symphony, and you say it's unfinished. I don't get it."

"Mike, get this. Shut up already."

So I subsided for the duration of the concert, which I must admit was exciting, especially at the last when they filled the playing field with singers for Beethoven's Choral Symphony. After numerous curtain calls and bravos my companion and I wended our way out into the uncharacteristically cool July evening. "It was a great concert," I observed as I clasped her hand to mine. "But there's one thing I'm curious about."

"I'm almost afraid to ask," she responded suspiciously.

"It's the male singers in the chorus. Do you suppose they're like anybody else, and go out and tie one on once in a while?"

"Well, they're only human," she shrugged.

"Sure, and suppose they tie one on before doing the Choral Symphony sometime, and they come out on the field staggering all around, knocking the sheet music flying, do you think they might have to somehow secure the music to the stands, to prevent further chaos?" I seized her passionately in a bear-like embrace.

"I'm warning you, Mike," she said, extricating herself from my vice-like grip. "I'm not going to like this."

"All I meant was," I expostulated, "that if that ever happened, the manager would find himself in the bottom of the ninth . . ."

"Oh no," she moaned.

". . . with the basses loaded . . ."

"Oh shit," she groaned.

"... and the score tied," I concluded triumphantly.

After a moment's pregnant silence, during which I congratulated myself on plugging the gap with another *bon mot,* she said quietly, "Mike, I have good news for you, and bad news."

"Okay," I replied. "Let's hear it."

"First off, you are a certifiable, ready for detoxification baseball junkie."

"I guess you're right," I nodded. "I never realized it until tonight. It was always something that happened to other people. But it's nothing I can't overcome. Now how about the good news?"

"That was the good news, mister. The bad news is you're an asshole." And with that she turned and walked away, leaving me once again stranded on third representing the tying run. Oh well, I thought, as I wandered disconsolately through the darkness, there are plenty of other attractive, intelligent free agents out there; some day I'll sign one to a long-term contract. In the meantime, I resolved never again to attend a symphony concert in the company of a woman. Obviously, classical music makes them bitchy.

—M.K.
July 13, 1989

THE GERBIL STRIKES BACK

It was a remarkable and totally unexpected turnabout by the Cubs in the nationally-televised game of July 20 from Wrigley Field. The Giants had taken a seemingly commanding 3–0 lead into the bottom of the ninth, and Steve Bedrosian was on the mound to close the deal. But with the aid of a wind-blown fly ball misplayed by Brett Butler and an idiotic throw by Candy Maldonado, the Cubs rallied to tie and send the game into extras.

All that was exciting enough, but the real fun began in the bottom of the eleventh. Lloyd McClendon singled, and as Dwight Smith stepped in, Giant infielders began creeping in to field the expected sacrifice. Only there was no sacrifice; Smith grounded sharply to shortstop for an easy double play, and the inning was dead. In the meantime, the TV camera switched to Don Zimmer in the dugout and caught him in animated, angry conversation with a fan in the first row, who had loudly questioned Popeye's choice of tactics. It was only after Curtis Wilkerson singled to keep the inning alive that I saw the method in Zimmer's apparent madness. Because having cleared the bench of all substitutes other than catcher Joe Girardi, Zimmer had little choice but to let pitcher Les Lancaster bat. So had Smith sacrificed McClendon to second, the Giants would surely have walked Wilkerson to get Lancaster to the plate. In other words, Zimmer had a choice of batting his pitcher with two on and one out, or getting the needed run out of the first three batters before the pitcher threw everything out of whack. I think he made the right choice, I'll wager Roger Craig thinks he made the right choice, and upon reflection, I'll wager even the vociferous front-row fan saw the wisdom of Zimmer's action. Not that it ended up mattering, you may recall, as Lancaster, batting with a man on first and two outs, knocked all strategic thinking into a cocked hat with a line drive double that rattled about and died in the left-field foul area, giving the Cubs a near miraculous victory in a season that has seen more than its share of same.

After a near miraculous win, I suppose it's time to ask: Is this a miracle season in the making? I'm still inclined to think not. The pitching remains remarkably solid, but it's still easy to find the fault lines in both the offense and defense, plus Andre Dawson's trick knee could finish him for the season at any moment. So I don't look for an NL East Championship this year, but then neither do I look for another classic late season fold as has become almost expected in the Windy City these past two decades. I think more likely than a fold is a can't quite get over the hump, just a couple of horses short performance, such as the Mets turned in '84; a harbinger, if you will, of things to come.

The reason I think this team wouldn't fold, and to me he's a major story of this season, is Don Zimmer. I'm not ashamed to admit that I used to laugh at this guy—I had plenty of company. Whereas resident geniuses like Sparky and Weaver get written up and immortalized by the likes of Angell and Boswell, Zimmer's public image has had the misfortune of coming directly from Spaceman Bill Lee. Of course, there's also the matter of the classic '78 Bosox collapse, when under Zimmer's reins a thirteen-and-a-half-game lead melted away to a three-and-a-half-game deficit seemingly overnight. But what almost everyone conveniently forgets is that the Sox battled back from the dead to force that now-famous playoff, and if not for Lou Piniella's literal blind stab of Jerry Remy's base hit, Zimmer might today be credited with fueling the most unlikely resurrection since Lazarus. It simply was not to be, and instead he became "The Gerbil," a ridiculous figure to many, a buffoon, a laughingstock—who won over ninety games three years running, and had nothing to show for it.

You know when we should have known better? When Roger Craig hired him to be third base coach. Sure, plenty of coaches are hired just to keep the manager company, but there's no reason to believe that Roger Craig operates that way. Behind the avuncular "humm baby" facade, Roger Craig, like another famous Giants manager, comes to kill you. If he wanted Don Zimmer to be his third base coach, it should have occurred to us that perhaps Zim had a keen mind perched atop his bloated body after all. Maybe it would have if not for the fact that he was suddenly spirited away to manage the Cubs by none other than his old high school chum Jim Frey. Was ever a managerial appointment greeted with so much derision, this side of Steinbrennerland?? Don Zimmer obviously hasn't had terrific luck all his life, what with the metal plate in his head, and losing that never-to-be-forgotten playoff, but here he is being promoted to one of baseball's elite jobs, and already people are snickering. (Naturally, it must be borne in mind—and once again I plead guilty on all counts—that the same people who have been

contemptuous of Zimmer tend also to be card-carrying Jim Frey detractors, in spite of his undeniably impressive credentials.) Sure, the old boy network strikes again. Recycle Popeye one more time; anything to avoid hiring Billy Williams or some other minority candidate. The Cubs are hopeless anyway. At least Zimmer will be good for a few laughs.

Well, I guess there's no doubt who's laughing now, and he also has the strategic advantage of laughing last. And between chortles he's managed to put together a pitching staff that need take a backseat to no one, as well as work around injuries to his entire starting outfield by phasing in the young talent that Dallas Green went to the headsman insisting was already in the pipeline. And if you've been fortunate enough to see many Cubs games, you know that "The Gerbil" has suddenly become the master of strategy. When he calls for a pitchout, the runner breaks. When he puts on the hit and run, the batter always makes contact. When an intentional walk is given, the next hitter always fails. At least for '89 we should retire those other nicknames and call him "The Rotund Tactician," or better yet, simply "Midas." It would be appropriate for a man who's living a fairy tale season, a man who's outlasted those of us who so wrongly thought his only touch was fecal rather than golden.

—M.K.
July 21, 1989

In retrospect, I don't know why it took me so long to believe in the Cubs. It may be that I watch them so often, most every day, and familiarity builds if not contempt at least a sense of ordinariness. The season virtually ended in Chicago on September 18, and after that series with the Mets, which was split, there could be little doubt that the Cubs were the better team.

I think my reluctance to believe in the Cubs came from focusing too much on two key members of the team: manager Don Zimmer, and reliever Mitch Williams. Zimmer is most interesting when talking about building a winning team. I'm paraphrasing a pregame show, but I remember one day Zimmer said that "We knew we'd be criticized for trading some people, but I didn't like for the younger players to walk into the locker room in August and see signs saying 'So many days to hunting season.' I thought we had to get rid of that kind of thing."

So I was wondering who had the sign up in the clubhouse, saying how many days it was to hunting season . . . let's see, Lee Smith, no, Rafael Palmeiro, no, Manny Trillo, probably not, Jamie Moyer, doubt it. It's got to be one of two people—Jody Davis, or Goose Gossage.

I can understand that, and I'd have to agree with Zimmer; if it was my ball club and somebody put up a sign like that, I'd get rid of him, too. I mean, you can tell him to take down the sign, but he's going to be the same person anyway. I give Zimmer and Frey a good deal of credit for reading their players and doing a kind of "intensity triage."

As a game manager also, there was about Don Zimmer going into 1989 a sense of the freedom of impending death. I think Zimmer recognized on some level that this could be his last season on the field, and that therefore he was going to do things *his* way, and if people didn't like it the hell with 'em. I have never seen a manager do so many things in a season which exposed him to second-guessing, and I have never seen so many decisions which seemed irrational at the moment they were made look brilliant an inning later. I'm not betting on this to continue another year.

But the Cubs were not lucky. They were a better team than the Mets, a lot better. The difference was more than the six games by which the Cubs beat the Mets. The most striking contrast is in the right side of the infield, where the Cubs throw Grace and Sandberg against Magadan and Jefferies. It is as difficult as choosing between Kirstie Alley and Bea Arthur. Grace and Sandberg are wonderful defensive players, hit home runs, steal bases, hit .300, and walk more often than they strike out. Magadan and Jefferies are inexperienced, mistake-prone, and will never be as good.

Sandberg and Grace were also the only Cubs players who played regularly, the only ones with 500 at bats. The thing about Zimmer in '78, where he can be faulted, is that in '78 he had eight regulars, and he wrote their names in the lineup every day right up to the debacle and then right through it. Few people will see it, but injuries often do work to a team's advantage. Injuries gave Walton and Dwight Smith and McClendon and Wrona and Girardi a chance to play, and they played well—but equally important, injuries gave Dawson and Berryhill and Dunston a little time off.

When the Cubs had no lights there was a dispute about whether this was a detriment to the team, in that it contributed to fatigue. I always believed that the pattern of evidence, fairly stated, was more consistent with the belief that there was a "sun fatigue" than with the belief that there wasn't. But what happens when an obstacle to success is removed? Of course; the team which had had the obstacle before is going to spurt forward.

It was a cool summer in the Midwest, and that may also have been a factor.

Can the Cubs win again in '90? I'd bet against them winning, just as I would have all last year—but I would bet that they do remain in the race. I don't believe in Mitch Williams as a relief ace. I don't believe Zimmer is a managerial genius. The Cubs don't have a left-handed starter, and they don't have as much power as they ought to have to play in Wrigley Field.

But Jerome Walton is going to have a better year this year than he did last year. I don't believe that any of the young players—Grace, Dwight Smith, Berryhill—did anything in '89 they can't improve on in '90. I don't believe Bielecki is a fluke, although you never know if he'll be healthy or not. I see the Cubs as the second-best team in the division.

QUICKIE

On Friday, July 28, at Royals Stadium, two teams which desperately needed a win went at each other tooth and nail for thirteen innings.

In front of me was a family with a deaf father. A small girl sat on her mother's lap and signed "I hug you," and then did. She asked for some chewing gum, or at least so I understood; her mother said no. It seemed at the moment a vastly better way to communicate than by making noise.

The game was a scorer's nightmare in which runners were caught off base, occasioning wild throws, bringing about further advancement of the runner, leading to future mistakes by fielders. This happened twice. Wathan and Robinson engaged in a duel to find the most irrational situation in which to order an intentional walk.

Willie Wilson singled in the ninth to tie the game. "Give me five," signed the deaf man. The little girl slapped his outstretched palm in glee.

The Royals gave the O's a gift run in the thirteenth. "They ain't no thirty-eight thousand here now," an old man said to his middle-aged son on the way out.

"Wish I'd gone home," grumbled the son.

Some went home early, and some went home surly.

LET'S GET FAMOUS FLOYDS

As the Cubs make their improbable run at the NL East title, and all eyes—and dials—are presumably turned to WGN, Chicago's very own Channel 9, a couple of things puzzle me. First, if the Cubs are such a hot item, why don't we see more real commercials during their broadcasts? Surely you've noticed the high percentage of what I consider vanity plugs, *i.e.* commercials touting their own insipid selection of reruns. If I had a dollar for every time they've run their "Famous Floyds of History" (with no mention of Floyd Bevans or Floyd Bannister) spot for *The Andy Griffith Show*, I could now retire. This week I have memorized the plug for *Let's Get Harry*, which I gather is a third-rate action movie rather than an insidious plot for revenge by Milo Hamilton. You see my point, don't you? If the Cubs are suddenly all the rage—and they are—why can't WGN sell more commercial time? You don't expect me to believe that they choose to tout their own schlock for nothing, do you?

Which brings me to another—and more important—point. If WGN (like the Cubs, part of the *Chicago Tribune* empire) can't—or won't—sell the maximum commercial time when the Cubs are at their zenith, then what was the sense of fighting to the death for lights at Wrigley Field? Certainly not to stimulate attendance. During the summer, win or lose, day or night, the Cubs are going to draw. Night games in April and September might help attendance, but not if the weather refuses to cooperate, as it

often doesn't, and anyway it's apparent that most night games are being reserved for the warmer months. So what then, I ask you, is the purpose of prime-time play at Wrigley if not to sell the more lucrative evening commercial time, and make the *Tribune,* the players, and Harry all richer and happier? And why isn't it happening? I've tuned in at night, and seen just as many "Famous Floyds" as during the day. This doesn't make sense. Did every advertiser in the world read the pre-season line and decide that, since the Cubs were no contender, it would be a waste to buy time on their broadcasts, day or night? I can see that, sort of, but what about now? Shouldn't eager admen be lined up for blocks, waving six and seven figure certified checks in their hands, begging for a chance to get their products hawked between innings? And you don't mean to tell me that WGN turns them down, that they plan all their advertising prior to the season, and will not deviate from it by so much as one iota, even with millions of dollars up for grabs? That they can't get by with just a few less "Famous Floyds" in exchange for megabucks? Oh, wait a minute! Of course, I get it now. That's how you get sponsors for insipid reruns of *The Andy Griffith Show* to begin with, promise them that you'll plug the show beyond all endurance during ballgames. How fiendishly clever. Well, God forbid that advertisers for the insipid *Andy Griffith Show* be offended, but there are probably a few baseball fans in Chicago who feel that the destruction of the noble tradition of day baseball only in the friendly confines was a rather steep price to pay for a result no more significant than keeping schlock TV pitchmen satisfied. Wouldn't it seem much more

in keeping with the times if we were at least being sold down the river for corporations that are the targets of leveraged buy-outs?

—M.K.
August 9, 1989

THE BUCS STOPPED

Did some despondent Pittsburgh Pirates executive, deep in the dark days of 1985, strike a deal with the devil that promised an almost miraculous turnaround, but which, unbeknownst to the exec, would expire suddenly in August of '88, leaving Satan in charge for an indeterminate length of time? You remember the situation that existed at that latter date, don't you, even if it now seems pre-history? Thanks mostly to the Mets spinning their wheels, the Buccaneers were still in the pennant race, GM Syd Thrift was acclaimed a mastermind, and the recently moribund franchise's future seemed brighter than a thousand suns. That was in early August; by the end of the month the aroused Mets had drawn clear of the outmanned Corsairs, which was not a major surprise, and Thrift had apparently lost interest in running the club, which was. When I say he'd lost interest, I mean he seems to have made up his mind that he wanted out, but preferred to leave in the guise of a sainted martyr pilloried by infidels. How else to explain the late August deal (with the Freebooters by then comfortably out of the race) that sent legitimate prospect Tommy Gregg to the Braves for declining, high-salaried veteran Ken Oberkfell? I don't know what more Thrift could have done to enrage the Pirates owners; paying Oberkfell's salary would tax the generous spirit of Saint Francis of Assisi. But it was an opportunity, apparently, for El Syd to scream from the very rooftops about owner interference, how after single-handedly refloating the sunken Pirates ship, he was being made to operate with hands tied behind his back, hamstrung by greedy profiteers who knew nothing about baseball, and by God he would not stand for it, and didn't. Well, the folks who own the Pirates may have an excessive interest in the bottom line, and they may indeed know next to nothing about baseball, but how much of an expert do you have to be to realize that the acquisition of Ken Oberkfell, with nothing at stake, is literally hundreds of thousands of dollars pissed away? If Syd Thrift threw down the gauntlet and declared "I have the right to trade for a Ken Oberkfell whenever I want, and you have no say in the matter," then I can only conclude that he wanted—and richly deserved—to be fired. The irony, of course, is that he landed on his feet, working for a man who would never dream of interfering in the day to day operations of a ball club—George Steinbrenner.

And Thrift's departure, it seems, was only the beginning. He surely planned on leaving a martyr, but I wonder if even he understood the extent to which, less than a year later, he could shout "After me, the deluge." For a deluge it has surely been. Spec Richardson's record for incompetent trades in the early Houston years is probably still safe, but Thrift's replacement, Larry "The Sixteenth" Doughty is trying to give Spec a run for his money. The Pirates need help at first base, but Randy Milligan is cleverly palmed off on the wretched Orioles. The Mariners never do anything right; if they're willing to trade Rey Quinones for Mike Dunne and some prospects, make the move before they change their minds. So what if it's the second shortstop you've traded for this season; just because Jay Bell couldn't win the job in shortstop-desperate Cleveland is no reason to think he can't do it here. And when catching help is needed, it's always best to turn to a thirty-seven-year-old, about to be cut loose veteran like Alan Ashby, even if you have to dispose of a seven years younger starting outfielder in exchange. In fairness it should be acknowledged that the deluge that has inundated Doughty has done more than a little structural damage to Thrift's reputation as a mastermind. Mike Dunne, it turned out, was a one year wonder, and for this year at least Andy Van Slyke is just an ordinary ballplayer. And Jeff Robinson, while eleven years younger than the departed Rick Reuschel, may need every one of those years to match Big Daddy's accomplishments in the past three.

Yes, of course, there are some things that no one can be blamed for. What can you do when Jim Gott blows out his arm in the first week? Or when Van Slyke and Mike LaValliere go down shortly thereafter? But Bill Landrum has emerged as a capable closer, Van Slyke and LaValliere are now healthy, and the team is not appreciably better. I'm reluctant to drag Jim Leyland into this, but while we're at it, what is it going to take to convince him that Bobby Bonilla is no third baseman? On the other hand, if he's waiting for Doughty to trade for a hot cornerman before making a move with Bonilla, he probably has every right to pray that the status quo holds. Because for one full year now, every change the Pirates have made has been an unmitigated disaster. Leyland can be forgiven if he just wants to hunker down for the rest of the season, ride out the storm, and start from scratch in '90. Surely the curse that's hanging over this club will be lifted by then. Everything can go wrong for only so long—ask the Baltimore Orioles. Unless someone in the upper echelons of the organization really did make a deal with the devil, and the devil insisted on a long-term, no-cut contract.

—M.K.
August 10, 1989

The indicators series says that the Pirates have to be better in 1990, and the logic here is unassailable. The Pirates figure to improve because, in order of importance:

1. They have a young team,
2. Teams which decline sharply in one year tend to come back the next, and
3. They played better late in the season.

The Pirates are a classic illustration of why a team which declines one year should improve the next. When a team has a good year, they don't address their remaining weaknesses. When they have an off year, they clear away the dead wood and redouble their efforts. A year ago, when Sid Bream did pretty much nothing at first base, the Pirates told themselves that he was a good glove and really all right as a hitter. They won't do that again. Instead, they have already signed two free-agent pitchers to improve their odds.

When a team drops off by ten games, generally several players have off seasons, and generally some of them come back the next year. Andy Van Slyke and Jose Lind, possibly Jim Gott if he returns, will contribute more to the Pirates in 1990 than they did in 1989.

When a team has an off year, they will still generally get something out of it. When Jim Gott was hurt, the Pirates had to take a look at Bill Landrum, and found out that he could pitch.

I got to wondering who would likely be the "Kevin Mitchell of 1990," who might explode on the league. The best candidate, in my opinion: Bobby Bonilla.

All of that makes it extremely likely that the Pirates will have a better year this season. That doesn't mean that I like the team or think they know what they're doing. The front office hasn't done anything that makes any sense since Syd Thrift left—or actually, as Mike points out, for a month before.

I'm not criticizing Jim Leyland, but he hasn't impressed me yet, either. The Pirates used twenty-three pitchers last year, which basically tells me that Leyland doesn't know what it is he is looking for in a pitcher.

Look at this lineup, which Leyland used on August 26 against Cincinnati:

Hatcher, rf
Bell, ss
Van Slyke, cf
Bonilla, 3b
Bonds, rf
Redus, lb
LaValliere, c
King, 2b
Pitcher

Billy Hatcher, whose on-base percentage was .277, led off.

Jay Bell, a right-handed hitter who strikes out in almost twenty percent of his at bats, batted second, as he did most of September; his on-base percentage was .307.

Andy Van Slyke batted third; his on-base percentage was .308, but I can understand that because he's a better hitter than that, particularly against a right-handed hitter.

Bobby Bonilla batted cleanup; his on-base percentage was .358. Barry Bonds batted fifth; his was .351.

Then comes Gary Redus. Redus is an awesome leadoff man—in fact, he and Tim Raines are the only players in the majors who have "leadoff skills" comparable to Rickey Henderson. He draws walks, hits doubles and triples and homers, and steals bases. He's not as good as Rickey—nobody has ever been as good as Rickey—and he's had trouble staying in the lineup because of his defense, but he is truly a phenomenal leadoff hitter. Last year his on-base percentage was .372. He was hitting sixth.

LaValliere was hitting seventh; his OBP was .406.

That's right—taking his first seven spots, Leyland had done an almost perfect job of concentrating all of the people who don't get on base at the top of the order.

In mid-August, Leyland moved Barry Bonds out of the leadoff spot, and began searching for a new leadoff man. His leadoff men day by day beginning on August 17 were John Cangelosi, Bonds, Billy Hatcher, Hatcher, Hatcher, Hatcher, R. J. Reynolds, Reynolds, Hatcher, Hatcher, Reynolds, Hatcher, Reynolds, Reynolds, Hatcher, Reynolds, Albert Hall, Hall, Hatcher, Hatcher, Hatcher, Hatcher, Cangelosi, Hatcher, Cangelosi, Hall, and Hall. Then he gave up and went back to Barry Bonds.

Redus was in the lineup almost all of that time—he was hitting third, sixth, seventh. Leyland was desperately searching for a leadoff man, and he had Rickey Henderson Redus in the lineup, and he never thought to give him a look.

I don't know, but I don't think this is a good sign.

I've got to pick the Pirates to have a better year, because they're a better team than they were last year and Bobby Bonilla is terrific—but I'm not picking them to win anything.

SOUR MUSIC

The story of the '89 Minnesota Twins is the story of Frank Viola and his multimillion dollar contract, and not surprisingly, it's a story without a happy ending. Don't get me wrong: Even if Viola had improbably agreed to pitch for less money and avoided controversy, the Twins would almost certainly have been no factor in the AL West race; Allan Anderson and Shane Rawley faltered out of the gate every bit as badly as Viola—the pitching in general was a shambles. But in exploring the brouhaha over Viola's contract, what's interesting is that no matter what angle you examine it from, whether your sentiments tend to lie with management or with the players, no matter how accurate your hindsight, it seems impossible to arrive at a definitive answer as to what the Twins and Viola should have done to make themselves, or someone—anyone—happy.

Part of the problem would seem to be that neither the Twins nor Viola were fully in control of their own destiny. The signings of first Dwight Gooden, then Roger Clemens and Orel Hershiser to long-term megabucks contracts previously unheard of for pitchers automatically upped the ante, as Viola had every right to consider himself the equal of those three Titans. As Casey Stengel would say, you could look it up. And since Viola was unquestionably their equal on the mound, it was not exactly illogical of him to conclude that he should be treated as their equal at the bank. Never mind that some disinterested observers thought the contracts

awarded the Gang of Three outlandish, if not potentially ruinous to their teams, and forget that sudden arm trouble for Gooden and Clemens must have Joe McIlvaine and Lou Gorman shaking in their boots, could Andy MacPhail reasonably have said: "Sorry, Frank, but the money being paid to those other guys is ridiculous. We know you're as good as they are, but we're simply not prepared to match that outrageous standard."? Okay, MacPhail *could* have said that, and it certainly would have simplified things for everyone, but remember that he's still operating in the very large shadow of the Ghost of Parsimony Past, Calvin Griffith. Griffith said approximately the above to many players, watched them depart for greener pastures, won no championships in the free agency era, and came to be abominated by most Twins fans, who voted with their feet by staying away from the ball park in droves. Given those circumstances, I don't see how MacPhail could have refused to negotiate seriously. So in the end it seemed that both sides were locked in: Viola by salaries paid to his contemporaries that he had no hand in negotiating, and MacPhail by a team history that he had no part in creating.

In the meantime, what of the attitude of the fans? Here's where another layer of complexity is added. Because what the fans want is to win. Right now. This year. And yet at the same time, they rail at the huge salaries that even mediocre players command. They want some sanity returned to the wage scale. Is it surprising then that the club owner who most wants to win right now and damn the expense, George Steinbrenner, and the owner who tries hardest to hold the line on salaries,

George Argyros, are both objects of scorn and derision? And given those contradictory attitudes by the people who after all pay both MacPhail's and Viola's salaries, is it any wonder that both sides waffled when it finally came time to strike a deal?

In this case, after Viola spurned a 7.9 million offer that reportedly equaled Hershiser's deal, the fans turned on him savagely. Rightly or wrongly, he was now perceived as a greedy mercenary. The fact that he was from New York, and had none too subtly expressed an interest in Met and Yankee long green didn't help. By the time he'd gone 0–4 out of the gate, the situation was probably beyond salvaging, although both sides tried, and a deal was eventually hammered out. But you never got the impression that any faction was truly satisfied; not MacPhail, not Viola, certainly not the fans, who watched Sweet Music continue to struggle. Even the players professed themselves disconcerted, and not surprisingly considering that Kirby Puckett and Kent Hrbek faced possibly a similar ordeal at the end of '89. Only pennant contention could have cleared the air, and when the last hope of that faded in late July, Andy MacPhail elected to cut his losses and play for the future. No one much blamed him.

Does anyone have any solutions to the problems herein enumerated? How can an owner get off the accelerating salaries escalator without seeming an Ebenezer Scrooge? How can a player demand a salary equivalent to that of his peers without seeming like a bloodsucking parasite? How can the fans register their opinion without seeming like a herd of nattering, know-nothing yahoos? I don't know the answers, I only know this: In the case of the Minnesota Twins vs. Frank Viola, there was no winner. Everyone involved ended up looking at called strike three. Can't we do any better than this?

—M.K.
August 11

IGNORE THIS ARGUMENT

May the Designated Deity strike me dead, but I have finally thought of an argument for the Designated Hitter Rule that almost makes sense. I've never for a moment bought any of the standard rationalizations in its favor. Yes, it stimulates the offense, but—assuming that the offense needs to be stimulated—there are approximately six million better ways of doing it: Bring in the fences, lower the mound, squeeze the strike zone, diddle with the ball. I've never found the mere act of a pitcher batting to be terminally mind-numbing, as some claim, but if it is, why not, as Craig Wright suggested in *The Diamond Appraised,* simply eliminate the pitcher from the batting order and go with an eight man lineup? This would surely boost the offense, yet at the same time remove the superfluous player with no defensive responsibility. Of course it can be argued that the eight man batting order would quickly produce wholesale chaos in the record book, and that's unquestionably a valid point; in the end it comes down to which do you prefer, an eight man lineup that makes a mockery of the hallowed records, or a designated hitter, that makes a mockery of the game? Not that we have to have either.

But after a summer of watching the Kansas City Royals struggle to put nine healthy bodies on the field at any given time, I began to think back to the halcyon days of Hal McRae, and how their use of the DH has evolved since then. Remember when the Royals were the envy of the American League for almost ten years running because they could write in the name Hal McRae at DH, and forget about it? No other team has been able to find anyone resembling a ten-year DH, although it should be noted that many were content to use the slot as a safety net for an aging star (*e.g.,* first Yaz, and later Jim Rice in Boston). The use of the DH to prolong the careers of superannuated sluggers was an argument both for and against it when the rule first appeared (you still hear sentiments such as "too bad Johnny Bench couldn't have DHed and had a longer career" expressed regularly; "too bad Dave Kingman was able to DH and have a longer career" is more in line with my feelings) but no one, then or now, seems to have noticed that what the DH is really good for, especially in the era of the lively disabled list, is getting injured players back into the offense sooner. The '89 Royals had hoped to write Pat Tabler in at DH, and forget about it. As it turned out, casualties necessitated his blundering about in the outfield almost from the first, while the DH became basically a rehab slot for whoever was recovering from their latest injury: first Brett, later Bo Jackson, and as I write, Danny Tartabull. A Hal McRae even in his DH prime would be siphoning valuable at bats away from the rotating wounded stars. And if you look around the American League, you'll see the same thing happening elsewhere. Dwight Evans, rebounding from back trouble, is DHing in Boston; Matt Nokes and Dan Pasqua, fresh off the DL, are getting some licks at DH; so did Kent Hrbek and Jose Canseco earlier. In fact, an all-inclusive list of players easing back into the lineup via the DH would prove lengthy indeed. And it makes perfect sense. What

manager wants to leave his luminaries on the sidelines any longer than he has to? And yet why risk injury reoccurrence by forcing them into the field prematurely, especially in the age of artificial turf? The designated hitter rule seems perfectly designed to resolve this dilemma.

The question remains, however, will the dilemma always exist? Is the trend toward fifteen- and twenty-one-man disabled lists, one of the most remarked on stories of '89, irreversible, or is it merely a fluke, like '87 was for home runs? My opinion is that, for whatever reason, the lively DL is here to stay, much to the disgruntlement of those who remember the good old days when a player would routinely shake off four broken ribs, a separated shoulder, a dislocated toe, and a mild case of beriberi to go four for four in the big game. If I'm right, the trend in DHs should be toward Pat Tabler types, who can help out—after a fashion—in the field while a not quite recovered regular flails away at DH, and away from Greg Luzinski and Dave Kingman types, who cannot. One final question: Now that even the baseball establishment is beginning to concede that artificial turf is harder on the body than grass, and given the fact that the preponderance of rugs are in the National League, can't it be argued that the wrong league is utilizing the designated hitter? Remember the shock when the '60 Tigers and Indians pulled off the first ever manager's trade? Maybe the time has come for the first ever inter-league rules trade.

—M.K.
August 16, 1989

THE YOUNG AND THE DEFENSE-LESS

At the outset of the '89 season, three teams committed themselves to live or die with young pitchers. The three were the Baltimore Orioles, Atlanta Braves, and Chicago White Sox, and as it turned out, none of them backed off. Sure you see a Jerry Reuss here, a Dave Schmidt there, but basically these are young staffs, especially the rotations. The results the three teams obtained, though, differed radically, and in retrospect it's easy to see why. The Orioles obtained outfielders such as Brady Anderson and Mike Devereaux who, whatever their offensive shortcomings, can run down any ball; went with slick-fielding rookie Craig Worthington at third base (resisting the impulse to transfer Cal Ripken, Jr., and risk unproven Juan Bell at short); and stayed with defensively adept but offensively dubious Billy Ripken at second. The result of a hungry young staff (unexpectedly supplemented by the long-abandoned Kevin Hickey) supported by a superb defense has been unexpected pennant contention.

The Atlanta Braves have probably the best young pitchers of the three, but the defense backing them has its weak spots. The Braves could not resist the temptation to switch power-hitting Ron Gant to third base, which resulted in both offensive and defensive disaster, hardly mitigated on the occasions Darrell Evans subbed for him. I yield to no one in my admiration for Lonnie Smith's accomplishments, but he still is not a good outfielder.

And returning Dale Murphy to center was surely a mistake; one recognized and addressed nicely with the mid-season trade for Oddibe McDowell. If Jeff Blauser can settle in comfortably at third, and Oddibe has at last found a home, the Braves should see considerable defensive improvement. And the stock of Glavine, Smoltz, Lilliquist, *et al.,* should continue to rise.

And then there were the White Sox, with more generic young pitchers than they knew what to do with, and no defense to support any of them. Who else has so many natural designated hitters? Kittle, Calderon, Walker, and arguably Pasqua; the irony being, of course, that until Harold Baines was traded, none of these born DHs ever DHed. It's almost as if Larry Himes thought that a radical rule change was about to be instituted, allowing teams to put their nine best hitters in the batting order and their nine best defenders in the field—platoon baseball. Along with the problem of too many DHs was the long-running drama of no third baseman, the curse of Buck Weaver if you will. Eddie Williams started the year there, but soon proved unacceptable despite a decent batting average; Carlos Martinez occupies the hot corner now, but it's generally conceded that this is but a holding action until Robin Ventura is ready. Steve Lyons and Fred Manrique had their chance at second base; the arrival of Scott Fletcher has probably plugged at least this hole long term.

But Larry Himes is never likely to plug many holes until he realizes that he has to make choices, and that he seems unwilling to do. Now that he's traded Baines, he's down to a mere three or four DHs; is it asking too much for he and Jeff Torborg to pick out one and dispense with the rest?

Carlton Fisk can conveniently spell whoever they keep. And maybe they could quit yanking pitchers back and forth between Chicago and Vancouver. (Is this what Torborg learned in a decade of coaching for George Steinbrenner?) if they would put a defense on the field that could decently support any of them. There is some evidence that Himes might be beginning to see the light; the arrival of Fletcher is a good sign. Daryl Boston, too, has been logging more time in the outfield; I've given up hope that he'll ever hit, but he certainly improves the defense. And now the highly touted Lance Johnson has been recalled; reportedly he will not aid the defense, but his raw speed on a conspicuously slow-footed club is badly needed regardless.

I can't escape the feeling, though, that Himes and Torborg will find some way to gum it all up again. Calderon, after a brief trial at first (Greg Walker has seemingly never bounced back after his seizure), is again cluttering up the outfield.

Maybe Himes is just biding his time until the offseason, maybe we'll all come out of hibernation next spring and gaze with wonder at an outfield full of legitimate fly chasers, and, miracle of miracles, only one designated hitter. But don't spend your long winter's nap dreaming about it.

—M.K.
August 18, 1989

As an analyst of the game I believe absolutely in two contradictory statements: one, that the basic responsibility to prevent the opposition from scoring runs has got to fall on the shoulders of the pitcher, and two, that a great deal of what people think is pitching is actually defense.

When those two articles of faith come into conflict, I know in my own mind where to draw the line. I would have difficulty producing any systematic evidence to support what I believe, but what the hell—who in baseball, other than me, feels the need to produce systematic evidence to support anything he says? In choosing when to use a glove man and when to use a hitter and take a defensive risk, what I believe is

1. A good defense means more to a finesse pitcher than it does to a power pitcher.
2. A good defense is far more critical to a young pitcher than it is to a veteran.

Once more, since young pitchers tend to be power pitchers and old pitchers tend to be finesse pitchers, my resolution of the issue is self-contradictory.

One of the hardest things for a baseball team to do is to make the transition from having young arms, as Atlanta and Baltimore and the White Sox have, to having young pitchers. There are lots of guys with good arms, but very few of them ever become outstanding pitchers. Obviously, the Orioles did the right thing last year in going with their best defensive option. To me, the biggest reason that was the right thing to do is confidence—not the cheap, transitory thing that announcers talk about, the thing that a player has today because he had two hits yesterday, but the genuine article, the knowledge that you can succeed because you know *how* to do the job. If a few balls scoot by a fielder's glove, a young pitcher is going to start to feel that he has to make perfect pitches, that he has to hit the black. He's going to overthrow, he's going to work behind the hitters, and he's going to be out of the league. If you can convince that same young pitcher that his defense will take care of him, then sometimes just that knowledge will be enough to knock a run off his ERA. That, I believe, is what happened to Jay Ballard last year—simply that he went from being a pitcher who believed that he had to make perfect pitches (8–12, 4.40 ERA) to being a pitcher who realized that he didn't (18–8, 3.43).

Now if it's Bobby Witt, that's a different story; Bobby Witt is going to win a lot of games before he learns to rely on his defense. If it's a veteran finesse pitcher, like Bud Black or Jerry Reuss, that's a different story; those guys have got to be expected to deal with the defense they've got without forgetting how to pitch.

I can't justify keeping a glove man who doesn't hit, like Jose Lind or John Shelby, in the lineup—for most teams. I don't think that the runs they save on defense make up for the runs they cost you on offense. But for a team like Baltimore, Chicago, or Atlanta, which is trying to put together a pitching staff—different rule. Then I think you *can* justify keeping those guys in the lineup, because the runs they save afield will pay a dividend in getting the young pitchers over that terrible hump.

If the White Sox are going to build a pitching staff, then, they have to get some of those damned DH's off the field, and go shake the glove tree. When Melido Perez was in the Southern League in 1987, he walked only twenty men in 134 innings, a fairly astonishing control record for a twenty-one-year-old. In his first year in the American League, 1988, his control record was decent. Last year he walked ninety men in 183 innings.

What has happened to his control is obvious; he has come to feel that he has to make perfect pitches. If the White Sox would put a defense on the field Melido's control would mysteriously return, and his ERA would drop from 5.01 down to the threes. Hillegas would benefit to a similar extent.

As a relic of my previous career, I have a series of six indicators which I use to help predict how teams will do in 1990. The six indicators are based on six known and demonstrable facts, four of which are

1. Everybody tends to gravitate toward the center. Losing teams tend to improve; winning teams tend to decline.
2. Resistance in baseball is much stronger than momentum. A team which improves in one year tends to decline in the next. A team which declines in one year tends to recover in the next.
3. Young teams tend to improve. Old teams tend to decline.
4. Teams which play well late in the season tend to carry over that performance the next year. The teams which played poorly late in 1989 will, as a group, play poorly in 1990.

The other two indicators are more difficult to explain, but they have to do with detecting luck. I get the other two indicators by comparing each team's *won-lost record* with their *team ability as measured in their other stats*. For example, the Dodgers are likely to improve this year, because their other stats show that they were a better team last year than their won-lost record reflects, and the Houston Astros are *very* likely to decline in 1990 because their other stats show that they weren't as good a team as their 86–76 record shows. Teams tend to gravitate toward their true level of ability.

There is only one major league team this year for which all six indicators agree. All six indicators agree that the Chicago White Sox in 1990 should be better than they were in 1989.

While all six indicators agree that the Sox will probably be better, four of the six indicators are weak, so the overall indication for improvement is not as strong for the White Sox as it is for two other teams, the Pirates and the Mets. Let's run a chart of the indicators:

Team	1990 Indicators
1. Pittsburgh Pirates	+ 20.3
2. New York Mets	+ 15.4
3. Chicago White Sox	+ 14.6
4. Detroit Tigers	+ 14.2
5. Los Angeles Dodgers	+ 13.3
6. Cincinnati Reds	+ 11.8
7. New York Yankees	+ 10.4
8. Toronto Blue Jays	+ 9.1
9. Cleveland Indians	+ 8.7
10. Minnesota Twins	+ 7.5
11. Philadelphia Phillies	+ 7.3
12. Boston Red Sox	+ 6.1
13. Seattle Mariners	+ 5.8
14. Atlanta Braves	+ 4.2
15. Milwaukee Brewers	+ 1.9
16. San Diego Padres	0.0
17. Texas Rangers	− 9.7
18. San Francisco Giants	− 11.2
19. Oakland Athletics	− 11.5
20. Chicago Cubs	− 12.1
21. St. Louis Cardinals	− 12.3
22. Montreal Expos	− 13.3
23. Kansas City Royals	− 17.4
24. Baltimore Orioles	− 18.2
25. Houston Astros	− 22.6
26. California Angels	− 25.1

A couple of words about the indicators:

1. The indicators are going to be right, over a period of time, a little more than three fourths of the time, and

2. That statement means considerably less than it might seem to.

Surprising as it may seem, being able to project whether a team will be better or worse next year and being correct in those guesses about eighty percent of the time is almost useless in terms of being able to project a pennant race.

Take the first fact listed above—that all teams tend to gravitate toward the center. This one fact alone will predict the direction of a team's movement 65% of the time. That is, 65 percent of teams that finished over .500 in 1989 will probably decline in 1990, and 65 percent of the teams that finished under .500 will probably improve. So just use that and you can predict the direction of movement with 65 percent accuracy—but in terms of predicting the pennant race, this information is completely useless; all it says is that the top teams will be down and the bottom teams will be up.

The same with the second point—it's right 65 percent of the time, but it's useless in predicting a pennant race.

OK, when those facts are combined with other things, like the team age, that information becomes a little more useful in predicting a pennant race. But if *all* of the predictions of direction were correct, you could still miss every pennant race. You could say that Toronto won last year and they'll be up so they should win again, but what if somebody else in the division is *way* up?

And if just one indicator in a division turns out to be pointed in the wrong direction, that's going to screw up your championship prediction most of the time. Most of the time, the team that *doesn't* perform as expected is going to be either the team that wins, or the team that was supposed to win—and either way, you're out in the cold.

Now, I won't make predictions that fly in the face of these indicators, because I know that if I do I'm going to be wrong most of the time. If the indication is strong—plus or minus more than ten—the direction indicated will probably be the direction the team moves over eighty percent of the time. There are sixteen teams in 1990 which have strong indications, and it's a good bet that thirteen of them will move this year in the direction shown. Even if the indication is weak, as for the other ten teams, the indicators are still going to be right fifty-five to sixty percent of the time.

I have six indicators—but if I had time to study the issue long enough, I could find more; I'm sure I could find fifteen or twenty, although most of those would be minor. If I had one guess of what the seventh indicator might be, it might be the performance of the team's AAA and AA players. The White Sox AA and AAA teams have a good number of players who could help—Adam Peterson, Jeff Bittiger, Tom Drees, Jack Hardy, Lance Johnson, Steve Springer, Richie Amaral, Robin Ventura, Wayne Edwards, Buddy Groom, Grady Hall, Tony Menendez.

So the "seventh indicator" would also be in the positive column, and I have to pick the White Sox to be better in 1990, no matter how much they might irritate me.

The White Sox in recent years have executed several series of moves of just staggering stupidity.

• In 1987 the White Sox won 77 games, finished very strong. That winter they traded away their top three starting pitchers, without getting an established pitcher in return.

• Their best young starter at that time was Jose DeLeon, who was traded for center fielder Lance Johnson, the American Association's Most Valuable Player. To make room for Johnson, the White

Sox shifted their incumbent center fielder, Kenny Williams, to third base.

Williams in 1987 was twenty-three years old. In 116 games he had hit .281 with 11 homers, 21 stolen bases, and 50 RBI—numbers that projected, even given no improvement, to make him one of the better-hitting center fielders in the league. He is a *fine* outfielder. He had never played an inning of third base in his professional career.

Williams, of course, stunk up the joint at third base and stopped hitting, which we all knew he would. Then, to complete the pratfall, they sent Lance Johnson to the minor leagues! In sum, the GM from Bozo-land had converted a twenty-five-year-old starting pitcher and a twenty-three-year-old center fielder into essentially nothing.

OK, he did pull Shawn Hillegas out of a side pocket of the deal. It is still the definitive Glass Naval sequence of the late 1980's.

• Steve Lyons in 1988 played 146 games as a five-position utility man, and hit .269. His best position is third base, so do the White Sox figure they have finally solved their third base spot?

Why, no, they shift Lyons to second base, a position that it is obvious to almost everybody that he can't play.

Even if they keep doing this stuff, the White Sox will win 75 games this year, a six-game improvement. If they'll cut it out and act normal, they'll win 85 games. And at 85 wins, the White Sox will be one of the success stories of 1990.

SOME HEROES AND GOATS

There are still forty games left to be played, and all of the pennant races are still up for grabs. In spite of that happy fact, it is not too early to single out individual players who have had a significant impact—whether for good or ill—on their team's performance this year. Some of these players include:

PHIL BRADLEY—ORIOLES. Remember a few years ago when Dick Williams called him a cancer on the Seattle Mariners? I don't know what the Phillies said he was, a syphilis or an AIDS virus, probably, but I know they didn't like him either. I was beginning to wonder: Here's this guy who puts up terrific offensive stats every year, is always in the lineup, and yet nobody much wants him. Is there something I hadn't heard? That all changed this year; the same old excellent offense, plus one third of a revamped outfield that could easily be nicknamed "Death to Flying Things." (Actually, the '88 outfield might have had the same nickname, since Orioles fly, and Lord knows their outfield killed them.) As the O's struggle to maintain a narrow lead down the stretch, Frank Robinson has inserted him into the leadoff spot, and if he maintains his usual production, the Birds will not fall short for lack of an offensive catalyst. If Bradley is a cancer, O's fans may be forgiven for hoping that he spreads quickly, and cannot be removed.

WADE BOGGS—RED SOX. It didn't bother me particularly that Margo Adams trashed Wade Boggs, the man, at every possible opportunity. He asked for it. What did

bother me was the way more than a few baseball people took the opportunity to kick him while he was down by trashing his reputation as a baseball player. A singles hitter who can't run, went the litany. Take him away from Fenway and he's shit. Yeah, take him away from Fenway and watch the Red Sox do a bigger belly flop than they already have. Tell me, how many singles hitters have slugged .485 after seven years in the league? How many hitters of any kind sport a .448 on-base percentage? Sure, Fenway helps him, it helped Teddy and Yaz too. It helps everyone. Show me any player, of any era, who's posted numbers anywhere near those of Boggs, who is not considered a great player, who is not comfortably ensconced in the Hall of Fame. Give Boggs some credit. He swallowed his pride and kept his composure amidst all the sound and fury. Trade rumors swirled around him and he produced. He had a contract hassle with Lou Gorman, and produced. More power to him, I say. If you want to denigrate Wade Boggs the man, fine. But lay off Wade Boggs the ballplayer.

BERT BLYLEVEN—ANGELS. They're touting him for Comeback Player of the Year, which I don't think is right, since he's only been gone one year. (Now Kevin Hickey, there's a guy who's been AWOL for a while. A comeback by Judge Crater would be no less likely.) On the other hand, he's an excellent candidate for the Cy Young Award. Don't ask me how he's doing it; if I'd been Andy MacPhail I'd have taken what I could get for him too, and good riddance. Who was the last pitcher to have ERA's above four for three years running, and then come back and have this kind of season? I guess in retrospect you can say the Metrodome wasn't suited to his style of pitching, but a quick check

of his home/road stats show no great disparity. What really interests me about Blyleven these days is his reputation as a great prankster and wit, much beloved in the clubhouse, who keeps everyone loosey-goosey. Quite a turnabout from the self-centered crybaby who quit the '80 Pirates in mid-season because he was not getting enough complete games, earning the enmity of even insouciant Chuck Tanner. Crybaby or comic, he's helped three different clubs (the '70 and '87 Twins don't count as the same) to the post-season.

SCOTT FLETCHER—RANGERS. If I'd known prior to the season that somewhere along the line the Rangers would need a scapegoat, I'd never have guessed it would be Fletcher. I thought—I still think—he's a terrific ballplayer, but there's no denying that for '89 the numbers have not been there. It still puzzles me that they didn't conclude "Well, he's having an off year, he'll bounce back in '90." Were they really so desperate for an established DH that they had to deal off an established shortstop? (My cynical opinion is that they already have an ideal DH; his name is Pete Incaviglia and he clutters up left field.) If Fred Manrique or Jeff Kunkel can fill Fletcher's shoes I'll be astounded. Was management particularly embarrassed by his sub-par year because they had just signed him to a lucrative long-term contract? I don't know the answer to that, but it appears management could be just as easily embarrassed by the performance of their anointed leadoff man, Cecil Espy; the continued inconsistency (which is putting it mildly) of Bobby Witt, and the failure of the catching corps *sans* Gino Petralli. But it was Fletcher who had to be dealt, and I'll be interested to see who has the better '90 campaign: anybody for the Rangers at shortstop, or Scott Fletcher, at second base, in Chicago. I'm betting on Fletcher.

BOB BOONE—ROYALS. You figure this guy out. I thought sure his .295 average (.352 OBP) at age forty was the fluke of the century; so far in '89 the BA is down, but the OBP is actually up slightly. He's on a pace to catch 130 games, and is still a bitch to run on. It's getting to be kind of a long-running fluke.

CARNEY LANSFORD—A's. You remember his '88 campaign, don't you? On June 6 he was over .400; he finished the year at .279, and was no factor in the World Series. He was also in the unfortunate position of being over thirty, and baseball men, like hippies of twenty years ago, tend to distrust those over thirty who can't hit their weight in the second half. You can be sure that *Carnivorus Lansfordus* (I prefer to refer to him by genus species) heard the whispering: is he washed up? Is it time to trade for a third baseman? How's that kid at Double A looking? As far as I know, *Carnivorus* kept his counsel and bided his time. When the '89 season began, the Athletics were obviously not the offensive juggernaut of '88; Canseco was injured, and Dave Henderson tailed off after a career year. Another quick offensive burst from *Lansfordus* was required, and he provided it. The dog days of summer arrived, Canseco returned, but still the Athletics could not draw clear; continued punch from *Lansfordus* was needed; there was no room for a second half fade away this year. He knew what he had to do for both the team, and his career. And he has done it, with a vengeance. As I write, a second batting title is not out of the question. The Athletics still have not broken away, and if they do, it may well be on the strength of dingers by the so far only sporadically

heard from Bash Brothers. If so, I hope the folks who were so busy whispering last winter about the imminent demise of *Carnivorus Lansfordus* will remember who held the fort until the bruisers were ready to assert themselves.

JIM EISENREICH—ROYALS. *"The most notorious ill-fortune must, in the end, yield to the untiring courage of philosophy"*—Edgar Allan Poe

Poe, a lifelong Royals fan, was not referring to George Brett's legendary battles with hemorrhoids, nor to Bo Jackson's decision to pursue football as a hobby; rather, he was describing the "notorious ill-fortune" that befell the Royals when Billy Gardner became manager. Gardner was a nice, well-meaning man who couldn't do anything right, much like the small time hoodlum Horace "Turd" Turner in John Gregory Dunne's brilliant novel *True Confessions*, who "When he got a contract, he hit the wrong guy."

Likewise, when Gardner called for a bunt, he got a pop-up. When he ordered an intentional walk, the next batter, invariably hitting .196, would crank his only homer of the year. Gardner, like the luckless Turd, was eventually dispatched, but not before performing one undeniably good deed; that is, recommending that the Royals sign Jim Eisenreich, then out of professional ball, apparently hopelessly in the throes of a mysterious nerve disorder. You know the rest of the story: how a new diagnosis by different doctors enabled Eisenreich to resume his career with the aid of medication. How he tore up Double A and was called to the majors, where he struggled until '89, when he exploded. For all the headline hogging by the overrated Bo Jackson, Eisenreich is now arguably the Royals best player.

What I like best about him,

though, and what is not much commented on, is this blatant Teutonism. Aside from his name, he looks like an early twentieth century German ballplayer, like Honus Wagner, at least facially. Why the stadium organist doesn't play "Deutschland Über Alles" every time he steps to the plate is a mystery. Also, given his obvious ethnic background, I think he should be allowed to wear the iron cross on his back rather than a number, as well as a spiked batting helmet. One more suggestion: remember when Germans used to be called "Boches"? Now that Eisenreich often follows Bo Jackson in the order, shouldn't he be nicknamed "Boche," giving us a daily double of Bo and Boche?

JOHN KRUK—PHILLIES. Kruk has been both hero and goat this year—goat in San Diego, hero in Philadelphia. I thought his decline in Padreland (which actually began in '88) was attributable to being stationed in the outfield full time, where he has the range of a brontosaurus, but since moving to Philly he has been inserted regularly in left, while at the same time exploding offensively. What interests me about Kruk, however, are his scientific theories on hitting, which happily are nonexistent. It's reported that, when the Phillies batting instructor attempted to discuss philosophy with him, Kruk shrugged and said that he just stepped in and commenced to hacking. Imagine, a ballplayer in the modern age who doesn't have a concept, who never studies slow-motion videotapes, who doesn't measure his stride with a micrometer. What in heaven's name does he say when broadcasters interview him? I suppose I shouldn't be so happy about Kruk's anti-intellectual approach to baseball; he's no future Hall of Famer;

maybe he would be if he studied the game intently. But somehow I find it refreshing that someone still holds to an existential view of the national pastime. If he wrote a book purporting to give hitting instruction, would he call it *Swinging and Nothingness?* Please, keep Walt Hriniak away from this man at all costs.

JAY HOWELL—DODGERS. Here's a guy whose luck is definitely not the greatest. He's having as stellar a year as a reliever can fantasize (ERA under a buck as I write) and no one knows he's alive. On the other hand, maybe he enjoys laboring in relative obscurity; look what happens every time he's thrust into the limelight. Who can forget the '87 All-Star Game, with its "What is Jay Howell doing on the AL roster?" controversy smoldering prior to the game, and bursting into open flame when he was the loser in the fifteenth inning. The disgruntlement was valid; Howell was having a terrible year (4.41 ERA at that point—it got worse), and would have been more aptly utilized on an All-Stink team. But think about how he must have felt. It wasn't his idea to be an '87 All Star; he didn't lobby for the spot. It was someone else's hallucination, and what was Howell to do, tell John McNamara to quit tripping acid? Tell him he didn't feel like pitching with the game on the line? It was a legitimate controversy, but one which Howell can be forgiven for thinking had little or nothing to do with him.

Then, of course, there was his pine tar controversy in the '88 NLCS, and once again Howell proved to be in the wrong place, at the wrong time. George Brett's '83 overdose of pine tar will perhaps be the most fondly recalled incident of his career—he even managed to convert it into a nationwide commercial. Joe Niekro,

his career hanging by a—fingernail?—earned a last gasp of notoriety after being suspended for possession of emery boards. And everyone has always loved and respected Gaylord Perry, not in spite of, but because of his dastardly moist deliveries. It doesn't appear to have worked out so well for Jay Howell. Caught red-handed with pine tar on his glove (no one claimed he was applying it to the ball) and nursing a narrow lead that eventually evaporated, Howell was ejected, suspended, and humiliated. No one rushed to him with offers for endorsements, or contracts for books. He was simply a miscreant.

It didn't get much better at the World Series. Before a pitch was even thrown, Don Baylor scared up some headlines by calling him gutless. Then when Howell started making his pitches, Mark McGwire deposited one in the bleachers for the Athletics' only victory. He rebounded the next night to earn a save and put the Dodgers in the driver's seat, but this would be quickly—and understandably—forgotten in the rush to lionize Orel Hershiser and Kirk Gibson. All in all, Howell had a winner's Series share, a new ring, and, undoubtedly, a feeling of great relief that the season was finally over. There'll be no Series share or ring in '89, but who can blame him if perhaps he'd just as soon toil in anonymity for a year?

PETE INCAVIGLIA—RANGERS. Have the Rangers finally given up on him? They say they want Harold Baines to be their DH for the next five years, and they wouldn't let Inky bumble about in left for that long, would they? Unless he starts showing some offensive improvement, he'll be lucky to bumble about anywhere. Even a one-dimensional slugger of the Dave Kingman variety should draw enough

walks to get his OBP above .300, but in '89 Incaviglia was not equal to the task. Also for the past two seasons he's been unable to stay in the lineup. Texas is justifiably proud of its "Murderers Row" offense of Palmeiro, Sierra, Franco, and Baines, but think how potent that offense could have been had Incaviglia come through; they'd have called it "Serial Murderers Row." The joke trade rumor of '89 was Incaviglia to the Cardinals, where he would replace Vince Coleman in left. Coleman may deserve replacement, but not by a three-toed tree sloth. I do look for Inky to go somewhere, though; Tom Grieve of late has shown limited patience with those who don't produce, and soon, as Oddibe McDowell, Jerry Browne, and Scott Fletcher can attest. Aren't the proper Bostonians always on the lookout for players of his ilk?

ROB "OFFICER" DIBBLE—REDS. He couldn't have picked a better year to become a star: The Reds desperately needed someone whose performance—and antics—could take people's minds off Pete Rose, even momentarily. And what a power performance; Dibble is striking out more batters per inning than Goose Gossage in his prime. The antics, apparently, rank with the best, too. I can see why the league fined and suspended him for throwing that bat on the screen, but why were the Reds so exasperated? Why wouldn't a publicity-loving owner like Marge Schott exploit Dibble's tantrum to the utmost by organizing bat-throwing-onto-the-screen contests, replete with vast herds of Little Leaguers descending upon the home plate area prior to game time, each dreaming of matching Dibble's Olympian standard in war club tossing. Where is Bill Veeck when you really need him?

On a more serious note, the emergence of Dibble as a dominant reliever makes him too valuable to be kept in the set-up role, which means that the highly desirable left arm of John Franco likely will be marketed. Isn't that the way it usually works? For all the talk of the importance of the set-up man, no team seems particularly interested in keeping two star quality relievers, one to set the table, the other to clear. Remember when Whitey Herzog, briefly, was the proud possessor of both Bruce Sutter and Rollie Fingers? He didn't dream of retaining the pair, and I've always assumed that the Pirates would have worked harder to sign Gossage for '78 had they not felt—correctly—that set-up man Kent Tekulve was ready to assume the closer role. The '78 Yankees did try, after a fashion, to operate with two bullpen stalwarts, newly-arrived Gossage and incumbent Sparky Lyle, but this turned out to be an unacceptable arrangement, especially for Lyle, who was dealt at the close of the season. At any rate, if and when Franco departs, Dibble will be left at center stage, and given his proclivity for grabbing headlines in a supporting role, one shudders to contemplate the show once he becomes top banana. It should be a very interesting 1990 in Cincinnati.

—M.K.

RAINBOW

A light rain stops the game at 8:05. Suddenly it is raining hard. For a half hour the delay seems unable to exhaust the grounds crew's repertoire of things to do to a turf while it rains. They form a diagonal file and stomp forward like a Prussian rolling pin, forcing the air under the billowing plastic into a corner from which it can escape. Harder it rains; they line up across one side of the field, remove the sand bags, and, on count, give that side of the tarp a coordinated yank before hustling on to the next baseline. Another side, another rolling pin, then they start at the center and march out, and it rains yet harder.

The rain comes now in droplets the size of bowls, solid rain, three-dimensional rain. At last the brave groundsmen are driven from the field, abandoning their quest for a perfectly flat surface. The PA operator plays "Have You Ever Seen the Rain?" and "Raindrops Keep Falling on My Head," but the thunder and the roaring chatter of thirty thousand fans jammed under the overhang leave one unable to discern the lyrics; no one seems aware of the songs. The wind seizes umbrellas from the crowd and hurls them bouncing across the infield, a neat three-hopper to short and on to the warning track. The air is white with rain. The rain blows even to my seat, fifty feet beneath the overhang. The crowd, at first irritated by the delay, is overcome by surges of excitement as the storm becomes spectacular. The PA announcer, scarcely audible through the noise and static, asks the brave souls who paid for upstairs seats and are still sitting in them to please take cover, for their own safety. Anyone still out in this is the kind of person who would take off his shirt at a December football game. Rain . . . have I ever seen it rain like this? I remember a rain in the summer of '67, when I was building a fence and took refuge in the doorway of a barn. Now hail begins, huge hail, hail the size of . . . hail that should have stitches. The murmur of the crowd mixed with the crack crack of the falling stones leaves one barely able to talk to one's neighbor. Now it rains again, perhaps not harder than before, but there is some subtle distinction between the rain before and the rain now which makes this seem as new and thrilling as the other. The water on the tarp forms a pattern of creeks and streams, visible from the seats. Water rolls down the aisles toward the field and spews over the rim of the seats in small Niagaras.

The rain slackens. Someone . . . Saberhagen? . . . in Bo Jackson's uniform and a white mask from a mad slasher movie comes out and slides into the "bases," fields imaginary ground balls, falls in the pools of water and splashes his arms like a one-year-old in the kitchen sink. By 9:01 it is raining no harder than it was when they stopped the game almost an hour ago. The grounds crew reemerges and begins pushing water into drains with push brooms and squeegees. The "water spectacular"—the fountain—begins its timid and orderly waterplay. Fans clamor back to their seats, or perhaps begin to claim the good seats abandoned by those with more money than faith. No one tonight will get a bigger cheer than the grounds crew, or earn one.

It takes only three minutes to pick up the tarp and dump the water, but then the flattening ritual must be repeated before the tarp can be folded and rolled. Although tommorow is the first day of school for many people, the crowd seems almost as large after the deluge as before.

By 9:20 the players are out loosening up; at 9:33 the game resumes with lightning in the distance. Mike Witt throws two ridiculously wide pitches before limping in with a near miss, then two called strikes. White, finally freed to swing, grounds a single up the middle at 9:36.

WISHING UPON THE STARS

At the risk of seeming to kick the New York Mets while they're down (and Lord knows they still have time to regain their feet and kick back), it's hard to look at their season so far and not think that there is something terribly wrong, and not just with the team on the field. Maybe we should have sensed it last spring, when they desperately tried to make the sure-to-have-been-ruinous Sid Fernandez and Howard Johnson for Mark Langston trade. It's easy to see what they thought at the time: Langston is better than Fernandez, and we've got Gregg Jefferies ready to take over at third and he's going to be a star. When the deal fell through, that was okay after all; just plug in Jefferies at second and never mind that he's woefully inexperienced at that position. Well, you see the result: Jefferies may yet become a star, but this year he's struggled, while HoJo has become a one-man highlight film, quite unexpectedly, much like the long-since departed Kevin Mitchell. (No, I'm not going to throw that one in Frank Cashen's face; anyone would have given Mitchell and Shawn Abner for Kevin McReynolds.) But the point is, the Mets seem to have become so obsessed with the acquisition of star players that they no longer see any value in keeping role players. How else to explain the Len Dykstra and Roger McDowell for Juan Samuel trade? I think it's simple: Dykstra is a solid, hard-nosed ballplayer, but no star, whereas for some reason the Mets thought Samuel had star quality. Did they keep looking at his inflated

'87 stats (28 homers, .502 slugging percentage) and convince themselves that a reprise was on the horizon? And what about his in-progress transfer to center field? Did they think two players enduring on-the-job training at new positions would have no effect on the overall defense? That it didn't matter because they were going to be stars anyway?

All right, maybe I'm kidding myself. I suppose you can say that all the incumbent offensive stars had to do was play up to their usual level and no one would have even noticed that Jefferies and Samuel were struggling. Yes, Keith Hernandez's injury was a blow, but his replacement, Dave Magadan, was ready, and is now the superior offensive player. No one can replace Gary Carter, but his decline had been pronounced enough that the Mets had to envision the collapse; I'm surprised that Sandy Alomar, Jr., was not obtained once the Langston deal fell through; he's another player with star written all over him.

But as it turned out, a different star was needed, a replacement for the brightest star of all, Dwight Gooden. And who better to replace the brightest star than the Betelgeuse of the American League, Frank Viola. I wish I could decide what I think about that trade. As a quick fix, it is obviously lacking, as Sweet Music has continued just slightly off-key, as in Minnesota; no Doyle Alexander instant turn around here. The long-term prognosis, though, is excellent: no more contract hassles, pitching at home, still in his prime—I think the Mets will get good value. And yet . . . assuming Doc comes back one hundred percent, what are they going to do with six starters? Trade one, for another star no doubt. But whatever happened to promoting from within, which is what brought them back from

obscurity to begin with? Okay, they tried David West, and he flopped, but did you see what Tom Kelly had to say about that when West arrived in Minnesota? How his mechanics were all fouled up, and they had to practically conduct a kindergarten to correct his delivery? What does that say about player development in New York? And even after West failed, there was still Rick Aguilera, temporarily in the bullpen, but with plenty of high-pressure starting experience under his belt. I don't know, I'm usually in favor of packaging any number of warm bodies to get a still youthful star, i.e. the deal the Yankees made to get Rickey Henderson. But this time I have qualms. In their quest to remain at the admittedly lofty pinnacle which they've achieved by dint of hard, aggressive work, I think the Mets may have lost sight of the big picture. There's another owner in New York who decided he had to have stars, at any and all costs, and verily, stars he had, but now his empire lies in ruins. Is it possible that the organization which throughout the mid- and late eighties seemed baseball's smartest is heading for a similar fate?

—M.K.

To write anything about the Mets, after so much has been written, is a bit daunting; my friend says that adding words to what is said about the Mets is like sending money to Japan. On the proposition that something has gone fundamentally wrong with the Mets, I vote "No." It is a backhanded compliment indeed to the Mets organization to say that Dave Johnson should have been fired after a season like 1989. In an era in which hardly anybody else can put two decent years together, are the Mets so dominant that even when nearly everything goes wrong, they must still be expected to win? Let us inventory briefly the Mets' 1989 problems:

1. Doc Gooden, one of the top pitchers of the generation, missed half the season,
2. Darryl Strawberry, the Mets' top slugger, had a miserable year, broke a toe and hit .225.
3. Gary Carter, the outstanding catcher of his generation, reached the absolute end of the line.
4. Keith Hernandez, the Hal Chase of the eighties, reached the end of his line.
5. Gregg Jefferies, projected as a super-rookie, took four months to get his bat going.
6. A big trade didn't work out.

So did the Mets lose a hundred games? No, no—they won eighty-seven games, had the fourth-best record in the league. Isn't that kind of amazing?

Mike is right about one thing: The Mets have lost sight of the value of role players. But he is dead wrong about another thing. It *wasn't* primarily players promoted from within who brought the Mets back from obscurity. It was trades precisely like the big trades of 1989, the Viola and Samuel trades. Since 1984, the Mets have packaged players who *could* be outstanding and players who could contribute on some level—and

money—to get stars. They got Strawberry and Gooden and a few others from the system, but they got Carter and Hernandez and McReynolds and Ojeda and HoJo and David Cone and Sid Fernandez by trading a package of white chips and red chips for a blue chip—exactly as they did last year for Samuel and Viola.

And that has always been a solid strategy, because talent in baseball is a pyramid. If you give away a white chip—a role player—you can come up with another one.

You remember a couple of years ago I urged you to think about Gooden and Strawberry as the Whitey and Mickey of the eighties? Maybe you don't remember—I always assume my readers are the same from year to year. Well, to me, the Mets' 1989 season was a great deal like the Yankees' 1959 season. Mantle didn't have a good year in '59, drove in only 75 runs. Whitey Ford was fairly good but that's all (16–10), and nobody picked up the slack; the Yankees couldn't come up with a Bob Turley or a Johnny Kucks that year. Moose Skowron missed half the year with a back injury, Hank Bauer hit the wall at thirty-six, the role players didn't have a good year. The Yankees won 79 games and finished third, and a lot of people wrote that there was something seriously wrong with the Yankees.

Of course there wasn't.

To me, there were only two basic things that went wrong here, beyond luck. The Samuel trade *was* a mistake—not a stupid trade, not a dumb thing to do, but a mistake all the same. It was a mistake for two reasons:

1) Samuel just isn't that good, and
2) Oddibe McDowell was available at a fraction of the price.

The Mets traded for Samuel on June 18, giving up two good players. Just two weeks later, the Atlanta Braves got Oddibe McDowell for Dion James. Compare the two of them.

Who gets on base more—McDowell or Samuel? Oddibe.

Who has more power? Samuel, but it's close.

Who is a better base stealer. They're essentially even.

Who is a better outfielder? McDowell, by a mile.

Who is younger? McDowell is two years younger.

So what kind of sense does it make to trade two good players for Juan Samuel, when McDowell is available for 30 percent of the cost?

The second basic problem was that the Mets forgot about defense. Now, I am *not* an advocate of placing too much emphasis on defense. I think that offense and pitching+defense in baseball are the same thing, merely seen from a different angle, and that therefore it is silly to say that baseball is more than fifty percent pitching+defense.

I think that the basic responsibility to prevent runs from scoring has to fall on the pitcher—at least 75 percent of defense is pitching. That means that defensive play at all eight spots is no more than 12 or 13 percent of the game. I think that one of the strengths of the Mets organization over the decade has been that they have had the courage to accept criticism for their defense, and keep playing players like Howard Johnson and Wally Backman.

But there is a limit. It's only twelve percent of the game, but it still counts. The Mets defense has crossed that line from "poor" to "unacceptable."

So what would I do, were I running the Mets?

1) Try to make a trade for a catcher. It's hard to believe that the Padres wouldn't have given up Alomar for the package that the Mets gave up for Samuel. Since that didn't work out, they've still got to find a catcher.

2) Don't panic. Too many major trades, coming too quickly, disrupt the

fabric of the team to where you don't know what you have anymore. Another major trade now and the Mets are going to get into next August and find out that they're missing some little part of the team that they'd forgotten about.

3) Build a defensive bench. You know the old saying—you can shake a tree and a dozen gloves will fall out. Well, the Mets need to shake that tree.

If Gooden and Strawberry come back, the Mets will win in '90. If they don't, the era which began in 1984 is over, and the question will be whether the Mets have moved from one outstanding team to another.

GREAT EXPEC-TATIONS

We hear a lot, these days, of how the pressure of playing big league ball in New York, in front of unforgiving crowds, beneath the magnifying glass of a hyperthyroid fourth estate, and (in the Bronx at least) under the thumb of an owner who knows not the meaning of the word patience, can, and often does, eat a young player alive, Greg Jefferies being the latest conspicuous example. Well, maybe. But it appears to me that this year, to find the prototypical player who couldn't stand the heat, we must look not to the Big Apple, but rather to Milwaukee, where Gary Sheffield, touted as the leading candidate for Rookie of the Year, failed to produce, lashed out at his teammates, and was returned to the minor leagues in the midst of what looked like—at that moment—a failed season for the Brewers.

How to apportion blame in the Sheffield fiasco? I think Walt Weiss—inadvertently—deserves his share of the burden. For Weiss was the rookie shortstop who stepped into the lineup, unproven, and proceeded to do more than his share in thrusting the '88 Athletics into the Series. The Brewers, after a near miss in '88, with Dale Sveum sidelined indefinitely, and the example of Weiss before them, decided that a similar performance from Sheffield could be their ticket to the post-season. I don't want to say that the Brewers were wrong to have such great expectations, but in dwelling on the similarities between Weiss and Sheffield, they neglected to note some significant differences, such

as Weiss's age when stepping in (twenty-four), and his four years of experience in big time college ball, as well as three years in the minors. Sheffield, by contrast, was just three years removed from high school. (Were the Brewers haunted here by the ghost of Robin Yount, age eighteen, landing the regular shortstop job? If so, they also forgot that tyro Robin was not expected to spark the '74 Brewers to a pennant.)

But there were problems beyond the—excessive?—pressure the Brewers placed on Sheffield to succeed in '89, and they had to do more with culture than with baseball. Simply put, Sheffield did not like his teammates, the vast preponderance of whom are white. He publicly denounced the entire pitching staff (none of whom are black) as lily-livered, and even though at least one sportswriter essentially agreed with that assessment, all he accomplished was to put still more pressure on himself. He accused management of plotting to shift him to third base (which he played on occasion in the minors) to make way for Billy Spiers, in the opinion of some a better glove man at short. In sum, he did everything that a rookie should not do in attempting to establish himself in the bigs. He didn't say so out loud, but you also got the impression that he loathed and despised the city of Milwaukee, and felt as if he was playing in a foreign land. I know, there is an irresistible temptation to say, "For Chrissakes, Gary, grow up!". After all, Henry Aaron, another southern black, seemed only too happy to be in Milwaukee; it was Atlanta that he initially shied away from. But Aaron grew up in a Jim Crow South that he was eager to escape; Sheffield did not. In the early fifties, blacks were grateful to be in the major leagues at all; the present generation has greater expectations. If it seems like I'm alibiing for him, I guess I am, but you see, I live in the Midwest, and have known over the years any number of people who have grown up on either coast, and, transplanted by either job or educational opportunity, arrived in the heartland and were almost instantly repelled. My friend Cristi Hansen, for most of her life a Californian, but now like me a Kansan, has made similar observations; perhaps all that's needed now is a demented psychologist to label it a syndrome and give it an eye-catching title.

All right, I agree, in exchange for likely riches beyond most people's wildest dreams, Sheffield should unquestionably swallow his distaste for his teammates and the Midwest and play ball. But it may already be too late; he possibly burned a very large bridge when he called the pitchers yellow-bellies. Worse, when he was sent down the team was in a tailspin; pennant contention seemed a distant memory. Without him, they have battled back into the race, and no matter how the season turns out, you can be sure that come 1990 his teammates will remember who was present and accounted for when they made their move, and who was not. Does this mean that I'm calling for Harry Dalton to unload him? Not at all. One spring training with a buttoned lip (and a hot bat) might affect a remarkable reconciliation. But neither will I second guess Dalton if he decides that, for the good of all concerned, Sheffield is better off achieving his long-predicted stardom somewhere else—somewhere other than the Midwest.

—M.K.
August 20

The interesting question about Gary Sheffield is how one distinguishes between immaturity, which a player will outgrow, and being a horse's ass, which a player rarely does. I don't have an answer to this question, but I don't like the odds. Baseball isn't *about* being bigger and stronger and faster and meaner than everybody else, like football; it's about learning what you can do and what you can't. One doesn't want to prematurely write a guy off because he doesn't know when to button his muzzle, but is it premature to suggest that there is something seriously wrong with a young man who criticizes major league pitchers because they don't do things the way his high school team did?

Sheffield is never going to be a shortstop, and it seems in retrospect curious that the Brewers failed to see something which was so obvious once you put him on the field. Maybe it's one of those things that wasn't obvious until you put him up against major league competition. I can't recall seeing anybody who pulled quite so many rocks. The impression I had of him, watching him play, is that he would field a ground ball and then look around to see if there was anybody on base. But then, I've never had much sympathy either for people who moved to the Midwest and wanted to tell me how awful it was because it wasn't the Coast. . . .

THE SAME OLD TRIBE

That the Indians were pretenders for a few months in baseball's weakest division should not obscure the fact that this is still, all advertisement to the contrary, the same old hapless Tribe. Remember as recently as '86, when they had the most potent offense in the American League, and the most impotent pitching staff? In true Indians fashion, they have turned that around in just three years—both ways. The staff, while not on a par with California or Oakland, is now eminently respectable, with an excellent rotation anchor (Greg Swindell) and closer (Doug Jones), but wouldn't you know it, now the offense, in spite of the presence of supposedly-feared sluggers Joe Carter and Cory Snyder, is punchless, and leads only the anemic Sparkmen in run production. How did this double turnabout come to pass? The same way everything happens in Cleveland, for in spite of all protestations to the contrary, nothing has changed in the front office; all that's been accomplished is a reshuffling of the same old deck that Gabe Paul had worn to the nub ten years ago.

In fairness to Paul, his caretaker administration did depart in a blaze of glory with the trades that bought Carter, Mel Hall, Brook Jacoby, and Brett Butler to the wigwam. But why do the Indians have to eternally obtain their young talent from someone else's organization? Aren't they ever going to start producing their own? (Don't talk to me about Swindell; he's a product of the University of Texas organization; a cynic might say that pitching only eighteen innings for an Indians farm is the reason he's so good—they didn't have enough time to ruin him.) Yes, it's wonderful to have a kid like Jerry Browne on your roster, but it would be even more wonderful if you hadn't coughed up Julio Franco to get him. Sure you can make an out and out steal once in a while, and actually the Tribe has made more than its share lately—Jacoby and Butler for the remains of Len Barker; Tom Candiotti and Doug Jones for absolutely nothing—but the down side is that you inevitably get stolen from too; anybody remember who the Indians exchanged for Bert Blyleven?

—M.K.
August 31, 1989

Alfred Hitchcock once said that self-plagiarism is the essence of style. The Cleveland Indians style was defined perfectly by the mid-winter signing of Candy Maldonado, an outfielder whose only decent major league season was the year everybody hit. The signing of Maldonado enabled the Indians to trade Dave Clark, who is a better player than Maldonado, which brought in Mitch Webster, which enabled them to trade Joe Carter, who is certainly a better player than Mitch Webster.

The Indians' moves this winter seem somehow uniquely pathetic; I can't quite say why, but I wince in sympathy when I hear each one announced . . . the signing of John McNamara as manager, the signing of Maldonado and Guante, the acquisition of Mitch Webster. Tired blood for an anemic offense; Hank Peters is reliving his youth. For Christ's sake, if you want players like this, just wait 'til the end of spring training, and other teams will cut them loose.

I've rarely seen a major league manager who was in as far over his head as Doc Edwards was, and I assumed that the Indians would improve after Edwards was gone just if they could find someone who would know enough not to kill Swindell every May. Now even that seems less than safe, and all that remains is to wait for things to hit bottom again and begin again an infusion of new blood, a new manager (Mike Hargrove?) with a new idea.

THE NEW WARDEN

Is David Letterman the Angel of Mercy, or just the new warden? The late-summer announcement that the Seattle Mariners were to be sold must be, to a Mariners fan, almost like a parole hearing; there is a chance here that we're finally going to escape our assigned hell, but we'll have to wait and see. Cleveland Indians fans thought they had been paroled when the last owners of that team, the invisible men, sold out to the Jacobs brothers, who at least have money. Nothing has changed; the Indians this winter traded Joe Carter for a minor leaguer and signed Candy Maldonado as a free agent. That's sort of like saying to the Indians fans "You didn't get a release date and we're closing down the rec room, but we do have a new guard on Cellblock D." The Indians have become the best argument going *against* ownership leaving the team in the hands of professional management.

I'm sure the Mariners fans figure their new owners can't be any worse than Argyros, which is not literally true but a reasonable guess. I've written many times that the Mariners were on the verge of a sudden improvement, and I've always been wrong, so I'm not going to write that any more. I'll still say that *the possibility is there* for a sudden improvement; the talent reflected in Briley, Griffey, Buhner, Schooler, Randy Johnson, Mike Jackson, and Eric Hanson, plus the three or four established players that the Mariners do have (Alvin Davis, Harold Reynolds, Scott Bankhead) is obviously enough to bring the team past .500.

I don't know what to make of Jim Lefebvre. Bringing in old Penitentiary Face is a classic Cleveland Indians move—hurts the team immediately if he has a bad year, hurts the team in the long run even if he has a good year. He had a good year, if you consider it that, so it will take a while for the move to hurt the team. I mean, I know Lefebvre was unhappy with Brantley's approach to the game and I can sympathize with a manager saying "If you don't want to play this game right, go play for Calgary", but the fact is that *if* the Mariners are going to get a championship team put together, Jeffrey Leonard isn't going to be a part of it.

Lefebvre did several other things which raise questions about his ability to recognize a ballplayer when he sees one. He gave Henry Cotto 295 at bats. He continued to play Jim Presley, the majors' longest-running disappointment, at third base instead of a younger and better player, Edgar Martinez.

He liked Presley's attitude. He gave interviews about Presley going with the pitch, learning to hit to right field. Presley hit .236. I'm suspicious of managers who want to make personnel decisions based on attitude. My favorite quote about managing is Billy Martin's crack that you've got your mules and your race horses, and you can kick a mule in the ass all you want to and he ain't going to win the Kentucky Derby. Part of a manager's job—the part that Billy Martin was good at—is setting fire to the tail of a lazy race horse. What Lefebvre did instead was to get rid of the lazy race horses—Brantley, Quinones—and play the mules. I don't think you can win that way.

But, hey, lots of successful managers start out slow, and I wish him luck. It is said that the Mariners are going to push out their fences this year, making it no longer a cheap home run park; don't you always love it when new management has a fresh idea about how to build a winner? If that happens there will be dramatic improvement in the Mariners

"pitching" this year. Randy Johnson, I'd guess, will win 15 games with 200 strikeouts and an ERA not much over three unless it's a hitter's year, and Scott Bankhead if healthy could lead the league in ERA. Add Erik Hanson, Brian Holman, and one of Swift, Dunne, and Harris, and the Mariners will have the most improved starting pitching in baseball.

It is equally likely, assuming the fences are out, that Jeff Leonard will hit .231 with 12 homers, that Presley and Valle will continue to struggle, that one other hitter will have a disappointing year and that no hitter will have a surprisingly good year. When Smulyan and Browning checked into a Seattle hotel during the purchase negotiations, the new owners of the team registered as "Rainbow Trout" and "Ruppert Jones." If they have a sense of humor that has to help a little, right? A sense of humor is usually a sign of self-confidence and intelligence, although what does it tell us that there have been four comedians in history who owned baseball teams, and two of them have owned the Mariners? If it doesn't work out, well, hang in there and we'll have another parole hearing for you in a couple of years. Try not to strangle any more of your cellmates, all right?

DODGING BULLETS?

The '88 Los Angeles Dodgers, seemingly dead and laid out on the undertaker's table after forty years as a quasi-dynasty, with the obituarist's typewriters already pounding away, proved after all that reports of their demise were greatly exaggerated. The question before us now is what are we to make of these '89 Dodgers, who again appear remarkably inert, with no discernible pulse or respiration. Are they finally ready for the formaldehyde and the eulogies, or are we likely to see them unexpectedly quicken with life in the nineties?

I think this time it's safe to send the flowers. Set aside the pitching staff, and you've got enough over-the-hillers and never-wasers to stock the '88 Orioles. Okay, the Dodgers play better defense, but offensively they're probably worse, and with nowhere to go but down. Face it, if Eddie Murray couldn't manage a resurgence in '89, when will he ever? Willie Randolph has been acceptable, but his always impressive OBP was desperately needed in the leadoff spot, which for some reason he could not fill. (The Randolph-Steve Sax switch is Steinbrenner's only cause for happiness in '89.) Alfredo Griffin raised his average fifty points and was still worthless. And what an outfield minus Gibson: Mickey Hatcher, Franklin Stubbs, John Shelby *et al.;* perfectly obvious why they didn't need Mike Devereaux.

You know, we often hear it said that baseball is a business rather than a sport. All right, it's a business in that it generates increasingly huge revenues, but almost every year the

World Series winners prove that at heart they're maudlin sentimentalists rather than hardheaded bottom liners. Do you think Peter O'Malley and Fred Claire really felt their Series triumph proved that Hatcher and Stubbs and Mike Davis were valuable ballplayers who could help them win again? Or that, in Kansas City after the '85 title, Ewing Kaufmann thought the retention of Lynn Jones and Greg Pryor would keep the Royals on top? Sure, some of these players were under contract, but implacable business tycoons are notorious for swallowing unfavorable contracts and cutting their losses, and the public be damned. Frankly I'm glad that the morals of the marketplace don't totally control baseball, but Dodgers fans can be forgiven if they wish that Fred Claire had asked himself, what can these players do for me next year? (Or maybe not; the one strictly dollars and cents decision made in the off-season led to the untimely departure of Sax.)

Anyway, as long as we're talking business, what, from a shareholder's point of view, is the future prospectus for the Dodgers? A healthy Kirk Gibson is desperately needed—and highly unlikely. Without him, no functional outfield exists. The right side of the infield is elderly; the left side will never hit. Mike Scioscia behind the plate is terrific, but Rick Dempsey is—finally—washed up, and there's no Sandy Alomar, Jr., in Triple A. Juan Bell was a solid prospect, ditto Mike Devereaux, but all they produced were Murray and Mike Morgan, a good but redundant pitcher. There are enough talented arms to exchange for improved offense, but Claire's first '89 move in that direction was not encouraging: Of all the outfielders available, he chose Kal Daniels, the only under-thirty player whose knee operations can't be counted on fingers and toes. Did Claire think he could get a two-for-one special on lame outfielders at the local hospital? Happy surgery hour?

The more I think about it, the more it seems that the '89 Dodgers are in the same position as the '84 Orioles: starting the inevitable decline after one last gasp championship. Maybe they won't sink so far as the Birds, maybe the quality pitching will at least enable them to keep their noses above water, but pitching was always thought to be the Orioles long suit, until one day they woke up and it wasn't, and then there was nothing left. After the turnaround the '89 Orioles accomplished, it would be foolish to write off any team until all vital signs have been extinguished, but increasingly the world champion Dodgers remind me of Samson in the temple of the Philistines, summoning all of his strength for one last unexpected moment to crush his adversaries—but also himself.

—M.K.
September 3, 1989

How many players were there on the Dodgers last year who played in the American League in the 1970's? About a dozen, I think . . . Willie Randolph, Eddie Murray, Alfredo Griffin, Rick Dempsey, Kirk Gibson, Mike Morgan, John Tudor. A lot of these guys, I remember they played in the American League but I'm not sure exactly when . . . Mickey Hatcher, Mike Sharperson, Mike Davis, Billy Bean, John Shelby, Jay Howell, Ray Searage. It's too bad John Castino got hurt; he'd be playing third base for the Dodgers now.

I suppose it is dangerous to write off the Dodgers; I know I didn't think they could win anything in '85 or '88, and still don't really understand how they did. The Dodgers draw upon resources that ordinarily mismanaged franchises, like the Mariners and Indians, can't match—a massive attendance base and polished public relations effort which keep the money coming in, a network of old scouts, the magic name "Dodgers." John Wetteland, I expect, will take over the league in '90 or '91, and Kal Daniels if he should happen to get healthy is a nice acquisition for the offense. Alejandro Pena could again become an outstanding pitcher.

It is, in many respects, a God-awful team, but the pitching is still good enough to keep them in the race and even win it if nobody pulls away. I pick them third, but with one caveat. If the pitching crumbles, they lose a hundred.

STRETCH DRIVE NOTES

*S*ept. 5—It's amazing what an aroused Jack Clark can do: seven RBI's in yesterday's 10–9 comeback win over Atlanta, which moved the Padres to within seven games of the front-running Giants. With Houston suddenly faltering ("Scott and Deshaies and pray for rain" was never destined to work, especially in the Astrodome), it appears that if there is to be a race to the wire in the NL West, San Diego will have to provide it. Credit Jack McKeon with—finally—making two bold moves: putting Bip Roberts in the leadoff spot (his OBP is light years ahead of any other candidate) and inserting Double-A sensation and number-one draft choice Andy Benes into the rotation. It's probably too late, but at least McKeon has done something; it seemed for a while that he had resigned himself to the second division. Now, who knows? It's been a long time since any Giants starter went down in a heap—almost three weeks. If the Padres continue to rally, and come up just two or three games short, I think Trader Jack will spend a long, cold winter thinking of what might have been. History has recorded that, on his deathbed, Robert E. Lee called again for one of his generals: "Tell A. P. Hill he must come up." It's not difficult to imagine McKeon, in a similar delirium years from now crying: "Tell Alomar and Benes they must come up—from triple A."

Despite suddenly wretched starting pitching, Cubs stock may have risen on Labor Day with the news that Cardinals ace reliever Todd Worrell has injured his elbow and is at least temporarily on the shelf. Whitey Herzog, who already makes daily choices between Tony Pena and Todd Zeile behind the plate, and among Vince Coleman, Willie McGee, and Milt Thompson in the outfield, must now ponder another decision: Who gets the ball with the game on the line: steady Ken Dayley or resurrected Dan Quisenberry? Both are battle-tested in pennant races, but for Quiz to suddenly, after a four year hiatus, again become the bullpen ace has a sort of storybook quality to it, don't you think? It was Herzog after all who first brought Quiz to the majors (although it took Jim Frey to make him a closer); it was the Rat who was in turn ruined by Quiz's clutch relief effort in the sixth game of the '85 Series, and it was Whitey who kept Quiz's career alive, and gradually revived it, after the humiliation of the last two years in Kansas City. I'm sure Herzog doesn't give a shit for storybook endings (he'd let Rumpelstiltskin take the baby if it would mean five more wins), but if he does decide to hand the ball to the ex-Royals ace when the money's on the line, "The White Rat and the Quiz" may yet be added as a supplement to the next edition of *The Fairy Tale Book of Baseball.*

Sept. 6—Brad Komminsk, center fielder for the Cleveland Indians, has never had an easy time of it. He was the Braves number one prospect of the early eighties, and when he unaccountably failed to hit, they just as unaccountably decided to convert him into a third baseman, with the usual result. Traded to Milwaukee, he appeared in but seven major league games in '87, and none at all in '88. He had all the appearance of a classic washout. But the Indians decided to take a chance on him, and if there's one thing the Tribe excels at lately, it's rejuvenating cast-off Brewcrewers. Komminsk proved no exception; in part time play he has raised more than a few eyebrows by hitting for both average and power. It's probably too late for him to have a standout career; he'll be twenty-nine when the bell rings in '90. In fact, he may have already missed his best chance at immortality when he failed to hold Cal Ripken's blast as he tumbled over the center field fence in Baltimore. I'm sure you saw the replay from various angles; he clearly dropped the ball on the way down. But there are some aspects of the play that I don't understand, such as how did the umpire know what to call? He certainly couldn't see through the fence, and he was in no position to peek over it. I'm told he received all manner of assistance from the nearby Orioles bullpen, but naturally they'd say it was no catch, he wouldn't take their word, would he? What then was to prevent Komminsk—had the ball not disappeared beneath a tarp holder—from quickly retrieving it and showing it to the umpire as though he had it all the way? That, many people claim, is exactly what Washington Senators right fielder Sam Rice did in the 1925 World Series, when he crashed into the bleachers in pursuit of Earl Smith's long drive, disappeared, and eventually emerged clutching the ball. The umpire, who could have had no idea what transpired while Rice was lost from sight, nonetheless ruled it a catch, and the Pirates lost by one run, although they eventually triumphed in the Series. In Rice's case, there was one major difference from Komminsk, and that is that those right field bleachers were occupied—by Senators fans, and it was the contention of the infuriated Bucs that a hometown fan had conveniently slipped the ball into Rice's glove, an option not available to the luckless Komminsk, who was on the road and anyway crashed into no-man's land.

But I would like to examine the Komminsk non-catch from a more speculative angle, if I might. Suppose the Indians and Orioles had not been playing a game that was meaningful only to the Birds, but rather a playoff to decide the AL East title. And suppose that the exact same play occurs, only this time Komminsk is able to quickly retrieve the ball and claim a catch, which claim the umpire upholds. And suppose that the Indians go on to win by one run? They win the division, while every TV set in the country is showing replays which prove conclusively that Komminsk dropped the ball. What then? I know, baseball has a hard and fast rule against using replays to overturn umpire's decisions. I know, the replays showed beyond question that Don Denkinger and Lee Weyer made bad decisions at critical moments in the '85 and '87 World Series, and nothing was done. But wouldn't turning an obvious home run into a harmless out, with millions of fans as witnesses, and the right to play for the league championship on the line, be possibly too much for even the league brass to swallow? Is it possible that, for the first time in baseball history, the instant replay could be used to make, and win, an appeal?

There's one other aspect of the Komminsk incident that I'd like to discuss. I've bitched and moaned about this before, but at the risk of seeming like a crank, don't you think

it's wonderful that we still have some ball parks with fences low enough to vault over and create an unforgettable baseball moment, and perhaps even a controversy? Naturally, Memorial Stadium is considered obsolete, and will soon be supplanted by a ball park featuring all of the latest appurtenances, but lacking—what do you want to bet?—fences that outfielders can climb. Well, maybe we should be grateful for any kind of fence, as long as we can avoid Plexiglas facades, or, worse yet, mammoth walls with abstract impressionist yellow lines above which lies home run territory. Absolutely the most useless controversy of the season was the one in Houston over whether someone's drive swerved over the yellow line, and was a homer, or whether it careened below, and was in play. Tell me, how do you want your games decided: by balls hitting above and below perfect geometric lines, or by Brad Komminsk, racing for the fence, measuring the flight of the ball, leaping at the last instant, and disappearing from view—with the ball in his glove?

Sept. 10—Can any team win the NL East? I'm beginning to wonder. The Cubs, Mets, Cardinals, and Expos all had chances this week to put one or more of their foes on the canvas, but none could land anything resembling a knockout blow, and there is little reason to believe that future head-to-head combat will produce a clear-cut, foot-on-chest winner.

It was the Cubs who came closest to going down for the count: In the first of their two games with the Mets, Rick Sutcliffe turned in probably the worst five innings by a winning starter of the '89 season. The bases were constantly jammed; hits and walks accumulated in profusion, but so did

breaks for the Cubs, most particularly the line drive off Luis Salazar's glove that deflected directly to Shawon Dunston, and was converted into an out. After escaping New York and Philadelphia with splits of two game series, the Cubs returned to Wrigley Field, opened a 7–1 lead on the Cards, and proceeded to blow the game 11–8, in large part due to the Dunston's butchering of an easy double-play ball, and wind blown homers by Pedro Guerrero and Terry Pendleton. It seemed the next day that the script for the fold was ready for rehearsal, but fortunately some Cubs neglected to study it. Dunston appeared to have learned his lines when he let Guerrero's eminently playable ground ball skitter past him to trigger a two run rally and give the Cards a one run lead, but fortunately Dwight Smith came up with some inspired ad-libbing in the bottom of the eighth when he singled to right, and, instead of meekly retreating to first when Tom Brunansky fielded the ball, paused between first and second, confusing Brunansky, and then broke for second and easily beat the befuddled outfielder's throw. This became a play of tremendous significance when, after Mark Grace was retired, Andre Dawson lashed an inning-ending double play grounder to short that was not a double play after all, thanks to Smith's daring, and Brunansky's rock. Luis Salazar, a last minute acquisition from the Padres, followed with a game-tieing single; Paul Assenmacher, a last minute acquisition from the Braves, held the Ratmen in the tenth, and then Salazar won the game with a one out double that scored Dawson. The Cubs may yet lose this race; the state of their rotation makes Spahn and Sain, etc., look like a cornucopia of starters. But I think that, thanks to a bold play by

Dwight Smith, and a bonehead play by Tom Brunansky, a bend, staple, and mutilate fold of the type last seen in '69, is now out of the question.

—M.K.

PHILADEL-PHIA

There is always hope. There is always hope because it is the nature of baseball to draw out hope from within us, whether or not there is a foundation for hope. If a teen-aged boy was trapped on a desert island with Shelley Winters, he would fall in love with Shelley Winters and probably be forever after fixated on three-hundred-pound banana slugs, simply because his need to fall in love is so strong that it will certainly find an object.

What is the starting point of the Philadelphia Phillies next championship team? Let's do a little systematic analysis of the Phillies, look at who they have and ask one question: Is it likely that this player can be a part of a championship team in Philadelphia some time in the future?

C	Daulton	No way
1B	Jordan	Well, maybe
2B	Herr	Forget it
3B	Hayes	Slim chance
SS	Thon	No
LF	Kruk	Probably not
CF	Dykstra	Could
RF	Hayes	Not likely
SP	Howell	Possibility
SP	Cook	Good possibility
SP	Carman	No
SP	Mulholland	Humm . . .
RP	McDowell	Sure
RP	Parett	Could

Boy, that's an awful picture, isn't it? Herr, Thon, and Carman are simply too old to last long enough to be part of a championship team, at least given their limited ability. Daulton and Mulholland aren't going to be part of championship teams because they can't play. Kruk and Hayes are good hitters but a little bit

unlikely, in view of their age, to still be productive four or five years from now. That leaves

1B	Jordan	Well, maybe
3B	Hayes	Slim chance
CF	Dykstra	Could
SP	Howell	Possibility
SP	Cook	Good possibility
RP	McDowell	Sure
RP	Parett	Could

Not one of whom has more than a fifteen percent chance of being a star, or better than maybe a forty percent chance of even being a regular four or five years from now. I'll cover their chances for development individually in Section III so I guess I shouldn't hit that now. . . .

This, in short, is a desperate situation, an awful team without any good young players. The front office's solutions this winter have been to sign Carmelo Martinez and offer a fortune for Mark Davis, whom they hope to convert to a starting pitcher, which is a dumb idea.

Competitive balance any more is such that one can see the possibility of any team winning their division two or three years down the road—any team, except Montreal and the Phillies. While the other divisions are being compressed, the NL East gives every indication of pulling apart over the next two or three years, with possibly two teams winning nearly a hundred games, and two teams losing nearly a hundred. We know which camp the Phillies are going to be in if it goes that way, and I'm sorry to say it. Phillies fans will find a reason to hope, but this is a Shelley Winters of a ball club if I've ever seen one.

A CUBS FAN SHARES HIS QUIET SAT-ISFACTION

Doctor, you're fired! I don't need you any more. This is it, the millenium, nirvana! Just three days ago, when they blew that 7–1 lead against the Cardinals, I knew it was coming, the inevitable fold. We just didn't have any pitching. Forget about the fourth starter, all we had was Greg Maddux; even Mitch Williams was none too steady anymore. The offense was holding up; apparently Jerome Walton and Dwight Smith are too green to know when to choke, but the big surge by Andre Dawson is never going to come, and when you get down toward the bottom of the order . . . What worried me most, though, was Shawon Dunston. The Shawon-O-Meter was no longer rising, and that sure double play ball he let go through his legs in that first Cardinals game was like a knife in the back. And then Saturday, when we're finally getting a good performance out of Sutcliffe, Dunston misplays Guerrero's sharply hit grounder, and the Cards turn it into two runs and the lead. I don't mind telling you, Doctor, I was despondent at that point. I called the suicide prevention hotline, but all I got was their answering machine; the counselor was out hanging himself. I didn't have any rope handy, or sleeping pills, not even—like a fool, having always been an advocate of gun control—any firearms lying about. So I decided to finish the game, and then go out to the garage and carbon monoxide myself. After the seventh inning, I made sure I had the car keys in my pocket, and before the bottom of the eighth I ran out and quickly checked the battery, belts, and hoses. No problem, my self-destruction was going to go off without a hitch. Well, I don't have to tell you what happened next, Doctor; how Dwight Smith made the nerviest play of the season. (Did you hear Harry screaming "Get back, get back!"?) to set up the tie, and how Luis Salazar drove in the game winner in the tenth. I went from the depths of despair to the apotheosis of ecstasy in less than three innings. And then yesterday, when they won the rubber game, and the Mets and Expos both lost, giving us a daylight lead over every one, I was so excited that I went out and sold my car, and threw away all my steak knives and razor blades, so that I would be sure to never commit suicide again. Because there's no way they'll back off now, Doctor. They've had their slumps, the pitching has bottomed out and rebounded, and they've proved they can win on any surface, in any park. I know, they still don't have four starters, but there's not enough games left to need that many. I tell you, it's a lock, you charlatan. Cubs win! Cubs win! Holy cow! And you said I was neurotic, you quack; you're the one that's neurotic. You didn't believe, you lack all faith, that's your problem. I tried to tell you but you wouldn't listen. You're a sick man, Doctor, and I feel sorry for you. But just to show that there's no hard feelings, can I settle the bill by giving you my spare World Series ticket?

—M.K.
September 11, 1989

STRETCH DRIVE NOTES

Sept. 14—You know things are breaking your way when even your liabilities suddenly turn into strengths. Last night the Padres were trailing Atlanta 2–1 in the bottom of the eighth, man on first, nobody out. Benito Santiago stepped to the plate. Now Santiago is still considered by many to be a first-rate player, strictly by virtue of his defense. They ignore the fact that offensively he is an out-making machine. No average, no on-base percentage, and, luckily for the Padres, no ability to sacrifice. After failing twice to advance the runner via bunt, Santiago golfed a game-winning homer into the left field stands that kept Padres hopes alive. Andy Benes chipped in with seven plus strong innings, and Mark Davis—summoned atypically while San Diego still trailed—was as usual untouchable. Tonight Ed (Still Having a Career Year) Whitson takes the mound; Friday brings the suddenly significant three game series in Frisco. If anything means nothing in baseball (pardon the Yogiism), it's momentum: The Padres could easily get swept out of Candlestick—and out of the race. But it's difficult to feel totally pessimistic about a team that's going so good that even failure to execute the sacrifice turns into victory.

Sept. 15—Just when it looked as if it might be safe to anoint the Blue Jays as AL East champs, they go into the Metrodome and get swept, three rookie pitchers (David West, Kevin Tapani, and Mark Guthrie) doing the honors. Is another late season collapse in the offing? Hard to say, but there are aspects of this team that don't inspire confidence. Tony Fernandez has never gotten untracked since recovering from his early season beaning, and went so far as to unilaterally pull himself from a game after being hopelessly overmatched against Bret Saberhagen. (This would have been headline news under Jimy Williams. With Cito Gaston at the helm, it caused barely a ripple.) Gaston undoubtedly deserves the credit for bailing out the sinking Blue Jays ship, but it's difficult to understand how he can continue to play Lloyd Moseby, much less bat him leadoff, without taking on more water. Fred McGriff has been in a slump, and George Bell is capable of commencing one at a moment's notice. And what if Mookie Wilson wakes up just in time to recall that he's not an All-Star after all? What does look good enough for the duration is the pitching, particularly the bullpen, which was totally immersed when Gaston took charge. Maybe it doesn't even matter; Baltimore is showing signs of handing it to the Gast House Gang by default: The 3–0 loss Wednesday night at the hands of the mighty White Sox and Cy Hibbard was either a wakeup call for the rest of the season, or taps. We'll soon find out which.

—M.K.

BOSOX BASHING— EACH OTHER

Ah, this is more like it. The '88 Red Sox, with their battle-back-against-all-odds spirit, their one-for-all attitude, their rallying behind the newly-minted manager in his confrontation with a fading star, those Red Sox, I say, were a distasteful sight to those of us born and bred on the more typical Bosoxian blend of egotism, recrimination, and out and out crybabyism. Not to worry, the '89 Sox quickly made it evident that, like Warren G. Harding before them, they preferred a return to normalcy. Bob Stanley, buried in the bullpen with an ERA excessive even for Fenway, let it be known that he "hated" Joe Morgan. Joe Price was even more candid. After allowing Devon White to steal second, third, and home, he responded to some understandable reproof by suggesting that Morgan perform the usual anatomically impossible act. These were only the most obvious signs of unrest among the natives, unrest management had earlier attempted to quell, not very successfully, by extending Morgan's contract through the '90 season.

I would not, however, wager my life's savings that he will manage 162 games in '90. But whether ousted sooner or later, I suspect he'll go down in history as another classic example of the Bob Lemon Syndrome, i.e., a manager who inherits a chaotic, desperate situation (such as Billy Martin left behind invariably), and calms the waters by saying something

like "The season begins today, just go out and have fun," and, perhaps, makes one or two lineup adjustments that seemed obviously necessary to everyone but the departed manager—in Morgan's case, benching Spike Owen in favor of Jody Reed—and sits back and basks in the praise for "clearing the air in the clubhouse." Now, if you're intent upon hiring managers like Martin and John McNamara, men like Lemon and Morgan become extremely valuable. The problem is that after they've unclogged the previous manager's backed up sewer, they seem without a clue when their own plumbing runs foul. Cito Gaston, who successfully mucked out a fetid Blue Jays clubhouse, has reflected that perhaps he should return to his old hitting instructor's job in '90, no matter how well the Jays fare in '89. Undoubtedly, most observers scoff at this, but I wonder if Gaston doesn't sense that, like Lemon and Morgan before him, he is better suited to cleaning up other people's messes rather than his own. If Toronto wins the AL East we're likely to find out, for surely he will be offered a managerial contract that, with the best will in the world, he cannot refuse.

In fairness to Morgan, the mess he was expected to clean up in '89 was possibly more Lou Gorman's (and Margo Adams's?) than his own, and its extent might have taxed the managerial ingenuity of John McGraw and Connie Mack. When Bruce Hurst departed for San Diego he left a hole in the rotation that was never adequately plugged, although John "the Balking Man" Dopson was far from a failure. To reach serious contention, Morgan must have known he'd need banner years from Roger Clemens, Mike Boddicker, and Oil Can Boyd. Instead, Clemens was good, not great, Boddicker mediocre, and the Can injured. Mix in a horrifying start by closer Lee Smith, and you wonder how the Bosox hung about the fringes of the race in even the AL Least.

The offense, as usual, was among the leaders in run production, but with the pitchers yielding an equal number, it hardly mattered. Nick Esasky (a born Fenway player) was a major improvement over Todd Benzinger, but Jim Rice finally proved to even his most stubborn partisans that he was washed up. The pity is that he used up over two hundred at-bats in doing so. Mike Greenwell, Ellis Burks, and Dwight Evans are a fine outfield, but Burks went on an injury tear, and Evans, bothered by a back ailment, was relegated to DH late. Given those openings, it's difficult to understand why Carlos Quintana has not seen more action; as I write, he has no more at bats than Sam Horn, who's seen entirely too much action.

But Gorman and Morgan and everyone should have known that the season was shot when always reliable second baseman Marty Barrett tore cartilage in his knee—three seconds after signing a long-term contract. He was back in August, seeing sporadic duty, and although the Sox didn't say so out loud, the talk of keeping Jody Reed, shifted to second in the wake of the injury, at that position, and making offensively anemic Luis Rivera the regular shortstop would indicate that Barrett did not return as good as new. Did something like that happen to Rich Gedman, only an accumulation of lesser injuries rather than one major disaster? How else to explain the complete collapse of his career? It's a foregone conclusion that the Sox will—reluctantly—dip into the free agent market for help behind the plate—and, of course, in the rotation. All the money in the world spent

on free agents, though, will not alleviate the curious malaise that seems to eternally infect the Fenway clubhouse. And in this respect Lou Gorman, who has succeeded by and large in his other major objectives of putting a winner on the field and expunging the long-standing Red Sox racist tradition, has run up against a stone wall. Doesn't most hardcore clubhouse discontent have an obvious source that, if removed, or at least tempered, allows the return of something resembling amity? In Oakland in the seventies it was Charles O. Finley; until recently in Toronto it was Jimy Williams, and in New York at the moment it may be Darryl Strawberry. But who's the culprit in Boston? They change players, managers, even owners, and—except for brief intervals when they win so frequently that not even W. C. Fields could reasonably grouse—nothing happens: The clubhouse remains a cacophony of contumely. Is there anything Lou Gorman can do to effect a change, or is it a hopeless task as long as the Sox play in a park that seems to increase self-centeredness as surely as it increases batting averages?

—M.K.
September 16, 1989

The world waits for something to happen in Fenway Park which is truly new, and not alone the recycled news of twenty or thirty or fifty years ago—inflated batting stats through the lineup, inflated ERAs in the pitching staff, unhappy stars, a team which contends but doesn't win, brain-dead managers, and an irresponsible media which sharpens its teeth on the ankles of superstars. . . .

The Red Sox play a summer game in a winter city. This is not a city built for hot near-naked afternoons where the wind strolls down buttermilk sands without a dollar in either hand or a pocket to put it in. Summer is for optimists, for endless possibilities and the snarl of traffic that they bring. This city sees optimism as arrogance and naïvete.

But optimism yields to gloom and finally the season of despair, and the city comes into its own. This is a place people go to study. This is a city built for the things you do in winter, huddled together in warm small restaurants, theaters lighting up the too-early nights, the dead ocean lying safely out of sight. A city that has rattled through three centuries does not despair merely because the wind turns to the north, but sees despair as cowardice and naïvete.

The Red Sox play perpetually out of season, in a town where people truly believe that baseball is designed but to break your heart. And what will they have in 1990? Why, what they had in 1950, of course: inflated batting, inflated ERAs, unhappy stars, a team which contends but doesn't win, brain-dead managers, and an irresponsible media which sharpens its teeth on the ankles of superstars. They are a third-place team which will finish second because the division has no second-place team, and the city will enjoy the experience but certainly never trust it.

STRETCH DRIVE NOTES

*S*ept. 17—The situation called for desperate remedies, and John Wathan went with a generic drug. In the Saturday night game at Baltimore, the Royals had battled back to tie the score in the top of the eighth. Oakland had already blundered its way to another loss in Boston, and the Wathmen had a chance to pull within two-and-a-half-games of the lead. So in the bottom of the eighth, when the Orioles put two men on with one out, I was sure Wathan would summon his ace, Jeff Montgomery, in a non-save situation, to fight tooth and nail for a victory that was clearly within reach. It didn't happen. Steve Farr, recently off the DL, was called in and proceeded to fan Craig Worthington. But slumping Bob Melvin singled home two runs, and the Royals were beaten. I still don't understand it. Montgomery was fresh, he'd only pitched once in the last week. I know you don't want to use your closer in anything but a save situation if you can help it, but going into the final two weeks, with an opportunity to gain desperately needed ground, this was a situation if there ever was one to show some flexibility. Wathan instead chose to hold hard and fast to the rule, and it may have cost him a game in the standings he'll have no easy time making up.

Sept. 22—It isn't often that news of a defensive play dominates the first seven paragraphs of a reporter's overnight story, but Mel Antonen for *USA Today* was on the money when he gave Mark McGwire's game-winning homer second billing to Tony Phillips's brilliant robbery of Kirby Puckett. It must have turned up on every highlights show in the country, but in case you missed it, Dan Gladden was on first when Puckett grounded sharply up the middle. Phillips raced behind the bag, made a diving stop, and rolled off his belly in time to backhand the ball to Mike Gallego for the force that may have saved the game, eventually won by the Athletics 2–1. I don't expect to see a better infield play all year, and a tip of the cap to Antonen for knowing what's important, even if it doesn't show up in the box score.

That's the good news; the bad news is why don't Antonen's bosses, who routinely inundate us with every possible offensive statistic on a weekly basis, publish comparable defensive statistics that would allow us to put Phillips's gem in perspective? I mean, how good a second baseman is he? I've seen him play maybe six times this year, how can I judge from that? I've seen McGwire those same six times and he's never homered; should I conclude that he lacks power? Maybe I would if his offensive numbers weren't in the public domain. I know this much: At the end of the '87 season, in which Phillips appeared at second eighty-seven times, the Athletics decided to sign free agent second baseman Glenn Hubbard, who logged most of the time in '88. Was this in fear of Phillips's offense, or defense, or both? In any case, Hubbard did not meet expectations, was released in '89, and the job fell to Phillips. The offensive stats we are inundated with show that he's hitting and reaching base about as much as can be expected, but again, what about the defense? How many assists does he have? How many double plays has he turned? What about total chances per nine innings? All we know for sure is how many errors he's committed—in the opinion of fallible human beings. Maybe I should count my blessings; I can remember the good old days when all I had access to were a player's batting average, home runs, and runs batted in—we've come a long way in a relatively short time. But now that we know the importance of—and are duly offered—slugging average and on-base percentage, when will *USA Today*, or *The Sporting News*, or someone give us regular access to the information we need to decide if, one brilliant play notwithstanding, Tony Phillips is, or is not, a first-rate second baseman?

STRETCH DRIVE NOTES

Sept. 20—It could still happen to the Blue Jays, the choke I mean, but if it does, won't someone please try to remember their September 19 thrilling, extra innings comeback against the Red Sox? In the bottom of the tenth, trailing 5–4 and down to their last out, with nobody on, George Bell—surging after a bitter summer of discontent and trade rumors—singled, and was replaced by Tom Lawless, who moved up on Greg Harris's wild pitch. Then Joe Morgan decided to go against the book and in an odd manner: He ordered right-hander Harris to intentionally walk left-handed hitting Fred McGriff, which violated the hoary rule against putting the winning run on base, but could probably be justified if a platoon advantage was thereby gained. It was not. The next batter, solid lefty swinger Ernie Whitt, foiled the strategy by singling in Lawless to tie the game, and switch-hitting Tony Fernandez had the opportunity—but failed—to win the game with another single. If this is a typical example of Joe Morgan strategic thinking, no wonder numerous Boston boosters have been heard to mutter that he's gone daft.

It didn't seem to matter, though, when the Sox broke through for a run in the top of the thirteenth against recently invincible Tom Henke. But in the bottom half Morgan was still, strangely, going with Harris. (*a digression:* Harris is the pitcher you may have heard about who wants to, and reportedly has the ability to,

throw ambidextrously. The Sox, grand traditionalists that they are, are not eager for him to do this, but as long as Morgan figured to leave him out there all night, wouldn't it have been nice to rest one of his arms by switching periodically? And anyway, isn't the very concept of an ambidextrous pitcher wonderful? I don't understand why the baseball establishment, which routinely acquiesces to such perversions as the DH and artificial turf, is reluctant to approve switch pitching; they should be actively encouraging it.) He stayed with him despite a leadoff walk. He stayed with him despite a one out single that put the winning run on base. After a wild pitch advanced the runners, the drawn-in Boggs was able to convert Gruber's grounder into a putout at the plate. One out away from victory. But Lee Mazilli (OBP since arriving from New York .425) coaxed a walk, loading the bases, and still Harris remained in the game. Nelson Liriano was down to his last strike before doubling to deep right to win the game and preserve the Jays two game lead over Baltimore. It also gave them a 12–4 record in extra inning games; is that a symptom of a team that's likely to choke it all away?

Understand, like most fans with no personal involvement in the AL East, I'm rooting for the miracle Orioles. I hope it all comes down to those last three head-to-head clashes in the Sky Dome, and that the Why Not-ers emerge victorious. But I most emphatically do not want to hear it said that the Blue Jays gave it away for lack of intestinal fortitude. And yet if Baltimore does win the division, it is almost inevitable that the Jays be derided as folders. I thought it was a bum rap in '87, and I think it would

be a bum rap in '89, but there it is.

Sept. 21—The San Francisco Giants are simply not going to back off. Three remarkable rallies in one month, with yesterday's resurgence from a 7–0 deficit against the Dodgers the most improbable of all. Down 7–3 going to the ninth, they faced NL ERA leader Jay Howell and took belated batting practice: seven consecutive hits, five runs, no outs recorded. You get the feeling they'd have scored as many runs as needed, no matter how astronomical the deficit. If '87 was the year of the lively ball, could it be that '89 is the year of the lively comeback? Early on the Phils rallied from a ten run deficit to hand Jim Rooker his walking papers, and the Blue Jays inflicted an identical humiliation upon the Bosox. Then the Cubs climbed out of a 9–0 hole to edge the Astros, and of course the Giants overcame an 8–0 Reds lead—after Roger Craig cleared the bench in concession. It now appears that two of the teams that engineered remarkable reversals will meet in the NLCS, and of course, in beautiful Wrigley Field. Anyone think there's much chance of some exciting playoff action?

Now that Cubs-Giants is a lock, the major issue in Chicago is undoubtedly *not* obtaining playoff or Series tickets, but rather protecting the Belmont Park statue of General Phil Sheridan and fiery war-horse from Giants miscreants. As reported early in the summer by Mike Royko, it seems that whenever the Craigmen invade the Windy City, one or more of their number venture out in the wee hours and paint the genitalia of the general's horse orange. Repeated pleas by outraged city fathers to Giants officials have fallen on deaf ears: Twice a year in recent seasons a city employee has wasted valuable hours, at taxpayers' expenses, scraping paint from the reproductive organs of Sheridan's noble charger.

Now, vandalism by immature West Coast airheads visiting the City of Big Shoulders is bad enough, but when these same airheads suddenly stand between the Cubs and their first pennant in over forty years, it becomes an intolerable state of affairs. My question: how many die-hard Cubs fans have gathered themselves into vigilante groups, posses if you will, lynch mobs if we're lucky, to stand twenty-four hour guard over General Phil and his mighty steed, and woe betide the effete Giant who comes near with a can of spray paint? Not that it should be allowed go at that: Revenge must be exacted for past insults, so I suggest that a Johnny Bench look-alike be commissioned to infiltrate the Giants clubhouse, under guise of taping one of his award-winning Krylon commercials, and before anyone is the wiser, spray painting Pat Sheridan's testicles blue, with cameras rolling, all the while solemnly intoning "no runs, no drips, no errors."

—M.K.

WHAT WE WON'T REMEMBER ABOUT THE '89 ORIOLES

Years from now, baseball fans may look back on the odyssey of the miracle '89 Orioles—I don't see them as any less miraculous simply because they didn't clear the final hurdle—and reflect that it all fell into place for them; that they knew from the start which young defenders to blanket the field with, which untested pitchers to send to the mound, and then sat back and allowed these players to carry them farther than anyone would have thought possible. In truth, they never had it figured out, and throughout the season were constantly groping for answers just like any other ball club. At the most inopportune times they were bedeviled by injuries, slumps (hitting, pitching, and yes, even fielding), and bad umpiring. They had their share of breaks—most conspicuously, playing in the AL East—but it was never a jog in the park; on the contrary it was what a 162-game season usually is—a fight-desperately-not-to-spit-out-the-bit marathon.

Years from now, will anyone remember that the Orioles came dangerously close to stubbing their toes terminally in spring training, when shifting Cal Ripken, Jr., to third to make way for phenom Juan Bell seemed a viable option? Thankfully—for them—Bell was not ready, and International League MVP Craig Worthington erased all

horrifying memories of Floyd Rayford, et al., with his glovework, and surprised many by making a solid offensive contribution. (Does this mean that the idea of moving Ripken is finally dead and buried? Cross your fingers.)

Years from now, fans will hark back to opening day, 1989, and reflect that they knew something was in the wind when the Birds unexpectedly pummeled the Bosox and Roger Clemens. It was an excellent burst out of the gate, but in another sense it was extremely costly, as right fielder Steve Finley, an unheralded rookie who earned a trip north by burning up the Grapefruit League, smashed into the fence and was immediately relegated to the disabled list. When he returned, he was no longer on fire, and it became a season-long struggle to raise his average to its final .249 mark. Another starter that day, center fielder Brady Anderson, was expected to key the Orioles offense from the leadoff slot. He drew the walks you require, his stolen base percentage was excellent, and he was brilliant in the field, but he did not hit. Robinson waited and waited and waited, but finally was obliged to pull the plug. Anderson's unexpected failure had long-term consequences, for his replacement, Mike Devereaux, a quality pick-up from the Dodgers, seemed uncomfortable at the top of the order, and Phil Bradley, thought by many to possess quintessential leadoff qualities, turned in an atypically lackluster performance when hitting first.

Years from now, fans will discuss the young pitchers who—still wet behind the ears—almost carried the Orioles to an impossible dream: Jeff Ballard, Greg Olson, Pete Harnisch,

Bob Milacki. They will conveniently forget that the opening day starter was Dave Schmidt, who in '88 had posted a remarkable 3.40 ERA—with no defense behind him, remember—mostly in relief, but in '89 could not make the transition to starter, even though backed by brilliant defense, and rang up an eventual 5.69 ERA before being (his word) "buried." Will anyone remember that Jose Bautista, the most experienced of the young pitchers, made ten dismal starts before mercifully returning to Triple A? Will anyone remember that, at the same time Bautista faded out, a sub-journeyman (31–47 lifetime entering '89) named Jay Tibbs resurfaced and promptly went 5–0 with an under-three ERA in eight starts, only to blow out his shoulder in early July and disappear onto the DL? And Years from now—perhaps sooner—the name Ben McDonald may be spoken in hushed tones of reverence presently reserved for Mike Cuellar and Jim Palmer, but will anyone remember that in '89, with a miraculous division title within one more live arm of becoming a reality, contract negotiations dragged on interminably, to the point that when he finally signed, it was far too late to help the Orioles in their desperate battle?

And last, and unquestionably least, let us fervently pray that years from now fans will have forgotten the mid-season acquisition of Keith Moreland.

What we'll remember, years from now, is a team of mostly no-names who, given the opportunity, took the bit between their teeth, and refused to relinquish it—despite more than their share of adversity—even at the last. Or will we? I've heard it said that no one long recalls a team that finished

second, but then how many runners-up have come from dead last (hell, embalmed last) to within a hair's breadth of garnering all the marbles in one year? I think that more than any other aspect of the '89 season, the Baltimore Orioles are worthy of our remembrance.

—M.K.

To me, the Baltimore Orioles of 1989 bore an uncanny resemblance to the Orioles of 1959–60. The Orioles after moving to Baltimore in 1953 had never finished over .500 or in the first division, and in 1960 Paul Richards decided it was time to push the old guys out of the way and take a look at a whole bunch of young players. Only a few of those young players were hot prospects—really, only one. Brooks Robinson had been the Orioles regular third baseman in 1958, had struggled and been sent out. When he came back in mid-1959 he was ready to play.

Surrounding Robby, though, were a bunch of guys who were just happy to be there. Jim Gentile in 1960 was a slugging first baseman who had been trapped in the Dodgers minor league system for years, and who even when traded to the Orioles had expected to open the season watching a veteran (Bob Boyd) play first base. Randy Milligan in 1989 was a slugging first baseman who had been trapped in the Mets and Pirates systems, and who even when traded to the Orioles had been slotted to sit and watch a veteran (Bob Horner). Each got a chance to play, and each played well.

The parallel at the other positions is not as perfect, but Gentile and Milligan characterize both teams. Both teams were chock full of players who very well could have spent the season in the minor leagues. For the 1960 Orioles, that list included Marv Breeding, Ron Hansen, Dave Nicholson, Steve Barber, Chuck Estrada, and Jack Fisher. For the 1989 Orioles, that list included Mike Devereaux, Brady Anderson, Craig Worthington, Greg Olson, Bob Milacki, Pete Harnisch, and a few others.

Both teams had a few reclamation projects to fill in the spots where no young player was available, and both teams had a benchful of veterans who probably weren't all that happy to be watching the younger players.

And both teams won. The 1960 Orioles won eighty-nine games, finishing second behind the Yankees. The 1989 Orioles won eighty-seven.

The 1960 Orioles are the true beginning of the great Oriole teams that followed. After 1960 the Orioles were contenders. They won ninety-five games in 1961, with the aid of an expansion, and pushed the Yankees to the wall in 1964, although they didn't win until 1966. I don't expect the 1990 Orioles to win ninety-five games—but I do think that they can hold most of the ground they picked up last year.

What these teams prove . . . well, prove is too strong a word, because these two teams will not convince a skeptic. What these teams demonstrate, to me, is that the number of players who can play baseball is greater than the number of major league jobs available to them, and that therefore a lot of talent is trapped in the minor leagues. They're not great players, but they're as good as some of the guys who have been kicking around for years. They were there in 1960, and they were there in 1989, and if the major leagues expand to serve the forty or fifty cities that deserve major league baseball, the talent is still going to be there.

I've explained before why the major leaguers don't want to believe that. The people who have jobs work hard to sell the idea that the players at the next level are light years behind them, that only the exceptional ones can make the leap necessary to move up. But you know, there's another reason I hadn't thought of, which you see from the perspective of the front office. If there is talent always available, then there is no excuse for failure, is there? If a team which finishes last can wring its hands and say that the talent to do better just isn't there, then the GM is off the hook; he can go on hauling in Candy Maldonados and Joel Youngbloods and say "Well, I did the best I could with what was available." The Orioles, in a sense, are a threat to those people, because they prove that that just isn't the case.

BRAVES NEW WORLD

I'm a little disappointed that the Braves are on the verge of regaining respectability; I so enjoyed the jokes that made the rounds when they were God-awful. Remember the one about the Brave who was so determined to improve his game that he injected himself with cork and filled his bat with steroids? Or the three Braves who were disgusted with all the losing and decided, out of frustration, to become abusers of intravenous drugs? The first Brave shoots up and passes the dirty needle to the second Brave, who likewise mainlines, and passes the even dirtier needle to the third Brave, who, a trifle reluctant, says, "Aren't you guys scared of getting AIDS?" to which the first two Braves reply, "Hell no, we're wearing condoms."

I thought, when the '89 season began, that there would be plenty more jokes of that ilk, as the Braves still looked to be in desperate straits. Imagine, they actually thought that thirty-three-year-old Lonnie Smith, coming off a .237 season, could be their left fielder. And they were bringing in the superannuated Darrell Evans for one last go around. They were also, as spring training wound down, desperately scanning the waiver wire, picking up their starting second baseman, Jeff Treadway, at the last possible moment, and also adding Toronto castoff Mark Eichhorn to bolster a bullpen that, among other things, lacked a proven closer. Was this any way to run a ball club? I couldn't wait for the punch lines to start zapping me from all directions. But a funny thing happened on the way to another sojourn in the cellar—the organization started to toss hints that it knew what it was doing. I still think Evans was a mistake, and Treadway not much more than a stopgap until Mark Lemke is ready, but with Dale Murphy still in the throes of a premature decline, Lonnie Smith's greatest year was desperately needed. Have you compared Smith's stats with those of the rest of the Braves? No one else—save the late-arriving Oddibe, more on him later—reached base regularly, no one else posted a decent slugging average—Lonnie Smith, almost by himself, was the Braves offense, and the fact that Bobby Cox alone thought he could play is a tribute to his willingness to go against the conventional wisdom.

Another tribute to Cox—and Russ Nixon—is their willingness to wait for the young pitchers to develop. Tom Glavine and Pete Smith were forced to take their lumps in '88 with a pitiful team behind them, but this year it was payback, at least for Glavine (Smith, for some reason, has taken a step backward), while the arrival of John Smoltz, Derek Lilliquist, and later, Marty Clary, completed a rotation that can only improve, although it is likely that September call-ups Tommy Greene and Gary Eave will have something to say about the composition of said rotation in '90. In the bullpen, journeyman Joe Boever suddenly was as good as anyone's closer for the first four months; his collapse in the later stages has opened the door for flame-throwing Mike Stanton.

(And now a pause for the presentation of the *Chickenshit of the Year Award:* To Al Rosen and Roger Craig, by acclamation, for whining to NL president Bill White that Atlanta shouldn't be allowed to start late-season additions Greene and Eave down the stretch against contenders—*runner-up for the award:* Bill White, for promising to investigate, rather than telling Rosen and Craig to stick their complaint where the sun doesn't shine. Forget for a moment their unmitigated gall; haven't they been around long enough to realize that pitchers no one has ever seen before—especially ones with solid Triple-A credentials, like Greene and Eave—often are extremely effective, at least the first time around? Did they really want Nixon to keep sending Pete Smith out there, *ad infinitum?* What a disgraceful controversy, and one which Rosen and Craig do not deserve to walk away from unscathed.)

If Cox and Nixon have erred, it's in not making a more forceful effort to surround their young pitchers with a solid defense—such as the Orioles' young pitchers have been surrounded by all season. They let erstwhile second baseman Ronnie Gant butcher the hot corner (and in consequence, his offense) for far too long. Moving Dale Murphy back to center was probably also a mistake, and while Lonnie Smith has been the team's offensive savior, he has never been a quality defender. Andres Thomas, on the other hand, has never been an offensive asset, but until '89 he could play defense. The complete and total collapse of all aspects of his game makes a trade a foregone conclusion, and as I write, Jeff Blauser, who solidified the defense at third when Gant departed, is being tested at shortstop—if he's at least competent he'll be a major improvement. But the best news of the year—offensively and defensively—was the arrival of Oddibe McDowell, who provided the Braves with a leadoff man (.358 OBP) and a replacement for Murphy in center.

Oddly, given McDowell's unqualified success since arriving from Cleveland, the speedily rehabilitated Gant has been seeing action in center; does this portend a platoon arrangement in '90?

In sum, even though this team made no progress in the standings, and barely discernible progress in wins and losses, there can be little doubt that it is much improved, and may even startle some people in '90. There's no quick ladder to the top, such as the Orioles found in the AL East, but at least Atlanta can take comfort in the likelihood that from now on, when someone tries a Braves joke, the typical response will be a frown and an "I don't get it."

—M.K.
September 25, 1989

YESTER-DAY'S WEAPONS, TODAY'S WAR

It's easy enough, with the usual twenty-twenty hindsight, to see where it all went wrong for the Montreal Expos. In race track parlance, they kept their eyes on the wrong horse. How can you blame them? The Mets beat them by nineteen games in '88, a state of affairs hardly calculated to cause inordinate fear of the Cubs. And since the Mets perceived strong point was their executioner's row (for mowing down murderer's rows) starting rotation, it's not difficult to see why Dave Dombrowski and Buck Rodgers highest priority was pitching, hence the deals that produced, variously, Kevin Gross, Mark Langston, and Zane Smith. Their strategy was successful, too; with the season almost concluded, the Expos have posted a 3.45 ERA, the Mets a 3.37. The only problem is that, in reality, the Expos staff was virtually a match for the Mets in '88: Montreal rang up a 3.08 ERA, New York a 2.91. They finished far back because the Mets out-scored them by 75 runs, and they've faded in '89 because the Cubs, with an almost identical staff ERA, have likewise far outpaced them in run production. In other words, the Expos spent all season trying to cure bronchitis of the pitching staff, while ignoring the cancer that ravaged their offense.

Did the offense suffer in part because Expos honchos began to believe that Buck Rodgers really was a genius, who, like Whitey Herzog, would find a way to haul in the pot no matter what kind of hand he was dealt? I thing Rodgers has proved he can manipulate his cards as well as anyone, but how many Damaso Garcias can you draw and still walk away winners? It wouldn't seem so disturbing except that Junior Noboa was absolutely destroying Triple A pitching all season; why won't anyone give him more than 80 at bats in the bigs, especially if Garcia and Tom Foley are the only alternatives? Unfortunately the roster seemed overburdened with makeshift players of their ilk, some better (Spike Owen), some worse (What possible excuse can there have been for giving Otis Nixon 250 plus at bats?), but none better than average. Sure, you can win with average players if you mix in a few standouts in the right places, but sadly for the '89 Expos their designated standouts (Raines, Wallach, Brooks, Galarraga) did not stand out enough. All right, Tim Raines did, but even his production may have been compromised by an extended sojourn in the cleanup spot. I can see absolutely what Rodgers had in mind, break up all those righty power threats with a man who can swing from the left, and it makes sense, except that in the meantime the Expos were left without an outstanding leadoff man, and Raines of course is a great one.

As for the rest of the designated standouts, time seems to have finally caught up with Hubie Brooks—his season was thoroughly mediocre, and with his contract running out there's no excuse for inviting him back. Tim Wallach plays hard and rebounded somewhat from a sub-par '88, but it appears he'll never again be a major long ball threat. Andres Galarraga has become a victim of Dickens' Disease (Great Expectations). It's not his fault: Remember the first half of '88, when he was ringing up Ruthian numbers, how players, managers, and journalists were falling all over themselves to concoct the most outrageous superlatives? Even the compulsively rational Whitey Herzog suggested that they order his plaque for Cooperstown. What a crock! He was twenty-seven years old in '88, suddenly he's going to become a great player? I feel badly for him; after all the hype, 20-plus homer seasons, with 80 to 100 RBI, plus good glove work, will never be enough.

And neither will the Expos offense ever be enough as it's presently constituted. Help may be on the scene already: Noboa was belatedly promoted, and Larry Walker, Jeff Huson, and Marquis Grissom will have the opportunity to win jobs in '90. I don't think Dombrowski and Rodgers can be fooled twice; they know now which aspect of the team needs to be upgraded. Re-signing Mark Langston would unquestionably help, but if this club is going to make its long-awaited breakthrough in '90, the kids out of Triple A will have to contribute.

—M.K.
September 27, 1989

The indicators series lists the Expos as one of the teams most likely to decline in 1990. The indicators don't know that Mark Langston, Bryn Smith, and Pascual Perez have flown the dome. What is going to happen to the Expos is obvious—even if not as inevitable as it now appears. There have been teams which seemed likely to collapse and instead came together suddenly, but obviously nobody including me is going to bet on it. There is almost no limit to how many games the Expos can lose in 1990.

SCHOTT DEAD—MARGIN-ALLY

Well, if you run your ball club like a car dealership, you have to expect that there will come a year when all your models get recalled, and your top salesman gets caught rolling back odometers. I have to admit that I reveled in the collapse of the Cincinnati Reds; it made my day watching Marge Schott seethe as the ongoing judicial process prevented her from giving Pete Rose his conge (a quaint, archaic expression; look it up in your Funk and Wagnalls).

But leaving aside all prejudice, if possible, it's difficult to imagine even the most vengeful deity inflicting his/her wrath so indiscriminately on one franchise. Why not just make it rain for forty days and forty nights on Riverfront Stadium and be done with it? I assume there have been longer injury lists than the one the Reds put together in '89, but don't most clubs manage to stagger them a little better? I mean, one day you woke up and there were Eric Davis, Paul O'Neill, Kal Daniels, Barry Larkin, Chris Sabo, Danny Jackson, and Jose Rijo all on the disabled list together, or so it seemed. The problem, it seems to me, with having your season destroyed by injuries—besides not winning—is that it becomes that much harder to evaluate your chances for next year. The Braves, for example, big losers this year but relatively healthy, needn't waste time asking themselves what X might have done if not for his mid-season cranial rectalotamy.

The Reds, though, will be pondering such questions all winter. Can Larkin, with his damaged elbow, again be a quality shortstop? And if he can't, and they move him to the outfield, can Luis Quinones or Mariano Duncan fill his shoes? Will a healthy Danny Jackson instantly revert to his '88 form, or was that his career year? I don't envy Murray Cook (or someone) having to sort it all out, but there remain, happily, some certainties that can be addressed with confidence. One is that Todd Benzinger remains a thoroughly mediocre ballplayer. What did they see in him to begin with? The offensive stats he posted in Fenway were strictly run-of-the-mill; how could they think he'd better them in a more realistic setting? (I've heard that Ted Williams was a longtime Benzinger proponent, and of course Pete Rose did not like Nick Esasky.)

Another certainty is that Rick Mahler has become an exact reflection of the team he's pitching for, nothing more, nothing less. He became a big loser in Atlanta when the Braves became big losers, but it was supposed to be different in Cincinnati, and I'm sure it would have been had the team won. Count on it, if the Reds rebound and win in '90, so will he, and considerable talk is sure to focus on Mahler's resurrection as a cause, rather than an effect. A more likely cause of a Reds resurgence might be Rob Dibble, temper tantrums and all, with his almost four to one strikeouts to walks ratio in '89, and, I assume, the closer's role in '90. (Did anyone else notice that John Franco began to falter slightly when he was linked peripherally to the Pete Rose scandal? In fairness, the entire team faltered with him.)

But the biggest uncertainty, and perhaps the key to the Reds future, one way or another, is Eric Davis. Bad hamstrings and all, Davis is still a fantastic player—the complete power and speed package that beats you offensively and defensively. He wants off the artificial turf, though (who can blame him?), and to that end has vowed to become a free agent after '90. This puts the Reds in the same quandary as the Mets with Darryl Strawberry; trade him now and get something, or hope for a great year in '90 that will carry them to a pennant. As I write, trade rumors are flying; the latest sends Davis to San Diego for Benito Santiago and, I assume, other warm bodies. It makes sense; Cincinnati needs catching, The Padres need a center fielder, and Eric the Red needs grass under his feet. But Lord, what an offensive downturn the Reds will face without Davis. Santiago is worthless with the stick; I don't see how his vaunted defense can cut off enough runs to compensate for the loss of Davis's firepower. Of course, solving the problem sensibly by tearing out the Riverfront rug is a heretical thought; better to wave adios to a franchise player than contemplate that. Does anyone else find it ironic that a car dealer is forced to dispose of her most luxurious model because its wheels can't handle the local roads?

—M.K.
September 27

One of the things that probably irritates you from time to time is that having been a baseball fan for a good many years, almost everything that happens reminds me of something else that happened one time. The 1989 Mets to me are a reprise of the 1959 Yankees, while the 1989 Orioles are reliving 1960.

But I have *never* seen this before. I have never seen a team's talent base deteriorate as quickly as the Reds did in 1989. Have you? We have all been saying, all us professional talkers, that the Reds had the best young talent in the National League, and we were so much in the practice of saying that that at the end of the 1989 season people were still saying it—but it just isn't true anymore. The talent has evaporated, as if into air. Several people got hurt. A couple didn't develop. A couple of others did develop, but didn't turn out to be near as exciting as ballplayers as they were as prospects. Look at the team now:

Catcher—They have nobody proven. The kid Oliver is probably pretty good.

First Base—Todd Benzinger. The new Dave Stapleton. He's a goddamned joke, to be frank.

Second Base—Nobody. Job belongs to the veteran Ron Oester, who was never very good and hasn't gotten any better with the injuries, and Mariano Duncan, who has the potential to lead the league in strikeouts and errors if he plays enough.

Third Base—Chris Sabo. He's all right, but he's an ordinary player. He's no star.

They've got one great outfielder, who is threatening to vault, one good starter (Browning), one good infielder and a good bullpen. That's it. Other than that they're ordinary everywhere.

For an individual, the label "great talent" is often more of a curse than a blessing, and one suspects this may work for teams, too. The Reds could be better off without the excess of potential that they seemed to have a year ago. They're no longer dealing with a pie-in-the-sky super-team somewhere down the line; they're in the business now of getting a real team put together. Lou Piniella is probably a good manager and there isn't anybody in the division who'll scare you, so the Reds have a chance to win.

But I'll tell you this: This is one job I sure wouldn't want. If I was a thirty-eight-year-old managerial candidate, this is one job opening I'd let pass. It's a great little city and the Reds have some of the best fans in the world, but the expectations here are just grossly out of line with the talent. If Piniella wins in 1990, it's a hell of an accomplishment.

STRETCH DRIVE NOTES

Sept. 28—Now the table is set: Three games to go, the Blue Jays lead by one. The Orioles must win two of three in Toronto to force a playoff in Baltimore. Any doubt as to which team is feeling the pressure? There is simply no way the Blue Jays can lose the division without being labeled chokers or Blow Jays, or something equally cruel. They didn't exactly take a step toward getting the monkey off their backs with that ninth-inning loss to the Tigers on the twenty-sixth. Leading 3–1, Duane Ward struck out the first batter, then threw Scott Lusader's bunt past first for an error. You could probably conclude that he was shaken by this, for he proceeded to walk Matt Nokes and plunk Doug Strange, loading the bases and producing Tom Henke. Then, broken bat singles by Gary Pettis and Alan Trammell cleared the bases and left the Jays in stunned defeat, a defeat that will linger long in the minds of their fans if the Orioles win the division by one. I repeat, I don't believe these Blue Jays are folders. They're quite capable of losing three out of four to Baltimore because they are not a standout team. Only Dave Stieb and Jimmy Key have been reliable starters down the stretch, and the present outfield is a far cry from the "greatest ever" of the mid-eighties. They can easily lose on talent alone, but again, I realize that no one will accept that.

—M.K.

STRETCH DRIVE NOTES

*O*ct. 1—In the end, everyone was satisfied. Sure, it's too bad it didn't go down to the last day, or better yet, to a Monday playoff, but no one, player or fan, can claim they didn't get their money's worth out of the Blue Jays-Orioles final weekend showdown. Cal Ripken, Jr., was probably exaggerating when he said: "There's no World Series game that was ever as exciting as these two," but I think these teams earned the right to hyperbolize. At the outset though, cynics who predicted all along a Gast House Gang choke must have thought themselves prophets of Biblical dimension when Phil Bradley slammed Todd Stottlemyre's first pitch over the fence. What were the odds that this none-too-steady-throughout-the-season youngster could right himself and allow no further damage for five innings? Not that it would have mattered had not Tom Lawless manufactured a run in the bottom of the eighth by stealing second, advancing to third on a grounder, and scoring on Greg Olson's two-out, two-strike wild pitch that Jamie Quirk nobly shouldered the blame for. Meanwhile, the Jays bullpen, a shambles when Cito Gaston took over in May but now among the league's best, resolutely repulsed every Baltimore scoring bid. In the bottom of the eleventh, with a runner on second, Frank Robinson elected to walk second-half disappointment Junior Felix, and pitch to entire season disappointment Lloyd Moseby. Far from outrageous strategy, especially since it set up force plays, but the Ebony Ghost foiled it with a game-winning off-the-wall single.

I thought the Orioles dead in the water after that, and when I learned that scheduled Saturday starter Pete Harnisch had stepped on a nail and been scratched (by Robinson, not the nail; the nail dug into his foot and tore it all to hell), I assumed it was the final—literal—nail in the coffin, since Harnisch's replacement, Dave Johnson, had not pitched effectively in more than a month. And in the first inning, a leadoff walk to Moseby and a two-out single by George Bell gave the Blue Jays a quick 1–0 lead with Jimmy Key on the mound. But hold the funeral oration: Johnson steadied himself and surrendered nothing more, while Key was not himself; the O's, aided by a bad call at first base, produced three runs and drove Key from the game. His replacement, Grover Cleveland Wills, proved untouchable, however, and when Johnson tired in the eighth, relievers Kevin Hickey and Mark Williamson were not equal to the task, and the much-derided Blue Jays eked out their second straight come-from-behind victory, silencing, at least temporarily, the prophets of doom who had spent the final month dutifully practicing the Heimlich maneuver.

You know what was refreshing about the Orioles-Jays race? It seemed so satisfyingly unspectacular. Both teams battled doggedly, yet carefully, down the stretch, not unlike soldiers advancing through a minefield. There were no monster streaks, winning or losing. No dominant player took control, carrying his mates on his back, and by the same token, no player went abysmally into the tank, earning major league goat horns. The race didn't build to anything resembling a crescendo of a climax, such as Bobby Thomson gave us in '51. It was simply two modestly-talented teams, one attempting to make history, the other to bury it. It may have been deficient in heroes and goats, and thus in thrills and chills, but I have moments when I wonder if the price exacted of players and managers in enduring excruciating defeat in the media age isn't a trifle high, even as I acknowledge the stupendous salaries they now earn, and even as I take vigorous exception to Brian Downing's reprehensible assertion that journalists and fans colluded to kill Donnie Moore. In sum, I'm glad that this year at least the pain seems to have receded for the Orioles much faster than is likely for some other star-crossed ballclub in the post-season.

—M.K.

HERZOG'S BELLOW

I expect Whitey Herzog's latest book to land in the stores any day now, and I'll be surprised if it's not a bestseller. No, it's not *The White Whale* or *Rat Redux;* it won't even have much to do with baseball. I think a more likely title is *Whitey Herzog's Guide to Deportment, Etiquette, and Discretion,* with a foreword by Miss Manners. I expect this book because it is obvious Whitey has turned over a new leaf, and will no longer automatically say what he thinks when asked; that diplomacy has become a large portion of his repertoire—so much so that I'm surprised he hasn't been appointed ambassador to Panama. Since everyone else who has revamped their life unexpectedly is writing a book, why not the erstwhile candid, pull-no-punches Herzog?

It's been a remarkable metamorphosis. I remember Whitey from the old days in Kansas City, when, not content with dominating the AL West—he had this insane desire to ride roughshod over the entire league—he complained frequently that the conservative Royals management would not wheel and deal for the players he needed to put Kansas City in the World Series. Without consulting higher-ups he informed the world that John Mayberry would never again play for him after the '77 ALCS. Eventually, his candor contributed in no small measure to his dismissal, but the Rat remained uncowed. Signed by the Cardinals and given *carte blanche* to rebuild, he did not hesitate to inform a St. Louis institution, Ted Simmons, that his catching was not up to snuff, and that in the future he would be

first base, or be gone. Likewise, when Keith Hernandez became a conspicuous cocaine abuser, Herzog immediately Mayberried him to the Mets, and took the heat without complaint when the deal quickly moved onto the charts as one of the worst of all time. Oh yes, and along the way, the Cardinals, moribund in the seventies, reemerged as one of baseball's best teams, making three trips to the Series in the eighties. But also along the way, Herzog shed his general manager's hat, and when he did, the block-buster off-season trades that sent name players scurrying all across the baseball map came to a halt. Bruce Sutter was seduced away by Ted Turner; would Herzog have let it happen? That loss turned out for the best, but three years later, perceiving that he was getting the runaround from the Cardinals front office, Jack Clark unexpectedly signed on as a Steinbrennerian. As if that wasn't enough, Redbird brass responded to this wholly avoidable defection by courting Japanese exile Bob Horner. The Rat erupted in fury: Horner was worthless, he stated recklessly (and correctly), and damned if he wanted him cluttering up his roster. The tirade fell on deaf ears, Horner was duly signed, and Whitey, like a presidential press secretary, rendered his previous statements inoperative, and with Horns beginning the '88 campaign at first, the Cardinals sank like a stone.

And since then, seldom has been a discouraging word heard from Whitey Herzog. There was really nothing to say about the '88 Cardinals—they stank. But '89 was a different story. The outlook was dismal initially; Greg Mathews and Danny Cox went right to the all-season disabled list, and Willie McGee might as well have. But strange things began to happen in the NL East. By mid-season, it seemed

obvious that the Mets, everyone's choice to obliterate the field, were not after all invincible, were in fact on a collision course with self-destruction. Meanwhile, if the pieces were not exactly all falling into place for the Cards, neither were they being scattered to the four winds. Joe Magrane and Jose DeLeon provided an excellent one-two punch in the rotation (One wonders: What if DeLeon's wife had waited 'til the off-season to divorce him; his mid-season slump coincided with being served the papers.) and Scott Terry had his moments, as did the late-arriving Ted Power. The bullpen was first rate, with castoffs Frank DiPino and Dan Quisenberry providing invaluable support for the always reliable Ken Dayley and Todd Worrell. The offense, predictably, was nothing to write home about. Vince Coleman steals better than anyone since Willie "The Roadrunner" Sutton, but he simply does not reach base often enough; reportedly Herzog has run out of patience and wants him unloaded. More difficult to understand is why Whitey never ran out of patience with the injury-plagued McGee. Milt Thompson was excellent offensively, but wound up sitting at critical moments when McGee was given yet another chance to salvage his season. The man who almost single-handedly salvaged an otherwise feeble attack was, of course, Pedro Guerrero, who forever silenced those who doubted he could produce in spacious Busch.

But the burden was too great for one man, and GM Dal Maxvill had to realize it, yet he did nothing to lighten it. I'm sure he didn't see his team as a contender at the outset; a strategy of ride it out and wait for '90 made perfect sense; it was surely the same strategy employed by Jim Frey, until he woke up one morning, realized the

Cubs could win after all, and set to work accordingly. Maxvill, though, never seemed to get his wake-up call. Ken Hill, after a promising start, faded badly, Terry was disabled, and who arrived to fill the void? Power and Ricky Horton. All right, Power was respectable, but Horton—in a starting role—was worthless, and you get the feeling that they were acquired not to fill any particular role, but because they were available dirt cheap. No minor league talent to be surrendered, no hefty salaries to be picked up. If you didn't know better, you'd think Maxvill was George Argyros's GM. That's what I can't understand; how can Maxvill dare to pretend he's hamstrung by a shoestring budget when Busch Stadium is packed every night? Who's in charge of the pursestrings these days, and why are they operating as if Augie Busch planned on taking it all with him? I mean, I understand why the Angels let opportunity pass them by; they just go irrational every now and then. But I thought, even in the wake of the Clark-Horner fiasco, that this was still a sensible organization that wanted to win. Now I have to wonder.

Which brings me back to Herzog. The irascible White Rat I remember from KC would never have gone down with his ship quietly, particularly if lifeboats were so obviously accessible. Yet in '89 he accepted his watery grave without a whimper. What's happened? Has he finally mellowed with age, or is he just tired, too tired, even, to seek out another managerial post if fired by the Cards for excessive candor? Or does he honestly feel that he can accomplish more by practicing subtle diplomacy? That he can outlast Maxvill, and that the pursestrings will eventually be loosened, enabling him to once again win with first-rate talent? If Whitey is consciously playing

it cool, I hope it works for him, and the Cardinals, but he was considerably more entertaining in the old fulminating days, and I will always be nostalgic for them.

—M.K.
October 18, 1989

If a cliché can be profound, my favorite is that you're never as good as you look when you win or as bad as you look when you lose. This is more true of managers, I think, than anyone else. A pitcher in winning will still give up hits, walks, and homers, but a manager in winning does only one thing: He Wins. In November 1988 I could have read you a list of the clever things Tommy Lasorda had done to help push the Dodgers over the top with an under-manned team, and last year was Don Zimmer's turn. When a manager wins, everything that he does is connected to the win; when he loses, everything becomes a cause of the defeat.

Whitey Herzog has won more than most managers, and more than that has won while doing things in his own way, disdaining big hitters and superstar starters for wheels in the outfield and five-deep bullpens with everybody working. Two years ago, with Herzog's genius at its zenith, I wrote that I thought Whitey Herzog had probably won his last championship with the Cardinals. I have yet to be proven wrong, and that's the most dangerous thing for a person who does this every year. When you're wrong you get careful; when you're right you get cocky. You wind up booming from the mizzenmast that the Dickson has lost it and the Zephyrs will never win again, and then they do and you look stupid.

Well, Whitey Herzog didn't WIN last year, but he was still winning, and still drawing kudos (what? on the bath-room? where?) for having the Cardinals in contention despite a rash of injuries to the pitching staff. In case any of the media should forget that the Cardinals had had a rash of injuries to the pitching staff, Herzog reminded them daily. What tended to be obscured was that the Cardinals had the healthiest eight-man lineup in the major leagues. Their only serious injuries were in the outfield, and with a fourth outfielder on hand who was as good as any of the other three, the injuries in the outfield weren't critical. In addition to having eight men they could count on, the Cardinals' top two starting pitchers, Magrane and DeLeon, were both healthy most of the year, and both having the best years of their careers.

That's why I'm sticking another year with my prediction that Herzog has won his last title in St. Louis. The Cardinals are getting long in tooth, some of them anyway; an injury to Ozzie Smith, now thirty-five, would be far more critical than the 1989 injuries to Willie McGee and Danny Cox. I doubt that the team will be as healthy in 1990 as they were last year. I'm not saying they'll collapse, but I'd pick them to contend until about the first of August, and then drop to maybe fourth.

ANGELS NOT YET ON HIGH

If you can explain the California Angels in the eighties you deserve an honorary degree in abnormal psychology. What other franchise has been so utterly unpredictable, rising to the highest peaks one year, sinking to the lowest valleys the next (and not always waiting even that long: You'll surely remember that the '86 edition was one strike away from reaching the summit of Everest, only to inexplicably lose its footing and crash to the very bottom only three days later); making brilliant personnel decisions one day, committing the most egregious blunders the next. Is it any wonder that, after almost thirty years in the

American League, this franchise, to the vast majority of baseball fans nationwide, is still totally lacking an identity?

You might recall that the Angels concluded the seventies by winning their first division title before succumbing to a superior Orioles team in the playoffs. Then, setting the tone for the eighties in many people's minds, they allowed Nolan Ryan to depart via free agency, and imported Fred Patek by the same route to plug their undeniable shortstop hole. In all fairness, it must be conceded that in '79 Ryan was not a consensus immortal, but it should be similarly acknowledged that signing an obviously washed-up Patek to a big bucks three-year deal was an act of folly worthy of Spec Richardson, especially when you consider that Patek's diminished presence cast a long shadow over a developing young infielder, soon to be traded, named Dickie Thon.

Some organizations might have spent ten years reeling from such a double dose of dimwittedness, but the Angels are nothing if not resilient. By 1982 another over-the-hill, but at least still competent shortstop, Tim Foli, was in place, and, more significantly, by cleverly exploiting the petulance of certain owners embittered by the '81 strike (and apparently intent upon venting their spleen by discarding their highly visible player reps), obtained Doug DeCinces in an absolute steal of a trade, and Bob Boone for cash. And if you think the simultaneous signing of Reggie Jackson as a free agent was a no-brainer, that it was just a matter of ponying up the money, think again. Reggie was thirty-six years old coming into '82, and had just completed the worst season of his career. The Angels didn't outbid Steinbrenner for his services, Steinbrenner simply didn't

THE HITTERS

The two best hitters in the National League in the 1980's, with apologies to Tony Gwynn, have much in common. Both are enormously strong and slow, at least now; they were faster ten years ago. Both started as outfielders and are now first basemen. Neither was a good defensive outfielder, and neither is a good defensive first baseman. Both have battled constant injuries, and both have taken criticism for not wanting to stay in the lineup.

Both have spent their careers in poor hitter's parks, and for that reason neither has gotten full recognition. Each has lost about forty home runs in his

career to the parks he has played in, plus some points off his batting average. If you had put Jack Clark in Wrigley Field in his best year, he could have hit .330 with 50 homers, 150 RBI. Guerrero in Wrigley in his best year could easily have won the triple crown.

I guess the odd thing is that *all* of the best hitters in the National League in the eighties have played the majority of their careers in pitcher's parks, preventing them from piling up the numbers. Dawson played his best years in Montreal before they put the roof on. Gwynn has won four batting titles in a park that cuts his average several points. Strawberry has played his career in Shea Stadium, which cuts his power *and* average. None of the people who *could* have rung up heavy numbers in Wrigley or Atlanta or maybe Philadelphia or Pittsburgh ever got the chance.

want him anymore; he thought the Candyman washed-up. If the Boss had proved right, the Angels would have run out of towels to wipe the egg off their collective faces. Mention should also be made of the arrival, a year earlier, of Fred Lynn. It's convenient nowadays to denigrate Lynn's post-Fenway career (I do it myself, constantly), but the fact remains that he came to Anaheim at no great cost—Frank Tanana in career crisis, the hulk of Joe Rudi—and in '82 contributed a stellar year, which he culminated with one of the greatest catches in history, smashing into the left-center field fence to rob Amos Otis of a home run, said thievery ultimately costing the Royals the game, a two-game swing in the standings, and finally, the division title.

So the Angels were, unexpectedly, on a decision-making roll, but arguably the smartest decision of all was the hiring of legendary—or notorious—skipper Gene Mauch, who molded this veteran aggregation into the unit that edged out the favored Royals and advanced to the ALCS. (*Mauch Serious Aside:* I may murder the next know-nothing who pillories Mauch as the only man to manage for six million years and never win a pennant, etc. Doesn't common sense inform anyone that since most of his career has been spent in the divisional play era, it is twice as hard to win a pennant as it was for Casey, or Marse Joe, or the Fordham Flash? All right, you're competing with less teams initially, but the fact that, even after you've beaten off all challenges within your division, you have to meet another champion in a playoff for the right to move on to the Series, doesn't that strike anyone else as a considerably increased level of difficulty?) And then, disaster. The Angels won the first two playoff

games (with only three victories needed), but lost three in a row after Mauch, tempting fate yet again, shortened his rotation. The defeat, all the more galling for being so unexpected, seemed to colaterally short-circuit the carefully rewired decision-making process, for in an act of petulance worthy of Charles O. Finley, Mauch was held personally responsible for the playoff loss, and allowed to resign in favor of John McNamara. Meanwhile, many of the incumbent veterans began to falter, and less valuable imports, such as Ellis Valentine, resurrected the Fred Patek free-agent tradition. As the Angels closed out '84 with an 81–81 record, they seemed an aging and tired ball club, a club with nowhere to go but down.

But two seasons of John McNamara's managing, apparently, will assuage even the most terminal petulance, for Mauch was restored in '85 and found himself stirring a full-bodied veteran broth spiced by the youth of, among others, Mike Witt and Gary Pettis. He also found himself serving, as the *piece de resistance* bullpen ace, Donnie Moore, who, miracle of miracles, had arrived not as a free agent, but as free agent compensation for the no-longer-valuable Fred Lynn. Had the Angels finally begun to learn from their past mistakes?

The '85 Halos just missed winning the division, but the '86 edition, spurred by the arrival of Wally Joyner, moved on to the ALCS handily, only to be so memorably destroyed by Dave Henderson's fifth game home run. It was time for at least a partial changing of the guard in '87: Bobby Grich retired, but Mark McLemore, was waiting in the wings. Reggie moved on to Oakland, but Brian Downing was ready to become the

DH, with Ruppert Jones or Jack Howell manning left, and Devon White taking over in right. The Angels, it seemed, were finally in a position to plug holes without frantic free-agent acquisitions or panic trades. Or so it appeared until, heavily involved in the '87 race, they made the frantic/panic moves that netted Bill Buckner, Tony Armas, and Johnny Ray, and sank into the second division. They seemed once again the same old irrational Angels.

The '89 season promised more of the same. Past his prime, thirty-eight-year-old Bert Blyleven arrived via seemingly meaningless trade, as did injury-riddled Lance Parrish, and thirty-four-year-old Claudell Washington signed on for three years, guaranteed, as a free agent. But the big fish, Bruce Hurst and Nolan Ryan, got away, so most saw little reason for optimism. How wrong they—we—were. Blyleven had possibly his finest year ever, Kirk McCaskill rebounded from two years of injuries, Chuck Finley suddenly emerged as a quality starter, and, astonishingly, Jim Abbott proved that he was capable of stepping into a major league rotation. The offense, once you recovered from the shock of this team actually winning games, bore a remarkable resemblance to the offense of '86: low average but high power. It seemed, in many ways, a classic Earl Weaver team: pitching, defense, and three-run homers. Wait a minute, defense? These guys? Chili Davis in left, Claudell in right, they are great defenders? Ray at second? He's there for his offense, everyone knows that. Schofield is okay, but no one considers him among the best in the league, and as for catching, they let their defensive specialist, Boone, leave for Kansas City. So how can this team have played great defense? And yet, how can the stats lie? The best pitchers in the world cannot ring up an ERA of 3.28 without quality defensive play, and there is the matter of committing the fewest errors in the division. Yes, errors are an overrated indicator of defensive prowess, but since the miracle Orioles also kept the flubs to a minimum, they seem to have meant something in '89.

At any rate, between the pitching, defense, and three-run homers, plus miraculously good health early on, the '89 Angels emerged as a serious threat to win the division. And then, in August, the injuries began to catch up with them. Dick Schofield broke his hand, Chuck Finley damaged his foot. Bill Schroeder was sidelined with an elbow problem, leaving the battered and bruised Parrish to grit his teeth behind the plate. No adequate replacements were on hand for any of these players, and yet incredibly, Mike Port, who had so eagerly—and futilely—wheeled and dealed during the '87 race, this time never made a move. Not one. He forced Doug Rader to use Kent Anderson (.265 slugging average) at short, and to thrust Terry Clark (4.91 ERA) into the rotation. When outfield help was needed, there was no one to turn to but venerable Max Venable (admittedly, he was an asset offensively). I absolutely cannot understand it. Was Port afraid his acquisitions would burn him again? Well, there's a simple solution to that: Don't make any stupid acquisitions like Bill Buckner. Is that asking so much? Every year GMs in pennant races make late season deals that produce players ten times better than Buckner. The Jays landed Mookie and Mazzilli for diddly; Assenmacher and Salazar didn't cost the Cubs the crown jewels; surely Port could have done something. It's as if suddenly, after proving beyond question that he was

right, and we naysayers wrong, that Blyleven, Washington, and Parrish could make a difference, he lost his nerve, and abandoned the climb, even as the summit loomed before his very eyes. It makes no sense, but what about this franchise does? As the Angels close the books on the eighties, they can look back on two division titles, and one near miss, and reflect that many major league teams have less to show for the decade. But they might also find it hard to avoid the conclusion that just slightly better judgment, coupled with a coherent, long-range plan of action, and, yes, a little better luck, might have seen them scale the same mountain that teams no better than their best—the '85 Royals, the '87 Twins—planted their flags upon so memorably.

—M.K.
October 2, 1989

The Angels' signing of Mark Langston at the start of the winter meetings is sure to provoke a knee-jerk pick-the-Angels-to-win movement next spring, and the Angels may yet win. Langston isn't a great pitcher, but he is a good pitcher who could become a great one, and as to the point that the Angels with four good starters didn't address their needs, the odds are overwhelming that they wouldn't have gotten through another full year without opening up a hole in the starting rotation.

The indicators series shows the Angels to be down next year, way, way down. With the exception of the Langston signing, I think all of the other early free-agent movements have tended to reinforce, rather than contradict, the indicators. The Pirates, who figured to improve themselves, have signed a couple of people. The Expos, who figured to be down sharply anyway, have suffered devastating losses to their pitching staff. The Braves, who figured to be up anyway, have signed Esasky.

There is a reason for this. A large part of what the indicators measure is the emphasis that each team will probably put on solving its problems. The teams which have had poor years will tend to concentrate on solving their problems; those which have had good years won't. That's why free agent movements tend to *emphasize*, rather than negate, the movements indicated.

Langston is irrelevant to the Angels' problems. He was signed not because he was *needed*, but because he was brilliant and available.

Will Langston counteract the other forces, and enable the Angels to have a good year? Not on your life: The Angels are going down the toilet in 1990, and Langston will just be along for the ride. The team is ancient—Washington, Armas, Chili Davis, Parrish, Johnny Ray, Blyleven, Downing. There's no way there won't be a collective decline among those players. A good many of them are second-year Angels, and players like that often give a team one good year but not two.

There's no way the Angels' starting rotation is going to be any better in 1990 than it was in 1989, even with Langston. You think Blyleven is going to go 17–5 again?

The Angels' basic problem is that they're just not as good as the way they played last year. They won ninety-one games; they ain't that good. And remember this: Doug Rader was a big hit his first year in Texas, improved the team by thirteen games due to a terrific performance by the pitching staff. The next year he got erratic. I know they say he's a changed man, but you put him under pressure and you've still got a fifty-fifty chance of finding that same old hardass Doug Rader.

Where will they finish? If the Angels hadn't signed Langston, they'd finish fourth.

Since they signed Langston, they'll finish fourth.

PLAYOFF POND- ERINGS

Oct. 9—I'm beginning to remember why I used to think Don Zimmer stupid. Am I the only one being driven stark raving mad by Popeye's compulsion to intentionally walk the bases loaded whenever the opportunity arises? I know there's general agreement that he was hallucinating in the first game when he ordered a free pass to Brett Butler, juicing the bags, and worse, mandating an at bat for Will Clark unless Rob Thompson hit into double play. You may recall the result of Thrill's at-bat. But I haven't heard much complaint about the two first inning IWs in game three that contributed mightily to three Giants runs on one ball hit out of the infield. You can't accuse Zimmer of inconsistency, though; in spite of two games worth of self-immolation, he was back for game four with a full can of gasoline. And he liberally doused himself in the third inning when, with two outs and first base open, he felt compelled to walk Kevin Mitchell and watch Matt Williams light the match with a two run single.

On the other hand, how can you blame him for his pyromania when the really serious second guessing begins only after he fails to order an IW? That was in the fifth inning of game four, with Clark on second, and one out. Fire starter Williams was again at the plate, and with southpaw Steve Wilson on the mound, and lefties Terry Kennedy and Pat Sheridan due next, articulate Vin Scully could not understand for the life of him why Williams was being pitched to. After

all, first base was open! Lord, is that what baseball is coming to? Every time first is unoccupied, and a batter slightly more threatening than John Shelby is due, he's going to receive the IW? Has this been the conventional wisdom ever since the '85 NLCS, when Tom Lasorda sensibly neglected to walk Jack Clark with first base open, yet was rewarded with defeat and an avalanche of second guesses? I know that in the present climate—Zimmer's obvious faux pas in the first playoff game notwithstanding—you can issue IWs until the cows come home and never receive serious criticism, even when you put the winning run on base, which was once a sin more unpardonable than any contemplated by Nathaniel Hawthorne. And really, how can you argue against this trend? Yes, Earnshaw Cook, in *Percentage Baseball,* railed against the IW over twenty years ago, and Bill James, in various *Abstracts,* has taken issue with this strategy, but the major impediment to arguing against free passes is that you cannot prove what the passee would have done if allowed to swing. To the opposing manager, it's obvious that any intentional walkman was likely to smack a 500-foot homer, so of course he had to be avoided; the opportunity for the on-deck batter to inflict equal damage with a 150-foot bloop double being shrugged off as less probable (which it probably isn't), but if it happens, well at least you didn't let the opposition's best beat you, as if who beats you as opposed to whether they beat you makes an iota of difference.

I don't know; it's been suggested throughout the history of baseball that rules changes be implemented that would effectively abolish the intentional walk. The fans, you know, become frustrated when their favorite slugger merely trots to first in a tight situation, and shouldn't something be done about it? My opinion has always been that the fans should learn to live with it, but now I'm beginning to wonder if such legislation wouldn't be desirable, not to please the crowd, or make the game more exciting, but simply to save managers from self-inflicted third degree burns. If such a rules change ever comes to pass, I have the perfect name for it: the Don Zimmer Smoke Detector and Fire Prevention Rule.

Oct. 10—Did anyone honestly feel that the Blue Jays had a chance to upset the Athletics in the ALCS? The talent disparity was so glaring that only brilliant pitching from Dave Stieb and Jimmy Key could possibly have altered the outcome. And yet, there were moments when it seemed the Jays might be in the hunt after all. Remember that uprising in the third game, after Dave Parker's second homer of the series had staked Oakland to a 3–0 lead? You could practically see the stream coming from Jays ears as they suddenly manhandled Storm Davis in the bottom of the fourth to take a 4–3 lead. It was as if witnessing a second slow motion home run slither from the corpulent Cobra was finally, absolutely, too excruciatingly much to be borne, and it was either explode, or suffer terminal boilover on the spot.

But while blowing your collective stacks may net one desperately needed win, it is an unlikely prescription for long-term success, especially when the causes are as relatively insignificant as Parker's pace and Rickey Henderson's mincing dance step into second on an uncontested steal. If that's all it takes to infuriate the Gast House Gang,

what do they do when a pitcher hits one of their mates? (I'll tell you what they do: Diddlyshit—ask Tony Fernandez, whose jaw was broken while the Jays went meekly about their business.) At any rate, when the moment seemed propitious in the fourth game for another eruption of Vesuvian proportions, with the Jay trailing 3–0 in the bottom of the fourth, but with the bases loaded and none out, the steam went unexpectedly out of the rally, only one run was plated, and the series was as good as over. Temperatures were elevated only once more, in game five, when Cito Gaston, evidently weary of contemplating the huge sums he might squeeze out of Pat Gillick to remain as manager, decided to accuse Dennis Eckersley of defacing the ball. As a serious controversy, this was a non-starter, but it did perhaps give the Blue Jays a victory in the get-bent-out-of-shape-over-nothing sweepstakes almost as one-sided as the Athletics' triumph on the field.

I don't know why the Jays couldn't take their licking like men. What is so disgraceful about a clobbering at the hands of probably the best team in baseball? The Athletics are beginning to remind me of those great Yankees teams of the fifties and early sixties, or rather what those teams would have been like if they'd needed speed as well as power. If they have a weakness heading into the fall classic, I can't find it. Unlike in '88, no one tailed off drastically in the second half, and Parker and Carney Lansford, not to mention Mike Gallego and Tony Phillips, are particularly improved. The addition of Rickey Henderson, in the last year of his contract, speaks for itself. The Giants will surely find that the Athletics can shuffle in more effective pitchers, day after day, than any National League team, and while

Giants bats may find a way to shuffle them out again just as quickly, there is little likelihood of their own pitchers doing to the Oakland offense what Orel Hershiser, *et al.*, did in '88. If Athletics batters do end up circling the bases in profusion, I hope the Giants find something better to do than timing their trots or measuring the accuracy of their steps.

Oct. 13—The harshest—yet not inaccurate—comment on the NCLS was Tom Weir's, who noted that in the Series ". . . the Giants will be playing without their real MVP from the playoffs, Don Zimmer." He forgot to mention the runner-up for the award, Andre Dawson. If the Orioles-Blue Jays showdown was distinguished by its lack of heroes and goats, the NLCS seemed made up of nothing but. Dawson's inability to connect with 17,000 men on base did not surprise me; he'd struggled through a horrible year (a just reward for his widely publicized off-season mutterings that Mark Grace should have been dealt to Texas instead of Rafael Palmeiro), but Zimmer suddenly going 0 for 20 in major managerial decisions after batting close to a thousand all season was a shocker. By the fifth game I was resigned to the reflexive intentional walking, and could even tolerate the hell-bent-for-leather baserunning that always backfired; it had, after all, succeeded all year, and managers love to discourse upon dancing with those who escorted them (forgetting that post-season choreography can be radically altered), but another long-term ballroom partner of Zimmer's had been the quick hook, and in the eighth inning of the final game, with Mike Bielcki obviously weakening, the hook suddenly became a wallflower, and by the time Zim realized he'd stood up Ginger Rogers, the music, and the Cubs' season, had ground to a halt.

But debating who lost the NLCS, and how, is a little like the old argument over who lost China. The Giants, like Mao and the Red Army, won because they made the plays. Sure, Zimmer played into their hands with all the intentional passes, but they still had to produce the hits in back of those walks. The fielders had to make the on-the-money throws that cut down rampaging Cubs base runners. The relievers had to hold narrow leads against an offense that was still potent despite the absence of Damon Berryhill and the feebleness of Dawson. Of course, it also helps to have arguably the finest offensive player in the game, Will Clark. He appeared as unstoppable in the NLCS as Rickey Henderson did in the ALCS; if either team can put a collar on one of them, they'll have taken a major step toward one more champagne bath.

—M.K.

It isn't your first thought that you have put your life on hold and come two thousand miles to blunder into the path of a natural disaster. It had been a tense, pressure-filled afternoon, trying desperately to get to the ball park in time to do my TV spot, fighting backed-up traffic and parking facilities at one time unfamiliar to me and inadequate to the conditions. I thought at first that I was fainting, that the pressure had gotten to me, and then I looked at Susie and she looked like she was fainting, too, and then I figured that it wasn't just me.

I wish I had a good story about the quake. A lot of guys I know, they'd go to an earthquake, they'd come home with hair-raising anecdotes from here to Alaska. That's a useful trait to a writer, helps you get on the Johnny Carson show and stuff.

It had been my intention in the spring to follow the Oakland A's with some care, to see them play in the spring and the summer and the fall, to see them play thirty or forty times if I could. I couldn't, and by the time the World Series came around I was too far behind on the book schedule. I had decided I couldn't go, turned down several offers to get out there one way or another.

And then Harry Fuller, news director of KGO-TV in San Francisco, asked me if I wanted to come out for the series. They were doing pre- and post-game specials for the World Series games, and they wanted me to be a part of them. He offered money. He said I could bring my wife.

The magic words . . . well, it's just two days, it's just like taking a weekend off, right? Besides, I'm a baseball writer; I'm *supposed* to go to the World Series.

I almost experienced my first earthquake on live television. I was on KGO with Dan Lovett and Joe Morgan when the show ended at 5:00. Susie was supposed to be picking up the tickets at will-call, and I went to try to find her. It turned out that our tickets for the game had been provided by a gentleman from a law firm in the Bay area, and Susie was talking to this gentleman when I found her. We were standing outside Candlestick, and you know how you are when you first meet someone, you try to give them your undivided attention.

There was a plane flying over, but the roar from the plane grew louder and louder, too loud. I thought a big truck was going by, but where? There was no place for a truck. I looked at the concrete walkway over my head, thinking perhaps a piece of heavy equipment was being rolled down it.

I didn't see the things that people reported. I didn't see the cars bouncing up and down in the parking lot, although I could see the parking. People say it lasted fifteen seconds; it seemed to me more like five. There was no sudden jerk at the end. I put my foot out in front of me to retain my balance, and by the time I strode out it was over. A policeman guarding the press gate came over and motioned to us to get away from the overhead walkway.

The crowd cheered and whistled. I had no idea about the severity of the quake. I knew it was an earthquake, but if nobody had told me any different I would never have guessed that it was a big one. This only applied for a few seconds, because immediately after that Californians began telling me that that was a big one. Bay dwellers are garrulous, open people anyway, at least compared to Kansans, and the moment of danger had cut loose an impulse to share, and so people kept rushing up to us, talking to us for a second and rushing on. They all told us that that was a big one, the biggest they had ever felt. Several people told us stories about other earthquakes, lightning quick. We ran into Dan Lovett, whom I had done the TV interview with; he seemed genuinely shaken by the event, and was the first person to tell me about seeing cars bouncing up and down in the parking lot. Within a couple of hours Lovett would be on nationwide TV, helping the network provide the nation with coverage of the disaster, but at that moment neither he nor I had any thought of that.

In fact, in retrospect, that was what was strangest—that so few people understood the import of what had happened. All of these people, all of the Californians, knew that that had been a big quake—but none of them realized immediately, or really for a half hour or more, that if there was a big earthquake there had to be serious damage around the cities. "It's just an instinct," Steven Copley explained to me later. "You look around. You're OK, your wife is OK, all these people are OK, the stadium is OK, so . . . well, that was a close one, wasn't it?" Within a minute of the quake, just after talking to Dan Lovett, I saw a plume of smoke rising at some distance. Disoriented, I thought the smoke was coming from Oakland; I later learned it was the Marina district. A few people were emotionally shaken. A little girl was crying, and a man in a half-assed clown costume was trying to comfort her, further frightening her; the girl's mother was trying tactfully to get the clown to go away.

We walked back to the car. A couple of men shouted to a policeman, said that they had heard that power was out all over town. The policeman said no, there were just a few lights out. But before we got to the car, somebody had a small TV, and the TV showed the Bay Bridge. . . .

Even then, it would be two hours before we had any idea about the extent of the damage. Susie and I sat in the car for a half hour in confusion. With the power out the PA system was out, so we heard no announcement that the game would not be played. Egress from the parking lot choked almost immediately to a standstill. They had parked us in a dusty cow pasture, anyway, and cars sat in long lines with their engines running, awaiting a chance to edge out of the lot. The news on the car radio turned bad and then worse, eventually frightening. Reports of deaths started out at two or three, and grew into the hundreds. A police spokesman came on the air frequently, pleading with people not to go downtown, not to go to the financial district.

Reporters and citizens called the radio station from all over the area giving damage reports. Not being from the Bay area, we didn't know where any of these places were. The hardest hit area was the Marina district. Were we in the Marina district? We didn't know. We were staying a few blocks from Fisherman's Wharf, so it *could* have been the Marina district, but was it?

Reports were heard on the radio about roving street gangs preying on the situation. One incident in which a man and his small daughter were attacked by a gang of hoodlums was discussed over and over. Although the city—and the media—later went out of their way to downplay such reports and to pat the city on the back for behaving so well during the crisis, the reports from the dashboard at the time were very different, and painted a much darker picture from the streets.

The highway leading from Candlestick back to the hotel was closed; if we had intended to drive back to the hotel (if we had been able to get out of the parking lot) we would have had to take back streets. Driving through the back streets of an unfamiliar city, with the street lights and traffic lights all out, trying to feel my way to the hotel on a night like this . . . no thanks; even without the street gangs, I think I'd pass. We began to think about what we could do . . . sleep here in the back of the car? Head south, away from the city, try to get a motel maybe fifty miles south of town?

And then you wouldn't believe what happened.

We got out to walk around a little bit, and I heard somebody yell "Bill?" Now, I'm a little bit famous, and I had been on TV a couple of hours earlier, so I just figured somebody had recognized me—but how, in the dusk?

It was Steven Copley and Craig Wright. Steven and Cathy Copley are good friends. I mentioned earlier that I had been turning down all offers to come to the World Series. Cathy had called several times, saying, "Bill, why don't you come out? We've got a big house, and we'll figure out a way to get tickets somehow. Come on out." I hadn't planned to come and stay with them, but we were planning to meet them at a restaurant after the game—this game. Now, in the gathering nightfall of a disaster setting two thousand miles from home, I had by sheer chance bumped into Steven, and he had recognized me. Cars stretching for miles in parking lots and pastures and the sides of streets—and he was parked thirty feet away.

Steven and Craig and Susie and I sat in Steven's car and listened to the radio for some time, and then Steven went to try to call Cathy. This proved impossible. There were long lines of people waiting to use very few phones, and portions of the phone system were down all over town; Steven wasn't able to call his wife. By this time the initial feeling of safety had long since passed, and Steven still had no way of knowing whether his wife and baby and their home had been involved in the quake.

Steven offered us the use of his spare bedroom, assuming it was still there, and we accepted gratefully. The quake had hit at 5:04, and it was 9:00 before the traffic trying to leave the parking lots had cleared up. We eased out onto the highway heading south, following the tail lights of Steven's car. Traffic at times was slow; at other times it didn't move at all. At one point Craig Wright opened the door and stepped out on the highway to see if we were still behind him. We honked. A forty-five minute drive to the Copley house took over two hours; it was near midnight when we arrived. The Copleys live over in Fremont, on the east side of the Bay; the bridge we drove over was inspected the next day and found to have suffered damage, and was closed for a couple of days.

The power was still off in Fremont, but Cathy and Lanie and the house were fine, and from then on it was kind of fun, sitting around the house for a couple of days with Craig Wright and Steven and Cathy and the baby and Susie, talking about baseball. Eventually we would run out of baseball to talk about and spend ten minutes talking about Mike Dukakis, but then we'd go back to baseball. I was driving a vehicle belonging to KGO television, and I knew in a situation like this they would be needing it, so I tried to get it back to them, but between the phones being out and everybody scurrying around like bugs on a skillet, it was twenty-four hours before I could get anybody at the station on the phone. We tried to make arrangements to fly out earlier, even drove to the San Jose airport to talk to the airlines there, but with some flights canceled the others were maxed out, and that also proved impossible. We called our hotel; they urged us not to come if at all possible. They had no power, and the area was hard hit. We stayed with Steve and Cathy, leaving our luggage at the hotel.

We came home on our originally scheduled flight on Thursday morning, a day and a half after the quake, and watched the end of the Series on TV with the rest of you.

There were suggestions, of course, that because of what had happened the final World Series games should not be played. Those suggestions, to be frank, irritate the living hell out of me. To begin with, it's hypocrisy. It's advocating for us—for baseball—a set of values that no one else is going to live by. Nobody else cancels anything, even their routine events. The movie theaters stayed open the very evening of the quake. Nobody was there, but they were open. The restaurants stayed open, the amusement parks. TV stations continued to broadcast insipid sitcoms—yet baseball, for some reason, was supposed to surrender its most treasured event to demonstrate our sensitivity to the tragedy!

More irritating than being singled out among public amusements, though, is that this suggestion attempts to force upon baseball a set of values that *no one* is going to observe in his own life. Tell me—if your next-door neighbor dies on Monday and you have a date on Friday night, do you cancel the date out of respect for your neighbor? Not unless you're dating his daughter, you don't. If your vacation is scheduled to begin on June 13 and two of your co-workers in the office are killed in a car wreck on June 10, do you cancel your vacation out of respect for the dead? Of course you don't. And that is hypocrisy—telling baseball that *we* must observe a set of values that you don't intend to observe yourself.

And nobody does that, because *it wouldn't make any sense to do that.* If you lived that way you'd live your whole life under the shadow of someone else's tombstone. Hell, 150 to 250 people die every day in the Bay area. When somebody in your life dies, you go to the funeral, pay your respects to the family, and then you get on with your life.

Sports *need* their championship games. Sports are about trying to be the best. Cutting off the last two World Series games would decapitate the season. Look at it from Tony LaRussa's standpoint. This man has worked for twenty years to get a World Championship ring on his finger—not only him, but Dave Duncan, and Mark McGwire, and Kevin Mitchell and all of the other players and managers and coaches on both sides, to a greater or lesser degree. Did you ever meet an athlete who had been a part of a championship team twenty years before, and see that ring? That ring is one of the anchors of an athlete's existence. Many of these people will never get another shot at one. To deprive them of perhaps their only chance for a championship is a terrible sacrifice to ask from them . . . and for what?

I'll tell you what: because some guilt-ridden, self-important, frustrated, constipated sportswriter wants to make the statement that sports aren't *really* important. That's what this flap is all about; people who want to say that sports, despite all the attention we give to them, despite all the newspaper space they occupy, despite all the money that is poured into the sports world, aren't *really* important.

Well, dammit, if sports events aren't important to you then *don't go.* Don't watch. Don't read. Don't spend your money. For a sportswriter to argue that World Series games aren't important enough to bother to play is like a politician arguing that elections don't matter, or a movie star arguing that the movie shouldn't be finished, or a cop arguing that drug-dealing is really no big deal. It reveals, among other things, appalling insensitivity to the lives of the athletes. OK, if you don't think sports are important, then *find something else to do for a living.* But don't tell me that the World Series isn't that important.

The idiots who write things like this are the same people who write articles about how athletics have become too important to colleges. A college isn't supposed to be a front for a professional sports team, they say, it's supposed to be first and foremost a place where people are educated. That's true enough, but the consequence of the refusal to admit that sports *are* important is that college athletics have become a moral quagmire in which the athletes are shamelessly exploited by a set of rules which says, very simply, that everybody in the world can make as much money as possible out of the games except the athletes, who are not allowed to make anything. A real decision is made based not on what the values of our society *are,* but upon somebody's idea of what our values *should be.*

Driving to Steven's home in Fremont, Susie noted that the expression on every driver and every passenger's face was just the same. With the traffic as it was you might drive beside another car for twenty minutes. Everybody had the radio on, listening to the news. No one had a tape on. No one was in a hurry, no one impatient with the crawling traffic. That struck me, somehow; I have often noticed that the roles we play at moments of death are unfamiliar ones, uncomfortable. When someone dies we don't know what to do or what to say or what is and isn't appropriate— but in this emergency, although we were not immediately threatened, everyone knew exactly how to behave.

The people who so stupidly advocated that the World Series be canceled probably didn't mean any harm; they were just uncomfortable with the roles they were playing in the face of death.

I don't like to say that sports are important. I don't mind saying that it is important for people to learn to enjoy their lives. Most of the evils of the world are created not alone by shortages or hardships or natural disasters, but by all of those things working together with people who never learned to enjoy their

lives, and turned to politics or greed or some other form of vicious self-delusion to create problems for their neighbors. When people die, we don't stop eating, do we? We don't stop going to work. We don't stop educating our children.

Maybe I could have made my point with a simple question: If you were killed in an accident on October first, would *you* want them to cancel the World Series out of respect for *you?* Would that make you rest easier? Respect for the dead does not mean that we give up enjoying our own lives.

SERIES SOUNDINGS

Maybe they should have halted the World Series after all. Not because of the quake, but rather because the Giants were on the ropes, and obviously defenseless; it would have been the equivalent of the referee mercifully stopping a boxing match, the first TKO in Series history. To carry the metaphor one step further, the '89 Athletics were baseball's answer to Mike Tyson, so clearly superior to any and all opposition that every post-season contest seemed a boring mismatch. Yes, I wish the Series had been more exciting too, but to complain about it excessively is to, in essence, blame Oakland for its very superiority. People affect to yearn for those halcyon days of dominant teams, the Murderer's Row Yankees of the late twenties, and later Casey's Bronx Bombers, and of course Sparky's mid-seventies Big Red Machine. What they seem to forget is that these teams demonstrated their greatness by winning some of the most one-sided Series in history. The Yankees '28 whitewash of the Cardinals had all the drama of your first trip to the bathroom in the morning, ditto the Reds '76 triumph over the Steinbrennerians. We simply cannot have it both ways. If we really prefer every Series to be a seven-game nailbiter, we had better borrow some more parity from the National Football League; great teams find a way to eliminate the excitement early.

Speaking of greatness, are there many out there unwilling to concede that the Athletics are indeed a great team? I suppose you could cavil that one World Series triumph is not evidence enough; their seventies brethren, after all, took three in a row, and the previously noted Yankees and Reds teams racked up multiple world championships. Yes, but after scuttling the Pirates in '27, the Ruth-and-Gehrig-led Yankees stood exactly where the Athletics stand now: two consecutive Series appearances, one unexpected loss, one lopsided win, and did anyone not think those Pinstripes one of greatest teams ever? Right, they went on to confirm it in '28 with another walkover Series win, and the Athletics could clinch their case by doing approximately the same in '90, but for the here and now I am more than willing to add my voice to the chorus acclaiming the '89 Athletics as great.

And besides, there were some interesting moments in the ballgames themselves; not exciting, but interesting. Will Clark landing in Fay Vincent's lap after running down a foul pop was one, but I confess that my favorite came in the ninth inning of the third game when, with the Giants hopelessly out of it as usual, pinch hitter Bill Bathe stepped to the plate with two men on. I'd forgotten that Bathe was on the post-season roster (let's be candid: I'd forgotten he even existed), but you have to hand it to the ABC graphics department—they were ready for every possible happenstance. Thus, when Bathe cranked his homer, and circled the bases to the wild acclaim of shell-shocked San Franciscans, and the cameras zeroed in on an attractive young woman, practically beside herself with ecstasy, and obviously the slugger's better half, this caption quickly appeared: THE WIFE OF BATHE.

—M.K.

THE 1990 FINAL STANDINGS

AMERICAN LEAGUE EAST

Toronto	94	68	.580	. . .
Boston	86	76	.531	8
Milwaukee	82	80	.506	12
New York	79	83	.488	15
Baltimore	78	84	.481	16
Cleveland	78	84	.481	16
Detroit	66	96	.407	28

AMERICAN LEAGUE WEST

Oakland	93	69	.574	. . .
Kansas City	84	78	.519	9
Minnesota	84	78	.519	9
California	79	83	.488	14
Texas	78	84	.481	15
Chicago	77	85	.475	16
Seattle	76	86	.469	17

NATIONAL LEAGUE EAST

New York	95	67	.586	. . .
Chicago	87	75	.537	8
Pittsburgh	84	78	.519	11
St. Louis	80	82	.494	15
Montreal	74	88	.457	21
Phil	71	91	.438	24

NATIONAL LEAGUE WEST

San Diego	89	73	.549	. . .
SF	87	75	.537	2
LA	84	78	.519	5
Cincinnati	81	81	.500	8
Houston	75	87	.463	14
Atlanta	65	97	.401	24

TWO

.

PEOPLE

_____

BILL CLARK

JACK ETKIN

With his pick of any space in the small parking lot, Bill Clark drives toward the back, away from the baseball diamond. He's not positioning his Chevrolet to beat the traffic, which will be minimal at this Missouri high school game. There are certain things you do at a ball park after twenty years as a scout, even before getting the lineups and making the first of many observations, and parking adjacent to and facing the field is not one of them.

"Even though it's a company car," Clark says, "one of the most uncomfortable things is to drive with the wind coming through the windshield."

The car belongs to the Atlanta Braves and was new in November 1988. While driving through southern Minnesota the following May, Clark, who scouts eight midwestern states for the Braves, watched the speedometer register twenty thousand and noted, "We're just getting it broke in." The Braves would be happy their first-year employee has an eye toward the machinery. They would be mildly shocked if Clark, perchance, were to appear on the Atlanta scene in their rust-colored Celebrity that looks as if the owner has been dispossessed save for what he could cram inside the car.

Boxes of files cover the entire back seat, topped by a road atlas. Styrofoam cups are neatly arrayed along the back window, eighteen in all. And Clark has seven more cups piled vertically in a slot near his seat. "I drink tea," says Clark, who drinks nothing stronger, "and rather than throw them away, I let them pile up. I take them home and my wife grinds them up and recycles them. Hell, they don't break down if you throw them away. They're not biodegradable. You need a lid for something or a cup for something, well, I always got a cup here. You never know what you'll need out here."

Part of Clark's preparation includes rubberized binoculars and copies of *A Field Guide to Wildflowers* and *A Guide to Field Identification of the Birds of North America* within easy reach on the front seat. One of Clark's projects is to photograph all of the wildflower species in his native Missouri, although state boundaries are no restriction when it comes to seeking natural beauty in the open spaces. He keeps lists of the wild flowers and birds he has seen by state. In fact, Clark belongs to the natural history of Audubon societies in every state he travels, as well as two Canadian provinces, and tries to coordinate their meetings with his scouting.

When Clark went to work for the Braves after eighteen years with the Cincinnati Reds, the Braves told him not to bother with North Dakota or South Dakota and to omit all but the eastern portion of Nebraska. Clark felt otherwise. He reminded the Braves about pitcher Gary Niebauer. He had gone from Scottsbluff in far western Nebraska to the University of Nebraska and in 1966 to the Braves; three years later, he was in their bullpen. Major leaguers don't come along often in these areas, Clark admitted, but they occasionally pop up.

Like Dave Collins, a twenty-third-round draft pick out of high school in Rapid City, South Dakota, whom the Reds couldn't sign in 1971 when they offered twelve thousand dollars, and Collins adamantly insisted on fourteen thousand. And Roger Maris, who grew up in Fargo, North Dakota. The Braves listened to this reasoning by Clark, who also knew "one of the major perks of my job was being jeopardized," and relented. "If they don't let me go to those states," he says, "they're taking away a part of my life—that is, my summer trips into the wildlife areas in those states. If you fight the highways, if you become singular in your direction, if baseball is your whole life, if you become a soul centered on one thing, you're only a part of what you should be. Too many people that are scouts, if they don't go the ball park, they might as well sit down and die; that's their whole life.

"I don't feel that way. Baseball's just simply part of it. You love the game. A grown man can sit and cry watching *Field of Dreams* because he loves the game. But it's not everything in life. So you got to have something else to do. I've involved myself in far too many things."

Clark has been a sportswriter and was a basketball referee until the winter of 1987–88 when his knees gave out. His interest in weight lifting led him to organize a national masters' competition for weight lifters over forty and to publish a newsletter for which he does all the typing and mailing. Visiting a son and daughter in the Peace Corps in Guatemala and Mali has been so eye-opening that Clark is thinking seriously of joining that organization. Much of what he does, as well as information about his wife, Dolores, and their five children—Patrick Sean, Michael Seumas, Kelly Kathleen, Kerry Maureen, and Casey Connor—and assorted pets goes into a family newsletter Clark sends to about six hundred people at Christmas.

"It's become a tradition," says Rick Mathews, the baseball coach at Muscatine [Iowa] Junior College and a roving minor league instructor for the Kansas City Royals during the summer. "I'll ask [his wife] Mary, 'Did Clark's letter get here yet?' We get it and just sit right down and read it. He's the most interesting guy I've ever been associated with."

"He documents everything," says Jim Van Scoyoc, formerly the baseball coach at Norway [Iowa] High School and still one of Clark's bird dogs, or recommending scouts. "I've never seen anybody like him. We had one hundred sixty-eight kids at a tryout camp this year. I was in charge of the pitchers, so you could weed out about sixty. Bill was in charge of the other hundred, and they all have just numbers. After we're all done working them out, he remembers practically everything about them as far as their baseball performance goes. He's just extremely good at what he does."

That was Van Scoyoc's basic message to Paul Snyder, the Braves' scouting director, when they met at Oneonta, New York, last summer. Van Scoyoc's son, Aaron, was playing shortstop there for the New York Yankees Class A farm team. "I told Paul I would like to have a full-time job with your organization," Van Scoyoc says, "but I hope you wouldn't expect me to do what Bill Clark does because I don't think anybody could match him. His energy level is extraordinary. I couldn't imagine being around him when he was younger."

His youthful enthusiasm notwithstanding, Clark will be fifty-eight in August. "I may age," he says, "but I don't want to get old. There's a difference. Aging takes its toll. But if you look forward to what you're going to do each day, you'll never get old."

Ronnie Miller is the reason Clark has driven to Belton, Missouri, just south of Kansas City. He's the senior shortstop for Ruskin High School, which is playing Belton. "He's bowlegged," Clark says. "He might could run a little bit."

Clark is speaking to Gene Baker, a good friend who scouts for the Pittsburgh Pirates. Baker played for the Pirates after breaking in with the Chicago Cubs in 1953. His route to the majors took him to the Kansas City Monarchs and a chance encounter with Clark. At age sixteen, Clark umpired one of the Monarchs games in his native Clinton, Missouri. Clark would soon go to umpire school, develop his skills and eventually work in three minor leagues. But when the barnstorming Monarchs came to Clinton, Clark was groping behind the plate.

"Connie Johnson let loose with the first pitch," Clark says, "and I never even saw it. Gene said I was so bad at umpiring he still remembers me."

The two scouts' first order of business, writing the lineups for both teams on their scouting cards, sparks the initial observation of the afternoon. "Maybe some of these Beltons can play," Clark says. "They're all juniors. Might be a good day."

"You never know," Baker responds.

With Belton's infield practice underway, Clark says, "Gene, all those juniors—we may have struck out."

Clark will grade position players for their arm, fielding, hitting, power, and body control. The Braves use a rating system that ascends from two through eight with five considered major league average. Clark, seeking finer gradations, continues to use the Reds' twenty through eighty system so "you can kind of paint the picture." Pitchers are graded for the movement on

their pitches ("sink, tail, slide, ride"), for their fastball, curveball, slider, changeup, and any other pitch in their repertoire, and for their control.

Clark sits behind the backstop, a better vantage point to see if Miller's front foot is bailing out. He'll move to the first-base side after two at bats to focus on any hitch in his swing; if he's scouting catchers, the first-base angle allows Clark to look into their faces.

"You can tell if they blink or flinch," he says, "and can see how they set up and can see the hands. If they throw, you can see if they come out of the chute to throw or they stand straight up."

Miller grounds to third on his first at bat and is timed at 4.33 seconds running to first, right at the average (4.3) for a right-handed hitter. Average time for a left-hander is 4.15. "What I like to see is 4.1 and four flat," Clark says. "Bo Jackson off the right side may be as fast as anyone in history. I got him in 3.65. No one wanted to admit they had that time. Everyone looked at everyone else and said, 'I missed that one.' "

After the game, Clark and Baker line up Miller and two of his teammates for a sixty-yard run. "What you want," Clark says, "is a guy who can burn—6.5." Miller barely breaks seven seconds. "You wanted to see him run better," Clark says. "But you see some things in this kid. Even though he's crude, he's got some [good] actions. His hands are soft. He may put his knee down on grounders, but we can correct that. And he can throw. He's got a quick bat; he gets fooled a lot, but there's guarded

Bill Clark

optimism. This kid might someday play in Atlanta or Pittsburgh or whoever takes him."

Clark has made this assessment after a dinner at Wendy's. He's drawn by their Super Bar, where pasta salads and tacos embellish the traditional all-you-can-eat salad bar. On daily meal money of twenty-one dollars, including three dollars for tips—which raises to twenty-seven dollars if he's scouting in a major league city—the Super Bar is a scouting staple.

Major league scouts, Clark's brethren who rove about the American and National League, know nothing about the competition in the fast-food arena that has generated this particular marketing ploy by Wendy's. These scouts pile up frequent-flier miles like other businessmen and check in at a Hyatt or Westin or Marriott or some other big-city hotel where a uniformed bellhop carries their luggage.

Clark has his own favorite spots like the Comfort Inn in Raytown, Missouri, or the Silver Saddle Motel in Ames, Iowa, or the Westfield Inn in Iowa City, Iowa. What they all have in common is travelers can drive right up to their rooms, an essential for Clark. Toting those file boxes for the work he will do in his room is a lot easier if stairs and lobbies can be avoided. Such is life in the baseball outback where the species Clark calls the mud scout toils.

To such men, the major leagues are a distant echo. Clark scans the box scores at breakfast. At night, the miles might roll by with a ball game on the radio. Clark has set his stations on 720, WGN in Chicago; 750, WSB in Atlanta; and 1120, KMOX in St. Louis, giving him listening options on the Cubs, Braves, and Cardinals, and knows he can pull in the Royals on 580, WIBW out of Topeka, Kansas. The major leagues may fade in and out on the airwaves but aren't as far away as they seem.

"It's not remote because in all the years I was with Cincinnati you did everything like we saw today where there's one ballplayer on the field who might have a chance to play professional baseball," Clark says. "Whether he'd ever be a big leaguer or not, who knows. In the period of a year, we look at that kid; we look at the all-America high school and all-America college player. Then we look at the Rookie leagues and the A leagues as a part of our coverage. I covered Triple-A ball for years. I'd see the guys just before they're coming to the big leagues or coming back down out of the big leagues. Then you work at the big league level.

"And it's all such a progression, all in a hodgepodge, mixed-up season, that you look at the young guy we saw today and it's no problem projecting him to the big leagues. It's all a part of the same picture. Now guys who don't have high minor league coverage, then the major leagues do become a remote area to them. They like to go to a major league game just to renew acquaintances with what the major league average is as far as

tools. If you don't cover all aspects of the game over a period of a season, you do have to take time off and renew your acquaintances with the big leagues because you lose sight of what you're looking for. You become a comparative scout."

Clark is a burly 240-pounder who tends to acknowledge correct statements by saying, "You got that right." He has a round face topped with a crew cut and walks with an arthritic limp. "My knees are bone on bone," Clark says. "The right knee's worse because when you're refereeing, you do all your pivoting on the right knee."

Years of scouting have given Clark occupational reference points at just about any turn in the road. The miles don't just whiz by in a monotonous blur; they bring memories. While going north on Interstate 35, heading toward Ames and a night at the Silver Saddle, the Des Moines city lights off in the distance bring to mind that this was where Clark signed Billy Turner. "I go to the house, and there's not a window in the house," Clark says. "The glass is gone. They're all cardboard. I knock on the door, and I go in. Here's this guy sitting in nothing but a pair of dirty undershorts, no other clothes on. Got a pint bottle of whiskey in his hand. And he's only got one eye. Got an ugly looking hole in his head, needs a patch over it. And he looks up at me, and he says, 'You Clark.' I said, 'That's right.' He says, 'You a fat fucker.' And thus began our negotiations." They were not pricey. Clark was offering a $1,500 bonus but finally came up to $2,000 after some protracted arguing. When the elder Turner and his wife left the room, Clark was left alone with Billy. "He said, 'What do you think of our windows? We had glass in here until yesterday. My old man and the guy living in that house right across the street got in a big argument. They ain't got no windows either, notice. They shot 'em out. They shot at each other across the street and shot the windows all out.'

"The kid had a great arm. He was a pitcher-second baseman. This was in 1969. He went out to Billings, a Seattle Pilots farm club, and he got into an argument over something. Somebody called him a nigger, and he beat up about half the ball club and broke his thumb. The manager liked the kid. He realized it'd been a bad situation. He didn't want to let the kid go, so they sent him home. That winter Seattle released about seventy-five minor league players because they couldn't pay them, and they released him. Shame, 'cause he had a good arm. I signed him as a pitcher with the idea don't release him until you make sure he can't play a position. But Seattle released a lot of them that year."

Seattle was the second stop on Clark's scouting sojourn. He had been working in the parks and recreation department in his hometown of Columbia, Missouri, and was its acting director for about five months when a first-year scout for the Pirates named Chet Montgomery wrote, seeking a place he could hold a tryout camp. Clark had umpired in the Nebraska State and Pioneer Leagues and been a bird dog for the Milwaukee Braves. In return for use of a Columbia park for a tryout camp, Clark asked Montgomery to make him a Pirates bird dog. The first tryout camp Clark was ever involved with was in Columbia in June 1963.

"It worked out that Chet Montgomery didn't know Joe Blow from anybody in the Midwest," Clark says. "Well, I'd been involved with weight lifting and boxing for a number of years, and those were my first baseball contacts in Kansas, Missouri, Nebraska, Iowa—my weight-lifting friends. They didn't know anything about baseball, but at least in those communities, they did know who did know about baseball. So I led Montgomery to sign some more bird dogs, through the weight lifters, and we developed a very strong friendship, me and Chet, both on the field and off."

Montgomery, now the scouting director for the Cleveland Indians, began giving Clark more responsibility. After about three years, he made Clark a part-time scout for the Pirates, giving him five hundred dollars a year and a limited expense account. That arrangement lasted two seasons until late in 1967 when Montgomery followed Pirates scouting director Rex Bowen, a Branch Rickey disciple, to the Reds.

The Pirates offered Clark the full-time position as Montgomery's replacement. He was working days in the parks and recreation department and nights at the *Columbia Tribune* where his sportswriting duties included writing a bowling column and organizing high school coverage.

"In recreation, I had applied for a number of jobs and didn't have a professional degree," Clark says. "I remember I applied in Kansas City. I applied in Ann Arbor, Michigan, and I couldn't be hired because I was not a professional in that field of public recreation. My degree was in journalism.

"I loved to see thousands of people playing thousands of games on hundreds of fields and loved to sit and put all this mass of humanity together and watch it work. It became obvious that I was not going to get a job out in the recreation field. And this fact came at about the same time that Pittsburgh offered me a chance to go into professional baseball. If I'd have been able to have gone ahead and gotten a master's degree and stayed in public recreation, I probably wouldn't have gone into scouting. I would have loved to have kept that a part-time relationship." Clark became a full-time scout for the Pirates in 1968 but worked for them just one season. They had promised him a raise of a thousand dollars in salary for 1969 but subsequently told him he could pick that sum up in additional expenses. Meanwhile, Seattle Pilots scouting director Art Parrack approached

Clark with an offer of a three-year deal that included a raise of $1,500, not $1,000, from what he had been making with the Pirates. "Boy that was big time," Clark says. "You were making eight thousand dollars; they were going to jump you to nine thousand five hundred dollars. That was big money in 1968–69."

Clark spent 1969 with the fledgling Pilots, who were undercapitalized and reborn as the Milwaukee Brewers in 1970. Parrack was fired, but Clark and several other scouts were untouchable because they had three-year contracts. Rex Bowen, the Pirate scouting supervisor now with Cincinnati, contacted Clark at the end of the 1970 season, thinking his contract was for two years. An agreement was reached. Milwaukee was glad to rid itself of someone under contract for another season; Clark joined the Reds in the fall of 1970 and began an eighteen-year association with the Reds by unexpectedly receiving a ring that year from the National League pennant-winners. The Big Red Machine had begun rolling, with Clark not just along for the ride.

After Clark's second season, Reds general manager Bob Howsam acted on his input to get reliever Tom Hall from the Minnesota Twins for Wayne Granger, who had led the National League with ninety appearances in 1969 and thirty-five saves in 1970. "I had a bird dog down at Joplin, who had a son, Steve Luebber, who had come to the Twins that year" Clark says. "I knew Steve since he was a little itty-bitty kid because of his dad, Kermit Luebber, who still bird-dogs for me. I knew Steve pretty good and said something about I saw Tommy Hall pitch and for a guy who's supposed to have a sore arm, he threw all right.

"Steve said, 'Ain't nothing wrong with his arm. He and [Twins manager] Bill Rigney cannot get along.' He said Rigney really treats the guy bad, won't tell him when he's going to start him. He'll put him in the bullpen and forget him. Hall knows it, so he says, 'Hell, I can play that game, too.' When Rigney calls him up, he says, 'Can't pitch, Skip. My arm's sore.' Steve said, 'I'll guarantee you there's nothing wrong with the arm.'

"I picked up the paper at the [1971] winter meetings, and I looked down and said, 'Oh my God. I'm fired. They traded the fireman of the year for a guy that supposedly has a sore arm.' But Howsam never flinched. He believed in his people. And what I never knew was that Granger had the sore arm. The Twins didn't know that. The Twins didn't have a friend on the ball club to tell them the truth. Hall was 10–1 in relief, and we won the pennant in '72 and Hall was one of the main reasons why."

Howsam, whom Clark calls "the greatest baseball man that I ever met" inspired a reverential loyalty among Reds employees. When he left after the 1978 season, the Reds, in the 1970's, could claim World Championships in 1975 and '76, two other

National League pennants in 1970 and '72 and a division title in 1973. Under frugal Dick Wagner, the Reds plummeted to last place in 1982 and 1983, a season that at least brought Clark some hope when Wagner was fired and Howsam returned to the Reds.

The hope was short-lived. Marge Schott, who had been a limited partner in the Reds since 1981, became their general partner in December 1984. Howsam left the following season but not before he gave Clark and several other scouts three-year contracts with salary increases that ran through the 1988 season. Schott believed scouts were more superfluous than necessary and did little to enhance the bottom line. "All they do is go to baseball games," she said in a telling statement.

"You knew where you were headed at the end of '88,' " Clark says. "I got cross-wise with her. She tried to mend fences. She wanted to know if we had anything that was for the good of the order. At the end of the '87 season, I wrote her a little letter for the good of the order which basically said why the hell don't you get out of baseball. I don't think she thought very much of me from that point on. I explained to her that her scouting staff was not a bunch of guys who had to grovel in the dust in front of anybody because they had to have money. I said your scouting staff happens to be populated by people most of whom are college educated and many have master's degrees and they'd be highly successful in any business besides baseball. I said they've chosen baseball because they love it.

"From what the secretaries said, she raved up and down the hall about who is this guy and how can he say that to me. I told the secretaries, 'Tell her to call me. I'll be glad to talk to her.' Couple of the other guys who were going to get fired, they tried to hang on. I told them to go look for a job; get the hell out of there. Consider it an honor for her to fire you. If Howsam had fired me, it would've crushed me.

"Atlanta offered me a job at the end of the 1987 season. I had another year at Cincinnati, and I really thought that Howsam would appear out of the mist again and take back over that ball club. Sixty thousand miles became thirty thousand, and you really didn't give a shit whether you saw another ball game or not. And that can't be helped. Quite frankly, it took a little bit to rejuvenate myself after the last two years to get excited about going back and pushing hard again. When you kind of gave up on things with Marge, it's taken the better part of this year to where I want to go out and hammer again."

With the June free-agent draft one month away, Clark's itinerary is hectic. Players must be seen and analyzed. But no matter how strong the inner drive to see more games and evaluate more players, Clark must fight two harsh forces. Scouting in the Midwest in the spring puts him at the mercy of weather that makes his schedule fragile. And unlike southern California and Florida, where baseball is played year round, there are far fewer professional prospects, let alone those who rise to the majors.

"You can go weeks up here and not see a big league ballplayer," Clark says. "And the players that you do sign, so many times, they're projections, and if anything happens to slow up that projection, they're released."

Because of their success, the Reds were traditionally drafting below most teams while Clark worked for them. He can count only catcher Don Werner, pitcher Bruce Berenyi, and Collins—who ultimately got his fourteen thousand dollars from the California Angels a year after the Reds drafted him—as players he was able to draft who made the majors. Indeed, there have been some stellar players from Clark's territory. Paul Molitor, a St. Paul native, came out of the University of Minnesota as the Brewers' number-one pick and the third selection overall in 1977. That same school sent Dave Winfield, another St. Paul native, to the San Diego Padres in 1973 as the fourth pick in the draft. Joe Carter was at Wichita State when he was taken second in the country by the Cubs in 1981. Kirby Puckett had played at Triton [Illinois] Junior College when the Minnesota Twins made him the third overall pick in the January 1982 draft.

The odds are overwhelmingly against seeing someone like this, or even a Steve Jeltz, whom the Philadelphia Phillies drafted out of the University of Kansas in the ninth round in 1980. Most of the players Clark watches will end up with the notation "NP" written very quickly next to their name, indicating they are not professional prospects. When coupled with the endless miles, nights in motels, restaurant food, separation from his family, and minimal chances of seeing someone like a Ronnie Miller who can play well enough to pique some interest, Clark's job seems to offer only glimmers of hope that fade quickly and a collusion of unsympathetic elements that never leave. Clark views matters differently.

"Scouting is a profession of optimism," he says. "And if you're not optimistic, if you can't go to the ball park every day and say, 'Today is the day I find the new Johnny Bench,' you might as well stay back in your room or you might as well get a job punching a clock and digging a ditch.

"As a scout, if you don't have that optimistic outlook, you're dead. When I go to the field, I'm looking forward to seeing maybe not a new bird; I've got enough species on my life's list that I don't see a new bird very often anymore. But always when I'm in the field, I'm thinking, 'Gee, this is warbler migration time right now. I might just stumble onto one of these warblers in migration that I've never seen before.' And if I don't, no big deal, I'm going to see lots of other beautiful birds, and I'm going to be out away from the damn phone and I'm going to be out where I can kind of smell the roses a little bit and I'm going to enjoy it."

The only smell outside the Silver Saddle on this morning is rain. Clark is as dependent on the weather as a farmer, so the day is already in jeopardy. His plan is to drive about four and a half hours to La Crosse, Wisconsin, where shortstop Trent Petrie of visiting Menomonie High School will play. Clark had Petrie in a tryout camp the previous summer. Because his father is a coach at Stout State in Menomonie, Petrie is fundamentally sound and, to Clark, "looks like a California player." There will have to be less projecting about Petrie's potential development than with Miller.

Clark learns from the secretary to Petrie's father that Petrie is healthy, and that it's cloudy but not raining in Menomonie, which is at least an hour north of La Crosse. A call there informs Clark the weather is also cloudy at nine A.M., which is no indication the game will be played that afternoon. Clark makes a few backup calls in search of a game that's worth seeing and won't be affected by weather.

There are no games that day in Nebraska, where Clark would like to see a couple "very marginal" players in Lincoln. "Neither one of them ran that good," Clark says, "but they have enough ability you'd like to see them if they were playing, and hopefully they'd be playing. But they weren't." He tries Simpson College in Indianola, Iowa, and discovers they have a tarp on their field. Simpson has a pitcher, of whom Clark says, "If I see him, that's fine. If I don't see him, that's equally fine. At most, he's an organizational type player. But as an optional game we would go there rather than not go anyplace. Maybe he got better."

This process of elimination has left Clark continuing on toward La Crosse in violation of one of scouting's meteorological precepts. "You learn to drive backwards," he says. "We're going the wrong way; we're going with the rain. Normally you turn around and go where the rain came from. But frankly there's no place to go where the rain came from; there's nobody playing where the rain came from today." His decision is to continue on to Albert Lea, Minnesota, and from there make another call to La Crosse. If he then learns the Menomonie game has been postponed, he can turn around and head for Indianola. "We're what's known as having all the direction of a blind dog in a packing plant right now," Clark says. "We can smell the meat out here, but we can't seem to find it."

Clark has not had to deal with Wisconsin in years. It's one of eight states he scouts for the Braves, the others being Kansas, Nebraska, Missouri, South Dakota, North Dakota, Minnesota, and Iowa. He had Arkansas in place of Wisconsin in his final years with the Reds. The weather wasn't the only thing better in Arkansas. "I lost players," Clark says. "Arkansas is always a good place to be." It seems even better when Clark finds it raining in La Crosse and the game postponed. Madison is just over one hundred miles away and the best remaining option to put Clark near upcoming games. He tried new lodging, a Marriott Fairfield Inn. Rooms go for $32.95. Naturally, there's parking right outside the door.

The day has been a series of phone calls, misguided plans and, of course, the usual dose of miles, all of which reminds Clark of a poster in a doctor's office. A large toad was in the foreground, while in the background and less distinct was a prince. The caption read: YOU MUST KISS A LOT OF TOADS TO FIND YOUR PRINCE CHARMING. "A scout kisses a hell of a lot of toads in a year to find a Prince Charming," Clark says. "Yesterday, we kissed a toad. We may not have found Prince Charming, but at least we had a chance."

The literary public knows him as W. P. Kinsella, author of such books as *The Iowa Baseball Confederacy* and *Shoeless Joe*, which was adapted into the movie, *Field of Dreams.* To Clark, he is Bill Kinsella, a friend who shares a love of the game and a certain belief in the mystical.

At the suggestion of his oldest son, Patrick, Clark read *Shoeless Joe* in about 1983. "I was absolutely intrigued by it," Clark says. "What a strange but wonderful book." Kinsella lives in Canada, so Clark sent the book to Ray Belanger, his lone part-time scout who helps him in Canada and lives in Weyburn, Saskatchewan. Belanger also enjoyed the book and used his connections to find out that Kinsella was living in White Rock, British Columbia. Some six months after writing Kinsella, Belanger heard from him.

"Ray sent me the letter," Clark says, "and I just simply sat down and wrote Kinsella a friendly personal letter back. And it wasn't very long until I got an answer. We seemed to be on the same wavelength a lot.

"We've just developed a good friendly relationship since then. No particular reason other than a little hero worship on my part, and I have a feeling that in a reverse manner a little hero worship on the part of Bill Kinsella. Not for me personally but for the fact that here actually in all his field of literature and baseball notoriety, here is his one contact with professional baseball. He doesn't have any other contacts in professional baseball, as far as I know. Other than he's a season ticket holder with the Mariners. But nobody [at the Kingdome] knows Bill Kinsella. He found out that [former Mariner] Phil Bradley was from my hometown, Columbia, and Phil Bradley was his favorite player because he knew a fellow that knew Phil Bradley." Kinsella would appreciate Clark's faith in white-crowned or white-throated sparrows. Seeing one of them before a ball game, Clark maintains, is a good omen. "At least three times in the last three or four years," Clark says, "we go into a ball park, and if I see a white-crowned or white-throated sparrow, the kid we went to see is a prospect. Never has the white-crowned or white-throated sparrow failed us."

Clark had always been intrigued that the white-throats and white-crowns might nest around Ball Club, Minnesota, which is on the Leech Lake Indian Reservation about a hundred miles northwest of Duluth. The combination of these birds and the town's name convinced Clark that if he held a tryout camp, a great ballplayer would turn up in Ball Club. "This is another Shoeless Joe," Clark says. "Shoeless Joe will be there, but he'll be in the flesh. I think you have to believe to go and look for him. But I think you'll be able to see him; even the nonbelievers will be able to see him once they're there."

About two weeks later, Clark made the pilgrimage to Ball Club. He reported his findings in a telephone message that was typically thorough and expressive:

I made it to Ball Club, Minnesota, and it was a tremendous disappointment. Two things. One, I found sparrows in the bush, and I thought, 'This is a great deal.' And they were house sparrows. I could not find a white-throated sparrow anywhere.

Not only that, but when I got to Ball Club, I couldn't find a ball park anywhere. Not even a softball diamond. There is absolutely nothing in Ball Club. The only thing that's flat and could be used for a workout area is an Indian ceremonial ground. Right in the middle of it, there are some permanent wooden structures, kind of like a Chatauqua area. And that eliminates any possibility of a workout in Ball Club.

It is an Indian community, almost totally. They play in Deer River, which is where I happened to see a high school game that same day. That's six miles, eight miles east of there. So there's no place in Ball Club where we could even set up a workout.

The Ball Club tryout camp fell through. Here once again, the white-throated sparrow dictated. Not a white-throated sparrow to be found. Really a place that didn't show much hope. Despair in Ball Club probably far outreaches baseball.

This disappointment might have been inevitable after the stroke of fortune Clark stumbled upon in Milwaukee. That was his destination after the futile day which had ended in Madison. Clark's focus in Milwaukee is Joe McLin, a tall power-hitting first baseman for Riverside University High School. Billy Bryk, a Pirates scout and close friend of Clark's, has summed up McLin nicely. "When he hits it," Bryk said, "the ball gets small quick." McLin actually ended up signing with the Pirates, who took him in the twelfth round, and will allow him to play basketball at the University of Wisconsin-Milwaukee.

By stopping in Whitewater, which is on the way to Mil-waukee, Clark can catch a few innings of the game between Wisconsin-Whitewater and Stevens Point. It is a gusty afternoon, sunny but too cold to really enjoy the bleachers. Clark has on his Braves cap but is wearing a Reds jacket over his sweater. At a high school game, a student noticed that combination and asked Clark, "You having an identity crisis?"

The Major League Scouting Bureau, which services all twenty-six teams, has recommended that center fielder John Andreoli of Whitewater be followed up on from last year. He's batting ninth, not a good sign. In infield practice, Clark watches him throw and notices, "The wind stopped his ball when he threw it home." Stevens Point has two seniors with above-average power—Chris Kohnle and Mike Ruechel. Kohnle, a right-handed hitter, gets a ball up into the wind that blows over the left field fence for a homer. "Bat speed OK," Clark writes in the book that he will open for notations such as this and then immediately close. Other players have been categorized with KR for can't run; CTB, Clark type body to paraphrase Chet Montgomery; a parachute sign to indicate he bails out on pitches; or TSH, signifying toilet seat hitter because he bends in his stance like someone going to sit, yes, on a toilet.

The left-handed hitting Ruechel follows Kohnle by driving a 1–0 pitch over the right field fence. "Power OK" writes Clark, who has noticed that first baseman Ruechel seems to have soft hands. "It looks like he's got a strong butt," Clark says, "which might mean he's able to run." Clark would like to see more of Ruechel but must leave after two innings for Milwaukee. "I hate to bail out on games like that." Clark says. "It's not good. It's an insult in a way. But the alternative is don't come." Even with a good reason for leaving, Clark is still somewhat disturbed. "To those kids," he says, "and those coaches and those fans, I was here. That's where I should have stayed."

Early on, these unavoidable departures made Clark realize something about his on-the-move profession. Day games. Night games. Here. There. Today. Tomorrow. "The scout is truly a ghost," Clark wrote in 1971 in *The Badger Baseball Review*. "He comes unannounced. He sees a boy in a pre-game workout. He sees him at the plate and watches the pitchers work and makes some basic judgments. He is sitting next to you one minute; the next minute he has resolved his judgments and is in his car rolling on to the next game."

That's the plan as Clark pulls up to Pumping Station Park in Milwaukee where Riverside University is supposed to be playing Technical at 3:45 in the afternoon. The field is empty. As Clark parallel parks, a man comes toward the car from across the street. He is middle-aged, wearing a parka, and looks a bit beaten down. "Bill," he says. "Bill Clark?"

"Who the hell is that," Clark wonders.

It is Murray Denemark. He lives in Milwaukee and scouts

part-time for the Cubs. Once a part-time scout for the Royals, Denemark explains that Riverside University and Technical played a day earlier. Sure enough, the line score is in the *Milwaukee Journal,* showing Riverside University won 10–3 and McLin homered. Technical asked that the game be rescheduled to avoid a conflict with its senior prom, Denemark says. Clark had found out none of this when he made his standard morning call to the athletic director's office at Riverside University to ask if the game was still on.

Another day appears to be disintegrating. It's now 3:30 P.M., and all Clark has done is see two meaningless innings at Whitewater. He asks Denemark if Martin Luther King High is playing. There's a better chance that a black school will have a jangler, as Clark calls the loose-limbed types that catch a scout's eye. Denemark has a preferable plan. Milwaukee Lutheran High is playing at 4:15 against visiting St. Catherine's High of Racine. LeRon Rogers, Lutheran's second baseman, is worth seeing, Denemark says. He leads the way out Capitol Drive. Clark is heading to his next game and following the scouting tapestry right back into his past.

"The first guy I ever signed lived on Capitol Drive," Clark says. "Name was Chris Charnish. Signed him out of Wisconsin-Platteville. I believe he was a defensive back. I gave him three thousand dollars. He went down to spring training, and they were going to be put him on the Tampa roster in A ball. They broke camp, and he disappeared. He went to Canada and decided to play Canadian football and kept our money. I thought, 'Shit, I won't be working for the Reds very long.'

"Then he got released from Canadian football and called and wanted to go back to the Reds. I said, 'See you later. I don't know who you are, baby.'"

As he writes in the lineups of Milwaukee Lutheran and St. Catherine's, Clark says, "We're putting together a day, anyway." It will soon take a nice turn. LeRon Rogers has soft hands but seems to sling his throws to first base. Clark wonders about his arm strength and would like to work Rogers out at shortstop to see if he can throw. It appears he can when he catches a foul pop-up behind first base and throws to the shortstop covering second base. "See that throw right there," Clark says. "He got up on top. He had some drive. Damn."

Clark detects "a little bat speed there" when Rogers, a switch hitter, lines to left on his first at bat. He lines a single to center the second time up, and Clark notices he has no hitch in his swing and is aggressive at the plate. "He's a better player than I thought he would be," Clark says. And within weeks, the Braves will draft Rogers in the fiftieth round. While Rogers opted for Oklahoma State, the Braves retain the rights to him until a week before the 1990 free-agent draft. Clark might not

have seen Rogers had Denemark not made his unexpected appearance.

"He was like a character in a Bill Kinsella novel, right out of the corn field," Clark says. "Maybe the baseball gods realized we were cheated out of our white-throated sparrow and sent Murray Denemark."

Some forty years ago, Clark's playing ambitions reached a dead end. He went to a three-day Cardinals tryout camp in Carthage, Missouri, and was cut after the first day. Clark was a decent outfielder, with a keen instinct for getting right to fly balls that helped compensate for an arm that was adequate. He could run a hundred yards in eleven seconds, not bad considering he had no track coaching, and he could hit a breaking ball. But Clark had one glaring fault. "I was living proof of the old saying, never throw a bad hitter a changeup," he says, "because that was the speed I could adjust to. You threw me a fastball, I had no chance, and I knew that. But I wanted to be a part of baseball."

Clark began umpiring in the Central Mexican League in 1956, the same year that the Mexican Leagues were made a part of organized baseball. He lost thirty pounds, wasn't making any money and had been married less than a year. Clark came home and within a week was hired by the Nebraska State League.

"They liked me in the Nebraska State League," he says, "and by then my wife had accepted the fact that I wanted to be an umpire. Everything was looking up, and then she got pregnant. She didn't want to have a baby alone, and I didn't blame her. I went and finished my degree in journalism at Missouri, went to work at the newspaper in Lexington, Kentucky, and came back to Columbia as the manager of circulation for the *Kansas City Star.* I probably had the most money I've ever had in my life in relation to the lifestyle."

Three children and three and a half years later, Clark realized "baseball is still in the blood." Dolores was willing to work and support the family, and Clark went to umpire school in Daytona Beach, Florida. He signed a contract with the Pioneer League, then a Class C league. It looked promising. It wasn't.

"I had to borrow money to report on," Clark says. "I had spent all my money going to umpire school. After I'd been out there a month, I had what's known as had it, so I quit. I had to borrow money to get out to the Pioneer League and quit after a month. That reduced me as low financially as I've ever been in my life. This was 1962. I came home. I had no job. I thought I was done as far as professional baseball. I'm a quitter. I'm a loser, and I know that.

"I come home and get two jobs. I get a job working as recreation director in the city of Columbia. Paid thirty-six hundred bucks a year. Not very much money. I worked from eight to five. Then I'd go to work at eleven at night in an all-night restaurant. Me and the Indian cook. We'd sling hash and sober up drunks 'til seven in the morning. I'd go home and take a shower, and I'd go back to the city and go to work again. I slept between six and ten at night when I could. I'd go sometimes three or four days at a shot without ever going to bed.

"I had to do that for over a year, I guess a year and a half. I worked seven days a week in that restaurant. I never had a tougher time of it financially than I did then. I guess you either had to be strong or dumb or both to survive that. My wife had to be strong too, I guess, to put up with me. Baseball about did everything in at that point."

That probably would have been the end of Clark in professional baseball had Chet Montgomery not written, seeking a field in Columbia for his Pirates tryout camp. More than two decades later, Clark has crisscrossed his scouting territory so much it has undergone a global melding. While angling across Wisconsin, he savors Bob Collins in the morning on WGN just like a Chicago driver headed for work on the Lake Shore Expressway. Dr. Marshall Saper dispenses his psychological advice to callers from KCMO in the morning, with Clark listening from Iowa as curiously as Kansas Citians heading toward the Country Club Plaza. For five-state weather two times an hour, it's best to locate 570 where WNAX is beaming from Yankton, South Dakota. Spinning the dial takes Clark somewhere else. Somewhere he undoubtedly has been. Somewhere he knows people well.

"You develop friendships out here that go beyond baseball, friendships that you cherish," Clark says. "The friendships come from the ball park but go deeper than who won or lost the game. I enjoy those things; they make the long hours short.

"I'm afraid most of the younger scouts don't develop friendships beyond baseball, and I'm sure most of them don't have any love for their territory. And to put that in perspective, I'm sure it doesn't make one damn diddly bit of difference in the performance of their duties. But it sure as hell makes life a lot easier to live."

Occasionally, Clark will see the parade of mile markers and wonder about alternatives. He'll think about scouting major leaguers, not because the life would be more glamorous or because at better hotels he wouldn't be carting his belongings from the car into the room. "I think one of the problems with scouting a territory your whole life is that your decision-making is done at a lower level," Clark says. "The longer you're around, the more you like the challenge to make the higher decisions.

"You'd like to be able to say, hey, I helped build the Atlanta Braves, not through a long drawn-out process of scouting for ten years down here, but to make some of the decisions at the top level that affect the ball club from day to day. It would be kind of a tradeoff in that it took away from some of your birding days but it would be worth it. It's not going to take them all away. But it'd be saying, hey, we're the National League champions, and I helped make some of the decisions that made us the champion."

The Braves signed Clark to a three-year contract and then, during the 1989 season, extended him another season through 1992. That multi-year deal brought Clark welcome security; the horizon when he left the Reds was filled with labor uncertainties in 1990. However, after he signed with the Braves, Montgomery asked Clark to be the Indians assistant scouting director. He would have been a cross-checker in the central part of the country, one of three people making final draft decisions, and would have set up tryout camps which the Indians have never had. Snyder, the Braves' scouting director, even gave Clark permission to talk to Montgomery. In the end, Clark told an astonished Montgomery he was going to stay with the Braves.

"I probably made a mistake," Clark says, "but I always felt your word is as valuable as your life. And once you've given your word, particularly to a guy like Paul Snyder who showed his interest in you as a person. . . . When I said yes to him, it was for three years."

Which means that Clark is still making quick stops, like the one at a coffee shop in Janesville, Wisconsin. There he handed two Braves' bumper stickers and one Braves' cap to Bob Suter, the baseball coach at Craig High School in Janesville. They became friends in 1980 when Suter had a player named Ross Kingsley who, of all things, was a shortstop and catcher and ended up being drafted in the ninth round by the San Francisco Giants. Suter became one of Clark's bird dogs when he was with the Reds; he has submitted his name to the Braves office and now, with the handing over of these Braves items, Suter has officially shifted allegiance and become one of about seventy bird dogs Clark has carried with him to the Braves.

He has included Kinsella in that group, having sent him the standard bird dog contract with the advice to be on the lookout for players in Canada. ("He made the comment to Canadian baseball people that this sealed the doom of the Atlanta Braves in last place.") Like Clark's other bird dogs, Kinsella will receive one hundred dollars if a player he recommends is signed by the Braves and plays sixty days at any level, another five hundred dollars if he plays sixty days at Double-A and an additional one thousand dollars if the player makes the majors and stays sixty days.

"The bird dog if used properly becomes your lifeline," Clark says. "I never ask a bird dog to make a final judgment.

I've got two or three that I will because they've been around a long time and they're probably smarter than I am, but have just got better jobs and couldn't leave. But what I want a bird dog to tell me is who are the best players in a general geographic area. Or if he happens to be a legion coach who travels over several states in the summertime, just tell me the best players you saw.

"And they know if they tell me about someone, I'm not going to drop what I'm doing to run in and see that guy immediately. With seventy bird dogs, if they tell me Joe Blow can play and he's a senior, I can't drop a player I know can play and run in and see a bird dog's player. And they've all learned that. Consequently, they start telling me about the sophomores and juniors, and they don't worry about the seniors so much. They tell me about a sophomore or a junior, then I've got a chance to get him in a tryout camp. Then I make the judgment whether I want to see him when he's a senior.

"I didn't have this base in Wisconsin the last few years because I didn't travel the state. I come up here, I'm bouncing around running down names, seeing guys who can't play, who can't run, hoping that I won't miss anybody. Next year, it'll be a little different than that. I'll have my bird dogs back in operation, and hopefully we'll be able to know where the better players are and what they can do."

Clark was actually going to give up scouting and not worry about using his time more efficiently in Wisconsin or what the weather is like in Iowa or just when that certain pitcher in Missouri is going to throw. Had he not lost money in a weight lifting gym in Columbia, Clark and his wife were going to go into the Peace Corps. Their son, Mike, spent three years in Guatemala with that organization and two additional years there with CARE. Clark made five trips to Guatemala, as well as two to Mali, where their daughter, Kerry, was a Peace Corps volunteer until June 1989. Seeing Peace Corps workers live with the villagers and become part of their communities intrigued Clark.

"It was interesting to watch how the Peace Corps kids had culminated two years of their experience over there to eventually building a dam to expand the rice paddies," Clark says. "And when they leave, they're going to leave that community much richer than they found it and didn't give anybody anything except their expertise and their kindness. You'd kind of like to do that."

There were other pleasures abroad, too, for Clark. He got to immerse himself in what he calls his "field of dreams," something he regards as "my magical fantasy." He went birdwatching. "I logged one hundred seventy-seven species in Mali," Clark says. "And I'm proud of that because I had to ride bicycles out in the countryside and walk through the desert or walk through the savanna or whatever and spent countless hours trying to figure out what the hell I'm looking at. I've got a field guide that's got pictures; I've got birds in winter plumage which don't look like birds in breeding plumage that are in the book. I have to read a lot and use seat-of-the-pants judgment as to what I'm seeing. Same thing applies in the United States, but at least I'm familiar with the birds here in the United States. It was a challenge, and hell, I was as proud of finding one hundred seventy-seven species of birds over there as you are of finding a big leaguer here in the United States. I probably worked harder at it over there."

Bobby Szymkowski was the last person Clark expected to see roaming the lobby of the Holiday Inn in Muscatine, Iowa. Like Clark, he was trying to piece together a lost weekend at one of the four subregional junior college tournaments in Iowa. Szymkowski had arrived in Muscatine, which is on the Mississippi River in southeast Iowa, on a crisp Saturday to learn the games had been canceled because of wet grounds. He and Clark exchange scouting horror stories. Bad weather. Long trips. No games. Szymkowski scouts for the Reds, working a territory once combed by Clark that includes northern Illinois, Wisconsin, Iowa, Minnesota, Nebraska, North Dakota, and South Dakota. He lives in Riverdale, Illinois, just outside of Chicago, and started as a bird dog for Clark on the South Side of Chicago. In the fall of 1986, the Reds made Szymkowski a full-time scout.

He will turn thirty-one in October and first met Clark in 1977. Szymkowski was an outfielder at what then was called Thornton Community College—it's now South Suburban Community College—in South Holland, Illinois, where the coach was Billy Bryk. Clark held a tryout camp at Triton Junior College in River Grove, Illinois, and it was there as an anonymous hopeful that Szymkowski first saw Clark.

"Bill was starting the camp," Szymkowski says, "and I took a look at him and saw a serious individual. He's got the crew cut. What was running through my mind was, 'I'll bet you this son of a gun knows everything about baseball and nothing about everything else.' Talk about being a poor scout; I had him dead wrong.

"We went birding down in Galveston, Texas. It had rained for two or three days straight, and all the priority games there to see were rained out. It's just amazing to see how quickly he can look out and identify the different things. I have a master's degree in environmental biology, and I'm just amazed at his knowledge of wildlife. It far surpasses mine, and I've had a training in it."

Szymkowski's scouting education came from Clark and included both overview and nuance. He explained that post offices sell stamped envelopes in lots of five hundred at slightly less than they would cost elsewhere; the main benefit, though, is it becomes unnecessary to lick stamps. There was instruction in running a tryout camp, developing contacts and camaraderie with coaches and other people in a scouting area and communicating with them by letter and telephone. Clark explained the importance of sending out a newsletter to your bird dogs two or three times a year; in it, Clark reveals his judgment—good and bad—about players in the territory and every year or so logs all the players from the territory on the forty-man rosters and thus makes these vital links in the scouting chain feel appreciated as well as informed. Clark stressed the importance of developing some hobby or other interest to occupy time on the road; for Szymkowski, a computer buff, it's reading computer magazines.

Szymkowski has been such a good pupil that Clark feels "like I'm competing against myself out here."

Clark has come to Muscatine to watch two of their freshmen, right fielder Shane Simon and catcher Tim Boge. In 1988, Clark drafted Boge out of high school for the Reds, but he opted for junior college. Boge is six feet two and 185 pounds, rangy for a catcher. Szymkowski has come to evaluate him, and the Reds, who could have signed him before the 1989 draft, eventually ended up redrafting him.

Simon ran sixty yards in 6.4 seconds, making him the fastest of about 150 players at Clark's 1988 tryout camp in Norway, Iowa. But at that camp, he appeared to throw better. Simon is six feet and 170 pounds, yet Clark thinks he has matured, unlike Boge who has "got a chance to develop into a stronger person than he is today. I don't see that in Simon."

In four at bats, Simon grounds a double inside third base, homers over the center field fence that measures just 345 feet, walks on four pitches ("Shit, I didn't come up here to see a guy walk"), and flies out. Clark knows that what he has seen hasn't been quite enough.

"Something has to click in a scout's mind before you spend money," he says. "I can't tell you what that trigger mechanism is. I guess it's all players are guilty until proved innocent; all players are NPs until they're not. I never got Simon to do with the bat what I wanted him to do. He's a guy you noticed that as he's matured in the last year's time, there's a slight stoop-shoulderedness about him. I think it affects his throwing. I had him in tryout camps for two years and have not seen the projection I thought would occur. He could still run; he seems to be able to play the outfield. He's an intelligent kid who does have some academic possibilities. I think it may be immoral to sign him. If I don't feel confident this guy's got a chance to play high in the pros, above Double-A, I may be doing an immoral thing by signing him to a contract where he's programmed to fail.

"You've got to look at it this way: I'm a father of five children; you've got to treat this kid as a sixth child. I think you're wrong if you don't approach it that way. I've lost some good players; probably the best example is Bobby Dernier. I gave Bobby Dernier good advice by his own admission to take a scholarship to Kansas, and he didn't take it.

"Simon's looking for a school [and ended up enrolling at Howard County Junior College in Big Spring, Texas]. I'll help him get into a program where the weather's good enough that he can play every day. Next year, if he makes the progress that I projected for him a year ago, then whatever it is that clicks, clicks, and your approach to his future is one hundred eighty degrees different if you go after him. But if it doesn't click next year, the worst that happens is you've helped Simon get an education through baseball and get a good start outside baseball through a good education. That can give you a sense of satisfaction, too. Although that's not what you're paid to do."

Clark is making these observations while heading east on Interstate 80. His destination is Bill Zuber's Restaurant in Homestead, Iowa, one of the seven Amana Colonies. Zuber, who died in 1982, pitched for the Cleveland Indians, Washington Senators, New York Yankees and Boston Red Sox from 1936–47. Baseball pictures from that era fill the walls. Clark isn't drawn just by the decor. The restaurant serves family style, meaning ample amounts to eat, and their boast that "No one ever strikes out when they come to Bill Zuber's" is accurate. After not getting to see games in two of the last four days because of the weather, Clark is enthused by more than a good meal.

"Today is a day like we should have had every day," he says. "It's decision time. You are to baseball what the cattle buyer is to the livestock industry. In our own way, we probe the back fat."

As he leaves Zuber's, Clark heads north on Route 151, the wrong direction to get back to I-80. Norway is about fifteen miles away, a worthwhile side trip to Clark. It is a town of six hundred with deep baseball roots. Hal Trosky came from Norway and had some hugely productive years at first base for the Indians in the 1930s. More recently, Norway sent pitcher Mike Boddicker and catcher Bruce Kimm to the big leagues and had five other players drafted since 1976.

The Class 1A Norway Tigers compiled a record of 896–238 under Jim Van Scoyoc, who coached them from 1971–88 and is Boddicker's brother-in-law. He guided them to five state championships in fall competition, which ended in 1985, and five in summer play. A semipro town team, the Norway Bandits, attracts players "all the way up to forty years of age," Van Scoyoc says, "sometimes more."

Clark points out red-winged blackbirds and cowbirds sitting on fence posts and flying by as he nears Norway. A pheasant is standing sentry in a plowed field where the highway curves west leading into town. The sky is a swirl of clouds, streaked with orange and yellow. It is Sunday evening, and as Clark drives down Railroad Street, peaceful and deserted, he points out a few landmarks.

"That's where Boddicker's mother lives," Clark says, passing a house at Railroad and Union. "Bruce Kimm's father lives up this street. Jim Van Scoyoc's house is right up there; we won't stop or we'll be there for hours. There's the grain elevator where Boddicker worked."

It's now the Amana Co-op elevator but used to be owned by Jerry Pollock when Boddicker held an off-season job there. Boddicker broke through with a 16–8 season as a rookie in 1983 for the world champion Baltimore Orioles. That October, as the playoffs were beginning, Pollock was asked if everyone working at the grain elevator was wearing Orioles caps. "No," Pollock said. "We wear them in church."

At the end of Railroad Street is immaculate Tuttle Field, the small-town jewel where Clark holds an annual tryout camp. *Field of Dreams* was filmed near Dyersville, Iowa, about an hour from Norway, and the soft evening light makes it easy to imagine the outcast Black Sox in their baggy flannel uniforms showing up at Tuttle. Except their path wouldn't be through a cornfield. Soybeans grow beyond right field, leading to the Chicago-Northwestern tracks and the trains that now speed by Norway without stopping.

"I love being a part of Norway," Clark says. "My tryout camp means a lot to the town, just as the state championships do and just as Mike Boddicker does. My tryout camp is part of the baseball aura; consequently I personally get to share in the baseball scene in Norway."

Iowa poses some scouting problems. The high school baseball season doesn't begin until track season ends. With time needed for practice, it's almost impossible to start the baseball season before May 25, or about one week, two at the most, before the June free-agent draft. The state tournament isn't played until the last weekend in July.

"Most of the scouts detest Iowa," Clark says. "I love this state. Baseball still means something in this state. In places like Norway and Clarinda, baseball is still played because it's baseball, not because it's the thing to do or because it's the product of Little League parents. It's played here for the beauty of the game to be rather corny about it. It's pastoral still; it's about one step removed from the New York Knickerbockers and Alexander Cartwright in many respects."

By eight P.M., Clark has zoomed back into the twentieth century on I-80. He will drive four hours to Kansas City where he'll stay at the Comfort Inn in nearby Raytown. His plan is to leave early the next morning for Joplin, Missouri. The drive is only about a hundred and fifty miles, and the game Clark wants to see is scheduled for mid-afternoon. He's built the extra time into his schedule to visit Prairie State Park where the wildflowers are worth seeing.

"The whole scouting thing is you become a trained observer," Szymkowski says. "Bill's at the point where he's observing the world. I guess that would be the way to put it."

TONY MUSER

JACK ETKIN

Pitchers and catchers had already gone through three workouts, and spring training for the Milwaukee Brewers was about to ease gently forward on February 27, 1986, with the arrival of the rest of the squad. By nine o'clock, the morning calm was a memory, shattered by a natural-gas explosion that turned the new clubhouse in Chandler, Arizona, into a disaster scene and changed the life of Tony Muser.

He was then the Brewers' third-base coach. Muser had gone over that day's schedule in a twenty-minute coaches meeting in Manager George Bamberger's office. Leaving the meeting, Muser thought about stopping in the trainer's room for some sun screen for his nose and the back of his neck before taking the field on what promised to be another ninety-degree day. Instead, Muser, who wasn't wearing a shirt, went back to his locker.

"There was a young plumber on a crate in a corner of the coach's locker room," Muser says. "I'm about six lockers from the heater. Deciding not to go into the trainer's room, I reached for a T-shirt out of the top of my locker and made kind of a quarter turn with my arm kind of extended in the air when the heater blew.

"It blew me into the wall. Hit the wall and went down to my knees. Kind of opened my eyes and the room was still full of fire. And it was such a weird looking fire. It was a pale orange that you could see through, but I remember two eight-to-ten-foot blue snakes running through it, which was the hot, hot part of the fire.

"Not knowing I was hurt at that particular time, I crawled on my knees to another opening which led into the manager's office. When I got to that opening, I stood up, and it blew again. But it didn't blow with the impact that the first one did; it was kind of a mediocre pop, but I could feel the compression push me back through the doorway. When I went through the doorway, the young plumber was right next to me screaming, 'God, please help me! God, please help me!' The back of his head was on fire. He had a red-and-white-checkered wool shirt on with blue Levis. His shirt was on fire, and he collapsed right in front of me. I'm thinking now, 'I've got to get the fire out on this guy.'"

The eternal optimism of the Cactus League notwithstanding, it was supposed to be a good spring for the Brewers. Never mind that they were coming off a 71–90 season and a sixth-place finish in 1985, just a four-game improvement over 1984 when they were last in the American League East. The Brewers had moved from Sun City, Arizona, where they were a symbol of vibrant youth in a retirement community, to better facilities in Chandler, about twenty miles southeast of Phoenix.

Muser traveled that distance by helicopter on the fateful morning, leaving behind an unfinished clubhouse undergoing the final touches of construction and painting and fields that were being resodded. When he returned the following February, Muser found everything completed or rebuilt but the past looming. "It was hard going into the clubhouse the next spring," he says.

"It's funny how time cures a lot of things. It's like I don't think about it anymore, but I'll always remember it." Muser's recollections were more than three years after the explosion that brought him months of anguish. He was in the visitors' dugout at Royals Stadium near the end of April. It was a chilly afternoon, and Muser was wearing a royal blue Brewers windbreaker that covered the scars on his left arm and back. Eight members of the Brewers were injured in the fire, none worse than Muser, who suffered second- and third-degree burns.

He saw Brewers general manager Harry Dalton, bullpen coach Larry Haney and Bamberger put out the fire on the plumber's back and heard Dalton shout "Call 911! Call 911!" Muser was on his hands and knees, leaning against the wall with his right shoulder and now very aware that his back had been burned.

"Harry said, 'Stay right here, I'll be right back,'" Muser says. "As soon as he left, the lights went out. I could hear a voice outside of the building screaming, 'Call 911! Call 911! Get out of the building! Get out of the building!'

"With the lights out, I panicked. I didn't want to be in there by myself. I crawled into that opening in the hallway on my hands and knees. My hands felt numb, so I kind of rested my elbows on the Astroturf hallway. My hands were still so hot from the fire that the skin was peeling off and resting up on my wrists. I got scared. I felt like, 'Oh God, any movement at all, the skin's just going to fall off of me.' So I laid face down in the hallway."

Before trainers John Adams (see "Biographic Encyclopedia") and Freddie Frederico appeared, Muser took quick stock of his situation. He didn't have any idea about the psychological and physical hell that awaited him before he would, amazingly, return to the Brewers that June. Muser couldn't foresee the pain or the degradation or the doubt that ultimately would lead him into making an either-or proposition with God: Let me heal or let me die. While lying on the floor of a new clubhouse that had just blown up and made him part of a national news story, Muser glimpsed the worst-case scenario and resolved that, no, events were not going to take that awful turn.

"The first thing that came to my mind was who's going to take care of my three kids if I die," Muser says, "and who's my wife going to marry. The next thing was I might miss a whole season of baseball. I don't want to do that.

"I don't want anybody else being a father to my children. I don't want anybody else marrying my wife. And I don't want anybody else doing my job in baseball."

Standing next to the batting cage, Muser offers an occasional word of advice to the Brewers' batters. "Let it go now, B.J.," Muser says to catcher B. J. Surhoff, who is slumping and having a miserable time in batting practice. "Spank on one." When Joey Meyer, a beefy first baseman-designated hitter, lines a ball off the left-field wall, Muser says, "Way to get to it, Jo Jo. Push yourself to the back, and then let it fly."

The messages do no more than skim the surface. Step-by-step explanation, theory, and any delving into nuance are omitted by design. "Say too much," Muser says, "it's just fucking garbled."

Muser won't be saying anything this season; the Brewers reassigned him after 1989, making him a minor league instructor and scout. Picked to contend in the American League East, the Brewers were a disappointing 81–81 and fourth in 1989. The Brewers made 155 errors, more than any team in the league, which put pressure on a pitching staff torn apart by injuries. They also finished ninth in hitting with a .259 average and sixth with 707 runs scored, totals that cost Muser his job.

"From what I understand from the organization, we didn't win the pennant because we didn't hit," he says. "That's disappointing to me because that's part of my job title with the club, and if I'm guilty, I'm guilty. I feel bad about it. I respect the decision that the Brewers made. I don't agree with it, and I don't like it.

"To have been let go and be put out of uniform in this organization hurts my pride, but it can't compare to what I went through in 1986. It can't compare to it, and it's not even in the same ball park.

"When you talk about getting out of bed, being able to comb your hair, having a face to look at in the mirror in the morning, being able to walk and mow the lawn and go shopping and all those things we take for granted, see there's no comparison in that. There's just none. I think what I went through in '86 strengthened me, and I think this will strengthen me also."

The 1989 season that ended with such uncertainty for Muser brought him change at the outset. He had been both the third base and batting coach for the Brewers in 1987 and 1988. Last season, Duffy Dyer, a minor league manager for five seasons, was promoted from Class AAA Denver and became the Brewers' third base coach.

The Brewers had finished tied for ninth in the American League with an average of .257 in 1988 and were also ninth in the league with 682 runs scored. They felt Dyer merited an advancement, and Muser, by being in the dugout when the Brewers were batting, wouldn't be splitting his responsibilities. "It's better for the hitters," Muser said, "but it's harder for me because I'm still adjusting to it. Sometimes you go to bed with this in your mind. You see swings in your sleep."

Better swings, then the nightmares that tormented Muser. Those terrifying visions had nothing to do with fire. He would wake up sweating, having dreamed of plane crashes, automobile accidents, loud noises, and being in uncontrollable circumstances. "Not driving the car but being a passenger," Muser says. "Flying at night with turbulence. But that's a lot better now." Only Muser, among those injured in the explosion, had to be airlifted to the burn unit of the Maricopa Medical Center in Phoenix. While the paramedics were asking him informa-

Tony Muser

tional questions such as the name of his employer, his job, the names of his wife and their children, they strapped him to a board and carried him outside. Muser was having trouble breathing. Ted Simmons, then a catcher and designated hitter for the Brewers, stayed with him.

"They cut the uniform off me and took my shoes off me and tried to get an IV in my right ankle, but it wouldn't go," Muser says. "They put oxygen on me. Teddy kept saying, 'Tony you're going to be OK. Hang in there. You're going to be fine.' "

Somehow, Muser injected some levity into the situation. He had been something of a comic as a player, particularly at Baltimore in 1975–77, where he was a backup first baseman, a left-handed bat on the bench and a wisecracking thorn to Orioles manager Earl Weaver.

"I used to get all over Weaver and scream," Muser says. "I used to scream like he did. I was what I call a turd. I wasn't a regular. Maybe the regulars could scream like Boog Powell or Bobby Grich or [Mark] Belanger. But they never did it openly; they would always yell and scream at him behind his back.

"I did it openly. I did crazy things. I knew [umpire Ron] Luciano and Weaver didn't get along good, and when Luciano was umpiring third base [near the Orioles dugout at home], I'd scream at him just like Weaver. Luciano would look in the dugout and get all ticked off.

"One time I went in the training room and got the eyechart and taped it up on the [dugout] wall and yelled, 'Hey, Luci, Weaver wants you to read this.' He ejected me from the game. Weaver got all pissed off at me. 'We lose this game because we don't have a left-handed pinch hitter, I'm sending you to Rochester.' "

On the morning of the explosion, Brewers pitcher Pete Vuckovich was late getting to the Chandler clubhouse. He arrived just before nine A.M. and found the injured Muser with Simmons waiting beside him. Vuckovich has bad acne on his back, a condition that soon became topical. "Tony's face was flashed and half his moustache was singed off," says Simmons, now player development director for the St. Louis Cardinals. "He said, 'Hey Vuke, how do I look?' Vuke looks at him and says, 'About like my back, but you'll be all right.' "

Once the paramedics told Muser a helicopter was on its way just for him the joking ended. "I said, 'How come I'm going to the burn unit?' He said, 'Well, Tony, you're burned a lot worse than these guys.' I said, 'Shit.'

"They loaded me on the helicopter. There was a female nurse there. I kept asking her about my face. 'Is my face right?'

" 'Your face is fine. You're going to be OK.' "

In the *Baseball Encyclopedia*, Tony Muser is listed just before Stan Musial. They are not contemporaries, since Muser was born Aug. 1, 1947, in Van Nuys, California, when Musial was in the fifth full season of what would become a Hall of Fame career. Other than the fact that both Muser and Musial batted and threw left-handed, they shared little. Muser bounced from the Boston Red Sox to the Chicago White Sox to the Orioles and finally to the Brewers. In nine seasons he had a .259 lifetime average, four points above the level to which Musial sank at age forty-two in 1963, his final season. Well before then, Musial had made an indelible impression on Muser.

"I saw Stan Musial take a swing on a sports commercial," Muser says. "I think it was Gillette. Look sharp, feel sharp, be sharp or whatever that commercial was. They showed a picture of him swinging in that commercial. I never forgot that swing; I was about eight or nine years old."

Musial's wasn't the only swing that touched the young Muser. His boyhood hero was slugger Steve Bilko, who averaged 49 homers, 143 RBIs and a .330 average from 1955–57 for the Los Angeles Angels of the Pacific Coast League. That output brought Bilko back to the big leagues in 1958, first with Cincinnati and then with the Los Angeles Dodgers.

"He could hit a ball as far as anybody," Muser says. "I was sitting in the LA Coliseum one day in dead center field on the other side of that screen where Wally Moon hit all his home runs. I was about ten rows up from the fence, and Bilko hit a ball that a kid caught right in front of me. That's something I'll never ever forget. It was a line drive.

"I mean it was just a monstrous blast, and I can still remember the bat angle and how the ball jumped off the bat and was halfway to me before I could hear the crack of the bat because I was so far out."

Muser transferred that visualization skill to his own game and believes "that was one of the reasons I was able to play professional baseball without a whole lot of ability." Just as he did with Musial and Bilko, Muser tries to break down the elements of a swing but in such a way that the batter too can "picture that swing and try to emulate it."

That's not to suggest that Muser's batting doctrine is based simply on some mental slide show. His approach with major leaguers has been to weigh the hitter's pluses and minuses and give each player a realistic plan, a timetable for implementing alterations, and the admonition to be patient because it will be a while before the changes and the positive results are in place.

"It's not going out there and grabbing them and saying, 'Hey, you've got to do this,' because then they go backwards on you" Muser says. "You've got to move 'em in the direction real, real slow without screwing up those pluses because they have to feel good about themselves. And you must allow them to express themselves because all hitting is an expression.

"But I also know I cannot change some of the gross things

that happened in that swing. So I study it, and I say, 'Well, how can we get around this negative without screwing up the plus?' That's the number one thing I will never do to a hitter, is ever screw up the plus to correct the minus.

"Because if there is bat speed there, I'm sure in heck not going to tell a guy to do something to influence that bat speed to slow down. I think bat speed and being able to wait on the ball are the most important, more so than any of the mechanics or the set-ups or any of that other physical stuff you talk about. Great hitters wait great. Good hitters wait good. And poor hitters don't wait at all."

When Muser arrived at the burn unit of the Maricopa Medical Center, a male nurse told him that they couldn't give him anything to relieve his pain before first doing a physical. That meant having a catheter inserted in his penis. "My guts felt like they were coming out," Muser says. "I started crying. I'd never cried until then." It wouldn't be the first time the ordeal reduced Muser to tears.

Muser's left arm had been burned badly. He was finally given some morphine and told he was going to have an escharotomy, a procedure that involves making a controlled incision to release the fluid buildup that otherwise could cut off circulation in the arm.

"The doctor explains to me, 'Keep feeling your fingertips in both hands,'" Muser says. "'Once you start feeling numbness, I want you to call me.' I felt like I dozed off. First thing I did when I woke up—I don't know how long I'd been out—I felt my fingertips. I couldn't feel them. I looked down, and the only thing I could see because of the bandages was the ends of my fingers and my thumb. They were swollen and about as blue as my jacket. I had no feeling in my arm at all. I couldn't move it. So I started screaming.

"The nurse came running in. She called the doctors. Now I had to go back into emergency and have this escharotomy done. When you have morphine in you, everything is slowed down. It's like they were all going in slow motion, and I was screaming, 'I don't want to lose my arm! I don't want to lose my arm!' I felt they weren't working fast enough, and I was cussing."

The escharotomy left Muser with two "ungodly incisions," running the length of his arm, one on the outside and one underneath. There were also two incisions in his left hand. When he awoke, Muser noticed that the swelling had gone down and saw that his wife Nancy and brother Timmy had arrived from California and were at his bedside.

Muser soon heard the elating news that he was going to get his first bath. "My hair still stunk from that smoke," he says, "and I felt grubby, rotten. They put me in a wheelchair and wheel me down, and I'm just thinking, 'bath.'" Muser found

himself on a little seat being cranked up and over a whirlpool and then being dipped into ninety-degree water. He sat in bubbling water for twenty minutes.

"The initial insertion into this water is pretty painful," Muser says. "A male nurse came in and took scalpels and brushes to start cleansing you and scrubbing and removing skin. You sit in there for twenty minutes. And the next twenty is just screaming."

The hydrotherapy treatments continued twice a day for the next three and a half days. Muser was then flown to the University of California-Irvine Medical Center in Orange, California. It was closer to his home in Los Alamitos, so Nancy could visit. "I only had to have one bath a day there," Muser says. "That was nine in the morning. But it was a bigger burn unit and a lot more people and a lot more pain and a lot more screaming."

Plenty of it by Muser. The hydrotherapy nurses, for whom Muser has respect combined with a disbelief at how they do their job, would sedate him and remove his bandages to reveal white spots, the first sign of skin growing back. "But the nerve endings hadn't started repairing themselves yet," Muser says. "So I didn't know what kind of pain I was yet to be in because the nerve endings were gone. The nurses would talk to me, and they'd put me in the pool. But I'd be so cold. I'd be shaking, just vibrating, and I couldn't stop. I felt like a spastic. And you're standing there naked in front of women. I mean, you're demoralized, man."

With the restoration of nerve endings came an itching and more pain. Coupled with his own misery, Muser was in a room "with four other people that were dying. Literally. Had a man in there named Helmut who had sulfuric acid thrown in his face. Ate an eye away. Ate an ear off his head. Had Lorenzo, who was directly next to me, who was burned on 96 percent of his body. Had his genitals burned off. It was horrifying, and I'm feeling guilty of feeling sorry for myself and looking at those people who were trying to live. What an experience."

It was at UC-Irvine, while the slow improvement seemed imperceptible, that Muser made his appeal to God. He had initially been banking on his toughness to get him through his torment. Fearing he would become addicted to morphine, Muser tried to go without it for nearly two-hour periods. A psychiatrist, who had been consulting with Muser, told him he was stupidly trying to be a hero. He decided he couldn't do it alone and vowed to listen to the doctors and nurses.

"I tried as hard as I could try," Muser says. "But it wasn't working, man. It just wasn't working."

"I've always believed in God. I just said, 'This is ridiculous. Come and get me. If you want me, I know you come and get people when you want them. If you want me, come and get me because I can't take it anymore. I can't. Or show me just a little sign that I'm getting better.' Because every day I was getting worse and worse."

The San Francisco Giants drafted Muser in January 1966. He turned down their twenty-thousand-dollar signing bonus to stay at San Diego Mesa Junior College. In 1967 Muser wasn't drafted, and Boston Red Sox scout Ray Boone signed him for fifteen thousand dollars. He went off to Waterloo, Iowa, in the Class A Midwest League and batted .283. With the Vietnam War raging, Muser joined the Marine Corps Reserves and had to do six months of active duty, limiting his 1968 season to thirty-three games at Greenville, South Carolina, and seven at Winston-Salem, North Carolina. But after a good showing in the Florida Instructional League, the Red Sox put Muser on their forty-man roster and brought him to big-league spring training in 1969. He was twenty-one.

"There was George Scott and Tony Conigliaro and Billy Conigliaro and Rico Petrocelli and Mike Andrews and Jim Lonborg and Reggie Smith and Carl Yastrzemski," Muser says. "Here I am on the same field stretching with these guys and dressing with them and taking batting practice with them and playing a few ball games and getting an opportunity to pinch-hit for Ken Harrelson. It really wasn't a dream come true; it was kind of a very big ego trip for myself just being there."

Muser's ultimate destination in 1969 was Class AAA Louisville where he hit .282 and drove in 62 runs. The Red Sox recalled him in September, and Muser played his first big-league game at Yankee Stadium, facing Mel Stottlemyre. Third baseman Syd O'Brien had left the team to be with his wife, who was going to give birth. Red Sox manager Dick Williams told Muser on Saturday night that he would play first base the next day and George Scott would move to third.

"I didn't sleep," Muser says. "I just stared at the ceiling all night and had a serious case of bowel trouble and came very, very close to telling Dick my stomach is killing me.

"First time up, Stottlemyre threw me a forkball or a split-fingered or whatever the hell he threw, and he got me to a three-and-two count and I hit a line drive to the shortstop for an out. Second time up, I tapped back to the mound. Third time up, he struck me out. Fourth time up, I hit a lazy fly ball to left. I was evaluating those four at bats, and the man never threw me anything on the decent part of the plate to hit. He was always around the plate with a lot of movement. And I said to myself, 'Man, if this is the standard of pitching in the big leagues, I'm going to have a rough time.'"

Just how hard soon became evident to Muser. In the ninth inning of that game, with the Yankees leading 1–0, the Red Sox had runners on first and second with two outs when Muser came up against reliever Jack Aker and lined a game-tying single to right field. "I had just gotten my first big-league hit and my first big-league RBI in my first game," Muser says. "I couldn't even feel my feet on the ground. Here I am in Yankee Stadium, where the greatest players of all time have played."

While Yankees manager Ralph Houk visited Aker, Williams and his coaches Eddie Popowski and Bobby Doerr conferred in front of the Red Sox' dugout. First base coach Doerr told Muser that when he winked at him it meant run on the pitch, stop halfway to second and get in a rundown. Muser even spotted a pebble in the basepath that about marked half the distance to second.

"Aker had a pretty long delivery, so he was fairly easy to get a jump off of," Muser says. "So I bolted to that pebble, and I put on the brakes and looked up. The crowd starts roaring. Here comes Aker [after making his delivery and cutting the throw off from the catcher] charging at me with the ball.

"I don't understand how he got the ball, so I'm confused. But I'm jockeying back and forth. Aker circles me to the first-base side and gets my momentum going toward second base. But he's not coming at me real hard. So I'm just kind of loping toward second base, and I know I'm close enough to where if I make a quick move and make a head-first dive, I could be safe. And that's exactly what I did. But as I make my dive into second base, I hear the crowd roar."

While Muser was taking second, rookie Luis Alvarado was caught off third base to end the inning. A double by Roy White and single by Thurman Munson gave the Yankees a 2–1 victory in the bottom of the ninth. Unaware that he had done anything wrong, Muser went back to the clubhouse. Lonborg patted him on the back and praised him for his hit. Doerr came by with the news that Williams wanted to see him.

"My immediate reaction was he wants to congratulate me," Muser says. "The door was open. I poked my head in there. 'Dick, did you want to see me?' He grabbed me by the shirt and flung me down in the chair and started screaming at me about how we went over this play a hundred times in spring training. Anytime the pitcher reaches up and cuts the throw off, you're supposed to coast on into second base. Well, I'd never gone through any of these plays, never covered it in Triple-A or A ball. Because we never did much of that stuff.

"He's yelling at me. And he more or less told me this is major league baseball, and if you can't make those kind of decisions on the bases, you can take that Red Sox uniform off. I don't care if you ever wear it again or something like that.

"I had tears in my eyes. He says, 'Now get out of here.' He slammed the door when he pushed me down into the chair. The door didn't slam shut, so it was open a little. There was ten or twelve reporters outside the door, and they're writing all this down. I come out with tears in my eyes and go and sit down at my locker and was feeling pretty bad. I said to myself, 'If this is major league baseball and this is the pressure you play under, I really don't want to play this game.' "

Muser made it to the majors for good in 1972 with the White Sox and stayed in the big leagues through the 1977 season. The Orioles released him just before spring training the following year. He signed a Class AAA contract with Spokane, a Brewers farm club, and spent 1978 in the minors until the Brewers recalled him for the final month of the season. After a difficult time playing in Japan in 1979, Muser came home to Los Alamitos in August to face a career decision.

"Nancy and I have a little tent-trailer," Muser says, "and never had gone on a family vacation, all of us together. So we drove up to Oregon and camped at all the campsites on the coast and had a real good time. Nancy and I talked, and I said, 'Look, if I'm going to get out of baseball, this is the time to do it. You've devoted your whole life to me running around the country chasing a dream, and it's been a good life. If it's over, it's over.' My wife told me, 'I want to be married to a happy man. You're never going to be happy outside of baseball.' "

Hallucinating might have been a nice release from the daily misery of his rehabilitation had Muser floated through strawberry fields forever. He didn't. As part of a process known as debridement, where dead tissue is removed in preparation for skin grafting, he was given a powerful drug known as ketamine. A side effect is it can cause hallucination.

"I went on a trip, man," Muser says. "I was in a tube about ten feet in diameter. The tube was so thin; it was about the thickness of a bubble that you blow. And on the outside of the tube was colors beyond your imagination. I was in some kind of vehicle, although I couldn't see it, and I was traveling suspended through this tube.

"It felt like a thousand miles an hour, like I was in a jet. I was passing other objects in this tube, and some were passing me. But there were also some coming at me, weaving and bobbing at a thousand miles an hour and coming close to having an accident or crash every half second. It was horrifying, man, and it lasted and it lasted and it lasted."

After enduring skin grafting, Muser was finally discharged from the hospital and began walking for exercise. "The first time, I made it around the block," he says. "I thought it was a major accomplishment. I told Nancy, 'Don't come looking for me. And don't come and get me. I'm making it around this block.' " He also made it back to the Brewers when they opened a three-game series with the California Angels at Anaheim Stadium on May 9, 1986—seventy-one days after the horror of Chandler.

After Muser's doctor told him he could rejoin the team, a disbelieving Harry Dalton heard Muser pass on this news. "He hadn't seen me since the first night in the hospital," Muser says. "And I know he thought I was maybe not going to make it or at least be out for the season. I said, 'The doctor released me to get back to work, Harry.'

"He said, 'You're not ready to do anything.'

"I said, 'I'm ready to throw. I'm ready to swing a fungo. But I can't stay in the sun very long.' I said it would be about a week before I could coach third base."

"He said, 'What's your doctor's number?' He called the doctor. He didn't believe me.

"They wouldn't let me do anything the rest of the year, but I came back. It was the happiest day of my life."

On September 25, 1986, Bamberger resigned and was replaced the following day by Tom Trebelhorn. He had been the manager of the Brewers' Class AAA team in Vancouver and had managed in the minors for seven seasons. Muser had managed in the Brewers' system for five years when he made it to the majors in 1985 as a coach under Bamberger. Before the clubhouse fire, Muser had been the heir apparent for Bamberger's job. After 1989, the career path that once was taking Muser onward and upward had left him in limbo.

"I kind of scratch my head from where I thought I was starting in 1980 and going through 1984 and managing in the minor league system," Muser says. "In 1985 when George Bamberger brought me to the big leagues as a coach, I felt real good about having the chance to manage on the major league level, whether it would be in Milwaukee or someplace else.

"Since 1985, I've worked myself downhill and not uphill. I feel in my heart that I still want to manage. I feel the uniform is the best place for me to be in right now, and it just hasn't happened that way. I've just moved backwards; I haven't moved forward. I don't know where my career will lead."

Wherever he goes in baseball, Muser will stay rooted to UC-Irvine. He hasn't confined his experience there to a dark corner of his memory. At Christmas, Muser returns for a party and reunion with people who were patients when he was there. Muser also sees current patients whose lives changed in a frightful instant and who are going through what seems to be an endless amount of unspeakable suffering, waiting and hoping to somehow get on with their lives like he did. Muser looks around at people he doesn't know and realizes he actually knows them all.

"There's a camaraderie with that group that's beyond the normal. This is tight," Muser says of baseball, "but it's not as tight as those people. They've been through something that nobody's been through. I know a lot of people don't experience being on a big league ball club, but this is different."

Muser is no longer sitting in an empty dugout. The Brewers

have filled in, awaiting the start of batting practice and creating a background noise as soothing as cicadas on a summer evening. As games of catch start, balls pop into gloves. There's the spitting of tobacco juice and the rumble of wood as players rummage through the bat racks near the entrance to the dugout.

The Royals have been taking their swings accompanied by some vintage rhythm and blues wafting out of the loudspeaker in center field. "My Girl" and "Since I Lost My Baby" by The Temptations and "Midnight Hour" by Wilson Pickett were popular in the mid-sixties when Muser was launching his professional career and the future had no horizon. He played on four second-place teams but never realized his dream to play on a pennant-winner and in a World Series. He embarked on an-

other career path in 1980 as a manager at Class A Stockton, California. Any chance Tony Muser had to become a big-league manager might have ended in a horrible Arizona moment, whose aftermath was revealing.

"It's relaxed me more," he says. "There's always a game tomorrow. Life could end at any moment, but there's always a game tomorrow. There's another season. And things are not that bad. When you're in a slump, you're so close to getting out of it. All you got to do is relax and look around you a little bit.

"Look how nice it is to put this uniform on. Look how great it is to come out here and field ground balls and work at a craft—to have the opportunity to be involved in a winning cause on a major league ball club. There ain't nothing like it."

JOHN MORRIS

JACK ETKIN

The workday begins with after-noon back exercises, a conditioning regimen that serious surgery imposed upon John Morris. Then the winds through a visualization process with the game underway, then more warming up with careful watching by his manager, and then maybe a chance to hit. Usually just one chance.

Baseball is the sport of redemption, with another game usually just a day away. Go hitless tonight, and there's always tomorrow to ward off the angst. Pinch hitters have less luxury. They don't revel in four at bats a game, making necessary adjustments along the way if necessary. They are baseball's lottery players, bucking big odds in search of a payoff that rarely comes.

Not surprisingly, a pinch hitter can develop an all-or-nothing outlook to his craft. Morris has been coming off the bench for the St. Louis Cardinals since 1986—and last year, finally healthy, spent his first full season in the majors. When he explains what he does, it is in absolutes without tailing off into gray areas. In the Cardinals' 1989 home opener, Morris went to right field in the eighth inning, part of a double switch. He came up in the bottom of that inning and hit a two-run homer against David Cone of the New York Mets, his roommate in 1982 when both were Florida State League farmhands of the Kansas City Royals.

"He's a fastball pitcher, and I'm a fastball hitter," Morris said. "If you hit him, you hit him. There really is no explanation for it. There are guys with a lot less ability than him who could roll the ball up there and get me out."

Morris is an outfielder by trade. Mostly, he is a left-handed bat on the Cardinals bench and a decent one. He averaged .220 as a pinch hitter last season, going nine for forty-one. Nine hits could easily have been thirteen or fourteen, but that's not the worst of it. Morris went without a pinch hit for what seemed an eternity, thankful then he had Denny Walling, thirty-five years old and in his eleventh season, as a teammate "to help mentally; oh-for-twelve for [Tom] Brunansky or [Terry] Pendleton takes three days. For a pinch hitter, oh-for-twelve takes a month."

Overuse was never a problem for Morris. For the entire year, he batted just 117 times and finished at .239. He's had better seasons and some that were much worse. In some ways, though, Morris had a very fulfilling 1989. "My number-one goal coming into this season was to stay off the disabled list," he says. "As far as my back is concerned, I wanted to erase that as a question in my mind and in other people's minds."

Cardinals manager Whitey Herzog believes Morris would not be an embarrassment if he played more often in the outfield and is certain there are a plenty of regulars in the National League with less ability than Morris. But his fate, with outfielders like Vince Coleman, Willie McGee, Milt Thompson, and Brunansky on the Cardinals, has been to deal with the tugs and pulls of succeeding off the bench.

"I would still like the opportunity someday to be a platoon player," Morris says. "Maybe my back injury has allowed me to prosper in this role. Maybe my back won't allow me to play every day; I don't know that, but I am able to go out there and contribute.

"I still think that at twenty-eight, I'm a little young to be doing this. I mean, I started when I was twenty-five, and usually this stuff is reserved for guys who are a little more advanced in their careers—Greg Gross, Ken Griffey, Joel Youngblood, and those guys who really know how to do this stuff. But I am very proud because it is one tough job to do. It really is. The hardest thing to do is accept it. Because before you became a pinch hitter, you were once an everyday player, and that's a tough thing to let go of."

The inherent difficulties of pinch hitting don't overwhelm Morris because of advice he received from Hal McRae and Steve Braun, two players who had immense success in that role. Morris went from Seton Hall University to the Royals as their number one pick in the June 1982 free-agent draft and the tenth pick overall. Before Morris was traded to the Cardinals for outfielder Lonnie Smith on May 17, 1985, he spent three years in the Royals system, enough time to go to big league spring training with the Royals and hear McRae expound on hitting.

When he was a young player with Cincinnati, McRae was used as a pinch hitter. As his career wound down, McRae returned to pinch hitting. In 1986, he set a Royals record with a league-leading fifteen pinch hits, batting forty-seven times in that role for an average of .319. McRae had four pinch hits in eleven at bats in 1987, his final season.

"I remember talking to him about pinch hitting a lot," Morris says, "and I remember the first thing he ever told me was that if you go two for ten as a pinch hitter, you're doing a great job, and he really meant it. And I started to think about, well, two for ten is only two hundred, and that is not really that good, but if you think about it, the fact that you have been sitting on the bench for seven innings and you're usually coming in against a closer, that's a difficult situation to be put in.

"McRae used to hold court with the hitters, and he would just talk over situations and what to look for, and he always impressed upon me to hit the first good fastball."

Braun made more of a career out of pinch hitting than McRae and did it remarkably well. With 113 pinch hits, Braun is seventh in history, and he piled up those hits in 402 at bats for a .281 lifetime average as a pinch hitter. Like Morris, Braun batted left-handed, although he did have five seasons where he batted more than 400 times.

Then at age thirty, Braun, playing for Seattle and the Royals, saw his at bats drop to 211. His fate became that of an extra man. He played until 1985 when he was thirty-seven and spent the final five seasons of his career with the Cardinals. Sixty of Braun's 113 pinch hits came with the Cardinals, giving him the club record. Braun then became the Cardinals minor league hitting instructor, which is how he met Morris, and after the 1989 season, Braun replaced Johnny Lewis as the Cardinals hitting coach.

"Braunie got me to really relax my mind, and he really believed in visualization, also," Morris says. "He would always encourage me to cloud my mind with positive thoughts and even in a negative at bat to find something good out of that. Like if I struck out, maybe I had one good swing when I fouled the ball straight back. He always tried to encourage me to dwell on that, and by talking to him over and over again, I felt like he was sincere when he said these things to me."

Help has also come from Lewis. Morris arrived in the majors holding his bat straight up and with a long, looping swing that caused him to hit a lot of balls in the air. Lewis made Morris a more economical hitter. "What Johnny has done for me is he has made my swing as uncomplicated as it can possibly be," Morris says. "I have very little movement, which means less things can go wrong and which means that my swing is consistent. And coming off the bench, you can't allow for a large margin of error because it is tough enough having a consistent swing when you're not playing that much."

By the time he does appear in a game, Morris has gone through a ritual of preparation. He always watches from the dugout for three innings, getting a feel for both teams and the starting pitchers and trying to sense an early flow that could hint at a later situation that might involve him. If any Cardinals outfielder is playing with an injury, Morris will pay attention; he might have to be ready to enter the game "out of nowhere."

In the top of the fourth, Morris will go into the clubhouse and "start to gradually picture who I might be seeing later on in the game." Namely, a right-handed relief pitcher. It might be Steve Bedrosian if the Cardinals are playing the San Francisco Giants; Jeff Parrett or Roger McDowell of the Philadelphia Phillies; Tim Burke of the Montreal Expos; Dave Smith of the Houston Astros; Les Lancaster of the Chicago Cubs. "I can always recall instances where I have hit off of these guys," Morris says, "and I'll put myself in that situation once again."

Once the fifth inning rolls around, Morris begins to loosen his legs and do some of his back exercises. Come the sixth,

Morris is in the tunnel leading from the Cardinals clubhouse. He's able to see the game as Herzog sees it and, after playing for him for parts of four years, anticipate his managerial moves. "When I first came up in '86," Morris says, "I didn't know what a double switch was because I had always been a full-time player in the minor leagues. And we always had a designated hitter, so you never had to worry about the pitcher having to hit. The first time Whitey told me we were going to double switch, I literally had no idea what the meaning of that was."

At that time, Morris didn't have to begin his baseball day at home and on the road with thirty to forty-five minutes of back exercises starting about three P.M. There are exercises for the stomach, quadriceps, and hamstring muscles, buttocks and upper back; the purpose is to increase the major muscle groups around the lower back to increase its strength and stability.

Morris began having back problems in 1986 when he was playing at Class AAA Louisville. Trying to run down a drive in the gap in right-center, Morris stepped into a hole in the worn-out artificial turf. "I felt something big pop in my back," he says, "and I missed about two weeks. I was fine for a while. It was a situation where with my lower back problem, it comes and goes. I was able to play the remainder of that year. Then in '87 around the All-Star break, I started feeling things. That was when the problems started becoming more serious."

Morris also had to worry about more than his back that year. In April, his mother, Grace, underwent a mastectomy. On June 17, former Royals Manager Dick Howser, who had given Morris a chance to make his team in 1984, died of brain cancer. That same day, Morris learned his seventy-nine-year-old father, John Matthew, had lung cancer. When a sportswriter broke the news about Howser to Morris, he broke down. "He couldn't understand why," Morris says. "It was just a combination of him and my mom and dad."

The elder Morris died that September. Morris left the Cardinals for three days to attend his father's funeral on Long Island and returned to St. Louis and the pennant race on September 20. His career-high four RBIs helped the Cardinals beat the Cubs 10–2 that Sunday afternoon.

"That day is without a doubt the most special baseball event that's ever happened in my life," Morris says. "It was just a strange, strange day from the moment I woke up. I remember getting up at four-thirty in the morning and going to my six o'clock flight, which was canceled. And I didn't leave New York until about ten-thirty and got here about noon. Whitey waited for me. For a one-fifteen game, he hadn't made out the lineup yet.

"When I walked into the clubhouse, I figured I'm not playing, but Whitey wanted to see me. And when I walked into his office, he had two lineup cards. He said, 'Kid, I know there is nothing more trying than a funeral, and I am going to leave it up to you. What do you want to do?'

"I said, 'Well, as long as I'm here, I might as well play.'

"He said, 'Go out there and get a few hits for your father.'

"And all the conditions considered, I really believe God made that day for me to give something back to my father. It was seventy-five degrees. There were forty-five thousand people in the stands. There was not a cloud in the sky, and we were a game and a half ahead of the Mets and playing the Chicago Cubs. It was everything my father always loved about baseball; the only thing that was missing was grass. And it was just a very, very special day for me."

Morris flared a two-run single to center against Greg Maddux to put the Cardinals ahead 2–0. On his next at bat, Morris grounded out against left-hander Mike Mason, scoring a runner from third to make it 3–0. Facing Mason again with runners on second and third, Morris singled home a run. He then lined out and finished his two-for-four day with a walk.

"I remember calling home that night," Morris says. "Everybody was happy that we all had something happy to think about again. And for some strange reason, I think my dad was part of that. I think he had the best seat in the house."

Morris decided to use baseball as an outlet, a way to take away some of the sadness and aid in the grieving process. He couldn't have picked a better year. The Cardinals drew three million people for the first time, won the National League pennant and went seven games before losing the World Series to the Minnesota Twins. When the Series ended, Morris lost more than his emotional buffer.

On December 1, 1987, he had surgery to repair a ruptured disc in his back. "I wish I was a little more patient making my decision [to have surgery]," Morris says. "However when you're dealing with pain and the pain was getting progressively worse over a period of time, you just want to get rid of the pain. After seeing two noted doctors in St. Louis, we determined it was best that I have the surgery, so that I would be ready by spring training. Isn't it funny how it turned out? I was ready for September."

In 1988, Morris didn't play until August 17 when he began an injury rehabilitation at Louisville. The Cardinals recalled him September 2. His entire season consisted of seventy-eight at bats, half with the Cardinals. It had been a lost year for Morris, who finished the season by going to the Florida Instructional League. He had first been there in 1982 after receiving a $100,000 signing bonus from the Royals and completing his initial professional season in Fort Myers, Florida. Morris was in ascent then, focusing on getting to what, after a medical detour, had finally become a happy place.

"When I got to the major leagues, I was expecting every-thing to be fantastic and it was," Morris says. "But there was still this emptiness inside of me. And I didn't know what it was. In light of everything that's happened, I think I just got away, understandably so, from just really appreciating the game of baseball. And since I got back, I just try to have more fun with it. I try to not take it so seriously. I'm now looking at it more again as I did when I was eight or nine years old playing in Little League. And if it were all to end tomorrow, I can honestly say I could really walk away from the game and not be devastated by it, whereas three years ago, if I was released, I would have been psychologically crushed.

"Every time I start to get on myself for a poor performance, I think about where I was in '88, not even close to being able to play and just hanging out in the training room. People look at you like, 'What is wrong with you? How come you're not getting better?' People constantly asking, 'How is your back?'

"I remember in the spring of '88 when I was in the training room getting two and three treatments a day. I remember walking out of the training room and just seeing media types, whether it'd be Jack Buck or Mike Shannon or Al Hrabosky, coming in my general direction and turning around and walking back into the training room to hide and not wanting to see these people. I was just crawling back into my own little hole; I didn't want to really deal with it. It was a devastating thing for me to deal with because I never had anything serious happen to me, and I couldn't understand what was happening."

There are far fewer unknowns these days. Morris will enter the 1990 season with twenty-four career pinch hits in 88 at bats, an average of .273. Since he turned twenty-nine in February and seems to have found a comfortable niche, Morris could challenge Braun's pinch-hitting records. How far he climbs and his place in pinch-hitting history are matters for the future, something that's become of much less concern to Morris.

"Years from now, I may have to have a second surgery to clean out some more stuff in there," he says. "I really have learned in the last year to live in the moment. I don't care about what happened last week. I don't care about last year. And I certainly don't care about a week or two weeks from now. I have really learned to focus on what's happening right now, and that's allowed my concentration to improve. It's also allowed me to appreciate what's happening right now; I could honestly say that I love watching that guy hit because he has the funniest stance in baseball."

Morris is sitting in the Cardinals dugout at Busch Stadium and speaking about Willie McGee, one of several players he can skillfully mimic. Having watched McGee over four seasons, Morris wondered, "Man, how is a guy hitting with that stance because it looks like he is sitting on a toilet seat." Morris began doing a secret imitation of McGee and, when he got to know him better, unveiled the batting caricature in Dodger Stadium. "Both teams were watching and loved it," Morris says, "and Willie was on the floor dying with laughter."

Morris moved on to former Cardinal Tommy Herr, emphasizing the facial contortions and squinting Herr goes through at the plate and how his top hand is corkscrewed around the bat. Imitations followed of Kirk Gibson and Jack Clark, a former teammate he came to like in 1987. With Gibson, it was a takeoff of his 1988 World Series home run, a hilarious imitation of his one-handed swing and limping tour of the bases, punctuated by some fist-pumping along the way. With Clark, there was no swing in the shtick, just Clark walking away from home plate after taking strike three to end an inning and tossing away his batting gloves followed by his helmet.

"I remember one time Jack struck out on a pitch," Morris says, "and he started walking down to first and he's leaving this trail of clothing down the first base line. He had the bat boy behind him picking up all this stuff. It was hysterical.

"Jack struck out a lot that year. He also had a lot of home runs. What I loved about Jack was that he was always so good to the guys who weren't everyday players. He was good to [Jim] Lindeman and [Curt] Ford and [Steve] Lake and myself in '87; he really made us feel like such an important part of the team. I really miss him a lot."

Morris let Bob Costas tape his repertoire for a pre-game show on NBC-TV last season. A ceaseless flow of material passes before Morris, giving him the chance to expand his act. Philadelphia's John Kruk with an odd stance in which his hands are held unusually high intrigues Morris. So does Pittsburgh's Bobby Bonilla, a switch hitter, who whacks himself in the back with his bat while getting out in front of breaking pitches. But for someone like Morris, curious about how hitters carry themselves, one player presents fascinating possibilities.

"Clark would be an interesting guy to work on," Morris says, "because he does everything so unorthodox. With his back foot pointing toward the catcher, bat up and then back. Did you know he used to be a fencer?"

John Morris leaned back and laughed. At his own joke, at the joys again coming from baseball, and most of all at the moment.

HAL MCRAE

JACK ETKIN

In his final years, as the at bats dwindled and his skills eroded, Hal McRae resorted to cheating. He didn't cork his bat or otherwise blatantly defy the rules framing the confrontation between batter and pitcher. McRae savored that one-on-one duel too much to do anything as flagrant as hollowing out the end of his bat. But he had passed his fortieth birthday, and he knew that what once was reasonably natural had become a burdensome combination of analysis and work.

That's the way it was in 1986 when he batted just 278 times with the Kansas City Royals and again in 1987. He was a player-coach that season, until the player part of his title was yanked away July 20 and he finished the season as the Royals batting coach. When his career came to a sudden end that July, McRae was ten days past his forty-second birthday. The bottom line on his final season shows just 32 at bats but 10 hits, one of them as a pinch hitter in the ninth inning in a June game at Milwaukee.

"Dan Plesac was pitching," recalls Royals outfielder Danny Tartabull. "He's just throwing gas. He's blowing everybody away. Mac's been sitting on the bench joking all game long and goes in to pinch hit. I'm on first base and saying, 'This guy's going to blow Mac away. Here's a guy throwing ninety-two, ninety-three miles an hour. This is not going to be pretty.'

"Mac gets up there. First pitch he throws him a fastball up in the strike zone. Base hit. I just said, 'I don't believe it.' I could not comprehend how easy it was for him to do something like that."

It wasn't all that effortless. McRae had taken a survivalist approach to the art. He forgot about what was no longer possible, discarding blocks of knowledge and plenty of technique. McRae knew what pitchers like Plesac were thinking, how they sized him up with a gunslinger's bravado. For McRae, who finished with 2,091 hits, less became more. He resorted to one hitting ploy.

"I went from trying to cover thirteen, fourteen inches [of the plate] to trying to cover four to five inches," McRae says. "They said he's old, so we can try to throw the ball by him. I started my hands early. I started my hips early. If they threw me a breaking ball or a ball away, I was dead in the water. That's why I ended up pinch hitting .319 [15 for 47] in '86 and hit .313 in '87. They went by the theory, we can pound the ball inside and by him. I was vulnerable to a lot of pitches, but I wasn't vulnerable to a fastball inside."

The players McRae coached in 1988 and 1989 were susceptible to most everything and couldn't bank on his pragmatism or realm of experience. McRae was the minor league hitting instructor for the Pittsburgh Pirates for two years, before returning to the majors in 1990 as the Montreal Expos hitting coach. While roaming throughout the Pirates system, McRae spent the bulk of his time in Bradenton, Florida. That's where the Pirates have spring training, their extended-spring program, their instructional league entry and their team in the Rookie Gulf Coast League. Pirate City, the team's minor-league complex, is a fifteen-minute drive from McRae's home and a full-circle journey from his baseball roots.

McRae grew up in Avon Park, Florida, about seventy miles east of Brandenton. His professional career in the Cincinnati Reds organization began in 1965 in Tampa, forty miles north. McRae played at Pirate City. The Reds took him to the Florida Instructional League at McKechnie Field, the vintage Bradenton ball park where the Pirates Gulf Coast League plays its home games.

"There are a lot of memories in what I'm doing," McRae says. "And that makes it a lot more satisfying and a lot more enjoyable. But the key is I got to remember I played, and I got to remember that, 'Hey, you did the same things. And you were as naive, as dumb as they seem to be on certain plays.' And now you sit back and say, 'How in the hell could you do that?' I did it for the same reasons they did it. I don't know why I did it. I just did it."

Bradenton is the bottom rung on the Pirates ladder. McRae takes his hitting tutorial to Class AAA Buffalo; Class AA Harrisburg, Pennsylvania; Class A Salem, Virginia; Class A Augusta, Georgia; and to another Rookie League team in Princeton, West Virginia. But at Bradenton the skills are the rawest; the players are making their entries into professional baseball, and the telltale sign that crudeness abounds is an audible one. There's a muted ring in the air at Pirate City. The ball comes off the bat with none of the rich crispness that signals action and is so taken for granted in the major leagues.

"Occasionally it'll have that sound," McRae says. "But I guess the amplifier is not as powerful. You've got a lot of guys coming from aluminum [bats] to wood. With aluminum, you can get some deceleration and hit the ball hard. With wood, you've got to accelerate to the ball. It's not as kind as aluminum.

"Rookie League players are not very good. In A and AA, the ball comes off the bat a lot livelier. After being here, it's good to hear that sound."

Hearing again what had become a faint echo is just a side benefit of traveling throughout the Pirates system. Making the rounds lets McRae view works in progress, something a teacher in any field would appreciate. He can have more input, perhaps see vast improvement, and isn't operating in an instructional vacuum. "You help players, and players help you." McRae says.

"So it's not a one-way deal. A guy that maybe you started with when he was nineteen and maybe he's twenty or twenty-one and he's at Buffalo and maybe he has a little minor problem where he hasn't been swinging the bat well. And you go in there and work with him one day, and he hits the ball well while you're there. That's a big pick-me-up right there. If it was just the kids getting satisfaction], then you give and you give and you give out. You give most, but they got to fill the tank for you."

The input at Bradenton comes mostly as glimmers of hope, vague outlines with the future largely indeterminate. Bradenton is baseball in a bell jar. The games begin at noon, usually before no more than a handful of people. It's always hot and humid. The fields are hard. Indeed, McRae calls it the toughest place to play. His job is to make it just a little easier. "The whole thing is communication," McRae says. "And you got to get to the guy's level to teach. If he doesn't understand you, it doesn't matter how much you know if you can't communicate to him. You aren't supposed to be over their heads. If you are over their heads, you're in the wrong place; you're in the wrong business because the kids are our future.

"You're here to reach these guys, not to say they dumb or they stupid. Maybe they are. But as long as they here, you got to reach them."

After the 1978 season, McRae had surgery on the rotator cuff in his right shoulder. That operation enabled him to play again as a designated hitter and play well, but his outfield days, which had already ebbed, virtually ended. Throwing batting practice is part of a coach's job. McRae does it from about forty-five feet, setting a protective screen in front of the mound and delivering pitches to players like Willie Greene. A shortstop and the Pirates first round pick in the June 1989 free-agent draft, Greene soon was promoted to Princeton. While he was at Bradenton, McRae did little but throw balls outside to get Greene to hit to the opposite field.

"You make him do some things," McRae says, "but you don't tell him. I don't want him to be conscious of nothing. He's in his own little world. It's exciting to watch him drive the ball. I watch and enjoy; I enjoy the ride.

"All I gave him was conversation, not instruction. I'd tell him to keep his head down. I gave him attention. He was fun to work with. You need some easy guys. You don't need a project every day."

The prodigies are few. As McRae throws batting practice or stands by the batting cage, he chisels away at the flaws. The bottom line, McRae believes, is a player either can or can't hit. What he feels he's able to do is give someone a chance for his ability to come into play. To Joe Ronca, an eighteen-year-old outfielder from Cantonment, Florida, McRae says, "Two fin-gers, Joe. Two fingers and a thumb." Ronca, the Pirates ninth-round pick, has a dominant top hand and tends to pull everything. By getting Ronca to grip the bat in batting practice with just the index and middle fingers and thumb of his left hand, McRae hopes to strengthen Ronca's left hand and get the right-handed hitter to hit more to the opposite field.

Michael Brown, a seventeen-year-old first baseman who is six foot seven and 225 pounds, is hitting balls into the netting and getting more frustrated with each swing. "You're trying to kill it," McRae tells Brown, a fifth-round draft choice from Vacaville, California. "Just hit a line drive. You're falling off the ball, using a lot of arms. That's why the ball won't go nowhere."

"Sometimes I don't think I'm doing too well," Brown says. "He just says, 'Swing the bat. It'll come to you. It'll all fall into place.' He said he'd like to see me more before he starts to change anything."

Any adjustments will be tailored to the individual. McRae doesn't want his pupils to have a recognizable style, some patented mannerism that stamps them as disciples of McRae. He doesn't tinker, refine and, in the end, turn out clones. "Everybody does something good," McRae says. "That's why they were signed. I try to find that and improve upon it. I believe in working with individuals not groups, so why should everybody look alike? Everybody should do the same thing, but everybody shouldn't look the same because everybody is different."

Much of what McRae teaches he learned from Charley Lau. Lau was the Royals hitting coach when McRae and pitcher Wayne Simpson came to the team in 1973 following an off-season trade that sent outfielder Richie Scheinblum and pitcher Roger Nelson to the Reds. McRae, who had spent the past three seasons as a part-time player on Reds teams that won two pennants, began his American League career by hitting .151 through June 17. He was twenty-seven and worried about being released. McRae sought out Lau for advice and batted .318 for the rest of the season, and .290 for his career.

What Lau preached was a stance with the weight on the back side, relaxation through the body and using the entire field. Lau believed in going from a firm back leg to a firm front leg, hitting through the ball and finishing high.

"To me the most important thing for a hitter is getting started," McRae says. "So we work a lot on that. I believe that in the stride, seventy-five percent of the weight should be on the back side. You don't want your upper body and hips to drift to the pitch. The head is attached to the upper half, so if the head moves to the pitch, the eyes are going to move and that's going to speed the ball up.

"You don't want your hips to drift because you want the hips to be on the back side so now you can explode through the baseball. At contact, actually the head should go down.

"When we do drills, we emphasize the upper half of the body is upright. That allows your hands and hips to work through the zone. Your hands open your hips. The hands go back, then we stride. The hips are closed, and the weight is on the back leg. When we hit, we take a stride and rotate the lower half. When I keep it under me, I've got power and I've got bat speed. We have no bat speed and no power when our ass is not under us, and we can't incorporate the lower half into the swing."

McRae demonstrates as he explains, bent slightly forward in the stance he used as a player. He stops and starts his swing at various points, making movements that are defined and forceful. McRae is not particularly muscular but does have a compact strength, notably from the waist down. The short stride, the weight shifting from the back side to the front and the hands—the trigger mechanism—moving slightly back and then forward are freeze frames of a process that has layers of intricacy.

"It's like dancing," McRae says. "You've got to coordinate the parts of the body and get them to work together, although at times they're going in a different direction."

Actually hitting often goes beyond the synchronization of dance. There are times when the batter is a jazz musician, deviating from the melody and just making an uncharted reach.

"The two-strike approach would be improvisation," McRae says. "You choke up on the bat. Look for a ball in the middle of the plate to away. On an inside pitch, you fight like hell to put it in play, but you must swing because you got two strikes. You protect against the breaking ball. Try to hit the ball in the middle of the field to right field."

McRae's gift is that he can do more than understand the tenets of hitting and more than talk about them. Quite simply, he can reach people, whether they are major leaguers making megabucks or the rawest professionals in the Gulf Coast League, and has a way of getting to the essence of any matter. Before a game in 1987, McRae stood by the batting cage and dropped this simple truth into the pre-game banter: "You know your wife loves you if you met her before you got to the major leagues."

At Bradenton, McRae's manner is cajoling and cutting, blunt but never vicious. He also leavens any sarcasm with a huge smile that often boils over into a cackling laugh. The young Pirate farmhand who knows McRae's ways best is Scott Bullett, a twenty-year-old outfielder. Bullett is a lanky six two, 190, and one of the better Bradenton prospects. The Pirates drafted him in 1988 but didn't sign him until later in the summer. He played twenty-one games at Bradenton in 1988 and returned there for extended spring training and more seasoning in the Gulf Coast League.

At Sarasota against the Minnesota Twins farm team, Bullett makes a diving catch in left-center. "What a thrill," says Bruce Kison, the Bradenton pitching coach, who muses that Bullett sometimes seems to be in another world. "You know something is there," McRae says. "Whether you going to get it out of him, you don't know." McRae theorizes that Bullett's lack of attention and concentration might stem from his Martinsburg, West Virginia, roots where he didn't play that much baseball.

Bullett finishes an outstanding day by going three for four and stealing three bases as Bradenton loses 3–2. As he begins walking from the field with his teammates, Bullet hears the gentle taunts of McRae. "Does that mean I don't expect nothing from Bullett tomorrow because he played good today?" McRae says. "Bullett going to be a true Rookie Leaguer, good one day and horseshit the next."

"No way," Bullett says.

He realizes that if McRae wasn't concerned about his welfare, the mild razzing would cease. "Basically you've just got to listen to him," Bullett says. "If you listen to him, it'll pay off because that's how good he is."

At the big-league level, no one was immune from McRae's needling. At Bradenton, he picks his targets more carefully. The joshing is reserved for players with whom he has developed a rapport, a smaller circle that includes Bullett, Brown, and Tony Mitchell, an eighteen-year-old outfielder from Detroit.

After a victory over the Montreal Expos farm team at McKechnie Field, McRae has a parting word for Mitchell. McRae has been managing the Bradenton team while Manager Woody Huyke was trying to shake a virus. Mitchell let a catchable ball go over his head in left field but later made two nice running catches. "He said don't be scared to turn around and go back and get the ball," Mitchell says. "Feel for the wall. Look for it and go back and catch it. He told me not to play scared because I thought I was going to run into the wall."

"It's like a father talking to you, telling you what's wrong and what's right. He's trying to make me better. What he told me definitely helped."

The following afternoon McRae has a related message for Mitchell, who has soft hands, decent bat speed and, McRae feels, is a prospect. Earlier in the year, Mitchell and six of his Mumford High School teammates were in a convenience store while it was robbed. One of Mitchell's friends was shot and killed. Mitchell took a bullet in his left arm. The bullet's still there. Mitchell has numbness on the left side of his left hand and has been telling this story on the bench. McRae is within earshot.

"How'd you get shot?" McRae asks.

"In a store."

"Were you robbing it?" McRae kids, a big grin on his face. "They caught me and a buddy and he died."

"You're lucky. So you should have nothing to fear out there on the field during a game. You should just say, 'Fuck it.' "

After the 1986 season, the Royals, in need of more offense, made a trade that brought Danny Tartabull from Seattle. He had hit 25 homers and driven in 96 runs for the Mariners and would better that output playing in more spacious Royals Stadium. Part of the reason was McRae. He constantly goaded Tartabull, telling him he had come from Seattle, where the Kingdome is a home-run palace, and belittled what Tartabull had done.

"He'd say, 'You guys are losers,' " Tartabull remembers. " 'You guys ain't got no flags.' All that kind of stuff. He'd just get all over me, and he had a way. No one's ever talked to me like that. No one."

No one ever gave Tartabull the mental insight into hitting that McRae did in 1987. "He talked to you about the game," Tartabull says. "Not so much about telling you what to do up at the plate, but to give you an idea of what to anticipate. I used to stand up there and look for a pitch and get that pitch that I was looking for."

What Tartabull encountered in McRae was a pillar of the Royals clubhouse. Before the 1989 season, veterans George Brett and Frank White were named co-captains by Royals manager John Wathan. The move was designed to provide the Royals with at least titular leaders. When McRae was around, there was no need to bestow rank. "Hal McRae is the consummate team leader," says Dan Quisenberry, a Royals reliever from 1979–88 before going to the St. Louis Cardinals. "He had the unique ability to get on everybody on the team and get away with it because of his years of service, his ability, and his aggressive style of play."

As much as any Royal, center fielder Willie Wilson felt the barbs of McRae's humor. Wilson is high-strung and mercurial, McRae easygoing. McRae is from central Florida, an out-of-the-way part of the state that doesn't attract tourists. Wilson grew up in Summit, New Jersey, in integrated surroundings and just a short drive from the big-city flash and dazzle of New York. What they shared as teammates was the desire to win.

"Mac would get me *so* mad before a game," Wilson says, "because he knew I would go out there and play better because I was mad. Every day, he would just piss me off. Every day. Then I'd get go out there so mad and I'd play good, and he'd just sit there and smile. He did it, and after a while, I caught on. Then I'd say, 'Forget you, man. I ain't playing that game no more.' When I caught on, he'd do something else. I wanted to fight him a lot of times."

"Then he'd turn around," Tartabull says, "and say something funny, and you couldn't fight him. He'd say, 'You can't fight me; I'm undefeated.' "

"He knew when to stop," Wilson says. "He'd do it to a point, until you got so pissed. Then when you got mad and you started yelling, he'd just sit there and let you yell at him. Then he'd say, 'You finished now, nigger? Are you done?' "

Injured Royals would have to endure a particularly humiliating McRae gesture. They were dead to the team, so he would shoot them in full view. Teammates who were sick or otherwise begged out of the lineup heard McRae tell them to just phone it in and go home, something McRae picked up from Cincinnati veterans like Tony Perez, Lee May, Joe Morgan, Pete Rose, and Johnny Bench.

"We used to say if you were hurt, we didn't want you at the ball park," McRae says. "So if you're hurt, go home. You can't help nobody hurt, so why even show up. We kind of kidded around with that, as if to say, 'We're here to win, and if you can't contribute because you're hurt, let's get somebody in here who can because we can't use a hurt player.' "

What Quisenberry calls McRae's "Samurai code of playing hard" was part of the Red's ethos. McRae calls his days with them "probably the most important three years of my career," even though he wasn't playing as much as he wanted. Only when he came to Kansas City, a fifth-year team still trying to leave their expansion moorings and become a contender, did McRae realize the value of his time with the Reds.

"The whole aspect of being a big-league ballplayer was learned in Cincinnati," McRae says. "Those guys played every day. They wanted to play every day. They didn't count the days of the schedule. They didn't count how many days you're going to have before you get an off day. There was a game, and I was in it; that was the attitude that they had. So I tried to be the same way when I came to Kansas City as those guys were in Cincinnati.

"A lot of things happened in Cincinnati that if you were attentive enough, you could learn from them. There was a lot of kidding and jiving around, but there was a message in all the kidding and jiving around almost every day. So all you had to do was listen and kind of apply what they said to playing the game."

With the Royals, McRae was more than a clubhouse quipster who could inspire his teammates. Beneath his lighthearted veneer was the sensitivity of a caring friend. "When I got into my trouble with cocaine," says Wilson, who was sentenced to ninety days in jail before the 1984 season, "Mac came over to my house, and we sat down and we talked. I wanted to quit. He wouldn't let me quit. He just sat there and talked to me like I was his son. He talked to me real sensitive, and he told me about some of the things that hurt him in the game. If he hadn't of talked to me, I would've quit.

"The way he made it sound was that's what they want you to do. He put it in such simple language that anybody could understand it."

It didn't take a crisis such as Wilson's for McRae to render judgment. He developed the reputation of being a good listener, a sounding board who could weigh any situation like a statesman and inevitably offer good advice.

"He wasn't a guy who would ever BS you or blow any smoke," Quisenberry says. "As only Hal McRae can do of anyone I've ever met in baseball, he just had a unique way of describing the game and chiseling away all the stuff around the game and getting right to the heart of the matter in whatever you're doing. Whether it's pitching, hitting, fielding, negotiating a contract—he just understood baseball.

"He also would hold court in the hotel bar. It was never called. He never said, 'I'm holding court tonight.' You just knew Mac was going to be there if you needed to talk about baseball or something. Hitters would go up to him and say they were struggling with a pitcher or their swing or something off the field. Or pitchers—I can remember going up to him about how to pitch to Don Baylor because Baylor was hitting me well in the early eighties. I couldn't figure out how to get him out. Mac would describe to me what exactly Don Baylor was trying to do at the plate. He was a student, not so much of how to pitch people but of what hitters were trying to do, and he could explain that to pitchers.

"He would say as a hitter Don Baylor is looking in this zone off you, so he's going to dive into anything in that zone and try and juice it. So he said to make him stop doing that, you need to stay out of that zone. At that time, I was trying to stay away from him. He was jumping over the plate, wrapping it all over the ball park. So then I had to change to the inside, and from then on, I did pretty well against Baylor."

Ed Smith Stadium, the new spring home of the Chicago White Sox in Sarasota, is off in the distance, giving the practice fields an on-the-outside-looking-in feel. The Bradenton Pirates have come to one of these diamonds for a game with the New York Yankees Gulf Coast affiliate. Other than a Saratoga sportswriter and the parents of one of the Bradenton players, the only other spectator is Buzzy Keller, the Pirates minor league field coordinator and admirer of McRae. "He gives them a little block out of the bale of hay," Keller says, "instead of the whole damn bale. Hal gives them just as much as they can digest."

McRae has made out the lineup, which includes nineteen-year-old Tim Williams from Springboro, Ohio, in left field.

Williams has a scraggly goatee and long hair tumbling from the sides and back of his cap.

"You go to the mall," McRae says, referring to Bradenton's De Soto Mall, a primary recreational diversion for the players, "you want to look like a ballplayer. They know ballplayers hang out there, so you don't want to them to check out your ID."

McRae had an alternative to kidding with marginal talents. He could have sidestepped these poorly played games in front of empty bleachers on blazing afternoons. He could have managed the Royals.

When they fired Billy Gardner on August 26, 1987, the Royals turned to McRae and offered him the job for the final thirty-six games of the season. Uncertain of their intentions and how well he would mesh with the hands-on approach of Royals General Manager John Schuerholz, McRae asked for a three-year contract. The Royals hired John Wathan, who had been in their organization since 1971 and was then a first-year manager at Class AAA Omaha.

When McRae declined the Royals offer, Frank Robinson was in the Baltimore front office and Cito Gaston was a Toronto coach. Earlier that season, Al Campanis had lost his job as the Los Angeles Dodgers general manager for his televised gaffe that blacks lacked the necessities to manage. That blunder brought about an affirmative-action push in baseball, and McRae would have been the only black manager in the majors had he taken the Royals job. Trailblazing was never a motive for McRae when it came to managing.

"I think about it, but I don't have any regrets," he says. "I knew I did the right thing, and my gut feeling said not to take it. I have a tendency to follow that as much as I can.

"The whole situation was very confusing to me. It was like a runaway freight train. It was moving too fast. I saw it and decided to step out of the way before it ran over me."

There was subsequent talk about being the Royals hitting coach, but the Royals offered $50,000 and McRae wanted $100,-000. The next discussion was about being their minor-league hitting coach in Baseball City, Florida, a two-hour drive from Bradenton. The Royals offered $30,000. McRae sought $50,000. He went back to Bradenton, and in December 1987, moved his family into the five-thousand-square-foot home he built. Convenience has its price. The Pirates came along with their offer to McRae, who was tired of traveling and longed to end the whirl of airports and hotels. McRae opted not to take a singular trip in July 1989 when the Royals inducted him into their Hall of Fame. He stayed in Bradenton, saying it was too soon to return to Kansas City. McRae was happy for the honor and would have been disappointed had he not been voted in on his first year of eligibility. But to him, the thrill was in being elected, not making an appearance where he didn't feel comfortable. To those who knew McRae, his decision to remain in Florida, despite two telephone calls from Royals president Joe Burke, wasn't a surprise.

"One of my favorite things McRae had," Quisenberry says, "is a cliché and doesn't sound like anything. He'd always say, 'A man's got to do what a man's got to do.' He'd just always say that at the right time. And he did, he lived by that rule, and I can't think of any teammate I've respected more than him."

Instead of being feted at Royals Stadium, McRae went about his work with the Bradenton Pirates. He's not naive enough to make any judgments about his managing talents as Huyke's fill-in at Bradenton. "I got a free run," McRae says. "I'm not accountable for nothing." While McRae won't pursue a managing job because he "can be content with what I'm doing," he does wonder whether he'll get the chance to manage or if he even wants it.

"I think the best thing for me to do is just work" ' McRae says. "Then one morning you'll wake up, and you'll have a clear-cut idea as to what you'll want to do. So I'm waiting for that morning to wake up and either say what you're doing is the thing to do or what you're doing is not something you want to do another five to ten years.

"But I want a clear-cut reason to change. I don't want to just rush in and do something. It's sort of like getting married. One day you say, 'This is what I want to do.' You're scared, but you say, 'This is what I want to do.' "

Should he opt for managing, McRae would approach the job thinking it has far less to do with strategy than dealing with people. That insight came from Sparky Anderson, for whom McRae played at Cincinnati.

"He told me the players come first," McRae says. "They got to know they come first. Although you don't take a lot of BS from the players, you got to let them know we're here to make it easy for you to play. We're here for you to express yourself on the ball field. And that's what I try to do."

"It's really weird," says Joel Pitcavage, a twenty-two-year-old outfielder from Sewickley, Pennsylvania, who would soon move from Bradenton to Princeton. "In a sense, he watches each individual and decides what his action will be in the process, which is pretty outstanding because you have to know how to read people. Which he does.

"He's very laid back. I've never seen him get in an argument with anybody. I've never seen him get upset or raise his voice, which is important with kids of a young age. You want to encourage them, not discourage them, which is something he

does very well. He doesn't try to intimidate you. He's always down at your level."

Pitcavage is standing behind the visitor's bench at Twin Lakes Park in Sarasota. This complex used to be the Royals minor-league base and where they once had their baseball academy until they consolidated their major and minor-league operations and moved to a state-of-the-art facility at Baseball City for spring training in 1988. By then, McRae had departed the majors where his pleasures had been reduced to disproving those who doubted him and seeking an occasional thrill. "I was intrigued with the ability I could do what they didn't think I could do," McRae says, "but the party was over. I only enjoyed hitting with the game on the line. At the end, that was the only thing that got my blood flowing, my heart pumping—if I could determine the outcome of the game."

That's not possible at Bradenton where instruction yields less finite results and the pleasures are mostly vicarious. When he's not traveling about the Pirates system, McRae is dwelling in a small, comfortable world. Road games mean a twenty-minute trip from Pirate City to Sarasota. Late-afternoon traffic is minimal as McRae leaves Pirate City and drives home. There's dinner with his wife, Johncyna, whom he met when both were students at Florida A & M, and the promise of another tomorrow at the ball park, where the pleasures, while abundant, no longer include taking a few practice swings and staring out at the pitcher to await another wonderful frenzied do-or-die moment. "I don't ever feel the adrenaline flowing, the excitement as a coach that I did as a player," McRae says. "But then again, I can no longer play, so I realize that. And I have no desire to play.

"But that feeling, you don't ever get that again, I don't think. There's nothing I can do, nothing I can sensibly do. Maybe fly an airplane. Or maybe drive a car three hundred miles an hour or climb a mountain. Maybe you can recapture that [that way]. But that is something I don't think I'll ever regain again. And that is an important part of me as a person because that made me feel good to be under the gun again.

"You can't recapture that. You know that's gone. And I think a mistake would be to try to find that again. Even if you were to manage in the World Series, the ultimate is to play. You don't ever recapture that, and I don't think I should try because if I try I could probably screw a lot of people up.

"Sometimes I get bored. And sometimes I miss it. But then again, you don't dwell on it. It's in the past. So hopefully all the regrets and all the things missed are in passing. And you give it four or five minutes or two or three minutes or whatever it takes, and go on to something else."

MATT WINTERS

JACK ETKIN

By the last week of the 1989 season, the daily autographing had become rote for Matt Winters. Pick up a ball. Find an empty spot. Sign it quickly. Go on to the next one. And when you're done with the entire box, cross out your No. 17 on the cardboard flap and repeat the whole process. These baseballs are a clubhouse staple, there to greet major leaguers before every game.

Winters had to endure eleven full years in the minors and part of a twelfth before surfacing with the Kansas City Royals at the age of twenty-nine. When initially adding his signature to that of other major leaguers, Winters did a happy double take because yes, finally, the long wait had ended. Some two thousand baseballs later, a self-effacing reality accompanies Winters' hasty scrawling.

"I'm sure some little kid at home is going to get the ball," he says, "and go, 'Oh, Matt Winters? Who's this?' Or he's not going to be able to read my last name. They won't be able to read Saberhagen's last name, either, but they'll see 'Bret' and know who that is. With me, they'll probably have to look it up or something."

What they'll find in the *Baseball Encyclopedia*, where only major league statistics are listed, is one line of data: 42 games, 107 at bats, 37 hits, a .234 average. There will be no hint of how Winters was a first-round pick of the New York Yankees in June 1978 or that his first 1,255 professional games were in the minor leagues or that there were seasons when he seemed to be running in place in outposts like Greensboro, North Carolina, and Columbus, Ohio, and his dreams seemed to be slipping away.

A September call-up was all Winters was hoping for when he began the 1989 season at Class AAA Omaha. On May 30, center fielder Willie Wilson was placed on the disabled list, and the Royals summoned Winters, then on a road trip in Pawtucket, Rhode Island. He was hitting .248 but leading Omaha with 9 homers and 39 RBI. The Royals wanted some left-handed power and turned to Winters, who was then mulling a hitless game when Omaha Manager Sal Rende gave him the unexpected news in Pawtucket's Howard Johnson hotel.

"I wasn't in a good mood," Winters says. "Sal came down and knocked on the room and said, 'Hey, you're going up.' I said, 'You're kidding me.' He goes, 'No, I wouldn't kid about that.' I don't think he would because Sal's kind of like me. He got kind of buried down there like me and never got the chance [to play in the majors]. There are a lot of guys who never got an opportunity. Maybe I'm kind of like the guy who stuck it out long enough."

Once the call finally came, getting to Kansas City was an ordeal. Winters' flight from Providence was an hour late taking off, causing him to miss his connection in Chicago. When he finally arrived in Kansas City, it was 4:15 P.M. His wife, Vicki, had driven down from Omaha to meet him. It's thirty minutes from the airport to Royals Stadium. At best.

Winters didn't know the most direct way to Royals Stadium. He and his wife mistakenly ended up downtown in rush hour traffic. When he arrived at the ball park, it was 5:45 P.M., and Winters said to his wife: "Well, it took me twelve years to get here. Why should it be easy now?"

By contrast, getting his first hit in the majors was a snap. That same night he joined the Royals, Winters pinch hit a double in the ninth inning against Roy Smith of the Minnesota Twins. He was cruising toward a 7–1 victory and started Winters off with a curveball for a strike.

"I was hoping the next pitch wouldn't be a curveball," Winters says. "It wasn't a great double, but it was good enough. He came with the changeup. I got it on the end [of the bat] and pulled it down the line.

"It just kind of capped off the whole day. And what made it even nicer was the guy playing shortstop, Greg Gagne, was an old teammate that I played a couple years in Greensboro with and a good friend. He was out there to congratulate me. It was kind of fitting. Another ex-Yankee [farmhand] and all of a sudden here we are on different teams in the major leagues."

Royals first-base coach Bob Schaefer, who had managed Winters for three seasons in the minors, says, "When he finally made it, he was a very mature player and wasn't awed like a lot of rookies get awed." Nevertheless, Winters was surprised to learn that the perks in the majors extend to the smallest detail.

"I got here and was getting ready to mark my stuff" he says, "and I just asked for a marker. Next thing I know, all my stuff is marked for me. You just don't really have to do anything except go out and play the game. It makes it a lot easier, but some things, like marking your clothes, you feel like, 'Hey, I can do *this.*' But you have somebody doing it for you."

In the majors, that's the norm. Two days after joining the Royals, Winters' first big league road trip took him to the Doubletree Hotel near Anaheim, California. His baseball life had taken Winters through an indistinguishable blend of lobbies, coffee shops, and reception desks, a routine that hardly varied. Something new came to Winters at the Doubletree, courtesy of Royals manager John Wathan.

"First trip to California, we were waiting for our bags," Winters says. "I was getting mad because we fly in, and I'm ready to change into some sweats. I went down to the lobby to see if our bags had got there, and Duke [Wathan] says, 'Just call down to the bellhop or tell the bellhop to bring your bags up because you can't be carrying them. They'll get all over you if they see you carrying the bags.'

"I used to carry equipment [bags]. How many years did I dress at a hotel and ride the bus over like a Legion game?"

The summers always seemed to bring Winters two guarantees. He would hit about twenty homers somewhere. And the box scores showing his production would be obscure to his friends back in Williamsville, New York, a suburb of Buffalo. By the end of the 1989 season, Winters had 190 minor league homers. He could also boast of two with the Royals, off Richard Dotson of the Chicago White Sox and Buddy Black of the Cleveland Indians.

Tom Dodd, a thirty-one-year-old teammate of Winters at Omaha in 1989, also finished that season with 190 homers in the minors. His one trot around the bases in the majors came with Baltimore in 1986. Inevitably, Winters and Dodd were compared to Crash Davis, the slugging catcher and career minor leaguer Kevin Costner played in *Bull Durham*.

"We got a little ink out of that," Winters says. "But we both realized that it is one kind of ink that it's nice to have, but it also is sad to have because it means we spent a lot of time in the minor leagues. The only thing was, Susan Sarandon wasn't waiting after games to try to help us with our swings."

Winters' parents never suggested he stop playing baseball. Neither did Vicki, whom he married after the 1983 season, the first of three he spent at Class AAA Columbus; Winters uses the pronoun we, automatically including Vicki when discussing his baseball plans and travels. Nonetheless, when Winters would return to Williamsville after another season in the minors, friends would question his logic. Quit, they told him. Get on with your life. Quitting simply wasn't an option for Winters. "I always believed in myself," he says. "I wasn't going to give up. I've seen too many guys give up baseball, and it's something that I've had a goal in life since I was eight years old to get to the major leagues. All of a sudden it came. A lot of people along the way said, 'Naw, you're never going to make it. You're not good enough.' But it's a situation where I'll stick it out as long as they keep giving me a uniform. Once they take the uniform away, then I'll decide what we got to do.

"I'll go back and finish school if I can't get a job in baseball—look out in the real world and maybe just be starting a little bit later than I would have before. But I'll always have something that they can't take away."

Winters received a more tangible jackpot after the 1989 season. He signed with the Nippon Ham Fighters in the Japanese Pacific League. The Tokyo-based team gave Winters a signing bonus of $187,500 and salary of $350,000 for 1990. Winters will received $450,000 from the Ham Fighters to play in 1991

or be bought out for $150,000. At worst, he will earn $687,500 for one season in Japan.

"My mother can't believe it," Winters says. "She's going, 'I can't believe they're paying you that much to play baseball.' I said, 'Mom, there's guys making three million dollars a year in the States.' She goes, 'I know, but I've never seen [such] a contract.'

"I look at it as a reward for the twelve years. Finally, somebody's giving me a reward."

Back in June 1978, Winters didn't think twelve years of perseverance would be a requisite for making the majors. That's when the Yankees made him the twenty-fourth pick in the country and gave him a signing bonus of about $50,000. He was the second of their three first-round draft choices that year, following infielder Rex Hudler and ahead of pitcher Brian Ryder. After the 1977 season, the Yankees lost pitcher Mike Torrez to the Boston Red Sox through free agency and used Boston's number one pick to select Winters.

His maximum salary in the minors was $26,000, but he was making nowhere near that much in 1980 when he went to Greensboro in the Class A South Atlantic League. Winters played there three seasons, the first two for Schaefer. He suggested that Winters, an outfielder whom Schaefer says "wasn't bad, but wasn't great and had to make it with his bat," consider catching. "He said, 'The day they ask me to be a catcher is the day I go to college and play basketball,'" Schaefer says. "If he could've caught, I think he'd have been in the big leagues for a long time."

Instead, Winters was reunited with Schaefer at Class AA Memphis when he came to the Royals organization in 1987. Schaefer now jokes with Winters about batting behind Don Mattingly at Greensboro in 1980 and Jim Eisenreich at Memphis in 1987, both of whom went on to establish themselves in the majors.

Winters did more than protect Eisenreich in the Memphis order in 1987. That season was Eisenreich's first in the Royals organization and marked his return to professional baseball after leaving the Twins early in 1984 because of a neurological disorder subsequently diagnosed as Tourette Syndrome. Eisenreich roomed with Winters in '87 and hit .382 in 70 games, which earned him a promotion to the Royals.

"He was a great influence on Eise on and off the field," Schaefer says. "He's outgoing, and Eise's introverted. Most people don't know how important Matt was for Eise. It was tough enough for Eise to come back as a baseball player, but it was Matty who helped him come back as a person. He brought him out of his shell and helped him relax again."

By then, Winters had happily escaped the Yankees organization where he felt doomed. In 1983, his sixth season in the minors, Winters thought that leading Columbus with 29 homers and 99 RBIs and batting .292 would earn him a September call-up to the majors. When Columbus manager Johnny Oates called Winters into his office at season's end, it wasn't to relay the news of a promotion. All the Yankees wanted was Winters' off-season phone number.

"I just basically knew after that '83 season I wasn't going to get a shot with them," Winters says. "And I think that kind of took a little bit of the competitiveness out of you. Because no matter how much you try to say, 'Hey, I'm going to gear myself up,' when you reach what you think you've done the best that you can do and you can't get there, then all of a sudden it's, 'Well, what do I have to do? Do I have to hit one more home run and one more RBI?' "

As it turned out, Winters had to spend three more years in the Yankees system. They released him after the 1985 season, after he refused an offer to return to Columbus, and he became a minor league free agent. Winters took a pay cut and signed with the White Sox because their Triple-A team was the Buffalo Bisons. He started doing promotional work for the Bisons that winter and was astonished to learn he had been sent back to the Yankees on February 13, 1986, in a seven-player deal that brought catcher Scott Bradley and reliever Neil Allen to the White Sox and catcher Ron Hassey to the Yankees.

Winters ultimately did start the season on loan to Buffalo where he went three for thirty-four (.088) in limited action. He returned to Columbus and finished the season at Class AA Albany when the Yankees wanted to make a roster move at Columbus.

"I said, 'I'll go to Double-A if you let me call some other clubs, and if I can get a Triple-A job, I can have a Triple-A job,' " Winters says. "They said. 'Sure.' I called around, talked to this one guy I knew from Syracuse. He said, we don't have any openings now, but I'll give you a call back if we do. About a week later, he calls back and said, 'Hey, we need some players.' I called the Yankees up. They said, 'We can't release you now. There's three weeks left.' So I was basically stuck there. It just screwed up my whole year. When wintertime came around, I couldn't get an offer because I really didn't have any stats or numbers put up."

Off the field, Winters also seemed to be sliding. After the 1985 season, he had done promotional work for the Bisons, who are owned by Bob Rich. Following 1986, when Winters had a combined six homers, 28 RBIs, and .202 average in 84 games at Buffalo, Columbus and Albany, he again worked for Rich. This time, on the assembly line at Rich Products.

"I kind of went from the penthouse to the outhouse," Winters says. "Well, not the outhouse, but I went from working with a suit and tie, going around talking to people and repre-

senting the Bisons. Next thing I know, I'm wearing a hairnet and packing Rich Whip and going on ten-minute breaks. I was making nine dollars an hour, so that wasn't bad."

Better baseball times came in 1987 after Winters wrote to John Boles, formerly the Royals player development director and now the Montreal Expos field coordinator, and got his first firm offer for that '87 season. Boles had managed in the White Sox organization before joining the Royals in 1986 and sought out information about Winters, mostly from White Sox people. "This is one terrific guy," Boles says. "Every coach, every manager who's ever had him, they want this guy on the club."

The job offer from Boles was to return to Class AA and play at Memphis. Winters took it and hit .268 with 20 homers, 88 RBIs. That was good enough to earn Winters a promotion to Omaha, where he thought he would play in 1988. Instead, the Royals had to send Winters back to Memphis.

"The tough time was '88 because we wanted him back," Boles says. "He wanted to come back. We had anticipated Gary Thurman making the big league team because Thurman came up in September of '87 and did great. Because of Thurman going down to Triple-A we had to move a guy down.

"I asked Matt, 'Would you go back to Double-A?' He said he would. I said, 'This is a favor to me.' It was tough because he wanted to play in Triple-A. When he went back to Memphis in 1988, he did things as an organizational guy to help that club. He lead that ball club. He was the most valuable player in the league (hitting .275 with 25 homers and 91 RBIs). He could have been a malcontent, and he wasn't.

"With Matt and somebody like Tom Dodd, these are guys when their playing time is over, you keep their names written down, and you offer them a job in some other capacity."

The joke in the Winters family was that Matt would have to get to the majors and uphold the family name by doing better than Clarence. In 1924, Clarence Winters, a pitcher whom Matt says was a great-great uncle, came and went with the 67–87 Red Sox, a seventh-place team. Clarence Winters did his small part to contribute to the Red Sox woes. He appeared in four games, including two in relief, and was 0–1. Alas, he allowed 22 hits and 16 runs in seven innings, disappeared from the majors and faded into history with a 20.57 ERA.

"That was the only Winters to ever get there," Winters says. "My grandfather played sandlot ball in Detroit; in fact, from what people have told me he was one of the best catchers there and had great power. He must've because he worked at a factory there but didn't have to really do anything. He played on the factory team and had kind of a cushion job. But he never got a chance because they said he was too small. My dad—the war came around, so he never got a chance.

"There's a lot of baseball in the family. That was kind of the joke. They always told me I'd have to get up there and get better stats than Clarence did because somebody had to try to downplay that 20 ERA."

Winters had to do it in three separate stays with the Royals in 1989. He was optioned to Omaha on July 10, just before the All-Star break because the Royals had to play five games in four days following that hiatus. They recalled him July 20 but again optioned him to Omaha on August 6 when Eisenreich came off the disabled list. On August 31, the Royals recalled Winters for the balance of the season.

The best summer of Winters' life actually brought misery for his wife. Darby, the Winters' first child, was born March 30, 1989, in Greensboro. Winters made the eleven-hour drive from Baseball City, Florida, where the Royals have their spring training complex, and arrived "fifteen minutes before Darby came out. Perfect timing."

When the Royals recalled Winters, he kept his apartment in Omaha, thinking he would soon return there. Vicki drove to Kansas City where Winters stayed for the most part at a Howard Johnson near Royals Stadium when the team was home. In July, most of Winters' second stint in Omaha came when that team was on the road.

"Before I got sent down the second time, we figured we'd just get a place in KC," he says. "We felt kind of sure we'd probably get called up in September, and when I got sent down, she would just go home. We were all set to do that, and I got sent down from Minnesota like two days before we were supposed to move down here. Then we started a long homestand in Omaha, so we just decided to keep the place up in Omaha."

So without an apartment in Kansas City, Winters returned to Howard Johnson when the Royals recalled him for the season's last month. Vicki joined him for about four days and then returned to Greensboro. "Finally she decided she'd had enough," Winters says. "She wasn't going to stay in a hotel the whole time, and she needed to see her family. I can't blame her for that.

"I think my major disappointment this year is that I don't think we could enjoy it as well as we could have with the moving back and forth. I know it's been hectic on my wife. She goes, 'I know this is the best thing for you and everything else.' She's like calling it the worst year she's ever had."

Reaching giddy heights caused Winters to do some reeva-luating. His elusive objective had been to simply make the majors. "All of a sudden you reach it," he says, "and you're sitting here going, 'Well, now what do I go for?' I think we'll have to go for the goal of trying to make the club out of spring training. You work twelve years to get here. And you can't be happy with this. Because if you just get happy with this, then you're not going to be here very long."

At the outset of the season in Omaha, Winters thought a productive 1989 could be a stepping stone to Japan for 1990. Experiencing the big leagues was all Winters needed to leave the Orient Express. He ended the season looking at 1990 and thinking about a full year in the majors, something Clarence Winters never enjoyed. But a fly-ball hitter? In spacious Royals Stadium?

"Being in the big leagues two years now," Schaefer says, "I know Matt's better than a lot of guys in the big leagues. He may not be ideal for us because he's a power hitter who doesn't run that well. I think he can play in the big leagues, maybe on a second-division team but maybe with us."

The Royals didn't make a concrete offer to Winters, a six-year minor league free agent after last season. They instead decided to re-sign Jeff Schulz, like Winters a six-year free agent and left-handed hitting outfielder, but a little younger. Schulz will be twenty-nine on June 2. Winters was to be in Japan when he turned thirty on March 18. He did some chronological reckoning of his own before he and his twenty-eight-year-old wife opted to cross the Pacific Ocean.

"It was a tough decision," Winters says. "I told Vicki if we were twenty-five years old, we'd be staying in the States right now. But we're not. It's just an opportunity now that we can get a house and get settled and put some money away in the bank." Winters' bottomline in the big leagues might be forever fixed at ninety-one days of service time. He didn't determine that figure himself by flipping pages and counting on a calendar but learned it when the Royals met to discuss post-season shares.

"That's ninety-one more days than I ever thought I would have," Winters says. "I could say that if I don't play baseball again at least I've reached it; I've obtained it. I think that one of the things that kept me going was all the people saying, 'You'll never make it.' This is something that nobody can ever take away.

"They might say, 'Well, he only played ninety-one days.' Yeah, but that's ninety-one more days than a whole lot of people who ever dreamed about playing."

THE DOWD REPORT

The great dead heart of the 1989 baseball season was the Dowd Report, special investigator John M. Dowd's report to the commissioner on the secret life of P. Edward Rose. I'm going to start here by trying to give you what I wanted someone to give me when I was working on this: a clear summation of the sequence of events which led to Pete Rose's being banned from baseball, with a limited and intelligible cast of characters.

Tommy Gioiosa had been a friend of Pete Rose's for several years, a kid who was introduced to Pete by his son, Peter junior. Gioiosa lived with the Rose family before Rose's marriage broke up in 1980, and with Pete after that. Gioiosa had no obvious means of support through most of the early eighties; Rose said that he bought Gioiosa's food and provided him with a car and a place to live.

In June, 1984, a bodybuilding center called Gold's Gym was opened in a Cincinnati suburb. Shortly after that, Pete Rose returned to Cincinnati as a player-manager, ending his five-and-a-half year exile in Philadelphia and Montreal. Gioiosa hung around the gym and brought Pete to work out there, and in early 1985 Gioiosa became manager of Gold's Gym. From then on Pete Rose's life began to get entangled with the lives of a variety of questionable characters, which is not to say that he hadn't known an occasional armpit before then.

The business partnership which operated Gold's Gym also was involved in some other activities, such as dealing cocaine, and Gioiosa, a none-too-stable young man with a drinking problem, also is alleged to have played a role in that end of the operation. Through Gold's Gym, Gioiosa also made contact with Ron Peters, a local bookmaker. In the fall of 1984, Gioiosa began placing bets on football games with Ron Peters—ten games a weekend, $2,000 a game.

The money bet on football games was Pete Rose's; no one seriously disputes this. Gioiosa boasted about being a professional gambler, and told a number of people that the bets he was making were made on behalf of Pete Rose. In the basketball season, Gioiosa and Rose put down bets running to thousands of dollars every night. 1985 was the year that Pete Rose chased down and finally broke Ty Cobb's hit record; his face was on the cover of every sports paper quite regularly. It was also the year, if you believe Ron Peters, that Rose began betting on baseball.

In 1985, Rose began dealing with another young man, Mike Bertolini—we'll call him Fat Mike, to give the story a proper gangster feel and try to avoid confusing you with names. Fat Mike, a New York native, managed Pete's card-show and memorabilia enterprises, and also ran bets for Pete Rose, placing his bets with a bookie in New York. In this sequence of bets Rose was particularly unlucky, almost certainly ringing up losses over the course of a year or so of more than $200,000. Some of these losses Rose paid off, and some of them apparently remained as debt. Dowd is convinced that Rose ran up this debt betting on baseball (among other sports), but he has *no* evidence to support this belief other than the allegations of Rose's two chief accusers, whose knowledge of the events is second- or third-hand. Fat Mike Bertolini, the only person who really knows what the bets dealt with, has never talked willingly, and his "unguarded comments" in a taped conversation provide no evidence that the "Bertolini bets" involved baseball.

The events which would lead to the unraveling of Pete Rose's life really began in October, 1986, and reached their culmination in May, 1987. During the 1986 National League playoffs, Gioiosa introduced Rose to the man who was to become his chief accuser, and who was to produce, directly or indirectly, almost all of the evidence against Pete Rose. Paul Janszen was a young bodybuilder who worked out—and distributed steroids—at Gold's Gym. Janszen and his girlfriend, Danita Marcum, quickly became friends with Pete and his wife, Carol. From October through December, 1986, Janszen and Marcum spent a considerable amount of time at the Rose house.

In the same time frame, Ron Peters alleges that Rose refused to pay him $34,000 owed from gambling losses. Tommy Gioiosa told Peters that Rose was unable to pay because he (Rose) was trying to catch up in payments to a Mafia bookmaker in New York.

On January 16, 1987, Rose, Gioiosa, and Janszen went to Turfway Racetrack, where somebody bought a $2,000 "Pik-Six" ticket. The ticket required the purchaser to pick the winners of the last six races correctly. They did, and the ticket was worth $47,646. Gioiosa signed for the ticket, telling the IRS that he was the sole owner of the ticket. Paul Janszen says that actually Rose owned 75 percent of the ticket, and the other two split the other 25 percent; Gioiosa claimed the whole thing because he was in the lowest tax bracket. The Pik-Six tickets are more or less irrelevant to the case against Rose as to betting on baseball. The IRS investigation helped to expose Rose's other activities, and the bets are part of the case against Pete Rose as being a slimeball, but they don't have anything to do with baseball.

In late 1986 and early 1987, Rose and Gioiosa began to quarrel. Pete had a private room at Turfway, but Gioiosa, apparently drunk, caused an incident at the racetrack in late January, and the track officials closed the room. On March 12, 1987—the day the NCAA basketball tournament began—Rose ordered written a $34,000 check to Gioiosa, which Gioiosa was supposed to use to pay off gambling debts; exactly which debts this covered, and whether Gioiosa applied it as it was intended, is in dispute. Rose and Gioiosa went their separate ways, and Rose became closer to Janszen. Janszen would run Rose's bets for him. Janszen and his girlfriend stayed with Pete and Carol during spring training, 1987.

Again, Rose began to build up serious debts to the bookmakers in New York, losing $67,900 (or more) to them in just over a month. Some of the bets made here involved baseball. The most critical point in the entire dispute is whether or not Paul Janszen could have been laying off his own bets under Rose's name. Dowd is convinced that Janszen could not have been doing that—and from that conviction, it follows that Rose was betting on baseball. There is good evidence that the bets were made; the only thing that can be disputed is that they were Pete's bets. Anyway, Rose was supposed to settle up on Mondays, but several Mondays came and went, and Rose had excuses, rather than money. In early May, 1987, the Reds traveled to Gotham for a series against the Mets. Rose had a meeting there with some gamblers, where his debt was discussed.

Rose has claimed that he stopped betting at that time, apparently to catch up on the payments—yet the "baseball bets" continued to be made. It has been suggested that when Rose got seriously in debt by betting on football and basketball, he started betting on baseball in a desperate attempt to get even. Dowd doesn't advocate this interpretation, because Dowd believes that Rose was betting heavily on baseball in 1986. In any case, rather than stopping, the betting action continued in New York until the New York bookie refused to take any more action. Dowd says that this happened because of the debt, that Rose had exhausted his credit with the New Yorkers, but there is another possibility—that the New Yorkers stopped accepting these bets in mid-May because they realized that it wasn't Rose's betting anymore, that Janszen was making the bets and couldn't cover the losses. Janszen, by his testimony, took all the money he had out of his safety deposit box and borrowed additional money to try to keep the New Yorkers from exposing Rose's gambling; all in all, he claims to have put out $44,000 of his own money toward Rose's gambling debts, believing that Rose would eventually pay him back.

After the New Yorkers cut them off, the gambling action shifted back to Ron Peters, who had been mollified by being shown a $34,000 check. Paul Janszen insists, and Ron Peters fervently believes, that the bets on baseball placed with Peters were placed on behalf of Rose. The debt in New York went unpaid, and the collection agency became impatient. A threat was made on Paul Janszen's life.

In June, 1987, there arose among Rose, Janszen, Peters,

Gioiosa, and the New York bookies a large-scale, complicated dispute about who owed money to whom and for what. It was directly as a consequence of this dispute that Pete Rose's life fell apart some two years later. Peters claimed Rose owed him $34,000, Janszen claimed Rose owed him $44,000, Rose claimed Peters owed him $45,000 or thereabouts, Gioiosa had dropped from the scene with a number of people angry at him and the New Yorkers were applying pressure on the other parties to get the bookkeeping straightened out and the money flowing.

The friendship between Janszen and Rose ended sometime in second half of 1987. Janszen says that it broke up over the money Rose owed him; he kept asking Rose about the money, and Rose kept putting him off. Rose says he dissociated himself from Janszen when he found out that Janszen was involved with drugs. One story is that Janszen and Rose quarreled in Cleveland when Rose took a girlfriend to a card show. When Carol Rose found out there was a nasty scene, and Rose and Janszen split as part of the fallout. At some point late in 1987, Danita Marcum was kicked out of the Rose house. Janszen became furious and apparently vowed to get even with Rose.

Janszen by now was involved in the sports memorabilia business. By early 1988 Janszen was in trouble with the law over steroids and taxes. He was dealing with the FBI. Unbeknownst to the FBI, Janszen met with Rose's lawyer, Reuven Katz, and told him that Rose still owed him a lot of money, and that he needed the money to hire a lawyer. By his own testimony, he offered to "protect" Rose with the federal authorities. Katz told him, on behalf of Rose, to do what he had to do, but their relationship was over. Katz talked to Rose; they gave Janszen a check for $10,000, marking it as a loan but not asking for security. Trying to get more of the money back, Janszen got Rose to sign a bunch of baseballs, bats, shirts, etc., which he could sell through his memorabilia business.

Janszen began cooperating with authorities in a number of investigations. He wore a wire to a meeting with Ron Peters; Peters was arrested and charged with conspiracy to distribute cocaine. Janszen tape-recorded conversations with his former friends—Bertolini, Gioiosa, another intermediary to New York—and began assembling his case against Pete Rose. He wrote a letter to Rose's lawyer, demanding the additional $33,850 that he claimed was owed to him, and saying that "For years I heard the stories that Mr. Rose didn't like paying his debts and had left several people hanging out to dry. Well they certainly were true."

If you had heard stories for years that somebody didn't like paying his debts and had left several people hanging out to dry, would you put up $44,000 to cover that man's gambling debts? Moving right along . . . before that letter was written, in all probability, reports that Rose had been betting on baseball had reached the ears of the major leagues' director of security, Kevin M. Hallinan. As more former Rose associates were hauled into court on one charge or another, it became apparent that word of the allegations would eventually reach the public. In January, 1989, Paul Janszen pled guilty to filing a false income tax return, stemming from his failure to declare his income from the sale of steroids.

On January 25, 1989, Rose was part-owner of an even bigger Pik-Six ticket at Turfway Racetrack. This time, a former groundskeeper for the Reds signed for the ticket, which had cost $2,680 and paid $265,669.20. The IRS, looking into ownership of the ticket, focused yet more judicial scrutiny on Rose and his circle of mischievous urchins.

On February 23, 1989, Ueberroth retained John M. Dowd, a Washington lawyer, to investigate the charges against Rose, and issue a report on what he found.

Ueberroth left the commissioner's office on April 1, leaving the investigation in the hands of Giamatti. A few days later, Tommy Gioiosa was indicted on five felony counts, involving drugs, taxes, and claiming Pik-Six tickets that you don't own.

I think that John Dowd probably went into the investigation of Pete Rose with a presumption of innocence. Early in the investigation, however, he talked to Paul Janszen, reviewed his records, and found that Janszen told a story that was essentially plausible and consistent, which was backed by substantial documentation, and many elements of which checked out on further investigation. Then, on April 20 and 21, he talked to Pete Rose, and Rose slimed him. Rose, not fully appreciating the gravity of the situation, lied to Dowd about

1. His gambling on other sports,
2. His association with unsavory characters,
3. His knowledge of the improper activities of his friends and associates,
4. His debts, and
5. His income and taxes.

At least. He may have thrown in a few gratuitous whoppers about some other subjects, like how many girlfriends he had around the country. Rose apparently claimed that he hardly knew Paul Janszen—an unfortunate choice of a lie, since Janszen could easily prove the opposite.

Dowd, naturally enough, lost all faith in what Pete Rose told him.

Unfortunately, to my way of thinking, he began to place increased—I think unhealthy—confidence in the stories told by Paul Janszen and Ron Peters.

On May 9, 1989, about a month into the baseball season, Dowd delivered his report to Commissioner Giamatti. The commissioner scheduled a hearing for May 26. Rose's representatives, seeing a copy of the Dowd report, went into shock. They requested a one-month delay before the hearing; the delay was granted. The situation became interminable, in part because we had expected a resolution so much sooner. The first *Sporting News* of the season, the one that carried the opening-day game box scores, referred to the Rose situation as "the Cloud over Cincinnati, a cloud that won't go away." When the commissioner's office was so indiscreet as to write a letter to a judge stating that they believed that one of Rose's accusers was telling the truth, Rose's attorneys filed a motion requesting a restraining order which would prohibit Giamatti from summoning Rose to a hearing on the case. The restraining order was granted on June 25. In the course of the battle over the restraining order, the Dowd report, and all of the damning allegations about Rose's life, became public.

> **The Dowd report is biased against Pete Rose to an almost bizarre extent. Every piece of evidence is interpreted against Rose to the maximum possible extent, even if to do so it must be twisted around to where it makes no sense.**

The crack investigative staff of the *The Baseball Book* has obtained a copy of this report (I stumbled across it at a card show). Like most of you, I suspect, I didn't understand what Pete Rose's representatives were doing in trying to prevent the ultimate resolution of the issue. Like most of you, I had confidence in Giamatti's ability to conduct an impartial hearing of the issue, and give a fair judgment—until I read the Dowd report. Now I see things in a different light.

The Dowd report is, in fact, biased against Pete Rose to an almost bizarre extent. Every piece of evidence is interpreted against Rose to the maximum possible degree, even if to do so it must be twisted around to where it makes no sense, and even if Rose's explanation is far more plausible. The Dowd report is bloated with irrelevant information, distorted by strange characterizations and interpretations, and systematically denuded of any material or explanation which would tend to support Rose or cast doubt on his accusers.

Convinced that Rose was guilty of betting on baseball, Dowd utterly abandoned the pretense that he was an impartial investigator, and set out to build a case that would convince everybody who read it that Rose was guilty. Dowd piled onto the real evidence mountains of unsupported allegations, marginalia and irrelevancies which tended to portray Rose in the worst possible light. Dowd looked the other way from the inconsistencies, lies, and contradictions in the story told by Rose's accusers, and used tainted and spurious allegations to build up the evidence that Pete Rose had bet on baseball.

And he succeeded. He succeeded in convincing the commissioner and the reporters who read the report—and thus, ultimately, in convincing the public—that there was overwhelming evidence against Pete Rose, when in reality there is not.

By so doing, he deprived Pete Rose of a fair hearing on the limited issue of whether or not Rose had bet on baseball.

Now, don't get me wrong; I am *not* arguing that Pete Rose was innocent; in fact, I'm not sure that the words "Pete Rose" and "innocent" should be used in the same sentence. Certainly Pete Rose, even if he did not bet on baseball, deserved to be banished from the game for some period of time for other reasons. But I am saying that

(1) Pete Rose, regardless of what kind of characters he associated with, regardless of what lies he told on other issues, regardless of what other kinds of arrogance and improper conduct he may be guilty of, is still entitled to a fair hearing on the limited but crucial issue of whether or not he bet on baseball games, and

(2) the evidence against Pete Rose on that limited issue, which has been repeatedly described as overwhelming, is, in fact, not at all overwhelming. It is distinctly underwhelming.

There is a *prima facie* case to show that Pete Rose bet on baseball. You know what that means—that if this case is presented and there is no rebuttal, it appears that Rose is guilty. But what does that mean? There must be a couple of thousand lawyers reading this book—isn't it your experience that, if you could present a case and the other side didn't get a chance to speak, you could *always* build a case, so long as there is some outline of improper conduct to build on?

And to that *prima facie* case, Dowd piles on volumes of damning but fundamentally irrelevant material, material which goes to establish and reestablish and re-reestablish points which are not in any dispute.

The facts which do not appear to be in any serious dispute are

That Rose in 1986 through 1988 bet heavily on football, hockey and other sports.

That Rose's friend Tommy Gioiosa became heavily involved in gambling, and at one point was placing bets of thousands of dollars a day.

That Paul Janszen also became heavily involved in gambling.

That Paul Janszen placed large bets on baseball games.

That Janszen says that he was placing those bets on behalf of Pete Rose.

That Ron Peters accepted bets from Gioiosa and Janszen upon the belief that these bets were being placed on behalf of Rose.

That several of Pete Rose's onetime friends were guilty of a number of types of illegal and boorish behavior.

Since these facts do not appear to be in dispute, any portions of the Dowd report which simply go to establish these facts are not of any real interest.

This covers the great bulk of the report. If you take the Dowd report and draw a big red X through those portions which simply go to establish that which we know anyway, you'll find that you've eliminated somewhere between ninety and ninety-seven percent of the report. A few examples:

Pages 24 and 25 of the report document an incident in which Rose tried to pay Peters with a $24,000 check, but the bookmaker refused the checks and demanded cash. Rose instead wrote three checks for $8,000 each to get cash, and Dowd found the checks in question in Rose's bank records.

Dowd is delighted to find the supporting evidence—but then you get to the date of the checks in question. The checks are dated February 5, 1986. The incident obviously has nothing to do with the critical question of whether or not Rose bet *on baseball*.

Page 27 of the report discusses (to what purpose I'm not exactly sure) a Corvette given Rose when he broke Ty Cobb's record. The car was actually given Rose by General Motors, but Rose alleges that Marge Schott manipulated the press to make people think she had given Rose the car. This is a kind of a gossipy insight behind the scenes of major league baseball—but again, it has nothing at all to do with the question of whether Rose bet on baseball.

Page 30 tells us that Ron Peters called Rose's lawyer, and an associate called him back and *didn't ask who he was.* Down reads great significance into this—almost an entire page is devoted to this, and then the fact is again cited on three other occasions—but what does it really mean? The fact that somebody named Robert Pitcairn returned Ron Peters' call and didn't ask Peters to identify himself means absolutely nothing, and illustrates very well what I object to in the Dowd report: the accumulation of marginal, irrelevant information into a pattern which is presented as damning.

Pages 101 to 105 of the report deal with Rose's friendship with a man named Joseph Cambra, who has been charged with being a bookmaker. There is a lot of talk about Rose's 1975 World Series ring, which Barry Halper has, and about a copy of the World Series ring that was made for Cambra. Cambra wouldn't say if Rose ever placed bets with him, but stated emphatically that Rose *never* bet on baseball with him. The five pages contain no evidence of any kind about whether or not Rose bet on baseball, other than Cambra's statement that he did not.

To Dowd, Rose revealed "a good deal of personal knowledge of how bookmakers operate"—like, for example, he knew what vigorish is. Well, I grew up in a small town in Kansas, and I've never placed a bet with a bookie in my life, and I've known what vigorish is since I was eleven years old, so what the hell does that prove? Rose's knowledge of bookmaking reveals nothing at all; it's another half a page wasted on irrelevant padding.

Seventy-four pages of the report are devoted to the "Rose Betting Chronology", a set of day-by-day logs that look like this:

> On June 6, 1987, the Reds played the Dodgers in Cincinnati at 7:05 P.M. and won 5–2. . . . Ten calls were placed from Pete Rose's home to the sports line between 9:31 P.M. and 11:57 P.M. Between 12:13 A.M. and 8:14 P.M., Janszen called the sports line eight times.

As presented in the Dowd report, the phone calls from Rose's home to the sports line are evidence that Rose was intensely interested in the outcome of sporting events, and thus that he may have bet money on them, as Paul Janszen's records show. But read it a little more carefully. If the Reds played a game starting at 7:05, could Rose have been home at 9:31? Of course he could not have been; the earliest he could have gotten back to his home is about 11:30; in this edited version you probably see that right away, although it is less obvious in the original. The phone records show that *someone other than Pete Rose*, calling from Pete Rose's house, is unusually interested in the progress of sporting events. At midnight, about the time that Rose probably would arrive home after a night game, the calls STOP at Rose's house, and sixteen minutes later they START from Paul Janszen's house.

So what do the phone records of June 6, 1987, really indi-

cate? They indicate not that *Rose* was intensely interested in the outcomes of the games, but that *Paul Janszen* was intensely interested in the outcomes of the games. Thus this record, presented as supporting the case against Rose, actually supports Pete's version of events as well as or better than it supports Paul Janszen's. I'll explain better what I mean by that in a moment.

Not that I'm particularly satisfied with calls to a sports line being used as incriminating evidence, anyway; I think if you start using common behavior as evidence of improper conduct, you can convict anybody of anything.

Many other pages of the "Rose Betting Chronology" show exactly the same thing—Paul Janszen, not Pete Rose, was making repeated calls to the sports line. Page 183 details a long string of phone calls made from Pete Rose's home (Rose was in San Francisco at the time) to Ron Peters, to Candlestick Park, to the hotel where the Reds were staying, to the sports line; altogether there are sixteen phone calls. Then there is a tag line which completes the section: According to Peters' records, Rose did not bet on this day.

Well, draw a line through that page. Maybe I'm dense, but if it isn't alleged that Pete Rose made any bets on this day, I don't understand what the significance is of there having been phone calls made from his house just three thousand miles from where he was staying to the sports line.

Four pages of the report are devoted to explaining the "Guiding Legal Principles"—mostly taken from instructions to juries, the legal precepts which instruct you as to how much credibility should be attached to the testimony of persons in various degrees of legal pain.

As mentioned, Dowd reads an awful lot into the $10,000 payment by Rose to Janszen to help with Janszen's attorney's fees when Janszen was facing criminal prosecution. To Dowd, the payment of this $10,000 by Rose is a tacit acknowledgment that the gambling debts rolled up by Janszen were in fact Rose's debts. While Rose characterizes this as a "loan" and Janszen as attempting to blackmail him, Dowd hones in the fact that the "loan" was given without any security and without requiring Janszen to sign an agreement, and that the correspondence between Janszen and Rose's attorney—again provided by Janszen, of course—discusses the money as a debt, not a loan.

Again, I don't see that this $10,000 means very much, and I sure as hell don't see that it makes any contribution to proving that Pete Rose bet on baseball. Look at the situation as it must have looked to Rose in the spring of 1988, when the check was written. Ten thousand dollars isn't very much money to Pete Rose. Rose knows that his former friend, Janszen, is guilty of dealing drugs. He knows that Janszen, if he starts talking, can tie Rose to a number of things he doesn't want to be connected with—associating with gamblers, turning a blind eye to Janszen's steroid business, etc. He may know that Janszen has used his (Rose's) name to cover his own baseball bets, and that the gamblers therefore *believe* that Rose is responsible for these debts. He has no idea how far he is going to be dragged into this swamp he is simply trying to put the whole relationship behind him.

So given the situation that Rose sees in the spring of 1988, he sent the $10,000 check. That doesn't prove anything to me beyond what is already known—that there was a relationship between Rose and Janszen, that Janszen was involved in illegal activities, and that Rose didn't want his knowledge of those activities to be brought to light.

A good portion of the report doesn't even accomplish that much. A good portion of it is just *there*, portraying Pete Rose's life in the least favorable possible light, but not doing anything to establish improper conduct beyond what is already acknowledged. For example, page 49 of the report tells us

1. That Danita Marcum, Paul Janszen's girlfriend, became a good friend of Carol Rose.
2. That when Carol Rose went with Pete on road trips, Danita Marcum and Paul Jansen would sometimes go along, too.
3. That Danita Marcum confirms that she and Paul Janszen were often invited to the Rose house in late 1986.
4. That Ms. Marcum says that at Rose's house she saw Rose, Gioiosa, and Bertolini placing bets—in December, mind you.
5. That she saw large amounts of cash in Rose's house.
6. That the boys would spend all of their time watching sports events on television.
7. That Marcum once worked as a clerk for Satellite Business Systems.
8. That Marcum is a part owner of Janszen's sports memorabilia business.
9. That Marcum has never been convicted of a felony.
10. That Marcum claims that she has never used drugs.
11. That in December, 1986, Janszen accompanied Rose when Rose went to New York to join Mickey Mantle in a card show.
12. That there was a photograph taken of Rose and Mantle with Janszen.
13. That Janszen gave Pete Rose a music box for Christmas, 1986.

14. That Janszen and Marcum also spent New Year's Eve with Pete and Carol Rose.

All of this, like most of the Dowd report, is rather interesting—gossipy, revealing of Rose's once-private life, and very different from the view of a baseball player that one normally gets off the sports page. But very little of it has anything at all to do with the investigation. So Pete Rose spent all of his time watching sports on TV—this is news? This is damaging? A year ago sportswriters wrote laudatory articles about Rose which stated exactly the same thing, but worked it into a pattern of Pete Rose as a hero.

So Pete Rose participated in a card signing with Mickey Mantle—so what? So Paul Janszen went to New York with him—so what? Is this incriminating? Does Rose deny this? So Paul Janszen gave Rose a music box for Christmas, so what tune did it play?

That portion of the page which does bear on the investigation—points four and five—only goes to reiterate that which is not contested and has never been in any real doubt: that Rose bet, and sometimes bet heavily, on other sports.

> A handwriting expert did identify the material as Rose's. A handwriting expert also stated that the Hitler diaries were genuine.

Beyond the silly shit like phone calls to the sports line, there is some real evidence that Pete Rose bet on baseball. The real evidence is

1. The testimony of Ron Janszen.
2. The testimony of Danita Jo Marcum.
3. The testimony of Ron Peters.
4. The betting records of Ron Peters.
5. The betting notebooks of Paul Janszen.
6. The comments made by Michael Bertolini in a tape-recorded telephone conversation with Paul Janszen.
7. The testimony of Jim Proctor, an acquaintance of Paul Janszen who claims to have overheard a phone call in which Rose made statements clearly dealing with baseball betting.
8. The three-page betting slip, believed in Pete Rose's handwriting, which lists major league baseball games (as well as other sports) along with Ws, Ls, and what appear to be gambler's notes.

Let's deal first with the betting slip. The "three-page" betting slip is, as far as baseball is concerned, a two-page betting slip; the third page is undated, but deals with college and professional football games. The third page doesn't have anything to do with baseball.

The first page of the betting slip gives the date "April 9, 1987," followed by four major league baseball games and four NBA basketball games, apparently in Rose's handwriting. Later it is reported (or alleged) that a gambling expert retained by Dowd has concluded that Paul Janszen's betting records match the records of these games.

On the second page of the "betting sheet," there are listings for April 10 and April 11 basketball and baseball games, including the Cincinnati game. On this page, there are also some notations in someone else's handwriting, unidentified.

Obviously, this is damaging evidence against Rose so long as it not challenged. If there had been a judicial proceeding, however, it is far from clear that Dowd's interpretation of this sheet would stand up. There are any number of other possibilities:

• The sheet could be a forgery. Remember, Rose is arguing that he is being framed. We're talking about two pages with probably a couple of hundred words on them. Someone else could have constructed the evidence.

A handwriting expert did identify the material as Rose's, but a handwriting expert also stated that the Hitler diaries were genuine. I don't know much about it, but I think handwriting analysis, where forgery is alleged, is an imprecise science in which disputes between experts are not uncommon.

• The "betting sheet"—so identified by Dowd—could have nothing to do with gambling, or the baseball portions of it could have nothing to do with gambling. It could be something as simple as a sheet on which Rose had recorded his bets, and when calling the sports line to check on his bets also jotted down a few baseball scores that he hadn't heard yet. Janszen could then have altered his own betting logs to make it look like they included the games that had incidentally been jotted down.

• It could have been written as a "what if" exercise. If you were betting on basketball games, and you were a baseball manager who therefore couldn't bet on baseball games, wouldn't you write down a few "what if" bets—if I *could* bet on these guys I would? I know I'd do that.

• It could be a basically legitimate document which has been altered in some way to make it appear more damaging than it is.

> **There was no date on which the reported pairings occured. The schedule is given for a non-existent date.**

I know that some of you will think I am reaching in trying to say that this document might not mean what it seems to mean, but I don't think you can forget this fact: that this document was provided for Mr. Dowd by the man who is Rose's chief accuser, the man who is, in one way or another, the source of virtually all the evidence against Rose.

I believe first of all that any document which has not withstood the scrutiny of partisan review should be regarded with some skepticism; one should not simply accept that it means what one side of the dispute *says* that it means.

I believe that that skepticism should increase five-fold when the document in question serves the purposes of the party which has provided it.

That's common sense, and I suspect, although I don't know, that it is also the law.

There is something else about this "betting log" which I wanted to call to your attention. At the bottom of the first page, there are three games listed, like this:

    Cin at Mont   W
    Philly at Atl.   L
    LA at Houst   L

These games are not associated with any date. When I tried to pin down the date, I noticed something odd: *There was no date, during the 1987 season, on which these three pairings occurred.* There was no date on which Cincinnati played at Montreal, Philadelphia was at Atlanta, and Los Angeles was at Houston—in fact, as best I can determine, there hasn't been a day in several years in which these pairings have occurred.

The time frame which is intended, however, is clear; the early-April period which the rest of the supposed betting sheet covers (April 9 to 11, 1987) is also the period which most nearly matches the schedule outlined. LA was at Houston on April 6, 7 and 8; Philadelphia was at Atlanta on April 7 and 9. While Cincinnati was not at Montreal as shown, Montreal was *at Cincinnati* on April 6 and April 8.

This is supposed to be Pete Rose's handwriting, and it does seem strange that Pete Rose would forget whether Cincinnati was at home or on the road. Someone else, looking at the schedule, could easily mistake a home game for a road game; one would think that the team manager would be less likely to. Still, it's a minor thing; anybody could write a game down backwards, even knowing where it was played.

But even so, there is no exact date of such a slate of games;

two of the games required were played on the sixth, two were played on the seventh, two on the eighth and one on the ninth—but never all three on the same day. (There were no rainouts which prevented such a schedule.)

There are other "glitches" or "holes" in Dowd's evidence which we'll deal with later, but that's not the fundamental problem. There are two fundamental problems with the report:

1) That too much of the report deals with the statements, activities, and actions of other people, other than Pete Rose, and

2) That Paul Janszen is, directly or directly, the source of way too much of the information which incriminates Rose.

To me, it seems like an obvious principle that *Pete Rose cannot be made guilty by the things done by other people.* Nothing that Paul Janszen does or Gioiosa does can make Pete Rose guilty of anything, unless it is proven that they did these things at Rose's bidding.

But Dowd argues that phone calls made to the Cincinnati clubhouse by other people show that Rose was participating in a gambling conspiracy. His argument for this is that "gambling is conducted in secret by its participants . . . payments are often made in cash by runners between the bookmaker and the gambler because cash is fungible and difficult to trace. The runners provide insulation and, thus, deniability to the gambler and the bookmaker." What Dowd says, by implication, is that because gamblers use others to do their bidding, the things done by others can incriminate the gambler himself. He doesn't say that directly, but he does present page after page of things done and said by other people as if they were incriminating to Rose.

In all of the secretly taped phone calls, Pete Rose's voice never appears. Is this considered by Dowd to be perhaps some slight evidence that Rose might not be as heavily involved as Janszen claims? Why no; in fact, this is more evidence that Rose was behind it all.

Nowhere in the report that I find is there even the allegation that Pete Rose made a phone call.

Of the thousands of phone calls detailed in the Dowd report, it doesn't appear that Rose himself made any; virtually all, if not literally every one, of these calls were made by other people. Dowd doesn't acknowledge this, but he also doesn't dispute it; he alleges that they were made on Rose's behalf. Or consider this one, which I alluded to before:

"Ron Peters called for Rose at Reuven Katz's office and received a call back from Robert Pitcairn, who, according to Peters, did not inquire who Peters was and did not dispute Peters' statement that Pete Rose bet with Peters."

Great. Pete Rose must be guilty because *Ron Peters* said so and *Robert Pitcairn* did not dispute him (according to Peters).

This quote is taken from page 219 of the report, but this is by no means the only time that the fact that Pitcairn did not dispute Peters' acquaintance with Rose appears; in fact, this singular piece of information occupies almost the whole of page 30 of the report:

> DOWD: Did he ask who you were?
> PETERS: No, never. Not one time. My opinion is he obviously knew who I was.
> DOWD: Was he friendly?
> PETERS: Yes, very friendly. He never asked who I was and is this a prank call or anything like that.
> DOWD: Which you would have expected since you'd never known him.
> PETERS: Right.
> DOWD: Like, "Who the hell are you?"

I drew a red X threw all that crap, too; that doesn't mean anything. But Dowd, not satisfied with twice, makes the point again on page 202 (Pitcairn returned Peters' call to Katz and made inquiries about the commissioner's investigation without asking Peters who he was and without disputing . . .) This simple fact, which to any fair-minded person isn't worth mentioning, is one of the minor pillars of Dowd's castle.

Pages 19 to 23 of the report deal with the testimony of a man named Dave Morgan, who worked with Peters and verifies (to Dowd's satisfaction) many of the things Peters alleges. At the end of these five pages there is a remarkable revelation-in-passing: Morgan has never met Pete Rose. His entire personal relationship with Rose is that he thinks he took a phone call from Rose one time during the football or basketball season, and handed the phone to Peters.

On page 96 of the Dowd report, Dowd says that in a phone conversation with Janszen, "Bertolini acknowledges Rose's debt"—leaving open the question of how Fat Mike knows what Rose's debts are and are not, and how *anything* Bertolini says proves that Rose owes Janszen money.

To Dowd, the repeated phone calls from Janszen to Rose are evidence that Rose is working with Janszen in arranging these bets—but that's not necessarily so. They could be evidence that Janszen was pumping Rose for information.

The comments made by Bertolini are, like almost everything else in this case, available by way of Paul Janszen. Dowd says that Rose's betting on baseball was discussed during the taped telephone conversation between Janszen and Bertolini—but only Janszen actually says anything about his betting on baseball. Pages 33 to 36 of the Dowd report are a transcript of a conversation between Janszen and Bertolini, a conversation secretly taped by Janszen. The character of the conversation can be seen by looking at Bertolini's first nine comments, as reported by Dowd:

> BERTOLINI: About what?
> BERTOLINI: Fuck'n, we're working it out and shit, I don't know, the fuck. Did you ever?
> BERTOLINI: So, he paid you about thirty-eight?
> BERTOLINI: How much, did he pay you anything yet?
> BERTOLINI: I hear you.
> BERTOLINI: Yeah.
> BERTOLINI: Yeah, I hear you.
> BERTOLINI: What, me or all together?
> BERTOLINI: Don't talk like that on the phone, I hate that.

You can tell what is happening—Bertolini is listening, and Janszen, taping the call, is trying to get Bertolini to join in incriminating Rose. Eventually, Bertolini does start to talk about Rose's gambling debts.

Review the list of the eight real elements of evidence against Rose:

1. The testimony of Paul Janszen.
2. The testimony of Danita Jo Marcum, Paul Janszen's girlfriend.
3. The testimony of Ron Peters.

Janszen was placing the bets with Peters. Janszen *could* have convinced Peters that these were Rose's bets when they were actually Janszen's. Peters is convinced that this is not so, but if he admits that it isn't then he has to admit that Janszen has made a patsy out of him—and most people are reluctant to do that.

4. The betting records of Ron Peters.
   Which list bets that Janszen told Peters were for Pete Rose, and which Peters recorded as being Rose's bets.
5. The betting notebooks of Paul Janszen.
   Which of course were provided by Paul Janszen.
6. The comments made by Michael Bertolini in a tape-recorded telephone conversation with Paul Janszen.
   Tape recorded by Paul Janszen.
7. The testimony of Jim Proctor, who claims to have overheard a phone call in which Rose made statements clearly dealing with baseball betting.
   Proctor is a friend of Paul Janszen's, who overheard a phone call in Janszen's car.
8. The three-page betting slip, believed to be in Pete Rose's

handwriting, which lists major league baseball games (as well as other sports) along with Ws, Ls, and what appear to be gambler's notes.

A notebook which Paul Janszen took from Pete Rose's house, and which was in the custody of Paul Janszen for more than a year before it became a part of the case.

Without Paul Janszen there is no case against Rose—and therefore fair play demands that we be very certain that there is something more going on here than Paul Janszen trying to get even with Pete Rose.

What all of the 1989 scandals in baseball are about is baseball players exploiting their celebrity status *to take advantage of the people who admire them.* Wade Boggs, based on Margo Adams' respect and admiration for him, her love for him, exploited her for sex and companionship. When she was finally able to accept that she was being taken advantage of, she set out to use the courts and the media to get even with Wade Boggs, bringing him pain and financial loss commensurate with her own suffering. This is also what happened with Steve Garvey—he used his celebrity status to exploit several women for sexual favors.

Just a few years ago, Pete Rose extended his career several years beyond its natural limits to pile up more hits than Ty Cobb had gathered. This was done in blatant defiance of one of baseball's most fundamental precepts: that in the effort to win, you put personal goals and statistics aside, and play the best players. Rose continued to play for several years although he was by far the worst first baseman in the league.

It was a selfish thing to do, but at the time we weren't supposed to notice. Rose took advantage of his position as a superstar *within* the sports world in exactly the same way that Boggs and Garvey preyed upon those from the outside who thought they were special. But if you wrote anything about it at the time, the reaction was who are *you* to criticize Pete Rose? Once again, we learn that we do no favor to the man himself or the world at large when we grant a man immunity from the rules the rest of us live by.

For money rather than sex, this may also be exactly what happened with Rose and Janszen; Rose tried to take advantage of Janszen, dumping him with a $44,000 debt, and Janszen decided to use the courts and the media to get even. If that's what happened I have no sympathy for Rose—but I'm not absolutely convinced that that's what happened.

The most critical point in the argument is whether Janszen, or Gioiosa, or both, were using Rose's name to cover their own bets. Rose, because it was known that he earned hundreds of thousands of dollars a year, had extensive credit with the bookies; Janszen and Gioiosa did not. A bookie would not have accepted $10,000 worth of bets on a given day from Janszen—but might have accepted the bets if Janszen said they were for Rose.

The practice of betting under somebody else's name to get credit is not uncommon; it's a persistent problem for bookies, what they call "ghost bets." Gamblers, frequently living on their last dollar and often perpetually convinced that they're luck is going to turn, will often suck up to somebody who has money, like Rose, and then to try to use his name to extend their own credit.

Dowd's argument—and this is the point on which I most seriously disagree with him—is that Janszen could not have been making the bets on his own, because he did not have the financial means to place large bets. This point is so essential to his argument that he tries repeatedly to sell it—on page 12, on pages 54–55, again on page 57, and again on page 62, and again on pages 65–67, and again on page 77, and again on pages 211 and 212. I may have missed a few.

Despite the repeated sales pitch, I simply don't buy it. Four points:

(1) Dowd can't possibly know enough about Janszen's and Gioiosa's finances to know what they were and were not capable of betting. Both of these guys, according to Dowd's report, were supporting themselves with the sales of drugs. Gioiosa was allegedly selling cocaine; Janszen was dealing in steroids. They were cash businesses—no big bank accounts, no IRS records. Despite his claims, Dowd has no way of knowing what their financial position was at any point in time.

(2) Since when are gamblers reasonable men? So Janszen couldn't afford to lose $10,000 on a weekend—does that mean he's not going to *bet* $10,000 on a weekend? Dowd thinks it does.

(3) During the early part of "the breach," the critical time frame when there is well-documented gambling activity on baseball by either Janszen or Rose, the bets were *winning*. According to Ron Peters, the Rose Bets were $27,000 *ahead* in May, 1987, and $40,000 ahead in June, 1987.

So even assuming that Janszen doesn't have a dime at the beginning of this period, why does his financial position prevent him from chasing a winning streak?

(4) The claim that Janszen is not financially capable of

placing these bets is contradicted several times by evidence that Dowd presents in other contexts. One informant, Michael Fry, insists that Janszen wasn't capable of betting $2,000 a game on major league baseball at the exact time when Dowd insists Janszen *was* betting $500 a game. How can Fry—or Dowd—know that Janszen *is* capable of betting $500 a pop on a string of baseball games, but *isn't* capable of betting $2,000 a game? I mean, if you could establish that Janszen was living hand-to-mouth, that's one thing—but to show that he isn't capable of betting $2,000 a game when your own evidence shows that he *is* betting $500 a game . . . well, that's drawing a fine line. And the financial records to show that that line is correctly drawn, despite what Dowd says, simply do not exist.

Pages 65–67 deal almost entirely with this issue. Dowd introduces a conversation by saying that Steve Chevashore, a contact to the New York gambling world, "acknowledged that Janszen could not have been betting on his own, for several reasons." What follows, however, gives only one reason—the same one Dowd gives, that Janszen didn't have the money to be making these kind of bets.

Although Dowd cites the comments of Steve Chevashore as proof that Janszen couldn't have been placing the bets for himself, Chevashore clearly doesn't know this. Although he *believes* that Janszen is telling the truth, this belief is tempered with doubt. Chevashore recognizes the other option in a taped phone conversation with Janszen, saying (page 66) "if you were the culprit and wrong, he is supposed to take care of it because we did everything under his merit . . . if you were doing something wrong, which *you're telling me* you didn't." (Emphasis mine.) Even Chevashore's statement that he thinks the disputed bets were Rose's is highly qualified. "Paulie," he says, "I don't know you, but to me I don't think [it was] you."

On page 57 of the report, Dowd writes that, "One incident which occurred during this period illustrates that Janszen indeed did not have the financial capability to place large bets for himself."

You know what happened in the incident described, which proves that Janszen didn't have the financial capability to bet $2,000 a game? Janszen bet $3,000 on the Reds in a game, and then when the Reds got behind 6–0 early tried to claim it was a mistake, that he had only intended to bet *fifteen hundred* dollars. I'm not joking—that's what happened. Janszen bet $3,000

> **The strongest evidence that these may have been Janszen's bets, rather than Rose's, is Janszen's own testimony.**

on a game, tried to claim that he'd only intended to bet $1,500—and Dowd uses this as evidence that Janszen didn't have the financial capability of placing large bets!

Another interesting thing about that exchange, which occupies 57–59 in the Dowd report, is that although Janszen now claims that this money was all his, Chevashore had been given a different impression at the time. According to the tape, Danita Marcum "said you and Pete wanted to bet three dimes on Cincinnati." Get it? The money was all Janszen's—but Marcum told the bookie when she made the call that it was for Janszen *and* Rose—evidence that Janszen *was* using Rose's name to cover his bets, at least some of the time.

Janszen, of course, has another interpretation for it; he explains that Pete had called with his picks and he (Janszen) had wanted to add his own bets to it (just $1,500) and Danita was calling in all of the bets and she got confused and she called in three thousand for Janszen as well as Rose. Dowd, of course, accepts Janszen's explanation.

When the New York betting was terminated and payment did not follow, someone called *Paul Janszen's* mother and threatened *Paul Janszen's* life—clear evidence that *the gamblers* may have concluded that Janszen was using Rose's name to lay off his own bets.

The strongest evidence that these may have been Janszen's bets, rather than Rose's, however, is Janszen's own testimony. *Although Dowd argues repeatedly that Janszen could not have afforded to place large bets on baseball games, he also reports that Paul Janszen paid $44,000 of his own money to cover these bets.* Forty-four thousand dollars. $44,000. Dowd argues that Janszen couldn't have afforded to place large bets on his own—but could manage to scrounge up $44,000 to cover Rose's bets!

One is tempted to say that anybody who is stupid enough to pay all the money he has on earth to cover a celebrity friend's gambling debts deserves whatever happens to him. It's tempting, but it's not right. People who are taken advantage of are entitled to the protection of society, regardless of whether they acted foolishly. If Rose really did allow Janszen to get stuck with $44,000 of Rose's gambling debts, then he deserves something worse than being banned from baseball.

What concerns me, though, is that Dowd completely ignores the evidence and the common sense which would suggest that Rose may be telling the truth, and chooses instead to interpret everything to Rose's disadvantage.

When Michael Fry, a part of the Gold's Gym ownership group, testifies that he was very familiar with Pete Rose's gambling, doesn't believe that Rose bet on baseball games, but does know that Paul Janszen bet on baseball games and would pump Rose for information about them, Dowd simply ignores this

(pages 11–12). Instead, he picks up on the side issue of whether or not Janszen had the money to bet two thousand a game on baseball—as if Fry was fully aware of the details of Paul Janszen's financial prospectus—and tries to use Fry's testimony to prove that Rose *did* bet on baseball.

When Rose was confronted with the accusations of Janszen, he named for Dowd some other people who could give information about Janszen's veracity. But Dowd, rather than attempting to use the people Rose named to evaluate the veracity of Janszen's testimony, simply asked them if they had any knowledge of Pete Rose's betting activity. When they said they didn't know anything about Rose's betting, Dowd just wrote them off.

On page 89 of the Dowd report, it is reported that Janszen volunteered to "protect" Pete Rose with federal authorities. Despite the obvious implications of this, Dowd says on page 225—almost the last paragraph of the report—that "the claim of blackmail arose after Rose was exposed to the evidence during his deposition on April 20 and 21, 1989." Obviously, this is not true, and obviously Dowd is being deliberately obtuse here.

While the transactions of a certain period of time are extensively "documented" (if you consider phone calls to the sports line to be documentation), the Dowd report is also full of allusions to baseball betting in other periods which is alleged by Janszen and/or Peters, but completely unsubstantiated.

Paul Janszen took a polygraph examination, and was asked whether he had placed bets on the Cincinnati Reds and baseball for Pete Rose. *He failed the examination;* the examiner concluded that he was lying. Undeterred, Dowd reported that he had subsequently learned that there was a disagreement between Janszen and the interviewer which had upset poor Paulie, and so Dowd arranged for a Janszen to be retested. Janszen passed the second examination, which is an excellent illustration of why lie detector results are not allowed in court; I'll guarantee you if Pete Rose could let *his* examiner test Janszen on the same issues, Janszen would get a failing grade.

One of the most key pieces of evidence against Rose is a $34,000 check, written to Tommy Gioiosa on March 12, 1987. Ron Peters' story is that Rose got $34,000 behind him, Peters stopped accepting Rose's bets, Rose showed him a copy of a $34,000 check to Gioiosa which was supposed to have gone to pay him off but didn't reach him, Peters accepted that Rose had made a good-faith effort to pay his debt, and Peters began accepting Rose's bets again.

Dowd buys that one—but it smells like dead fish to me. A gambler who wants $34,000 wants $34,000, not a photocopy of a $34,000 check that was supposed to be cashed and given to him but wasn't.

This check is important because it is one of very few pieces of physical evidence in the case, and thus one of the few things that can be tied directly to Pete Rose's hands. Rose's explanation was that the check had nothing to do with Ron Peters, but was written to cover gambling losses on the 1987 Super Bowl and the 1987 NCAA Basketball Championship. "But," adds Dowd sagely, "the NCAA Basketball Tournament had not begun before March 12, 1987."

Now, let's look a minute at who we should believe here. The key thing to me is the date of the check—March 12, 1987. The Reds are in the second week of spring training games. So far as I know, *nobody* bets on those games. There isn't enough interest in early spring training games to sustain any widespread betting, so somebody betting a significant amount of money on them would attract attention almost immediately.

The NCAA tournament, on the other hand, is gambler's nirvana, one of the three big betting events of the year—dozens of games one right after another, all of them on television. There are thirty-two first-round games; a gambler can put down 2,000 on each of about twenty games and figure that at worst he's probably going to come out down maybe 8,000 to 12,000.

Dowd is correct in saying that the NCAA Basketball Tournament had not begun *before* March 12, 1987. It began *on* March 12, 1987. That's right: *The check was written on the very day that the NCAA Tournament started.*

Does Dowd *really* expect us to believe that a check written early in spring training, and written on the very day that the NCAA Basketball Tournament began, had nothing to do with college basketball, but can be used to tie Pete Rose to betting on baseball?

Yes, he does; he believes that, and he expects us to believe it—but look:

(a) the check was written on the day the NCAA basketball tourney started,

(b) the check was written in the second week of spring training games,

(c) Pete Rose says it has to do with the NCAA Basketball Tournament,

(d) Paul Janszen says it was written so Rose could start betting on baseball again.

Who you gonna believe?

Dowd believes Janszen.

Shouldn't that tell you something?

It's obvious what happened here, isn't it? Rose wanted to place some bets on the NCAA tournament, and he called his bookie, or Gioiosa called on his behalf, and the bookie said

"Hey, your credit ain't too good, you know?" The conversation took an ugly turn; the bookie began making threats. So Rose had a check drawn to bring him up to even or close to even, so he could bet on the NCAA tournament.

Then Dowd asked Janszen if he remembered the check, and Jansen said yes (he very probably *did* remember it, since he may well have made a photocopy of it before it was cashed), and thus gave Janszen the opportunity to interpret the check however he wanted to. Janszen, of course, came up with an interpretation which supported his story.

Dowd's contortions reach comic proportions on page 223 of the report, when he assures us that Peters and Janszen had been "voluntary and forthright. Each has stood before the bar of justice and engaged in the most painful act of integrity—the admission of guilt to illegal acts. . . . None of them has anything to gain for his voluntary act of cooperation."

Wonderful, huh? If you have *any* doubt that Dowd has abandoned the impartial role and is acting as a prosecutor, read that. Pleading guilty to a felony has become "standing before the bar of justice and engaging in the most painful act of integrity."

Dowd is trying to use the fact that these assholes have pled guilty to various felony charges to *bolster* their credibility. Give us a break, huh? Janszen is a jailbird with a grudge. Even if we're willing to assume that Pete Rose ranks even lower on an integrity scale, that's not exactly testimony from Tip O'Neill.

Regarding Rose's betting in 1985 and 1986, Ron Peters says that, while Gioiosa almost always placed the bets, Rose himself placed the bets on a few occasions. He says that on one of these times, he tape-recorded the conversation, and then played it back to Rose as an insurance policy, to make sure that Rose would cover his losses.

The tape recording, guess what, can't be found; Peters left it with his wife and they got divorced and she can't find it. To me, this incident again has a strong smell of bullshit about it. Peters vividly recalls Rose calling him from the ball park five minutes before a game—but the investigation's exhaustive study of phone records, which details the exact minute of hundreds of calls to the sports line, conspicuously fails to document this event. This is the kind of thing that makes *me* wonder to what extent Peters can be trusted—but Dowd has no doubt; Peters is telling the truth, he's sure.

Apart from the bias of the report against Rose, there are a number of puzzling oversights or contradictions in the report, bearing upon its credibility.

Pages 63–64:

A phone conversation between Janszen and Chevashore makes reference to a $7,500 check given by Rose to a gambler that was no good. Dowd doesn't find the check. Is he deterred by this? No—he finds *two* checks that total up to $7,500, written to Tampa Bay Downs on different days three days apart. Did the checks bounce? No, the bank payed them, but they were marked "NSF" (non-sufficient funds), and Rose was charged $10 per check for the overdraft.

Dowd interprets these checks are supporting evidence—but obviously, the checks in question were *not* the one discussed. The gambler had referred to "a check for $7,500" several times, not "checks." Nobody is going to confuse two checks, cashed three days apart, with one check. But more important than that, what difference would it make to the payee whether the checks were marked non-sufficient funds? As long as they got their money, and they did, they're not going to know or care whether it causes Rose to be overdrawn. Again, the fact that Dowd believes that these checks were the $7,500 referred to shows how far he is willing to reach in his zeal to convict Rose.

Pages 83–85:

Dowd alleges that "Rose's betting on baseball was also witnessed by . . . Dave Bernstein." Bernstein is the source of the story about Janszen using hand signals to keep Rose in the dugout informed of how they were doing during games. He was a friend of Paul Janszen's, but never actually met Pete Rose.

Bernstein spent his Friday evenings with Paul Janszen, meeting him at Janszen's apartment. He testifies that "Every Friday night, without fail, Pete [Rose] would call and Paul would take down whatever he wanted to bet that night and then call Ron Peters with the bets." Bernstein answered the phone when Pete called, he testified, on several occasions.

Sounds impressive, right? Except for the time frame. The betting with Ron Peters began on May 17, 1987. Bernstein, according to page 83 of Dowd's report, moved to Chicago in *late May*, 1987; the date is unspecified, so let's assume it is May 31, 1987. In between those dates are exactly two Friday nights—May 22 and May 29.

John Dowd fails to notice.

In trying to reconstruct the scenario of events from Dowd's confusing back-and-forth wandering, one finds a huge gap on the time line. Although the first half of the 1987 calendar year is detailed day by day and almost minute by minute, the second half of the year virtually doesn't exist. There is *no* explanation of why and how Janszen and Rose split up, apart from one reference to Danita Marcum being kicked out of Rose's house.

Although Dowd states early in his report that "the product of gambling . . . is debt—enormous debt which leads to" corruption, he never establishes, never really makes any stab at establishing, that Rose's financial position had in fact become precarious. Rose claims that he is *not* seriously in debt, that his financial position remains strong. Dowd offers no evidence to contradict this.

Dowd was able to come up with three independent records of Rose's betting—the two pages in Rose's handwriting, Janszen's records and Peters' records. This is an impressive performance. Professional gamblers are so programmed to destroy paper records that federal investigators looking into gambling—armed with subpoena powers, sometimes able to search people's houses and places of business, frequently able to coerce testimony with the threat of a jail sentence—are often unable to come up with any paper documentation to support an indictment. Dowd, without subpoena power, without a search warrant, without the threat of jail, was able to get Rose's gambling records from three sources.

This is impressive—if the records are genuine. It also suggests the possibility of an orchestrated effort to burn Pete Rose.

Q. Who would orchestrate an effort to burn Pete Rose?
   Somebody who got burned on a big debt.
Q. Who would have the ability to do that?
   The Mafia.
Q. How would they do it?
   They'd talk to a few people—maybe five, six people, get them to say that they had seen Rose bet on baseball.

Just a theory, one way things could have happened among fifty that you can see.

If that is what happened, Rose might have, in a sense, no recourse to the law. What is that legal doctrine . . . is that what they mean by "clean hands"? For good reasons, the courts are unwilling to sort out disagreements among thieves. And certainly in one sense, that is what happened here: Rose could not go to court—could not face a hearing on the issue—because his hands were not clean.

Look, there are a lot of things here that nobody wants to say. Nobody wants to say that Pete Rose's blast at Giamatti on Tuesday, August 26, may have induced the heart attack that killed Giamatti. Because Giamatti is dead and glorified, nobody wants to say that in his last days Giamatti may have deliberately misled Rose's representatives. Nobody wants to say that Rose was cheating on his taxes.

I probably shouldn't, but I'm going to tell you exactly what I think happened, and if it hurts somebody's feelings that's tough tamales.

I think that Peter Ueberroth, hearing rumors that Rose was involved with gamblers, didn't want to believe them, and appointed John Dowd to check into them with the full expectation that Dowd would issue a report clearing Rose's name.

I think that John Dowd, early on in the investigation, was surprised by the strength of the evidence.

I think that Pete Rose, not realizing the seriousness of *these* allegations, lied to Dowd about several side issues.

I think that Rose then lost all credibility with Dowd, that Dowd became convinced that the allegations against Rose were true.

I think that Dowd then completely lost track of his assignment, that he ceased to be an impartial investigator of the charges against Rose and became instead Rose's prosecutor.

I think that Bart Giamatti, coming into an awful situation already in progress, became so immersed in the controversy that he was unable to get a clear conceptual handle on it, and wound up putting more faith in Dowd's report than was justified or appropriate.

I think that Pete Rose and his representatives, sensing correctly that Giamatti had more or less made up his mind, at first tried to arrange for an unbiased hearing of the charges against him.

I think that Rose and his representatives then realized that an unbiased hearing of the issues involved, even though it might clear Rose of betting on baseball, would reveal enough of the seamy underside of Rose's life to get him banned from baseball for other reasons.

I think that it took Rose and his representatives some time to come to grips with this reality, and that in the meantime, not knowing what to do, they simply tried to forestall a resolution of the issue, trying to find some way in which Pete Rose's legal rights would protect him from justice.

I think that this secondary battle—Giamatti trying to *end* the situation and Rose trying to *avoid* the end—made the situation thoroughly miserable for all parties involved on both ends of the phone line.

I think that Rose then realized that he could not actually win the primary battle—that even if he were to prove that he never bet a dime on baseball, that he still would have to be suspended for a period of time for some very real and undeniable offenses such as associating with known gamblers and a variety of other creeps and losers.

I think that Rose was also cheating on his taxes.

I think that Rose or his attorneys further realized that if Rose pursued justice with regard to the limited point of whether

or not he had bet on baseball, he would have to give testimony which might possibly hurt his position with regard to the tax court.

I think that Rose then saw a situation in which he could not possibly clear his name and remain in baseball, and I believe that he then accepted the inevitability of a suspension.

I think that Rose and his attorneys then tried to negotiate a surrender at the minimum cost. I think that they believed that as long as there was no official finding that Rose had bet on baseball, then there remained the possibility that the penalty extracted could be as little as one year's suspension.

I think that they had good reason to believe that, that that was a reasonable thing for them to believe under the circumstances.

I think that Giamatti deliberately and knowingly allowed them to believe that.

> **Was it proper for Giamatti to sign an agreement that there was no finding that Rose had bet on baseball, and then announce that *in his opinion* Rose *had* bet on baseball? Of course it was not.**

I think that when Rose accused Giamatti of stabbing him in the back, he was giving an honest and intelligent response to the situation as he had been allowed to see it.

I think that Giamatti carefully mouthed the same words to Pete Rose on Tuesday when the agreement was signed that he did to the public on Wednesday when it was announced—but made them come out different.

I think that Giamatti knew that.

I think that when Rose accused Giamatti of dishonesty, it induced enormous stress in Giamatti.

I think that Giamatti knew, on some level, that in his desperation to put this nightmarish situation behind him, he had allowed Rose's representatives to believe that there was a chance of the minimum punishment, when in fact there wasn't.

I think that Giamatti's internal knowledge that he had dealt less than candidly with Rose further increased the stress that he was feeling.

I think that that stress triggered Giamatti's heart attack, and that that heart attack killed him.

Am I looking into people's hearts, pretending to know what they were thinking? Sure.

Could I be wrong?

On some points, I'm sure I am.

I don't see any other way of making sense of this situation. Giamatti is dead, and Rose is unable for obvious reasons to tell the whole truth. You *can't* read this situation in the lines, so you *have* to read it between the lines.

Was it proper conduct for Bart Giamatti to sign an agreement saying that there was no official finding that Pete Rose had bet on baseball, and then immediately announce that *in his opinion* Pete Rose *had* bet on baseball? Of course it was not.

The irony of the resolution of the Pete Rose case is that within forty-eight hours people went from saying that Rose was dragging the case out beyond any purpose to saying that Rose must be guilty or he wouldn't have given up so easily. *So Easily!!*—people actually said that, wrote that, after six and a half months of sheer undivided hell, Pete Rose gave up *so easily* that he is obviously guilty.

The sainthood of Giamatti, in time, may be Rose's biggest obstacle in trying to get back into baseball.

What am I really saying, if I am not saying that Pete Rose is innocent? I am saying that Pete Rose signed an agreement under which he left baseball *with no finding that he had bet on baseball games,* and *he is legally and morally entitled to be dealt with on that basis.* If the commissioner wanted it to be a part of the record that Pete Rose did bet on baseball and did bet on his own team, then he had a reasonability to go through a process, respecting Pete Rose's rights, to establish that. He elected to take a shortcut; he elected to have Rose sign an agreement.

Like it or not, it is baseball's obligation to live up to that agreement.

I am saying that the presumption of innocence is not a legality, not a theory, not an abstraction; it is a very real thing, a right. I am saying that you and I, in our own time, will depend upon that right.

I am saying that for that reason, it is important to realize that the presumption of innocence does not reside in the law, but is a part of the agreement that you and I make among ourselves as participants in a free society.

Like it or not, it is baseball's obligation to recognize that the issue of whether or not Pete Rose bet on baseball *has not been resolved,* and to treat Pete Rose accordingly.

THE WAR BETWEEN THE LEAGUES

The new decade was greeted with old hostilities. The origins of the Players' League reach back many years before 1890. Since before the founding of the National League, the players and owners had fought about the rules by which salaries would be agreed upon and player movements approved. In 1885 the players formed a "Brotherhood"—a union—to represent their interests. After years of complaining of unjust treatment and a solid year of muttering about a strike, the players in November, 1889, announced an alternative measure: the founding of a new league, a "Players'" League.

The National League through the 1880's had competed for the public's respect and affection with the American Association. Although the American Association did well in the annual exhibition matches between the league's champions, the National League was the dominant league—older, more entrenched, better financed, and with more of the best players. By 1889 the National League controlled most of the biggest cities, although this had not always been true. The Brotherhood, formed of National League players, was never extended to include the American Association, in large part because the American Association owners and players, battling first to survive and then to reach even ground with the National League, tended to see themselves as being on the same side of the fence as their owners—against the National League.

The fence had several sides. In 1889 there were sixteen teams which are now recognized as having been major league teams—the eight in the National League, and eight in the American Association. It was at that time the most successful season in the league's history, "and the money fairly poured in," wrote Cap Anson in *A Ball Player's Career*. As a general rule the National League controlled the big cities of the East, and the American Association the growing metropolitan areas of the Midwest. The two leagues went head-to-head in only one city, Philadelphia; otherwise the National League had teams in Boston, Chicago, Cleveland, Indianapolis, New York, Pittsburgh, and Washington, and the American Association had teams in Baltimore, Brooklyn, Cincinnati, Columbus, Kansas City, Louisville, and St. Louis. In addition to these two leagues, there were many other leagues which were of somewhat comparable strength—the International Association, the Atlantic Association, the Western Association.

Historians, searching for things which can be readily identified among a confusing welter of wandering facts, have tended to represent the two sides of the dispute in two men: Albert Spalding and John Montgomery Ward. Albert Spalding, a pitcher, won forty-six games for the Chicago team in the National League in 1876, the first year of the league. Using his position as a star player to make himself a central figure in the player-management disputes of his own time, Spalding had helped to found the National League, and in consequence of that had gotten the contract to provide the league with baseballs and other supplies. Using this as a foundation, he had expanded his sporting goods business, and using that as a foundation, expanded into other businesses; by 1890 he was forty years old and a millionaire.

John M. Ward, ten years younger than Spalding, had started out along a similar path. At the age of nineteen Ward, then a pitcher, won forty-seven games for Providence in the National League. Ward, like Spalding, was a bright, ambitious man, the type which thrived in the rough-and-tumble era of range wars and hero outlaws in the Wild West, and robber barons in the civilized East. Listed in the encyclopedias now as "Monte" Ward, but more often referred to in 1890 as "John M. Ward," Ward had arm trouble after his big season in 1879, but remained in baseball, switching to the outfield and then to shortstop. He became one of the outstanding defensive infielders and one of the best base runners of the nineteenth century. He also became a lawyer, a graduate of Columbia Law School, and an outspoken advocate of players' rights in their never-ending battles with management.

Spalding became the largest figure in National League politics in his time, representing the conservative forces in baseball, the rich Republicans, the Walter O'Malley and Bowie Kuhn of the nineteenth century. Ward became the central figure in the players' movement, representing the liberal forces, the rich Democrats, the Marvin Miller of his time. Ward gave frequent and sometimes eloquent speeches about the players being treated as property, and issued written statements with astonishing regularity. Spalding spoke about the greater long-term good of the game, and generally preferred to work behind the scenes, studying the political dynamics and calculating how to make them rebound to his advantage.

The founding of the Players' League was the opening shot in baseball's civil war. The first result was a scramble for positions in the various leagues. In the second week of November, 1889—a week after the formation of the Players' League—the two existing leagues had their annual meetings in New York City, meeting at separate hotels a few blocks apart.

On November 13 the American Association, torn by an internal rift, held an all-day debate with continued ballots to try to select a new league president. Deadlocked, they were unable to reach agreement. On the way to the American Association meeting, the representatives of four teams had stopped off in Philadelphia for a "little caucus" with the Philadelphia Athletics. The other three members of the association were not informed of the little caucus. When Charles Byrne, representing the Brooklyn team, and Aaron Stern, owner of the Cincinnati team, found out about the "little caucus" in Philadelphia, they left the meeting and adjourned to their hotel rooms, where they decided to jump leagues. Walking down to the National League meeting in progress a few blocks away, they applied to join the National League.

The National League owners, with severe financial pressures on some of their weakest clubs and at the same time wondering where they were going to get the players to retain credibility in the face of the Players' League threat, accepted the application within a few hours. At six P.M. on November 13, 1889, as the American Association owners were still debating their next president, the National League announced that it had added the Cincinnati and Brooklyn franchises, making the league, at least for the time being, a ten-club circuit.

The Kansas City team in the American Association, which had been a part of a clique with Brooklyn and Cincinnati, dropped out of the American Association to join the Western Association. The Baltimore team tendered its resignation, and announced its intention to play the 1890 season in the Atlantic Association. It appeared that the American Association might collapse, that it might have played its last game.

Somehow, the association regained its footing. Syracuse, a strong team from the International Association, applied for admittance to the American; they were accepted quickly, and followed by teams from Toledo and Rochester, also from the International. The Baltimore team sought to rejoin the American Association, but the AA, feeling cocky, turned them down and filled out to eight teams by issuing a new franchise to Brooklyn.

All this happened, of course, over a period of months. There was a wild winter of speculation about who would have a team and who would not. Although the American Association went through a chaotic winter, by comparison its battle was straightforward, since after the defection of Cincinnati and Brooklyn none of the decisions of the American Association hinged upon what was to be done by the other two leagues. The Players' League and the National League, however, spent the winter in a left-footed dance, naming cities and denouncing them, waiting until the last possible moment. As of mid-March, 1890, the National League still had not worked out what to do about the teams added in November, which had given the league ten teams. The league announced a ten-team schedule, but did so with massive misgivings; all prominent league author-

ities commented on the inconvenience and expense that a ten-team schedule would create.

What the league wanted, quite simply, was for its two weakest franchises to crawl into a corner and die. The two weakest franchises were in Washington and Indianapolis. The Washington team was just trying to be agreeable; if the league wanted them to go away, they made it known they would be happy to go away. They weren't making any money anyway. John T. Brush, however, was the owner of the Indianapolis team, and he was having none of it. He insisted throughout the winter and into the spring that Indianapolis had a National League franchise and By God was going to field a team. Brush insisted that he had already sold $12,000 worth of season's tickets, and simply couldn't afford to just leave the league. Eventually he reached an agreement: Indianapolis, for $60,000, would not field a team in 1890, but would retain its franchise in the National League. It was an amazing bargain for Brush: Facing a year of almost certain heavy losses on a team which he had purchased just a few years earlier for $18,000, he had agreed to take $60,000 not to compete for one season.

The National League, just weeks before opening day, finally knew who would and would not be in the league. The Players' League was having equal problems, in part because they wanted to compete with the National League, and so wanted to go wherever the National League wound up. In mid-March, Secretary Brunell of the Players' League was still fielding questions about potential cities for competition. "What do you think of Detroit's proposition to join the brotherhood?" asked a reporter.

"That was a mere bluff at the league," Brunell confessed. "We couldn't think for a moment of taking Detroit. Why, that man Stearns has been known for the last five years as the greatest living barterer in baseball flesh and blood, and we would be going right back on our principles if we were to think for a minute of having anything to do with him. Besides all this, Detroit is no ball town."

And having dispatched Detroit, Brunell fielded questions about St. Louis, Washington, and other possible cities for the league—with exhibition games already being played in Florida. It was a war, A. G. Spalding recalled later, in which the guns and ammo were "printer's ink and bluff."

Other than John Montgomery Ward, the prime mover and shaker in bringing the Players' League into existence was Albert L. Johnson, a Cleveland streetcar magnate. Johnson was the brother of the mayor of Cleveland, Tom L. Johnson; the two were business partners, with holdings in St. Louis as extensive as those in their home city, and lesser interests throughout the

Midwest. Some sources say that Johnson was a baseball "crank" who liked to play poker with some of the players, and got involved in baseball out of friendship and anger at the injustice being done to the players. Other historians have portrayed him as a businessman who saw the loaded streetcars carrying fans to games on his competitor's route, and who wanted to establish a team on his own route to get the same advantages. That explanation seems a little unlikely to me, but in any case, Johnson was the chief organizer of the businessmen involved in the Players' League, backing the Cleveland franchise himself and arranging financing for most of the other teams in the new league.

The plan of the Players' League was to compete head to head with the National League—in short, to supplant the National League in its own cities. The National League at the moment was in Boston, Chicago, Cleveland, New York, Philadelphia, and Pittsburgh, so the Players' League placed teams in Boston, Chicago, Cleveland, New York, Philadelphia, and Pittsburgh. The basic idea was that the players on the National League team in Boston would jump to the Players' League team in Boston, the players on Anson's Chicago team would jump to the Chicago team in the Players' League, etc. The Brooklyn team, managed by John M. Ward himself, acquired the rights to the players from the Indianapolis franchise (although it was able to sign but a few of them). On March 11, 1890, the members of the New York *Players'* League club were given a banner symbolizing the championship of the *National* League in 1889; the members of the New York National League club, of course, were also presented with a banner claiming the same title.

Because this was a Players' League, and because the arbitrary "selling" of players without their consent was one of the central issues in the dispute with the owners, obviously it would have been inappropriate to restrict the players to one team; if a player wanted to leave the Chicago team and sign with Boston, he could apply to the league's governing board, and if they approved he would transfer without compensation to the team losing him. The league's governing board included a president, two directors, and one player and one capitalist from each team.

The one National League city which had no direct competition was Cincinnati, that team being instead in Buffalo, behind which, too, there is a story. Deacon White, a longtime National League star, had been a leader in the Brotherhood movement, speaking out against players being sold without their consent. After the 1888 season White and Jack Rowe had been sold by Detroit to the Pittsburgh team (White by way of Boston), as part of a "fire sale" distribution of the Detroit players. White and Rowe, rather than reporting to Pittsburgh, purchased an inter-

est in the Buffalo team in the International League, and announced that they would play for Buffalo.

This was not permitted by baseball rules of the time, just as it would not be now; a man who is reserved by one team cannot decide to play for another, even if he owns the other. The White-Rowe situation threatened to spark a legal war over the reserve clause—but John M. Ward was already planning the Players' League, and didn't want the Brotherhood's attention divided by a costly lawsuit over the reserve clause and the possible chaos that would result from a solid legal victory. To bring Rowe and White into line with the Brotherhood, he promised them that if they would report to Pittsburgh in 1889, when the Players' League started in 1890 they could bring the Buffalo team into the Players' League.

Rowe and White worked the Pittsburgh team in the National League for a better deal, and then reported. "We are satisfied with the money," White announced with unusual honestly when a deal with Pittsburgh was finally reached, "but we ain't worth it. Rowe's arm is gone. I'm over forty and my fielding ain't so good, though I can still hit some. But I will say this. No man is going to sell my carcass unless I get half."

Apparently, Ward and the other powers in the Brotherhood rather regretted the offer to White to allow Buffalo to come into the league, but being honorable men there was nothing they could do about it. The Buffalo team was the odd man out of the Players' League. It was the only team which didn't compete head to head with a National League team. It was the only team which had a prior history in another league. It was also, as the summer would show and many suspected all along, by far the weakest team in the league, destined to lose almost three fourths of its games.

There were rumors that the St. Louis Browns, an American Association team run by Chris Von der Ahe, would jump to the Players' League. Von der Ahe attended the Players' League meeting in mid-December, but St. Louis never jumped, perhaps because there was no room for them, all eight spots being taken. It was written that the Brotherhood wanted Rowe and White to get out so that Von der Ahe (and Von der Ahe's money) could come in, but if that was what was hoped for it could not be arranged, and there are also reasons to think that the Brotherhood might not have truly desired Von der Ahe's eccentric input.

If the scramble for teams was wild, the scramble for players was beyond anyone's comprehension. The American Association players were not members of the Brotherhood, so when the Cincinnati and Brooklyn teams jumped into the National League, they retained their entire rosters. Those two teams, which had jumped leagues, were almost the only major league

MESSERS COMISKEY AND ANSON
IN THEIR FAVORITE DUO,
"UP WE GO, DOWN WE GO."

teams which retained essentially the same personnel. As players from the National League jumped to the Players' League (and sometimes jumped back), the National League purchased the contracts of players from existing leagues—including the American Association—to fill their rosters. The American Association had to fill in for the players lost. Von der Ahe tried to buy a good minor league team to cannibalize their roster, but his offer was rejected. Players who had played in the majors sometimes years before were brought back from exile to the minors. Players who signed contracts with the Brotherhood were served with writs and injunctions threatening legal consequences if they played, and while these maneuvers in the end came to no effect, during the process they considerably darkened the waters.

And yet, somehow, when the smoke cleared there was the appearance of perfect order—three leagues, each with eight teams, the perfect number for a league. Challenged with head to head competition, the National League had established a war committee—Albert Spalding, Giants owner John Day and John I. Rogers, a lawyer who owned the Philadelphia Phillies.

The Brotherhood, as a courtesy to the National League, sent the NL a copy of their schedule as soon as it was settled, so that "the National League can, should it so choose, avoid

conflicting with our clubs in the cities of Boston, New York, Brooklyn, Philadelphia, Pittsburgh, Cleveland, and Chicago. May I also suggest," Secretary Brunell appended to the announcement, "that the National League adopt a resolution permitting its clubs to play against those of the Players' National League, before and after the championship season of both leagues."

The war committee, however, decided to engage the threat directly. Making what was perhaps the most critical decision of the war, the National League decided to schedule its games to directly conflict with the Players' League games. If Brooklyn in the Players' League was playing at home at 3:30 on June 22, the National League would schedule *their* Brooklyn team to play a home game at the same time. Because the Brotherhood had also intended to directly challenge the National League, the parks in most cities were separated by only a few blocks, if that; in a couple of cities they were across the street from one another.

The war committee's logic was simple: This was a war to the finish, a battle to the death. In the era of unchecked monopolies, the National League was not interested in dividing the market. If they had scheduled to avoid the Players' League they might have envisioned both leagues being able to survive, but they didn't want that; they wanted one league to win, and the other to die. Head-to-head scheduling minimized the chances of both surviving.

With twenty-two shuffled rosters among the twenty-four teams and a couple of hundred new players scattered around, no one had any clear idea on opening day, 1890, about what teams were and were not strong, although of course opinions on the issue were not hard to find. Historians of the era usually say that the Players' League attracted most of the best players, and I suppose this is literally true. Sometimes historians say that Anson was almost the only major star to remain in the National League, and this is certainly *not* true; the National League retained many of the League's veteran, established stars—Anson, Sam Thompson, Jack Glasscock, Tommie Burns, Charlie Bennett, Jeremiah Denny, Billy Sunday—plus a number of young stars (Mike Tiernan, Bill Hutchison, Amos Rusie) and was able to add a few other players of star quality from the American Association. Harry Wright, a superstar manager and figure in the game almost to rival Spalding, spoke respectfully of the Brotherhood but declined to join their league; in return, his players respected him so much that many of them refused to jump, and Philadelphia retained many of its players.

In general, however, most of the best players went to the Brotherhood—the young stars, the solid players, and some of the veteran stars. It was upon this fact that the Brotherhood rested its hopes—the expectation that the public would flock to the Players' League parks first because they wanted to see the best players, and second because the working public would identify with the "working men" of baseball rather than with the money men. In fact, organized labor did actively support the Players' League. Organized labor was in its infancy, but various guilds and unions enlisted volunteer help to organize a boycott of the National League games. (The Brotherhood was invited to join the national labor organizations, the American Federation of Labor and the Knights of Labor, but elected not to get involved.) For the league opener at Pittsburgh the NL retained a band, but when it was discovered that the band was a Knights of Labor band, the union sent an extra band free of charge to play at the Brotherhood opener down the street.

That was an appropriate beginning for the Pittsburgh season. While the other teams retained at least some portion of their talent, the Pittsburgh team retained only one significant player (Doggie Miller) from their 1889 roster. The organization didn't have the money to bring in any suitable replacements, and so the Pittsburgh team in the National League in 1890 was proclaimed by Cap Anson the worst National League team he had seen, and he had seen them all. It was, quite possibly, the worst team the National League would ever have.

Let's start with the story of Fred Dunlap, if we're talking about Pittsburgh. Just two years earlier, Dunlap had been the highest-paid player in baseball, earning $7,500 as a fancy-fielding second baseman who was also a good hitter. He fell off to .235 in 1889, despite which he retained a star's attitude. Signing with Pittsburgh in the Players' League, he clashed with the young manager of the team, Ned Hanlon; apparently he felt that he should have been given the job as Pittsburgh manager. He was given his walking papers. The Philadelphia Players' team wanted to sign Dunlap, but he demanded to be paid $8,000—$3,000 more than anyone else on the team was getting (or at least had been promised). His abilities didn't warrant that kind of a salary and the attitude wasn't really in keeping with the spirit of the Brotherhood, and so he wound up back in the National League, back with Pittsburgh.

Pittsburgh's unfortunate manager was Guy Hecker, who had had a good career as a pitcher-first baseman in the American Association. He and Dunlap didn't get along, either. After hitting .172 through seventeen games, Dunlap was released again. Dunlap, furious, said that his sister could play better than Guy Hecker, and also accused Hecker of winning the players' money gambling and being drunk during a game.

Billy Sunday, perhaps Pittsburgh's best player, supported Hecker on all counts, except that he did allow that he had never seen Dunlap's sister play baseball, and so could give no opinion as to her ability.

On May 7 it was revealed that the Pittsburgh club owed $8,000 for "ground rent." By late May the franchise was reported $65,000 in debt, and asked permission to cancel the rest of its schedule. Their players had not been paid in two weeks. The league voted unanimously that Pittsburgh should have to finish the schedule, despite the debt, but it appeared certain that the franchise was destined either to collapse, or to sell out to the Players' League. That, of course, would have been disastrous for the National League, and so several league owners put up money to enable Pittsburgh to meet its obligations, sort of, and continue to play.

They played. The *Chicago Tribune* reported on June 8 that "Billy Sunday, the Pittsburg outfielder, addressed a Gospel meeting of the Y.M.C.A. at Cincinnati yesterday. Sunday has had an opportunity to display Christian resignation this season. Any man who is compelled to remain with a team like Pittsburg deserves a martyr's crown." (Incidental note: that spelling of "Pittsburg" was common until World War I.)

No one came to their games. In late July Pittsburgh cancelled the rest of their home games, converting them all to road games. The players simply gave up; they began to go through the motions. In August Pittsburgh played 28 games, and lost 27 of them. Altogether they lost 113 games (reported at season's end as 114). They were presented with a "Booby" pennant to commemorate the feat, a beautiful blue silk flag with 114 stars sewn onto it—one for each loss.

Lest the Giants fans should laugh, they had to remember that it could have been them. The New York Giants, the defending champions, lost all of their key players except Mike Tiernan and Mickey Welch. Then as now, a good deal was heard about the importance to the league of having a strong franchise in New York, and so the Giants were awarded the rights to the players from the suspended franchise in Indianapolis. This included several players of quality—Pebbly Jack Glasscock, Amos Rusie—but they were not given to the Giants; the league charged them for the players, part cash and part credit, to offset the league's costs in buying off the Indianapolis owner.

In late June, the New York owners notified the National League that they were broke, financially unable to continue. John Day, principal owner of Giants, claimed that baseball had taken him from being a wealthy man to being a pauper in the space of a year. The league had to come to the rescue of the Giants. Albert Spalding purchased about $25,000 worth of previously undistributed stock in the Giants, some of which he resold to Cap Anson. Arthur Soden owner of Boston, also invested in the team, and John T. Brush, owed $60,000 by the league for sitting out the season, accepted $25,000 of Giants stock in lieu of the money; eventually he would become majority stockholder of the team. Other owners around the league also kicked in some money, and became part owners of the New York team, which with the aid was able to stumble through the season.

Pittsburgh was the bottom of the barrel, but there were other teams almost as desperate. The American Association had converted three minor league teams, and those teams were all right, but for their fourth new entry had created a team in Brooklyn out of whole cloth. With no real sources of talent to draw upon, the Brooklyn team in the American Association lurched from loss to loss. They were called the Brooklyn Castaways—players let go by other teams. They had twenty-six wins by late August, when they left the league. Their place was taken by the repentent Baltimore team, returning to the American Association after spending most of the season in the Atlantic Association. The Baltimore team took over the won-lost record of the Castaways, for which reason the *Baseball Encyclopedia* and *Total Baseball* consider the Brooklyn and Baltimore teams to have been one team, Bkn-Bal. or BB. It was a completely different team; Baltimore acquired the rights to the Brooklyn players, but chose not to retain any of them. The Brooklyn players were never paid for their last two month's work.

The Cleveland team in the National League, which also retained only a couple of players from 1889, staggered to a total of forty-four wins.

With many of the good ballplayers from the remaining teams jumping ship, the Cincinnati and Brooklyn teams, which had been two of the strongest teams in the American Association in 1889, became two of the strongest teams in the National League in 1890—in fact, both posted very similar records in 1890 in the NL to their records in the American Association the year before.

The race for the National League pennant was conducted among five teams: Cincinnati, Brooklyn, Chicago, Boston, and Philadelphia. The Phillies were seen as a strong team, having retained several of their key players such as Sam Thompson, catcher Jack Clements, and pitcher Kid Gleason. To this the Phillies had added an exceptional young player from the American Association, Sliding Billy Hamilton, and a fine young shortstop in Bob Allen. Drawn together and guided by baseball's most revered manager, Harry Wright, the Philadelphia team seemed well positioned to win the weakened league.

The Phillies started well, and held first place through May. This is how they stood as of May 31:

Philadelphia	20	11	.645	...
Brooklyn	18	12	.600	1½
Cincinnati	18	12	.600	1½

Anson's Colts and the Boston team had struggled getting away from the gate, and Philadelphia was in charge of the race.

In late May, however, Harry Wright went blind. Curiously, none of the major historians of the game seems to have noticed this period of blindness. Harold Seymour, Lee Allen, Fred Lieb, and Preston Orem seem entirely unaware of it, as do all of the minor and derivative historians; the *Baseball Encyclopedia* shows Wright as managing the Phillies for the entire season, although he was gone from the team for long periods of time. Robert Smith and David Voigt refer vaguely to Wright's "failing vision." *Total Baseball* does show the period of Wright's absence, so somebody is aware of the problem although I haven't seen it written up anywhere.

I looked to all of these sources, of course, trying to find the cause of the blindness. It appears that the blindness was a part of a degenerative disease which would kill Wright in 1895, but what exactly the disease was I do not know; two reasonable guesses would be diabetes and syphillis. In any case, the Phillies in Wright's absence were managed by Jack Clements and Al Reach, not very successfully, before turning to the twenty-two-year-old rookie shortstop, Bob Allen. But by the end of June Cincinnati had taken over first place:

Cincinnati	37	18	.673	...
Brooklyn	34	21	.618	3
Philadelphia	34	22	.607	3½

The Cincinnati team, as mentioned, brought most of its players with it from the American Association. Among their best players were:

Bid McPhee, a quiet, distinguished second baseman who, in these chaotic years in which players seemed to change teams almost as often as Steve Garvey changes girlfriends, played eighteen years at second base for Cincinnati, scoring over a hundred runs ten times. I sometimes argue that McPhee should be in the Hall of Fame.

Bug Holliday, who had a sensational rookie year in the American Association in 1889, hitting .343 with a league-leading 19 home runs. Holliday was a natural comedian, in the tradition of Rick Dempsey, Bret Saberhagen, and Nick Altrock; he liked to amuse the fans at odd moments in the game.

Long John Reilly, a Cincinnati native who had played first base in Cincinnati for ten years by 1890. He had led the American Association in home runs twice, in RBI at least once, and in 1890, at the age of thirty-one, led the National League in triples with 26. He also finished second in total bases.

Tony Mullane, the famous switch-pitcher, was with the team as a utility player and part-time pitcher.

Their top pitcher was Billy Rhines. According to Lee Allen (The Cincinnati Reds), "Rhines was the original submariner, author of a style of pitching later made famous by Carl Mays. Most underhanders get that way as a result of an accident that precludes their pitching in the normal overhanded fashion. But with Rhines it was his natural style, and one that proved perplexing to the batters." Of course, just fifteen years earlier *everyone* had thrown underhanded, so I don't know what it means to say that Rhines was the original.

Cincinnati at this time was the nation's central pork market; reporters sometimes referred to Cincinnati as "Porkopolis," and a Cincinnati-Boston series as "Pork and Beans." With the pennant in sight, Porkopolis added Arlie Latham, a deserter from the Players' League, to their roster. Latham was a great ballplayer and the most famous ballplaying cutup of his time, but he was also a hard-drinking, hard-living wild man. Earlier in the 1890 season, Latham was locked out of his hotel room at the Lindell Hotel in St. Louis as the attorney for "his most recent ex-wife" attached all of his belongings to cover unpaid attorney's fees. Latham spent several hours wandering around the hotel in a sweaty baseball uniform until his then-manager, Charles Comiskey, was able to find some clothes for him. The team discipline, a problem early in the season, deteriorated in the second half.

Cincinnati's moment in the sun passed. Philadelphia went on a tear while being managed by young Bob Allen, and at the end of July the Phillies were back in first place:

Philadelphia	55	28	.663	...
Brooklyn	53	29	.646	1½
Boston	53	32	.624	2½
Cincinnati	49	33	.598	5½

It is important to remember also that road trips were much longer in 1890 than they are now; a team could spend a month on the road, not infrequently three weeks. Cincinnati surged in June, when they were home most of the month, and collapsed in July, when they went on the road.

In any case, Philadelphia was back in front, and Harry Wright, having recovered some of his vision, came back to manage the team. Sportswriters all but pronounced the race over, but the Phillies seemed to become tentative and lose direction under their true sovereign. By the end of August Brooklyn had taken control of the race:

Brooklyn	71	36	.664	...
Boston	69	37	.651	1½
Cincinnati	64	41	.610	6
Philadelphia	65	42	.607	6
Chicago	60	47	.561	11

The Boston team, under rookie manager Frank Selee, would become one of the two dominant teams of the decade, but in 1890 they were a collection of too young and leftover over-achievers, kept in the race by three key pitchers—Kid Nichols, John Clarkson, and Charlie Getzien. Clarkson had been one of the great pitchers of the 1880's and Nichols would be one of the great pitchers of the 1890's, but in the year of the war it was all they could do together to keep Boston in the race for four months.

Brooklyn would face one final challenge. Cap Anson had lost almost his entire team, retaining only himself, Tommie Burns, and pitcher Bill Hutchinson. Despite the losses, Anson was optimistic in the spring. In a letter to Albert Spalding from St. Augustine on February 26, 1890, Anson wrote:

> Dear Sir:
> Replying to yours of Feb. 20, as to my opinion of the new players we have under contract, would say that upon the whole I am very much pleased with them. I think we have been exceedingly fortunate in nearly all of our sellections. We have great men in Cooney, Nagle, Wilmot and Carroll. I am very much pleased with O'Brien and Andrews and feel sure that they are going to please their Chicago friends by the showing they will make this season. I believe we have an excellent pitcher in Coughlin and a great little catcher in Kittredge. . . . Just at present I do not think we want to sign any more players, and unless I am much mistaken our old players will be little missed.

It could always be suspected that the letter was written for the benefit of the newspapers, but Anson's judgment of his young talent proved sound. Walt Wilmot, purchased from Washington, would lead the National League in home runs that season with 14, and was among the leaders in stolen bases with 76. Malachi Kittredge, the rookie catcher of whom Anson spoke so well, would play in the major leagues for sixteen years.

Anson worked hard at teaching his youngsters the tricks of the trade. In an exhibition game in Houston, Anson found himself trailing by two runs with two out and the bases loaded. Recognizing the inexperience of the opposition and the umpire, Anson found something to argue about, and began bellowing in his famous bullhorn voice. He argued "so fierce and long that he held the attention of the Houston players until all three Chicago baserunners had slipped home, the umpire having neglected to call time." Anson was a brave man, a reporter opined; men had been lynched for less in Texas.

The Colts, struggling early in the season, began to pick up in June. They were a fun team to watch, a hustling outfit that took chances; sportswriters began calling them the "Cubs." The term "cub" at that time refered to anyone who was inexperienced but enthusiastic in his profession; the term survives today in isolated usages, such as "cub reporter." (On the other hand, the Chicago team in the Players' League picked up the old nickname "White Stockings", and referred to Anson's men as the "Black Stockings.") Anson became "Pop." Lingering near .500 through July, the Cubs were the best team in the League over the last two months, going 41–15 after August 1. They moved from sixth place to second—but the eleven-game deficit to Brooklyn was too much to be made up.

The Bridegrooms won the National League in 1890 with almost exactly the same team which had won the American Association in 1889. It is a curiously unimpressive team, for a two-time champion, the only team to win consecutive pennants in different leagues. Oyster Burns, an outfielder, led the league in RBI with 128, not that anybody was counting at the time. Germany Smith, the defensive anchor of the team at shortstop, hit .161. Apparently no one on the team is in the Hall of Fame, and there are only a few players who might be. They had the famous combination of Bob Caruthers and Dave Foutz, who had been so devastating a few years earlier in St. Louis, but by 1890 neither was more than a shell of his former self. (Caruthers and Foutz, as pitchers, are one-two on the all-time list in winning percentage, at .692 and .690. In 1885 Caruthers won 40 games, Foutz 33; in 1886 it was Foutz 41, Caruthers 30. When not pitching they played the outfield. In 1887 each player hit .357.)

While Brooklyn had been favored to win their league and eventually did, the weakened American Association came up with a shocker. In 1889 the Louisville Cardinals were the worst team in the major leagues, winning only 27 games while losing 111. Four of the teams ahead of them, of course, dropped out of the league and were replaced with teams from the minor leagues; that automatically catapulted Louisville into the first division.

On March 27, 1890, a devastating tornado hit Louisville, killing seventy-six people and doing immense damage to the city. The team, previously known as the Louisville Colonels, began to be called the Louisville Cyclones.

The city rallied around the team, something to turn to in the face of the catastrophe. The Cyclones went on a long road trip through May, returning home at the end of May three and a half games behind the Philadelphia Athletics, two behind Rochester. Their record on the road trip was just 11–12, but for a team which had won only 27 games the entire season before, this was considered a wonderful accomplishment, and the team was met at the train station with a brass band, given a parade through the streets.

At the end of June Louisville was in third place, seven and a half games behind the Philadelphia Athletics. They won twelve straight games in early July, capped by a four-game series sweep of the Athletics, and moved into first place on July 12; they had wiped out a seven-and-a-half-game deficit in less than two weeks. By the end of July Louisville was three games ahead

of St. Louis; the Athletics had fallen to six games behind. By the end of August Louisville was solidly in first place, eight games ahead and twelve up in the loss column. In the end Louisville, in last place in 1889 with a record of 27–111, had won the league with a record of 88–44, a sixty-four-game improvement in one year. Although the record is no doubt wind-aided, it remains the only time in history that a team has vaulted from first to last in a single season.

What happened to them? An outfielder who was seriously overweight in 1889, Chicken Wolf, went on a strenuous walking program, shed the weight and hit .363, winning the batting title. Pete Browning, a veteran star who had hurt the team in 1889, left and was replaced by an ordinary but contributing player. Pitcher Scott Stratton, who was 3–13 in 1889, went 34–14 in 1890. Another pitcher, Red Ehret, jumped from 10–29 to 25–14. A couple of rookies came through for them. There was an opening there for an underdog to arise, and the Louisville team rallied to the opportunity.

It was a wild year to be a baseball fan, and in this strange hybrid, half major league and half minor, most anything could happen and probably did:

- After a game in Syracuse the grandstand collapsed as the crowd rose to leave, carrying fifty people into a pile of lumber and nails. No one was seriously hurt.
- Members of the Philadelphia and Rochester teams were arrested before the game one Sunday, charged with violating the blue laws, and fined individually as well as a fine levied on the team.
- Several teams kept Negroes as mascots, mostly young boys or very small adults. During one game, the Columbus team tossed their mascot from player to player like a rubber ball so roughly that one reporter said that "people wondered if he could survive." After being beaten up in a fight with a groundkeeper the next day, the boy resigned as mascot. (And you thought silly creatures with Styrofoam feathers were offensive, huh?) Clarence Duval, the mascot of Anson's Chicago Cubs, jumped leagues and served as mascot for the Chicago Players. The 1891 *Spalding Guide* presented the following note:

The Folly of the Mascot Idea
The steady influx of a more intellectual class of players into the base-ball profession, and the gradual weeding out of bummers and thugs, have worked wonders to raise the moral and intellectual standard of the game. There was a time when the base-ball profession was as prolific of superstition as a dog is of fleas in the summer time, but that time has passed. Had not the mascot been introduced many of them would have remained, but after the latter's inglorious fall a new era begun in base-ball history, as it marked the beginning

of the elimination of foolish ideas. The mascot was the most absurd invention, if such he could be called, of modern times.

- At a Fourth of July doubleheader in St. Louis, the owners of the St. Louis and Brooklyn teams set up a fine meal for the players after the morning game, rather than following the usual practice of playing a morning game, going back to the hotel to eat, and returning to the park for the afternoon game. The meal included a keg of cold beer, however, and several of the players made more use of the beer than the food. The quality of the second game suffered considerably, and the game eventually ended in a forfeit (which itself was subsequently overruled by the league) when the Brooklyn players left the field.
- A pitcher named Toad Ramsey, once a good pitcher with Louisville, was reaching the end of his line with St. Louis. Ramsey during the season was married, jailed on a paternity charge, and invented a new drink, which he called Ramsey's Cocktail. The entire recipe was not known, since Ramsey insisted on acting as his own bartender, but it could be observed that a part of the process was pouring a pint of whiskey into a pitcher of beer. Ramsey considered it important that he drink three of these a day, making himself so valuable to his team that Von der Ahe offered to sell him to a sportswriter for five cents. Ramsey wound up the year playing right field for Dallas in the Texas League.
- A Sunday game was scheduled in Syracuse in August. The police warned the players and umpires that they would arrest all present if the game was begun, which was enough to convince the umpire and the Louisville team not to go out to the park. The Syracuse players went out to the park, however, and when Louisville failed to appear a substitute umpire—appointed from the crowd—declared a victory by forfeit for Syracuse. The association, incredibly, allowed the forfeit to stand, and fined the umpire for his refusal to go out and work the game.
- The Columbus team on one occasion put on a prearranged show of discontent. When a call went against them all eight men in the field dropped to their knees and stretched out their arms as if in prayer. The ump fined them five dollars apiece.

The season was rich in comedy and pathos, but only one team in the association, the thrilling Louisville Cyclones, made money. Brooklyn, one of five "major league" teams operating in the New York metropolitan area, drew crowds of only a few

hundred a game, and rarely won. As mentioned before, they left the league in late August.

In early September the Philadelphia Athletics ran out of money. Several players sued the club for the balance of their salaries. The owners released some of the players, and recommended that the others operate the team as a cooperative, splitting whatever money they could come up with. The team had lost some money during the season, but people were puzzled about why the stockholders had permitted an investment which had made money over the years to go to pieces over a relatively small amount of money. Several key players, released by Brooklyn, signed with Baltimore in mid-September; among them was Wilbert Robinson, in time one of the most famous of the old Orioles. The Athletics at season's end were losing every game, and by large margins. Louisville clinched the pennant on October 9, and finished with a ten-game margin.

We come then to the Players' League, which was of course the real story of the season. This is not a history of the players' rebellion; that story has been told many times, by better historians than myself. This is a story about the season, the season one hundred years ago.

Albert Johnson had lined up financial backing from hither and yon. Each team was supposed to have established a fund of $40,000 or more to get them through the season. Some of the owners had put up this sum on their own (and some didn't), but each player had the right to invest in the team for which he was playing, and the players who had earned good salaries in the past were strongly encouraged to do so, the money being needed. Reportedly players owned as much as 40 percent of some teams.

From this account, money was to be spent in a specified order:

1. All ongoing expenses were to be met.
2. Player salaries were to be paid.
3. Each team was to contribute to a "championship fund." In theory a pool of $20,000 was to be set aside as a "winner's share"; the championship team would get $6,250, the second-place team $4,800, the third-place team $3,500 . . . on down to $400 for the seventh-place team.
4. The first $10,000 of profits—monies beyond those allocated on points 1, 2, and 3—were to go to the teams' owners, distributed according to shares owned.
5. The next $10,000 was to go to a pool of "players money," to be shared equally by all players in the league.
6. Any additional money was to be split equally among the

clubs and the players, and again was to be pooled by the entire league.

As noted loudly by the league owners, the salary arrangement wasn't all that generous. The players got paid only after other expenses, which somewhat insulated the investors against heavy losses. John T. Brush said that he would have been happy to employ players on the same basis, but of course that wasn't what the argument was about; the players wanted increased control over their careers. Players held offices in the Players' League which were more generally reserved for businessman. Tim Keefe, a New York pitcher and member of a sporting goods company (Keefe and Becannon) was awarded a three-year contract to supply the league with baseballs. Buck Ewing was head of the Playing Rules Committee. Players were responsible for discipline among themselves.

The league brought forward many innovations, some of which were later adopted by other leagues. Each club had eight flags, one for each team in the league. On game day, the team would fly two flags—its own, and that of its opponent for the day.

The Players' League assigned two umpires to each game, the first time this had been done in professional baseball. The umpires were outfitted in pure white uniforms.

In the Players' League the pitcher was one-and-a-half feet further from the plate than in the National, to increase the batting; their ball may also have been livelier.

A new playing rule in the Players' League allowed a team to make two substitutions in a game, instead of one as was previously allowed, and allowed the substitutions to be made any time during the game, rather than only at the end of an inning, as before. (Sources on rules conflict, so I could be in error somewhere here.)

But as soon as the season opened, it became clear that this wonderful new thing, this baseball Utopia, would have a mighty struggle to survive. April attendance was a shock; nobody was coming to the games. The officials blamed the April weather, and looked for better in May.

It didn't happen.

Quite simply, the public was turned off.

The public was confused.

The public had been asked to take sides in a bloody battle between workers and management, and the public had refused. When two teams offered to represent the city in the struggle for on-field glory—and like it or not, that is what spectator sports are about—neither team seemed like a true representative.

Since everyone lied about their attendance, there are no accurate attendance figures. It is generally agreed, however, that (1) the Players' League drew a few more fans than the National League, and (2) the two leagues together drew fewer fans than the National League alone had drawn in 1889.

Attendance shriveled throughout the baseball world. Every minor league except the Western League reported losses. Attendance even in Cincinnati, the one National League city which had no competition, was down dramatically. Several teams drew fewer than a hundred fans for some games.

Attempting to create the impression that they were winning the battle, both teams padded their attendance figures. Spalding posted men outside the gates of the Players' League team in Chicago to count their attendance, and then published his own figures to embarrass his rivals. A newspaper sent reporters to check out the attendance at the two New York parks on August 15, and found both teams to be over-reporting by about 150 percent.

Teams in 1890 did have other sources of income, such as concession sales and scoresheet sales, but all of these were based on attendance in one way or another. The Players' League teams had a heavy capital investment to start the season, in that they had to build several parks. This wasn't equivalent to building modern stadiums, of course, but neither was it cheap. The competition for players had escalated players' salaries, at least taking them back to where they had been in 1888.

Since the arrangement in the Players' League was that the players got paid after running expenses, the lack of paying customers hurt the players in the Players' League worst; the National League owners at least guaranteed the salaries of their players. So the NL policy of deliberately scheduling conflicts, splitting whatever crowd there was, hurt the players in a very direct way. Asked if there was any chance of the schedule being altered to remove the conflicts, Players' League secretary Brunell replied "I hardly think it will do either of us much good. We are all losing money. If a man's expenses are one hundred dollars a day and he is making a dollar per day he is in a bad way. If he doubles his earning and makes two dollars a day it is an improvement, but it does not do him much good. That is the base-ball situation."

The National League had originally hoped to win the war at the box office. When it became apparent that that was not going to happen, Albert Spalding switched to a scorched-earth policy: Make the cost as high as possible. Make the cost to both of us so high that the other side will be unable to continue the war.

Spalding announced that interest in baseball was dying out. Several other owners—coincidentally, of course—issued similar statements. If the game was to die, they figured the Players' League would die first, and they were simply trying to hurry the process along. John M. Ward replied that "The game will live if both leagues die."

Both leagues, but particularly the NL, left passes at barber-shops, distributed free tickets to charities and held innumerable "special days." At the league grounds in Cleveland, ladies were to be admitted free to all games except Saturdays. The public, of course, will not pay for that which they can receive free, and Spalding was counting on that to speed up the process of decay.

By mid-summer, then, it was apparent that the Players' League gamble could not succeed in the form originally envisioned. The Players' League made overtures to the American Association to merge their assets, to turn the two into some sort of an amalgamation. The American Association received these overtures more or less as a woman might receive a marriage proposition from a man with AIDS. Monte Ward was reported so cranky that "He was jumping at umpires like they were hack drivers or waiters."

Newspapers suggested pooling the two teams in each city into one, but the National League of course wanted none of that. A few players who had jumped to the Players' League went back to the guaranteed money of the National League, although in deference to the players one should note that it was surprisingly few in view of the desperate situation. "Deserters" were denounced by both sides and both sides said that they would not be taken back, but they always were.

In such a season it would probably have been impossible for a pennant race to catch the public's imagination, but the Players' League was not blessed with an exciting pennant race. The Boston team under King Kelly took an early lead and held it to the wire. No one enjoyed the Players' League more than Kelly, who ran the Boston team with a free hand. Waking up one morning with a sore hand, Kelly remarked how pleasant it was to be a Brotherhood official, gave himself the day off with a sore hand and went to the races. Despite his arrogance, irresponsibility, hot temper, and hard drinking, Kelly was a good manager and the most popular player in the world, presented by Boston admirers that summer with a fine house and lot, valued at $10,000, a horse and carriage, a billiard table, and a bowling alley. A band played "Slide, Kelly, Slide" as the pennant was raised in late October.

Throughout the league the teams tended to string along pretty much as they had played in the National League the year before. Cleveland, which had been sixth in the NL in '89 with a record of 61–72, finished seventh in the PL at 55–75. Pittsburgh, which had finished 61–71 in the other league, had almost the same record in the new league (60–68). Philadelphia, which had been 63–64, went 68–63. The Buffalo team, which had no business being in the league, finished a distant eighth. The Chicago team under Charles Comiskey was perhaps the league's top disappointment. With a good mix of defectors from Anson's Colts, including Hugh Duffy, Fred Pfeffer, Ned Williamson,

RIVAL BASEBALL CAPTAINS RENEWING THEIR YOUTH
Capt. Anson—"You dassent!"
Capt. Comisky—"Yes, I dast!"
Capt. A.—"Yah!"
Capt. C.—"Yah!"

Jimmy Ryan, and Duke Farrell, and players brought to Chicago with Comiskey from the great St. Louis Browns team (Arlie Latham, Silver King), the Chicago White Stockings seemed to have an established star at every position, an amalgam of the two great teams of the 1880's. Instead, they followed much the same pattern as Anson's team, starting slowly and having too much ground to make up late in the season. They finished fourth.

The surprise team was Brooklyn, managed by John M. Ward himself. The League had placed a team in Brooklyn because the National League now had a team in Brooklyn, and also because this gave both Ward and Buck Ewing, both leaders in the Brotherhood, the chance to stay in New York and manage their own teams. The Brooklyn players from the American Association weren't Brotherhood members, of course, so they didn't jump; Ward instead acquired in theory the rights to the players from Indianapolis. Indianapolis wasn't a very good team, and most of their best players elected to stay in the league (with

New York), so Ward had to fill in his roster with late pickups and minor leaguers. He did this exceptionally well, as he did most things, and the new Brooklyn team finished second, even making a run at Boston in August.

The Players' League batting champion was Pete Browning, who is worth a book in himself. Browning was known as, among other things, The Gladiator, Pistol Pete, Distillery Pete, Old Red-Eye, and The Inspector of Red Lights. The Gladiator and The Old War Horse were things that Browning called himself when he spoke of himself in the third person, which he often did, and he had been a great player in the American Association years earlier. By 1889 he seemed to be washed up, for reasons which should be obvious from the other nicknames.

For the 1890 season he had joined the Cleveland team in the Players' League. It was well known that he had spent the spring in Hot Springs, Arkansas, drying out; this was well known because Hot Springs was a favorite place for ballplayers to winter in that time. "I will slide this season if it breaks my leg or neck," Pete said before the season. "The Old War Horse is not played out as they say. If he don't keep some of the youngsters guessing, he knows nothing about baseball." A reporter added that Browning's pants were padded until he looked "like the fat man in the Dime Museum" but that otherwise he seemed to be in good shape and was staying clear of the saloons.

In addition to the drinking problem Pete was apparently nearly deaf, which caused him to react oddly to things that were said. When someone said something about the cyclone in Louisville, Browning thought they were referring to Jesse (Cyclone) Duryea, and passed the information that Cyclone had signed with Cincinnati. When someone referred to the "force bill" being debated in Congress, which had to do with compelling workers to abandon strikes, Browning began talking about Davey Force, who had played years earlier. He had been reported at various times in the 1890 season as fishing in a city gutter, trying to walk through a brick wall on a cloudy night, and trying to hire a hack driver to drive him around all night while he slept in the coach. He had many other documented eccentricities, even when he was sober.

In 1890 he was. In an interview with a newspaper in late July, Browning said "I never knew what it was to go to bed sober until the fourteenth of last August and, if I live until next month, it will be a year since I touched liquor. Some men know when they have plenty; I did not, and since I stopped drinking I feel like a new man. I sleep better, have an awful appetite, and hit the ball harder and more often than ever before."

The interview was widely reported, but always with a caveat. Newspapers, which had reported dozens of apocryphal Browning anecdotes with an absolutely straight face, felt compelled to cast doubt on the authenticity of this statement; "Pete couldn't talk that way to save his life," offered a Louisville reporter who had known Browning for years. Eventually it became apparent that the quote was genuine, as Browning gave similar statements to other papers.

Although everyone knew that Boston's team under Mike Kelly was the best in baseball, a World Series was arranged between the winners of the other two leagues, Brooklyn and Louisville. Brooklyn won the first two games, 9–0 and 5–3. Harry Raymond, third baseman for Louisville (his name at birth was Harry Truman) played very badly in the first two games of the series, going 0-for-9 and committing four errors. After the second game, Raymond and pitcher Red Ehret went out to Louisville's red light district, and got in a fight with a cab driver over how much he was owed for driving them from place to place. The dispute wound up at the police station.

Game three ended in a 7–7 tie, then Louisville rallied to win three out of four. Appropriately, the seven-game series ended in a tie, the Louisville players voting not to continue the series. The season ended without a world champion.

The defeat of the Players' League was apparent by June, and by August the bitterness of the previous years and the anguish of the failure had been replaced by acceptance. The National League was suffering almost as much; the ability of either side to sustain the war for another season was very much in question. John M. Ward and the other leaders of the Brotherhood turned their attention to salvaging something from the peace. The Brotherhood proposed a joint conference, which was set for October 9 in New York. On October 5, President Aaron Stern of Cincinnati announced the sale of the team, which had jumped from the AA one year earlier, to the Brotherhood, which at the time was seen to give the Brotherhood considerable leverage in the upcoming negotiations; the National League, remember, was still "carrying" two franchises. The New York and Pittsburgh franchises were being carried by the other six owners, which was now down to five.

On October 10, an agreement in principle was announced to merge the three leagues into two, a "50 cent league" and a "25 cent league" (that was to be the admission, of course). Boston, Chicago, and Philadelphia would have teams in both leagues, but otherwise the "50 cent league" would be in the bigger cities, and the "25 cent league" in the smaller cities. The Brotherhood wanted to drop both names and call it "United League," but the National League owners felt it was important to use the name which had been used since 1876, symbolizing a return to normalcy. Over this small issue and others, the meeting ended without a firm agreement in place, and the battle resumed.

Everyone stayed in New York; in coffee shops and conference rooms and offices around town, moguls from both sides met with players and player representatives in almost every imaginable permutation. Spalding's strategy was to drive a wedge between the players and the financial backers of the new league. Some of the money men had come into the league with their eyes open, but some of them had been recruited in part with the promise of large profits. No one had been offered the chance to lose a bundle.

Spalding focused on finding the soft spots, identifying the Players' League backers who were most ready to sell out. Perhaps inevitably, the Players' League financial backers began to waver. Edward Talcott, financial backer of the New York team, merged his team into the New York Giants; in essence, he was bought out.

Ward blasted Talcott for his selfishness and weakness; Talcott replied that he had put up $3,000 a month to keep the team going and had seen nothing for his money but "high-priced ball playing." Ward's outburst was perhaps ill-advised; it played into Spalding's strategy. Back in Chicago John Addison, owner of the Chicago team, sold out to Spalding himself, although the transaction was held up while an arrangement was worked out to pay off the players, some of whom had not lately received their salaries. When the Brooklyn Players' team capitulated to the Brooklyn Bridegrooms the battle was over. The Brotherhood had no base left to dictate any terms.

On November 22, 1890, Secretary Brunell and the officers of the Players' League club in Chicago were evicted from their offices in Chicago for nonpayment of rent.

Historians in writing about the 1890 season have focused on the war between the Players' and the National Leagues, and have by and large given little notice to the serious wounds—eventually mortal wounds—inflicted on an innocent bystander, the American Association. The Association lost two of its best teams to the National League, lost many of its best players to the Players' League, and suffered attendance declines as part of the fallout of the bitterness and the public's attendant anger. The association was forced into smaller cities with fewer big name players. Although the association survived through 1891, when it surrendered to the National League, the Players' League experiment clearly killed the American Association.

With teams in danger of collapsing in the middle of a war, some National League owners were forced to invest in their competitor's operations, and so wound up owning a piece of other teams. This laid the foundation for the system of "syndicate ownership" which was to be the curse of the 1890's, multiple teams being owned by the same individuals.

We hear talk now, a century later, of another league being founded by players' agents. If it ever comes to pass, it will end as this one ended—in financial ruin. A business which respects the rights of its employees is a fine thing. A business which is founded for the benefit of its hired hands has a foundation in quicksand.

I am struck by the fact that a season which at the time was regarded as a disaster seems, in retrospect, so fascinating. I am sure this reflects poorly upon me as a writer, but as I reach the end of the story I have a pageful of notes which I have been unable to place in my narrative. "The remarkable developments of the professional base ball season of 1890 and the many novel and interesting events which characterized the past year," wrote Henry Chadwick in the 1891 *Spalding Guide*, "call for largely increased space . . . for editorial comment. The past year may be said to have been one which developed base ball history at an exceptionally rapid rate." Herewith the notes:

• Abuse of the umpires was a growth stock in 1890. An umpire named Larry O'Dea developed a reputation for being able to squelch hecklers like a vaudeville comedian. When a fan yelled out "you're rotten, rotten, rotten!" O'Dea walked over and told him "Maybe I am, but you ought to see my brother." O'Dea, however, resigned from the league after he had been roughed up three times in a week, was mobbed at least a dozen times and acquired a reputation as the quickest umpire in the league to levy a fine.

• In a game in early May an umpire named Bob Emslie was roughed up by a crowd at Rochester when he blew a couple of calls, allowing two runs to score and Columbus to beat Rochester.

• Gus Weyhing, sitting in the bleachers, bellowed at the umpire in such an abusive fashion during one game that he was arrested on a charge of public intoxication.

• Ed Crane, New York pitcher, was arrested after a fight with police at a liquor store in Harlem.

• In a game in Brooklyn, Pat Luby of Chicago knocked the ball over the right field fence, but a policeman recovered the ball and flipped it back over the fence so quickly that Luby was held to two bases.

• All teams in 1890 wore white uniforms at home, but many wore bright colors on the road. The dull gray and brown uniforms which you associate with old-time baseball came along later.

• With the expansion of the major leagues from sixteen teams to twenty-four there was a tremendous demand for new players, and many young stars were discovered in 1890 who would play in the major leagues for years. Among those who got a break in 1890 were Cy Young (purchased by Cleveland after pitching .500 ball in the Tri-State League), George Davis (arguably the greatest player not in the Hall of Fame), and Jesse Burkett and Kid Nichols (who are in the Hall of Fame.)

• Cleveland (P) used a sixteen-year-old pitcher, "Kid"

McGill; he started twenty times for Cleveland, and was regarded as an impressive young pitcher.

• The substitute umpires rule was still in use. In several games, when umpires did not show up, players were used as umpires.

• Connie Mack had invested in the Buffalo team owned principally by Rowe and White.

• A quote from Cap Anson's biography:

> It has also been said that the plan of the Brotherhood was perfected by the ringleaders therein during the around-the-world trip, and it may be that this is true, but if such was the case the whole affair was kept remarkably quiet, for it was not until late in the season that I was aware of the intended secession of the players, I then being approached by John M. Ward with a proposal to join them, a proposal that I declined with thanks, giving as my reason that the League had always treated me fairly and honestly up to that time, and that such being the case I could see no reason why I should leave them in an underhand manner.

The suggestion that Players' League plans were hatched during Spalding's famous round-the-world tour has not been picked up by any modern historian, most of whom have suggested that, on the contrary, the National League used the absence of Ward on the tour to put over on the players the salary classification plan of 1889.

• The New York team in the Players' League reportedly loaned a player, Gil Hatfield, to Boston for three games, leading to protests by John M. Ward and others that this was taking the concept of "Brotherhood" too far. The encyclopedias list Hatfield as having played only for New York, and I did not get time to check box scores and see if Hatfield actually appeared in a game for Boston.

• Both terms for a team leader—"manager" and "captain"—were in use at the time. A "captain" was generally a player, what would now be called a player-manager. While the term "manager" was generally used for a nonplaying manager.

• A circular from National League president Nick Young, circulated on April 15, advised that managers "will be responsible for the neat attire and good conduct of players . . . The wearing of dark colored shirts about hotels or towns is to be discouraged. Managers are asked to avoid using the trains and hotels patronized by Players' League clubs at the same time."

Young was embarrassed by publication of the memo, which was meant to be private, and insisted that the request to avoid the hotels and trains of the Players' League was only meant to prevent fights from breaking out when players who had jumped the Brotherhood came into contact with their former companions. "It is a well-known fact," he said, "that Glasscock, Denny, Al Myers, Clements, Clarkson, Bennett, and others are not

disposed to tolerate any indignities that may be attempted by their former associates."

• A doubleheader between New York and Buffalo was advertised on May 19, but the Buffalo team didn't get the word that two games were to be played, and so didn't show up in time for the first game.

• On May 28 Secretary Brunell of the Players' League was hit in the head by a foul ball, and knocked senseless. He was bedridden for a couple of days before returning to the battle.

• The *Chicago Tribune* reported on June 26 that "The Cleveland papers are claiming a deal of praise for Zimmer because he acknowledged himself out at second a few days ago when Lynch, who was umpiring, did not see the play. That may read very well to the uninitiated, but to those who understand the game it shows that Zimmer does not take much interest in his work."

Zimmer caught 125 games of his team's 132, and at one point reportedly caught 100 consecutive games, an astonishing thing at the time. Buck Ewing, the greatest catcher in nineteenth century baseball, never caught more than 97 games in a year.

• Dozens of games appear to have been forfeited during the season for one reason or another. Anytime an argument developed, the team on the losing end was liable to pull its players off the field and go home to demonstrate how strongly they felt about the issue. I had never before appreciated what a problem this became, which is why to pull your players off the field now is one of the game's cardinal sins. Earl Weaver did that once, but if you do it about twice your career is over, because the league isn't going to stand for it.

• A National League game in Chicago on September 2 was claimed as a forfeit victory by both sides.

• In September, two teams of women played a game at Atlantic Park in New York City. Reported *The New York Times*:

"The usual disgraceful scenes occurred during the play. After the game the women had to be taken out through a side entrance to escape the crowd of 3,000, consisting principally of loafers." After another exhibition of women's baseball, the crowd stormed the field and tore down the fences. . . .

• The Kansas City team, which had dropped out of the American Association and into the Western Association, won the Western Association handily in 1890, finishing with a record of 78 wins, 39 losses.

• John M. Ward, returning to the National League, continued as a manager as long as he was an active player, then left the game. He later became relatively prominent in the world of golf.

(Other than contemporary newspapers, particularly the *Chicago Tribune,* the *Louisville Courier-Journal* and *The New York Times,* the first source of this article is *Baseball* [1890] *From the*

Newspaper Accounts, copyright 1967 by Preston D. Orem, published by Mr. Orem. Other important sources include Harold Seymour's *Baseball: The Early Years,* David Voigt's *American Baseball: From Gentleman's Sport to the Commissioner System,* and the 1891 *Spalding Guide.* Also of use were Cap Anson's autobi-

ography, *A Ball Player's Career,* and two of the Putnam histories, Lee Allen's *The Cincinnati Reds* and Franklin Lewis's *The Cleveland Indians,* and Peter Levine's biography of Albert Spalding, *A. G. Spalding and the Rise of Baseball.* My thanks to all.)

AGE 41
ALL-TIME ALL-STAR TEAM

POS	Player, Season	G	AB	H	2B	3B	HR	Run	RBI	BB	SO	SB	Avg
C	Chief Zimmer, 1902	42	142	38	4	2	0	13	17	11		4	.268
1B	Pete Rose, 1982	162	634	172	25	4	3	80	54	66	32	8	.271
2B	Honus Wagner, 1915	156	566	155	32	17	6	68	78	39	64	22	.274
3B	Bert Campaneris, 1983	60	143	46	5	0	0	19	11	8	9	6	.322
SS	Luke Appling, 1948	129	497	156	16	2	0	63	47	94	35	10	.314
LF	Ted Williams, 1960	113	310	98	15	0	29	56	72	75	41	1	.316
CF	Ty Cobb, 1928	95	353	114	27	4	1	54	40	34	16	5	.323
RF	Stan Musial, 1962	135	433	143	18	1	19	57	82	64	46	3	.330

		G	IP	W	L	Pct.	SO	BB	ERA	ShO	Sv
RS	Cy Young, 1908	36	299	21	11	.656	150	37	1.26	3	2
LS	Warren Spahn, 1962	34	269	18	14	.563	118	55	3.04	0	0
3S	Ted Lyons, 1941	20	180	14	6	.700	50	26	2.10	0	0
4S	Pete Alexander, 1928	34	244	16	9	.640	59	37	3.36	1	2
5S	Rip Sewell, 1948	21	122	13	3	.813	36	37	3.47	0	0
RA	Hoyt Wilhelm, 1965	66	144	7	7	.500	106	32	1.81	0	20

	Record at Age 41		Career Leader Through Age 41		Leader Among Active Players		Pace of Record Holder	
Games	Pete Rose	162	Henry Aaron	3213	Pete Rose	3099	Rose	3099
At Bats	Pete Rose	634	Pete Rose	12544	Pete Rose	12544	Rose	12544
Runs	Sam Rice	81	Ty Cobb	2245	Pete Rose	1995	Cobb	2245
Hits	Pete Rose	172	Ty Cobb	4191	Pete Rose	3869	Rose	3869
Doubles	Honus Wagner	32	Tris Speaker	793	Pete Rose	697	Speaker	793
Triples	Honus Wagner	17	Sam Crawford	312	Pete Rose	126	Crawford	312
Home Runs	Ted Williams	29	Hank Aaron	745	(Reggie Jackson)	530	Aaron	745
RBI	Stan Musial	82	Hank Aaron	2262	(Reggie Jackson)	1601	Aaron	2262
Walks	Luke Appling	94	Babe Ruth	2056	Pete Rose	1358	Ruth	2056
Strikeouts	Willie McCovey	70	Reggie Jackson	2385	(Reggie Jackson)	2385	Jackson	2385
Stolen Bases	Honus Wagner	22	Lou Brock	938	(Rickey Henderson)	573	Brock	938
Average	Stan Musial	.330	Ty Cobb	.367	(Rod Carew)	.328	Cobb	.367
Power/Speed	Honus Wagner	9.4	Willie Mays	444.8	(Reggie Jackson)	315.9	Mays	444.8
Wins	Cy Young	21	Cy Young	478	(Steve Carlton)	314	Young	478
WL %	Rip Sewell	.813	Whitey Ford	.690	(Tom Seaver)	.613	Ford	.690
Strikeouts	Phil Niekro	176	(Nolan Ryan)	4083	(Nolan Ryan)	4083	Ryan	4083
ERA	Cy Young	1.26	Ed Walsh	1.82	(Tom Seaver)	2.82	Walsh	1.82
Shutouts	Cy Young	3	Walter Johnson	110	(Tom Seaver)	61	Johnson	110
Saves	Hoyt Wilhelm	20	(Rollie Fingers)	341	(Rollie Fingers)	341	Fingers	341

Top Alternative Selections

POS	Player, Season	G	AB	H	2B	3B	HR	Run	RBI	BB	SO	SB	Avg
RF	Sam Rice, 1931	120	413	128	21	8	0	81	42	35	11	6	.310
LF	Zack Wheat, 1927	88	247	80	12	1	1	34	38	18	5	2	.324

		G	IP	W	L	Pct	SO	BB	ERA	ShO	Sv
5S	Jack Quinn, 1925	37	205	13	11	.542	43	42	4.13	0	0
5S	Phil Niekro, 1980	40	275	15	18	.455	176	85	3.63	3	1
5S	Red Ruffing, 1945	11	87	7	3	.700	24	20	2.89	1	0
RA	Earl Caldwell, 1946	39	91	13	4	.765	42	29	2.08	0	8

OTHER PLAYERS WHO COULD HAVE BEEN CHOSEN TO THE 41-YEAR-OLD ALL-STAR TEAM INCLUDE:
Catcher Rick Ferrell (1947; 37 G, .303), Second Baseman Rogers Hornsby (1937), Third Baseman Lave Cross (1907), and Pitchers Babe Adams (1923; 13–7), Mike Ryba (1944; 12–7) and Connie Marrero (1952; 11–8, 2.89 ERA).

MOST VALUABLE 41-YEAR-OLD:
Honus Wagner

WINNING TWENTY

Twenty wins began to become recognized as a standard of excellence, I believe, between 1910 and 1915, and by 1930 was a well-recognized plateau of success. This was relatively late; a three hundred batting average was a hallmark of quality in the nineteenth century, when pitchers were still posting won-lost records like 26–33, 21–25 and 32–28. Adonis Terry won twenty games as a rookie in 1884, but I doubt that anyone was unduly impressed; the man lost thirty-five. Even in the first years of this century, it was not terribly unusual for a pitcher to win and lose twenty games in the same season.

In the 1980's, we saw a dramatic reduction in the number of pitchers winning twenty games, and I wanted to discuss for a moment whether we are going to see, within a few years, the end of the twenty-game winner.

To many of you, the complete extinction of the twenty-win species is probably incomprehensible; you simply can't imagine that there won't be any pitchers winning twenty games. I want first of all to convince you that it *is* possible for such a thing to happen. Look at it this way:

In the early days of baseball history, pitchers won as many as sixty games—but that last happened in 1884.

A pitcher won fifty games in 1885—but that hasn't happened since.

During the 1880's, twenty-five pitchers won forty games in a season. Two decades later, only two pitchers won forty games—and no one has since 1908.

In the first twenty years of this century, about one pitcher per season won thirty games. But by 1935—just fifteen years later—that species of pitcher was essentially extinct, although as you all know there was one thirty-win season since—one in the last fifty-five years.

As recently as the 1960's, winning twenty-five games in a season was a common occurrence, accomplished eleven times in that decade. But by the 1980's, the twenty-five-win season was apparently extinct; no pitcher has now accomplished that in nine years.

Across the sweep of history, sixty-game winners, fifty-game winners, forty-game winners, thirty-game winners, and twenty-five-game winners have disappeared one by one. Wouldn't that suggest that twenty-game winners might be the next to go?

Or look at it this way: Before twenty-game winners disappear, one would expect there to be sharp decrease in their population—as, of course, there was for forty-game winners, thirty-game winners, dodo birds, and twenty-five-game winners before those became extinct. One would expect that if the species is healthy, then their numbers would continue at a relatively stable level.

In fact, there has been a sharp decrease in the number of twenty-game winners—from ninety-six pitchers winning twenty games in the 1970's, to thirty-seven pitchers winning twenty games in the 1980's. The same percentage decrease in the 1990's would leave us with fourteen pitchers winning twenty games in the ten years.

There are three factors contributing to the rapid decrease in the number of twenty-game winners in the last ten years, of which the most commonly cited feature—managers going to the bullpens earlier—is the second-most important. The biggest factor by far was the switch from four-man to five-man starting rotations, a shift which began in Los Angeles in 1972 and reached maturity in the late 1980's. In 1989, for the first time, every major league team used a five-man starting rotation through the middle of the summer, although many teams still used four-man rotations in April and some did in September.

The third factor, the most minor one, is increased competitive balance (see "The Parity Party," Section I.) When the best teams won two thirds of their games, it was almost a given that the best pitchers would win four fifths of their games or more. But the best teams now are around .600, so the number of pitchers with winning percentages over .700 is way down.

But while I would not be shocked to see twenty-game winners disappear entirely, neither do I believe that will happen. Six points:

1) While the five-man starting rotation is dominant right now, I am still not convinced that it makes sense. I still believe that managers could control the strain on their best pitchers' arms more effectively by using a four-man pitching rotation, but being more careful about going too long in a game. I think most starting pitchers could handle a 42-game, 260-inning workload *better* than they can handle the 34-game, 240-inning work loads that are common now. I think sooner or later teams will find that they can get more innings out of their starters over the course of the year by starting them more often, but not allowing them to work too long in any game.

2) The distribution of wins among different pitchers on a staff is butting up against roster limits. Rosters have been limited to twenty-five players for a long, long time, twenty-four players now, which is somewhat extended now because of liberal access to the disabled list. But if you've only got twenty-four men you can only carry nine or ten pitchers, and if you can only carry nine or ten pitchers there just isn't that much more you can do to spread the work among different pitchers. The historical drift toward equalization of workloads among the starting staff has a

limit imposed by the size of the squad, which is not expanding.

3) Competitive balance also has its limits. If every pitcher was in reality a .500 pitcher, some pitchers would still win twenty games by sheer luck. Competitive balance has already done nearly all that it *can* do to eliminate twenty-game winners.

4) It is quite possible that, over the next twenty years, we might see an increased reliance on pitchers with low-impact deliveries such as the knuckleball and/or throwing underhanded. In a logical world there would be more knuckleballers than there are, and though superstition and prejudice might rule for centuries, the accidents of history eventually tend to discover logical arrangements.

5) The development of biomechanics, and particularly the computerized study of how bodily motions create injuries, might over time lead to training young pitchers to throw in such a manner as to reduce the damage to their arms, shoulders, and elbows. Again, I have been surprised by how long it has taken this to happen.

6) The rules for awarding victories to pitchers are obsolete, out of sync with the way baseball is played today. They've been out of sync for sixty years, but the problem has grown more acute in the last few years. Consider the pitching lines for Boston last May 31:

Clemens	8	5	1	0	3	10
Smith (W, 4–1)	2	1	2	1	1	4

Clemens, who allowed the Oakland A's only one run in eight innings (that unearned), left the game after eight innings with a 2–1 lead. Smith allowed the tying run to score in the ninth, and then allowed another run to score in the tenth, but was credited with a win when Boston rallied in the bottom of the tenth.

Clemens, pitching one of his best games of the season, got nothing for his trouble, while Smith, by giving up a run as soon as he came in the game, became eligible for the win.

This makes no sense for two basic reasons: one, that a pitcher should not become eligible for the win by surrendering the lead, and two, that Smith doesn't care about the win, anyway.

This much should be obvious to everybody: that it is illogical to reward a player for failure. If Smith had done his job, he would not have been eligible for the win. He should not *become* eligible for the win because he surrendered the lead.

But as I said, Smith doesn't care about the win, anyway. Starting pitchers care about wins, because starting pitchers get paid according to their won-lost records—but relief pitchers don't. Smith isn't going to make any more money because he wound up the season 6–1 than if he had wound up 5–1, because won-lost records don't play any real role in evaluating relief pitchers for the purpose of salaries.

As you all know, that's not a particularly uncommon situation; "vultured wins" are pretty much an everyday occurrence in baseball. A more logical set of rules would say that:
1. The pitcher who contributes the most to the victory should be awarded with the victory.
2. A pitcher should not become eligible for a win by surrendering the lead, and
3. Who was last on the mound for Philadelphia when Philadelphia scores a run has nothing to do with anything.

There are all kinds of phrases you can use to outline what you mean . . . "A win may be credited to any pitcher who leaves the game with his team leading after the completion of the fifth inning," or "A win for which a relief pitcher becomes eligible only by surrendering the lead may be transferred to another pitcher at the discretion of the official scorer." But the current system makes no sense, and while there is no "fan movement" at the moment for a sensible system, in the long run I wouldn't bet against a more logical rule being adopted.

Under the current rules, by the way, starting pitchers get more losses than wins, and relievers get more wins than losses. I don't have exact data, but the overall winning percentage for starting pitchers is about .480, while that for relievers is about .545. This is illogical in principle, but it is especially illogical in view of the fact that relief pitchers really don't care much about wins and losses.

Creating a logical set of rules wouldn't change won-lost records dramatically; on average I think it would add about one half win per starting pitcher per season. But even so, that would make a twenty-win season a little bit more likely.

Twenty-win seasons are under pressure from large historical forces, forces which have extinguished one by one their nearest relatives. It is quite possible that twenty-win seasons will be the next to become extinct—but it is equally likely that in the twenty-first century there will be not fewer twenty-win seasons, but more.

MAJOR LEAGUE ALL-STAR TEAM 1980–1989

CATCHER	G	AB	R	H	2B	3B	HR	RBI	BB	SO	SB	CS	Avg	Slg
1. Gary Carter	8.1	592	77	156	27	2	26	99	62	67	1	2	264	447
2. Carlton Fisk	7.4	573	82	150	26	2	26	90	51	88	9	4	262	450
3. Lance Parrish	7.9	602	76	154	27	3	28	96	51	121	2	3	256	451

4. Bob Boone, 5. Ernie Whitt, 6. Jim Sundberg.
Silver Bat: Gary Carter
Gold Glove: Bob Boone

FIRST BASE	G	AB	R	H	2B	3B	HR	RBI	BB	SO	SB	CS	Avg	Slg
1. Don Mattingly	6.3	642	98	207	43	2	26	114	50	38	1	1	323	521
2. Eddie Murray	9.3	606	93	177	31	2	30	108	81	79	6	2	293	497
3. Keith Hernandez	8.4	589	89	177	33	4	14	88	89	80	8	5	300	438

4. Will Clark, 5. Pedro Guerrero, 6. Jack Clark, 7. Glenn Davis
Silver Bat: Pedro Guerrero (So sue me; that's still what I think.)
Gold Glove: Keith Hernandez

SECOND BASE	G	AB	R	H	2B	3B	HR	RBI	BB	SO	SB	CS	Avg	Slg
1. Ryne Sandberg	7.6	642	99	183	30	7	18	72	54	92	33	9	285	439
2. Frank White	8.7	590	66	153	33	3	15	70	32	79	9	5	260	401
3. Lou Whitaker	8.8	603	93	166	29	5	16	71	75	76	10	5	275	420

4. Willie Randolph, 5. Steve Sax, 6. Manny Trillo
Silver Bat: Ryne Sandberg
Gold Glove: Frank White

THIRD BASE	G	AB	R	H	2B	3B	HR	RBI	BB	SO	SB	CS	Avg	Slg
1. Mike Schmidt	8.1	569	102	158	28	3	38	114	100	114	7	5	277	540
2. George Brett	7.7	602	99	187	39	6	25	110	84	53	10	4	311	521
3. Wade Boggs	7.3	621	113	219	43	5	9	72	103	46	2	3	352	480

4. Paul Molitor, 5. Buddy Bell, 6. Carney Lansford, 7. Gary Gaetti
Silver Bat: Wade Boggs
Gold Glove: Buddy Bell

SHORTSTOP	G	AB	R	H	2B	3B	HR	RBI	BB	SO	SB	CS	Avg	Slg
1. Ozzie Smith	9.1	588	78	154	27	4	2	53	73	38	40	9	261	331
2. Cal Ripken	8.1	623	98	173	33	3	25	92	68	78	2	3	277	461
3. Alan Trammell	8.6	606	95	175	31	5	15	74	64	62	19	8	290	431

4. Julio Franco, 5. Tony Fernandez, 6. Dave Concepcion
Silver Bat: Cal Ripken
Gold Glove: Ozzie Smith

LEFT FIELD	G	AB	R	H	2B	3B	HR	RBI	BB	SO	SB	CS	Avg	Slg
1. Rickey Henderson	8.5	606	131	177	29	5	16	63	113	82	98	22	291	436
2. Tim Raines	7.8	619	111	187	33	10	11	63	90	66	74	11	303	442
3. Kirk Gibson	6.8	583	98	160	25	6	27	88	72	130	30	8	274	475

4. Jim Rice, 5. Jose Cruz, 6. George Bell
Silver Bat: Rickey Henderson
Gold Glove: Left Fielders don't win Gold Gloves

MAJOR LEAGUE ALL-STAR TEAM 1980–1989 (*continued*)

CENTER FIELD	G	AB	R	H	2B	3B	HR	RBI	BB	SO	SB	CS	Avg	Slg
1. Robin Yount	8.9	637	107	194	38	9	19	92	62	73	17	5	305	485
2. Dale Murphy	9.5	600	99	164	27	3	32	98	83	134	14	6	273	491
3. Kirby Puckett	5.7	674	95	218	35	7	17	89	33	86	15	9	323	469

4. Eric Davis, 5. Brett Butler, 6. Chet Lemon
   Silver Bat: Dale Murphy
   Gold Gloves: Garry Maddox, Brett Butler

RIGHT FIELD	G	AB	R	H	2B	3B	HR	RBI	BB	SO	SB	CS	Avg	Slg
1. Dwight Evans	9.0	591	106	165	34	5	28	99	102	113	4	2	280	497
2. Dave Winfield	8.1	614	99	178	32	5	27	111	68	89	12	5	289	492
3. Tony Gwynn	6.5	623	94	207	29	8	7	64	58	36	34	13	332	437

4. Andre Dawson, 5. Darryl Strawberry, 6. Jose Canseco
   Silver Bat: Dwight Evans
   Gold Glove: Jesse Barfield

STARTING PITCHERS	G	IP	W	L	Pct	H	R	ER	SO	BB	ERA	CG	ShO
1. Dwight Gooden	4.6	38	279	22	8	719	227	91	82	252	82	2.64	11	4
2. Roger Clemens	4.6	38	280	21	10	679	237	104	95	265	81	3.06	13	5
3. Jack Morris	8.7	38	280	19	14	577	253	124	114	186	98	3.67	15	2
4. Ron Guidry	6.4	40	258	17	11	607	251	113	105	177	65	3.65	9	2
5. Bob Welch	8.2	38	254	17	11	596	230	100	90	177	81	3.21	6	3
6. John Tudor	6.4	39	254	16	10	612	238	99	88	143	68	3.13	8	2
7. Orel Hershiser	5.6	42	262	18	12	605	223	91	78	182	78	2.69	10	4
8. Teddy Higuera	4.0	38	269	19	11	639	234	107	98	213	82	3.28	11	3
9. Bret Saberhagen	5.0	41	264	18	12	601	247	104	95	173	51	3.23	10	2
10. Dave Stieb	8.8	38	264	16	12	562	229	108	97	157	94	3.32	10	3

11. Fernando Valenzuela, 12. Dave Stewart, 13. Tom Browning
14. Rick Sutcliffe, 15. Mike Scott, 16. John Candelaria
17. Jimmie Key, 18. Nolan Ryan, 19. Frank Viola
20. Sid Fernandez
    Silver Bat: Don Robinson
    Gold Glove: Ron Guidry

RELIEF PITCHERS	G	IP	W	L	Pct	H	R	ER	SO	BB	ERA	Sv
1. Lee Smith	7.8	75	107	6	7	467	92	39	35	107	43	2.96	30
2. Dan Quisenberry	8.4	76	119	6	5	552	120	39	35	43	18	2.67	29
3. Jeff Reardon	8.3	76	105	7	7	483	90	38	36	86	35	3.06	32

4. Dave Righetti, 5. Bruce Sutter, 6. Goose Gossage

MOST VALUABLE PLAYER OF THE EIGHTIES: Mike Schmidt
CY YOUNG AWARD FOR THE DECADE: Dwight Gooden
ROOKIE OF THE DECADE: Cal Ripken
MANAGER OF THE DECADE: Whitey Herzog

Records given are the player's stats for the eighties in seasonal notation.

BIOGRAPHIES

A **Henry Aaron,** who hit more home runs than any other player in major league history.

Henry Louis Aaron was born February 5, 1934 in Mobile, Alabama, the third of eight children of Mr. and Mrs. Herbert Aaron. Years before Henry's birth, Herbert Aaron's father, a country preacher, had told Herbert that one day he would have a family which people would read about to the end of time. Meanwhile, survival; Herbert was employed as a rivet bucker by the Alabama Drydock and Shipbuilding Company, a job which involved bracing sixty-pound rivets against the steel hull of a ship while the rivets were locked in place from the other side. In the depression of the 1930's this work paid sixteen cents an hour when it could be had. "I bucked rivets and whatever else the man wanted me to do," Herbert told Alex Poinsett of *Ebony* magazine in 1974. "I was just workin' whenever they had somethin' in there to work on. Sometime I'd go two or three months without pay. I just lived anyhow." He lived by his wits and his garden. If the family needed wood for the cookstove, an abandoned house could be stripped for firewood. "Bird don't have no money," Herbert Aaron said, "but their babies gotta eat. I knew I was at least as smart as a bird."

Henry was addicted to sports almost from the time he could walk. As a small boy he got "a good whuppin' " when, displaying his father's ingenuity, he cut the head off his mother's new mop to make a bat. Though Herbert Aaron had no time to play catch in the backyard with the boys, he would roll rags together and tie them with string to make a baseball. When not working in the garden Henry worked on the back of a neighborhood ice truck, horsing twenty-five-pound blocks of ice with tongs, and played "strikeout" with his brothers and buddies. Strikeout was played with a broomstick and pop-bottle caps, which explains a little about the hitting style of the mature Aaron.

In 1947, when Aaron was thirteen, Jackie Robinson broke in with the Brooklyn Dodgers, and immediately jumped to the head of Henry Aaron's list of heroes. His high school did not field a baseball team, but Aaron starred as an end and halfback on the football team. In the spring of 1950 Jackie Robinson and the Dodgers visited Mobile for an exhibition game. "Henry," asked Herbert as they left the park, "do you think you can play like Jackie Robinson one day?"

Henry replied that he would be in the major leagues before Jackie was gone.

Mobile in that time had a strong city recreational program, funded in large part by the Senior Bowl football game. This is part of the reason, if you've wondered, why Mobile produced so many major league baseball stars between 1950 and 1975. Henry played softball in the city league, and one day in 1950 a neighbor named Ed Scott asked Aaron if he would like to make some money playing baseball. The sixteen-year-old boy who would turn down this offer has yet to be born, but the Mobile Bears played on Sundays, and Henry knew that his mama wouldn't hear of playing baseball for money on Sundays. Scott was persistent, and several Sunday visits to the Aaron house persuaded Mrs. Aaron that this was an important opportunity.

A 140-pound infielder batting cross-handed, Aaron proved that he could play semipro baseball, and the determination to make the major leagues became an obsession. That spring he began cutting school. Going by a poolroom one day, he saw that the Dodgers would be playing and the game would be on the radio. His daddy caught him, and they had a long talk about it. "I was listening to the baseball game," Henry explained. "I'll learn more about how to play second base from Jackie Robinson than I will in a schoolroom."

Herbert Aaron didn't agree. Once in awhile one of the black teams of that time would barnstorm through Mobile and play the Bears. After a game against the Indianapolis Clowns in 1951, a man named Bunny Downs, their traveling secretary, asked Aaron if he would like to play for the Clowns. Aaron didn't take the offer seriously at the time, but the next spring a contract arrived offering Aaron two hundred dollars a month to play for the Clowns. "You can't imagine how big that looked to a poor boy in Mobile, Alabama," wrote Aaron in his autobiography with Furman Bisher. "It even looked big to my mother." Aaron had received offers to play college football, but in May, 1952, three weeks before graduating from high school, he left for Winston-Salem, North Carolina, where the Indianapolis Clowns were conducting spring training.

By 1952 the remnants of the Negro Leagues were hanging by a wire from a third story window. "The Clowns didn't live in Indianapolis," recalled Aaron in *Aaron*, "they lived in that bus. I never did see Indianapolis." In Winston-Salem the team stayed in a cold, foul-smelling hotel over a poolroom. The older players greeted Aaron, he recalled, as if he were a disease. Aaron coped with the animosity by hitting. In a matter of weeks Syd Pollock, owner of the Clowns, received an offer for Aaron from the New York Giants. Pollock wrote a letter to John Mullen, farm director for the Braves. The letter ostensibly discussed other matters, but Pollock tagged onto the bottom:

"P. S. We got an eighteen-year-old shortstop batting cleanup for us."

And hitting over .400. With the Clowns playing in Buffalo, the Braves sent Dewey Griggs to check out the shortstop. Griggs talked to Aaron about his cross-handed batting style, told him that major league pitchers would knock the bat out of his hands if he tried to hit that way. Aaron said he would try it the other way, with his right hand on top. The first pitch they threw him he hit over the right-field fence. Later in the game he hit one over the left-field fence. Griggs was impressed; Aaron never went back to hitting cross-handed.

The Giants thought they had an agreement to sign Aaron, but since the Negro Leagues were not a part of organized baseball, Aaron could sign either with the Giants or the Braves. At the time he didn't fully understand what that meant, at least in terms of negotiating power. The Braves beat the Giants' offer by fifty dollars a month, and paid Pollock ten thousand dollars to steer Henry to the Braves. Pollock gave Henry a cardboard suitcase.

Henry Aaron's first plane ride took him to Eau Claire in the Northern League. He was named the league's All-Star shortstop less than three weeks after reporting. It wasn't because of his defense; Felix Mantilla was regarded as the top shortstop in the system. When Mantilla and Aaron became teammates at Jacksonville in 1953, Aaron was moved to second. Aaron was assigned to relive—at a lower level—the experience of his hero: Aaron, Mantilla, and a center fielder named Horace Garner broke the color line in the South Atlantic (Sally) League.

Black players were being accepted throughout baseball, but this was the South;

fans in Montgomery still yelled "nigger" and "coon" at the three young men. Aaron, Mantilla, and Garner could all play, and Jacksonville walked off with the Sally League. On the team's first day in Jacksonville after breaking camp, Henry met a student at a local business college named Barbara Lucas; he says that he spent as much time at the Lucas house that summer as he did at the ball park. Aaron led the league in nearly everything, although a second baseman named Tommy Giordano, wherever he may be today, can tell his grandchildren that he hit more homers that summer than Henry Aaron. On October 6, 1953, Henry Aaron and Barbara Lucas were married.

The Braves thought that Henry would eventually make the majors as a second baseman, but that his path would be shorter as an outfielder. Aaron was asked to take his bride to Puerto Rico and learn to play the outfield. Mickey Owen, managing at Caguas, worked with Aaron that winter. When spring training opened in 1954, Aaron was in the big league camp, in condition and ready to hit.

The Braves had made a big trade in the winter, giving up Johnny Antonelli (see Antonelli) to bring Bobby Thomson into left field. On March 13, 1954, Thomson hit a line drive off the left field fence, and slid into second base. He didn't get up. His ankle was badly broken. The next morning Charlie Grimm picked up Aaron's glove, threw it to Aaron and told him the left field job was his until somebody took it away. Jackie Robinson was still with the Dodgers.

Aaron had a fine rookie season in 1954, drawing one vote for Rookie of the Year. His season was ended on September 5, oddly enough, in the same way that his major league career began: Like Bobby Thomson, he broke an ankle sliding into a base. (It was third base in his case. Incidentally, two oft-quoted "facts" about Aaron's rookie season are that he finished second in the Rookie of the Year voting—he did not—and that he had hit five home runs in the week before the injury occurred. In fact, he had hit only one home run in the previous five weeks.)

Aaron had been assigned the number five in 1954, that being the type of number you give a young superstar. But that fall, Aaron approached Donald Davidson, Braves publicity director, and said "Hey, Donald, how about me trading number five for two numbers?"

"Like what?" the little man asked.

"You're so skinny, I don't know how a little bastard like you could carry two numbers around."

"I don't mean just any kind of double number," Aaron answered. "I mean like 22 or 33 or 44, something like that." Stars of the future would fight over the number 44. Willie McCovey and Reggie Jackson are among those who have adopted the number, as have superstars in other sports. When my coffee gets cold—this is Bill James breaking into the narrative—I stick it into the microwave and punch "44," a small tribute to Henry Aaron. Wearing number 44 in 1955, Henry Aaron began the kind of career that can claim the language.

Aaron spoke quietly and played baseball with a businesslike efficiency (one biography reports with a straight face that the Braves front office nicknamed him "Hank" to make him more colorful), and in the early part of his career the press didn't know exactly what to make of him. A minor league manager had said about Aaron that "No one can guess his IQ because he gives you nothing to go on." In a spring training game in 1954, Aaron hit a home run and a triple off of Curt Simmons, one of the best pitchers in the National League. Asked about it after the game, Aaron said, "Oh, was that Simmons? He didn't show me much." The remark laid the cornerstone for Aaron's public image in his early years. It became a commonplace to hear that Aaron never knew who was on the mound. Once he received a wire from Commissioner Ford Frick notifying him that he was being fined for reporting too early to spring training. When he stuffed the telegram into his locker Charlie Grimm told him,

"Better look at that thing, Henry. It's from Ford Frick."

"Who's he?" asked Aaron.

Of course Aaron knew who the commissioner was; he just hadn't caught the name—but when the story hit the newspapers, it didn't come out that way. In a society which would soon reach Montgomery, people were comfortable believing that Aaron was just a simple kid with an unnatural ability to launch a fastball.

Stung by a media image which projected him as a simpleton, Aaron worked for many years to reveal to the media a literate, thinking man. Though according to his own biography he had not been a good student, he would later describe his childhood for a reporter by saying that "I hung around home

a lot, and read books at the library." In an interview with Ray Robinson in 1964 he discussed at some length the works of James Baldwin. For a photo accompanying a magazine article, he posed in his home in the middle of an enormous library.

Inside baseball, there had always been tremendous respect for Aaron's abilities, even before those abilities matured. By the end of 1955 dozens of people were on record predicting greatness for Aaron. The lead story in the December, 1955, edition of the *Baseball Digest* was "Aaron: 1956 Bat Champ?" probably the only such predictions in history to come true. Aaron's teammates and the Milwaukee press knew Aaron to be a quick study and the possessor of a sharp wit, and tried without much success to convey this to the public. In his second year in the major leagues, he bluffed a bunt against Jackie Robinson, playing third base for the Dodgers; Robinson moved not a muscle. "How'd you know I wasn't going to bunt?" Aaron asked Robinson.

"Henry," said the aging hero. "Anytime you want to bunt, we'll give you first base." Aaron decided to forget about bunting. Robin Roberts in 1955 described the twenty-one-year-old as "the only hitter I know of who catches up on his sleep between pitches", and already by that time every article written about him discussed the exceptional power in his wrists. Curt Simmons said that trying to sneak a fastball past Henry Aaron was "like trying to sneak a sunrise past a rooster."

The press frequently cited his consistency; at the time they were talking about his in-season consistency, the fact that he never seemed to go into a slump, but the comments in retrospect are startling—almost as if they were telling us that he was Henry Aaron before he was Henry Aaron.

The Sporting News in 1956 named Aaron the National League player of the year, an award which he would win only one more time despite having many better seasons. Early in 1957 Red Schoendienst said that the twenty-three-year-old was "the greatest right-handed hitter I've ever seen, and he has more power than the greatest left-hander, Stan Musial." That season he set the standard for a Henry Aaron year: 44 homers, 132 RBI, .322 average. For the next fifteen years it seemed as if those were his numbers every season. His forty-third homer, in the eleventh inning of a game against the Cardinals on September 23, clinched the pennant for the Braves, and was often cited before 1974 as the biggest hit of Aaron's career. (Some accounts have even described this as a Thomson-type home run, but this is a gross distortion, since it occurred with a week to go in a race won by the Braves by eight games.) He had led the league in RBI despite batting second in fifty games, the power spots being occupied by Eddie Mathews, Joe Adcock, and Wes Covington.

Topping off his first great season, Aaron hit .393 with three homers in the Series against the Yankees, while the rest of his team hit below two hundred. The pivotal moment of the '57 World Series occurred in the tenth inning of Game Four, with the Yankees holding a one-run lead in a game which could have given them an advantage of three games to one. The Nippy Jones shoe-polish incident ignited a rally, and with one out the Braves had the winning run on second base, Eddie Mathews at the plate and Henry Aaron on deck. With a right-hander on the mound and the left-handed slugger Eddie Mathews at the plate, first base open, a year earlier—probably even a month earlier—the Yankees would have walked Mathews to get the platoon advantage and set up a possible double play. Instead, the Yankees pitched to Mathews, and Mathews hit a game-winning home run. The moment marks Aaron's emergence as a superstar, a distinction made official weeks later, when Aaron was named the National League's Most Valuable Player—an award which, remarkably enough, he was never to win again.

When we soar too fast the Lord likes to touch our feet to the ground. Just weeks after the MVP Award was announced, the Aarons had twin sons, born prematurely. One, Larry, was severely asthmatic from birth, so much so that he was unable to live with the family in Milwaukee, staying with his grandparents in Mobile. The other was born dead. Henry and Barbara had three other children over the years.

After winning their second pennant in 1958—the Yankees got even that fall—the Braves began a series of oddly frustrating seasons. From 1954 through 1963 the Braves had three Hall of Famers at the peak of their powers—Aaron, Mathews, and Warren Spahn. It is doubtful that any other team ever had three players of the same caliber for an entire decade. Beyond those three the talent core was formidable: starters Lew Burdette and Bob Buhl, reliever Don McMahon, catchers Del Crandall and Joe Torre, first

baseman Joe Adcock, second basemen Red Schoendienst and Frank Bolling, shortstops Johnny Logan and Roy McMillan, outfielders Wes Covington, Bill Bruton and Lee Maye. From 1959 through 1961 the National League was ripe for the picking; the 1959 Dodgers, 1960 Pirates, and 1961 Reds are three of the weakest champions in the history of the league.

The Braves somehow frittered away the opportunity. When Red Schoendienst developed tuberculosis in 1958, the Braves used over a dozen second basemen in two and a half years, most of them inept, before trading for Bolling; they even ran Aaron back to second base for a few games, and in the winter of 1959–1960 talked seriously about moving Aaron to second. Aaron campaigned against the idea. "When I played second base before," he told *The Sporting News,* "I couldn't make the double play. I was afraid of the runners coming in. It's the hardest position on the field. The runners come in and you've got your back to 'em. If he [Charlie Dressen] tells me to, I'll go there. All I ask is that I play there from the start of spring training. I don't want to go there in midseason and be made a fool of at the position." In jest, Buzzie Bavasi said if the Braves played Aaron at second base he was going to sign 294-pound football star Big Daddy Lipscomb as a pinch runner. "Big Daddy would only have to run for me once and I'd pay him for the full year. We'd send him in as a pinch runner and they could begin to pick up Aaron's pieces." Funny man, that Buzzie.

With astonishing consistency for fifteen years, the Braves would string along a young pitcher from age eighteen to twenty-five, refusing to give him a full shot at a starting job, and then would trade him at the very moment when he was ready to take over; this left them perpetually short of starting pitching behind Spahn and Burdette. With a bench full of veterans who couldn't play the field anymore and didn't hit what they were expected to hit, the Braves had very little ability to withstand an injury. After 1953, the Braves could not do what a quality organization has to do, which is to fill in the holes with good young players that other organizations have not been able to find a spot for, and thus there was a constant expectation that the Braves would win next year and next year and next year, and eventually the Dodgers and Giants and then the Cardinals put outstanding teams together and took over the league.

In a sense, Aaron's reputation was held hostage to this; many of the sportswriters of the era always thought that Aaron would be the big story next year. As a player, Aaron was the embodiment of the idea of playing within yourself. He was not a man of great size or obvious strength, but he had strength where he needed it to hit. "Like a pool hustler," wrote Jim Murray, "he never tries the impossible shot. If a hitter has just hit a double, Henry gives it to him. But he NEVER plays a double into a triple. He is 'Mr. Percentage.' He makes Willie Mays look like he's learning the business."

As Dave Kingman demonstrates the inefficient use of strength in baseball, attempting to overpower the game, Aaron represents its efficient use, generating uncanny bat speed with an apparently easy flip of the bat head. This was true of his skills in all areas. When he came to the major leagues he was not regarded as possessing great speed, and in fact an odd way of running back on his heels earned him the nickname "Snowshoes," convincing many people that his speed would become a problem for him. But when Bill Bruton was injured in 1957, Aaron moved to center field and filled in well enough that the Braves just continued to win, and when Manager Bobby Bragan told Aaron that the reason Willie Mays had a reputation as an all-around player and he didn't was that Mays stole bases, Aaron began stealing bases, too, stealing twenty-five bases a year while hardly ever being caught.

He had few nervous mannerisms, at the plate or on the bases or in the field. He cradled each catch with a nonchalant gesture which was as much his signature as anything. He wasn't a long-distance thrower; he just threw the ball as far as it needed to go, throwing out twelve to fifteen base runners every year and leading the league several times in runners doubled up. On the bases he took every base he could get and made it look easy. To give a modern fan a sense of what he was like, he was in a manner of speaking the exact opposite of Juan Samuel: a player who had few impressive physical attributes, but who somehow could do whatever he was asked to do.

The Milwaukee era came to a bizarre end in 1965 when the Braves owners decided they had pumped all the money they could out of Milwaukee, and it was time to move on to Atlanta. The Milwaukee fans had supported the Braves extremely well, but with Chicago just to the south, a lake to the east and Minnesota to the north and west, the team's ability to draw fans from long distances was limited. The owners hoped that a team in Atlanta would capture the entire South, drawing fans in from Miami to Memphis. Milwaukee fans organized a boycott, and the Braves, still a strong team in 1965—every Brave team in thirteen years in Milwaukee was over .500 and in contention—began playing before an empty stadium. As recalled by Merle Harmon in *Voices of the Game:*

"There were baseball people deathly afraid we were going to win the pennant, and that we'd wind up in the World Series and County Stadium would be half-deserted." On August 18 in St. Louis, with the Braves holding a narrow lead in a four-team pennant race, Aaron batted against Curt Simmons. "With his herky-jerky motion and great change-ups, Curt had driven Hank crazy for years . . . in fact, it was a running joke that Curt had thrown Hank exactly one fastball in his life, and Hank had promptly hit it over the roof at Busch Stadium." Aaron took an outside changeup and hit the pitch out to right field—but umpire Chris Pelekoudas disallowed the home run and called Aaron out; in his desire to get at the changeup, he had hit the ball with his foot on home plate. "That one moment really demoralized the team," said Harmon. "It was all downhill from there."

Twenty-five years have twisted the memory just a bit; actually, the Braves came back to win that game and remained in contention until shut out in ten innings by Dick Selma on September 12, a game which Aaron did not play. Not to hammer Harmon, but the mis-memory is very illustrative of one of the systematic distortions of oral history: the tendency to think that *striking* and *memorable* events were also *important* and *pivotal* events. Because the human mind is always searching for explanations of an overpoweringly complex reality, and because the mind only actively retains a small portion of what happens, the mind tends to link together that which it retains with causes and effects, making the remembered events into turning points. In any case, the season degenerating quickly after Selma's shutout, and the Milwaukee era stumbled to an end.

Throughout his Milwaukee career, Aaron had set goals of tremendous difficulty, and annexed those goals with apparent ease. He had said he would play against Jackie

Robinson, and he did. In 1956 he told a reporter that he had three goals in baseball: to win the Most Valuable Player Award, to lead the league in hitting, and to play in a World Series. By the age of twenty-three, he had done all of that. Although he did talk occasionally about hitting .400 or hitting sixty homers, marks which he was never to approach, by the early sixties he was quoted as saying that the only goal that he had left in baseball was to get 3,000 hits. Although he didn't actually reach the mark until 1970, it was apparent for three years before that that he would clear 3,000 with ease, and since he remained one of the best hitters in baseball, he naturally began to look around for other challenges.

No statistic in baseball had a greater mystique than Babe Ruth's career total of 714 home runs. Jack Webb, a baseball fanatic, had used 714 as his badge number on *Dragnet.* (Webb, incidentally, was a friend of Fred Haney, Aaron's manager for several years, and would hang around the Braves clubhouse when they came to Los Angeles.) When I was in high school, I wrote a paper for a math project explaining why it was impossible for this record ever to be broken.

It is outside the purview of this book to deal with park effects, but it is important for you all to understand this: Throughout most of his career, Henry Aaron's batting stats were hurt—not helped, but hurt—by the ball park he played in. Although the dimensions of Milwaukee County Stadium are relatively short, some games in Milwaukee are played in cold weather, and cold weather helps a pitcher. Aaron, year-in and year-out, hit more home runs on the road than he did in Milwaukee, as did Eddie Mathews and Joe Adcock and the Braves team as a whole. Had he been playing in another park—not Ebbets Field or Wrigley, but just any other park—Aaron would have hit many more home runs in his prime seasons than he did, and in fact it is likely that had he played his best seasons in a true home run park, he would have challenged the sixty-homer mark. From 1953 through 1961, Milwaukee County Stadium was the most difficult park in the National League for a hitter.

In 1966 Aaron went from a park which was taking several home runs a year away from him to a park which was giving him the same edge. Thus, although Aaron from 1966 through 1973 was not, in fact, as good a hitter as he had been in his prime, the statistical record, taken at its face value, shows no

decline; Aaron's best five-year home run stretch *began* in 1969, when Aaron was thirty-five years old.

By June 21, 1966, Aaron had hit 24 home runs, a National League record for home runs by that date. Thus, within weeks of arriving in Atlanta, the fact that one could hit boxes of home runs here was apparent. Aaron began to focus on his career home run total. Within a couple of years of moving to Atlanta, Aaron realized that if he kept himself in shape and continued to hit, he could possibly break Babe Ruth's unbreakable career-home-run record. And he began to concentrate on doing that, working hard in and out of season to stay in shape, and, as a hitter, consciously trying to pull the ball. By 1970 it was apparent to everyone that Aaron had an outside chance to break the record. In 1971, age thirty-seven, he hit a career-high 47 home runs—and suddenly it was just a matter of time.

Aaron's pursuit of Ruth's career home run total was an event tailor-made for hype—a battle enacted over a sustained period of time, giving every reporter with a ballpoint or a Nikon a shot at the story. It was a "chase" with an inevitable winner, a black man pursuing the treasured record of a beloved white man in a nation which at the time was obsessed with race. Aaron was playing for a bad team with very little else to talk about. The pressure that was focused on Aaron as he grew near the record is a difficult thing to comprehend. His face was on countless magazine covers. His face stared down at Atlanta from numerous billboards, leaving him bereft of the anonymity a man needs to do ordinary things. Children's books about his life were churned out. Sightseeing buses regularly pulled up in front of his home; tourists spilled out, pens in hand, and sometimes a bold traveler would march up to the doorbell and see if Henry could come out and chat. Photographers snapped his picture from morning to night, and every morning and evening TV talk show in every big and little city wanted just a moment of his time before he broke the record. Letters came in by the thousands, containing a measure of racist abuse and indiscriminate hatred along with a burdensome crush of hero worship. Death threats became a part of his routine, routinely forwarded to the FBI, and not taken all that seriously unless they perhaps were directed at a specific member of his family or gave a specific date or method for his prospective murder. On road trips Aaron had to be registered under an assumed name and smuggled into his hotel room, where he would hide out until it was time to go to the ball park. His sixteen-year marriage broke up under the pressure, leaving four children with a divided family, and in that spotlight he conducted a courtship of talk-show hostess Billye Suber Williams, whom he married in Jamaica on November 12, 1973. (His second marriage has now lasted almost as long as did the first.)

One final controversy arose in the opening days of the 1974 season, when Commissioner Kuhn ordered the Braves to play Aaron in road games, ruling that for the Braves to hold Aaron out so he could break the record in Atlanta would in some manner attack the integrity of the game. Having contributed this to the discussion, Kuhn then declined to break a previous engagement to be in Atlanta when the record was broken; Aaron sniffed that if the record was being broken by a white man, Kuhn would be there. On April 8, 1974, with Al Downing on the mound, Aaron hit his 715th career home run. "Thank God it's over," he said after the game.

Aaron returned to Milwaukee after the 1974 campaign, playing two seasons with the Brewers; the park worked its predictable effect on his stats, creating the impression that he lost it suddenly in 1975. His next goal was to move into the front office, to have a career as a baseball executive, as Carl Hubbell and Hank Greenberg had, which complemented his Hall of Fame accomplishments on the field. He had laid the groundwork for this as early as the winter of 1963–64, working with the Braves front office in the off-season, beginning by helping to sell tickets. In 1976 he returned to Atlanta to become vice-president in charge of player development for the Braves, where he worked closely with his former brother-in-law, Bill Lucas, Braves director of player personnel, until Lucas's death in 1979.

Though Aaron in his prime years did not speak out often, he had an impact when he did. In the spring of 1961, a controversy arose when black players on the Yankees complained about their Florida accommodations. Braves manager Birdie Tebbetts said that he thought that Milwaukee's black players were satisfied with their living situation. Aaron told *The Sporting News* about the place he was staying. "Sometimes the place is so crowded that they have guys sleeping in the hall. They have five guys living in two

rooms. They put two beds in one room, two more in the hall and another bed in a smaller room. They got a room over the garage, they call it the penthouse. At the most you can put four people in there and they have eight. They said this place was carefully selected for us to stay. Carefully selected from what? There isn't one decent place in this town for us to stay." The comments from Aaron, Aaron the Quiet, had an impact because of who had spoken them.

In November of 1964, when the Braves were rumored to be moving to Atlanta, Aaron and teammate Lee Maye spoke out against the move, both saying that they would play in Atlanta but would never move their families to the South. A trip to Atlanta to see conditions there reassured Aaron somewhat, showing him that life in Atlanta was very different from life in rural Georgia, yet Aaron still approached the move with some apprehension. And, inevitably, everything that Aaron did in his first years in Atlanta was presented to the public as the accomplishment of the South's first black superstar, a presentation which invited the bigots to respond.

Among the rewards that Aaron earned by his superstar stature was the friendship of Jackie Robinson, with whom he spent a good deal of time in the last years of Jackie's life. Jackie told him to keep speaking out, to keep talking about whatever made him unhappy. But as the owner of one of baseball's most prestigious records—not to mention a page or two of other records—Aaron's status within the game changed in ways that were sometimes difficult for him to anticipate or deal with. Suddenly, everything he said was news. A controversy arose in 1974 when Aaron expressed some pique at not being offered a managerial post. Aaron had said repeatedly that he was not interested in managing *unless he had the opportunity to become the first black manager.* Of course no one was going to hire him to manage under those conditions, but Aaron was apparently miffed to discover this. This petty controversy set a pattern for Aaron; to this day he is quoted occasionally on the suitability of pitchers winning MVP Awards or some similar thing, and frequently he finds himself isolated on no particular side of these debates except his own.

His career as an executive has not been one of great success. Aaron was director of player development for the Braves for thirteen years, during which time the perform-

ance of the Atlanta farm system cannot be defended. (The Braves 1989 media guide says that "Dale Murphy, Zane Smith, Gerald Perry and Andres Thomas are just a few of the current Braves who came up through Atlanta's farm system under Aaron's direction." Dale Murphy was in the majors before Aaron retired as a player, and the other three guys had all played themselves out of a job by the end of the 1989 season. Aaron has recently been "promoted" to vague duties in the Atlanta front office.) When the commissioner's job became open at the end of Bowie Kuhn's command, Aaron campaigned for the job, proposing interleague play, realignment of the divisions, a salary cap like the NBA, and a system of revenue sharing. Although he was the only announced candidate, the search committee looking for Kuhn's replacement failed even to acknowledge his interest, starting another controversy. In the end, Aaron established only that no one really knows how one gets to be commissioner.

The basic personality outline for Henry Aaron is that of a school principal—a serious man, a man who asks for respect from those around him and gets it up to a point. Though the years of confronting racism have left him super-sensitive and inclined to whine a bit—Jackie might have done him more of a favor if he'd told him to keep his peace once in awhile—Aaron is respected for his accomplishments, respected for his work habits, respected for his work with charities, respected for an intelligence which carries off the notion of competence if it fails to soar. Considering the shadow that young men of talent have so often cast over the rest of their lives, this is no mean accomplishment. Contrast the 1990 Henry Aaron with the pathetic end of Pete Rose, the financial tribulations of Harmon Killebrew, or even the drifting *just being there* of Willie Mays and Johnny Bench, and one concludes that Aaron has done damn well.

Tommie Aaron, whose destiny it was to live out his life in the shadow of his older brother.

As a youngster in Mobile, Tommie played for the same Mobile Black Bears for whom Henry had starred several years earlier and played well enough to draw a flock of scouts. One of those scouts, Ivy Griffin of the Cubs, watched the Bears in one game and immediately reported to his employers that the real prospect on the team was an outfielder named Billy Williams. When Tommie was signed by the Braves, Henry told reporters that "I've never seen him play, so I can't tell you much about him. The only thing I know is he runs back on his heels like I do."

Great; Billy got the wrists, Tommie got the heels. Tommie began his pro career by playing for the same two teams his brother had played for, Eau Claire in the Wisconsin League and Jacksonville in the Sally League. Though not approaching his brother's accomplishments even in the minor leagues, Tommie blasted 26 homers at Eau Claire and had consecutive seasons of .299 with good power at Cedar Rapids and Austin (Texas League), earning him a job backing up Joe Adcock with the Braves in 1962.

With the Braves Tommie roomed with his brother. On July 14, 1963, in a hotel in St. Louis, the air conditioner in the Aarons' room burst into flames; the room was destroyed. Hank said he'd never been so scared in his life. He went three for five that night, with a tape-measure home run. Tommie started too; he went hitless in three tries. Well regarded as a glove man, Tommie failed to hit in the major leagues, but returned to the minor leagues time and again to battle his way back by hitting around .300 with some power in the minors. In an exhibition game against Detroit in 1965, he hit the first home run ever hit in Atlanta–Fulton County Stadium.

In 1973 Tommie became player-manager of the Savannah team, and began to chop his way back through the system as a manager. He managed in the Braves system for six years, leading Richmond to the International League Championship in 1978, and then joining the big team as first base coach. By 1982 he seemed on the verge of breaking into the managerial ranks, but late that summer was discovered to have leukemia. He died of the disease at Emory University Hospital on August 16, 1984, his life over at age forty-five.

Don Aase, contemporary pitcher.

Signed out of high school by the Red Sox in 1972, Aase put in a five-year apprenticeship in the minor leagues, and began his major league career by pitching extremely well for Boston over the second half of the 1977 season. Traded that winter to the California Angels in an odd move (it is very unusual for a young pitcher to be traded before he has struggled in the major leagues) Aase found himself forced to the rear end of a rotation anchored by two stars, Ryan and

Tanana. With shaken confidence and an inept defense behind him, Aase struggled for two and a half years to find himself as a starting pitcher.

Banished to the bullpen in mid-1980, Aase liked the transition to relief, and pitched well for the rest of the 1980 season. "I think that for myself," he told John Strege early in 1981, "it helps being in a situation where I come in and throw as hard as I can for as long as I can." As long as he can usually has been about two months; then his arm blows out. In Cleveland on July 17, 1982, Aase "felt something pop" in his right elbow, plunging him into a six-year battle with the disabled list.

Blessed with a ninety-plus fastball and two decent breaking pitches, Aase has pitched well most of the time when healthy since 1980, but has had to work around an elbow operation (October, 1982; out two years), and a shoulder scope (July, 1987, ineffective for a year and a half). His two-year absence from the Angels following the elbow problem was painful for both Aase and the club. At a Kiwanis luncheon in 1983, an Angels executive said "I'm here on Don Aase watch. If I see him raise his hand above the table, he'll be back in the bullpen." Aase kept his arm down, and was on the disabled list for another year before returning to the bullpen. Joining Baltimore as a free agent in 1985, Aase had his best season in 1986, saving 34 games plus the All-Star game. Aase had 29 saves in early August that year, leading the major leagues, but was slowed late in the year by a twisted back.

Aase appears to be a quiet person who doesn't draw a lot of ink. In 1978, when Dick Miller was writing the Angels column for *The Sporting News*, he almost managed to make it through the entire season without so much as mentioning Aase's name—a rotation starter—finally including Aase in September when he missed a start after being shaken up in a three-car accident near Anaheim Stadium. To this day, I don't believe *The Sporting News* has done an article of any substance on Aase, anything that went beyond "Aase pitching well," or "Aase coming back from latest injury." Obviously, Aase is well enough liked by his coaches and managers, because a player who isn't well liked doesn't get as many chances to come back as Aase has had. His career appears to be near an end.

Ed Abbaticchio, a National League infielder from 1897 to 1910, best remembered

today as the first significant baseball player of Italian descent.

Born in 1877 in Latrobe, Pennsylvania, Abbaticchio in 1895 played for what is generally considered to be the first professional football team. On September 4, 1897, he made his major league debut as a second baseman for Philadelphia, then managed by George Stallings. The next spring Stallings shifted Nap Lajoie to second base, which pushed Abbaticchio to third, where he made five errors in his first game, an exhibition game. Though Abbaticchio hit well early in the season, his defense was awful, and his offense collapsed under the pressure.

After spending several years in the minor leagues, Abbaticchio resurfaced with the Boston Braves in 1903, and after a year's detour to second base became one of the top shortstops in the league in 1904–05. By 1906, however, Abbaticchio had become the owner of a hotel in his hometown of Latrobe, and the hotel had a liquor license. Pennsylvania law at this time required that the proprietor of any establishment with a liquor license could not reside out of state for more than three months at a time, so Abbaticchio would have had to surrender his liquor license to play another season for the Braves. When he refused to do this, preferring the long-term income of the hotel to the short-term advantages of a baseball career, the Braves gave Giants owner John T. Brush permission to negotiate with him. Brush, however, was also unable to attract Abbaticchio back to baseball, and so he simply sat out the 1906 season. This episode gave Abbaticchio a wonderful nickname, "The Latrobe Boniface," a boniface being an innkeeper; he was also known as Abby and Batty.

In 1907 the rights to Abbaticchio were passed to the Pittsburgh Pirates, for whom Abbaticchio could play without losing his license. Because of a fellow named Honus Wagner, Abbaticchio was shifted back to second base, and gave the Pirates two solid years as a second baseman. You may remember that the 1908 National League pennant race was perhaps the greatest pennant race of all time, and that in this race the season came down to its last regularly scheduled date (Sunday, October 4) with three teams still having a chance to win. It was on that day, as the Pirates lost, that the most famous event of Abbaticchio's career occurred (see Tracers).

Abbaticchio was a bench player in 1909 and out of baseball a year later. (This article

TRACERS

*In 1908 Pittsburgh finished a single game behind the Cubs
. . . Pirate fans of that day still argue that a mammoth boner
by a plate umpire did the Pirates out of the National League
championship.*

*[Ed Abbaticchio hit] an apparent grand-slam home run in a
late-season game in Pittsburgh with the Cubs. If the four runs
had been allowed, the Pirates would have claimed the
pennant. . . . A feminine fan then sued the Pittsburgh club
because the ball clouted by Abbaticchio struck and severely
injured her. She produced her ticket stub in court as part of
the evidence.*

*The news made Pittsburghers groan . . . her rain check
showed that she was seated in fair territory!*

—Dick Meyer
January, 1953, *Baseball Digest*

This story also appears in Arthur Daley's 1950 classic *Inside
Baseball*, which adds that the play in question happened on the
last day of the season and that "scrutiny of the location charts
revealed that her seat had been in FAIR territory," and in
Okrent and Wulf's 1989 *Baseball Anecdotes*, which adds that the
court ruled against the woman *because* "it was conclusively established that she had been sitting in fair territory at the time."
Because the accounts given in these three places conflict on
several key points, it's obvious that there are intermediate
sources as well, but I don't know what they are.

Anyway, Mike Kopf, whose life revolves to an unhealthy
extent around the 1908 pennant race, naturally drew the assignment of checking this one out. This proved to be a difficult thing
to do, because the lawsuit in question didn't arise at the moment, but at some undetermined point after the season was
over. In fact, we're not even sure that the lawsuit was ever filed
at all, but that's getting ahead of the story.

• The game occurred on October 4, 1908 at West Side Park
in Chicago.

• Abbaticchio batted in the ninth inning with the Pirates
trailing 5–2.

• There was one runner on base, Honus Wagner, who was on
first.

• Abbaticchio hit a drive down the right field line, *not* into
the seats but into the overflow crowd standing in the outfield.
The base umpire, Cy Rigler, signaled that the ball was a double,
but plate umpire Hank O'Day overruled him, and said that the
ball was foul.

So if Rigler's call had stood, the Pirates would have had
men on second and third with no one out—but they would still

have trailed, 5–2. Instead, Abbaticchio struck out, and the Pirates did not score. The Pirates after the game were gracious in
defeat, and made no issue of the foul-ball call.

Enough was made of the fair/foul controversy at the moment that we're essentially certain this was the play in question.
Everybody got *parts* of the story right; Okrent and Wulf had the
game in Chicago (the other sources had it in Pittsburgh) and
had the ball hit to right field (Daley had specified that it was hit
to left). Daley correctly reports the game as being on the last day
of the season, while Okrent and Wulf have it being played in
late September (the two teams did not meet in late September).
Daley correctly identified the umpire in question as Hank
O'Day, as did Okrent and Wulf, but Daley specified that
"O'Day's hesitation was too momentary to be noticed. He
gulped hard and intoned, 'Foul ball!' " an obvious fictionaliza-
tion of the incident. No one had a second umpire involved in
the play.

But everybody has it as a grand slam home run which would
have given the Pirates the pennant, when in reality it was just
a double that would have made the game a little more interesting. We could find no record of the lawsuit. Since the event in
question occurred in Chicago, a lawsuit would also have been
played there. Mike scoured the *Chicago Tribune* microfilm for
the entire off-season, and could find no mention of such a suit.
He went through *The Sporting Life* for the same period; no luck.
The 1909 *Reach* and *Spalding* guides make no mention of such
a lawsuit. This doesn't necessarily mean that there was no such
lawsuit, but there is something else a bit unlikely about it. Mike
Kopf's description of the scene:

*A throng of 30,647 is shoehorned into the park (this is six thousand
above and beyond any previous crowd in the park), and as was custom
at that time, allowed to overflow into the outfield. Except that on this day
the overflow is a tidal wave. Minutes before game time the cranks have
surged to within spitting distance of the infield. The police are called upon
to force the crowd back, which they do (not without casualties), but when
the action begins, at least half of the outfield belongs to the spectators, who
incidentally are not, as was often the case, roped off.*

It seems just a little bit unlikely, does it not, that the ticket
stub could prove where the woman was actually standing? She
was sold a ticket to stand in the outfield, remember, and while
this ticket might have specified where she was *supposed* to stand,
the crowd was out of control. For the umpires to have disagreed
on the call, she obviously would have had to have been standing
within a foot of the right field line, one way or the other. When

a line drive was hit at her, she presumably would have attempted to jump out of the way, wouldn't she? Might have, anyway. It seems enormously difficult to believe that it could ever have been proven that the woman was standing in fair territory, regardless of what the ticket stub said and regardless of what witnesses said, and since it wouldn't have made any difference to the trial whether she was fair or foul anyway, the whole business about her bringing in affidavits and testimony about where she was standing just doesn't ring true.

If anyone can find a record of the lawsuit, or any mention of the lawsuit printed before 1920, we would be very interested to see it.

---

researched by Mike Kopf, primarily from newspaper microfilm.)

Bert Abbey, National League pitcher in the 1890's.

Abbey was a graduate of the University of Vermont, where he was taught to throw a curveball by an older teammate—Amos Alonzo Stagg, later a great football coach. While pitching against Johns Hopkins in 1892, Abbey was seen by Arthur Irwin, manager of the Washington Nationals, and signed to a contract. Though he seems to have pitched reasonably well with Washington, he racked up an ugly 5–18 record with a bad team, and began bumping around the National League, playing for Cap Anson in Chicago and Frank Selee in Brooklyn before leaving the league. Out of baseball by 1899, Abbey was a farmer and also organized the first telephone company in Vermont. He lived to be ninety-two years old, and was for a short time before his death in 1962 recognized as the oldest living ex–major leaguer.

Charlie Abbey, an outfielder with the Washington Nationals in the 1890's, who drove in over a hundred runs in 1894 and scored over a hundred the next year.

After a five-year major league career, Abbey was released by Washington on August 21, 1897. "The Washington team is fourth on the list in point of salaries, and eleventh in the race," announced the team's business manager, "and I was convinced there was something radically wrong." Abbey's place on the roster was taken by an eighteen-year-old pitcher named Roger Bresnahan.

A Nebraska native, Abbey drifted out of contact after his career, and is one of comparatively few players whose date and place of death have not been located by SABR's biographical researchers.

Bud Abbott, vaudevillian and star of B movies. Abbott and Lou Costello perfected baseball's most famous comedy routine, "Who's on First," performing it so often and so well as to eventually make it their own, as DeWolf Hopper had for "Casey at the Bat."

Fred Abbott, a good-field, no-hit catcher in the first decade of this century, perhaps best remembered for engaging in a pretty damn good fistfight with Dan McGann of the Giants in the opening days of the 1905 season.

Glenn Abbott, former major league pitcher who is now a coach for the Tidewater team in the Mets system.

Signed by the Oakland A's in 1970 after a year at State College of Arkansas, the six-foot-six right-hander went 18–8 in the Pacific Coast League in 1973 to earn a look with the perennial World Champions. The A's were not exactly short of pitching, and Abbott never got the full attention of the team—in fact, Alvin Dark in his autobiography referred to Abbott three times as "Gene" Abbott. On the last day of the season in 1975 Abbott took part in the famous four-pitcher no-hitter started by Vida Blue, but he never received a full shot at a starting job until taken by the Seattle Mariners in the 1976 expansion draft.

Abbott won twelve games for the Mariners in their first season (1977), easily the most on the staff, and gained an added measure of satisfaction when the Mariners finished one game ahead of the A's, suddenly denuded by free agency. Drawing the assignment as the home team's starting pitcher in the first game of the 1978 season, Abbott pitched six strong innings to become the first major league pitcher at 1–0. "Dear Abby: You were great," cooed a Seattle paper; *The Sporting News* headlined "M's Abbott Starting Fast in His Bid for 20 Victories." Abbott didn't win again until June 18. Though unable to meet his own projections, Abbott remained one of the Mariners' best pitchers for several years, and held the team record for career wins (44) until passed by Mike Moore in 1986.

Knocked almost out of baseball by tendinitis in 1979—at one point he was driven to try acupuncture on his arm—Abbott went on a Nautilus program in the off-season, and had his best major league season in 1980

(12–12); this earned him his third opening-day assignment in 1981. That season, however, slogged down in a morass of problems which seemed certain to end Abbott's career and perhaps to threaten his life. Abbott had surgery to remove bone chips from his elbow, then had a bout with viral meningitis, during which he lost twenty-three pounds, lost 20 percent of the hearing in his left ear, spent a month in bed and had several months of blurred vision. To the amazement of everyone, Abbott fought back again to the major leagues, going 7–4 in 1983. "I thought I'd have to go to his funeral when I saw him last fall," said pitching coach Frank Funk. "I couldn't believe he would ever pitch again."

On his game, Abbott threw ground balls; his basic pitches were a slider that broke down and away from a right-handed hitter and a fastball which didn't "sink" so much as it died of exhaustion about the time somebody hit it. The psychological portrait which emerges from Abbott's clippings is more interesting. Early in his career his constant optimism bordered on self-delusion, and you could almost laugh at this man who in 1978 was sure that he would win "at least" fifteen games, and who always thought that this year would wind up his best year, no matter where it seemed to be headed. You could almost laugh—until this incorrigible optimist came back from staggering odds to take on major league hitters with a fastball which at the end of his career went about seventy-five miles an hour. He wasn't a great pitcher, but you've got to think that if anybody's earned the right to make a living as a pitching coach, he's earned it.

Jim Abbott, sensational young pitcher of the California Angels, who at the age of twenty-two has proven that he can pitch major league baseball despite the absence of his right hand.

The basic outline of the Jim Abbott story is well known. He was born September 19, 1967, with a right arm ending about half way between the elbow and wrist. At the age of four, he was fitted with a hook-type prosthesis, which he despised; after a year his parents agreed to let him live without it. When he developed an interest in sports, his parents (Mike and Kathy Abbott) at first tried to guide him toward soccer, the only sport which doesn't require two hands, but when Jimmy said that he liked baseball and football better, they bought him a baseball glove and hoped for the best.

Abbott learned from an early age to shift the glove on and off his left hand as a part of the natural motion of his delivery. In high school he was a multi-sport superstar. As a senior he hit .427 with seven home runs, pitched four no-hitters with many strikeouts and played the outfield when not pitching. As the quarterback on the Flint [Michigan] Central High Football team, he led the team to the state playoffs. His coach there, Bob Holec, said that "He's a tremendous competitor, but not because of his handicap. Jimmy doesn't think he has a handicap."

A central theme in the Jim Abbott story; from high school to the present, Abbott has insisted that "I don't think people should make so much of it. I was blessed with a good left arm and a not so good right one." Drafted in the thirty-sixth round by Toronto, Abbott passed on a fifty-thousand-dollar bonus offer to attend the University of Michigan. At the time his fastball was clocked in the low- to mid-eighties, enough to make Michigan coach Bud Middaugh think that Abbott could start as a freshman for the Big Ten team.

After going 18–5 in his first two years at Michigan, Abbott was selected for Team USA in the Pan Am Games (1987). It was there that he began to take over the media. He started out as a curiosity, but after going 8–1 with a 1.70 ERA and more than a strikeout per inning against tough international competition, writers began to realize that Abbott was perhaps the best player on the team. After Team USA beat the formidable Cuban team in Havana, Fidel Castro came down from his box to congratulate the team and particularly Abbott. (Asked later what he thought about Castro, Abbott joked that Fidel seemed to have a lot in common with Bo Schembechler.) For his performance he won the 1987 Golden Spikes Award as the outstanding amateur baseball player in the country, and became the first baseball player to win the Sullivan Award as the outstanding amateur *athlete* in the country.

Abbott returned to the University of Michigan for his junior year, where he had a less than spectacular season (8–3), and was confronted with some surprise when the California Angels made him their first-round draft choice, number eight in the country, in 1988. The Angels were looking for a left-handed pitcher, and all of their scouts agreed that Abbott had the best combination of qualities—intelligence, arm, athletic ability, poise—of any left-hander in the country. By this time the radar guns showed him throwing ninety to ninety-four miles an hour. "He's the only guy we ever drafted," said minor league director Bill Bavasi, "that we knew going in what he had inside." Before joining the system, Abbott went to pitch for the Olympic team, where he again performed impressively. "I thought he was a polished pitcher with fair stuff," said Olympic coach Mark Marquess. "He's the hardest thrower on my staff." Slogging through a schedule of day-in, day-out competition and relentless travel, Abbott led the Americans to a gold medal in the Seoul Olympics, including a spectacular defensive play in his championship-clinching performance, which incidentally came on his twenty-first birthday.

Capping this run of success, Abbott went to spring training in 1989 with the California Angels, ticketed for AA ball, but pitched so well that he opened the season in the Angels starting rotation. By season's end he had established a record for major league wins by a pitcher in his first professional season.

The burden of being a special athlete no doubt becomes tiresome for Abbott from time to time. In every city children with handicaps are brought to shake his hand and talk with him a minute. By all accounts, Abbott has played the role assigned to him with grace and dignity, but it is clear that he wants nothing so much as for the handicap to be put under a dim light. He is making remarkable progress in accomplishing that. Watching Abbott pitch, his lack of a hand slips automatically into the background; I find that if I try to focus on the motion of slipping on the glove, I can't do so for more than a few pitches before my attention shifts back to where it ought to be. The longer Abbott is around, the less conscious we become of the difference between him and the other athletes.

Symbolism is by its nature heavy handed. In one of F. Scott Fitzgerald's novels—I think it was *Tender is the Night*—he has a character who says "I am here as a symbol of something. Can you figure out what I am a symbol of?" The temptation to convert Jim Abbott into a symbol of *something* is irresistible, even if we may have difficulty saying exactly what it is. To many people Abbott is a symbol of courage, to others of determination. When Abbott played in Korea, Cuba, and Italy people told him that in their countries a little boy with one hand would never be allowed to play competitively. Jim Abbott the symbol of America, the symbol of the country in which everyone, no matter what his starting point, has the right to take his best shot.

I'm not sure that it takes any more courage to play baseball with one hand than it does with two, and if Jim Abbott is a symbol of America, maybe George Steinbrenner is, too; after all, what other country grants a central role in the sports world to fat, mouthy middle-aged men with lots of money and no respect for sportsmanship? But sports are symbolic by nature, spectator sports I mean. I saw Abbott pitch three times in 1989, and each time seated near me I could see three or four little boys with a hand missing or some very similar condition; you don't see them near the dugouts, but up in the cheap seats, where people wind up who don't come to the ball game very often, there you see them all around you; there must have been two or three hundred in the park each time Abbott pitched, maybe more. This is what sports are about, the forming of symbolic connections; we choose players to root for because they wear our colors, but also because they went to our high school or our college or because we share with them a religion or a hobby or some portion of an experience or simply because we like them. These connections are easily formed and easily broken, and owners and agents and often ballplayers, by stripping sports of their annoying symbolic gingerbread, and sportswriters by cooperating with them, put a mighty effort into destroying them. Serious, thinking sportswriters demystify the athletic world by drawing the human failings of athletes into the foreground, focusing the story on money and therefore greed, eating away at the symbolic hitches that pull us obediently behind the games.

But the connection between Jim Abbott and those boys at the ball games—that can never be broken. It is unfair to make him carry this burden, but the success of Jim Abbott enriches the sports world in a thrilling and irreplaceable way, not only for those boys but for all of us; it is truly a wonderful thing just to see him on the mound. All of us who are less than perfect have to wish the best for Jim Abbott.

Spencer Abbott, winner of 2,180 games as a minor league manager, and once targeted by Wilbert Robinson to be his successor as manager of the Brooklyn Dodgers.

Born in Chicago in 1877, Abbott's astonishing managerial career began in 1903 with Fargo in the Northern League, and ended in the Tri-State League in 1947. His story of how he became a manager:

"I was a pitcher, but my arm petered out and so I went about the country trying to land a job of any sort. Finally I hit Fargo, North Dakota, and that team needed a first baseman. I hit pretty well, and got to be manager of the club. George Tebeau, who owned the Kansas City club, heard something about an Abbott and he supposed it to be some youngster. I had known him earlier and he had concluded I had quit when my arm became useless. Kansas City acquired me by the draft route, Tebeau paying three hundred dollars, a good deal of money in those days. I won't forget the look on his face when I walked into his office.

" 'Why, how are you, Abby, old fellow,' he said. 'I thought you were dead. What are you doing?' " Abbott told Tebeau that he was the new first baseman that Tebeau had just paid three hundred dollars for, and Tebeau hit the roof. Abbott compounded his predicament by making a costly error in his first game with KC, but after a while he had a good game against Topeka, and the Topeka team bought him to be their manager.

Abbott managed in various small leagues in Kansas from 1904 through 1911, managing Topeka, Hutchinson, Wellington, and Lyons, Kansas, in the Missouri Valley League, the Western Association, and the Kansas State League. In his first ten years as a manager he almost always had a losing record. "When I first started out I had a bad failing," he would recall years later. "During games I would lose my temper. I found out how it was to the players at times, and started trying to curb it." Probably another reason he didn't win many in those first years was that he continued to play first base, and generally he didn't hit a lick, although he would steal some bases.

Abbott drifted out of the managerial racket by 1914, returning to it with Tulsa in 1919. He had a good ball club in Tulsa, and the American Association at that time was an exciting league, with many players just a step away from the major leagues. In 1920 the lively ball era came, and a catcher named Yam Yaryan, who had been playing for Wichita for several years without impressive results, hit .357 with 41 home runs. Leading Wichita 8–5 in the ninth inning, Abbott saw Yaryam come to the plate with the bases loaded. "Now I get a flash of genius," Abbott would say. "I tell my pitcher to give Yam an intentional pass. It forces in a run, of course, but we get the next guy out and win, eight to six. Now I'm expecting I'll get a pretty good write-up for my strategy. Know what the headlines said next day? YELLOW ABBOTT WALKS YARYAN! Shows you how one-sided home-town papers are."

After winning the Western Association with Tulsa in 1920, Abbott jumped to Memphis in the Southern Association, where he hit big again, finishing with a 104–49 record. A part of a minor league manager's job in that time was to hype his players to help sell them to the higher leagues, and Abbott was a master at the task. In 1924, managing a rather poor Reading team in the International League, Abbott's top star was a slugging outfielder named Shags Horan. In an exhibition game against the Dodgers, Horan belted a pitch through the window of a schoolhouse beyond the left-field fence. "Does it all the time," Abbott yelled to the Brooklyn writers. "They've got a special monitor in the class room who watches the game from the window and yells, 'Under the desks, kids, Horan is up!' "

Abbott was able to sell Horan and a veteran pitcher (Al Mamaux) to the Yankees and infielder Rhodie Miller to their top competitors at the moment, the Senators. "One of the best deals I ever made," he said. "I got about seventy thousand dollars all told for the three of them in August and had them all back in Reading with me the next spring." Abbott got fired a couple of months into the 1925 season, but then it was on to the next job, Kansas City in 1926.

Though he settled down some after a fiery start, Abbott never became an easy man to play for. Tom Meany wrote that he "probably put verbal blowtorches to even more players than John McGraw." When he was hired by the Kansas City Blues in the spring of '26, a KC writer wrote that "The average fan has the conception that Spencer Abbott is a driver, a despot hard upon his men, a ruler whose scepter is wielded savagely."

"I want a manager who will make the players work," said Blues president George Muehlebach. That summer Kansas City lost a game as the tying run was picked off first base when the batter had a 3–0 count on him. Abbott yelped and leapt off the bench, forgetting that the dugout had a low ceiling; he was knocked cold. "Let the old sonuvabitch lay there," said a veteran when a younger player tried to revive him. "At least we'll be able to dress in peace."

"There have been times when I would have liked to commit murder," Abbott acknowledged. "At that, I believe they should pass a rule permitting a manager to carry a shotgun." Abbott lasted one year in Kansas City and then on to the next job, Jersey City in 1927. He managed in the top minor leagues almost continuously from 1919 through 1943, though he never spent more than three years in any job, and usually only one. When Wilbert Robinson left the Dodgers in 1931 he recommended Abbott as his replacement, but Abbott was only a few years younger than Robinson, and the Dodgers chose Max Carey instead. In 1935 Abbott coached with the Senators, then back to the minors. Managing Williamsport in the early war years, Abbott lost three second basemen in one year to the draft. "I guess they're going to fight this damn war around second base," Spence concluded.

Out of baseball for three years, the sixty-nine-year-old Abbott returned as manager of Charlotte in the Tri-State League in 1946, leading that team to a rout of the pennant race with a 93–46 record and a win in the playoffs. Retiring as a manager after 1947, Abbott was hired as a scout by the Washington Senators, and died in Washington in 1951.

(Abbott's managerial record is outlined in *Minor League Baseball Stars, Volume II,* from SABR. Several stories about Abbott, which may be apocryphal but which are repeated here anyway, are told in *There've Been Some Changes In the World of Sports,* 1962, by Tom Meany. Additional material for this entry taken from 1926 articles in the *Kansas City Star.*)

Robert B. Abel, president of the Western International League in the forties and fifties.

Ferdinand Augustus Abell, a gambling hall owner and professional gambler who was one of the organizers of the team which became the Brooklyn Dodgers.

In the summer of 1882 three gentlemen named Harry Taylor, Charles Byrne, and Joseph Doyle decided that Brooklyn should have professional baseball. They enlisted the aid of Abell because Abell had money, and with his help they built Washington Park. When a member of the group learned that the Camden Merrits, leading the Interstate League, were in danger of folding for lack of attendance, they bought out the Camden team and transferred it to Brooklyn, thus winning the Interstate League in their only season in the league in 1883.

In 1884 the club joined the American Association, and solidified itself by buying several players from the Cleveland team. It still took them several years and several more player purchases to reach the top of the American Association (a major league), but this was accomplished in 1889. In the chaos of that winter the Brooklyn team, by now known as the Bridegrooms, joined the National League (see "The War Between the Leagues"). The Grooms won the National League in 1890 with almost exactly the same team which had won the American Association in 1889. In 1891 the Brooklyn National League and Players' League teams consolidated.

In time Joseph Doyle sold his interest in the club and Charles Byrne died, and Abell became majority stockholder in the club. Abell brought Charles Ebbets, who began as a team secretary and operations manager, into the ownership arrangement and made him club president. In 1898 the Brooklyn and Baltimore teams merged, and Abell wound up owning (at one time) 40 percent of Brooklyn, 40 percent of the Baltimore Orioles and 10 percent of the New York Giants, whose owners he had loaned some money in 1890.

The deal with Baltimore had also brought Ned Hanlon into the ownership arrangement. The team under Hanlon, the Superbas, won the National League in 1899 and 1900, but with somewhat disappointing attendance. The American League in 1901 challenged for "major" status, and another price war began. Abell, long regarded as a generous owner, was by now in his late sixties and growing crotchety. He refused to match the salary offers coming from the American League, lost almost all of his players, and shortly thereafter pulled out of the team's ownership, leaving Hanlon and Ebbets to battle over the remains.

Abell, who once told a reporter that he always checked his wallet and valuables at the hotel desk before he went to a meeting of the National League owners, died at his estate in West Yarmouth, Massachusetts, on November 8, 1913.

(The primary source for this entry is an article by Abe Yager in the 1914 *Reach Guide*. All histories of the Dodgers which I own, and particularly Lee Allen's, are surprisingly weak on material about the original owners.)

Al Aber, American League pitcher of the 1950s.

A native of Cleveland, Aber in 1945 (age eighteen) turned down a $1,500 bonus from the Yankees to sign with his hometown Indians for $225. After going 24–8 in the Tri-State League in 1949, Aber's major league career began with a nifty five-hitter against the Senators on September 15, 1950, but he was drafted into the army a few days later, making a two-year wait before he could try to build on this. Al Rosen once described Aber as a "left-handed Bob Lemon," meaning that every pitch that Aber threw did *something*. Aber didn't develop, and spent most of his career in the bullpen. Ted Williams, in *My Turn at Bat:* "The Tigers brought in a left-hander, Al Aber. He had a sidearm, kind of crossfire delivery, tough for a left-handed hitter."

Ted Abernathy, a major league relief pitcher from 1955 to 1972, whose delivery was so underhanded that he sometimes scraped his knuckles on the pitcher's mound.

Born in North Carolina in 1933, Abernathy in high school was a straight overhand pitcher until he hurt his shoulder, then dropping down to a three-quarters delivery. He entered baseball as a big (six feet four inches, two hundred pounds) hard-throwing right-hander with a conventional delivery coming from ten o'clock. His first minor league season, at Roanoke Rapids in 1952, was terrific: 20 wins, 293 strikeouts and a 1.69 ERA. He was drafted early in the '53 season, and out of the army the Senators brought him straight to the major leagues, where he was beaten senseless throughout the 1955 campaign. Pitching better early in 1956, he blew out his elbow, and missed almost the entire year. In 1957 he finished 2–10 with a 6.78 ERA, and required another arm operation. The doctor told him that he could throw any way he wanted to, but it was going to be two or three years before his arm was strong.

"Now I figured this out," Abernathy told the *Kansas City Star* in 1970. "I was going to have to be a reliever, and a reliever with something unusual going for him is at an advantage. So I went to the submarine pitch. I got it from Dick Hyde, who was with Washington when I was on that club."

It took Abernathy several years in the minors to acquire good control with his new delivery, and once he acquired the control it was several years more before the major leagues' persistent need for pitching outweighed their skepticism about people who do things a little different. The Cleveland Indians finally took a chance on him in '63, and he pitched well for one year, then not so well in '64.

At the end of spring training in 1965, Abernathy was sold to the Chicago Cubs. Bob Kennedy, "head coach" of the Cubs— by 1965 the coaching rotation had almost relapsed into a traditional arrangement—put Abernathy in the game the first day of the season, and Abernathy retired everybody he faced. Impressed, Kennedy began using Abernathy three or four times a week. "He pitched me the way I like to work," Abernathy said. "Not too long any one day. I can go for seven or eight days in a row if I don't have to work over a couple innings at a time." In 1965 Abernathy was a quiet sensation, breaking the major league record for game appearances with 84 (the record moved several times in the sixties), and saving 31 games, which in retrospect is the most up to that time although saves were not an official stat at the time, and at the time no one had any idea what the record would have been. He was named the National League's Fireman of the Year by *The Sporting News*.

The arrival of Durocher in Chicago in 1966 sent Abernathy diving for cover, and the good year was followed by a bad one, but the bad one was followed by a great one: With Cincinnati in 1967 Abernathy led the NL in game appearances, 70, and posted a 1.27 ERA with 28 saves; again he was named the Fireman of the Year. In 1968 he led the National League in game appearances for the third time, with 78, and again posted a good ERA.

Abernathy launched the ball from the lowest point possible, but not with a conventional underhanded delivery like a softball pitcher. He was actually throwing more or less sidearm, but with his upper torso twisted severely to the right, so that his head was almost pointed toward third base, and an arm coming out of the side of his body was pointed at the ground. He threw a fastball, a curve, and a knuckleball as a change of pace. He spun the fastball off of his fingertips, with tremendous forespin; it started at the ground, rose to about the belt, and then began burrowing for the knees. If you hit it, it began burrowing toward shortstop. His curve ball rose; if this is impossible, as physicists claim, at least it *seemed* to rise. In any case it was an unconventional pitch that tended to get him pop-ups and strikeouts, particularly from left-handers. His threw hard, certainly much harder than Quisenberry, Tekulve, or Eichhorn. He was an *athlete,* a powerfully built man using a delivery which demanded flexibility and agility as well as strength.

As he aged, the delivery began to cause him control problems. Beginning in 1969, Abernathy had a series of frustrating seasons in which he posted consistently good ERAs and hit ratios, but could not command the confidence of his managers because of the control problems, and so bounced from team to team. Always a pitcher who thrived on a heavy workload, Abernathy argued that his control would return with more regular work. He joined the Kansas City Royals in mid-summer, 1970. After saving 35 games with excellent ERAs in a year and a half, Abernathy lost his job as the bullpen closer. After posting a 1.71 ERA in 45 games in 1972—even his control record was good—he was released in spring training in 1973, and no one picked him up.

Abernathy, now fifty-seven, resides today in Gastonia, North Carolina, and works for Summey Products.

Woody Abernathy There are two Woody Abernathys in baseball history, the pitcher Virgil Woodrow Abernathy, who pitched for the Giants in 1946 (he pitched all right but for some reason didn't stick), and a minor league slugger named Thomas Woodley Abernathy, who belted 42 homers with a .309 average for Baltimore in 1936. T. W. Abernathy also led the International League in homers in 1934, and was an outstanding hitter from the beginning of his career in 1928 (hitting .358 in the Cotton States League) through 1939, when he hit .332 with 103 RBI in the Southern Association.

Cliff Aberson, an outfielder with the Cubs in the late forties, who also played pro football; he was a running back with the Packers in '46.

Dick Beverage in *The Angels,* his book about the Los Angeles Angels of the Pacific Coast League:

"[Aberson] was not a good fielder and

his arm was merely average, but it was hoped that he would improve in Los Angeles. There didn't seem to be any question about his hitting. He had a good eye at the plate and had immense power." Aberson hit extremely well with Des Moines the first half of 1947, hit well with the Cubs the second half of that year, and had a fantastic season in the Pacific Coast League in 1948 (.329 with 34 homers, 103 RBI in 116 games), but for some reason suddenly stopped hitting in 1949.

Harry Ables, a legendary Texas League and Pacific Coast League pitcher and personality, who also pitched briefly in the major leagues.

Born in Terrell, Texas, in 1884, Ables attended and was a pitching star at Southwestern University in Georgetown, Texas. In the fall of 1904 the Corsciana Oilers of the North Texas League found themselves short of pitching in the middle of a marathon nineteen-game playoff with Fort Worth, and hired Ables to help pitch them through the playoffs.

A huge southpaw who could wrap his fingers completely around a baseball, Ables joined the Dallas team in 1905, and began to compile his remarkable list of freak accomplishments. Working with a young catcher from Ohio named Branch Rickey, he won seventeen games with a 1.93 ERA, with nine of the seventeen wins coming against Fort Worth, the league's best team. On the Fourth of July that year, Ables pitched both ends of a doubleheader against Ft. Worth, pitching two shutouts and allowing a total of only five hits.

His performance earned him a look by the St. Louis Browns late that year. He was unsuccessful with the Browns, and so apparently returned to college; in any case his only known appearance in organized baseball in 1906 was one game for Dallas, which he won. In 1907, joining Dallas in mid-season, he went 12–5 with a 1.77 ERA. In 1908 he pitched briefly for Birmingham in the Southern Association, and then joined the San Antonio Broncos, going 15–6 with a 2.04 ERA, helping the Broncos to their first Texas League pennant.

Wealthy patrons of the San Antonio team, delighted by the championship, treated the San Antonio players to a formal banquet at one of the city's finest whorehouses. Each player was presented with a fine meal, a huge engraved trophy, a hundred-dollar bill, and other rewards not announced to the public.

In 1909 Ables went 19–12 with 259 strikeouts in 293 innings, and earned a more prosaic reward: another shot at the big time. Ables pitched well with the Indians in late 1909, but was not invited to return. Back with San Antonio in 1910, Ables enjoyed or suffered through the most eventful summer of his career:

- On July 5 he pitched 23 innings in a game which ended in a 1–1 tie. Ables allowed a first-inning run, then pitched 22 scoreless innings, striking out 17 men.
- On August 8, he struck out the first 10 batters that he faced.
- He wound up the season with 325 strikeouts, a Texas League record which still stands. (The only other Texas League pitcher to strike out 300 men was Dizzy Dean in 1931.)

Overshadowing these performances, though, was a scandal and league crisis which erupted when Ables reported that a player from the Houston Buffaloes had offered him a bribe to throw a game. A league meeting was held, and although no players were suspended the league threw out the results of seven games, including four Houston wins, which forced the schedules to be packed for the rest of the season, which gave rise, among other things, to

1. an appeal to the National Association, governing body of the minor leagues,
2. a scheduled triple-header of three five-inning games,
3. a forfeit which resulted when one team left the field in the middle of the third game, and
4. a disputed league championship, eventually squared by declaring two teams to be co-champions.

After another look by a major league team early in 1911, Ables joined Oakland in the PCL in time to go 22–11 with 218 strikeouts. The next year, 1912, he led the PCL with 25 wins and 303 strikeouts, but the 363-inning workload apparently caught up with him, as Ables was never effective after that season. After three losing seasons, he called it quits.

In 1925 Ables, now forty years old, purchased a controlling interest in the San Antonio team. As a gate attraction, the old star pitched one game for San Antonio in 1925 and another in 1926. In his two years as president he built the San Antonio team into a contender, but the minor league system at that time was in a painful transition from entertainment to training ground, and Ables sold his stock and moved on to other pursuits. He died in San Antonio on February 8, 1951.

(Information for this article derived from *The Texas League,* by Bill O'Neal, and Volume II of *Minor League Baseball Stars,* by the Society for American Baseball Research, as well as from contemporary guides.)

Shawn Abner, the first player taken in the 1984 draft after hitting .580 as a senior in Mechanicsburg, Pennsylvania, but still attempting to establish himself as a major league outfielder.

Seth Abraham, at one time a special assistant to Bowie Kuhn.

Al Abrams, a Pittsburgh sportswriter from 1926 to the 1960s, and founder of the "Dapper Dan" club.

The Dapper Dan club began almost as a gag in 1936 when Abrams, a sports columnist with the Pittsburgh *Post-Gazette,* printed the names of various gentlemen that he knew around Pittsburgh, calling them "Dapper Dans." One of the Dapper Dans suggested that they get together for a banquet, and they did; they sent out 500 invitations, and 457 people showed up to start the organization, which was chartered as a philanthropic organization in 1939, and remains an active one today. They put on a banquet, give awards, run golf matches and bowling tournaments for charity.

Abrams became sports editor of the *Post-Gazette* in 1947, and was perennial president of the Dapper Dans. He typifies a generation of sports editors who filled a unique role in their cities—part civic leader, part fan, part organizer, well-liked or even beloved, drawing on his connections not only to keep abreast of what was happening but also to promote sports in his city. Branch Rickey came to Pittsburgh in the mid-fifties. Unlike the New York sportswriters, who regarded Rickey with suspicion but generally promoted the idea that he was a genius, Abrams was harshly critical of Rickey as an executive, but liked him as a person and had a good relationship with him.

Cal Abrams, outfielder with five major league teams between 1949 and 1956.

Abrams was born in 1924 in Philadelphia, the son of a Russian immigrant father who was in the trucking business. His family moved to Brooklyn, where Cal attended James Madison High School and signed with the Dodgers upon graduation. Three weeks after reporting to the Pony League, however, Abrams was drafted; he would be out of baseball for almost four full years, serving in Greenland and the South Pacific.

Resuming his career in the Three-I League in 1946, Abrams had five straight outstanding minor league seasons, hitting .331 to .345 each year. He had a cup of coffee with the Dodgers in 1949, and joined the team as a pinch hitter and spare outfielder in mid-season, 1950. In the bottom of the ninth inning on the last day of the 1950 season, Abrams was involved in the most famous play of the season. As described by Red Smith:

"The Dodgers put their first two batsmen on base and Duke Snider lashed what had to be the deciding hit into center field. Richie Ashburn fielded the ball on one hop, threw swiftly and superbly to the plate, and Cal Abrams, coming home with the winning run, was out by twelve fat feet."

This play, which is described in at least fifty books, *was* the pennant in 1950; if Abrams had been safe the Dodgers and the Phillies would have wound up in a tie. Ashburn, who had a bad-arm reputation, apparently made a hell of a throw, and no one blames Abrams for attempting to score or for failing to score, although he has been criticized for failing to slide.

In any case Abrams, despite playing extremely well in 1951, could not break into the Dodger outfield of Pafko, Furillo, and Snider, and in early 1952 he was traded to Cincinnati, then to Pittsburgh, where he had his best year in 1953. Cincinnati made him part of a package for Gus Bell, one of the trades on which Gabe Paul built his reputation in the early fifties.

Abrams, who drew cartoons as a hobby, was never really able to break through as a regular, but he was the kind of player that I, as an analyst of the game, was always very fond of; had I been a general manager in the early fifties, I would have wanted him on my team. He hit for a decent average, had some power, ran above average, and had an above average arm. And he drew a tremendous number of walks. In his last major league season, 1955, he hit just .243, but had an on-base percentage well over .400 because of the walks. Had he not missed the four critical years in his youth, he would certainly have developed into an exceptional player. He didn't, and he left baseball in 1956 after a year at Miami.

(Additional information about Abrams can be found in the *Jewish Baseball Hall of Fame,* by Erwin Lynn.)

Jesse Abramson, longtime sportswriter for the *New York Herald-Tribune,* best known for his writing about track.

Eufemio Abreau, catcher with the Cuban Stars, 1920–30.

Bill Abstein, first baseman for the World Champion Pittsburgh Pirates of 1909. In the first *Fireside Book of Baseball,* Honus Wagner recalled that during the rough-and-tumble of the 1909 World Series a "Tiger runner hit Bill Abstein, our first baseman, in the stomach with his fist. Abstein folded up and Ham Hyatt had to take his place." Although this event never actually occurred as told here (Abstein played every inning of the 1909 World Series at first base), some similar event may have happened during the course of the season.

Ralph Acampora, vice-president and general manager of the Albany-Colonie Yankees.

Felipe Acevedo, a scout for the New York Yankees.

Hector Acevedo, a scout for the Cleveland Indians.

Jim Acker, a relief pitcher now with the Toronto Blue Jays.

Acker, who has ping-ponged between Atlanta and Toronto since 1980, is a Texas native and was a part of the awesome UT baseball program from 1977–80, becoming a first round draft pick in 1980.

Acker's number one pitch has always been a hard sinker or sinking fastball, which he throws 90–92 miles an hour. After some arm problems, he was allowed to pass off the Atlanta roster just one year ago, but came back in 1989 to have his best major league season, pitching 73 games with a 2.43 ERA. His best years may still be ahead of him.

Acker's brother, Bill Acker, played professional football for five years.

Tom Acker, a big relief pitcher nicknamed "Shoulders."

Acker, a New Jersey native, entered pro baseball in 1948, and pitched unimpressively in the minor leagues until 1955, when he gained some measure of control. Always a starter in the minors, he pitched well in relief for the Reds in 1956 and 1957, but never moved into a key role.

Carl Ackerman, a scout with the California Angels from their start-up until the early seventies, and later with the Chicago White Sox.

Cy Acosta, American League pitcher in the early seventies.

A native of El Sabino, Mexico, Acosta began his career in the Mexico Central League in 1966, and led the league in losses his first two seasons (6–15, 6–13). Acosta fought his temper as well as his control for several seasons (he was suspended twice by the Mexican League) before turning the corner. Acosta pitched brilliantly with the White Sox in 1972 and 1973, but lost his career to arm trouble in 1974.

Eduardo Acosta, a Panamian pitcher with the San Diego Padres in the early seventies.

Acosta was a starter all the way through the minor leagues, and pitched his way to the majors with a 2.72 ERA in 172 innings in the International League in 1971. Traded to the Padres on August 16, 1971, he pitched a shutout in his first major league start on August 24; he wound up the '71 campaign with a 2.74 ERA and only seven walks in 46 innings.

In the spring of '72 the Padres decided to switch Acosta to the bullpen. He was ineffective in 1972, and released after the season. Despite pitching well in the PCL in 1973, Acosta never got another shot at a major league job.

Jose Acosta, brother of Merito Acosta. A 134-pound right-hander, Acosta struggled to ten wins with the Senators in the early twenties.

Acosta is listed in all encyclopedias as still living, although if alive he would now be ninety-nine years old, causing one to suspect that biographers have lost track of him in Castro's Cuba.

Balmadero "Merito" Acosta, a Cuban outfielder who was among the first players signed by Clark Griffith after he came to Washington in 1912.

The signing of Acosta, who was as dark as Ozzie Smith or Amos Otis, rekindled hopes that the coming of Cuban players might mean a grinding away of the color barrier (see Rafael Almeida).

Teolinda Acosta, a player who, like many others, missed his generation. In 1961 Acosta, an outfielder in the Cincinnati Reds system, led the Sally League in hitting (.343) and also stole 40 bases with an excellent strikeout to walk ratio. In 1961 the major leagues weren't looking for outfielders who could hit singles and run. Acosta got thirteen games in the PCL in 1962, and then went back to Sally League.

Acosta, who never played major league baseball, had 2,724 hits in the minor leagues, with a lifetime .328 average. About half of his hits were in the Mexican League (1968–76), about half in the American minors. He won five minor league batting titles, hitting .369 in the Pioneer League, .343 in the Sally League, and .354, .392, and .366 in the Mexican League.

Bill Acree, traveling secretary of the Atlanta Braves.

Edward J. Acton, owner/operator of the Peninsula Pilots, the South Bend White Sox, and the Welland Pirates.

Roy Acuff, announcer for the San Antonio Missions.

Bill Adair (actually Marion Adair), one-time minor league second baseman and manager, now a scout for the Philadelphia Phillies.

Adair's playing career, which involved not a game in the major leagues, began in 1935 and lasted until 1956, and included some outstanding offensive seasons for a middle infielder—.329 with 113 RBI with Montgomery in 1940, .356 with 120 RBI in 101 games with Owensboro in 1949, 29 homers for El Dorado in 1953. His managerial career lasted even longer; it began in 1949 and lasted until 1973, and included seven first-place finishes and a nine-game stint as interim manager of the White Sox in 1970, before Chuck Tanner arrived. He also coached at the major league level with the Braves, White Sox, and Expos.

Adair was Henry Aaron's first minor league manager. Aaron wrote twenty years later that "a guy couldn't have asked to break in under a better manager than Bill Adair. He was from Montgomery, Alabama, and I think that because he was a southerner he was even a little more understanding of the little black kid he had playing beside him. He was a lot more than a manager to me." Actually, Adair was born in Mobile, like Henry.

James Aubrey "Choppie" Adair, a long-term minor league infielder who played eighteen games for the Cubs in 1931.

Employed in baseball all of his adult life, Adair coached with the White Sox in 1951–52, and later scouted for Baltimore, Oakland, the Kansas City A's, and Royals.

Jerry Adair, American League infielder from 1958 through 1970.

Adair, a native of Sand Springs, Oklahoma, went to Oklahoma State University at Stillwater on a basketball scholarship, play-

ing for the legendary Henry Iba. He was a starting guard for the Cowboys as a sophomore and junior, their second-leading scorer each year.

Before his senior year he signed a forty-thousand-dollar-bonus contract with the Baltimore Orioles, and began his professional career with eleven games at the major league level in 1958. Although Adair did require a minor league apprenticeship, he made it a brief one—one year in the Texas League, one year at Miami. In 1960, when Adair was the outstanding shortstop in the International League, the Orioles regular shortstop was Ron Hansen, who was a year younger than Adair and the American League's Rookie of the Year. Adair earned a place on the Baltimore roster in 1961 although there really wasn't a job waiting for him, and got a chance to play when both Hansen and second baseman Marv Breeding had disappointing years with the bat.

Like many middle infielders, Adair hit well his first two seasons in the majors, but failed to develop as a hitter due to interrupted playing time from injuries. He was, however, an outstanding defensive player either at shortstop or at second base, where he set a number of defensive records:

- Fewest errors in a full season at second (5),
- Consecutive errorless games at second base (89),
- Highest fielding percentage at second (.994),
- Consecutive errorless chances at second (458).

Adair's manager in his first years was Billy Hitchcock, and the two had a number of run-ins; as I understand it, Adair bitched whenever his name was not in the lineup. He was a hard-nosed, hustling, aggressive player. In a doubleheader in 1964 he was hit in the mouth by a bad throw in the first game; the injury required eleven stitches, but Adair got it sewed up, went back to the park, and played the second game. All of it. With Adair at second, Brooks Robinson at third, and Luis Aparicio in between, the Orioles developed the league's best defense, and became perennial contenders.

In the spring of 1966 Adair was moved out of his regular job by a kid named Dave Johnson, now the Mets manager. He was furious; in his opinion this simply wasn't the way things were done in baseball. "I lost my job in spring training," he said, sounding shocked a year later. "I was their regular second baseman and, if you're an established regular like I was, you don't lose a job in spring training." He was quickly at odds with another manager, Hank Bauer, and began to travel around the league.

On June 3, 1967, Adair joined a miracle in progress. For four months Adair was a regular without a position for the 1967 Red Sox, and he was one of the most valuable men on the team, hitting .291 in 89 games while splitting time almost evenly among second, short, and third. On August 20 the Red Sox got behind California 8–0; Adair hit a run-scoring single and a home run to cap a comeback and deliver a 9–8 win. The game came one day after Conigliaro's beaning, and Adair's home run in the opinion of many was the Sox' biggest hit of the year, the hit that made them believe they could win. Adair finished fifteenth in the voting for the American League's MVP Award.

Taken by Kansas City in the 1969 expansion draft, Adair gave the Royals a solid second baseman in their first year. In the spring of 1970, however, Adair's life was jolted by the discovery that his young daughter was suffering from terminal cancer. Absent from the team during much of spring training, Adair was pulled off a team flight in late April and informed that he had been released. Predictably, and justifiably to some extent, Adair ripped the Royals for their insensitivity as well as for not allowing him a chance to play his way back into shape. The little girl died a few weeks later.

Not knowing exactly what else to do, Adair played a year in the minor leagues to get back in shape, then spent a season with the Hankyu Braves in Japan. In 1972 Dick Williams, who had had Adair as a player in Boston, hired him as a coach with the Oakland A's. He was a coach for all three World Championship teams, then left to follow Dick Williams to Anaheim.

Cancer, however, was not through with him. In the late seventies Adair's wife, Kaye, began a battle against the disease, a battle which, though ultimately successful, consumed several years of their life, and then it was Jerry's own turn. On May 31, 1986, in a hospital in Tulsa, Oklahoma, Jerry Adair died of cancer of the liver. He was forty-nine years old.

Robert Adair, Houston railroad executive who was the first president of the Texas League (1888).

John Adam, trainer for the Milwaukee Brewers, and the only former player among current trainers.

A pitcher, Adam was drafted out of high school in 1972 by the Baltimore Orioles, and pitched briefly in the Orioles and Angels chains. An injury brought him into the office of Dr. Frank Jobe. "I was overwhelmed by his knowledge of the human body," Adam told Mike Bryan in *Baseball Lives.* "It sparked an interest." Forced out of baseball by the injury, Adam earned a degree from Cal State at Domingus Hills, and after passing his California boards as a trainer began working his way up the Milwaukee system. He has been the Brewers head trainer since 1984.

Randy Adamack, director of communications for the Seattle Mariners.

Erwin Adamcewicz, an outfielder in the Cardinals system who died of wounds received while fighting in Korea, 1952.

Jeannie Adamo, accounting manager for the San Francisco Giants.

Ace Adams, relief pitcher with the New York Giants from 1941 to 1946, and once the holder of numerous records for relief pitchers.

Ace, to begin with, was not a baseball nickname; that was his real name, Ace Townsend Adams. He goes on a team with Fielder Jones. Ace began his professional career in the Evangeline League (Louisiana) in 1934, and pitched in various leagues throughout the South for several years, originally as a starter; he won twenty-six games in the Georgia-Florida League in 1937. Up to Nashville in 1939, Adams was hammered as a starter early in the year, and moved to the bullpen by owner-manager Larry Gilbert just to give him some work. He pitched much better in relief than he had as a starter, and in 1941 Bill Terry brought him to the Giants as a mop-up man.

With the coming of World War II, there was of course a shortage of quality pitching, and managers began to experiment with the use of more relievers. In the years 1942–45 Adams, Gordon Maltzberger, Joe Berry, Mace Brown, and Joe Heving were among the first pitchers to have outstanding seasons as relief pitchers. In 1942 Adams set a major league record by pitching sixty-one times in relief, posting a 1.84 ERA. In 1943 he pitched seventy times, sixty-seven times in relief; he broke records for games finished and innings pitched in relief. In 1944 he pitched in sixty-five games, again leading the National League. Though the other pitchers

named also had fine seasons, Adams was the outstanding reliever of the era.

What I should know, but don't, is why Adams was 4-F, why he couldn't be drafted. In any case, in late 1945 the "real" major leaguers, who had been off fighting the war, came back, and Adams's effectiveness slipped suddenly. In the spring of 1946, representatives of the new Mexican League approached many of the top players in the major leagues, starting with the New York Giants, flashing a roll of hundred-dollar bills and offering big money to play in Mexico. Adams was among the players who accepted their offer; on the morning of April 26, 1946, Adams and Harry Feldman, a starter, cleaned out their lockers and left the Polo Grounds. "I understand," Mel Ott told the press, "that they were flashing a roll of bills totaling about fifteen thousand dollars. Well, I'm missing nothing."

The Mexican League adventure turned out badly for most of those involved; the big money ran out, and the players who had jumped contracts were banned from organized baseball for four years. The careers of Sal Maglie, Danny Gardella, Mickey Owen, and others were severely damaged or ended by their decision.

Adams, on the other hand, probably did all right on the deal. Facing stiff competition for jobs from the returning soldiers, Adams had an ERA of 16.88 through three outings. He was thirty-four years old, and his "stuff" was never all that good. Adams career was over, but the money he took from the Mexicans was probably more than he was going to make if he'd stayed in New York.

Emery "Ace" Adams, pitcher with the Baltimore Elite Giants and other Negro League teams, 1932–45.

Bill Adams, director of ticket sales and operations for the San Diego Padres.

Babe Adams, hero of the 1909 World Series, winner of almost two hundred games in the major leagues, and one of the greatest control pitchers in the history of baseball.

Charles Benjamin Adams was born on a farm in Tipton County, Indiana, on May 18, 1882. In 1896 the Adams family, which was very poor, moved to St. Louis, and apparently some three or four years after that, as Adams was almost grown but not quite, he left his family to live with a farmer named Lee Sarver in Mount Moriah, Missouri. Putting in long days walking behind a plow, Adams grew to be a strong six-footer, and when a local barber named Fred Coffman was organizing a baseball team he asked Adams to give it a try. Adams had pitched in high school and could throw harder than anybody else there, and so wound up as the pitcher.

Early in 1903, Adams was beaten badly by a team from a neighboring town. After the game a shortstop on the opposition team showed him how to hold a baseball to make it curve. Adams was fascinated with the idea, and spent a good part of the summer throwing curve balls against a barn; within a year he was unbeatable in local competition.

In the fall of 1904 the old Missouri Valley League changed its name to the Western Association, and concentrated on moving into larger cities; this created an opening for a new league, and a new league formed using the old name, Missouri Valley League. The league hired a Missourian named Ham Hamilton, who was an umpire in the Pacific Coast League, to scout players for the new teams, and Hamilton recommended Adams to play for the Parsons team, which was called the Parsons Preachers. (A paper from a rival town, picking up on the fact that an asylum was located in Parsons, preferred to refer to them as the Parsons Asylumites.)

On May 11, 1905, Adams pitched his first game as a professional player, which was also the first game played in the new Missouri Valley League. He inaugurated the league and his career in style, pitching a one-hit shutout, the one hit being a seventh-inning single. The entry on Adams in the *Biographical Dictionary of American Sports* says that Adams won 30 games for the Preachers that summer, but the league printed no statistics, and my review of the box scores for the league shows that Adams probably won not many more than 15; the team, after all, played only 101 games. However many he won, he made an impression, and at season's end was purchased by the St. Louis Cardinals.

After starting one game for the Cardinals early in 1906, Adams was sold back to the minor leagues, to Denver of the Western League. (*The Sporting News "Daguerreotypes"* shows Adams as pitching for Parsons in the Missouri Valley League in 1905 *and* 1906; however, there was no Missouri Valley League in 1906.) After an unimpressive 1906 season with Denver, Adams apparently pitched better in 1907 (that league didn't figure pitching stats for 1907, either) and was purchased by the Pittsburgh Pirates late in the year.

TRACERS

On August 24 [1921] Pittsburgh arrived in New York for a five-game series ... the Giants were losing, 3 to 0, in the seventh inning of the opening game. Babe Adams was pitching serenely for Pittsburgh, until the Giants suddenly filled the bases with Kelly batting. The count rose to three balls and no strikes.

"I almost don't bother to look," Stengel said, "because I know McGraw will flash the sign to take the next pitch. But I nearly fell off the bench. McGraw is giving him the sign to hit, and Kelly hits a grand-slam home run.

—Joseph Durso
The Days of Mr. McGraw

This story also appears in a slightly different form in Noel Hynd's *The Giants of the Polo Grounds;* Hynd tells that it happened with "a man on base" and "the game still close," but describes it as "one of those plays upon which a season can turn." It's a Casey Stengel story, remembered by the authors from the way Casey had told them from the way he remembered it from thirty years earlier, and since the two diverged on details, we got to wondering what the original facts were.

Babe Adams came into the game with a winning streak of nine straight games, and several essential facts are correct in both versions of the story:

- The Pirates were seven and a half games ahead on August 24, 1921,
- They did go to New York for five games,
- Babe Adams did pitch the first game,
- George Kelly did hit a home run off of him, and
- The Giants did go on to sweep the doubleheader and the series, sparking their drive to the pennant.

The New York Times reported the next day that "George Kelly bobbed up to bat. That was what he was there for—to bat, and he did it with some fervor and abandon. He put the old K.O. on the unfortunate globule and it went through the ropes into the far stretches of the crowd in the left field bleachers."

In fact, though, the bases were not loaded at the moment when Mr. Kelly put the old K.O. on the unfortunate globule, nor was it even a two-run shot; the bases were empty. The home run changed the score of the game from 3–2 to 4–2, and it wound up 10 to 2. The *Times* summary reported the next day that "George Kelly got his 22nd home run of the season in the first game, but George wasn't the whaling hero of the pastime. That honor fell to Emil Meusel."

No story of the game mentions that the count was 3–0 when the home run was hit, but since this was why Casey remembered the incident at all, it's a good bet that that detail is accurately recalled. The home run had some importance, but did the season swing on it? Hardly. Casey's memory illustrates again the point I made with regard to Merle Harmon's recall of Henry Aaron's lost home run: that the memory enlarges that which it saves.

In 1908 the Pirates farmed Adams out to Louisville, where he won 22 games and a nickname. Adams nickname—Babe—was given him by female fans at Louisville, who screamed "Oh, you babe!" when he pitched. Tom Shea, who wrote a pamphlet in the 1940's on baseball nicknames, wrote that yelling "Oh, you babe" was a 1908 equivalent of "hubba hubba," leaving us to wonder what the 1990 equivalent might be; in any case, the origin of Adams's nickname is a matter of some interest, in part because Adams was the only important "Babe" in baseball before George Ruth. Bob Creamer, in *Babe*, listed among the background elements for the nickname that "The Pittsburgh Pirates' baby-faced righthander, Babe Adams, was then in his sixth season in the major leagues."

Creamer in describing Adams as "baby-faced" was probably following Fred Lieb, who in his history of the Pirates wrote that Adams was given the nickname because of his youthful looks in comparison with the other Pirate pitchers. Adams *did* look younger than his age, more markedly so as he got older than when his career began—but I would never describe him as baby-faced. He was an exceptionally handsome man; one might say that he had a James Bond-type face, except that with his deep-set, piercing eyes thrown into a permanent shadow beneath heavy brows, he looked just a bit too menacing to play Bond; anyway, Dr. James Skipper, leading authority on baseball nicknames, says that the "Oh, you babe" story is the most credible explanation for the nickname, and I agree. Adams's brilliant pitching at Louisville—he walked only 40 men in 312 innings—earned him an invitation to spring training with the Pirates.

"The first time I went to training with the Pirates, we were at Hot Springs, Arkansas," Adams recalled years later. "We would take hot baths in the morning and in the afternoon we would hike about eight miles over those Ozark hills and trot a lot of the way." The Pirates in 1909 had about as little need for another pitcher as any team will ever have. With a staff headed by Howie Camnitz (25–6), Vic Willis (22–11), and Lefty Leifield (19–8) as well as Nick Maddox (23–8 in 1908, still effective in 1909 although with fewer wins), Pirate veterans Sam Leever and Deacon Phillippe had been forced into minor roles even though both were still extremely effective.

Somehow, Adams made the team, and on

Charles "Babe" Adams

May 4, 1909, earned his first important victory—an eleven-inning, 1–0 shutout over the defending champion Chicago Cubs, winners of three straight pennants; the Pirates moved into first place the next day. Combining formidable pitching with an excellent offense and a tight defense, the Pirates of 1909 won 110 games, the same number as the 1927 Yankees, and never surrendered the lead which they took on May 5. The 1909 Pirates had separate winning streaks of 14 and 16 games, the 16-game streak beginning September 9, and beat the three weakest teams in the league 56 out of 64 games. Adams got only 12 starts and 13 relief appearances during the season, but pitched brilliantly, winning 12 of 15 decisions with an ERA just over one—in fact, his 1.11 ERA is the best ever by a rookie, although ERA was not an official stat until 1912 and the term "rookie" didn't become common until the late thirties.

The whoopla surrounding the 1909 World Series before it was played centered around the matchup between the two best players in baseball, Honus Wagner of the Pirates and Ty Cobb of the Tigers. The people who were "doping out" the World Series for the newspapers paid no attention to Adams; no one even thought he would pitch. Several things combined to fool them. First, there was Adams's pitching, which strengthened his role on the team as the season progressed. On August 28 he shut out Brooklyn, 3–0. On September 6 he struck out six straight batters, tying a record at the time; this was done against the New York Giants, one of the best teams in the league. On September 21 he started against Boston and pitched a three-hit shutout. On September 27 he started against the Giants, and delivered another three-hitter, although he gave up a run.

While Adams was brilliant, Leifield and Willis struggled some in the closing weeks of the season. Then, just before the World Series, Howie Camnitz, the ace of the staff, came down with "a severe attack of quinsy" (probably tonsilitis), and was unable to pitch. Even so, Adams was not thought to be high on the list of candidates to replace him.

In the middle of the 1909 season, National League President Harry Pulliam had committed suicide. He had been replaced by John Heydler, who is sort of a hero of mine, one of my favorite people in baseball history. Heydler had a business in Washington which he had to tend to until he could get it sold,

and while in Washington in September he saw a game in which Dolly Gray, a mediocre pitcher for the Senators, had stopped the great Cobb and hog-tied the Tiger team. Heydler thought that Gray's pitching form was extremely similar to that of Babe Adams, except of course that Adams threw harder and had a sharper curve and better control. Fred Clarke knew Adams to be a solid, unshakable young man, and thought that he would handle the World Series pressure well. When Heydler, whom he respected, weighed in with his support for Adams from a different perspective, Clarke decided to start Babe Adams in the first game of the World Series.

Well, as they say, the rest is history. Within a few weeks, Babe Adams's name "immediately became a household word throughout the nation" (Fred Lieb). Adams allowed a run to the Tigers in the first inning of Game One, but settled down to pitch a six-hitter, beating the Tigers 4–1. Camnitz tried to start the second game but was shelled, Maddox staggered to an 8–6 win in the third game, and Leifield was hammered in the fourth. Adams came back in Game Five with another six-hitter, striking out eight men and walking only one. The score of that game was 8–4, but two of the runs were cheap home runs over a temporary fence put in for the World Series, and another run scored on an error. When Vic Willis pitched poorly and lost the sixth game, Clarke decided that Adams on short rest (two days off) was still the best thing he had going. Adams pitched another six hitter, this one a shutout—and the twenty-seven-year-old rookie was a national hero.

His strategy for pitching to Ty Cobb was never to throw him a fastball, to mix up off-speed pitches with off-off-speed pitches, frustrating Cobb by refusing to challenge him. It worked; Cobb was one for eleven against him in the series—and never got a chance to redeem himself, playing nineteen more seasons in the major leagues. In the book *My Greatest Day in Baseball*, published several times in the forties and fifties based on a long-running series of magazine articles, only one game was chosen twice, the game of October 16, 1909—chosen by both Babe Adams and Honus Wagner as the most memorable of their careers.

Adams had been married on March 2, 1909, to a Mount Moriah girl named Blanch Wright, but had not yet had a chance to set up housekeeping; he still resided with Lee

Sarver on the farm near Mount Moriah. Several friends from the Mount Moriah area traveled to Pittsburgh and Detroit for the series, and the Sarver household kept up with the World Series by exchanging constant telegrams with these friends. Fans from all over central Missouri converged on the Sarver house for news of the series. "Come out and see me," said a telegram after the seventh game. "I'll pay all expenses and show you the best time of your life." Christy Mathewson had pitched better in 1905, but Adams, the surprise hero, may have been the biggest sensation in the young history of the World Series.

"As the last man went out," Adams told Herbert McDougal years later, "we raced for hacks that were to take us down to our hotels, where we dressed. The crowd was rushing, too, and here came my friends from Missouri pushing roses at me. There was a pin in the handle of the bouquet and it ran into the back of my hand, deep. I guess I was thinking more about that than the game as the hack started downtown. I was wondering if it was going to keep me from the barnstorming tour we were going to make." Before heading back to Missouri, Adams went by Pittsburgh to get his belongings and take part in the victory parade. When he reached his home there was a crowd of about a thousand people milling around in his yard and in the street in front of his house; a reporter wrote that, by actual count, 463 of the thousand were women who had come there hoping to give him a kiss. Adams snuck in the back door. His winner's share of the World Series: $1,825. It was more than he had made during the season—but less than he would make barnstorming after his series triumph.

Adams settled in after that to several years of what might be called ordinary excellence; he won 18 games in 1910, 22 in 1911, 21 in 1913. He had five quality seasons behind him and was pitching well early in 1914 when, on May 17, 1914, Adams hooked up in a historic pitchers' duel with Rube Marquard of the Giants. The two teams were battling for the league lead; the Pirates were in first place, the Giants in second. The game was tied 1–1 after three innings, and it was still 1–1 after nine, after ten, twelve innings, after fifteen, after seventeen, after nineteen, twenty. When they moved to the twenty-first inning it became the longest game in the thirty-eight-year history of the National League—with Marquard and Adams both still on the mound, and the score still knotted at one. With two out in the top of the twenty-first, Adams gave up a two-out single to Bob Bescher, who then stole second. Laughing Larry Doyle hit a drive to center field. The center fielder dived for the ball and missed it—Adams always insisted that it should have been caught—and Doyle circled the bases, being credited with a home run. The game ended 3–1 in twenty-one innings; Adams had walked not a single batter in twenty-one innings, a record which we can safely assume will never be broken.

Perhaps I am wrong to say this, but in retrospect it was foolhardy of the Hall of Fame managers, McGraw and Clarke, to allow Adams and Marquard, their best pitchers, to pitch twenty-one innings in a game. Marquard, coming off seasons of 24–7, 26–11, and 23–10, *lost* twenty-two games in 1914—in fact, Marquard's ineffectiveness is what opened the door for the Miracle Braves of 1914; had Marquard remained sharp, the Giants probably would have retained their title. He remained ineffective in 1915. Adams's career took an even more serious turn for the worse; he dropped to 13–16 in 1914, as the Pirates season came apart. The Pirates, who had had a winning ball club since 1899 and were several games ahead of the pack early in the 1914 race, dropped out of first place on May 30, two weeks after the long game, and then fell apart; they finished seventh. Adams pitched .500 ball in 1915 but in 1916 was driven out of the league, posting a 2–9 record with an unsightly ERA. On August 3, 1916, Babe Adams was released by the Pirates to St. Joseph (Missouri) of the Western League. He refused to report—his career apparently over at the age of thirty-four.

Over the winter, however, his arm began to feel better, and he decided to give it a try, to go to St. Joseph and try to work his way back. Pitching for St. Joe and later Hutchinson (Kansas) in the Western League, Adams was way too good for the league, winning 20 games with a 1.75 ERA. This, however, was a low minor league, and minor leaguers who could dominate poor leagues were plentiful in 1917; Adams was sold to Kansas City in the American Association in 1918, a better league, but he remained a forgotten man. Adams pitched even more effectively for Kansas City, (14–3, 1.67 ERA), and fate intervened on his behalf. With the war in Europe, suddenly the major leagues were short of bodies; a veteran pitcher past draft age (see Ainsmith) who could win big in the minors suddenly looked awfully good. In August, 1918, two years after his release, Adams returned to the Pittsburgh Pirates.

Ballplayers in that time did not last as long as they do now. In the war year (1918) there were several older players who made it back to the major leagues for an extra cup of coffee, but other than Adams, they didn't stick after the war. Adams in 1919, age thirty-seven, was almost the oldest player in the league—and was one of the league's best pitchers. In 1919 he won 17 games, threw seven shutouts and posted a 1.98 ERA, fifth in the league. In 1920 he won 17 games, led the league with eight shutouts and posted a 2.16 ERA, second in the league behind Pete Alexander. Always blessed with good control, by this time he had phenomenal control, pitching 263 innings each year with only 23 walks in 1919 and 18 in 1920.

Again, as he had ten years earlier, Adams became a phenomenon. Fred Lieb wrote in 1920 that "there is no more remarkable player in baseball today than Babe Adams." In 1921 Adams, now the oldest player in the league, was perhaps the most effective pitcher in the league. His 14–5 won-lost record tied for the league's best winning percentage, and his 2.64 ERA missed leading the league by five hundredths of a run. That season, however, ended in terrible disappointment for the Pirates, to which Adams contributed. The Pirates, in command of the pennant race since April, held a seven-and-a-half-game lead on August 24, when they went to New York for a five-game series against the Giants. Adams pitched the first game of the series and was hit hard (see Tracers), triggering a five-game sweep for the Giants, who then pushed the Pirates aside in September.

We can assume that Pittsburgh wasn't a happy place to be that fall, and Adams announced after the season that he wanted to leave the Pirates. He had received an offer from the Los Angeles club of the Pacific Coast League, and he thought that the warm Los Angeles weather would be good for an old man's bones. It may have been a negotiating position; anyway, Barney Dreyfuss convinced him that the Pirates could win the pennant in 1922, and Adams returned to the fold. The Pirates started slowly and didn't win, and Adams, though pitching well, had a tough-luck season and a losing record for the first time since 1916. Again that winter he talked about retiring; this time he said he would like to play for an independent team at Kenosha, Wisconsin. He said they had offered him as much money as he was making with the Pirates, and he'd only have to pitch once a week and wouldn't have to go traveling all over the country.

Again, he returned to the fold in 1923; by now he was the oldest player in all of baseball. Again he pitched well, winning thirteen games and losing seven. Sunday, June 30, 1923 was Babe Adams day at Forbes Field; he was presented with presents and showered with tributes and affection. "I cannot explain my lasting much longer than many other pitchers on any other theory than this," he told a reporter. "I always take things easy, and I never worry. I discovered many years ago that when I exerted myself I was not so effective, for the mere effort of trying to be uncommonly good distracted my mind from the simple task of pitching." He also took the occasion to correct his age; for many years his year of birth had been incorrectly reported as 1883, when it was actually 1882. "I am forty-one years old, and rather proud of it," he explained.

Again the Pirates finished third in 1923, and again Adams returned for 1924. He pitched well in 1924—1.13 ERA in forty innings—but missed most of the year with a sore arm. Again the Pirates finished third, and again Adams returned for 1925.

By now this finishing third every year was getting tiresome, and the Pirates' front office was edgy. In early season, 1925, Fred Clarke was named vice-president of the Pirates, put on a uniform and took his seat on the bench. Clarke, the Pirates' old manager, was a minority stockholder in the team. It was a rather odd arrangement. He wasn't a coach, he was an executive, a front office man—but there he was on the bench, sharing his advice with Bill McKechnie, looking over McKechnie's shoulder and taking whatever he learned back to the front office. The arrangement seemed to work. The Pirates won the World Championship in 1925.

I pass over this World Championship rather lightly, as Adams had no major role in it (see Vic Aldridge.) He pitched one scoreless inning in the World Series. It would have been a wonderful way to end his career, with that inning in the World Series, but unfortunately the participants didn't have the sense to let it end there; Adams wanted to come back, and Barney Dreyfuss, by now convinced that Adams was a good luck charm and could probably pitch forever, wanted to have him back.

In early February, 1926, Adams signed a contract. "It has frequently been said that sentiment cuts no figure in baseball," opined the Pittsburgh *Telegram*.

> Yet when Barney Dreyfuss made out the contracts for 1926 there was one for Charles ("Babe") Adams, the glorious old veteran of the Pirates. And though Adams won only six games for Pittsburgh last season, and pitched only a pair of complete games, the handsome Kansan will receive the same salary in 1926 as he did in 1924 and 1925. . . . Adams will be forty-four on his next birthday. There have been few active players in the majors at forty-four. All baseball is pulling for Adams to go another half dozen years. He was a fine looking chap at the National League's "Golden Jubilee" dinner, and could have been taken for a man ten years his junior.

Unfortunately, almost tragically, Babe Adams in 1926 became a central figure in one of the most famous player mutinies in baseball history. The incident revolved around Fred Clarke, the front office executive-assistant manager. It had been ten years since Clarke had departed as Pirates manager, and only two veterans remained with the Pirates who had played for him—Adams, and team captain Max Carey. Both liked Clarke well enough, and had welcomed him back—but as the 1926 season progressed, some members of the team began to feel that Clarke was undercutting McKechnie, angling to get back in the manager's chair, and that this was undermining the team's morale.

The Pirates were playing well, holding first place, but in Boston on August 7, they were shut out in a doubleheader by the Braves, a bad team, and after that the situation came to a head. Clarke had been lobbying McKechnie to bench Max Carey and put somebody else in center field; anybody else, he eventually said, "even the batboy." Carey talked to the members of the team, and found that several were harboring ill feelings toward Clarke. Carey asked Adams if he thought it was appropriate for Clarke to suggest lineup changes for McKechnie—a loaded question under the circumstances, but Adams gave him an answer. "The manager is the manager," Adams said. "Nobody else should interfere." Acting as team captain and spokesman for the players, Carey asked that Fred Clarke be removed from the bench. Adams and Carson Bigbee, a veteran outfielder, stood with him publicly on the issue.

Carey clearly felt that he represented the majority of the players if not all of them, and that as team captain he was acting properly as a spokesman for the players in support of their manager, Bill McKechnie. They met with McKechnie before going public with their statement. McKechnie at first seemed to appreciate the support, but then studied the situation and found himself between a rock and a hard place. He was forced to denounce the players' attempt to meddle in the administration of the team. Fred Clarke met with the press, and announced that he would not return to the bench until heavy penalties were inflicted upon the offenders.

The World Champion Pittsburgh Pirates were in chaos, and the story was all over the newspapers. Barney Dreyfuss was vacationing in Europe, leaving the club in the hands of his son Sam. After exchanging telegrams with Europe, the Pirates front office met August 12 in a crisis atmosphere, after which they scheduled a meeting the next day with the players. The players held their own angry meeting, and while it is not clear exactly what happened, there was no consensus in support of the dissidents; reportedly, a resolution to demand the removal of Clarke was supported by only six players.

Sam Dreyfuss, hated by the Pirates players, began the meeting of August 13 with the announcement that "I'll do all the talking." Bigbee and Adams were given their unconditional release. Max Carey, too good a player to release, was put on waivers and suspended without pay; Pie Traynor replaced him as team captain.

Expecting support from two sides, the dissidents had been cut off at the knees when neither arrived. Meeting in Pittsburgh on August 15, the three appealed to Commissioner Landis for a hearing of their grievance; WE HAVE BEEN UNJUSTLY TREATED AND PENALIZED WITHOUT A HEARING, they said in a telegram to the commish. Landis agreed that there should be a hearing, but asked National League president John Heydler to conduct the hearing, which was held in Pittsburgh on August 17. "I cannot go back of the right of the officials of a league club to release, suspend or ask waivers on any of its players, nor would I wish to do so if I had the right; but it is my opinion, after a most complete and thorough hearing of this case, that none of the three players—Carey, Bigbee, and Adams—has been guilty of willful subordination or malicious intent to disrupt or injure his club," Heydler announced after

the hearing. In effect, he had cleared the players' names but refused to reinstate them.

The historical import of the controversy is twofold: first, that it obstructed the development of a dynasty in Pittsburgh, and second, that it helped to define the roles played by coaches and executives in the modern front office. The Pirates, hopelessly divided by the turmoil, collapsed to a third-place finish. (They had been in the lead on August 7.) McKechnie was fired after the season, and Clarke removed from the bench. In view of the fact that the Pirates were World Champions in 1925 and added several outstanding players to their roster in the next few years (including the Waner brothers), it may well be that the crisis prevented the Pirates of the late twenties from becoming one of the game's great dynasties. The rift deprived the Pirates of an outstanding manager in McKechnie; he was replaced by Donie Bush, who had continued conflicts with the players.

The modern front office in 1926 was at a critical point in its evolution. Branch Rickey moved into the Cardinals front office in 1925; Billy Evans in 1927 became the first man to wear the title "general manager." Baseball was leaving the era of the major league owner-operator, the guys who ran their own teams with a treasurer, a secretary, and a couple of scouts; soon enough there would be farm directors and scouting supervisors and executive vice-presidents with Rolodexes and reservations for lunch. Never again would there be a coach-vice-president; the dangers in that had been exposed. In effect, the incident built a wall between front office and field level management, a wall through which the manager was—and is—the only door.

Carey moved on to the Dodgers, where he played, coached, and managed for several years, but the major league careers of Bigbee and Babe Adams had come to an end. "A series of misunderstandings," Heydler said, which were beyond his power to repair.

Adams throughout his career had invested his money in farmland, and by the end of his career owned two large farms as well as some other real estate in Missouri and Kansas. He was well fixed, but this was no way to end a baseball career. In 1927 Adams signed on as player-manager of the Johnstown (Pennsylvania) team in Mid-Atlantic League. Forty-five years old and disabled by injuries, he was able to pitch only two games for Johnstown, and though he won both games the team played poorly the rest of the time. He resigned from the Johnstown job on June 4, replaced by Chief Bender. Moving closer to home, he signed with Springfield, Missouri, of the Western Association, where he pitched brilliantly in seven starts late in the season. Springfield wanted him back and he thought hard about it, but in mid-March, 1928, he notified Springfield that he would not return. His career was finally over.

As a pitcher, Adams was probably more like Bert Blyleven than like any other contemporary pitcher. Like Blyleven, he threw hard as a young man but used a big breaking curve as his best pitch. Like Blyleven, he started out with good control, and it got better. His control record is surpassed by only one other pitcher, his onetime teammate Deacon Phillippe. He was a left-handed hitter and a pretty good one, with a lifetime average over .200. He was an excellent fielder, and obviously he kept himself in shape. He was a quiet man with unshakable composure; probably the last thing he would have ever expected was to find himself in the middle of a player rebellion. He once said that he spent eighteen years in baseball without opening his mouth, and then when he answered a question for a teammate all hell broke loose. Perhaps because of the way he left the game, he hasn't been selected for the Hall of Fame, yet he certainly was as good a pitcher as several who have been.

Out of baseball, Adams farmed for several years, then, apparently sometime in the 1930's, took a job as a sportswriter. An avid hunter, he was known into his sixties as the finest rifle shot in the county. During World War II he went to the Pacific as a foreign correspondent; in the Korean War, nearing seventy, he went again. In 1958 Babe and Blanch Adams moved from the farm near Mount Moriah to Silver Spring, Maryland. People who knew him in Maryland say that until the end of his life, he remained a well-built man who looked years younger than he was. At Silver Spring, on July 28, 1968, Babe Adams died of throat cancer at the age of eighty-six.

(There is no primary source for this article. I would like to express my appreciation to Bill Deane and Tom Heitz of the Hall of Fame Library and to Clifton Cardwell and the Tipton County, Indiana, historical society for their assistance in providing research materials.)

Bobby Adams

Adams, Robert, was ready for a trial with the Cincinnati Reds when he was called by the Army. A product of the Reds farm system he worked his way up from the Pioneer League in '39 to Syracuse in 1942 and that fall was signed to a parent club contract before he went into service. He's a second baseman and played a lot of ball for Air Force teams while in uniform. Once hit two homers in a game while he was with the Santa Ana Army Air base team, driving in six runs. In '41 he led the Sally League in base hits, 195 good for 271 bases. He's fast, accounting for lots of two base blows.
—1946 *Street and Smith's Rookie Who's Who*

The outfield plays him straight away and average deep. The third baseman never in closer than even with the bag and most of the time average deep. He did attempt to bunt to beat it out one time, but that was all. Not even a fake. Strictly a fast ball hitter. The Chicago pitchers pitched him all breaking stuff low. Never anything up over the plate. They either pitched him high tight to show it to him and then breaking stuff away and low. He went fifteen times without a hit in these four games.

He can really run and a great infielder. Do not fail to tell your men to really run if and when he is to handle the ball. Quick as a cat and go both ways with ease. And I mean both ways.
—Scouting Report filed by Wid Matthews for the Brooklyn Dodgers, 1947

Robert Henry Adams (Bobby)
Born, December 14, 1921 at Tuolumne, Calif.
Height, 5.11. Weight, 170. Blue eyes and brown hair.
Throws and bats righthanded.
Ancestry—English
Married Barbara Jeanne Lowary, March 10, 1944.
Hobbies—Bowling, music and golf.
Led National League third basemen in double plays, 1953.
—1954 *Baseball Register*

Few people in baseball have known the satisfaction that [Bobby] Adams had in the conversion of [Ken] Hubbs from a shortstop into a second baseman who, within little more than a year, not only won the National League rookie award but shattered two all-time fielding records.

In his second season in the system, Hubbs hit .216 at Lancaster (Eastern) and he wasn't doing much better the first half of 1961 at Wenatchee in the Class B Northwest League. This happened to be the first year of the Cubs' all-coach system and one of the members of the ten-man board, Bobby Adams, was dispatched to Wenatchee to supervise the conversion of Hubbs from a shortstop to a second baseman.

Adams worked the remainder of the northwest League season with Hubbs, showing him how to play second base.
—*The Sporting News* March 21, 1964

(Adams continued as a major league coach for many years after this was written, and eventually had the opportunity to coach his own son.)

Buster Adams, a longtime outfielder in the Pacific Coast League, who had two outstanding years in the National League during World War II.

Though born in Colorado, Adams attended high school in Bisbee, Arizona, where a Cub scout named Roy Johnson (not the outfielder with the same name) saw him playing basketball, and liked his speed and athletic ability. Signed by the Cubs in 1932 on his seventeenth birthday, Adams played two years with the Catalina Cubs, a Chicago-supported semipro team which played in Wrigley Field, Los Angeles.

I don't exactly understand the legalities of it, but apparently the Cubs owned the rights to Adams although he was playing semipro baseball, not "Organized Baseball." Anyway, during the training camp in 1935, Adams hurt his arm, was released by the Cubs and wound up in the Cardinals farm system. In 1936 Adams was transferred to Sacramento of the Pacific Coast League, originally as a third baseman, later as a center fielder.

At this time Adams was regarded as a coming star. The manager of the Sacramento Solons was Reindeer Bill Killefer, the old catcher. The *Sacramento Bee* on March 17, 1937 reported that that Adams "is the fastest man on the squad and appears to be made for center field. The Solon manager is ready to bet that Adams will go up to the major leagues. 'He has everything it takes,' said Killefer. 'He can run, he can slug, he can field and he has a great spirit.'" Branch Rickey thought that Adams would be ready for the major leagues in one more season, and Willie Kamm, then managing the Mission Reds, named Adams over Ted Williams as the best young ballplayer in the league.

Adams's career began to go awry in the spring of 1938. The Cardinals at this time ran a kind of "meat market" minor league operation, not uncommon now but new at that time. They would bring in young players from all over the country, put them through spring training together, and then parcel them out to their sprawling minor league system at the end of the spring. Adams didn't want to have anything to do with that; he refused to sign his 1938 contract, saying he wanted to stay in Sacramento. The March 14, 1938, *Sacramento Bee* reported that

"Adams was given a 'going over' by Killefer and [Doc] Crandall, and now is en route to join the St. Louis Cardinals in Bradenton, Fla.

"Killefer impressed Adams with the fact that if he continues to refuse to sign a contract and report to the Cardinals he will be out of a job like 12,000,000 others.

"Adams feels he is not ready for the big tent and said he has his heart set on returning to Sacramento."

Instead, Adams got one at bat in the major leagues in April, 1939, and then was assigned to Columbus in the American Association, where he played poorly for half a season, and then was returned to Sacramento. Assigned to the International League in 1940, he again played poorly; back in Sacramento in 1941, he again played well.

Called for the draft several times, Adams was excused from service each time because of ulcers. In World War II, that made him a hot property—a solid bat, a solid glove, and a solid deferment. Called up by the Cardinals in 1943, he played well through the war, with the Cardinals and Phillies; interestingly, his wartime stats are extremely similar to his typical years in the Pacific Coast League before and after the war. On June 18, 1943, Adams hit a double and a triple in the same inning (he is one of less than twenty players to have done that), and in 1945 he drove in over a hundred runs.

Adams was the kind of player that I've always liked—a good defensive player with a balance of offensive skills. He wasn't exceptional in any area, but he could do several things—hit a lot of doubles and some home runs, draw fifty to eighty walks a year, run the bases. He lasted a couple of years in the postwar majors, and then went back to the Pacific Coast League until 1951.

Tired of the travel, Adams left baseball when he was through as an active player. He became a beer distributor in Palm Desert, California, selling the distributorship in 1965. Now retired, he still lives and plays golf in Palm Desert.

(The research for this article was done by A. D. Suehsdorf, who also wishes to thank Mr. Adams for his cooperation.)

Caswell Adams, a New York sportswriter best known for his writing about boxing.

Adams worked for the New York *Herald-Tribune,* the King Features syndicate and the New York *Journal-American.* A good friend of Red Smith's, Adams died young and was fondly recalled by Smith in several articles; it was Adams who used to say that when he got out of bed in the morning he read the obituary page. If his name wasn't on it, he shaved.

Charles F. Adams, vice-president and part-owner of the Boston Braves, 1924–36.

From *Who's Who in the Major Leagues,* 1935:

> Sports events of all classes have always appealed to Mr. Adams. In his youth he was a first baseman, batting left-handed, and played in his home town, Richford, Vt. He also has been prominently identified with ice hockey, a game which enjoys great popularity in Boston, where he became manager of the Irish-American team, an amateur organization, in 1920. He supplied the bankroll and the club developed into one of the best ever seen in the New England States.
>
> In 1924 Mr. Adams acquired a franchise for the Hub in the National Hockey circuit. In recent years he has won the Prince of Wales trophy five times. He obtained control of entire Western League in 1927 at an investment of $300,000.

One gets the impression, even from this polite note, that Adams was a man who liked to control things. After buying into the Braves in the early 1920s, Adams became antagonistic toward team president Judge Emil Fuchs, whom he apparently felt was a fool (it wouldn't have been hard to certify), and tried to rally the stockholders and take control of the team away from Fuchs. He was unsuccessful in that battle. In 1928, in the context of a fight over Sunday baseball, Adams alleged that a Boston city councilman had attempted to extort a bribe from the team in exchange for legislation permitting baseball to be played on Sunday; that kicked up a *real* ruckus, and the city council passed a resolution denouncing Adams.

Chuck Adams, vice-president of public relations and community affairs for the Chicago White Sox (1989).

Dr. Daniel L. Adams, president of the New York Knickerbockers Club in 1857, and also first president of the National Association of Base Ball Players.

Dan (Rube) Adams, Federal League pitcher.

A St. Louis native, Adams had pitched for several years with Hannibal, Galesburg, Ottumwa, and Muscatine in the Central Association before the Federal League offered him a shot at "major league" status. After the failure of the Federal League Adams pitched for two years in the Three I League before retiring.

Dick Adams, brother of Bobby Adams; played briefly with the Phillies in 1947.

Franklin P. Adams, a young columnist with the New York *World* in 1908, when he wrote baseball's second-most-famous poem:

These are the saddest of possible
        words—
Tinkers to Evers to Chance.
Trio of Bear Cubs and fleeter than
        birds—
Tinkers to Evers to Chance.
Thoughtlessly pricking our gonfalon
        bubble,
Making a Giant hit into a double,
Words that are weighty with nothing
        but trouble—
Tinkers to Evers to Chance.

Adams went on to a distinguished career as an editor and newspaper columnist. He was a part of the Round Table of the Algonquin, a friend of George S. Kaufman, Heywood Broun, Robert Benchley, Dorothy Parker, *et al.,* and wrote a kind of overblown gossip column called "The Conning Tower" for many years in the New York *World.* He was also involved with the *Information Please* radio program.

Gary Adams, head baseball coach at UCLA.

George "Partridge" Adams, nineteenth century outfielder.

The fact that Adams played only four major league games but has a nickname listed in the *Baseball Encyclopedia* obviously means that there is a story associated with him, but I do not know what that story is. I would assume that he was a well-known amateur or minor league player.

Glenn Adams, Minnesota's left-handed designated hitter, 1977–81.

Adams was originally signed by the Houston Astros in 1968. Like Mike Aldrete (see Aldrete), Adams was a left-handed line-drive hitter without speed. He spent four years in the Astros system, hitting .335 for their top two farm teams in 1971, after which the Astros released him. "I had a sore arm," he explained later; a simpler explanation would be that Spec Richardson was running the Astros at the time.

After a year out of baseball, Adams caught on with the Giants system, where he hit .352 to win the PCL batting title in 1974. As a rookie pinch hitter with the major league Giants in 1975, Adams hit .300 in 61 games (12/33 as a pinch hitter.) A natural DH, he wound up in Minnesota a year later, platooning for Gene Mauch. In his first American League season, he

(a) broke his wrist while sliding, missing six weeks,

(b) set a team record for RBI in a game, with 8, and

(c) hit .338.

He never had as good a year again, but he hit .280 throughout his career. He is now a roving batting instructor for the Minnesota Twins.

Herb Adams, outfielder with the Chicago White Sox, 1948–50.

Adams shot to the major leagues after a big year with Hot Springs in the Cotton States League, where he had 223 hits in 133 games. He hit fairly well with the White Sox, but had no power.

John Bertram (Jack) Adams, catcher with Cleveland (1910–12) and the Phillies (1915–19) listed in the encyclopedias as "Bert," but in contemporary publications as "Jack." From the 1916 *Spalding Guide:*

> Jack Adams, the third catcher of the Phillies, is a youngster, born in San Antonio, Texas, twenty-four years ago. He was drafted from New Orleans in 1914 by the New York Giants, but he never reported to McGraw. He was included in the trade for Lobert, going to the Phillies with Demaree and Stock. He is a big, strong ambitious fellow, anxious to work.

Karl "Rebel" Adams, pitcher with the Cubs in 1915.

Adams would have had the kind of APBA card that you'd set fire to if he was on your team. He went 1–9 with a pretty decent team, had an ERA 70 percent over the league norm, and as a hitter went oh-for-thirty.

Margo Adams, a mortgage banker from Santa Ana, California, who carried on a four-year affair with Wade Boggs, and sued him when the affair ended.

Margo Adams met Wade Boggs in April, 1984, just after Boggs's second major league season. Although Boggs was married, from 1984 through 1987 the two carried on a peculiar affair in which Margo traveled with the team, rode on the team bus, attended team parties, and generally took the part of Wade Boggs's wife while he was on the road. In the spring of 1988 the relationship broke apart when (a) Debbie Boggs found compelling evidence that Wade was still carrying on with Margo, and (b) Margo began to find out that Wade was still carrying on with other girlfriends.

At that point, as Margo tells it, she asked

Boggs to pay her $100,000 more or less to compensate her for wages she had lost following him around the country on the expectation that the two of them would eventually be married. Boggs called the FBI, and alleged that this woman was trying to extort money from him under a threat of revealing their affair to his wife.

This plunged the two of them into a lawsuit and public pissing contest which, over the course of a year or so, made Margo astonishingly famous. Margo sued Wade for $6 million—no, let's make that $12 million. To sustain herself until her ship came in, she turned to shoplifting and petty theft. In January, 1989, Margo pled guilty to running up $4,871 in charges on somebody else's credit card. In March, she was arrested for wearing a $258 coat out of department store without paying for it. She sold her story to *Penthouse* magazine, revealing that Wade Boggs's favorite form of pizza was double-anchovy; *Penthouse* insisted that she pose for pictures to accompany the story. She made the talk-show circuit, was a guest on Bob Costas and a superstar of afternoon television for a month or so.

Ballplayers have been carrying on with loose women for a hundred years or so and the republic still stands and three outs are still an inning, but surely there is something wrong with a society that makes a person like Margo into a celebrity. What is her talent? What is it that she does well? She's not very bright. She's not attractive. Her fame is based not on anything that makes her unique and certainly not on anything that makes her admirable, but upon her having slept with Wade Boggs and upon her willingness to talk about it. She's more than a sign that *something* is wrong with our society, more like a compendium of several things that are wrong, beginning with the simple fact that we create the belief that famous people are more real than the rest of us, more important, more worthy. The dividing of the world into the famous and the insignificant invites the famous to exploit the insignificant, creating a psychic middle ages of serfs and potentates. If Margo can tell the world that famous people are simply people, that if you make them into kings then, like kings, they will exploit you and abuse you, then perhaps that is a justification for her fame.

Mike Adams, a utility player in the 1970s, and the son of Bobby Adams.

Adams entered baseball as a middle infielder, and hit fairly well in the minor

leagues. His career was kind of messed up when the Tigers, who had originally signed him, traded him to the Minnesota Twins, and the Twins decided to shift him to the outfield because they thought Rod Carew was all the second baseman they'd ever need. Adams had a good year in the PCL in 1972 (.311, 21 homers), and went north in 1973 believing he was the Twins regular third baseman, only to be told an hour before the opening game that he was being moved back to the outfield.

"I've just always wanted to play the infield," Adams told *The Sporting News* in 1975. "They [the Twins] wouldn't even let me take ground balls in practice." Adams was traded to the Cubs in 1975, where he was able to work with his father, and after a good year in AAA earned another shot at the majors, but was never able to stick.

Red Adams, pitching coach for the Los Angeles Dodgers from 1969 through 1980, now a roving pitching instructor in the Dodgers system.

Adams pitched only eight games in the major leagues, none of them wins, but pitched in the Pacific Coast League seemingly forever (1942–58); he won 153 games in the PCL, plus 40 in other minor leagues. Wrote Tommy John:

"It was with the Dodgers that I became a full-fledged pitcher again, and I thank coach Dwight 'Red' Adams for that. When I joined the club [in 1972], I was still convinced that I had only a mediocre fast ball and that I was going to have to depend chiefly on my breaking pitches to win ball games." Adams worked hard to convince John that his fastball, though not overpowering, had good movement and could be used as an out pitch.

Ricky Adams, infielder with the California Angels, 1982–83, and San Francisco Giants in 1985.

Sparky Adams, National League infielder of the 1920s and 1930s, who died in 1989 at the age of ninety-four.

Adams is listed in the encyclopedias as being five feet five inches tall, but according to Lee Allen in *The Hot Stove League* he was actually only five foot four, the smallest player ever to play regularly in the National League. According to Allen, Rickey first saw him working out at shortstop, and jumped to his feet shouting:

"Get that bat boy out of the shortstop's position!"

"That's not a bat boy, Mr. Rickey," said one of his aides.

"Oh, it isn't? Well, who is he?"

"That's Earl Adams."

"Judas Priest," Rickey exploded. "Do you mean that is the man we paid seven hundred and fifty dollars for?"

Adams didn't stick with the Cardinals, but did stick with the Cubs two years later. For his first two years he was known as Rabbit Adams, but when Rabbit Maranville joined the Cubs in 1925 he said "We can have only one rabbit on this team and it's going to be me. You're a spark plug, so we'll call you Sparky."

Although he had no power and didn't reach the majors until he was nearly thirty, meaning that some of his speed was probably gone, Sparky Adams stayed in the majors by hustle, defense, and contact hitting until he was forty years old. Three unrelated notes about him, at least two of which can be considered relics of my previous career:

• Adams was the starting third baseman for the 1930 St. Louis Cardinals, the only team of this century for which all eight regulars hit .300.

• I once did a computer search to try to figure out which two players in major league history had the most similar career totals (among players with twelve hundred or more games). The answer I got: Sparky Adams and Dave Cash.

• Adams' major league career runs from ages twenty-eight to forty—very late compared to the average player—and he lived to be ninety-four years old. I have noticed many times that players whose "career center" is chronologically late are often players who live long lives, while players who bloom early and fade early are often destined also to die early. To some degree, the reasons for this are obvious: Adams, a tiny man, didn't fight his weight as a player and didn't put extra pressure on his heart as he aged, while somebody like John Mayberry, who was finished early as a player, is probably a hundred pounds overweight today and not likely to live to be ninety-four. I've never actually researched it, but on an intuitive level, doesn't it seem that a player who lasts a long time as an athlete could be expected to live a long time as a person? Wouldn't you think that the rate of aging as a person would mirror the rate of aging as a ballplayer? And if you established that this was true of *ballplayers*— that you could loosely predict how long they would live by their aging pattern as a player—then wouldn't it follow that it might be true of people in other professions—that

among executives or truck drivers or writers or secretaries or whatever, those who peak later professionally will live longer than those who peak early?

The Cardinals won the pennant, with Adams at third base, in 1930 and 1931. In '31 Adams led the NL in doubles with 46, but an ankle injury late in the season kept him on the bench through most of the '31 World Series.

Adams had pulled ligaments in his leg in 1932, and missed almost the entire season; at season's end he was thirty-eight years old. Still, he came back in 1933 to play regularly again. Sparky's pop-out to Bill DeLancey on October 1, 1934, marked the end of the 1934 National League pennant race, and also the end of Adams's career.

In retirement, Adams returned to the mining town of Schuylkill County, Pennsylvania, where he grew up, and took up farming. Later in life he ran a service station in Tremont, Pennsylvania.

Spencer Adams, a utility infielder of the 1920s.

Adams was in the major leagues only four years, but played for four different teams and four excellent teams—the 1923 Pirates (87–67; in first place until September), the 1925 Washington Senators (American League Champions), the 1926 Yankees (American League Champions), and the 1927 St. Louis Cardinals (92–61, second place; lost pennant in last days of season).

Todd Adams, executive assistant for the Charleston Wheelers.

Willie Adams, American League and Federal League pitcher, 1912–19; won only ten games in the major leagues.

Joe Adcock, slugging first baseman of the 1950s and '60s, best remembered today for hitting four home runs and a double in one ball game, but also the holder of many other small or "freak" records for unique batting accomplishments.

Adcock was born in Coushatta, Louisiana, reportedly in 1927. "The population of Coushatta," Adcock once said, "is a few pigs and cattle, and Clint Courtney has all the cattle." His father, Ray Adcock, was the sheriff of the Red River Parish for twelve years, and the whole family—the whole region, for that matter—rooted for the Cardinals; Adcock's boyhood favorites were Joe Medwick and Johnny Mize. In his senior year in high school, 1944, Adcock led his basketball team to the finals of the state tournament, and was named to the all-state team.

He received a number of scholarship offers as a basketball player, selecting Louisiana State, where he enrolled in the fall of 1944. In part, he played basketball as a youth because the town was so small that it was difficult to get together enough kids for a baseball game.

It may bother you a little that Adcock's reported date of birth is October 30, 1927, but he went to LSU in the fall of '44, when he would have been sixteen years old; it makes one suspect a "baseball age." In any case, Adcock starred as a college basketball player, even earning a place on some all-American teams as a sophomore in 1945–46. As it happened his first basketball coach at LSU was Don Swanson, who was the team's regular baseball coach, doubling as the basketball coach while the regular man was seeing duty in World War II. Swanson was looking for a first baseman, and asked Adcock, six feet four inches, and built like a horse, to give it a try.

Adcock at the time didn't own a baseball glove, but Swanson got a glove for him and assigned a teammate named Bert Kouns to work with Adcock on defense. Adcock started to hit as soon as he started to play, playing semipro ball in the summers to sharpen his skills. Playing for a team in Jena, Louisiana in the summer of 1947, Adcock received offers to turn pro.

During the depression, Adcock's father had lost the family farm; that's how he wound up as the sheriff. When he had a chance to play professional baseball, his father told him "You gotta play hard so you can make enough money to buy back our place. That should be your dream." Studying offers from the Yankees, Tigers, and Reds, Adcock selected Cincinnati because two of his buddies were already in the Cincinnati system and, he said, "The Yankees had about thirty-five farm teams and thirty-five first basemen, and they all had a jump on me. I figured Cincinnati was the quickest way to the major leagues."

The logic was sound, but what Adcock didn't know was that an Indiana University *foot*ball star, Ted Kluszewski, was already in the Reds system, and at the moment hitting .377 at Memphis. Anyway, Adcock spent two undistinguished years in the Sally League, playing for Gee Walker, and suffering the first of many broken bones he would have throughout his career, a broken leg at the start of the 1948 season. From there he moved on to Tulsa in the Texas League in 1949. Al Vincent, his manager at Tulsa, told him one day, "I'm either going to make you a ballplayer or ruin you."

"Fine," said Adcock. "Let's get started." His career took off from that moment. He drove in 116 runs in 1949 and hit an eleventh-inning home run to win the seventh and deciding game of the Texas League playoff.

This earned him a spot with the Cincinnati Reds in 1950. He opened the season watching Ted Kluszewski play first base. In Pittsburgh early in the year, Big Klu was chasing a pop foul near the stands when a small boy reached out for the ball. Trying to avoid crunching the little boy, Kluszewski jammed his wrist against the railing, and was out for a few days. Adcock played the next series in St. Louis and had a big series with the bat, and when Kluszewski came back manager Luke Sewell asked Adcock to go to the outfield. He did and hit well enough, finishing the season at .293 in 102 games; he was named to *The Sporting News* all-rookie team.

Kluszewski, however, was an immovable problem. It was almost exactly the same problem the Giants would have a decade later with Cepeda and McCovey: Although Adcock was a right-handed hitter and Kluszewski a lefty, the two players were extremely similar. Adcock and Kluszewski were probably the two strongest men in the National League at the time and almost certainly the two best hitters on the Reds, but both were dedicated first basemen. Kluszewski was in possession of the first base job, and Adcock couldn't move him.

As an outfielder, Adcock was in danger of becoming a joke player, like Willie Aikens or Smead Jolley. He had no experience in the outfield, having been a first baseman all of his life. With long, flapping arms, sleepy feet, and what Al Silverman described as "a kind of picture-book clumsiness," he had no ability as an outfielder. The first ball hit to him in the outfield went between his legs, and it wasn't the last one to get through there. He was the favorite target of bench jockeys throughout the league, known to turn red and lose his concentration upon hearing words like "busher," "hick," and "hayseed." As if that wasn't misery enough, he broke an ankle in 1951 and had an off year with the bat. In mid-season, 1952, Rogers Hornsby was hired to manage the Reds, and Adcock apparently didn't enjoy playing for Hornsby, which may be like saying that he didn't enjoy root canal. As recalled by teammate Dixie Howell in a 1960 article in *Sport* magazine:

It seemed like Joe would fall on his face every other day. My locker was next to his and all I'd hear from him was griping. One day he fell down twice and came in cussing and raising hell about the Reds putting a big-hitting first baseman out chasing fly balls over an obstacle course.

It got a little monotonous hearing the same thing every day, so I stopped him and said, "Joe, look out the window. Over there is the head man's office. Why don't you either go raise hell with him or shut up?"

Adcock took the advice, and after a meeting with Hornsby also talked to a reporter:

"I'll never make good money as an outfielder," he said. "But I can as a first baseman. Next spring I'm coming to training camp with a first baseman's mitt and no one is going to take it from me. If the Reds can't use me at first base, then they're going to have to trade me." When a rookie outfielder named Jim Greengrass drove in twenty-four runs in eighteen games in the closing weeks of the season, Adcock was history in Cincinnati. On February 16, 1953, he was traded to the Braves as part of a four-team trade; essentially, Adcock was traded for Rocky Bridges. Rogers Hornsby was pleased with the trade.

TRACERS

Ruben Gomez [hit] Joe Adcock of the Milwaukee Braves in the ribs with a pitch. When Adcock charged the mound from the first base line, Gomez threw the ball at Adcock again, hitting him in the hip. Gomez, terrified, then fled all the way to the Giants clubhouse in center field with the slower Adcock in hot pursuit. A few minutes later, Gomez attempted to reemerge, brandishing an ice pick.

—Noel Hynd
The Giants of the Polo Grounds

A network broadcaster also told this story a couple of years ago, as an "I was there one day when . . ." The key to the story is that phrase "all the way to the Giants clubhouse in center field"; the Giants clubhouse was four hundred feet from the pitching mound, and the image of the massive Adcock chasing the terrified little Latin across the open acres of center field is what gives the story its comic center.

Hynd says that the event occurred in 1956, which narrows the field immediately to eleven games, the eleven games that the Braves played in the Polo Grounds in 1956. A review of those eleven games finds no such occurrence, but in a story about one of those games Rob found a reference which gave us better directions. . . .

The incident in question took place on July 17, 1956, and several elements of the story are accurately reported: Gomez did hit Adcock with a pitch, Adcock did start for first and did charge the mound, Gomez did throw the ball at him again as he charged the mound and did hit him again, after which Gomez did turn and run, and Adcock did chase him. . . .

But not into center field. He ran into the Giants *dugout,* not their clubhouse.

And the incident did not happen in the Polo Grounds. It happened in Milwaukee.

The incident triggered a near-riot in Milwaukee; Gomez left the park under police guard. Gomez was fined $250 and suspended for three days for deliberately hitting Adcock with the pitch, an action described by *The New York Times* as "disgraceful" and "cowardly" (the "respectable" and "courageous" thing for him to have done, obviously, would have been to stand there and let the massive Adcock beat the crap out of him.) Adcock was fined $100 for charging the mound. Giant manager Bill Rigney:

"Gomez got excited. The incident is regrettable. It happened, now it's over and the less said about it the better." No mention is made of an ice pick in any contemporary account of the game, which doesn't necessarily mean that there wasn't one.

The Braves moved to Milwaukee, and Adcock began to compile his portfolio of fantastic hitting feats. On April 29, 1953, he hit the ball into the center-field bleachers in the Polo Grounds; in the thirty years since the Polo Grounds were remodeled in 1923, it had never been done before. Playing every game for the Milwaukee Braves in 1953, Adcock hit a respectable .285 with 33 doubles and 18 homers, although he also led the league in grounding into double plays.

Late in the 1953 season, at the suggestion of Red Schoendienst of the Cardinals, Adcock tried an odd grip on the bat, aligning his hands knuckle-to-knuckle, rather than the usual way, left knuckles aligned with the right finger joints (and vice versa). The grip seemed to release his wrist, and his hitting improved.

In June, 1954, Adcock scuffled in a Chicago restaurant with his teammate Lew Burdette. It was a two-day story, and blasted out of everyone's memory a month later.

At Ebbets Field on July 31, 1954, Adcock had one of the greatest individual days in the history of baseball. In the second inning Adcock homered off of Don Newcombe. Up in the third, facing Erv Palica, Adcock ripped the ball off the top of the wall in left center; it rebounded for a double, and Adcock has always said it was the hardest that he hit a ball all day. In the fifth, facing Palica again, Adcock hit the ball in the upper deck, his second home run. Off of Pete Wojey in the seventh, Adcock homered to left center. He came up in the ninth, facing Johnny Podres.

"Dusty Boggess was umpiring," Adcock recalled, "and the first two pitches were high and outside. Dusty said to me, 'Hey, kid, this guy ain't about to give you nothin' to hit.' I said, 'Well, I'm gonna hit somethin'.'" Adcock took a wild cut at a pitch over his head, and hit it into the center-field bleachers—his fourth home run of the game.

At the time it was reported that Adcock was using a bat borrowed from Charlie White, a 38-ounce bat; Adcock now says that that was not true, that he was using his own bat.

"I remember it was about ninety-five degrees," Adcock recalled. "It was brutal out there. I didn't take batting practice, because I was hitting the ball good, and I figured if you're going good, batting practice only gives you more bad habits."

The game set, or was part of setting, innumerable records, the most important of which was most total bases, game (18). Adcock had also had a big day on July 30, the day before (single, double, and home run), which created a whole slew of two-game records. In his first at bat on August 1, he dodged away from two inside pitches from Russ Meyer, then ripped another double, creating a few more records; his second time up Clem Labine drilled him in the head with a fast ball, putting him out of the game. Batting helmets were brand new at the time; Adcock had only been wearing his for about a month. Labine's fastball put a dent in Adcock's helmet, and many people who saw the pitch claim it might have killed Adcock had he not had the helmet. Adcock has kept the helmet as a trophy, and shows it to reporters whenever they stop by.

Back in the lineup for the fourth game of the series on August 2, Adcock hit another double; in the four-game series he hit 5 homers and 4 doubles. For the season as a whole, Adcock hit 9 home runs in the eleven games the Braves played in Ebbets Field, the first National League player to hit nine home runs in an opponent's park—in fact, Adcock hit 50 percent more home runs that year in Ebbets Field than he did in his home park in Milwaukee. "If I played for the Dodgers I'd hit thirty-five homers a year in this park," he said after the big game; it would prove to be an extremely conservative estimate. Adcock hit .395 against the Dodgers that year, with 9 homers, 22 RBI, and a staggering total of 64 bases in 22 games.

The four-homer game made Adcock a star. The front page of the Milwaukee *Journal* the next day was covered with a full-color picture of Joe Adcock. Adcock's picture appeared on the cover of the 1955 edition of *One For the Book*, from *The Sporting News*. His reputation for defensive play improved; although he caught the ball one-handed, which some people thought looked like a hot-dog play, he did catch the ball. Even Rogers Hornsby spoke up in his favor, saying how hard he had worked to improve himself. A new image of Adcock sprouted. Stories about his big ears and gangly appearance were replaced by stories about his ice-blue eyes and coal-black hair.

"As a young player," wrote Chris Stern in *Where Have They Gone*, "Joe Adcock was the National League's most eligible bachelor. He was big and friendly, dark, rugged, and possessed of a Louisiana drawl that melted women. But Joe was very shy except when it came to baseball." Ogden Nash wrote a poem about him, about his shyness. After one of his broken bones, Adcock met a woman named Joan James who worked in the office of the Braves team physician; they were married on November 16, 1956. His image marched on.

On September 11, 1954, with the Braves still in the pennant race, Don Newcombe directed another fastball at Adcock's head. Adcock threw up his arm in self-defense, and the pitch burrowed into his wrist, rupturing the blood vessels in the wrist so seriously that Adcock was unable to play the rest of the season—and the Braves, who had lost Henry Aaron a week earlier, were done for the season. Adcock, who still refused to say that the Dodgers were throwing at him, wound up the season at .308, his first and only .300 season, and set career highs with 23 homers and 87 RBI—in fact, it was the fifth time in five major league seasons that Adcock had established a new career high in home runs. He was named the Braves Most Valuable Player, and was given a "day" late in the season (a practice which got a little out of hand in the fifties). His family was flown to Milwaukee, and he was given a Cadillac, a motor boat, a good bit of money (which he donated to charity), and three hunting dogs.

On July 31, 1955—one year to the day after the four-homer game against the Dodgers—Adcock again was hurt by a pitched ball, this one thrown by Jim Hearn of the Giants (incidentally, the same pitcher against whom he had hit the ball into the center-field bleachers at the Polo Grounds). The pitch from Hearn fractured Adcock's right forearm, and he was out for the season. Adcock's patience was taxed; he had to put a stop to being used as a target. This set up another famous anecdote from Adcock's career, the incident in which Adcock allegedly chased Ruben Gomez from the pitcher's mound into the center field dugout (see Tracers).

Returning to the lineup in 1956, Adcock belted 38 home runs in just 454 at bats. On July 19, 1956, Adcock drove in 8 runs in a game. He also resumed his assault on the Dodgers:

- At Ebbets Field in 1956, Adcock blasted 7 home runs. He also hit one against the Dodgers in a game at Roosevelt Stadium in Jersey City, making a total of 8—just one short of the record he had tied two years earlier for home runs in an opponent's park.
- Playing only 17 of the 22 games against the Dodgers that year (one of

those as a pinch hitter), Adcock hit 13 home runs against the Dodgers, tying the league record.

Remember, the Dodgers were the team the Braves had to beat in 1956; this wasn't like piling up numbers against the Phillies or Cubs. Porter's *Biographical Dictionary of American Sport* also says that Adcock was the only player to hit a ball over the left-field grandstand at Ebbets Field; however, I do not know when this was done.

And yet, incredibly, Adcock that season lost his regular status. In the spring of 1956 a fancy-fielding first baseman named Frank Torre showed up in the Braves camp, and manager Fred Haney took a liking to him. Haney started using Torre as a defensive replacement for Adcock in the late innings, and occasionally giving Joe a day off. Adcock wasn't happy about it from the start. Early in the 1957 season he told a reporter "The only way Torre will get my job is for me to break my leg," and then damned if he didn't; on June 23 he slid into second base against the Phillies, and broke his ankle, the fifth serious injury of his career.

Adcock was out for two-and-a-half months, and Torre played reasonably well in the interim. When Adcock returned, Fred Haney announced that he intended to platoon the two first basemen. The Braves, perennial runners up, won the 1957 National League title, their first in Milwaukee. In the fifth game of the World Series, Adcock drove in the only run of a 1–0 game, helping the Braves to a seven-game victory.

That was his only highlight of the series, and Torre had a somewhat better series. Thus, when the 1958 season opened, Adcock found himself back where he had been in Cincinnati, fighting a left-handed hitter for playing time, and forced to go to the outfield to get some at bats. He was angry about the situation and spoke out. "I make my living swinging a big bat and a big bat wins games," he said. "The trees are full of good fielders." Relations between Adcock and Haney . . .

In May, 1959, Adcock played a central role in the bizarre finish of one of baseball's most famous games. For twelve innings that day, Harvey Haddix pitched perfect ball; thirty-six men up, thirty-six men out. It was perhaps the greatest one-game pitching performance in the history of baseball. Lew Burdette matched him with your ordinary thirteen-inning shutout, and the game was scoreless heading into the bottom of the thirteenth. Leading off, Felix Mantilla grounded the ball to third base, and the third baseman threw the ball away. Eddie Mathews bunted Mantilla to second, and Henry Aaron was intentionally walked to bring Adcock to the plate. The perfect game was gone, but Haddix still had a no-hitter.

Adcock hit the ball out of the park, way out, over the 394-foot sign in left-center. The fans screamed for Adcock and gave Haddix a standing ovation. The scoreboard operator put three runs on the scoreboard, and the game was over; Haddix's incredible performance had ended in a 3–0 defeat.

Except it didn't. Henry Aaron, knowing that the game was over but apparently not realizing that the ball had cleared the fence, touched second base, and then returned to the dugout as Adcock circled the bases. While the jubilant Braves caroused their way toward the clubhouse, a Milwaukee coach turned to the field and saw a chilling sight: the umpires. The Braves and Pirates had left the field, but the umpires had not. Why? In a flash, Haney realized what had happened. Aaron was rushed back to the field and completed his circuit, but Joe Adcock was declared out for passing Aaron on the basepaths, and the score was changed to 2–0.

That didn't stick, either; the next day the score was changed to 1–0. Frank Dascoli, the umpire who called Adcock out, ruled that since Aaron had left the basepaths voluntarily he was entitled to return and score his run; Adcock should be credited with a double and 2 RBI. National League president Warren Giles, however, ruled that because the ball was not a home run, the game ended as soon as the first run was scored. If the incident had happened with two men out—if Adcock's "out" had been the final out of the inning—the argument it provoked might never have been resolved. In any case, Haddix lost a ball game, Adcock lost a homer, and the media had something to talk about for the next fifty years.

It was, Adcock said, the only time all year that Fred Haney congratulated him. Speaking out in Cincinnati had been the right thing to do, in that it got the situation resolved, but speaking out in Milwaukee may actually have delayed Adcock's return to full-time play. Haney, forced to defend the platoon arrangement, became defensive about it and then became stubborn about it, perhaps even outrageously stubborn. While Torre did nothing, Adcock had a terrific 1959 sea-

son with the bat, including a twenty-game hitting streak—yet the two continued to share the position. The Braves and Dodgers wound up the schedule in a tie, and the Dodgers won the playoff. Facing Don Drysdale in the 156th and final game of a 154-game schedule, the Braves cleanup hitter was not Eddie Mathews (.306, 46 homes, 114 RBI) or Hank Aaron (.355, 39, 123) or Joe Adcock (.292, 25, 76) or Wes Covington or Del Crandall, but Frank Torre, a .228 hitter with one home run in 115 games.

Fred Haney resigned after the 1959 season, and Adcock finally had his job back. While the Braves' slide continued, Adcock, healthy and in the lineup at last, had a chance to hang up numbers indicative of his ability. He hit .298 in 1960, led the league in fielding percentage and was named to the All-Star team for the first time. His 1961 season was even better, probably the best of his career (.285 with 35 homers, 108 RBI.) On June 8, 1961, Mathews, Aaron, Adcock, and Frank Thomas became the first players in history to hit four consecutive home runs.

Battling injuries in 1962, Adcock still led the National League in fielding percentage (for the third time) and posted his seventh consecutive season with a slugging percentage over .500. With the Braves suffering another decent but disappointing season, Adcock—at season's end—was known to be on the block.

Gabe Paul had traded Adcock away in Cincinnati, at the urging of Rogers Hornsby, and had always regretted it. Now running the Cleveland Indians, he saw an opportunity to get Adcock back. Cleveland put together a package of kids, and Adcock became an Indian. Not wishing to be unkind, the sequence defines Gabe Paul perfectly: Trade a kid away when he's twenty-five, let him hit about 250 home runs, put together a package of kids and get him back when he turns thirty-five. Adcock spent one year with Cleveland, and moved on to California where he awaited retirement in a three-year holding pattern. At age thirty-eight, he could still hit. In his final season he hit 18 home runs in 231 at bats. Only one player, Ted Williams, had a better home run ratio in his final major league season.

Adcock in his career had only four seasons as an everyday player—yet he hit 336 home runs. The ten players whose career records are most similar to Adcock's are Roy Sievers, Greg Luzinski, Frank Howard, Willie Horton, Boog Powell, George Foster,

Norm Cash, Rudy York, Vic Wertz, and Gil Hodges. None of the ten is in the Hall of Fame or should be—but all ten were formidable hitters at their best, and Adcock may have been the best hitter in the group. He battled injuries, and perhaps even more significantly, he battled the parks in which he played. The bulk of Adcock's career was spent in parks that were taking several home runs a year away from him. When Adcock came up Crosley Field was the toughest home run park in the National League; in 1953, when they traded Adcock away, they also moved the fences in, causing Kluszewski's home run total to explode. In Milwaukee, Adcock lost several home runs a year to the park, as did Aaron (see Aaron)—but Aaron got a chance to play in Atlanta and get even. Adcock never did. Incidentally, in the nine years that Aaron and Adcock were teammates, Adcock homered 8 percent more often, per at bat, than did Henry Aaron.

In his career Adcock hit only 137 home runs in his home park, as opposed to 199 on the road, one of the lowest percentages of home runs at home of any player. Adcock probably lost more home runs to the parks that he played in than any player ever except Joe DiMaggio and Goose Goslin, and he lost almost as many as them. DiMaggio and Goslin were great players with multiple skills; a park which diminished their power simply emphasized their other skills. But Adcock was a slugger, pure and simple, and thus a player who needed to have a park working for him rather than a park working against him. He wasn't DiMaggio, he was Gil Hodges—but playing in the same park, if somehow the two of them could have both played first base for the Dodgers at the same time, Adcock would have outhomered Hodges by a wide margin, and that's what people don't realize. Hodges was a better fielder than Adcock and a better runner, and Hodges was better at staying in the lineup—but Adcock, despite what the stats seem to show, was a much better hitter than Gil Hodges.

In the fall of 1966 Gabe Paul decided that Joe Adcock would be a good manager. Adcock was the strong, stable type of individual who commanded the respect of his teammates, and Paul no doubt saw him as being in the mold of Walt Alston and Gil Hodges. He was intelligent, he had worked hard to learn the game, he was well liked; what else was there?

Alston, of course, was a schoolteacher who had spent ten years in the minor leagues learning how to manage, and Gil Hodges had gotten his brains beaten in for two years before his teams began to improve. Adcock began his managerial career with no experience, no real preparation, and it was a disaster. The Indians stumbled through a typical Cleveland Indians season. Like Hornsby, Adcock tended to expect his players to work as hard at the game as he himself had worked.

Adcock had always been one to sound off about what bothered him, but in his relationships with his peers this was kept in context; Adcock was a friendly, open, basically likeable guy who would complain a bit when things didn't go his way. In the manager's chair, the trait affected people in an entirely different way: Adcock was never satisfied. "Joe loves to correct faults," said Leon Wagner, "and that left me out. I've been trying to find a flaw that Joe could work on so that I could play more." Adcock's relationship with the press, which had always been good, was not good in 1967.

Adcock managed a year in the minor leagues then, at Seattle in 1968. Perhaps he realized that he needed to learn how to do the job; perhaps he hoped to get back into the major leagues when the four new teams were added in 1969. It didn't happen, in any case, and Adcock left the game.

What to do? Along the way, Adcock had made plenty of money to buy back the family farm in Louisiana—in fact, he'd accomplished that by the early fifties. "I've always enjoyed good animals," Adcock told Jim Molony of the Houston Post last summer. "We always had horses on our farm when I was growing up. We had a lot of Appaloosas, but my father told me, 'There's only one kind of horse to have and that's a thoroughbred.'" He went into the horsebreeding business, and he's been very successful at it; he's been Louisiana's leading breeder eight times. His Red River farm has grown to 640 acres (some stories say 1,000); the horses they have produced include So La Me, the Louisiana champion two-year-old in 1988, and Part Native, the three-year-old champion. His horses have won many, many races, although he will point out that most of the wins have been "down here in the pond with the perch, not up in the ocean with the sharks." Now sixty-two years old and with four grown kids, Adcock is in good health, working very hard and living the good life in Coushatta.

(For an exceptional account of Joe Adcock's early days in the major leagues, see the August, 1955, edition of Sport magazine, the article by Al Silverman. Other sources for this article include Sport, November, 1960; Where Have They Gone, by Chris Stern, and numerous contemporary newspaper accounts and annual publications.)

Bob Addie, Washington sportswriter.

Born in 1912, Addie entered World War II as a private, and came back as a captain. Addie covered the Washington Senators from the late forties until the departure of the second Senators team after the 1971 season; in twenty years assigned to the beat, he never missed a game. After stints with the Washington Times-Herald and the New York Journal-American and another two years with the air force in Korea, Addie joined The Washington Post in 1954, and worked for the Post until his retirement in 1977. For most of that time he also wrote a column called "Addie's Atoms" for The Sporting News, a scattershot, here's-what's-on-my-mind type of column which at its best was wonderful. One thing he would do was a column titled "Take Away the Uniforms and What Do You Have?"

It would have entries like this:

> **Gene Woodling**—Smokey the Bear with a heart of gold.
>
> **Jim Gentile**—The guy you see staring back at you in the hair tonic ads.
>
> **Don Gutteridge**—What happens when you ride too many horses before breakfast.

I don't know what that means, either, but it sure makes you think.

Addie, who was president of the BBWAA in 1967, was the kind of guy who would become friendly with the Senators manager. He wrote about kicking around Kansas City on an off day with Gil Hodges, visiting Indian graves. He would write about the Senators as "our" team, talk about what "we" need to do. In his generation this was not uncommon. "I wrote like a fan because I was a fan," he said.

Addie liked athletes—in fact, he was married to one; his wife was Pauline Betz, at one time the best woman tennis player in the world. Gentle, humane, vaguely erudite, Addie died in Washington on January 18, 1982.

Bob Addis, National League outfielder of the early fifties, never a regular.

On September 27, 1951, Addis scored from third on a ground ball, evading Roy Campanella with an outstanding slide, to put the Braves over the Dodgers 4–3. The Dodgers were positive the call was blown, and someone kicked the door on the umpires dressing room to pieces; Jackie Robinson, Campanella, and Preacher Roe were fined by the National League for the incident. The game played a critical role in putting the Dodgers into a tie with the Giants.

Charles Addison, nineteenth-century Chicago developer, owner of the Chicago Players' League team (see "The War Between the Leagues") and vice-president of the Players' League. Addison sold out to Spalding when the league folded, and maintained friendly relations with Spalding for many years, becoming an investor in the Cubs. Addison Street, which goes near Wrigley Field, is named after him.

Jim Adduci, contemporary first baseman who has been to Japan and back, and is still trying to find a major league role at the age of thirty.

Bob "Magnet" Addy, nineteenth-century outfielder.

Addy reportedly was one of the first players to slide into a base. The book *A Century of Baseball,* by A. H. Tarvin in 1939, reported that Addy "paralyzed the baseball world in a game in 1866 by negotiating a steal of a base by sliding into it. Such a thing had never been heard of before." Robert Smith wrote that "in the beginning, practitioners like Studley and Bob Addy . . . did their sliding by aiming both feet at the base and dropping to the seats of their pants, allowing momentum to carry them along."

Pete Adelis, a Philadelphia loudmouth fan.

Adelis and his brother were street vegetable merchants, guys who ran around yelling "Potatoes! Tomatoes! Get your juicy red tomatoes!" in voices loud enough to pull in housewives from a block away. They were also baseball fans, and merciless ones. Big Pete and his brother would sit on opposite sides of the field, one on the first base side and one on the third base side, and converse with one another about the shortcomings of the players and managers. They would heckle anybody—the umpires, the opposing players—but they particularly concentrated on the Philadelphia players. They were probably the greatest hecklers in the history of professional sports. They would find out personal things about the players—maybe the

guy had had a big fight with his wife—and bellow about those. Pete would wear a hard hat and bang on the hard hat with a billy club to emphasize his points.

The A's and Phillies nearly went nuts trying to control them. Other fans would complain about them. Mack reportedly offered them money not to come to the games. They declined. He offered to give them free tickets if they would come to the games but behave. They accepted the tickets for a few days, but decided it was too boring, and turned the passes back in.

It has been written in several books that in the late forties the A's and/or Phillies hired Big Pete to heckle the opposition. This was after his brother was dead, I think. . . . There are stories about his being hired to sit in the front row of the upper deck and berate Larry Doby and Jackie Robinson. Other stories are that the opposition gave him free tickets to get on the Phillies' players. How much truth there is in these stories is not clear to me.

Morrie (Smut) Aderholt, a bit-part outfielder during the war years.

A North Carolina native, Aderholt graduated from Wake Forest in 1938, signed with the Nats (Washington) system for 1939 and reached the majors at the end of his first pro season. In his first game in the majors in September of 1939, he hit a home run that was considered the longest hit that season at Griffith Stadium.

His career was all downhill from there; he hit only two more major league home runs, and even during the war years (apparently he was draft exempt due to a bad heart) he was never able to find a regular spot in the major leagues. He stayed in baseball after his playing career, however, and as late as 1951 had an excellent season with Roanoke Rapids in the Coastal Plain League (Class D), where he was a thirty-five-year-old player-manager. Retiring as a player, he moved up as a manager to the Carolina League (Class B) in 1952, and was with Scranton in the Eastern League in 1953 (Class A) when that franchise folded.

Shifting to a scout's role, Aderholt continued to work for the Senators, and was in Sarasota scouting the Red Sox during spring training when stricken by a heart attack in his hotel room, March 17, 1955. He died later that night at a Sarasota hospital.

Dewey Adkins, a pitcher in the forties. Pitched in thirty-eight games and won two of them.

Grady "Butcher Boy" Adkins, pitcher with the Chicago White Sox, 1928–29.

Dave Adlesh, a catcher with the Astros from 1963–68.

Adlesh had been paid a bonus by the Astros, and was a decent defensive player, so they pushed him through the system regardless of how he hit. In 1964 Adlesh hit .203 in the Texas League, with 96 hits and 156 strikeouts; the Astros brought him up for a look late in the year. He posted a lifetime major league batting average of .168 with a slugging percentage of .199, and had almost twice as many strikeouts as hits in the major leagues, but still he played parts of six seasons.

Troy Afenir, contemporary catcher; has gotten 20 at bats in the major leagues, and doesn't seem likely to get many more.

Tommie Agee, hero of the Mets miracle in 1969.

Tommie Agee was born August 9, 1942, in Magnolia, Alabama, the son of Carrie and Joseph Agee. The Agee family moved to Mobile, Alabama, in 1943, where his father worked for the Aluminum Company of America. There were eleven children in the Agee family, nine girls and two boys. Agee as a youth became fast friends with Cleon Jones, five days older than himself, with whom he was a teammate in junior high school, in high school, at Grambling College in Grambling, Louisiana, and later with the World Champion New York Mets.

Agee's mother wanted him to become a minister, but Agee had obvious talents as an athlete. In a sports-mad town, Agee shagged flies as a kid for Billy Williams, and then saw him start off to stardom. Agee was a multisport star in high school, drawing some attention by running the 100 in 9.8, and wanted to sign a pro contract out of high school. Pro scouts were not interested, concluding that Agee was poorly coordinated and had no grasp of fundamentals. Agee enrolled instead at Grambling, where the college president, Dr. Ralph Waldo Emerson Jones, was also the head baseball coach. Dr. Jones worked with Agee to cut down his swing and harness his raw ability. In his one year at Grambling (1961) Agee hit a conference-record .533. The Cleveland Indians paid him $65,000 to do what he would have been happy to do for free one year earlier: Sign a contract.

His star continued to ascend. After reporting to Dubuque in mid-season, 1961, Agee blasted 15 homers in 64 games, scoring

49 runs. A powerfully-built five feet eleven inches, Agee was the kind of athlete that major league scouts dream of seeing, and can never keep in perspective once the vision has arrived. In 64 games of Class D baseball, Agee also struck out 78 times, which might have suggested that he was a few years away from playing major league ball, or if that doesn't get your attention then how about that .892 fielding percentage in the outfield? Instead, the Indians began to see how fast they could push him through the system.

Agee in 1962 played for Burlington in the Carolina League and had a poor season—yet the Indians publicly proclaimed him the top prospect in their organization, and late in the year brought him up for a look. Agee played in 1963 with Charleston in the Eastern League, where he broke his hand in an on-field fight and had an undistinguished year—yet the Indians brought him up to have another look.

Tommy John, a teammate of Agee at several minor league stops, wrote that in those days people "still wanted black people to stay with 'their own kind'. Well, Tommie was my kind—a rugged, good-natured guy . . . who was built like a halfback and could run like a wide receiver. Tommie had as much raw talent as any ballplayer I ever met and he was always good company, ready to go anywhere and not given to quarreling. We often ate our meals together."

The 1964 season was a breakthrough for Agee. Despite suffering another broken hand while playing winter ball—Julio Navarro hit him with a fast ball—Agee hit .272 with 20 home runs and 35 stolen bases for Portland. The first time I remember hearing about Agee was in the fall of 1964 when I read a newspaper article about him. The article compared him to Willie Mays. That winter Gabe Paul, putting together a package of kids to bring Rocky Colavito back to the Indians, included Agee in the package, along with Tommy John (see comments on Gabe Paul, Joe Adcock entry). Sox manager Al Lopez, who had been in baseball for forty years, described Agee as "one of the most exciting players I've ever seen." Agee had nailed down a job that spring, but a few days before the start of the season he broke his right hand for the third time in his career, this time while sliding into home plate, and thus missed the chance to play for Al Lopez, who retired after the season. After a miserable year with Indianapolis in 1965, Agee finally reached the major leagues in 1966.

And he was sensational. With power, speed, and Gold-Glove defense in center field, Agee was a runaway choice as the American League's Rookie of the Year. Comparisons of Agee to Willie Mays now were commonplace; when Agee's name was mentioned, Mays's inevitably followed.

Strangely, he was to play only one more season in Chicago. Agee still had little concept of the strike zone, and his batting stats slipped badly. There were conflicts between Agee and Eddie Stanky, the firm hand at the White Sox wheel. "He was very difficult to play for," Agee told Maury Allen. "There was a lot of tension on that team." Agee also told Doc Young that the White Sox, worried about Agee's night life, had hired a detective to follow him around. This had been a common practice in baseball from the time of Anson through the 1950s, but by 1967 it was discredited, and the White Sox denied that they had ever hired the private dick. Agee claimed that he had made a deal with the detective to send him a once-a-week report on his activities which he could forward to the front office, and the rest of the time the detective would leave him alone.

In any case the White Sox, intent upon building a bad team, traded Agee while his value was down for Tommy Davis, coming off a .302 season with the Mets. A year later, they would let Davis go in the expansion draft.

New York writers, picking up on the Mays connection, nicknamed Agee the "Shea Hey Kid." On the first pitch of spring training, the Shea Hey Kid was hit in the head by Bob Gibson. He crumpled to the ground and lay unconscious for several terrifying moments; finally he was helped to his feet and staggered off the field. On April 15, 1968, the Mets played 23 scoreless innings, the longest scoreless tie in baseball history, before losing to Houston in the 24th. Agee went 0-for-10, plunging him into a streak of 34 straight hitless at bats.

On his first trip into Manhattan in 1968, Agee's car was stolen. Uncomfortable in the clubhouse, uncomfortable in the city, uncomfortable in the batter's box, uncomfortable with the New York press, Agee's season became a nightmare. He was criticized by his coaches for lunging at pitches, as if he hadn't been lunging at pitches for eight years, and by his manager for letting too many good pitches go by. He apparently was involved with a woman who had some emotional problems, serious ones. Playing about as

badly as one can play, Agee in 1968 was a fit symbol for the nation in 1968, spinning desperately out of control and headed toward a seemingly frightening future.

What saved him, as best one can see from this distance, were two people: Cleon Jones and Gil Hodges. Cleon, his roommate and lifetime friend, had an excellent year in 1968, and many people thought that, as badly as Agee had played himself, his presence on the team had been good for Cleon. Hodges had seen Agee play in the American League in 1966–67 and had wanted him for the Mets. After a rocky beginning, the two developed a close relationship; Agee would go into Hodges's office, close the door and try to talk through his problems. Hodges would listen.

Agee went to the Florida Instructional League in the fall of 1968, and regained his confidence somewhat by playing well there. The 1969 season, of course, was golden; Agee did everything that Willie Mays could do—not nearly as often, but still often enough to finish sixth in the MVP voting. In the August 2, 1969, edition of *The Sporting News,* there appeared this note:

Tommie Agee was singled out by both Ron Santo of the Cubs and Gil Hodges, the Mets' manager, as the difference between the second-place Mets of this year and the ninth-place Mets of last year.

"Agee has great desire and it shows," said Santo.

"If I had to pick out one man as the reason for our rise," said Hodges, "I'd have to say Agee. He makes the ball club move."

The Mets overcame incredible odds to win the National League pennant; Agee, despite batting leadoff most of the season, was the team leader in home runs and RBI. The team rallied around Gil Hodges, who had suffered a heart attack in September, 1968, and, in a sense, adopted Agee. When Bill Hands hit Tommie with a pitch, Jerry Koosman took the mound and drilled Ron Santo in the chest with his best fastball. "I would have done the same if any of our guys were hit," said Koosman. "It just meant a bit more because it was Agee and because he had gone through so much." On August 19, Agee homered in the fourteenth inning to beat Juan Marichal, 1–0, a fitting bookend to the beginning of Agee's nightmare in the 24-inning, 1–0 defeat sixteen months earlier.

In a three-game demolition of the Atlanta Braves in the first National League Championship Series, Agee hit .357 and homered twice, and although he hit just .167 in the World Series, he was nonetheless one of the keys to the five-game rout. In the third game of the 1969 series:

• Agee homed leading off the first to give the Mets the lead.

• With the Mets ahead 3–0, but with two men on in the fourth inning, Elrod Hendricks scorched a ball to the warning track in left-center. Agee got to the ball to make a tremendous running backhand catch.

• Leading off the seventh inning, Hendricks led off and drove the ball to deep *right-center*. Again, Agee ran the ball down.

• With the bases loaded and two out in the seventh inning, Paul Blair ripped the ball into right-center. Agee dived, slid on his belly, and made an impossible one-handed catch. The play is still seen regularly on television, emblematic of the Miracle Mets.

Agee had dominated the game, and the game had turned the series. Agee made several other outstanding plays in the series, as did Ron Swoboda and others.

Agee's 1970 stats were even better than his 1969 stats, rivaling 1966 as the best statistical season of his career. In mid-June, 1971, he began to have trouble with his knee; though he continued to hit well, he was frequently out of the lineup for the balance of the season. Gil Hodges died of a heart attack in spring training, 1972. The entire team was hurt, no one more than Agee. In mid-July, 1972, Agee was disabled by a pulled muscle in the rib cage. His batting average dropped like a lead weight, and his speed departed him, due to a combination of injuries and extra weight. Agee was traded to Houston in November of 1972, to St. Louis in August of 1973, to Los Angeles in December of 1973, and was released in the spring of 1974. His career ended at the age of thirty-one.

Frustrated by being unable to get back into baseball, Agee complained that he had been blackballed for some reason. In the early 1970's, Agee and Cleon bought a bar/restaurant near Shea Stadium, which they called the Outfielders Lounge. The club thrived for several years, Agee eventually becoming sole owner and proprietor. He married and had two daughters. By the early eighties both the bar and the marriage had run their course. Agee drifted from job to job, working for the city on recreational projects, occasionally trying to get back into baseball.

Agee remarried a few years ago (Cleon Jones was his best man), and is working in the insurance field. Tommie, who failed his draft physical in 1962 because of a heart murmur, is pushing fifty now and seriously overweight; one expects to read almost any day that the heart has failed him. In thirteen years of professional ball, Tommie Agee had three years as an outstanding player, and one moment of pure unforgettable magic.

(Sources for this article include *The Mets From Mobile*, by Doc Young, an article on Jones and Agee by Ray Robinson in *Baseball Stars of 1970*, and the numerous books on the Miracle Mets, most notably *After the Miracle*, by Maury Allen, although Agee was the only 1969 Met who refused to be interviewed for that book, and Stanley Cohen's *A Magic Summer*, for which Agee was also the only Met who refused to be interviewed.)

Harry Agganis, "The Golden Greek," a college football star who died suddenly in his second year with the Red Sox.

Born in Lynn, Massachusetts in 1930, Agganis played quarterback at Boston University. Although his college career was interrupted by fifteen months in the marine corps, Agganis was a football star of the first magnitude. He was, according to *The Sporting News*, "a great T-quarterback and forward passer. He was also a good punter, runner and a star defensive player as a safety man." Playing for Paul Brown in the Senior Bowl in Mobile, Alabama, in 1952, Agganis was named the game's outstanding player. Brown wanted Agganis for the Cleveland Browns, where he envisioned him succeeding the great Otto Graham.

Agganis, however, wanted to play baseball. Turning down an offer of $25,000 a year from the Cleveland Browns, Agganis signed with the Boston Red Sox. After one year in the minor leagues (he drove in 108 runs for Louisville, tying for the American Association lead) Agganis became the Red Sox first baseman. He had an unimpressive rookie season, and in 1955 the Red Sox opened the year with a massive rookie named Norm Zauchin at first base. Zauchin failed to hit in his first five games, and Agganis got the job back and went on a tear, hitting over .300 for the next month.

A big, strong left-handed hitter, Agganis was an idol in Boston second only to Ted Williams. He was a hometown boy, handsome, articulate, cultured. In the *Baseball Register* there used to be a listing for players' hobbies. In a generation where 80 percent of the players listed hunting and fishing, or occasionally bowling or home movies, Agganis listed "stage plays, recordings and interior decorating." How this image affected his teammates is anybody's guess; a Boston clubhouse attendant groused thirty years later that "I knew Harry Agganis and he was an asshole." In any case, Agganis got his degree from Boston University, and when in addition to all of this he began to hit well in 1955, his future seemed without limit.

In May, 1955, Agganis was hit with a bout of pneumonia, or at least what appeared at the time to be pneumonia. Slowly he regained his strength, but he rushed it; an hour after being released from the hospital, he was in uniform at Fenway Park, trying to get his stroke back. He started a road trip with the Sox in Chicago on June 1, and had three hits in two games; on what was to be his last at bat, he batted in the eighth inning with two on and the Red Sox down by two. He ripped a liner in short right-center, but was robbed of a hit on a circus catch by Jim Rivera.

In Kansas City on June 4, Agganis complained of chest pains and fever. The trainer, Jack Fadden, called GM Joe Cronin, and put Agganis on a plane for Boston. Cronin met the plane in Boston and rushed him to the hospital. The pneumonia had returned with a vengeance; on June 16, Agganis was put on the voluntarily retired list, meaning essentially that he was done for the season. Zauchin, Agganis's good friend despite their rivalry for first base, came to the hospital three times to visit, but was never allowed in to see him. On June 27, with Agganis health apparently rallying, the twenty-five-year-old physical marvel died suddenly from the effects of a "massive pulmonary embolism."

Hearing the news of Agganis's death, the Massachusetts House of Representatives adjourned for the day. Agganis's body lay in state for two days at the St. George's Greek Orthodox Church in Lynn; on the day of his funeral more than ten thousand people filed by his casket. Playing in Washington, the Red Sox carried on but held a memorial. Ted Williams said in his biography that he cried on the field the day they buried Harry Agganis.

Mike Agganis, president of the Canton-Akron Indians.

Joe Agler, first baseman in the Federal League.

Susan Aglietti, manager of club relations for the commissioner's office (1989).

Sam Agnew, American League catcher from 1913 to 1919.

A fiery player with an exceptional throwing arm, Agnew didn't hit but made himself valuable with his defense. He loved to throw to the bases, frequently catching runners off base. He was the type of catcher that an old catcher, as a manager, likes to have. The number-one catcher for the Browns from 1913 to 1915 (he played two seasons under an old catcher named Branch Rickey), Agnew was sold to Boston in 1915, and found himself competing for playing time with three other catchers—Pinch Thomas, Hick Cady, and Bill Carrigan, an old catcher who was also the team's manager. Starting out at number four, Agnew survived the other three, and was the most-used catcher on the team in 1917 and 1918, helping the Red Sox to a World Championship in 1918, although he hit just .166.

Late in the 1916 season, Agnew's first with Boston, a fight developed in Washington when Carl Mays hit a Washington player with a pitch. The player threw his bat, Agnew screamed at him, the benches emptied and Agnew punched out Clark Griffith, the Senators manager. He was arrested by the Washington police, had to pay a fifty-dollar bail to get out, and was suspended for five days by the league president. Griffith, who apparently didn't hold a grudge, purchased Agnew after the 1918 World Series, and Agnew's last major league season was spent playing for the man he had once been arrested for assaulting.

Juan Agosto, contemporary lefthander.

A Puerto Rico native signed by the Red Sox in 1974 at the age of sixteen, Agosto didn't come into his own until 1987, when he stepped into the role of setup man for Dave Smith in Houston. In between, Agosto pitched for the White Sox for three years and parts of six, pitched briefly for the Twins, and was signed by Houston after being released. Agosto, who throws a hard sinker, developed in Houston after pitching coach Les Moss helped remove some flaws from his delivery.

Paul Agosto, head baseball coach at Rice University.

Luis Aguayo, contemporary infielder.

Aguayo, five foot nine and weighing almost two hundred pounds, came through the Philadelphia system as a shortstop-second baseman, a tribute to the Phillies' stubborness. In 1980 he played 84 games in the American Association and led the league in errors (28), but the next year was called up by the Phillies. A hitter with some power and

a serviceable defensive infielder, Aguayo has now had a ten-year career as an extra infielder.

Jose Luis Gutierrez Aguilar, general manager of the San Luis Potosi Cactus Men.

Rick Aguilera, contemporary pitcher now with the Minnesota Twins.

Aguilera, a native Californian, was drafted out of high school in the thirty-seventh round by the St. Louis Cardinals *as a third baseman.* He elected to attend Brigham Young University instead of turning pro, and in his sophomore season at BYU was converted to a pitcher. A teammate of Wally Joyner at BYU, Aguilera went 7–3 as a junior, was drafted by the Mets in the third round, and joined the Mets organization.

Working through four levels in the Mets system in a little less than two years, Aguilera has pitched consistently well in the major leagues, but his career has been interrupted by constant elbow problems—a bone spur on the right elbow, a "sprain of the medial collateral ligament of the right elbow." In 1987 Aguilera made 17 starts and finished 11–3, but he was out from May 30 to August 10 with the elbow problem. 1988 was completely lost to arm problems, his career in jeopardy; he had arthroscopic surgery on the right elbow in July.

Used in relief in early 1989, Aguilera was a dominant pitcher, striking out 80 men in 69 innings with a 2.34 ERA. Although his best pitch has always been a hard, late-breaking slider, in '89 he was getting 60 to 70 percent of the strikeouts with a split-fingered fastball. Traded to Minnesota as part of the Viola package, he was returned to the rotation, and pitched fairly well.

Used as a pinch hitter four times in 1986, Aguilera reached base three times on two walks and an error. He has a lifetime batting average of .203.

Hank Aguirre, left-handed pitcher in the major leagues from 1955 to 1970, remembered as a "zany" left-hander who was an effective pitcher but a hopeless hitter.

Aguirre was born in Azusa, California, in 1932. Stories about him used to say that he "had Mexican heritage;" I never knew exactly what that meant. His family had been Mexican but had been in the country for several generations, perhaps? Some of his ancestors were Mexican but some weren't? I don't know. Anyway, he went to junior college for a year in East Los Angeles, and signed with the Cleveland organization in 1951.

As a young pitcher Aguirre, six foot four and weighing then about 190, was your basic hard thrower who had no idea of the strike zone. He walked over a hundred men in the California League in 1952, in the Three-I League in 1953, in the Eastern League in 1954 and in the American Association in 1955, but all the same rose steadily through the Cleveland system. A starting pitcher for a team which already had one of the best starting rotations in baseball history, Aguirre was traded to the Tigers in 1958, where he was converted into a left-handed short man out of the bullpen. It wasn't exactly a glamour job for a twenty-six-year-old, but it was a major league job, and he pitched in that role for several years during which his control gradually improved and he mastered a screwball which was to become his out pitch.

On May 26, 1962, scheduled starter Don Mossi reported to Yankee Stadium with soreness in his shoulder. Wanting to use a left-hander against the Yankees, manager Bob Scheffing decided to give Aguirre a start. Aguirre pitched brilliantly, beating the Yankees 2–1 with a complete game. He wasn't the story of the day; Al Kaline, off to a red-hot start, broke his collarbone on the last play of the game, crashing into the fence to make a game-saving catch. Kaline was out two months, but Aguirre was out of the bullpen. He finished the season with a 16–8 record and a league-leading 2.21 ERA, by far his best major league season.

Aguirre was most famous, at this time, as the worst-hitting pitcher in baseball. But unlike some pitchers, who just didn't care about their batting, Aguirre was obsessive about it. According to Craig Wright in *The Man Who Stole First Base,* Aguirre "took extra batting practice, studied books and films, and took all the batting advice he could get." A left-handed pitcher but a right-handed batter, Aguirre decided that he couldn't do any worse batting left-handed, and in mid-June, 1962, in the middle of a ball game, he became a left-handed hitter. He hit an RBI single his first try lefty, and got a standing ovation. It was to be his only RBI of the season; he finished 1962 at 2-for-75 as a hitter with 46 strikeouts.

In spring training, 1963, a stranger approached Aguirre and handed him an envelope. "$10,000 for ten hits in 1963," said the note inside, and there was a $10,000 check—signed by Santa Claus.

Well, defying all odds, Aguirre got the ten hits in 1963. He drove in six runs that year, which was more than he had driven in in his eight previous seasons. He began switch hitting in '63, and his hitting did improve some, enough to lift his lifetime average to .085. He never got the ten thousand dollars; Santa Claus can be hard to find when you have his name on a check.

After pitching fairly well in '63, Aguirre in '64 had repeated conflicts with his manager, Charlie Dressen; at one time he demanded to be traded. After thinking things over in the winter, Aguirre arrived in '65 determined to repair his relationship with Dressen, and did, building a solid relationship with Dressen and putting up a solid season as a starter (14–10).

"Maybe I wasn't serious enough on the field," he said later. "I was looking for laughs most of the time. But when I got on the mound, I was strictly serious. I guess people couldn't tell the difference."

In the spring of 1966 Dressen had the notion that Aguirre, as an older pitcher, would thrive by starting less often, maybe every six or seven days, and occasionally throwing an inning of relief in between. It was to be a tough year in Detroit. Dressen suffered a heart attack on May 16, and died later in the summer. His replacement, Bob Swift, was hospitalized in July with lung cancer, and he died, too, that October. Lost in the shuffle, Aguirre finished 3–9, and his career as a starter was over. He managed to hold on for four more seasons back in the bullpen as a left-handed short man, even posting a 0.69 ERA for the Dodgers in '68.

Aguirre was a very fast worker; he believed that working quickly was an obligation that he owed the fans. "I can't sit on the bench and watch a guy pitch slow," he once said. "It drives me crazy. So I work as fast as I can when I'm out there." In the off-seasons he worked as account executive for a company that made industrial motion pictures, and at last report was still involved in that business.

Willie Aikens, major league first baseman, 1977–85, now on the roster of the Bradenton Explorers in the Seniors Professional Baseball Association.

Aikens was born in Seneca, South Carolina, in October, 1954, a couple of weeks after the end of the 1954 World Series, and was named for the best player in baseball at the moment: Willie Mays Aikens. As a sophomore in high school Aikens weighed 258 pounds. Playing all three major sports, he worked his way down to 240 by the time he

graduated. Aikens attended South Carolina State College in Orangeburg, South Carolina, where he apparently lost his eligibility in mid-career, and was taken by the California Angels in the January, 1975, free-agent draft, the second player taken in that "off-season" draft. Signing with the Angels, he worked his way through the system with his bat, leading the Midwest League in RBI (and Errors) in 1975, the Texas League in home runs and RBI (and errors) in 1976, and the PCL in home runs (and errors) in 1978. In 1978 Deron Johnson benched him for five days for not hustling, and he would make about 25 errors a year as a first baseman, which isn't that easy to do, but the man could hit for an absolute fact.

Listed at six feet three inches and 220 pounds, Aikens was (and is) a left-handed hitter with a long, sweeping swing full of violent jerks and jolts. Sharing the DH job with Don Baylor in 1979 and playing first when Carew was hurt, Aikens drove in 81 runs in 379 at bats in his first full season. (You often read that Baylor in 1979 was "the first DH to win an MVP Award," but actually Baylor was primarily an outfielder that year.) With Carew out of the lineup with an injury, Aikens hit a grand-slam home run on June 13, 1979, in Toronto, and then hit another one on June 14; he is the only player in the last twenty-five years to hit grand slam home runs in consecutive games.

His season ended on September 18 when he tore up his knee attempting to slide into second base after having finished the Royals season. I remember the game like it was yesterday. The Royals had the lead in June of that year, but were swept by the Angels in KC the weekend of the SABR convention, and then fell almost out of contention in July, due primarily to the atrocious pitching of Rich Gale. I was ready to get Gale out of the pitching rotation about the middle of

TRACERS

Exactly a month to the day after the Copa Incident, Billy was traded to Kansas City. . . . A week after that, I was pitching against Kansas City and we were leading by about eight or nine runs. It was the eighth inning and Billy came to bat. I threw him a big slow curve and he took it for a strike. I got the ball back and said to him, "Same thing." I wanted him to hit it for a single or a double, but I threw another big slow curve and he wrapped it around the left-field foul pole for a home run. Now he was prancing around the bases, the son of a bitch. When I saw him prancing like that, I was sorry I did it. . . . The last thing Casey wanted to do was to be shown up by a player he had just traded away.

—Whitey Ford
Slick (page 139)

This story is also recalled in several other recent books about the Yankees, including *The Mick* (pages 167–168). The Copa Incident occurred on May 15, 1957; a group of Yankees, celebrating Billy Martin's birthday at the Copacabana, got involved in a post-midnight brawl, and a month later Billy Martin was traded. The trade happened while the Yankees were in Kansas City, and Martin did hit a home run in the series. . . .

But it wasn't the home run recalled by Ford and Mantle. The home run Ford remembered actually happened on July 30, Stengel's sixty-sixth birthday, but six weeks after the Martin deal. The Bombers, with four RBI from Yogi, led 10–3 after seven innings. In the top of the eighth (after thirty years Ford has the inning right) Martin concluded the evening's scoring with a solo home run off Whitey, who pitched a complete-game thirteen-hitter.

With the exception of having mixed up the time frame, Ford's memory of the game appears accurate.

May; Herzog would take him out but then he'd run him back out there, take him out and then give him another opportunity.

The Royals got back in the race and were three games behind California on September 17, with California coming in for three games. Leonard and Gura would pitch two games in the series, but who would pitch the middle game was up in the air—maybe Pattin would go, or maybe Gura would pitch Tuesday on three days' rest and Craig Chamberlain would come out Wednesday on three days rest. I remember driving to the game with Susie on September 18, she said she'd heard on the radio that Gale would start. I laughed; I thought she was just kidding me. When she convinced me that she really *had* heard that on the radio, I told her the announcer had screwed it up; Whitey wouldn't start Rich Gale, who hadn't had a good outing in two months, in a critical game like this.

So there it was, a matchup of two weather conditions, Frost and Gale. The Royals won the other two games of the series, and would have won this one if Pattin had started the game, but Pattin didn't get in until Willie Aikens's double had knocked Gale out with one man out in the first. Willie Aikens's *slide* knocked Willie Aikens out of the season, so they all ended more or less together—Gale's outing, Aikens's season, the Royals' chances, and Whitey Herzog's tenure in Kansas City.

Then that winter Aikens came to Kansas City. It was hard to believe what an awful first baseman he was. I used to write long articles in the *Abstract*, poking fun at Aikens's defense; in retrospect perhaps it is enough to say that he played first base like a man with a drug problem. He must have been uncoachable. I honestly believe that Aikens thought that it was his responsibility to cut off the throw to home plate if he could get to it; I don't think he had any idea that this was just an option.

Through the first two months of the 1980 season, Aikens was hitting .232 with 2 homers and 21 RBI. In a game in early June, Jim Frey removed Aikens for a pinch hitter. Aikens slammed his helmet off the dugout floor and screamed obscenities at Frey. The two had an angry meeting after the game, lasting an hour. The next night Aikens went 3-for-4 with a double, a homer and 4 RBI. His season turned around, and the Royals won the pennant. In the 1980 World Series Aikens homered twice in the first game, and then homered twice again in the fourth game; he is the only man to have two two-homer

games in a single World Series. After that game, Aikens spoke movingly to the press about his battle with a speech impediment. Returning home to Seneca, South Carolina, Aikens was honored with a parade.

You had to feel, at the moment, that Aikens was on the verge of breaking through. Jim Frey said he would hit 30 homers a year, but the Kansas City park took several home runs a year away from him (in 1980, when he hit 20 home runs and drove in 98, he homered only five times in Kansas City), and he never hit anything the first two months of the season in Kansas City, so with his defense he was always under fire from the Kansas City fans. In 1981 he started slowly, played bad defense and saved his season's stats with a late-season rush. In 1982 he started slowly, played bad defense and saved his season's stats with a late-season rush. In a typical year Aikens would hit close to .350 against right-handed pitching, but about .180 against left-handed pitching, and he was the slowest runner in the American League.

In April, 1983, Dick Howser decided that Aikens had to be platooned. Aikens expressed his opinion by skipping batting practice and infield drills (not that he'd picked up much in ten years of infield drills, anyway.) Dick Howser said that had better not happen again, and it didn't. Aikens pushed his batting average to .302 with 23 homers in just 410 at bats, but as the season progressed an ugly rumor emerged as fact: Aikens was one of four Royals indicted by a grand jury and subsequently convicted of possession of cocaine. Aikens was sentenced to three months in prison, and served his time in a federal prison in Fort Worth.

While Aikens was in stir, the Royals traded him to Toronto. In December, 1983, Aikens and his teammates were banned from baseball for the 1984 season by Commissioner Kuhn. An arbitrator, however, ruled that the commissioner's action was excessive, and that the players must be allowed to play as of May 15, 1984. In the Toronto lineup on May 17, Aikens hit a single and double and received a standing ovation from the Toronto fans. It probably wasn't his last good day of the season, quite. After hitting .205 with the Blue Jays in '84 and getting off to another slow start in '85, he was released by the Blue Jays.

I think some of Aikens's problems as a hitter were caused by being a hot-weather hitter; I just don't think he could get his bat untracked in cold weather. Signing to play in

the Mexican League in 1986, Aikens has now played four seasons in Mexico, and become a folk hero. With Puebla in 1986, Aikens had one of the greatest offensive seasons in the history of organized baseball, hitting .454 with 46 homers in 129 games; his slugging percentage was .863. Again in 1989, Aikens led the Mexican League in batting average, at .395, and narrowly missed the Triple Crown.

Obviously, Aikens at thirty-five is still a major league hitter, and you never know, he may yet get a chance to prove it. If not, the Seniors League may survive, and Willie may be the big star there. It's been an odyssey; in thirty years it may be the basis of a hell of a novel. We'll hope for a happy ending.

Danny Ainge, an NBA guard formerly with the Boston Celtics, who attempted for three seasons to play major league baseball.

Born in Eugene, Oregon, in 1959, Ainge was a three-sport star in high school, playing basketball, and football as well as—no, make that better than—baseball. In his last two seasons of high school basketball, he led his teams to a 52–1 record and two state championships, after which he signed to play basketball at Brigham Young. Later that summer, he was drafted by the Blue Jays in the fifteenth round; he would have gone much sooner, but most people felt he would stick to basketball.

The Blue Jays started Ainge out in AAA ball in 1978, as the starting shortstop at Syracuse. He was way over his head and couldn't play shortstop, notwithstanding which the Blue Jays brought him to the major leagues in 1979. They tried him for a year as a second baseman, then for a year as an outfielder, then for a year as a third baseman. He wasn't very good at any of those places and didn't hit a lick. For a while in 1980 he talked about switch hitting, and although the encyclopedias show him as a right-handed batter, he did bat left-handed in two games in 1980.

Ainge had said throughout his early career that he would not try to play both sports professionally, that he would choose one or the other and stick with it. The Blue Jays under Peter Bavasi had determined to their own satisfaction that Ainge would eventually be a quality major league ballplayer, and they felt that they were in a war with pro basketball to acquire Danny Ainge's future. Thus, although Ainge as a major league baseball player was (literally) out of his league, the Blue Jays continued to play him as a sign of their commitment to him as a baseball player. This generated inevitable resentment in baseball, where major league playing time is precious.

While he struggled in baseball, Ainge excelled in basketball. As a sophomore at BYU, he set a single-season scoring record with 632 points, leading the team to a berth in the NCAA playoffs. In his junior year he made some All-American teams; in his senior year he made them all. In his senior year he brought BYU into the Final Four by driving the length of the floor and hitting a lay-up with two seconds left to push the Cougars past Notre Dame. Still, in October, 1980, he announced that he had made the decision: He would play baseball. Ruling out a career in the NBA, he felt that he would progress more rapidly when he was able to concentrate on one sport.

Being young, Ainge tried to make that decision stick beyond the point at which it was clear to everybody else that he had made the wrong choice. When he struggled in baseball, Ainge felt that it was important to him not to accept failure, but to respond to the challenge by working harder and proving that he could so play in the major leagues. Eventually his teammates were able to talk some sense into him. They convinced Ainge that he would never be as good in baseball as he would be in basketball.

In August, 1981, Ainge decided to go to pro basketball. Then there was another holdup; Ainge had signed a contract with the Blue Jays saying that he would not play pro basketball, and had taken money from the Blue Jays for that agreement. In November, 1981, the Boston Celtics agreed to compensate Toronto for Ainge's release from a baseball contract, and Ainge's baseball career came to an end.

Ainge was not a great success in his early years in the NBA, taking criticism particularly for his defensive play. About 1984, the joke was that Ainge had proven so far that he couldn't play shortstop, second base, third base or the outfield, hit left-handed, hit right-handed, hit a jump shot, or guard Andrew Toney. He stuck with it in basketball, however, and turned his career around, becoming a respected member of a World Championship team.

Eddie Ainsmith, the player in the "test case" by which baseball players in World War I were determined to be engaged in nonessential conduct, and thus eligible for the draft.

Born in Cambridge, Massachusetts, in 1910, Ainsmith spent a year and a half with the Lawrence, Massachusetts, team in the New England League, and began his major league career in 1910 at the age of twenty. As a player he did little of note. He is remembered sometimes as being the man who caught many of Walter Johnson's games. On June 26, 1914, Ainsmith stole second, third, and home in the same game; he is the only catcher ever to do that. He ran very well for a catcher and had good enough defensive skills, but he wasn't a hitter, at least of baseballs. In August, 1914, Ainsmith was suspended for jumping into the seats to go after a heckler.

His moment of fame arrived in 1918, when America went to war. In July, 1918, Ainsmith was declared by his local draft board to be engaged in nonessential employment—baseball—and therefore to be eligible for the draft. The Senators, representing all of baseball, appealed to the War Department, basing their appeal on three grounds:

1) Baseball was a unique business, with large investments and property, the value of which would be utterly destroyed if the work-or-fight order was applied to baseball players.

2) Baseball players had unique and specialized skills. To close up baseball would automatically create a hardship on baseball players, who could not hope to find any comparable employment in war-related industries.

3) Baseball was the national pastime, the cessation of which would make a tiny number of soldiers available, but do great harm to civilian and military morale.

These arguments are similar to the arguments used by baseball in World War II to keep baseball alive, but remember they were not arguing here whether baseball could be played, but whether baseball players should be exempt from the draft. Secretary of War Baker rejected the arguments, ruling that

1) Many baseball players were beyond draft age, so baseball teams would *not* be put out of business.

2) Baseball players were young and healthy men, and should have no trouble finding employment in an "essential" industry.

3) The national need to make sacrifices took precedence over the need for entertainment.

Wrote Baker at the end of the Ainsmith case:

"The non-productive employment of able-bodied persons, useful in the national defense, either as military men or in the industry and commerce of our country, cannot be justified."

Later, baseball won a partial reprieve, in that the work-or-fight order was not to be applied to baseball until September 1, allowing the season to be brought to an orderly conclusion.

The war was over by the time the 1919 season was ready to start. In January, 1919, Ainsmith was sent to Detroit as part of a three-way trade; he may have been shipped out in part because of negative fan reaction in Washington to what was seen by some as a reluctance to do his patriotic duty. In any case, after eight years in Washington, Ainsmith began the nomadic phase at the end of his career. His batting improved markedly with Detroit, which played in a much better hitter's park, and improved even more with the coming of the lively ball era. With the Cardinals in 1922 Ainsmith, who had hit only 6 home runs in his twelve prior seasons of major league baseball, belted 13 home runs in one season, also posting a career-high .293 average. His career ended suddenly in 1924. From the 1925 *Reach Guide:*

CADORE AND AINSMITH DISMISSED IN DISGRACE

At Cincinnati, on August 16, Manager McGraw, of the Giants, took occasion to hand out a bit of severe punishment to a pair of erring Giants. Eddie Ainsmith and Leon Cadore, the bullpen artists, were shipped home by McGraw for violation of training rules. McGraw became tired of the way Eddie and Leon were cutting up and decided to ship them East, after asking waivers on both. "The violation for which these players have been dismissed from the camp is not their first, you may be sure," said McGraw. "I don't let players out when they fall down once. They have done it several times and I am in no mood to stand for their capers. I had taken both of these fellows when nobody else wanted them and gave them every chance to make good. I had tried out Cadore a couple of times and like the way he looked and might have been able to do something for him. Ainsmith, of course, had less of a future, but at least he could have remained with the club indefinitely to warm up the pitchers and help out in other ways. However, I expect when this club is paying a man's salary it is entitled to some return on its money, and neither Cadore nor Ainsmith was willing to play fair with it."

Debbie Aitchison-Brooks, general manager of the Sarasota White Sox.

Redskin Raleigh Aitchison, a southpaw who had a good year with the Brooklyn Dodgers in 1914 before hurting his arm.

This was the infancy of flight, and in the spring of 1915 an aviatrix named Ruth Law took several of the Brooklyn players up for rides in her primitive little airplane. Raleigh Aitchison refused to have anything to do with it, saying that it was his intention to die in a soft bed. His wife, however, called Redskin Raleigh a "scaredy cat," went up in the plane, and spoke movingly about the thrill of flying (see *Stengel*, by Robert Creamer). Perhaps provoked by this, Aitchison later may have gone up with Ms. Law, and may in fact have been the person who dropped the famous grapefruit that Wilbert Robinson attempted to catch, believing it was a baseball.

This was also the era of the players' fraternity. Aitchison, who had a $4,000 contract with the Dodgers in 1915, was released to Milwaukee, where he was paid only $1,325. With the support of the fraternity he sued Dodger owner Charles Ebbets for the $2,675 difference and won the case.

Jack Aker, longtime major league relief pitcher and coach, who was a central figure in the incident aboard TWA Flight 85 in 1967.

A California native, Aker was a high school football star, and went to the College of the Sequoias on a football scholarship. After a year there he was offered a scholarship by the University of California, but USC made it clear that he could not play baseball for them, only football. Aker knew that that would be end of his baseball career, and baseball was his first love, so when the Kansas City A's offered him a small bonus to sign with their organization in 1959, he did.

Beginning in the Nebraska State League in 1959, Aker stole 21 bases in only 52 games, but hit just .208. He was sent that fall to the Florida Instructional League, where A's director of player personnel George Selkirk watched him swing, and recommended he switch to pitching.

As a pitcher, Aker struggled for several years until he caught a break: The organization gave up on him. Aker had been with Lewiston (Northwest League) in 1961, then up to the Texas League in '62, then back to Lewiston in '63. Sensing that no one was paying any attention to him anyway, Aker began to experiment with a side-arm delivery. He found that the side-arm action gave him better control and a sinking fastball, and his career took off. He was 6–1 at Lewiston

with a 1.24 ERA, and a year later he was in the major leagues.

Called "Chief" by his teammates because he was part Indian, Aker in 1966 had a great season, one of the best seasons ever by a relief pitcher up to that time. He was the cover story of the July 30, 1966, edition of *The Sporting News*; the story dealt largely with his disappointment over not making the All-Star team, which he ascribed to not pitching well against the Minnesota Twins, whose manager selected the pitchers. He pitched well against everybody else; he wound up the year with a 1.99 ERA and 32 saves, the most ever up to that point (see Ted Abernathy). He allowed less than one batter per inning to reach base, hits and walks combined.

In 1967 he was not the same pitcher. On August 3, 1967, Aker was hit hard in a loss in Boston. On the flight back to Kansas City, he sat in the back of the plane with Ken Harrelson, and drank heavily. (Harrelson had "borrowed" a tray of little drink bottles from a stewardess and distributed the drinks among the team members.) The flight, an economy flight, made stops in Baltimore and St. Louis before returning to Kansas City, and apparently a number of players were well into their cups before the final touchdown. It hadn't been a bad road trip (the A's had split twelve games), and there were *no* immediate reports of disorderly conduct on the flight. Sid Bordman, a Kansas City reporter who was on the flight, saw or heard nothing unusual, but then, that's Sid Bordman for you; the man had a nose for news. Before the controversy exploded, fifteen to twenty players had signed a letter to TWA complimenting the stewardesses on the conduct of the flight, which the players then pointed to as a sign of a routine, satisfactory flight, and if you believe that one. . . .

In time, however, word got to Charlie Finley that players had been drunk and that stewardesses had been abused in some manner on the flight. Pitcher Lew Krausse may (or may not) have made crude remarks in the presence of a woman passenger and her child. Krausse had a history of problems, and Finley demanded that Alvin Dark fine Krausse five hundred dollars for his misbehavior.

Alvin Dark, who sat up front on flights because he didn't much want to know what was going on in the back, talked to several players, who all insisted that Krausse had done nothing improper on the flight, and so

Dark refused to levy the fine. Finley ordered that in the future, alcoholic beverages would not be served to players on team flights. He drew up a letter to the players to that effect; Aker, as player representative, was required to read the statement to the players.

Not even a beer? Not even a beer. The players were outraged. Aker drafted a statement on behalf of the players:

> We, the players of the Kansas City Athletics, feel that an unjust amount of pressure has been brought to bear on several members of the club who had no part whatsoever in the so-called incident on the recent plane trip from Boston to Kansas City.
>
> The overwhelming opinion of the players is that the entire matter was blown out of proportion. Mr. Finley's policy of using certain unauthorized personnel in his organization as go-betweens has led to similar misunderstandings in the past and has tended to undermine the morale of the club. We players feel that if Mr. Finley would give his fine coaching staff and excellent manager the authority they deserve, these problems would not exist.

Every player on the team signed the statement, and Jack Aker read it to the media. By "unauthorized personnel in his organization" the players meant Monte Moore, the team broadcaster; if you look up "lackey" in the dictionary there's a picture of Monte Moore, Finley's lackey. Word of the statement reached Finley in his hotel room at 1:30 A.M. In the midst of an emergency meeting with Dark and club executives, he demanded that Aker be brought to the meeting. Aker could not be found; he was out on the town, well past curfew. When he came in he was brought to the meeting, fined for his curfew violation, and told to retract the statement and apologize to Finley. He refused, of course.

Twenty years later, interviewed by Armen Keteyian for *Catfish*, Krausse said that Finley "had the story all screwed up. I was single. A couple of other guys were married. One of the guys, who was in the bathroom with a stewardess, he was married." The flight was to become as famous within baseball, wrote Bill Libby a decade later, as the trips taken by the *Lusitania* and the *Hindenburg*. As the upshot of it, Alvin Dark was fired, Ken Harrelson was released and made a lot of money out of the deal, and the young A's, on the verge of a breakthrough, were set back a couple of years. The players requested a hearing of their grievance by Commissioner William Eckert, and also filed a charge of unfair labor practices with the National Labor Relations Board. The hearing with the commissioner resulted in a compromise of all issues involved except the fine levied against Krausse. The request for an NLRB hearing was withdrawn by Krausse in a surprise move, perhaps because Finley reached an agreement with Krausse, or perhaps because Marvin Miller, wanting to challenge the owners' ability to levy fines indiscriminately, became aware of other incidents involving Krausse which might make him a less than ideal test case.

In many ways the incident is uncannily similar to the 1926 incident on the Pittsburgh Pirates (see Babe Adams)—the basic dislike of a skinflint owner manifesting itself in a trivial incident, the troubles created by people with loyalty to the front office interacting with the team, the support of a well-liked manager placing that manager in an untenable position, the oh-so-serious meetings in the front office and the ever-so-angry meetings in the clubhouse, the macho ownership asserting control of the team by fining and releasing those who spoke out, the appeal to the commissioner to sort things out. The time frame within the season is exactly the same; the Pittsburgh incident began on August 7 after a defeat in Boston and ended on August 17; the Kansas City incident began on August 3 after a defeat in Boston and ended with the firing of Dark and the release of Harrelson on August 21. Like the Pirates, the A's collapsed in September, winning only ten games in the last month and a half of the season.

Several players, again led by Aker, insisted that they would never sign another contract with Finley, but this was 1967 and they had no choice. Finley forced Aker to be the first player to sign his contract for 1968, a symbolic crushing of the opposition to him.

Aker had another poor season in 1968, and in October, 1968, the A's let him go to Seattle in the expansion draft. The '69 Pilots, you will recall, were Jim Bouton's team, the team portrayed in Ball Four. Bouton's most memorable insight into Jack Aker in 1969 was that Aker was just learning to chew tobacco, and hadn't figured out how to spit properly, so his uniform was always covered with brown spots. Again, he was the player rep for the Pilots. Traded to the Yankees in May, 1969, Aker regained his effectiveness. Although he never had a "workhorse" season as he had in Kansas City in 1966, Aker

pitched extremely well for the Yankees in 1970, posting a 2.06 ERA with 16 saves, and for the Cubs in 1972.

His playing career ended when he was released by the Mets in 1974, but Aker has remained in baseball as a minor league manager and major league coach. He managed in the Mets system for several years. In 1981, when the Mets cut him loose, they announced that they were doing so for Akers's benefit, feeling that it was time for him to move on. Though at age forty-nine Aker may have missed getting a shot as a major league manager, he was the pitching coach for the Cleveland Indians as recently as 1987, and remains a part of the pool of talent from which coaches and managers are hired.

(Accounts of the incident on TWA Flight 85 can be found in *Hawk*, by Ken Harrelson, *When in Doubt, Fire the Manager*, by Alvin Dark, *Charlie O. and the Angry A's*, by Bill Libby, *Charlie O*, by Herbert Michelson, *Catfish, My Life in Baseball*, by Armen Keteyian, *Catfish, the Three Million Dollar Pitcher*, by Bill Libby and the 1967 *Baseball Guide*, from *The Sporting News*, as well as in contemporary newspapers and in other books about players who were on the team.)

Bill "Dizzy" Akers, shortstop for Detroit, 1929–31, and third baseman for the Braves in 1932. Dick Bartell said of Akers in *Rowdy Richard* that Akers "had his own way of making a triple play on a ground ball. He would drop it, kick it and then throw it away. One of his pitchers asked him which side he was playing for."

Roy Akin, a longtime star third baseman in the Texas League.

Akin has the unique distinction of having both hit into and turned an unassisted triple play. He hit into an unassisted triple play in the Pacific Coast League on July 19, 1911, a play described in *Minor League Baseball Stars* as "the outstanding individual fielding play in minor league history, or at least the most sensational." With runners on first and second, Akin ripped a low liner into short center. The center fielder made a miraculous diving catch, somersaulted halfway to second base, touched second and then ran to first, doubling off both runners. This is the only unassisted triple play ever turned by an outfielder.

Akin got his unassisted triple play on May 9, 1912, back in the Texas League. He was playing third base with runners on second and third when the opposition manager attempted a trick play intended to score two

runs with a sacrifice bunt. The bunt was lined to Akin, who touched third and tagged the runner.

A glove man who rarely struck out, Akin played minor league ball at least from 1902 through 1914. On a road trip in 1908, members of the Houston club found a baby boy abandoned on the train. The players, led by Akin, made the discarded baby their own, passing the hat at games and doing other things to raise money for the infant's care. Akin eventually adopted and raised the little boy. (See *The Texas League*, by Bill O'Neal.)

Marv Albert, the best known of three brothers who are sports broadcasters. An older brother, Al, is the voice of the NBA's Denver Nuggets, and a younger brother, Steve, does play-by-play for the New York Islanders, which I think is a hockey team.

Born in 1943, Albert as a kid became an APBA freak and, for some unknown reason, the biggest Solly Hemus fan in the world, or if not in the world then certainly outside of St. Louis. He started a fan club; the newsletter was called the *Hemus Headliner*.

In 1957 Albert talked his way into a job as an office boy with the Dodgers; among his duties was listening to away games on the radio and posting the scores on the scoreboard. When not occupied, Albert and his brothers would sit in an auxiliary press box in right field and "broadcast" the games to each other. Eventually they became obnoxious enough to get thrown out.

"You have to understand that we were not into subtle, toned-down broadcasting," Albert wrote in *Yesss!*, his book about sportscasting. "We went at it hot and heavy." He did, and still does, using the one-word affirmative as his signature affirmation that something exciting has occurred. Though not assigned to baseball play-by-play by NBC, Albert for several years enlivened the peacock pre-game show with inflamed rhetoric, constant enthusiasm and offbeat humor.

At times Albert gives occasion for offense; when Bart Giamatti left the presidency of Yale University to become president of the National League, Albert asked Whitey Herzog if he was going to apply for the presidency of Yale. Herzog interpreted this as a put-down—I doubt that it was intended as one—and told Albert that he didn't think it was at all funny and the interview was over. Albert, apparently delighted, put Herzog's snit on the air.

Albert broadcasts like a man who has bet every penny he has on the game, and desperately needs for both teams to win. One suspects that Marv probably gets more irate mail than any other sports broadcaster around. He is sometimes careless about what he says, and can become more interested in provoking a reaction than in promoting understanding. In a world in which ever more announcers choose to rattle out sports events in a High Civic Duty Mono-Drone, Albert, God bless him, is more afraid of being boring than of stepping on toes.

Francis Alberts, Texas League batting champion in 1975 with a .342 average,

Gus Alberts, shortstop with Cleveland (American Association) in 1888; sort of a nineteenth-century Johnny Gochnaur.

Ed "Rube" Albosta, National League pitcher just before and after World War II.

Albosta's major league won-lost record was 0 and 8. I'm not sure, but I believe he holds the record for most losses, career, by a pitcher with no wins.

Nat Albright, broadcaster, who re-created games on the Dodgers radio network from 1950 through 1962.

A native of Dallas, Albright was working in Columbus, Georgia, when Buzzie Bavasi hired him, after hearing a tape, to do Dodger re-creations. While Red Barber and Vin Scully did live broadcasts of Dodgers games, Albright re-created the same games from a studio in Washington, D.C.; his re-creations were carried on more than a hundred stations for several years (apparently it was not economically feasible for some reason to mass-distribute the live broadcast). With an exciting team and a country torn by a racial division which the Dodgers symbolized, the Dodgers broadcasts had tremendous impact throughout the eastern part of the country, at times drawing higher ratings than the local teams.

Alex Albritton, pitcher with the Baltimore Black Sox and Washington Potomacs (Negro Leagues), early 1920s.

Vic Albury, pitcher with the Twins from 1973 to 1976.

A native of Key West, Florida, Albury's professional career got off to an extremely unpromising beginning. Signed as a first baseman by the Cleveland Indians, Albury hit .233 in the Midwest League, got into a disagreement of some kind with Indians officials, was suspended and then released.

And then drafted, drafted by the big team with the baggy green uniforms. Albury spent two years in the army including one in Vietnam. Back home, he arranged for a tryout with San Diego, but the man who arranged the tryout told him he'd have to switch to pitching. After an outstanding year with Charlotte in the Southern League in 1971, where he had a 1.73 ERA and a .354 batting average, Albury was drafted again, this time by the Twins, and sent to winter ball. After going 7–3 with a no-hitter in Puerto Rico, Albury seemed ready to make the show, got to spring training—and couldn't lift his arm. He had surgery to remove bone spurs from his elbow, and went back to fighting his way through the system.

After all that, Albury didn't have an outstanding career, but he did win 18 games in the major leagues before the elbow problems came back in 1976.

Santo Alcala, a pitcher who went 11–4 as a rookie for the Reds in 1976, and then won only three more games in the major leagues.

Luis Alcaraz, infielder with the Dodgers and Royals, 1967–70.

Alcaraz was an outstanding hitter for a second baseman in the minor leagues, and why he failed to progress more rapidly is a bit of a mystery. He didn't make many errors as a second baseman, but for some reason he spent four years in the California League, and by that time was too old to be a well regarded prospect, even when he won the Texas League batting championship in 1967 with a .328 average and 22 home runs. He played well for the Royals late in 1969, which was a factor in the decision to release Jerry Adair (see Adair), but then failed his only shot at a regular job in 1970, when he was twenty-nine years old.

Dan Alderman, pitcher with Notre Dame in the first decade of this century, who was killed in France in 1918. A native of Goshen, Indiana, Alderman starred at Notre Dame, pitched minor league ball and was for a time a sports reporter with the *Des Moines Register.*

Sandy Alderson, vice-president of baseball operations for the Oakland Athletics.

Now forty-two years old, Alderson played second base for Dartmouth in the sixties, went to Harvard Law School and joined a legal firm in San Francisco. In 1981 the firm was retained by the A's to prepare arguments for salary arbitration, and Alderson, because of his baseball background and fan's interest, was detailed to the duty. He impressed the A's owners so much that they retained his services as consul for the organization, and in 1983 Alderson became vice-president of baseball operations.

Not wishing to deprive Jose Canseco, Mark McGwire, Tony LaRussa, or anyone else of due credit, Alderson may be the critical man in the success of the A's in the late eighties. In an era in which many top executives resist modern analysis and cling to old-school bullshit, Alderson has accepted and advocates the basic tenets of offense advanced by sabermetrics: that scoring runs is essentially a function of getting people on base, that the surest way to score those who reach base is wall-to-wall power. In competition with GMs who insist on dumping a player when he has an off year, Alderson treats the trade market as he would treat any other market: Buy a player when his value is down, trade him when his value is up.

A class act from start to finish, Alderson keeps a low profile, sometimes going to absurd lengths to do so. The Oakland A's media guide has profiles of Ted Kubiak (manager at Southern Oregon), Frank Ciensczyk (equipment manager) and William Savarino III (non-roster player)—but nothing about Alderson, nothing beyond his name and title. In contract negotiations, Alderson is respected for fairness, honesty, and the maturity to keep the lines open and the negotiations proceeding—but by no means is he an easy mark. The fact that Alderson came into baseball because he could help prepare a salary arbitration is not *quite* just a happenstance; it means something. Better than anyone else, Alderson represents the modern baseball executive, the baseball executive drawn into the game in the 1980s because, with ballplayers being paid $3 million a year, it has simply become too expensive to make decisions carelessly.

Mike Aldrete, outfielder with the Montreal Expos.

A graduate of Stanford with a degree in communications, Aldrete worked his way through the San Francisco system by hitting .417 (Pioneer League), .339 (California League), .333 (Texas League), and .371 (PCL). When Aldrete hit .325 in his second year in the majors (1987), some people projected him as a star. Then reality set in; Aldrete is a line-drive hitter, no speed, not much power, and nothing in his previous record *really* suggests that he should hit .325;

.325 with the Giants would be about .410 with Phoenix. But if Aldrete is not the hitter who hit .325 in 1987, he's also a better hitter than the man who hit .221 in 1989, and his career is likely to rebound.

Vic Aldridge, the pitcher who opposed Walter Johnson in the seventh game of the 1925 World Series, the game once described by *The Sporting News* as "the best and worst game of baseball ever played in this country."

Born in Indian Spring, Indiana, in 1893, Aldridge attended Central Normal College, leaving there in 1915 to sign with the Indianapolis team in the American Association. Indianapolis sent him out to a lower level, but by 1917 Aldridge had earned a job with the Cubs. In his first start with the Cubs, on May 16, he pitched a shutout, beating Boston 8–0. He pitched reasonably well with the Cubs in 1917, but his ERA was a half a run over the league, and when the Cubs acquired Lefty Tyler and Pete Alexander in cash-added trades over the winter, Aldridge was squeezed out.

Sold to Los Angeles in the Pacific Coast League, Aldridge put in four solid seasons in the PCL, finally earning a ticket back to Chicago by going 20–10 in 1921 with a league-leading 2.16 ERA. With the Cubs in 1922, he began a run of four extraordinarily consistent seasons, winning fifteen or sixteen games each year with ERAs in a range of 3.48 to 3.63. At the end of that run Aldridge was with the Pirates, and the Pirates were in the World Series.

The Pirates had used five starters in 1925 of almost equal ability, so the pitching patterns for the World Series were pretty much up in the air. Aldridge started the second game, and beat Stan Coveleski, 3–2. He started the fifth game, again against Coveleski, and beat him again, 6–3; Aldridge went the distance in both games. What was to have been the seventh game was rained out, giving Aldridge two days rest, and so McKechnie elected to bring Aldridge back to start the seventh game against Walter Johnson; both Aldridge and Walter were trying to win for the third time in the series.

When the crowd assembled on October 15, 1925, to try again to watch the seventh game, they were met at the gates of Forbes Field by fog and drizzle. The low point of Commissioner Landis's reign, to this point and probably forever, was a World Series

game in 1922 which had been played to a tie, exposing Landis to a menacing mob and sustained criticism. Landis wanted no repeat; "If we start this thing," he said in a pre-game conference, "we're going to finish it come hell or high water."

What came was high water, although Roger Peckinpaugh might have argued it was the other. Aldridge was knocked out in the first inning after walking in a run; he was replaced on the mound by a steady rain. Washington was ahead 4–0 in what became a horribly played but hotly contested game. Walter Johnson called for dry towels on the mound, called for sawdust to be spread around the mound. He should have called for something to be spread around shortstop—holy wafers, perhaps. Two errors by Roger Peckinpaugh, who had eight in the series, let Pittsburgh back in the game, and the Pirates rallied for a 9–7 win.

This portrait of Aldridge appeared in the 1926 *Reach Guide*:

> Pitcher Victor Aldridge . . . was secured by the Pirates from the Chicago club in the big trade of last winter and after an indifferent start because of lack of condition, pitched pennant winning ball for the Buccaneers. . . . Besides being a hurler who is well-nigh unhittable when he is right, Aldridge is one of the hardest working pitchers in the National League. He has an admirable disposition for a twirler, never grumbles and takes breaks as they come.

Aldridge pitched two more years with the Pirates, winning fifteen games again in 1927, and being hammered once more in October by the 1927 Yankees. He held out in the spring of 1928, and was traded to the Giants for Burleigh Grimes, who was also holding out. The trade worked out badly for John McGraw, and because so many books about baseball are written from a New York point of view, Aldridge is most remembered today as the guy that the Giants got burned on in a trade; that, at least, is what I find most of the time when I spot his name in an index. Aldridge won four games for the Giants, and was finished at age thirty-four.

Chuck Aleno, reserve third baseman for Cincinnati during World War II.

Grover Cleveland "Buck" Alexander, pitcher in the Negro Leagues, mid-1920s.

Charles Alexander, professor of history at Ohio University, and the author of two baseball biographies.

Alexander is the author of six volumes of critical history, two on the Ku Klux Klan, two on the impact of nationalism on American intellectual life, and one each on the Eisenhower years and the Mercury project. His two baseball books are *Ty Cobb*, released by Oxford University Press in 1984, and *John McGraw*, from Viking in 1988. Alexander's works are scholarly, detailed, meticulously footnoted and indexed, and as such represent the definitive biographies of their subjects.

Alexander is currently at work on a one-volume interpretive history of baseball.

Chuffy Alexander, first baseman-third baseman with the Birmingham Black Barons and the Monroe Monarchs, 1928–32.

Clifford Alexander, scout for the Dodgers, 1950–67, and for the Reds from 1967 to his death in 1975.

Dale "Moose" Alexander, the American League batting champion in 1932, whose major league career was ended when he was accidently scalded by a primitive diathermy machine.

Born David Dale Alexander, Jr., on April 26, 1903 in Greenville, Tennessee, Alexander attended Milligan College in Greenville for two years, where he played basketball and starred in both baseball and football. In 1924 he entered professional baseball still in his home town, hitting .331 for Greenville in the Appalachian League. In four more years in the minor leagues Alexander had four more outstanding seasons, capped by winning the International League triple crown in 1928 with a .380 average, 31 home runs and 144 RBI. Toronto, which had purchased Alexander for $5,000, sold Dale and a pitcher to Detroit for $100,000 and several players.

Alex was a big right-handed hitter (six feet three inches, 215 pounds) with huge features which gave him the impression of having muscles everywhere—muscles in his nose, muscles in his jaw. He had dark, heavy eyebrows, as if maybe he had some muscles in his forehead, too. He bore a facial and physical resemblance to Jess Willard, the former heavyweight champion. Despite his build he was a line-drive hitter who hit to all fields, and although he was always suspect as a fielder he ran deceptively well until the accident. He farmed in the off-seasons, and he looked the part; a writer said that the country stuck to him. Despite being better-educated than the average player, he was quiet to the point of shyness, and played baseball without color or frills. George Stallings, then managing in the International League, nicknamed him "the Big Ox" but said that Alexander was one of the best natural hitters he had ever seen.

As a twenty-six-year-old rookie in 1929, the Big Ox tore the American League apart. He hit .343, which is usually listed as the American League record for a rookie (although a few people consider Joe Jackson to have been a rookie in 1911). He drove in 137 runs, a record at the time and still one of the highest totals ever for a rookie; was one of about a dozen rookies ever to hit more than 40 doubles; hit 15 triples, which is still the league record; hit 25 home runs; and led the American League in hits, with 215. He also led the league in errors, but Tigers manager Bucky Harris told a writer that "That big farmer boy over on first base is going to be one of the great stars of baseball—perhaps another Ruth," and The Sporting News in 1930 described him as "heir apparent to George Herman Ruth, Sultan of Swat and Emperor of the Hot Dog Eaters."

The Tigers had two sensational rookies that year, Alexander and Roy Johnson, who also had over 200 hits, 45 doubles, and 14 triples. Alexander's offense tapered off a little bit over the next two years, and with a team drifting miles away from the pennant race, his defense came under fire. By early 1932 he was on the bench, watching a glove man named Harry "Stinky" Davis play first base; he had only sixteen at bats in the first two months of the season. In early June, Alexander and Roy Johnson were traded to the Red Sox for Earl Webb, the outfielder who had set the all-time doubles record the previous year.

Alexander started to hit immediately upon joining the Red Sox, and soon enough found himself chasing Jimmie Foxx for the league lead in hitting. Foxx, trying to beat Babe Ruth's home run record, concentrated on hitting for power, and Alexander slipped ahead of him in average. After a seesaw contest in the closing weeks, Alexander won the batting title by hitting two singles on the last day of the season, giving him a .367 average. By the standards of today Alexander would not be considered eligible for the title, and Foxx, who hit .364 with 58 homers, would have won the 1932 triple crown.

In a game at Philadelphia on May 30, 1933, Alexander twisted his knee. In the clubhouse after the game, he was treated with a new machine, a "diathermy treatment." The water was too hot, and Alexander's leg suffered third-degree burns. Gangrene set in; he almost lost the leg. He got back in the lineup in August, but didn't hit the rest of the year.

"I couldn't run and I couldn't field," Alexander said a few years later, "and when I got hurt, that was the end." Despite a lifetime major league batting average of .331, the Red Sox dumped him.

Alexander returned to the minor leagues. He played for Newark, Nashville, Kansas City, and Chattanooga, and then down to the lower leagues on his way out—Sanford in the Florida State League, Thomasville in the Georgia-Florida League. He hit everywhere. At Minneapolis in 1935 he hit four home runs in one game. At Thomasville in 1940 he hit .388 with 96 RBI in 91 games. With Semla in 1941 he hit .438 in 56 games. His entire professional career is detailed in the SABR publication, Minor League Baseball Stars.

After his playing career Alexander stayed in baseball for almost twenty years as a manager and as a scout for the Giants and Red Sox. He married a hometown girl in Greenville in 1931, and raised two sons, one of whom became a minister. He lived to be seventy-five years old, and died in Greenville in 1979.

Dave Alexander, head baseball coach at Purdue.

Doyle Alexander, a contemporary starting pitcher who has won almost two hundred games in a career chopped up by repeated disagreements with his employers.

Alexander was selected by the Dodgers in the forty-fourth round of the 1968 free-agent draft. "My second year in the minors," he told The Sporting News in 1980, "Bob Shaw [the former White Sox standout] changed my entire delivery. It was the single most important moment of my career. I would have never made it the way I was going." He reached the majors in mid-season, 1971, and after half a season was sent to Baltimore in the Frank Robinson trade. He was able to crack the strong Baltimore rotation in 1973, but suffered the only arm trouble of his career during that year (tendinitis of the elbow), and lost the action on his sinker as well as some velocity off his fastball. He compensated by improving his changeup and curve. For the next two years he was used primarily out of the bullpen.

In 1976 Alexander again entered the rotation. The 1976 season was the beginning of the free-agent era. Free agency was known to be coming, but no one knew quite what it would do to their rosters. The Orioles, looking ahead better than most teams, unloaded the players they didn't think they could sign, and acquired a younger staff, and so Alexander was included in a ten-player trade with

---

TRACERS

You know you think of a lot of funny things that happened in baseball, sittin' around gabbing like this. I remember when I was with the Cubs, and I was with them longer than any other club, we were playing the Reds in a morning game on Decoration Day. The game was in the 11th when I went up to bat and I said: "If they give me a curve ball, I'll hit it in the bleachers. My wife's got fried chicken at home for me." They gave me a curve and I hit 'er in the bleachers.

—Pete Alexander in
My Greatest Day in Baseball (Page 234)

Not to confuse anybody, this event wasn't recalled by Alexander as his greatest day in baseball; it was just another game that came up at the end of the interview.

Alexander's memory is sharp. The event in question occurred on May 31, 1920, and it happened almost exactly as he remembered it—Decoration Day, large crowd, playing the Reds in the morning game, Alexander hit a game-winning home run in extra innings. He seems to have missed only detail, that being that the game was in the tenth inning, not the eleventh; the dramatic home run was hit off of Ray Fisher with two men out in the bottom of the tenth. The game gave Alexander an eleven-game winning streak on his way to a 27–14 season.

the Yankees. He won thirteen games in 1976, his major league high to that point, started one game in the World Series and became a member of the first "big bucks" free-agent class, signing a six-year, $900,000 dollar contract with the Texas Rangers.

Alexander won seventeen games with Texas in 1977, then had two off years, quarrelled with the Texas management, and was traded to Atlanta. The changing face of baseball's economics had converted his seemingly generous 1976 contract into chicken feed. Alexander demanded adjustments and, receiving no offers from Atlanta, exercised his right to demand a trade. He was traded to San Francisco, where he had a good year in 1981 (11–7, despite the strike). Demanding the trade, however, had wiped out Alexander's opportunity to reenter free agency after the 1982 season, and so as a substitute Alexander announced that he would retire rather than pitch for the Giants in 1982. "I'm being paid less than the median salary for starting pitchers," Alexander told Nick Peters, "I just can't understand it. . . . I am prepared to retire if I have to." At length Alexander and the Giants located an owner willing to meet his salary demands—George Steinbrenner.

The return to New York almost destroyed Alexander's career. He started the season of 1982 poorly, and on May 17, after giving up five runs in the third inning at Seattle (in a game that proved to be Gaylord Perry's three-hundredth win), Alexander entered the dugout and punched the wall, breaking a knuckle and sidelining himself for nine weeks. His final two months of the season were equally disastrous. The New York media got on him something awful, stating as if it were a simple fact that Alexander only wanted the money and didn't care about earning it. He wound up 1982 with a 1–7 record and an ERA over six. In 1983 Billy Martin was back at the Yankee helm, and on June 8, with a 6.35 ERA and no wins, Alexander was released.

He signed with Toronto and lost his first six decisions for them. His first win of the 1983 season came on August 27, and then in September he won six straight games, finishing with a 7–6 record for the Blue Jays. "I have to thank Al Widmar for working with me and advising me to make some adjustments," said Alexander. Al Widmar was (and is) the Blue Jays pitching coach.

"He was throwing too high," said Widmar. "His whole body would go up in the air on his deliveries. I told him to lengthen his stride off the pitching rubber by about a foot. That increases a pitcher's velocity." Alexander won seventeen games for the Blue Jays in '84 and again in '85, the best back-to-back seasons of his career, and helped pitch the Blue Jays to their first divisional title in 1985. In the playoffs in '85 Alexander was the victim of George Brett's monster game in Game Three, and was beaten by Brett and McRae again in Game Six; he gave up ten runs in ten-and-a-third innings in the playoffs, Brett scoring five of the ten runs and driving in four of them.

Alexander was eligible to become a free agent after the 1986 season. In early 1986, although still pitching well, Alexander gave an interview to the Toronto *Sun*, an interview in which he "charged the Blue Jays' front office [with] not being interested in winning and said as many as five or six other Jays wanted out." (TSN) Toronto, realizing then that they couldn't sign Alexander, traded him to Atlanta for minor league pitcher Duane Ward.

Finishing the season 11–10, Alexander again became a free agent—but this time no one was buying. The winter of 1986–87 was the high-water mark of collusion, the owners' attempt to cap salaries by conspiring not to sign free agents from other teams. Alexander turned down a two-year, $2.37 million offer from the Braves on January 8, 1987; the Braves under the rules of the time were unable to make him another offer until May 1, and because of collusion no one else made him any offer. When he was eligible to re-sign with the Braves on May 1, their offer was considerably smaller; Alexander finally accepted a contract from the Braves on May 5, at a base salary of $400,000.

Alexander through much of his career has acted as his own agent, and (not to editorialize) has become a classic illustration of why a player shouldn't do that. His timing on seeking a new contract has been consistently awful; his tactics have often been counterproductive. He has tried to renegotiate when his stock was down, and locked himself into contracts that he was unhappy with when he was pitching well. He signed a six-year contract at a moment when salaries were escalating dramatically, and two years later was looking at four years of being underpaid. By demanding a trade in Atlanta, he wiped out a chance to reenter free agency at a time

when salaries were again skyrocketing. He pitched well in San Francisco, but having punted his negotiating power, he tried to force the Giants into giving him a new contract by complaining loudly and holding out, and succeeded in exchanging an excellent situation for him, where he was thriving as a pitcher, for a nightmarish situation in New York. A good agent wouldn't have let him do that; a good agent would have told him to go out and have a good year for the Giants, and *then* worry about the money. He turned down a good offer in 1987 to back into collusion. By focusing on short-term dollars rather than what is in the best interests of his career in the long run, the agent Doyle Alexander has put the pitcher Doyle Alexander under enormous pressure and into difficult situations, resulting in constant trades, releases and free-agent departures.

Part of what an agent does for a player is to be the bad guy, to be the one who speaks out when the player is unhappy, to be the one who demands more money so that the player can shrug his shoulders and say, "Gee, I just want to pitch." Because he has acted as his own agent, Alexander has gotten himself portrayed as greedy and bitter wherever he has been, much as agents are often portrayed. But while he has been always portrayed as greedy and often as overpaid, he hasn't *really* made good money. He has used ineffective and largely discredited negotiating ploys like threatening to retire and blasting the team in the press. A good agent could have gotten Doyle 50 to 70 percent more money than he has made out of baseball, at least, just by knowing when to act, when to keep quiet, and what tactics to use.

Anyway, Alexander finally signed with the Braves on May 5, 1987. After two months of indifferent work he was traded to Detroit, where he pitched sensationally down the stretch, going 9–0 with a 1.53 ERA, carrying the Tigers into the post-season, where once again he got the bejeebers kicked out of him, this time by Minnesota. (Throughout his career Alexander has pitched *extremely* well in September, and equally poorly in October.) Another fourteen-win season for the contending Tigers in 1988 gave Alexander five straight winning records, but in 1989, as the Bengals collapsed around him, Alexander finished 6–18, creating the impression that he was getting shelled although actually his ERA and innings pitched were almost the same in 1989 as in 1988. Alexander was released following the 1989 season, but will surely be invited to spring training with somebody. Doyle has been reported working on a knuckleball for at least six years, and at a mere thirty-nine years of age it would surely be premature to write him off.

Alexander has won 194 games in the major leagues, and at least that many enemies. Alexander has been ripped by managers, general managers, fans, broadcasters, and sportswriters, all of whom have reported that he is a chronic malcontent, but still you have to respect the ability of a man who goes from being a marginal prospect with an 86-MPH fastball and from being the last pitcher on the staff who is given a chance to a career of almost two hundred major league wins. If baseball was a popularity contest his career would have ended a long time ago, but fortunately it isn't, and for all we know Alexander may still have several years left.

(—M.K. and B.J.)

Gabriel Alexander, baseball's second outside arbitrator, 1972–74; he was replaced by Peter Seitz.

Gary Alexander, catcher and designated hitter for three teams in the seventies, now with the Bradenton Explorers in the Seniors League.

Alexander, a consistent .300 hitter and power threat in the minors, was up for a late-season trial with the San Francisco Giants in 1976 when he caught John Montefusco's no-hitter. He hit .303 for the Giants in 1977, but was unable to establish himself as a regular due to his defensive shortcomings as a catcher. In March, 1978, Alexander was sent to Oakland as a part of the Vida Blue trade. Given regular work that year (both behind the plate and as DH) by the Athletics and later the Indians, he hit for power but threatened the league strikeout record, which he failed to break only because he wasn't able to stay in the lineup. Over the next three seasons (the last two spent with Pittsburgh) his at bats gradually diminished, although he did hit consecutive pinch-hit home runs on July 5 and 6, 1980. His major league career was ended by knee surgery on August 5, 1981.

(—M.K.)

Grover Cleveland Alexander, one of the greatest pitchers in National League history, the holder of innumerable pitching records, and a man once portrayed by Ronald Reagan in a film biography.

Alexander was born in Elba, Nebraska,

in 1887, the sixth of eight children of a farm family headed by William and Margaret Alexander. He was born in the Wild West. According to the 1916 *Spalding Guide,* Alexander was born "of a democratic family, both politically and otherwise. His parents were 'settlers' in Nebraska during the Indian times, and 'Alex' was born in a hut, miles and miles from nowhere. His early existence was one of hardship, he being of a race which could not shirk work of the hardest kind." He farmed as a youth, building up formidable strength, worked as a telephone-line repairman, and gained a measure of local fame as a pitcher in Sunday semi-pro leagues.

Alexander always drank. "My father . . . was a hard drinker before me, and so was my grandfather before him," Alexander told Fred Lieb in 1950. In 1909, age twenty-two, Alexander came to the attention of a minor league team in Galesburg, Illinois, which offered to pay him fifty dollars a month if he could pitch for them. He inquired about his expenses for the trip; they said sure, they'd pay those, too, and Alexander launched his career in the Illinois-Missouri League. He went 15–8 for a last-place team in 1909. According to later stories, Alexander was hit by a pitched ball during the season, knocked unconscious and had blurred vision for some time, apparently ending his career. (If you're in Illinois and can get to the microfilm of a Galesburg newspaper for the summer of 1909, it would be a public service if you could document this event.) In any case the problem eventually cleared up, and Alexander was drafted by the Indianapolis team in the American Association, one of the strongest minor leagues of the time. Unfortunately for them, they decided without ever looking at G.C. that they didn't need him, and sold him down to Syracuse in the New York State League.

Alexander won twenty-nine games for Syracuse in 1910, prompting his jump to the major leagues. (The other stats given for Alexander that season in "*Daguerreotypes*" and other sources are of unknown origin, and are obviously wrong. They may represent "as known" stats, figured from incomplete box scores. A. D. Suehsdorf in *Porter's Biographical Dictionary* says that fifteen of the wins were shutouts, but I don't know where this comes from, either.) According to Ira Smith in *Baseball's Famous Pitchers,* the manager of Albany in the New York State League, James Patrick O'Rourke, also acted

as a scout for the Phillies. One day in September, 1910, O'Rourke talked to the umpire before the game:

> "I'm going to claw the air and shout some dirty names at you over one of your decisions," O'-Rourke told the umpire, "but don't take it personal. I just want to get tossed out of the game so I can catch a train this afternoon and hustle down to New York." O'Rourke put on his act, was banished by the co-operative umpire and raced for the Albany depot.

O'Rourke met with Red Dooin, the Phillies manager, and convinced him that the Phillies ought to buy Alexander from Syracuse, and then Dooin convinced Horace Fogel, owner of the Phillies, to pay $750 for Alexander.

In the spring of 1911 the Phillies split their training camp into two squads, one managed by Dooin, and the other in the hands of Pat Moran, a veteran catcher. Alexander was in Moran's squad, the "B" squad. At the end of spring training Dooin wanted to cut Alexander and return him to Syracuse, but Moran insisted that Alexander had to be kept, telling Dooin, prophetically, that Alexander would turn out to be the "find of the decade."

Alexander as a rookie in 1911 led the National League in innings (366) and wins (28); he also struck out 227 men, an NL record for a rookie finally broken by Doc Gooden. One of the wins was a famous one-hit, 1–0 victory over Cy Young on September 8. This game, which is variously reported as lasting twelve innings and being the last game ever pitched by Cy Young, was remarkable enough on its own merits. What the hell; let's do a modern-style box score of it and run that:

PHILADELPHIA (N)	ab	r	h	bi		BOSTON (N)	ab	r	h	bi
Knabe 2b	4	0	0	0		Ingerton 2b	4	0	0	0
Paskert cf	4	1	1	0		Bridwell ss	3	0	0	0
Lobert 3b	3	0	1	1		Jackson lf	3	0	0	0
Magee lf	4	0	1	0		Donlin cf	3	0	0	0
Beck rf	4	0	1	0		Kaiser cf	0	0	0	0
Luderus 1b	4	0	2	0		Miller rf	3	0	1	0
Walsh ss	3	0	0	0		McDonald 3b	3	0	0	0
Carter c	3	0	0	0		Gowdy 1b	3	0	0	0
Alexander p	3	0	0	0		Tenney 1b	0	0	0	0
						Rariden c	3	0	0	0
						Young p	2	0	0	0
						Flaherty ph	1	0	0	0
Totals	32	1	6	1		Totals	28	0	1	0

```
PHILADELPHIA                    000        000        010—1
BOSTON                          000        000        000—0
```

LOB: Philadelphia 5, Boston 1.   SB: Paskert, Lobert.
Ejected: Donlin, Gowdy.

PHILADELPHIA	IP	H	R	ER	BB	SO
P. Alexander W, 24–12	9	1	0	0	0	7
BOSTON						
C. Young L, 6–5	9	6	1	1	1	2

Umpires: HP—Klem;   Bases—Brennan.   T: 1:27.

The 28–13 record earned him a $500 raise, to $2,000. In 1912 he was weakened for a good part of the summer by some illness, but Dooin, who like a good many managers of his time believed more in toughness than percentages, kept sending him to the mound anyway; he led the league in innings pitched and strikeouts, but finished 19–17.

The Phillies that Alexander had joined were traditionally about a .500 team, and in 1911 and 1912, despite the addition of Alexander, they failed to improve much. In 1913, for one season, Alexander was relegated to the number two spot on his own team, despite a 22–8 record with a 2.79 ERA. A young right-hander named Tom Seaton, one year younger than Pete and also from a small town in Nebraska, won twenty-seven games with a 2.60 ERA, and led the league in innings pitched and strikeouts. In 1914, when Seaton jumped to the Federal League, the Phillies dropped to sixth place, out of contention.

But in 1915, led by the slugging of Gavvy Cravath and an incredible season by Alexander, the Phillies vaulted to the pennant. Alexander won thirty-one games, pitched twelve shutouts and posted a 1.22 ERA. Alexander became Alexander; in that season he became what he would be for the next decade, indisputably the greatest pitcher in the game. On June 26, 1915, Alexander pitched a one-hitter in one hour and nine minutes, reportedly throwing only seventy-six pitches. He threw four one-hitters that summer, three of them in a space of thirty-one days.

Going into the World Series, many fans and writers expected Alexander to dominate the series; predictions were common that he would win three games for Philadelphia. "It is a fine thing to have friends who are confident in you," Alexander said later, "but I may say the responsibility of pitching in the World Series is enough in itself without the added consideration of living up to high expectations." Or was quoted as saying; sportswriters at the time unself-consciously quoted Nebraska farm boys as if they spent their spare time polishing articles for *Harper's Weekly*. Alex beat Boston in the first game of the World Series on October 8, 3–1. Babe Ruth, then a twenty-year-old pitcher, made his first World Series appearance as a pinch hitter against Grover that day, and grounded out, the Babe's only action in the 1915 series.

That win would hold as the only series game won by the Phillies until 1980. Alexan-der's second time out, Game Three on October 11, the game was tied 1–1 going into the bottom of the ninth. The Red Sox got a leadoff single, and after a sac bunt, an intentional walk to Tris Speaker and a groundout had runners on second and third with two out. Pat Moran, then managing Philadelphia, let Alexander choose whether to pitch to Duffy Lewis, at bat, or Larry Gardner on deck. Lewis was right-handed but a .291 hitter, the team's leading RBI man and four-for-seven against Alexander in the series. Gardner was left-handed but a .258 hitter and one-for-six against Alex. Alexander elected to pitch to Lewis, and Duffy hit a game-winning single over second base. Alexander was roundly criticized for his decision, and admitted that the call probably was the wrong one.

In the fifth game Alexander was expected to start again, even though he would have had only one day of rest. "The World Series was a disappointment to me," wrote Alexander in an article which appeared under his name in *Baseball* magazine that winter.

A great deal has been written about the fifth game. I was slated to pitch and, in fact, intended to pitch up till the last moment. I never wanted to pitch a game so much in my life.

But I knew when I started to warm up that I wasn't right. Once again I had to make a decision. I had to choose between my own instinctive desire to pitch and my knowledge that I was in no condition to properly represent my team. I decided to tell Moran how I felt. I must give him credit for taking this information without any great demonstration of disappointment.

"If you are not right, Alex," he said, "the rest of us will have to carry it."

As long as I live I will always wonder how I might have fared had I pitched that fatal fifth game of the '15 series. . . . No matter what anyone else may say, I know the reason I lost the 1915 World Series was that I was not in the proper physical condition to give it my best."

Moran started Erskine Mayer, his number two starter, Mayer failed to protect a 4–2 lead, and the series ended in five games. The subtext, of course, is that Alexander was suspected of being not in condition to pitch because he was hung over. There is no evidence that this is true, but his explanation for his stiffness in that article is odd. He says that on Labor Day, pitching a crucial game with a blister on his finger, "I unconsciously tried to humor that blistered finger. In doing so I brought the muscles of my shoulder into play in an unusual manner . . ." He didn't tell Moran that he had wrenched his shoulder, but the fact is that he went on to pitch very well throughout September, clinching the pennant with a one-hitter against the Braves.

In any case, Alexander rolled through the next two seasons in indomitable form, being by far the greatest pitcher in the world. In 1916 he won 33 games, pitched 16 shutouts and posted a 1.55 ERA. He pitched 38 complete games that year, and 389 innings. In 1917 he won 30 games, and pitched 388 innings with a 1.86 ERA. The Phillies, basically a .500 team without Alexander on the mound, finished second both seasons.

Physically, Alexander looked a great deal like Mike Scott, current-day pitching star of the Houston Astros, although he was thinner than Scott and had more freckles. As a pitcher, he had much in common with his contemporary, Babe Adams. Like Adams, he had incredible control. Like Adams, he traced his impressive physical strength to hours of walking behind a plow as a youngster. Like Adams, he would last forever, pitching and winning past his fortieth birthday. Like Adams, he was a quiet, soft-spoken man who consciously worked to remain on an even emotional keel. Like Adams, he wasted no effort on the mound. Burleigh Grimes said about him in *The Man in the Dugout* that he was "Smooth and easy—always smooth and easy. I used more effort winding up than he did in pitching nine innings. He threw a sinker and a curve. Always kept them down. He was fast, too. I'll say he was! That thing would come zooming in and then kick in about 3 inches on a right-handed hitter."

"I never saw a machine like him," said Jesse Haines in *The Gas House Gang*, by Robert E. Hood. "Every pitch he threw was the same. Low outside. To every hitter. The only thing he adjusted was the position of his infield and outfield. He'd shift the fielders around. He didn't care who the batter was. He'd pitch him low outside. Throw him the fading fast ball. Or curve him. I saw a lot of pitchers in my time, but I never saw a machine that worked any better than he did."

The memory simplifies the past; every pitch Alexander threw was *not* low and away, regardless of what Haines would remember forty years later. "Old Low-and-Away" is listed in some sources as a nickname for him, along with "Alex," "Pete," and "Alexander the Great." That was his stock in trade: Don't forget the basics. Throw strikes; get ahead of the hitter. Keep the pitch away from the hitter, where it's hard to pull. Change speeds. Think; don't react emotionally. Don't make the game harder than it is.

As Alexander's success accelerated, his salary requests escalated. America in the spring of 1918 was gearing up for war, and before the season Alexander was informed that he was high on the draft list. The Phillies, afraid of losing Alexander uncompensated, sold Alexander and Bill Killefer to the Cubs for $60,000 and two minor players. Alexander refused to sign with the Cubs unless compensated with a $10,000 bonus, but he did depart for California, where the Cubs were training. He disembarked in Kansas City to say hello to some friends, and talk to a young reporter for the Kansas City *Star*:

The mighty 'Alec' didn't sign a contract, but he checked his trunk through to California. Grover Cleveland may not sink his fins into any portion of that $10,000 bonus he is demanding for attaching his monogram to a Chicago contract, but he isn't passing up any free trips to California.

The article is unsigned, but according to George Monteiro in *American Literature*, the young reporter was Ernest Hemingway. Anyway, Alex eventually worked out some sort of agreement, and won two games for the Cubs early in the year before returning home to marry his longtime sweetheart, Aimee Marie Arrants, and report to the U.S. Army on May 31.

He was shipped to France with a field artillery outfit. The shells departing near him cost him a part of his hearing, and the whole experience to some degree shattered his nerves. He suffered epileptic seizures for the rest of his life, and nervous twitches which according to Fred Lieb were the result of a disorder related to St. Vitus' dance. His drinking grew worse.

Despite the problems, Alexander returned in 1919 to post a league-leading 1.72 ERA. In 1920 he won eleven consecutive games (see Tracers), won twenty-seven games and led the National League in wins, strikeouts, innings (363) and ERA (1.91). It was the fourth time in his career he had won the "Pitcher's Triple Crown," leading the league in wins, ERA, and strikeouts, an unmatched record although the concept of a pitcher's Triple Crown didn't come along for another half-century or so.

Although into his mid-thirties and less spectacular, Alexander remained one of the league's better pitchers through the early twenties. It was a peculiar time in America, with a growing temperance movement which would eventually bring about Prohibition, and sports reporters often attacked Alexander in moralistic essays for his drinking. He was not a popular man with the press in those years, despite his easy-going nature; he was inclined to the opinion that they might write more about his pitching and less about the drinking. Some writers did write as if the thirty-six-year-old drunken bum should apologize for going just 22–12 in 1923.

In June, 1926, Alexander was sold from the Cubs to the Cardinals for the waiver price, $4,000. "He was getting along in years then but still quite a good pitcher," said Joe McCarthy in *The Man in the Dugout*. "I had to get rid of him though. He didn't obey orders. Wouldn't go along with me. A fellow asked me one time if Alex followed the rules. 'Sure he did,' I said, 'but they were always Alex's rules.' So I had to let him go . . . but he was a nice fellow. Alex was all right. Just couldn't keep to the rules, that's all." McCarthy had taken over a last-place team, and knew that he faced a long building job which would be longer if the team lacked discipline and good work habits.

"Alexander may have been a problem for the Cubs and Joe McCarthy," wrote Rogers Hornsby in *My War With Baseball*, "but he wasn't for us. I didn't do any preaching to him or anybody else on the ball club about not doing any drinking." Alexander pitched well for the Cardinals, but he was just another pitcher on a talented staff during the season. The Cardinals played their last home game that year on September first, spending the entire last month on a road trip, and they left St. Louis in third place. Pittsburgh faltered in the grip of the Fred Clarke rebellion (see Babe Adams), and when Cincinnati also slumped in the last two weeks the Cardinals won the pennant at the wire, giving Alexander his first chance to redeem himself from the disappointment of 1915.

In the second game of the 1926 World Series, Old Pete stopped Ruth, Gehrig, Lazzeri, and company on a four-hitter, beating them 6–2. In Game Six, six days later, he beat them again, 10–2.

"After the game I told him to take it easy that night," wrote Hornsby. " 'You're the best we've got if we get into trouble, so get to bed as early as you can. You've got a long winter ahead when you can do whatever you please.' "

Alexander told Hornsby that he would be ready if he was needed. The Cardinals scored three runs in the fourth inning, and held a 3–2 lead entering the seventh inning. Pop Haines, pitching for the Cardinals, developed a blister from throwing the knuckle ball (which he actually held with his knuckles), and the bases were loaded with two out, Tony Lazzeri at the plate. Hornsby signaled for Alexander.

Walking to the mound, Alexander stumbled slightly. Hornsby left his position to meet Alexander at second base. "I wanted to get a close look at him, to see what shape he was in," said Hornsby. "And I wanted to tell him what the situation was, in case he'd been dozing." Alexander was fine, but the first pitch broke low; Lazzeri was up 1–0. Alexander hit the outside corner with a pitch, evening the count, and then Lazzeri strode into another outside pitch and sliced a tremendous drive to left field, just curving foul. "He's in a tighter fix than I am now," Alexander told himself, breathing a sigh of relief.

Alexander threw a curve ball low and away, a pitch so low, wrote James R. Harrison, that one of the Singer midgets couldn't have hit it. Lazzeri dived at the pitch and missed.

This became, and don't ask me why, probably the most famous at bat in World Series history, certainly the most famous strikeout. I wish I knew why. It may have been that tiny stumble, which made the fans think that Alexander perhaps had been drinking, which created incredible tension in the ball park. It may have been partly that this was one of the first World Series captured by newsreels and shown in theaters all over the country before the movie started. Generations of writers would write unashamedly that Alexander was hung over that day, but all of the participants in the scene say that he was not, that he got to bed early the night before.

Coming back to the bench, Alexander was mobbed by his teammates, who shook his hand, pounded on his back, and yelled into his ears. Alexander asked them to leave him alone, to let him think about what he needed to do.

"I just wanted to go over the Yankees lineup in my mind to see when Babe Ruth would be coming up," he said later. "I figured that if I got the side out in order in the eighth and got the first two men in the ninth, the Babe would be up there with a chance for me to strike him out for the last out of the series." All went according to plan for five batters, five infield outs, but Ruth worked Alexander for a walk. The Babe, however, took off for second base, and was nailed by Bob O'Farrell. The series was over, and Alexander was the hero.

The Cardinals became the last National League team in this century to win a title; the other seven teams had all won titles by 1920. The only *American* League team which hadn't won a title at the time was the St. Louis Browns. St. Louis went wild with the victory, giving the Cardinals a welcome home that set new standards for civic madness. Alexander, according to Hornsby, drank enough black coffee on the train ride home to float a battleship, trying to get in condition for the celebration, but reacted with characteristic disinterest to the hero worship.

"So they're calling me a hero, eh?" Pete asked. "Well, do you know what? If that line drive Lazzeri hit had been fair, Tony would be the hero and I'd be just an old bum."

Alexander was not through, as a pitcher; he won twenty-one games in 1927, at the age of forty. In 1928 he went 16–9 and helped pitch the Cardinals back into the World Series, although he was hammered in that World Series, won by the Yankees in four straight.

In 1929, at the age of forty-two, Alexander's drinking problem grew suddenly worse. With the Cardinals in Philadelphia on a road trip, Alexander met some of his old drinking buddies from his Philadelphia years, and went on a bender of massive proportions. The Cardinals, in another pennant race, had to send Alexander to a sanitarium to dry out. Alexander reported from the sanitarium in early August sober and clear-eyed, and pitched a shutout his first time back, but the Cardinals returned to Philadelphia, and Alexander went off the wagon again. At the time there was no Sunday ball in Philadelphia, and Alex put the day of rest to a poor use. Jimmy Wilson, Cardinal catcher, had to be sent looking from bar to bar to find him and bring him home. Bill McKechnie, managing the Cardinals, sent Alex home to St. Louis to meet with Sam Breadon, owner of the team, and Breadon suspended him. He finished the year with a 9–8 record, a good ERA; he was tied with Christy Mathewson for the NL career record for wins.

He couldn't do it. He couldn't stay sober long enough to get that last win. Imagine it—as if Henry Aaron, tied with Babe Ruth

with 714 home runs, couldn't function well enough to get just one more. Alexander signed with Philadelphia for the 1930 season, but early in the year, with no wins, three losses and an ERA of 9.00, Alexander was released by the Phillies. He went to the Texas League for a month, but he couldn't get anybody out there, either.

What to do? Alexander had nothing put away for the future. Baseball had no pension plan. In 1930 there was no card-show business, no jobs available as a TV or radio broadcaster. Alexander hooked on with the House of David team, a touring team from a religious colony which wore long beards and, as I understand it, mixed baseball playing with a little bit of gospel. They took it upon themselves to keep Alexander sober; Alex traded in his dignity for the service and a paycheck. He pitched regularly in those years against Satchel Paige. The Kansas City Monarchs, for whom Paige pitched, and the House of David would go through the small cities of the Midwest on separate barnstorming tours, each taking on (and defeating) a local All-Star team. Then the two would return to face each other in a "championship" exhibition, Alexander against Paige.

Alexander lived that way until 1938, giving it up at the age of fifty-one. His wife Aimee divorced him, they remarried and separated again. They had no children. His epilepsy and alcoholism worsened. When the Phillies won the pennant in 1950, their first since 1915, someone in the Phillies organization invited Alexander to the series, but apparently left him on his own between games. Alexander struck writers at the series as a rather pathetic figure. "You know I can't eat tablets or nicely framed awards," he told Fred Lieb, referring to his Hall of Fame election and other awards. "But they don't think of things like that." He died less than a month after the 1950 World Series, alone in a hotel room in St. Paul, Nebraska.

After his death, a world which had been embarrassed by his presence while he was among us tried to find more ways to honor him. Hollywood made a movie about his life, *The Winning Team* with Ronald Reagan as Pete and Doris Day as his wife. It is an awful movie, a *Reader's Digest* movie, rearranging the events of Alexander's life into a cliché. Ogden Nash wrote a little poem about him:

A for Alex
The great Alexander;
More goose eggs he pitched
Than a popular gander.

That he was never able to enjoy his life, that he was never able to build a life for himself outside of baseball or find work in the game, is a disgrace for which both Alex and the baseball world must share responsibility. We would like to think that this could never happen now, that we would never allow the heroes of *our* youth, Mantle and Mays and Musial and Williams, to die the way that Alexander died. Perhaps we wouldn't. Alexander may not have been the greatest pitcher who ever lived, and then again he might have been.

Hugh Alexander, legendary scout.
Signed as an outfielder by the Cleveland Indians in 1935, Alexander tore through the minor leagues in a year and a half, posting records which were almost as impressive as he now remembers them as being. After appearing in seven games with the Indians in late 1937, Alexander lost his hand that winter when a sleeve was caught in the gears of the equipment in an oil field. The Cleveland Indians—out of kindness, Alexander now says—offered him a job as a scout, and Alexander attacked. Working twelve months for six months' pay, Alexander stuck to the prospects in his mid-South region until he knew them better than their neighbors did. His first signee was a future star, Allie Reynolds; his second another, Dale Mitchell.

"I'm recognized in baseball as being the number-one scout that ever scouted the game of baseball," Alexander told Mike Bryan in *Baseball Lives.* After fourteen years with the Indians, helping to build the outstanding Indian teams of 1948–58, Alexander moved on to the White Sox, then became a scouting supervisor with the Dodgers. As scouting became more sophisticated, the scout's job evolved from *discovering* and evaluating young talent to evaluating and *signing* players in a competitive environment. Alexander, a born salesman, was in his element; he developed a bag of tricks that a used car salesman would envy, and in fact that is what several of his wives thought Alexander perhaps should do—quit spending 330 days a year on the road and get a good job as a salesman. To date Alexander has gone through six wives looking for one who didn't want to make road trips with him and keep him from working, and he still travels an estimated 150,000 miles a year.

In 1970 Alexander moved to the Philadelphia Phillies as a major league scout, remaining with them until 1987; he is now with the Cubs. "Scouting is not intuition and hunches," Alexander told Mike Bryan. "It's breaking the kid down. If I look at you and then get in a car and drive two hundred miles, I'm going to break you down right in my mind going at seventy mph: your arm, your speed, fielding, hitting, power—five things for a regular player. If you have two or three minuses, I'm going to walk away from you."

Jess Alexander, a one-armed black outfielder who barnstormed against teams with Pete Gray after the 1945 season.

Matt Alexander, one of six players employed by the Oakland A's exclusively as a pinch runner.

Charles O. Finley, owner of the Kansas City and Oakland Athletics for approximately twenty years, liked to think of himself as an innovator, a forward looking man who expanded baseball's horizons by daring to try new and different things. One of the new and different things he tried, or actually forced his ball club to try, was to keep a player on the roster strictly to be a pinch runner—in fact, in 1976 and 1977, the A's devoted *two* roster spots to pinch runners, the two men being Matt Alexander and Larry Lintz.

Alexander, a minor league third baseman and outfielder, played several years in the minor leagues, and reached the majors with the Cubs in 1973 after hitting .309 at Wichita; he stole only 20 bases that year in 106 games. He was very fast, however, and after sprinter Herb Washington ran out of chances to figure out major league baserunning, the A's acquired Alexander and made him their pinch runner.

Alexander wasn't dramatically successful as a base stealer, but unlike Washington and most of his other predecessors in the role, Alexander did score some important runs and did earn the respect of his teammates, in part because he was a baseball player who could be used in the field or at bat if the need arose. Chuck Tanner, his manager in Oakland, thought enough of him to take him to Pittsburgh with him, where he played the same role for the Pirates from 1978 to 1981.

Charlie Finley, who had said that a good pinch runner could win his team fifteen games a year, then insisted that his pinch runners *had* won their teams fifteen games a year, an incredible statement, since it meant that without their pinch runners the 1972–74 A's would have been under .500. In a sense, Finley was a victim of his credulity; when baseball men would talk about how speed could win so many ball games for a

team, Finley believed them. If speed was really as important as baseball men say it is, then it would make perfect sense to devote one or two roster spots to pinch runners—but baseball men instinctively know that it isn't; they know better than to believe their own hyperbole. Finley didn't know enough not to take all that stuff seriously. Anyway, Alexander, after leaving the majors in 1981, played several more seasons in the Mexican League before retiring. In 1983 he hit .312 for the Mexico City Tigers, stealing 73 bases in 116 games. If he had concentrated on stealing bases early in his career, he could probably have had a good major league career as a leadoff man.

Raymond S. Alexander, a minor league pitcher, and Grover's brother.

Ted Alexander, pitcher with the Kansas City Monarchs and other Negro League teams from 1940 through 1949.

Walt Alexander, a minor catcher from 1912 to 1917, at one time a backup for Sam Agnew (see Agnew).

While Alexander was with Kansas City in 1915, the *Kansas City Times* said that "he is full of the old pepper, has a regular pegging arm and, last of all, some brains."

Angel Alfonso, shortstop with the Cuban Stars and other teams, 1924 to 1930.

Carlos Alfonso, director of player development for the San Francisco Giants.

Mario Alioto, director of marketing for the San Francisco Giants.

Andy Allanson, catcher for the Cleveland Indians.

Allanson was taken in the second round of the 1983 free-agent draft, and after leading the Eastern League in batting average in 1985 (.312), jumped to the major leagues as the Indians number one catcher. Allanson is an odd combination, a big man with excellent speed but with little power—in fact, he never hit a home run in the minor leagues.

Allanson, picked by many (including Peter Ueberroth) as a coming star, didn't hit in 1986, and when Rick Dempsey was signed for the 1987 season Allanson was returned to the minors for seasoning. In July Dempsey was injured and Allanson returned. In 1988 he was again the regular, and caught the most games of any American Leaguer. He hits around .250, and with no other real pluses the Indians' acquisition of Sandy Alomar, Jr., creates a career crisis for him.

(—M.K.)

Barry Allen, sports information director (baseball) for the University of Alabama.

Bernie Allen, second baseman for the Minnesota Twins and Washington Senators of the sixties and early seventies.

Bernie Allen was a star quarterback as well as a baseball player at Purdue University. Calvin Griffith, in his first season in Minnesota, paid Allen a $50,000 bonus to sign with the Twins, and after just eighty games in the Sally League Allen catapulted to the majors in 1962. He had a wonderful rookie season, hitting .269 with good totals of doubles, triples, and homers (27, 7, 12), 62 walks, and very solid defense. *The Sporting News* on September 15, 1962 noted that Allen " . . . transformed a derelict Twins infield, along with Richie Rollins, into one of the most stylish in the majors. . . . Allen has wonderful range and can throw from any position, and is learning fast how to play the hitters." He helped the Twins move from seventh place to second.

It was to be his best season; his career degenerated rapidly over the next three years due to the types of injuries to which second basemen are prone, the most serious being a torn ligament in his left knee suffered when Don Zimmer crashed into him at second on June 13, 1964. By 1965, when the Twins won their first pennant, Allen was limited to nineteen games, and was not on the active list for the series.

In December 1966 Allen was traded to the Washington Senators, where he continued his comeback battle for three years. Ted Williams became the Senators manager in 1969, and Allen at first developed in his hands, showing greatly improved patience at the plate and a resulting increase in his other batting stats. Shortly after the 1969 season, Allen reinjured his knee playing a charity basketball game for a radio station, and the Senators management (Williams and Bob Short) thought he should retire. They thought highly enough of Allen at that time to offer him the position as manager of their AAA farm club in Denver, but little enough of him as a player that they traded for another second baseman, Dave Nelson.

Allen, however, thought he could come back and play, and rejected the offer. When Nelson hit .159, Williams began using everybody else at second base—Lenny Randle, Tim Cullen, Tom Ragland. Allen became unhappy with Williams, and, being a natural leader, became the leader of the clique forming in opposition to Williams. In August, 1972, at a mock ceremony at the home of Denny McLain, Allen was proclaimed the

Grand Wizard of the Underminers Club—a group of players jokingly but nonetheless avowedly intent upon undermining Ted Williams' rule. According to Shelby Whitfield in *Kiss It Goodbye,* Allen "was dead serious in his resentment of Williams and a number of his teammates even openly called Allen 'Wizard.' "

After the 1971 season Allen demanded a trade, saying that he would quit baseball rather than play another year for Williams, whom he said "ran a concentration camp and did not communicate with his players." He was traded to the Yankees at the beginning of spring training, and his career stumbled to an end in mid-season, 1973.

(—M.K. and B.J.)

Robert G. "Colonel Bob" Allen, Philadelphia shortstop in the 1890's, later the long-term owner of the Knoxville team in the Southern Association.

Born in Ohio in 1867, Allen began his professional career as a pitcher in 1887, but reached the majors as a shortstop in the talent crunch of 1890. In his rookie season he served for a month or so as player-manager of the team, while Harry Wright recovered his sight, and the team played well for him. A light hitter but a renowned defensive player, Allen in 1892 established a record for chances accepted by a shortstop; the record was broken by Rabbit Maranville in 1914.

Returning to the minors after a five-year stint with the Phillies, Allen turned to managing, and returned to the major leagues as manager of the Cincinnati team in 1900. He lasted only one year in that role. Out of baseball, Allen purchased the Knoxville team in the Southern Association, which he owned and operated for many years with great success. From Rudy York's letter to his son:

Somebody told Colonel Bob Allen in Knoxville about me. Allen asked me to meet the club in Atlanta for a tryout. That's how I got my start.

Knoxville signed me and kept me on the bench for about a month. Now, you'll run into all sorts of people in baseball, and you'll find them all, even the smart ones, making mistakes now and then. This Colonel Allen made one, and he was known as a smart baseball man. . . . But Colonel Allen made a mistake. He released me. If he had held onto me another year, he could have sold me for $50,000 or more.

Allen died in Little Rock in 1943.

Bob Allen, left-handed reliever with Cleveland in the sixties.

Allen was one of the first pitchers to be used exclusively as a left-handed middle reliever; he pitched 204 games in the majors, all of them in relief, was credited with only 19 saves and pitched only 274 innings. It's embarrassing to admit this, but we really haven't been able to find out a damn thing about him as a person, including why he disappeared from the majors after his best season in 1967. Basically the press never paid any attention to him.

Buster Allen, pitcher with several teams in the Negro Leagues, 1942 to 1947.

Clifford "Crooks" Allen, pitcher with Hilldale, the Baltimore Black Sox, the Homestead Grays and the Memphis Red Sox, 1932 to 1938.

Dick Allen, the American League's MVP in 1972, and one of the best and most controversial players of the sixties and early seventies.

Richard Anthony Allen was born in Wampum, Pennsylvania, a small steel town (about a thousand people) thirty miles outside Pittsburgh, in 1942. One of nine children, young Dick was a sensational basketball player at Wampum High School, teaming with brothers Ron and Hank (future major leaguers) to lead the school team to a state championship. He had also excelled in baseball since the Little League. His mother Era recalled that young Dick was constantly batting stones when a ball was not available. She remembered, she said, because "I was the one paying for new window panes all over the neighborhood . . . there were no baseball fields in all of Chewton or Wampum that could hold a stone if Dickie hit it good."

The Jackie Robinson stone, Dick remembered, was always the one that broke the window. Dickie was hounded by major league scouts, and was offered over one hundred college athletic scholarships. Allen's father had stranded his mother with the nine children, and so finances made professional baseball really the only option; Era was barely making ends meet by taking in sewing, ironing, and washing. She handled the negotiations with the scouts, and came to favor John Ogden of the Philadelphia Phillies. Ogden had earned her confidence in part by bringing the great Negro League star Judy Johnson to the Allen home for a visit. Mrs. Allen drove a hard bargain: Dick signed for $60,000, plus the promise of a contract for his brother Hank, and a Phillies scouting job for brother Coy. Dick recalled with pride

years later that much of the money went for a new house for his mother.

Playing mostly second base and shortstop, Allen rose through the Phillies system. In the Eastern League in 1962, Allen went into the last day of the season battling Jim Ray Hart for the batting title. As told by Gaylord Perry in *Me and the Spitter,* Allen suggested that the two of them go out for a couple of drinks the night before the last game, and Jim Ray said sure. Allen figured if he could get Hart a little out of form he could win the title, so he put twenty dollars on the bar and the two of them went to work on it. But about the time Allen was ready to go, Jim Ray "grabbed Richie's arm and put his own twenty dollars on the bar . . . Suddenly, Richie realized he might be in a little trouble. He was. The next day Richie went oh-for-four and Jim Ray went four-for-four."

Allen's autobiography recalls the same story, although in Allen's version he went four-for-six and Hart went six-for-six. It was a good year, anyway, and after the season Allen asked for a raise. As he told Tim Whitaker in *Crash: The Life and Times of Dick Allen:*

All I wanted was fifty bucks. I needed to feel I was making progress. But that was not the way [Phillies general manager John] Quinn saw things. He said if I held out for a raise, I would spend another season in the minors. I did, and Little Rock was the result.

The team was the Arkansas Travelers of the International League, and on opening night 1963 Allen became the first black man to play professional baseball for an Arkansas team. "When I arrived at the ball park," recalled Allen, "there were people marching around outside with signs. One said, DON'T NEGRO-IZE BASEBALL. Another, NIGGER GO HOME. They were the same signs that greeted me the day I arrived at the Little Rock Airport." After his first game, alone in the parking lot, he found a note attached to his windshield: DON'T COME BACK AGAIN NIGGER.

In retrospect, Allen was the wrong man to choose to integrate the Arkansas Travelers. Following the example of Jackie Robinson, most organizations had chosen to integrate holdout cities with exceptional players. Henry Aaron had integrated the Southern League without incident—but Henry Aaron had two black teammates to share the experience, and Henry was a southerner. He knew the rules. Allen was all alone, and he didn't know how a black man was supposed to live in the South. Allen by nature was solitary, shy, preferring to spend his time alone, and in this peculiar pressure cooker that solitary nature became a breeding ground for paranoia, which appears to have enormously exaggerated the abuse he saw coming toward him. When he heard gunshots in the middle of the night, he was certain they were intended as a message to him. Although there is no evidence to support the idea, Allen believed that many of his teammates hated him. Although no one else saw or heard very much abuse directed toward him, in Allen's mind it was omnipresent.

Quartered by the Travelers in the black section of Little Rock, Allen came to feel isolated from his teammates. He had married Barbara Moore early that spring, but on the advice of his mother had not brought her to Arkansas. According to some reports, Allen began that summer to drink more than was good for him. Finally he called his brother Coy and told him he was coming home. Coy, John Quinn, and John Ogden flew to Little Rock to assess the situation. Coy reminded Allen that if he went home to Wampum, he would wind up working in one of two places: the steel mill or the cement mill. Allen's wife Barbara joined her husband in Little Rock, and he agreed to stay. On the field, he led the league in home runs and RBI, and was selected by the fans as the Travelers' Most Popular Player.

Allen was promoted to the Phillies in 1964. The Phillies, moribund as recently as 1961, had quickly retooled under the tutelage of a young manager named Gene Mauch. They needed a third baseman. Allen had not played third since high school, but he accepted the challenge. Not surprisingly, he led the league in errors at his new position, but at bat he had one of the half-dozen best rookie seasons in National League history, scoring 125 runs while hitting .318 with astonishing power. He had 352 total bases as a rookie, a National League record. In mid-September, it appeared that Allen might be not only the Rookie of the Year, but the first rookie to be selected Most Valuable Player.

And then the Phillies folded, the most famous collapse in the history of baseball. Six-and-a-half games ahead on September 20, the Phillies lost the lead on September 27. The Phillies lost ten straight games, while the Cardinals won eight straight, the Reds won nine straight, and the Giants won seven of nine. On the last day of the season, Richie Allen, completing a fabulous rookie season, was booed by the Philadelphia fans.

Frank Thomas was a veteran National League ballplayer, and for ten years had been an outstanding one. He had joined the Phillies in August, 1964, in the hope that he could fill the first base hole. He hit extremely well after joining the Phillies until stopped by a broken thumb in the first week of September, one of the contributing causes of the Phillies disaster. While out of the lineup, Thomas had filled in as a morning radio personality on a major Philadelphia radio station. The Phillies had acquired Dick Stuart to play first base over the winter, however, and Thomas, subbing at first and trying not very successfully to play the outfield, was struggling to keep his spot on the roster. He wasn't a key player but he was very well liked at least by the fans, a guy who had once studied for the Catholic priesthood, had quit that to play baseball and become the father of seven children.

On July 3, 1965, Allen and Thomas were joking around at the batting cage; Allen and Johnny Callison were riding Thomas about his failure to get a bunt down the night before. The joking turned a little more serious, and Thomas made a remark that Allen interpreted as being racist. Allen punched him, and Thomas hit Allen with a bat.

Thomas hit a home run that day, and was put on waivers after the game; he went to the Houston Astros a few days later. Allen says that he pleaded with the Phillies not to release Thomas, because of his seven children—but Allen also refused to talk to the media about the fight. Thomas, who had many friends in the media, talked to them all, and his view of the event was a popular one. Allen says now that he was ordered by Mauch not to talk about the incident, and believes that this unfortunate order was the cause of many of his subsequent troubles. In the minds of the Philadelphia public, Allen had cost a white man his job. "I had to choose between a thirty-six-year-old and a twenty-three-year-old," Gene Mauch told a press conference. The next day Allen stuck his head out of the dugout and was greeted with booing and racist abuse. As long as he played in Philadelphia, the booing would never stop.

Allen was a wonderful player in those first years—fast, incredibly strong, smart, a good base runner. He was about as good a hitter as I ever saw. He swung a huge bat, forty to forty-two ounces, the heaviest in the majors perhaps since Ruth had retired. His stats are impressive now, but in the hitting-starved sixties they were more impressive than they look now. In 1966, despite missing almost a month after he dislocated his shoulder while sliding, Allen hit .317 with 40 homers and 110 RBI. Frank Robinson won the triple crown in the other league that year, but Allen actually had a better year per at bat than did Robby. His defense at third base improved a little, and the Phillies also began using him in the outfield.

His salary rose rapidly, to a reported $82,000 in 1967. The salaries were highly publicized. No other player had ever been paid so much so early in his career, and this also did not sit well with some of the Philadelphia fans—that a twenty-five-year-old black man was earning such an incredible salary. While the other Philadelphia players negotiated contracts with GM John Quinn, Allen negotiated directly with team owner Bob Carpenter.

On August 24, 1967, Allen was hitting .307 with 23 homers and 77 RBI. Pushing an old automobile (a 1950 Ford), he put his hand on a headlight. His feet slipped out from under him, and his hand went through the glass. "When I pulled out my hand," wrote Allen in his 1989 autobiography *Crash*, "it looked like it had been blown off by a land mine. Blood was spurting everywhere. Underneath the blood, my hand looked like spaghetti." He had severely cut two tendons and severed the ulnar nerve in the right hand. He was out the rest of the way, and the Phillies, probably destined not to win anyway, dropped out of contention. The Phillies, uncertain if Allen could play again, offered him a "conditional contract" for 1968—no play, no pay. A bitter contract dispute followed, during which, Allen once told a reporter, he decided "From then on, it was 'I'm for Dick.'" Finally Bob Carpenter, owner of the team, interceded to get Allen signed to a standard contract.

You might get the sense, in some of what follows, that Allen was not well-liked. At his best, he was extremely well-liked, a soft-spoken man of great charm. Younger teammates and fans, from the beginning of his career to the end, would idolize Allen and benefit from his counsel.

But from the moment his hand went through the headlight, Allen was plunged into an ever-darkening web of conflict with the Philadelphia management. It's so hard to explain, for those who are too young to remember it, what a strange time it was. The whole world was about race then; looking backward, it doesn't seem that there was any other news. At the start of the decade, there had been avowed racists, Ku Klux Klan members, in the United States Senate. By 1965 overt racism was in retreat, and black militancy in ascendance. Lynchings, tolerated in the South for years, suddenly exploded into massive news stories, as the rest of the nation sent the message to the deep South that this could no longer be tolerated.

"I wouldn't say that I hate Whitey," Allen told a reporter, "but deep down in my heart, I just can't stand Whitey's ways, man. I get to reading those novels and things and get right mad."

"What novels?" asked the reporter.

"I just got through reading—what was it—*Greengage Affair*, I think it was, about the life of a black cat who lived in Mississippi—I'm sorry—Tennessee. Cut off the cat's hand. He went to Detroit. It's a good book, but, you see, all this type of stuff makes me mad. And then I'm really aware of Whitey, man, really aware of Whitey."

Racists, backed into a corner, fought back with petty terrorism. In Philadelphia, they fought back by making Richie Allen their target—or perhaps Allen, by his own behavior, made himself the target of their abuse. Rocks were thrown and BBs were shot through the windows of his house. His lawn was torn up by cars driving across it, his car smeared with paint. His children were taunted on the streets; his wife received threatening phone calls.

In all likelihood, there was a relatively small cadre of racists who were behind the harassment of Allen, just a bunch of guys at a redneck bar somewhere who thought this was fun and kidded themselves that they were doing something to stop them people from taking over the world—but a large section of the city of Philadelphia supported those extremists at some level. Allen was booed wherever he went, the target of insults and objects thrown from the stands. Allen began wearing a batting helmet all game, the only player of his time who did that, to protect him from the things that were thrown at him during the games. (His teammates began calling him "Crash Helmet," later shortened to "Crash," which became his nickname.) As far as Allen was concerned, the whole white world was against him—the front office, the press, the fans, even (at times) the other players. Becoming increasingly frustrated and paranoid, Allen's behavior over the next few years became ever more irrational.

Allen delighted in being a nonconformist, in doing things *differently* than other major leaguers did them. He wore his hair in a "natural" style, the first black player in the majors to do so, and grew wide sideburns. It was his way of defying the racists—and it insured that he would continue to be the target of their abuse. He loved the horses, and he made no secret of that; he bought a race horse as soon as he could afford to, and eventually came to own half a stable. He once told *Ebony* magazine that the people who ran baseball didn't respect him or any other black man, so he didn't respect the rules and standards of baseball.

"My early mistakes were due to inexperience and confusion," he told *Ebony* in 1970. "I was a young man fresh from the country with a high school education, and I paid for those mistakes. But when things got exaggerated and people started harassing my family, I did a lot wrong to influence them to trade me." By his own peculiar lights, Allen was (and is) a religious man. He read the Bible regularly, prayed before every meal, said the Lord's Prayer as a part of his pregame ritual, and spoke of whatever would happen as being the Lord's will. He also drank excessively, spent most of his free hours at the race track, cheated on his wife, and lied whenever it suited his purposes to do so. Justifying his attitudes by the racism of the society, he raised selfishness to an art form. His preferred method of solving problems was to punch out whoever was bothering him; even now, according to his autobiography, he thinks the racist abuse could have been ended if he had just been allowed to slap a few people around.

A Philadelphia cop clubbed him to his knees after a routine traffic stop—Allen says only because he was slow to produce a driver's license, but the cop says after Allen made threatening comments.

Allen was accused, perhaps falsely, of slapping a small boy who asked him for an autograph.

He got into a fight with a spectator at a horse race.

TRACERS

Clyde Manion labored six years with the Detroit Tigers and never once succeeded in hitting a home run on the home field—not even during batting practice there. Traded to the St. Louis Browns in 1928—Manion returned to his former stomping grounds in Detroit when the Browns came there to play the Tigers for their first game of the season. But Clyde Manion's hopes of hitting a home run in the Tiger ballpark weren't bright, for he sat on the bench until he was sent in as a pinch-hitter in the ninth inning—and, you guessed it, Manion surprised everyone, himself included, by hitting a homer!

—Bill Stern
Bill Stern's Favorite Baseball Stories, (Page 152.)

Bill Stern, a popular radio and print sports "reporter" of the depression and post-war years, is famous for never allowing the facts to get in the way of a good story. Stern may have been the original for the sportscaster in Woody Allen's *Radio Days* who tells a heroic story about a pitcher who keeps competing despite the loss of a leg, two legs, an arm, both arms, an eye, both eyes . . . it's overdrawn for comic effect, but many of Stern's stories are wildly implausible.

This one, though, is largely correct; Manion played for the Tigers from 1920 to 1927 without hitting a single home run (he batted a little less than four hundred times altogether), but did hit a home run for St. Louis in Detroit on April 13, 1928. It was the third game of the season, not the first, but the home run was in the ninth inning and it was as a pinch hitter.

Fred Lieb should come so close.

"He'd show up late for batting practice, come in glassy-eyed and still hit the ball four hundred fifty feet," a teammate told the press. For a spring training workout in 1968, Allen arrived seriously intoxicated. His hand began to hurt again; on March 8, 1968, Allen jumped the team to go see his doctor. He was absent for three days, and was fined $500. Mauch began fining Allen almost every week—$1,500 for showing up late for a game, a thousand for drinking, $500 for missing batting practice. Most of the fines were not announced.

In May, 1968, Mauch accused Allen at a team meeting of not hustling. Allen came to the park the next day badly hung over, looking for a fight with Mauch. Coach George Myatt sent him home. For ten days beginning June 1, Allen was benched. Allen would spend the games in the bullpen, refusing to talk to his teammates. Several times he dressed before the game was over.

Gene Mauch was fired on June 15, 1968; once again, Allen was seen in Philadelphia to have cost a white man his job. As he had with Thomas, Allen went out of his way to say nice things about Mauch after the fact, about how he had never wanted Mauch to lose his job. Bob Skinner took over as Philadelphia manager, and met with Allen; they thought they had an understanding. Allen would call when he was going to be late; Skinner would try to help him deal with the fans and media.

To give the Philadelphia fans less opportunity to attack him, Allen stopped working out before home games.

On August 21, 1968, Allen got in a fight with the owner of a bar; charges were brought by the owner, and then dropped. For the 1968 season he hit just .263 (the first full season of his career in which he had failed to hit .300), yet despite all of the turmoil, despite the damage to his hand, two fingers of which were paralyzed, Allen played 152 games in 1968, hit 33 homers and drove in 90 runs.

Allen had asked to be traded after the 1967 season. After 1968, he was determined to make a trade happen. "I began to set my own rules," he said. "Before ball games, instead of going straight to the ball park, I started making regular stops at watering holes along the way." On May 2, 1969, Allen missed a morning flight to St. Louis. Instructed to get on an afternoon flight, he went to the wrong gate. Frustrated, he went home. He didn't appear In St. Louis until the middle of the next game. Skinner fined him $1,000.

Cookie Rojas, a veteran infielder, called a secret team meeting and blistered Allen, telling him that the other players didn't appreciate his attitude toward his work, that he was not hustling. The meeting turned to Richie-bashing, and several other players also ripped into him. The team divided into factions of Allen supporters and Allen critics.

Defiant, Allen never defended himself to the press or fans, never tried to tell his side of the story. On June 24, 1969, the Phillies were to play a doubleheader at Shea Stadium. Allen went to New Jersey in the morning to see a horse race, and got caught in traffic trying to get to the park. By the time he got to a phone to call Skinner, the game was underway, and he couldn't get through. Skinner announced between games of the doubleheader that Allen had been suspended. Skinner levied a fine on Allen of $2,500, but Bob Carpenter cut the fine in half. Allen jumped lanes in the Lincoln Tunnel, and was stopped by the police.

The indefinite suspension lasted twenty-six days, in large part because Allen did not feel he was ready to return. He rejoined the team only after extracting a promise that he would be traded at the end of the season. When he was finally scheduled to return and face his teammates and the fans, he steeled himself for the ordeal with approximately a dozen stiff drinks. At the clubhouse, he cleaned out his locker and moved his stuff into a small, stuffy equipment room. Skinner ordered the stuff moved back. "I don't care if he sits in there," Skinner explained, "but he'll dress in the clubhouse with everybody else." He didn't, though; for a week or so every day Allen would move his clothes to the equipment room, and Skinner would order them moved back. Eventually Skinner gave up, and Allen dressed in the equipment room the rest of the year.

I'm not a psychologist, but it seems obvious, in retrospect, that Allen was suffering from clinical depression, which today would probably be recognized and dealt with as a psychological illness. Often a person who is depressed just wants the world to go away and leave him alone. Allen expressed this in irrational ways—hiding in the equipment room, refusing to take batting practice at home. He told a reporter that "I wish they'd shut the gates and let us just play ball with no press and no fans. Like it was in Wampum when I was a kid." But at the time, no one said "This man is depressed. He needs help." They said "This man is acting like a jerk. He needs punishment." *Life* magazine in August, 1969, described Allen as "the most controversial and probably, the most disliked and unhappy player in baseball . . . [He] has been accused of being more thirsty than hungry and of swinging harder off the field than on it." *Life* described him as "a quick-tempered non-conformist."

He began scratching large words in the dirt at first base—"BOO" and "COKE"; he says the Coke sign just meant that he wanted to hit a home run over the Coca-Cola sign in left field, but it was subject to some misinterpretation.

In the midst of this erratic behavior, Allen hit five home runs in six days. Commissioner Kuhn, attending a game, saw the messages and ordered them to cut it out. Allen wrote "NO" in the dirt, and "WHY." (Incredibly, Kuhn also ordered Allen to shave his moustache, which he thought was inappropriate for a major league player.) On the last day of the homestand, Allen wrote "MOM," which he says meant that only his mom could tell him what to do. NL president Warren Giles notified him that he would be suspended by the league if he persisted in writing in the dirt.

In early August the Phillies had scheduled an exhibition game against their AAA farm team. Allen asked Bob Carpenter, team owner, for the day off; Carpenter said OK, but failed to notify Bob Skinner. Allen told Skinner he was taking the day off. Skinner told Allen he wasn't. Allen told him the management had already approved it. While Allen debated whether to go to Reading, Skinner resigned, charging that the Phillies front office had interfered in his attempts to discipline Allen. "Allen is a big factor in our losing and there is very definitely disharmony on the club," said Skinner.

Once more, Allen was seen to have cost a white man his job. Now he was booed wherever he went, home or road. He spent more and more time at the race track, the one thing he loved. He got into a fight with another spectator at a track. The press criticism accelerated.

In his early life Allen had always been known as "Dick". When he came to the majors, for reasons nobody knows, they began calling him "Richie", perhaps after Richie Ashburn. After accepting this for years, Allen began asking to be called "Dick."

" 'Richie' is a little boy's name," he would explain.

Playing only 118 games in the 1969 season, the center of his discontent, Allen hit 32 homers and drove in 89 runs. The Phillies traded him to St. Louis after the season, the trade supposed to bring Curt Flood to Philadelphia (Flood, of course, refused to report, and made history instead.) On opening day in St. Louis, Allen received a standing ovation from the Cardinal fans. He fought back tears and determined to have a good year. Someone asked Red Schoendienst if he was expecting any trouble with Allen. "If you're looking for it," Schoendienst said, "you'll find it. There's no need in anticipating those things."

Allen had fun that summer, fun playing ball and fun with the press. He talked to the writers before every game. Somebody asked him what he thought of artificial turf. "If a horse won't eat it, I don't want to play on it," he replied.

Allen's playing time was curtailed by a problem with his Achilles tendon and pulled muscles, so that he played only 122 games that year—yet he hit 34 home runs and drove in 101. In Busch Stadium. He was looking forward to returning in 1972, but just as the season ended he was traded to the Dodgers. Years later, Red Schoendienst was asked about the manager's role in making trades. "One year they asked me if I wanted Richie Allen on my team," Schoendienst recalled. "I said no, I didn't want him, because I had heard that he didn't hustle and was a bad influence in the clubhouse. They made the trade anyway. The next year they asked me if I thought we ought to trade Allen to LA. I said no, we shouldn't, that Allen had been no problem and had helped the team. They made the trade anyway."

Allen played 155 games for the Dodgers, and although the season was quiet he didn't have a great year, hitting .295 with 90 RBI. On December 2, 1971, Allen was traded to the White Sox for Tommy John.

Allen had decided, at that point, to retire from baseball, and at the beginning of spring training, 1972, had not signed his contract. The White Sox manager, Chuck Tanner, was a native of the same county in Pennsylvania that Dick was from; their families had known one another for many years. Tanner went to Wampum, and talked for hours to Era. Still trying to decide whether to play, Allen called his mother. "Listen, son," she said, "go help Chuck out."

Chuck Tanner, apart from his long acquaintance with the Allen family, had taken to heart Joe McCarthy's famous statement that if he couldn't get along with a .400 hitter, they ought to fire him, and so he set to work to get along with Dick Allen. He was the original schmooze manager, the manager of the seventies, the manager of the time of the sexual revolution and drugs-are-no-big-deal. He allowed Allen to pass up batting practice, home and road, and to report to the park only a half hour before game time. Tanner also had the sense not to ask Allen to play multiple positions, ending six years of shifting Allen from position to position by anchoring him at first base. The city of Chicago took him to heart. In Philadelphia, the PA announcer had persisted in calling him "Richie" even after he asked to be called "Dick", but in Chicago he was "Dick" from the day he arrived. Allen gave Tanner and Chicago a great season, leading the American League in home runs, RBI, walks, and slugging percentage. In a pitchers' year, when the American League's overall slugging percentage dropped all the way to .343 (one of the lowest ever), Allen slugged over .600. The White Sox, losers of 106 games just two years earlier, went 87–67, and finished second in the division. Allen won the American League MVP Award, by the widest vote margin in almost twenty years.

Although he tolerated Tanner better than previous managers, Allen was also disrespectful to Tanner at times, and told *Newsweek* that as far as he was concerned, a manager was "nothing but a big flunky." Allen continued to show some signs of depression—eating almost all of his meals in his hotel room, refusing to do interviews—but some of his natural charm returned, and Allen was generally well-liked by his Chicago teammates. He began demanding payment from newsmen for interviews. Tanner agreed that a star of Allen's magnitude should not have to do interviews.

In early 1973 Allen seemed on his way to perhaps an even greater season. On June 28, 1973, Allen dove for a wide throw at first base, and Mike Epstein stepped on his leg. The leg was broken, and Allen was in essence done for the year, although the White Sox team doctor (Hank Crawford) said that Allen was malingering, and could have played the last six weeks if he had wanted to.

Allen returned in 1974. Although statistically he hit nearly as well as he had in 1972, the magic was gone. The White Sox had ac-quired Ron Santo over the winter. With his inimical talent for making the worst of things, Allen engaged Santo in a divisive war for the team leadership, forcing Chuck Tanner eventually to say that there was only room for one team leader on the Sox, and that was him. On September 14, 1974, Allen announced his retirement. He had played 128 games that year, hit .301 and led the American League in home runs with 32.

With Allen retired and the White Sox tired of him, Chicago traded the rights to Dick Allen to Atlanta that winter for very little. Allen's goal in retirement was to raise horses, but Allen and his wife quarreled over the horses, among other things; Allen found life as a family man as trying as life as a ballplayer. Toward the end of spring training he began to talk about coming back. An attempt was made to get him through the National League on waivers, to trade him to the Yankees, but Philadelphia claimed him, and the waivers were withdrawn. Having retired, having been traded to Atlanta, and having publicly refused to report to Atlanta, Allen nonetheless charged that he was being "blackballed" by major league baseball.

In April, three Phillies visited Allen at his farm near Philadelphia. The three were Mike Schmidt and Dave Cash, active players, and Richie Ashburn. The three talked to Allen about returning to the Phillies. At first it seemed like a bizarre idea, but after a time the idea of making a triumphant return to the scene of his greatest anguish began to seem attractive. Atlanta charged that the Phillies were tampering with their ballplayer; Bowie Kuhn dismissed the charge. On May 7, 1975, Allen was traded by Atlanta back to Philadelphia.

Philadelphia, having completely rebuilt since Allen's departure, was ready to contend by 1975. Both Allen and Philadelphia seemed anxious, on his return, to make things right. Frank Rizzo, Philadelphia mayor, pronounced Allen's return "a splendid thing." A newspaper poll on whether he should be welcomed back went in his favor by a two-to-one margin. At a news conference at Veterans Stadium, he was cheerful and gracious. "I'm older, I guess a little smarter," he told reporters. "If they would have let me clear the air around here before like they did today, maybe I never would have had to leave." On his first at bat in Veterans Stadium on May 14, he received a standing ovation. In his first month back in a Phillies uniform he hit in the .180s—the first major slump of his career—and he waited almost a month before he hit a home run, but the fans stayed with him. On June 7 he hit two home runs against Los Angeles' Doug Rau; Philly fans gave him four standing ovations.

Allen by 1975 was thirty-four years old, and he had missed spring training, or most of spring training, every year for several years. He appeared to be pressing, trying too hard to make up to the Philadelphia fans. Apparently it just caught up with him. Hitting .234 at the All-Star break, Allen had his eyes checked and was fitted with new glasses, but he wound up the year hitting .233, seventy points below what he had hit with the White Sox, and with little power. Still, the younger Philadelphia players (Greg Luzinski, Mike Schmidt, Dave Cash) spoke glowingly of Allen as a teammate, and talked about how much they learned from having him around. Danny Ozark, managing the Phillies, had nothing but good words for Allen despite the off season. It was, Allen said at the time, his happiest season in the major leagues, and he announced late in 1975 that he was anxious to get to spring training and help the Phillies win in 1976. "I owe them something," he said.

Allen's bat returned in 1976. In May, 1976, Allen was put on the fifteen-day disabled list with a sore shoulder, and complained about that to the press; he was sure he would be ready to play in two or three days. On his return Ozark began platooning Allen at first base with Tommy Hutton. The Phillies were winning in 1976, running away from the division, and Allen was happy to be a part of it—working hard, keeping quiet.

And then—well, he was Dick Allen. On July 25, 1976, Allen collided at first base with John Candelaria, injuring his shoulder. On July 26 he called in, and received permission not to come to the park. On July 27 he didn't call, but stayed home with the injury. On July 28 he came to the park, but left the game in the third inning without permission. On July 29 he didn't show up. On July 30 he returned to the park, explaining to his teammates that he had been unable to play because of his shoulder. The love affair was over. Danny Ozark fined him two days pay plus an unspecified penalty, and—again over his objections—placed him on the fifteen-day disabled list, retroactive to July 26. Allen and Ozark talked about the situation, and seemed to have it patched up. But when

Allen returned to play after a five-week layoff with the shoulder injury, his timing was off, and he didn't hit.

Once more, Allen began to divide the Phillies into warring camps. Allen, hypersensitive to race, felt that the Phillies "were working a quota on us." Ollie Brown, a black, and Jerry Martin, a white, were platooning in left field; Allen felt that Brown should have the everyday job. He also felt that Bobby Tolan "wasn't getting the shot he deserved." Allen quarreled in public with Larry Bowa and Tug McGraw. With the team in Montreal, just hours away from clinching their first divisional title, Allen told a newsman that if the Phillies didn't put Tony Taylor on their eligible roster for postseason play, then he (Allen) wasn't going to play, either. Taylor, past his fortieth birthday, had batted twenty-three times all year, just filling in when other players (mostly Allen) were on the disabled list. When the Phillies clinched the title in the first game of a doubleheader in Montreal, Allen stayed in the dugout, not joining the team in the clubhouse celebration, and then Allen stayed in the clubhouse with Mike Schmidt and some of the black players on the team during the second game, holding their own private celebration.

After the series in Montreal, Allen jumped the team, returning to his farm near Philadelphia. Ruly Carpenter came in to smooth things over, as his father had so many years before. After visiting with Allen at his farm, he announced that Allen had apologized for his actions, and that Tony Taylor would be in uniform as a coach for the post-season series.

Allen was a free agent after the 1976 season. The Phillies were not interested in having him back. Only one team, the Oakland A's, selected him in that winter's free-agent draft. The A's, suffering massive free-agent defections, were desperate for talent. On March 15, 1977, Allen signed with Charlie Finley and the Oakland A's. Early in the year things went well. Mitchell Page, having a sensational rookie year, credited Allen for helping turn his career around.

Allen didn't want to be used as a designated hitter. According to Allen, Finley had agreed to this before signing him; according to Finley, he hadn't. Since both men lie a lot, you can believe who you want. Anyway, Jack McKeon in April wrote Allen's name into the second game of a doubleheader as a DH. Allen refused to do the job. They talked

about it, and agreed that Allen would not have to DH.

On May 25, McKeon made a defensive switch, taking Allen out of the game but forgetting to inform him. Allen went to first base to find Earl William already there. Allen stormed off the field screaming at McKeon, telling him he could "find somebody else to play first base the rest of the season," and told the press that he had lost respect for McKeon as a result of the incident. After a forty-five-minute meeting behind closed doors, the parties emerged and described it all as "a minor misunderstanding." McKeon was fired two weeks later for being a weak disciplinarian. According to *The Sporting News* (June 25, 1977), "Finley became disenchanted with McKeon within a day or so of [the] incident between McKeon and Dick Allen in Toronto."

As he had before with Mauch and Skinner and Frank Thomas, Allen spoke well of McKeon to the media after the firing, saying "I'm sorry to see Jack go. He was all right . . . I think it's a matter of getting everyone mentally prepared. You can't be in the ball game and be listening to it on the radio."

The new manager was Bobby Winkles. Winkles's first act was to have a long meeting with Dick Allen, after which he met with the rest of the team. Just days later, getting Finley's permission, Allen left the team for three days to "rest an aching shoulder." While he was gone he was photographed at a Chicago race track. "He is there with my blessings," said Finley. Allen returned, and said that he needed to platoon at first base, that at thirty-five he didn't think he could play every day. Winkles and Finley said OK, he could platoon. But the next day, Finley walked into the Oakland clubhouse in the sixth inning, to find Dick Allen taking a shower. Finley exploded, yelled at Allen, suspended him for a week and called an impromptu press conference. Red in the face, Finley shouted that "I've gone along with Dick Allen all the way. I gave him the benefit of the doubt. I wanted to show the world I could be the first to work with Dick Allen. I found out I was like all the other suckers."

As always, Allen apologized and expressed his willingness to talk through the problems. But when the week was up, Allen could not be found; even his mother said she didn't know where he was. A few days later, he called Finley, asking him to reinstate the pay he had lost during the suspension. Finley told him to go to hell. Allen wrote to the A's, announcing his retirement but hinting that he might play in Japan in 1978.

He didn't. On October 11, 1979, Allen's farmhouse in Bucks County, Pennsylvania was destroyed by fire. Allen, who had put almost all of his money into his horses, had no insurance on the house. The IRS was after him. Allen and his family moved into a cottage on the property which had been used by the stable hands. In 1980 he left his family, driving around California trying to collect his thoughts. He got a new girlfriend, and was divorced from Barbara in 1981. She went to court and got everything, even his baseball pension. "And she never once had to stand in against a Bob Gibson fastball. That's what's unfair," Allen whined in his autobiography. The book, with Tim Whitaker, was published in 1989; entitled *Crash,* it is one of the best baseball biographies of recent years. Near fifty, Allen retains his extraordinary ability to avoid responsibility for his own life, to create a rationale for behaving irrationally, and then to blame everybody else when faced with the consequences of his self-destructive behavior.

Allen's three children have remained close to their mother, leaving Allen, as he was born to be, isolated and alone. He worked for the Texas Rangers in the spring of 1982, as a hitting coach, and for the White Sox in 1985 as a roving minor league hitting instructor. "I wonder how good I could have been," he said in the book. "It could have been a joy, a celebration. Instead, I played angry. In baseball, if a couple of things go wrong for you, and those things get misperceived, or distorted, you get a label. After a while, the label becomes you, and you become the label, whether that's really you or not. I was labeled an outlaw, and after a while that's what I became."

Earl Allen, a part of the original ownership group of the Houston Colt .45s (now Astros), later treasurer and vice-president of the Astros.

Ethan Allen, who was George Bush's college coach.

Author, filmmaker, game designer, and major league outfielder from 1926 to 1938, Allen was born in Cincinnati on New Year's day, 1904. Ethan was a multi-sport star at Withrow High; he stayed in town to go to college, and received a B.S. from the University of Cincinnati in 1926.

After working out with Tris Speaker and the Cleveland Indians and John McGraw's Giants, Allen was signed off the campus by the local team, the Cincinnati Reds; according to Lee Allen in *The Cincinnati Reds* he received a bonus of $8,598.43. He never played a game in the minor leagues, reporting directly to the Reds, where he sat on the bench for the last three-and-a-half months of the season.

In 1927 Allen succeeded Ed Roush as the Reds center fielder. Although Allen hit consistently around three hundred and was the first player to hit a ball over the center field wall in Crosley Field, his primary asset was his speed; he was one of the fastest players of his time. He also had a good arm, and led the National League in fielding percentage in 1929.

In 1930 the Reds had a new manager (Dan Howley); Allen started slowly with the bat, and was traded to the Giants, where once again he succeeded Ed Roush in center field. When Fred Lindstrom was moved to the outfield in 1931 Allen became the fourth outfielder. While with the Giants, Allen earned a master's degree in physical education from Columbia University, marking him as one of the best-educated players of his day. For several years he was a part-time player.

In 1934 Allen landed with the seventh-place Philadelphia Phillies. Projected as a part-time player, Allen stepped into a talent void—the Phillies after the trade of Chuck Klein that winter had *no* outfielders—and won a regular job. He had a fine year in 1934, hitting .330 with a league-leading 42 doubles, and had another one in 1935, getting 198 hits including 46 doubles. "I finally learned to wait on the pitch and hit it the other way," he told *The Sporting News* in 1975. In 1935 he played in the major leagues' first night game. In early 1936 the Phillies decided that they had to have Chuck Klein back from the Cubs, and made Allen a part of the package. His career faded quickly; he wound up his thirteen seasons with a lifetime average of exactly three hundred, playing in a time and place where outfielders were expected to hit three hundred.

With his retirement as a player, Allen's life in baseball was just getting started. In his last years as a player he carried around a manuscript for a book on how to play baseball. He talked about the book often to reporters, so by the time it came out as *Major League Baseball* in 1938, the public was aware of it. Also an accomplished photographer, Allen had punctuated the book with photographs, some of them of the top stars in the game. Kiki Cuyler demonstrated flip-down sunglasses, Roy Johnson was pictured with "permanent" sunglasses, and Earl Averill was shown with glasses held in place with an elastic band. The book was a great success, and was republished annually for many years, eventually under the title *Baseball Play and Strategy.*

Allen went to work as a filmmaker for the National League, a position he held for four years. Later he made a series of ten instructional films on how to play baseball.

"When I came up, there was little teaching of the baseball fundamentals," Allen has explained. "You were supposed to pick up everything on your own. I wanted to help the young players learn the fundamentals more readily." A generation of Little Leaguers grew up on the fundamentals of baseball as explained by Ethan Allen. On the back page of the book there is a list of "Hints to Players." The number one hint is "Have good equipment. Wear clean undergarments."

Allen tried his hand as a game designer. He created "All-Star Baseball," which was successfully marketed in 1941, and was followed many years later (1969) by "Strategic All-Star Baseball." Eventually the games went off the market, when major leaguers began to demand to get paid for the use of their statistics to produce such games.

Ethan Allen became head baseball coach at Yale in 1946, a position he would hold through 1968. He produced five Eastern Inter-Collegiate League champions, and took his team to the College World Series in 1947 and 1948. It was there, of course, that he coached the future President. "When you asked him to bunt," Allen recalled, "he bunted." When Bush was nominated to be head of the CIA, somebody called doing a background check. "If he could fathom my signal system," Allen said, "he's qualified to do spy work." There's a famous picture taken when Babe Ruth visited Yale in 1948, three people in the picture: Ethan Allen, Babe Ruth, and George Bush. Allen still keeps in contact with his 1948 captain.

Upon leaving the Yale job at age sixty-five, Allen and his wife Jean moved to Chapel Hill, North Carolina, where Allen continued to be involved in a number of baseball-related enterprises, including local little leagues. Now eighty-six years old, Allen is still alive and well in Chapel Hill. We have heard through the publishing grapevine that he would like to write or collaborate on his memoirs, but hasn't been able to find a publisher who had an interest. If any of you reading are able to remedy this, we recommend that you act quickly.

(—R.N. and B.J.)

Frank Allen, who won twenty-three games in the Federal League in 1915.

An Alabama native, Allen was described by a contemporary reporter as a "chunky little rebel." Allen joined the Dodgers in mid-1912, as did Casey Stengel; Bob Creamer's Stengel bio reports on an incident in which Stengel, Allen, and Zack Wheat went to a restaurant and got sloshed on champagne. He was very ineffective with the Dodgers (15–41 over three years), and so wound up in the Federal League, where he was very effective, winning twenty-three games and throwing a no-hitter on April 24, 1915. Back in the National League in 1916, he was again sharp (8–2, 2.07 ERA), but disappeared after a poor 1917 season.

Allen died young (forty-three years old), but I do not know why.

Hank Allen, older brother of Dick and Ron, and an outfielder for the Washington Senators.

Hank and Dick Allen began their professional careers together at Elmira in the New York-Penn League before following separate paths. Hank was drafted out of the Phillies organization by the Senators and converted from a first baseman to an outfielder. He spent an undistinguished season and a half with Washington before Ted Williams arrived as manager in 1969.

Like his brother, Allen was regarded as a leader, not always in the best sense. "Hank Allen controls all the blacks on the team," Bernie Allen told Shelby Whitfield, the team's broadcaster. The Senators 1968 manager, Jim Lemon, did not have a good rapport with the team's black players—but Williams developed an excellent relationship with them. Allen, like most of the Senators in '69, hit for the highest average of his career. In 1970, again like many others, he reverted to his previous level and was traded to Milwaukee. Williams felt that Allen could have been an outstanding player, but lacked the necessary desire.

About sixty days short of a pension, Allen was activated by Chicago in 1972 as a part of their keep-Dick-Allen-happy campaign. Since leaving baseball he has become a successful trainer of thoroughbred race horses, saddling Northern Wolf for a sixth-place finish in the 1989 Kentucky Derby.

(—M.K.)

Johnny Allen, a hot-tempered right-hander who won fifteen straight games in 1937, setting an American League record for winning percentage.

On a scorching evening in the middle of the 1927 summer, Paul Krichell, a scout for the Yankees, checked into a tavern and rooming house in Sanford, North Carolina. When he asked the night clerk for extra fans for his room, the clerk delivered the fans and confided to Krichell that he was also a pitcher, pitched in a church league. The night clerk's name was Johnny Allen, and he signed with the Yankees the next day.

Allen worked his way through the Yankee system, fighting his control. At Toronto in 1931 he pitched for Steve O'Neill, longtime American League catcher, who was able to get some things straightened out; Allen won twenty-one games and joined the Yankees in 1932.

Joe McCarthy at this time was trying to put together a pitching staff good enough to stop finishing second every year despite a formidable offense. McCarthy gave April starts to Allen, Ivy Andrews, and Dusty Rhodes; Allen, with the hindrance of an outfielder, was pasted in his start, while Andrews pitched well. Ivy, however, came down with a cold in early May, giving Johnny another shot. He pitched a five-hit shutout, launching a string of four straight Yankee shutouts, and the Yankees were on their way to blowing away the league.

Allen won seventeen games as a rookie, losing only four; at one point he had a ten-game winning streak. Despite this, and despite continuing to win an enormous percentage of his games, Allen was never a favorite of McCarthy's due to his inability to control his temper and sometimes his pitches. He was often injured, struck by the flu, and had a chronic sore arm—in fact, Allen, who was one of the first pitchers to throw the slider, is also one of the pitchers who was the foundation of the belief that the slider caused sore arms. After Allen was injured during a key series against Detroit in 1935 McCarthy decided that he would never be a reliable starter. Steve O'Neill, Johnny's manager from Toronto, was hired to manage Cleveland in late 1935, and was anxious to have him back. A trade was arranged.

Allen struggled early in the year. "He had the temper of seventeen wildcats," wrote Franklin Lewis in *The Cleveland Indians.* Lewis reported that opponents would work on Johnny's temper by stepping out of the box, constantly asking the umpire to check the baseballs, and directly accusing him of throwing spitballs. Tiger coach Del Baker took the direct approach, accusing Allen from the third base coach's box of all kinds of chicanery; Allen had to be restrained from attacking Baker. The heckling became so intense that Cy Slapnicka, then the Cleveland general manager, wrote a letter to the league president charging the opposition with "poor sportsmanship," and asking for the umpires' help in controlling the complaints. This backfired, of course; the league president issued a communiqué publicly absolving Allen of throwing spitballs, and thereby intensifying the opposition's efforts to throw Allen off his game. By June 4 Allen was 4–5. That night, in the Brunswick Hotel in Boston, Allen exploded, tearing hell out of the bar and a couple of hallways, resulting in a three hundred-dollar bill for damages and fines. It turned out to be money well spent; with the anger out of his system, Johnny went on a tear, and wound up the season with twenty wins.

It was the only twenty-win season of his career. Bob Feller was a rookie for Cleveland that year. "He had a fiery fast ball," wrote Feller in his 1947 book *Strikeout Story,* "was master of the pitch called the slider, and had an extremely deceptive change of pace." Were it not for the temper and the injuries, his career would have known no limits. Jimmie Foxx named Allen as by far the toughest pitcher he ever faced.

Allen held out through most of spring training, 1937, but won his first four decisions before being stopped by an attack of appendicitis. Returning to action on August 15, Allen won eleven straight games in a month and a half, running his record to 15–0 going into the last day of the season. The American League record for consecutive wins in a season was sixteen, so Allen pitched on the last day of the season in an attempt to tie the record. In the first inning a single by Hank Greenberg scooted through the legs of Odell "Bad News" Hale, scoring the game's only run. Allen lost 1–0; it was incidentally Greenberg's 183rd RBI of the season. As Lefty Grove had when a misplay in a 1–0 game had ended *his* winning streak at sixteen, Allen threw a famous temper tantrum, almost resulting in a fistfight between Allen and Odell Hale on the train home. The 15–1 won-lost log was a major league record for winning percentage until Roy Face's performance in 1959, and remains the American League record.

Allen continued to pitch brilliantly in 1938, and continued to behave like a child. On June 7, again in Boston, he was ordered by umpire Bill McGowan to cut off a dangling piece of his sweatshirt that was distracting the hitters. Allen refused, and left the game instead. Ossie Vitt, the Indians' new manager, ordered him to cut off the offending cloth and get back in the game, and fined him $250 when he refused. This led to a celebrated confrontation between Vitt and Allen. Team president Alva Bradley eventually defused the situation by having his brother, who ran a department store, purchase the sweatshirt for $250 and display it in a glass showcase (the sweatshirt today is the property of the Hall of Fame).

Allen won twelve straight games again in 1938, was 12–1 at the All-Star break, pitched in the All-Star game and was hurt about then. Later reports said that Allen had injured himself while pitching to Ducky Medwick in the All-Star game, but Bob Feller wrote in *Strikeout Story* that "while taking a shower in his hotel room the evening before the game, Allen slipped in the soapy tub and struck his right elbow. Like Dizzy Dean . . . Allen's decline was directly traceable to the midsummer exhibition."

Allen was never the same pitcher again, although he lasted for six-and-a-half more seasons. Bounced out of Cleveland in the housecleaning following the Cleveland Crybabies incident of 1940 (a players' rebellion against Vitt), Allen began the nomadic phase which often occurs at the end of a player's career. Joining Leo Durocher and the Dodgers in late July, 1941, Allen helped pitch the Dodgers into the World Series. Durocher liked Allen, and for almost two years was able to spot him effectively; in 1941 he went 3–0 and pitched fifteen shutout innings in a game without getting a decision. In midsummer, 1942, Allen was on the mound when Pete Reiser suffered the first of his serious injuries in the outfield.

The most famous incident of Allen's career, other than perhaps the last day of the 1937 season, occurred on May 27, 1943, at Pittsburgh. In the bottom of the eighth, with the Pirates leading 8–5, Allen was called for a balk by umpire George Barr. According to Roscoe McGowen of *The New York Times:*

Promptly the enraged Allen wheeled and dashed at full speed to Barr, who was between first and second base. Johnny seized Barr by the shoulders, one hand apparently gripping the umpire's coat collar. Manager Lippy Leo Durocher . . . was first to reach the combatants. Aided by Coach Clyde Sukeforth, who was close behind, he wrestled Allen to the ground and the two held Johnny there for a minute or two until they thought he had cooled off.

He hadn't, though, for as soon as he was released he was up and making for Barr again. However, numerous Dodgers were then clustered around, as well as umpires Jocko Conlan and Lou Jorda, and Allen was kept away from Barr.

This incident, often distorted almost to the limits of recognition, is part of the myth of the game; for an entertaining fictionalized version of the episode, see *Nice Guys Finish Last.* Allen is also the apparent frame around which Philip Roth fashioned the terrible-tempered pitcher Gil Gamesh in *The Great American Novel.* Allen received a thirty-day suspension and a two hundred-dollar fine for his assault. It could easily have been worse. Jocko Conlan recalled in his autobiography that league president Ford Frick was considering as much as a one-year suspension. Conlan, who had played against Allen years before in the International League and later in the American League, told Frick "Allen's not a bad guy. He just lost his temper."

Branch Rickey, newly arrived as the Brooklyn GM, was not as forgiving, and traded Allen to the Giants. He didn't get along well with Mel Ott or pitch well for the Giants, and his career ended after the 1944 season.

His career in baseball, however, had one surprising turn left: He became an umpire, umpire-in-chief of the Carolina League. His umpiring philosophy was that the player "can say anything to me as long as he don't touch me. He puts his hands on me, he's gone."

On March 29, 1959, Allen died of a heart ailment in his longtime home in St. Petersburg, Florida; he was fifty-four. His obituary reported that he had been working in real estate.

(—M.K. and B.J.)

John Morrison Allen, a minor league shortstop who committed suicide in March, 1950.

John Allen, Jr., played for the Homestead Grays in the 1920s.

Lee Allen, author and official historian of the Baseball Hall of Fame from 1959 until his death in 1969.

Allen was born in Cincinnati in 1915; his full handle was Leland Gaither Allen. He became a serious baseball fan at the age of nine. He came from a wealthy family, which enabled him to pursue his interest to an unusual length in his early life. In high school, it became his habit to depart early for Redland Field whenever the Reds were playing at home. Allen recalled years later, "I just told [the principal] I couldn't go to class, and that we'd have to work something out." He served as an unofficial, unpaid pitch-counter for Reds beat writer Jack Ryder, and eventually obtained his first job in baseball, the Reds paying him seventy-five cents a game to phone scores of other National League games from the press box to the scoreboard.

Allen graduated from Kenyon College with a degree in psychology; as an undergraduate he knew Bill Veeck, also a student at Kenyon, and wrote a novel, which was never published. Allen moved on to the Columbia School of Journalism. In the spring of 1938 he abandoned Columbia in favor of a position as assistant to Gabe Paul, then director of publicity for the Reds. After a stint as a civilian employee with the navy during World War II, Allen took over Paul's job from 1944 through 1945.

After the war, he held a variety of baseball-related jobs. For a short time he was Waite Hoyt's broadcast partner. "He was around six weeks," recalled Hoyt in *Voices of the Game,* then he tried to get a raise, go the union route, and they canned him." He worked for *The Sporting News,* the Cincinnati *Enquirer,* the Cincinnati *Star-Times,* and the Herkimer, New York, *Evening Telegram.* His first book, *The Cincinnati Reds,* was published in 1948 as a part of the Putnam team history series; he would eventually author ten books.

In 1959 Allen was appointed historian of the Baseball Hall of Fame, replacing Ernest Lanigan, who had health problems (the man drank like a sponge). Allen's personal library of baseball books, records, and memorabilia weighed in at an estimated five thousand pounds when shipped to Cooperstown. At first it was a dream job for Allen, and he seemed happy for perhaps the first time in thirty years; later he began to quarrel with the powers at Cooperstown. Allen was an indefatigable researcher, being particularly obsessed with establishing the proper dates of birth and death for all major league players. He resented being called a statistician. "I care very little for statistics as such," he said.

"My concern is the players. Who are these men? What are they? What problems have they faced? Where are they? Statistics are a skeleton for the flesh."

He dreamed of writing a twenty-volume history of baseball, a series "appreciated by only a few. I don't care about the others or whether it ever makes a cent." Despite his reputation as the foremost authority on baseball, Allen played down his knowledge. "I'm amazed at what is not known, and as the years go on we know less and less. There are things that will never be found out and this infuriates me, along with the realization that we'll never be able to acquire complete knowledge of the game's past." The more obscure players were, the more he seemed to care about them.

Allen had an endless variety of anecdotes about baseball, best displayed in his 1955 book *The Hot Stove League*. He could entertain an audience by rattling on about baseball for hours at a time—weird stuff, macabre tales from baseball's forgotten past. He loved puns. When the Phillies broke their long losing streak in 1961, he put together a menu for the Cooper Inn in Cooperstown which was all Phillies puns, stuff like "Coker-Cola" and "Mauch Turtle Soup."

In World War II, Allen had been rejected for military service due to hypertension. Like his predecessor as historian, Allen fought the battle of the bottle, which gave him an interest in *ballplayers* with drinking problems, a subject he researched with his customary zeal. He was a chain smoker and chronically overweight. Friend and writer Ted Patterson recalled that "When we would walk down Cooperstown's main street we would often have to stop a minute or two because 'his ticker had to catch up with him.'" He worked long, long hours at Cooperstown, recognizing that he was risking his health. On May 20, 1969, while driving from Cincinnati to Cooperstown, Allen suffered a massive heart attack and died. "Who can say," asked Joseph Overfield in *The National Pastime*, "if it was the alcohol, the cigarettes or the work?" His final project, which had occupied him for twelve hours a day, seven days a week toward the end, became his memorial later that year. It was *The Baseball Encyclopedia*.

(—M.K. Lee Allen's books are *The Cincinnati Reds, The National League, The American League Story, 100 Years of Baseball, Dizzy Dean: His Story in Baseball, Babe Ruth: His Story In Baseball, The Giants and the Dodgers, The Hot Stove League, The World Series,* and *Kings of the Diamond.*)

Lloyd Allen, pitcher in the seventies for three American League teams.

After pitching briefly for the Angels in 1969 and '70, Allen became the club's main man out of the bullpen in 1971, racking up fifteen saves. He faltered a bit the next season, and after a terrible start in 1973 was traded to the Texas Rangers. His arm was still highly regarded; Rangers manager Whitey Herzog described him as "one of the best pitching prospects in the country," and immediately stuck him in the rotation.

Allen never got it going for the Rangers, and he finished his major league career with the White Sox in 1975. Allen went zero and ten his final three seasons, with ERAs of 9.42, 7.45, and 11.81. For several years after that he was a successful reliever in the Mexican League, but never made it back to the major leagues.

(—R.N.)

Jamie Allen, part-time third baseman for the Seattle Mariners in 1983.

Maury Allen, sportswriter and author of many baseball books, including books about Casey Stengel, Joe DiMaggio, Bo Belinsky, Jim Rice, Reggie Jackson, Catfish Hunter, Whitey Ford, and Ron Guidry.

Allen grew up in Brooklyn, but oddly enough grew up as a passionate Yankee fan. In David Halberstam's *Summer of '49*, Allen recalled that as a kid he was the local baseball bookie, taking dime bets from neighborhood kids based on who would get hits in a game, but he was wiped out of the bookmaking business when the Red Sox had a big day against the Yankees, and he wound up owing more than he had.

Mel Allen, voice of the New York Yankees from 1939 through 1964.

Allen was born Melvin Israel in Alabama in 1913. His first contact with major league baseball came during summer visits to an aunt in Detroit, where he sold hot dogs at Navin Field. Having learned to read long before entering school, he skipped grades and graduated from high school at the age of fifteen. He enrolled at the University of Alabama as a political science major. Intent upon earning a varsity letter but lacking athletic ability, he became an equipment manager for the football team, as well as public address announcer for home football games.

After earning his undergraduate degree, Israel moved on to law school. When the radio announcer for Alabama football games resigned, head coach Frank Thomas was asked to recommend a replacement. Years later, Allen told Curt Smith in *Voices of the Game* that "Thomas didn't know one announcer from another, and to that I say, 'Thank God!' Because, you see, he knew *me*, he knew I'd done P.A. work, and he didn't see any difference between that and broadcasting. So he asked me to audition for the job."

Israel got the job, and at age twenty became the Voice of the Tide over Birmingham station WBRC, a CBS affiliate. He was still planning a legal career, and after passing the bar exam in late 1936 went to New York City for a brief vacation. While there he visited CBS headquarters for an audition. The audition was a success, but Mel had to return to Alabama for a final semester as a speech instructor (he'd won a fellowship) before embarking upon his new career. It was at this time that, much against his father's wishes, he changed his last name from Israel to Allen, adopting as his last name the father's middle name in an effort to mollify the angry papa. He earned forty-five dollars a week as a staff announcer, plus fifty dollars a week more for introducing guests on the *Pick and Pat Minstrels Show.*

"The more broadcasting I did," Allen recalled, "the more I liked it. Things got to the point where I was covering political conventions, inaugurations, presidential elections." He abandoned all thoughts of a law career, and began to contemplate a baseball broadcasting career. He spent afternoons at the Polo Grounds and Yankee Stadium, practicing for an uncertain opportunity. He walked the streets of the city practicing his broadcasts; he discovered, he said, that New York was full of people who walked around all day talking aloud to themselves, and nobody paid any attention to them. The New York teams, at that time, allowed the broadcast of only opening day and World Series games. But in 1939 the Yankees and Giants signed a joint contract with CBS to allow broadcasts of all home games for both teams.

A Washington sports announcer named Arch McDonald was imported, and Allen was tentatively scheduled to replace McDonald as voice of the Washington Senators. At the last moment, however, Clark Griffith tabbed Walter Johnson for that job, and Allen was left temporarily out in the cold.

It turned out to be his biggest break of all. Early in the '39 season, McDonald's sidekick was pitching Ivory Soap between innings, and twice referred to it as "Ovary Soap." Allen became the replacement sidekick, and when McDonald returned to Washington after only one season, Allen was given the top job.

In 1943, Allen entered the army, and that summer, unable to find a sponsor, Yankee and Giant broadcasts went off the air. By 1946, when Allen was ready to resume his career, Larry MacPhail was running the Yankees. MacPhail determined that henceforth all Yankee games, home and road, would be broadcast live; no more sharing the same station with the Giants. The man he wanted behind the microphone for this great leap forward was his veteran Cincinnati and Brooklyn announcer, Red Barber. Surprisingly, Barber resisted MacPhail's blandishments and remained with the Dodgers. Allen, thinking he had no chance with the Yankees, had meanwhile given his word to owner Horace Stoneham that he would stay on board for Giants broadcasts. But Stoneham was having difficulty finding a station, and when MacPhail turned to Allen as his second choice Stoneham released him from his commitment.

By 1949 Allen was already something of a legend. David Halberstam, in his best-selling *Summer of '49*, described his technique:

> With a soft, almost silky voice, and a natural feel for the microphone, he not only brought the fan into the Stadium, but also projected a sense of intimacy with the players; Allen made the fan feel as if he were a part of the greater Yankee family.

Curt Smith wrote:

> For twenty-five years he owned the most fanatical following of any announcer in America. Zealous and seductive, he discoursed with almost maddening detail, and his exuberant narrative brought joy to provinces located time zones away from the Big Ball Park in the Bronx.

A bachelor and a perfectionist, Allen made broadcasting his life. After a game, recalled Jim Woods (one of his sidekicks), he would sit in the booth for a half hour and pick the broadcast apart—what had been said at the key moments of the game, what mistakes might have been made, how it could have been done better. He was not an easy man to work with.

As early as 1948 Allen had begun appearing on television, teaming with Curt Gowdy to broadcast games on TV and radio simultaneously. He was soon a regular for both the All-Star Game and the Rose Bowl, and between 1955 and 1963 covered all of the World Series but one. He coined the nicknames of many of the Yankees of the time—"Old Reliable" for Tommy Henrich, "The Springfield Rifle" for Vic Raschi, and worked these nicknames into his broadcasts often enough to keep them going.

Allen and Red Barber, in a sense, are the fathers of the two schools of modern sports broadcasting. Barber considered himself a journalist, was lyrical but forced and somewhat stiff, and thought it a cardinal sin to root for the home team in any way, shape or form. Allen was an unabashed fan, spontaneous, prizing his enthusiasm, glorifying his team. "When the crowd yells, shut up," advised Barber; Allen used the crowd noise as a background, as a part of his broadcast. Barber asked for the respect of his audience; Allen, for their affection.

Sadly, the Red Barber school of broadcasting since the early sixties has become increasingly dominant, and broadcasts as a result have become ever more boring. "We were first and foremost *newsmen*, not some jock announcer," said Bob Elson, as if proud of this. Vin Scully, a hack in love with the sound of his own drone, has been glorified as if he was some sort of a damned demi-God because he represents the Red Barber virtues so well. Scully is so thoroughly prepared and so dispassionate that sometimes you'd never know there was a ball game going on. Harry Caray is the last of the Mel Allen school still broadcasting regularly, a group that once included Bob Prince, Lindsay Nelson, and Dizzy Dean. The broadcast world has been overrun by Milo Hamiltons.

While broadcasting the fourth and final game of the 1963 World Series, Allen suffered an attack of laryngitis. As Mickey Mantle homered to tie the score in the seventh inning of the fourth and final game, Allen lost his voice completely. It was a tremendous professional embarrassment. Dick Young, heedless as always of who he would hurt, wrote that "They said he had laryngitis, but if it was, it was psychosomatic laryngitis. Mel Allen couldn't believe his beloved Yankees were losing four straight to the Dodgers. His voice refused to believe it, and therefore he could not report it."

Allen, of course, pointed out that he had broadcast many Yankee failures over the years, from Podres's shutout to Mazeroski's home run, without surrendering his voice. But after the 1964 season, Allen was suddenly fired, not even allowed to broadcast the 1964 World Series. Reportedly, Dan Topping thought that Allen talked too much. Another version of the story is that Allen was forced out by the financial troubles of Ballantine Beer, the chief broadcast sponsor.

Neither Allen nor the public was ever given any explanation for the firing. In the absence of a reason, ugly and unfounded rumors gained credibility. Depressed but determined to battle back, Allen landed a unique broadcasting job for the 1965 season: describing lame-duck Milwaukee Braves games to future fans in Atlanta. He felt he had the inside track for the permanent job in 1966, and was stunned again when the nod went to Milo Hamilton. In 1968 he turned down Charley Finley's offer to become the voice of the Oakland A's, choosing instead to commute between New York and Cleveland, signing to do forty-six TV games. While his partner, Harry Jones, attempted to talk baseball during a stultifying broadcast from Minnesota one night, Allen turned instead to poetry, reciting from memory the first thirty-seven lines of Longfellow's "The Song of Hiawatha." In the ultra-serious sixties he seemed passé, old-time. After that season, he was never again hired as a regular major league announcer.

The Yankees, showing the same kind of judgment on the field as in choosing broadcasters, went in the tank immediately after firing Allen. Millions still associated Mel with the glory days of the Yankees. He was in demand for commercials, banquets, and voice-overs. A survey taken years after his firing identified his as one of America's most-recognized voices. Neophyte broadcasters still solicited his advice, which he was consistently generous with. He became the voice of *This Week in Baseball*, and that more than anything else became his salvation. Using his longtime signature phrase "How about that?" and his unique and wonderful phrasing, Allen has become as familiar to young Americans today as he was forty years ago, if not more so. Allen broadcast the Yankee games for twenty-five years and was fired twenty-six years ago, but he remains, at seventy-six, one of the top names in his profession.

On August 7, 1978, Mel Allen and Red Barber became the first recipients of the Ford C. Frick Award for broadcasting excellence, and were inducted into what became the broadcasters' wing of the Baseball Hall of Fame.

(—M.K. and B.J. The best source of information about Allen appears to be Curt Smith's *Voices of The Game.*)

Neil Allen, contemporary pitcher.

Allen, a native of Kansas City, Kansas, was an outstanding high school athlete, and turned down a number of football scholarships to play professional baseball. "I was mainly interested in football and was going to go to college, except I didn't really like to study," he later said. The Mets picked him in the eleventh round of the 1976 free-agent draft, and before long Allen, with a rising fastball and a hard curve, established himself as one of the Mets' top pitching prospects.

Allen made the Mets roster in 1979, but got hit hard as a starter. About to be sent to the minors, he was instead sent to the bullpen (because of an injury to reliever Skip Lockwood), and a career was created; Allen pitched in relief for the rest of '79, and led the club in saves from 1980 through 1982, piling up fifty-three over those three years. (At the time, Jeff Reardon was the Mets' number two reliever, which was strange enough because Reardon was more effective than Allen was.)

Young, strong, handsome, and a star in New York City—what a combination! Allen was one of those players, like Mark Gastineau, Len Dykstra, and Gregg Jefferies, who got to be a lot more famous than he deserved to be by playing in New York, and the rest of the country kind of got sick of hearing about him. In 1983 after a controversial magazine interview, domestic problems, team fines, and some poor pitching performances, Allen told the Mets he had a drinking problem and needed help. The Mets sent him to an alcoholism treatment center, where a counselor decided that Allen *didn't* have a drinking problem. "Neil's problem appears to be the result of stress reaction and . . . Neil unfortunately and unwisely over the past few weeks used alcohol to excess because of that overstress," said the counselor. A doctor at the clinic put it more precisely. "The only thing wrong with you," he told Neil, "is that your curve ball is hanging."

On June 15, 1983, Allen was traded to St. Louis for Keith Hernandez. Whitey Herzog made him a starter in the second half of 1983, and he pitched well in that role over the second half of the season (9–6 in eighteen starts.) Despite this, he preferred to re-

lieve, and in 1984 he went back to the bullpen, where he was just fair. Allen's career kicked along until early 1989, hitting some terrible low points and no real high spots as he bounced from the Cardinals to the Yankees to the White Sox, back to the Yankees and finally Cleveland, with a few intermediate visits to the minor leagues.

Allen I think is a historical first of a type. It used to be that starting was the glamour job, and nobody wanted to pitch relief. Pitchers sometimes would screw up their careers by insisting on starting when they should have been pitching relief. But Allen is the opposite: He is perhaps the first pitcher to screw up his career by insisting on pitching relief when he obviously should have been a starter. Allen pitched well as a starting pitcher, in the minors, in 1983, and in 1986 when he started for half the season for the White Sox and went 7–2. But he constantly expressed the desire to pitch relief, and people went along with him although he very obviously didn't have either the psychological makeup or the stuff to be a relief ace. He spent almost a decade trying to get back to that magic moment at the beginning of his career, when he was young and a New York Met, and the world was his to command.

Newt Allen, a Negro League player of Hall of Fame or near-Hall of Fame quality, who played second base for the Kansas City Monarchs for twenty-three years.

Henry Newton Allen was born in Kansas City in 1902. He attended Western Baptist College for a couple of years, and worked summers as a "canvas puller" and ice boy when the Kansas City Monarchs were organized in 1920, being given a few baseballs and allowed to practice with the team in exchange for duties on the grounds crew. A high-school friend of Allen's made the Monarchs, and Allen tried out with the team, but the manager didn't think he was good enough, so Allen went with a semipro team in Omaha. It was a good team and Allen was their star player, and after playing well in an exhibition against the Monarchs he was given the job he wanted.

The Monarchs in 1921, their second year of existence, played a city championship series against the Kansas City Blues of the American Association. The Monarchs lost that series, but a year later, with Allen in the lineup, they beat the Blues five out of six games.

Nicknamed "The Colt"—physically there was something about him that re-

minded people of a young colt—Allen could be described as a Negro League Frankie Frisch or Eddie Collins. Like Frisch and Collins, he was a small man. (*Porter's Biographical Dictionary* and *Only the Ball Was White* say he was five seven and a half and weighed 170, dimensions which are of uncertain origin, and can't be right. One hundred seventy pounds is stocky for five seven; Allen was quite slender.) Anyway, like Frisch, Allen was a second baseman who could also play third and a little bit of shortstop. Like Frisch and Collins, he was a hot-tempered, intense player, a spark plug. Like Frisch and Collins, he was a great base runner. Like Frisch and Collins, he had a long career and was remarkably healthy for a second baseman. Like Frisch and Collins, he shuffled very little from team to team, spending almost his entire career with one team. Like Frisch and Collins, he was a player-manager late in his career. Like Frisch and Collins, his teams won many championships.

The difference between them, apart from race, is in the emphasis of their excellence. Frisch was a good second baseman and a great hitter (for a second baseman). Allen was a good hitter for a second baseman, but a great defensive player, regarded by many as the best defensive second baseman of the Negro Leagues. "He wouldn't even look at first base on the pivot," recalled Bill Drake. "He'd throw the ball to first under his left arm." Allen had an outfielder's arm and speed, but was assigned to play second base by the Monarchs because they had a strong outfield. In the first Negro League World Series of 1924, Kansas City against Philadelphia, the Monarchs turned six double plays in a nine-inning game. They won that series, but then lost the series in 1925.

Offensively, Allen was a number two hitter (like Eddie Collins), with a career average probably in the .280s. In four World Series he hit .272 (22/81) with nine doubles. He was fined frequently by the league and the team because of his quick temper. The league used home-town umpires, who tended to cause a good many fights. Once Allen needed eighteen stitches in his leg after a slide by Dave Malarcher; years later, he nailed Malarcher in the head with a relay throw to first. As he matured, Allen learned quicker ways to deal with enemy base runners, as he recalled in John Holway's magnificent *Voices From the Great Black Baseball Leagues:*

I learned that if they jump high, watch the leg that's in the air. If he's going to try to spike you with it, step aside and hook it with your arm. Sometimes your glove will catch a spike; or you want to hook your arm just past his shoes and pull. I could throw a man ten feet and break his neck almost. You do that to one or two bad sliders and you don't have any trouble out of the rest. Or hit two or three of them coming into second base in the chest with the ball—next time they'll run right out of the base path.

Allen played second base for ten championship teams. The Monarchs were champions of the Negro National League in 1923, 1924, 1925, 1929, and 1931, and of the Negro American League in 1937, 1939, 1940, 1941, and 1942. Satchel Paige jumped from team to team, but spent many years as Allen's teammate. "Kansas City is a good baseball town, if you're a winner," Allen told Holway "We used to draw 14 to 15,000 people during those times, 18 to 19,000 on Sunday, and ladies' night, my goodness, we'd have lots of people. We drew quite a few people, white and colored." As great as they were, they lived as much on the road, barnstorming, as on local support. In the winters Allen played baseball for teams in Cuba, Mexico, Venezuela, Puerto Rico, and California. Allen married young and had two sons, but his marriage broke up under the strain of his constant travel.

"It's hard," Allen recalled in *The Kansas City Monarchs.* "You know, you're playing, making good plays and you have admirers sitting up there in the stands. You don't even know them. Ball game's over, go to your hotel and get telephone calls asking for you—you don't even know who it is."

Traveling through Michigan, the team stopped at a small restaurant for some hamburgers. After they had ordered, the owner told the Monarchs that they couldn't eat in his restaurant, that they'd have to take their food and go. "We just all walked out," Allen recalled. "We left them with fifty-some hamburgers on the grill. It was one of those times when you even the score."

One winter in the mid-thirties Allen was part of a Negro League All-Star team which toured China, Japan, and the Phillipines, playing exhibitions against army teams and clubs from sugar plantations. According to Donn Rogosin in *Invisible Men:*

Many of the players considered the trip the high point of their lives. "You'd pay your money and get in that rickshaw, and ride wherever you wanted to go," recalled Newt Allen about Kobe, Japan. "It was fun."

Race relations with other ballplayers were never the problem, at least as Allen saw it. "Ballplayers—white and black—have a lot of respect for each other. They know they can play ball, and they know they're going to play with them or against them. You hear a lot of harsh words from the grandstand, but very seldom find prejudiced ballplayers." After his retirement, after the major leagues came to Kansas City, the semipro and minor league players who had been baseball in the area held an annual reunion, blacks and whites together.

In the early forties the Monarchs were thinking of signing a young shortstop from UCLA, Jackie Robinson. They sent Allen to evaluate him. "He's a very smart ballplayer," Allen reported, "but he can't play shortstop. He can't throw from the hole. Try him at second base." Second base, of course, was Allen's position; Allen was nominating Jackie Robinson to replace him. Robinson joined the Monarchs with that in mind, but when the Monarch shortstop Jesse Williams hurt his arm, Robinson broke in at short, teaming for a while with Allen.

In the war years the Monarchs were cut to a roster of nine men, while players like Robinson went to the army. Allen played with the Monarchs through 1944. A loyal and active Democrat, Allen got a political patronage job after his career, as foreman at the Kansas City County courthouse. He spent the last years of his life in a rest home in Cincinnati, and died June 25, 1988. His obituary in *The Sporting News* was two sentences.

(Sources for this article include *The Kansas City Monarchs,* by Janet Bruce, *Only the Ball Was White,* by Robert Peterson, and *Voices from the Great Black Baseball Leagues,* by John Holway. Almost every imaginable fact is in conflict among these sources and the others cited, including Allen's age, place of birth, the years in which he joined and left the team, the teams for which he played, whether he was a switch hitter or a right-handed hitter, how good a hitter he was, when they made the trip to the Orient, the years in which the Monarchs won the title, and what league they were in. I'm not an expert in the history of the Negro Leagues, and I've made the best guesses I could about what to believe.)

Nick Allen, catcher in the Federal League and later the National League, never more than a bit player in six seasons.

Ron Allen, brother of Dick Allen.

Twenty-one months younger than his most famous brother, Ron Allen received a degree in history from Youngstown University and turned down offers to play pro basketball from the New York Knicks and Cincinnati Royals. A switch-hitting first baseman, Ron was bigger than his brother, and nearly as strong. With Spartanburg in June, 1966, he hit a massive drive that reportedly traveled six hundred feet. He had some good minor league seasons, including 1967 at Tidewater (24, 100, .288), and 1969 at Reading (25, 97, .300), but he had only one hit (a home run) in the major leagues. He is now a partner with his brother Hank in a very successful stable outside Laurel, Maryland.

Todd Allen, a Negro League player of the World War I era. Allen played third base and managed the Indianapolis ABCs, the Chicago American Giants and the Lincoln Giants between 1915 and 1925.

Toussaint "Tom" Allen, first baseman with Hilldale and other Negro League teams, 1914 to 1926.

Wilbur P. Allen, president of the Texas League for a few years about 1910.

Gary Allenson, catcher with the Red Sox from 1979–84, and now managing in their farm system.

Gary Allenson was the International League MVP in 1978, as much for his defensive skills as his .299 average and twenty homers. He made the Red Sox the next spring, and with Carlton Fisk hurt saw substantial action behind the plate. His .357 average as a backup in 1980 may have been a contributing factor in the Sox' willingness to let Carlton Fisk get away; in any case Allenson got a chance to start, but never hit, leaving the majors in 1986 with a .221 average. He managed in the Yankees system for two years before taking over Boston's Lynchburg farm club in 1989.

Gene Alley, shortstop for the Pittsburgh Pirates in 1966, when the Pirates set a National League record with 215 double plays.

Alley moved through the Pirates system in tandem with Willie Stargell, even outhomering Stargell at Grand Forks in the Northern League in 1960, where Alley was the Most Valuable Player. He played mostly second base until arriving at Columbus in 1963, where he became a full-time shortstop. He received rave reviews for his work in the Arizona Instructional League that fall, his mentor, George Detore, reporting that Alley "could be a major league shortstop; at second base he's as good as there is and he is an outstanding third baseman." The Pirates at this time had Gold Glove winner Bill Mazeroski at second, with bonus baby/power threat Bob Bailey at third.

After spending 1964 backing up Dick Schofield, Alley became the regular in 1965. In 1966 and 1967 Alley was a tremendous player, hitting for average (.299, .287) with some line-drive power, excellent baserunning and defense. He won the Gold Glove both seasons, was named shortstop on *The Sporting News* post-season All-Star team both seasons, and started the All-Star game in 1967. The Pirates, who led the league in double plays every year anyway because of Mazeroski, turned even more DPs after Alley arrived, working 215 twin killings in 1966, which was (and is) a National League record. (The Pirates were in the middle of the league in terms of opposition base runners.)

In August of 1967 Alley injured his right shoulder while making an off-balance throw. He was never again the same player. He was in and out of the lineup throughout 1968, and although named to the All-Star team, had to give way to a replacement. His offense tailed off. He began the 1969 season on the disabled list, and Fred Patek became the regular shortstop, Alley seeing most of his action at second base in place of the aging Mazeroski. He regained the shortstop job in 1970, but was no longer a durable player, and his contribution to the 1971 World Championship was marginal. Two years later his career was finished.

Gair Allie, starting shortstop for the 1954 Pittsburgh Pirates.

A rookie in 1954, Allie set a major league record for the least number of hits (83) for a player with over four hundred at bats (418). He wasn't much as a shortstop, either, and his first year in the bigs was also his last.

Bob Allison, slugging outfielder for the Washington Senators and Minnesota Twins from 1958 to 1970, and the most feared base runner of his time.

As a high school athlete at Raytown, Missouri, a Kansas City suburb, Allison starred in football, basketball, and track; the high school had no baseball team. He played sandlot ball, however, and was well-known to major league scouts when he enrolled at the University of Kansas in 1952. He played varsity football and baseball for the seasons of 1953 and 1954 before signing with the Senators, turning down an offer from the Yankees in hopes of making the majors faster.

Allison didn't hit his first three years in the minor leagues, but set the teeth to chattering with a good year at Chattanooga in 1958. "Allison is like another DiMaggio," reported Sherry Robertson, the Senators' chief scout, perhaps a little overexcited. "He's a dream." The Senators' 1958 center fielder was Albie Pearson, and he was the 1958 American League Rookie of the Year, with sluggers Jim Lemon and Roy Sievers in left and right. Pearson reported to camp with a bad leg, however, and later battled a groin injury, while Allison was sensational in the spring. Calvin Griffith said that Allison had "the best arm we've had on this club since Jackie Jensen," and trainer Doc Lentz said that Allison was "the strongest boy I've ever handled." Allison won the job out of spring training, and was the Senators clean-up hitter on opening day.

In the minors Allison had been a line-drive hitter, hitting only 28 homers in more than 500 games. He began homering in bunches in the majors, however, and by August 30 had 29 home runs. The American League record for home runs by a rookie was 31, by Ted Williams; Allison seemed sure to break it, although he didn't, hitting just one home run in September. Harmon Killebrew, who wasn't a rookie that year but was a first-year regular, hit 42 home runs for the Senators; Killebrew and Allison were dubbed "Mr. Upstairs" and "Mr. Downstairs" for the length of their home runs. Allison and Killebrew had been teammates in the minor leagues, were roommates for years, and remain friends to this day. Allison played in the All-Star game as a rookie, led the league in triples, and was an overwhelming choice as the American League Rookie of the Year; he was the second consecutive Washington center fielder to win the award. After the season he appeared on *Home Run Derby*.

Allison was shifted to right field in 1960 to make better use of his arm. The Senators became the Minnesota Twins in 1961, and also became a good team, winning over ninety games in 1962 and 1963. Allison drove in more than a hundred runs in '61 and '62, had his best years in 1963 and 1964, but was overshadowed by the awesome slugging of his buddy Killebrew. In 1964, to clear

TRACERS

They [the Yankees] didn't act that way in 1947, my first year with them, though. I had 19 wins with two-and-a-half weeks to go in the season. But they wouldn't let me go for my twentieth win. They pitched me in relief. I had so many opportunities to win 20, if they had let me. . . . The truth, though, was that they didn't want me to win 20.

—Allie Reynolds
The Men of Autumn (Page 3)

Pure fiction. Reynolds started for the Yankees on September 7, 12, 17, and 23, winning his twentieth game on September 23—five days before the end of the season. He could have started one more time, on the Sunday marking the end of the season, but with the pennant long since decided and the World Series starting on Tuesday, what kind of sense would that have made?

Reynolds was out of action from August 23 until September 7 (missing one or two starts), but there are specific details of an injury on August 23—Reynolds "threw out his arm after tossing a ball and a strike to Bockman following passes to Jack Conway and Les Fleming with two away in the ninth. Lefty Joe Page had to amble out of the bullpen . . . the extent of Reynolds' injury was not immediately determined." There are followup reports on an examination by "Dr. Robert F. Heylad" (Dr. Hyland?) and quotes from Reynolds on the progress of his return, making it clear that this is not a plot to hold him at sixteen wins until it is too late to get twenty. Basically, Reynolds's memory has gone from "I could have won twenty games if things had gone right" to create a specific scenario that just didn't exist.

a spot for Tony Oliva, Allison was shifted to first base, which stranded Killebrew in left field. Harmon was as mobile as a park bench but didn't have as good an arm, so that defensive alignment didn't work out too well, and in '65 Allison went to left, with Killebrew coming to the infield. That clicked or something did, and the Twins won their first pennant in thirty-two years. It was to be an off-year for Allison, but it became notable for his brilliant, diving catch of Jim Lefebvre's drive down the left field line in the second game of the 1965 World Series. Allison made the last out of the World Series, striking out against Sandy Koufax.

Allison was a fierce competitor and a frightening base runner. "He looks like a locomotive when he's coming in to break up the double play," said an opposing second baseman. "He's gonna slide into somebody and send him to the moon one of these days." Any poll of second basemen or catchers taken in those years as to who they least wanted to see bearing down on them always started with Allison. Physically, Allison was quite similar to three other major league players—Bo Jackson, Reggie Jackson, and Jackie Jensen—all of whom had also played college football. Like those three, he was both big and fast, with a powerful arm. Although Reggie went farther than the other three, they were all quite comparable players, with almost interchangeable stats in some years except for Bo's poor strikeout and walk data. Another guy who was physically similar, and who could have played major league baseball if he had chosen to, was another Kansas University fullback a few years behind Allison—John Riggins.

Allison's 1966 season was ruined when he was hit by a pitch in June and suffered a broken bone in his left hand. He returned to full-time duty in 1967 and 1968, and pulled a conspicuous rock in the final game of the '67 season. On October 1, 1967, the Red Sox, Twins, and Tigers were all 91–70; Minnesota was at Fenway Park. Trailing 5–2 in the top of the eighth with runners on first and second and two out, Allison ripped a line drive into the corner in left, scoring a run. He tried to go to second, and Yastrzemski nailed him with a perfect throw, ending the inning (and for all intents the season) with the score 5–3. He saw part-time duty as the Twins won the first two AL West division titles in 1969 and 1970, 1969 being Billy Martin's first title as a manager. In *Number 1*, with Peter Golenbock, Martin recalled that

Allison "was my leader behind the leader on the bench, a beautiful buffer for me. I'd say to him, 'Bob, tell so-and-so about such-and-such when you get a chance,' and coming from Bob they wouldn't resent it nearly as much as if it came from me. If he wasn't in business now, he'd have made somebody an excellent coach."

Allison had a successful career as a Coca-Cola bottler in the Twin Cities for years after retiring from baseball, but in the last year has been stricken by "a mysterious disease," and has moved to Rio Verde, Arizona, near Phoenix, in the hope of regaining his health.

Doug Allison, regular catcher for the famous Cincinnati Red Stockings of 1869, the team which won all fifty-seven games that it played. Allison, though not an outstanding hitter, appears to have been one of the better players on the team, and is listed on some all-star teams as the outstanding catcher of the 1860s. He also appears as a minor character in Darryl Brock's new novel *If I Never Get Back* (Crown Publishers, 1990).

Mack Allison, a pitcher with the St. Louis Browns in the early teens.

Mack (that was his real name) debuted on September 13, 1911, and the St. Louis *Post-Dispatch* observed that, "Allison is a big fellow, who heaves with the right. He seemed to have a lot of speed, and a good curve ball." He was 6–17 in 1912, his only full season.

Arthur Allyn, Sr., longtime partner of Bill Veeck's in the ownership of the Cleveland Indians, St. Louis Browns and Chicago White Sox.

Allyn, an investment broker, first became associated with Veeck in 1946, when he was brought in as part of the syndicate involved in the purchase, masterminded by Veeck, of the Cleveland Indians. He and Veeck worked well together, and he remained a part of the team when Veeck brought the Browns in '51 and the White Sox in '59. Allyn died at the age of seventy-three on October 7, 1960, in Chicago; two of his sons later owned the White Sox.

Arthur Allyn, Jr., and **John Allyn,** brothers, one or the other of whom owned the Chicago White Sox from 1961 through 1975.

At the death of their father in 1960, his sons Arthur junior and John were left as partners with Bill Veeck and Hank Greenberg in a company called the CBC Corp, which owned the White Sox. The Artnell corporation, headed at that time by Arthur Allyn, bought out Veeck and Greenberg in

June, 1961, and, on May 4, 1962, purchased all remaining stock in the club from Charles A. Comiskey II, grandson of the team's founder, for $3.3 million. The total purchase price of the team was about $8 million. The acquisition was in the courts for a while, as the Veeck-Greenberg stock was the source of a lawsuit by a man named Bernard Epton, who claimed that he had made an agreement in May, 1961, to purchase the team.

According to *Voices of the Game*, Arthur Allyn was "a butterfly collector, amateur pilot, pianist, and former chemist [who] stunned the Cubs by signing a television contract with WFLD, Chicago's first UHF [ultra-high frequency] station. Channel 32, he said, would air all Sox' games, home and away." Phil Wrigley thought that Allyn had stabbed him in the back, thinking that he had a handshake agreement that neither would broadcast road games in Chicago while the other team was at home.

In 1964 the Sox offered Jim Brosnan a contract which would forbid him from publishing articles during the baseball season. The American Civil Liberties Union threatened to file a lawsuit, claiming that Allyn was censoring his employees (which of course he was).

"Balderdash!" was Allyn's reply. He claimed he just wanted Brosnan to concentrate on his pitching. Nothing came of the lawsuit.

Veeck was a tough act to follow—he would probably have paid Brosnan extra to fire off an occasional rocket—and Allyn was never a popular figure in Chicago. It didn't help that the Sox didn't win a pennant in the sixties. In 1969, Arthur junior sold the team . . . but it stayed in the family, because the new owner was John Allyn.

In the fall of 1975 John Allyn, exasperated with Harry Caray's unwillingness to gloss over the team's shortcomings, announced that if he owned the team in '76, Harry would be gone. Caray responded by releasing a statement which read, "I can't believe any man can own a ball club and be as dumb as John Allyn. Did he make enough money to own it or did he inherit it?"

Harry's job was saved when Allyn sold the White Sox to a group headed by Bill Veeck, completing an elegant circle. (Allyn did retain a 20 percent interest in the club.)

John Allyn suffered a heart attack and died at his home in Winnetka, Illinois on April 29, 1979. Arthur junior died in

Sarasota, Florida, on March 22, 1985, after a long illness.

(—R.N.)

Mel Almada, the first Mexican-born player to play in the major leagues.

Born in Hwatabampo, Sonora, Mexico in 1913 (according to current encyclopedias) or 1915 (which was the date given while he was active) Melo Almada came to Los Angeles with his family at the age of one. An older brother, Louis Almada, played in the Pacific Coast League, with the Mission team, and Mel took the same route, signing with Seattle in the PCL in 1932.

Almada was lightning fast, and his career began brilliantly. He hit .311 and .323 for Seattle, stole some bases and had over two hundred hits in 1933, earning a late-season look with Boston, for whom he hit .341 in fourteen games. Joining Kansas City in 1934, Almada hit .328 and was selected the MVP in the American Association; he beat out four bunt singles in one game. By 1935—age twenty or twenty-two—he was the Red Sox center fielder, and had a decent season, hitting .290 and scoring 85 runs.

It is interesting to compare the beginnings of Almada's career with those of Joe DiMaggio. Both were center fielders, of about the same age (Almada was three months younger according to contemporary sources). Both had older brothers who were Pacific Coast League outfielders, and both began their careers in the PCL in 1932. Almada was a regular that year; DiMaggio just played three games at the end of the year. Almada surfaced in the American League in 1933, more than two years before DiMaggio, and was a Red Sox regular while DiMag was still with the Seals. An interesting instruction on the value of premature evaluations of young players. . . .

In the mid-1930's Tom Yawkey bought the Red Sox, and began spending hundreds of thousands of dollars to purchase stars from other American League teams. Flit Cramer got Almada's job in center. Almada was a very nice-looking man, with a big wide smile like Luis Medina. He was fast, had a good arm, hit around .300 (.295 in '37, .311 in '38), struck out very seldom; it's hard to see why the package wasn't enough, but apparently it wasn't, because after losing the job in Boston he became a traveling center fielder. With the Browns in 1938 he hit safely in forty-seven of forty-eight games; he had an eighteen-game streak, missed one game, and then had a twenty-nine-game streak. He

scored 101 runs that year, and was out of the league the next season.

Rafael Almeida, a Cuban third basemen whose signing by the Cincinnati Reds in 1911 raised hopes for an erosion of the color line.

According to Robert Peterson in *Only the Ball Was White,* the signing of Almeida and his Cuban Stars teammate Armando Marsans led to speculation that

> ". . . it would not be surprising to see a Cuban a few shades darker than Almeida and Marsans breaking into the professional ranks, with a coal-black Cuban on the order of the crack pitcher, [Jose] Mendez, making his debut later on. Manager McGraw of the New York Giants is quoted as having said he would give a large sum of money for his release . . . if McGraw did not think he would raise too much of a racket he would sign Mendez today."

Almeida was to be a wedge, which split open a crack in segregation's armour. It didn't work out. According to Seymour's *Baseball: The Golden Age,* Reds owner Garry Herrmann had made inquiries in Cuba about the players' heritages. They were signed only after Herrmann had been assured that they possessed only "pure caucasian blood in their veins." Herrmann was hoping that the Cubans' "freakiness" would draw curious fans.

(—R.N.)

Bill Almon, the first player chosen in the 1974 amateur draft, and a major league infielder until 1988.

A native of Providence, Rhode Island, Almon starred at Brown University, received a degree, was named the College Player of the Year in 1974, was drafted by the Padres to start the first round, and signed with the Padres for a reported $100,000. Starting at the AAA level, Almon struggled with the bat for his first year and a half. On April 19, 1976 at Aloha Stadium in Hawaii, Almon had a scary accident at second base when he was creamed by the base runner and, a fraction of a second later, hit in the mouth by a throw from first base. Almon lay on the field unconscious for twenty minutes, moving his legs very slightly a couple of times; he had swallowed his tongue and suffered cuts on his face in the accident, described by *The Sporting News* as "a close brush with death." He was taken from the stadium in an ambulance, had twenty-eight stitches in his lip, and was back in the lineup within a month.

Almon's play improved dramatically in

1976, and in 1977 he became the Padres' regular shortstop. He had a good year for a rookie—11 triples, .261 average, 20 stolen bases, led the league in sacrifice bunts and putouts at short. A funny thing happened in the Padres camp the next spring: A fellow named Ozzie Smith showed up. "If I had lost my job to an inferior player," said Almon, "it would have bothered me a lot." This is probably the only time in my thirty years as a baseball fan I've ever heard of a young player losing his job, and admitting that the other guy was better.

Almon was shifted to second base, and played well there for about the first two weeks of the season. Then he went into a defensive slump, which anybody should have expected in view of his never having played the position before, and the Padres moved Derrel Thomas to second base, Almon to third. "The next thing they'll tell you," a friend of his suggested, "is that you don't have enough power to play third base." The friend, of course, proved a prophet; Almon hit .331 through late May, and hit the pines as soon as he dropped below .270.

This has always bothered me, to inject a personal note, that it was just *so* obvious what the Padres needed to do, and yet they couldn't see it. Almon was perfectly equipped to be a quality second baseman for twelve years if they could have suffered through the apprenticeship. He was a quick, agile shortstop who just didn't quite have a shortstop's arm. Instead, Roger Craig put him at third base, which exposed his arm and overmatched his bat, and screwed up Almon's future as well as costing the Padres a player.

Anyway, Almon played eleven more years in the major leagues, and never really did get reestablished. His best year was the strike year, 1981. Released by the Mets, Almon got on the phone and started calling people. Roland Hemond of the White Sox gave him a triple-A contract, and when Todd Cruz got hurt in spring training, Almon took his job away; he played almost every game at short for Tony LaRussa, and hit .301. Almon was thin (six feet three inches, 170 pounds), so of course people said that the reason he finished strong was that he needed the two months off in the middle of the year. He went through free agency several times after that, playing for the A's, Pirates, Mets, Phillies— altogether he played for seven teams, some of them twice. He adjusted his attitude; rather than a guy who expected to be a regular, he became the guy who was just happy to be in the majors, the guy who would go make an effort to catch when all the catchers were gone. He played every position in the major leagues except pitcher, took a real good living out of the game and gave an honest effort in return. He was a utility player and a nomad, but he was a class act all the same.

Luis Aloma, Cuban-born Chicago White Sox pitcher of the early fifties.

After six undistinguished years in the minors, Aloma caught on with the 1950 White Sox. According to Richard Lindberg's history of the White Sox, *Who's on Third,* Aloma made the majors initially to serve as rookie shortstop Chico Carrasquel's interpreter (Aloma was bilingual), and lasted an extra year to interpret for Mike Fornieles. He also pitched well. He lasted four seasons as a reliever, and would have had a hell of an APBA card in 1951—went 6–0 with a 1.82 ERA and a .350 batting average. He made only one start in the major leagues, that in 1951, and pitched a shutout. His career won-lost record was 18–3, which I think is the best winning percentage ever for a pitcher with more than ten decisions.

(—M.K.)

Roberto Alomar, contemporary second baseman with the San Diego Padres, son of Padres coach Sandy Alomar, and brother of catcher Sandy Alomar, Jr.

Sandy Alomar, a durable infielder of twenty years ago, and the father of two outstanding young players today.

One of nine children—three of his brothers also played minor league ball—Sandy Alomar signed with the Milwaukee Braves in 1961 for a bonus of over ten thousand dollars, an amount rarely given to a Latin player at that time (see Felipe Alou). A shortstop, Alomar ripped through the minors in good order, being named Player of the Year in the Pioneer League in 1962, and hitting 22 triples in the PCL in 1964. After nineteen games with Milwaukee at the end of the 1964, Alomar "made such a good impression . . . that Bragan has him classified as the [Milwaukee] shortstop." *(TSN).* Bobby Bragan, Braves manager, thought then that Alomar might be the best defensive shortstop to come along in years.

It didn't work out that way; Woody Woodward, a year ahead of Alomar in the system, won the Braves shortstop job in '65. Alomar

a) spent most of the next three years in the minor leagues, and

b) was traded three times in those three years, and

c) became a switch hitter.

Originally a right-handed hitter, Alomar became a switch hitter to take advantage of his speed (sure). He finally surfaced in the major leagues as a second baseman for the White Sox in late '67, and had his best years as a second baseman for the Angels beginning in '69.

Alomar was extremely durable, an exceptional second baseman and a good baserunner. Though he weighed just 140 pounds and played the second-most-dangerous position on the field, Alomar played 648 consecutive games for the Angels, the equivalent of four consecutive seasons, earning the nickname "The Iron Pony." He played in the 1970 All-Star game. He also had some major weaknesses as a player. The Angels in Alomar's prime were an organization with more money than sense, and they insisted on batting Alomar leadoff, which was just really dumb, since he had a career on-base percentage of .291.

Alomar was traded to the Yankees in July, 1974, and spent a year and a half as the Yankees second baseman before they came up with Willie Randolph. After that Alomar spent three years on the Rangers bench, and was through as a player.

Returning to Puerto Rico, Alomar ran a gas station for a while to make a living, and coached with the National Team. He wanted to get back into baseball, and in that effort he had two major assets: two sons who can play ball. Puerto Rican players are not drafted like Americans; they are free to sign with whoever they want. Alomar signed with the Padres as a minor league coach in 1984. His two sons signed with the system within a few months.

Once in the system, Alomar obviously impressed the Padres. He was named a major league coach in 1986 by Steve Boros, and has stayed on through the regimes of Larry Bowa and Jack McKeon. Having managed for several years in the winter leagues (and won a Manager of the Year award for his work with Santurce) Alomar now has the resumé of a major league manager, and may well get a shot to do that job. At forty-six, time is rapidly running out on him; few people get their first shot at a managing job after the age of fifty. He appears to be among the best-qualified minority candidates for a manager's job. (Sources for this article include the October, 1972 *Baseball Digest;* Ross Newhan's *The Cal-*

ifornia Angels; the *San Diego Padres 1989 Media Guide.*)

Sandy Alomar, Jr.

How you going to explain this guy in twenty years? Maybe I'd better put it on record now, in case it's that long before anybody gets around to the rest of his story.

While spending almost the entire season in the minor leagues, Sandy Alomar, Jr., became one of the central figures in the National League West in 1989. Alomar was the Most Valuable Player in the Pacific Coast League in 1988. With a desperate shortage of catchers around the majors, the Padres had not one, but two outstanding young catchers—Alomar, and Benito Santiago. From the beginning of spring training, rumors buzzed about which of the two would be traded and to whom. If you can believe the newspapers, several teams offered *more* than one good player for Alomar—a player plus a prospect, or two players. The Padres, for reasons no one can understand, decided to pass on all offers and hold Alomar for a year—and by so doing, they wound up finishing two games short in the National League West.

Alomar was traded to Cleveland after the year, for a star player named Joe Carter. We'll finish the story in about twenty years.

Felipe Alou, outfielder–first baseman for the Giants and Braves, oldest of the three Alou brothers, and the first Dominican to play regularly in the major leagues.

Alou was born and raised in Haina, the Dominican Republic, a fishing village twelve miles from Santo Domingo (the encyclopedias are apparently wrong on this point, having his place of birth as Santo Domingo). "Alou" was his mother's name, actually; in Santo Domingo the family was known by the name "Rojas." His father was a carpenter/blacksmith who made his sons' first bats. He could not make baseballs, so the Alou boys spent their early years swinging at lemons.

There was no high school in Haina, and Felipe was forced to live in Santo Domingo with his uncle Juan, an army captain, to continue his education. Instead of playing high school baseball he joined the track and field team, running 100 and 200-meter dashes and throwing the javelin (according to one source, his longest javelin throw was still a Dominican record in the early seventies). Alou continued to play baseball in summer leagues, and years later recalled his disappointment at just missing the batting championship in a league that offered the prize of a new glove. At sixteen, he went to work in a cement factory. He told John Devaney in *Where Are They Today?*:

> There was this machine in the factory. We called it Korea. What you did was pick up these big rocks and throw them into Korea. And as fast as you could pick up those rocks and throw them in, the machine broke them up. For eight hours you do that, always bent over, and at six in the morning, when our shift was over, you weren't good for anything.

After high school Alou enrolled at the University of Santo Domingo. He and his parents had long ago decided that he would become a doctor. He also became a star player for the university baseball team, and a trip to the Pan-American Games in Mexico City altered his destiny. At the last moment he was pulled off the track and field squad and placed on the baseball team. He played brilliantly and caught the eye of major league scouts as the Dominican team won the gold medal.

Alou was now in a quandary. One by one, his teammates from the Pan-American team began signing professional contracts. Still, he stuck to his decision to study medicine until fate again intervened. His father lost his job. His uncle had the audacity to disagree with Generalissimo Trujillo, and he was out of work, too. His family owed a grocer $400. Continuing his education was no longer an option for Felipe; he had to help the family financially. His coach at the university, Horacio Martinez, had become a scout for the Giants, and in December 1955 signed Alou for a bonus of $200, with the reluctant acquiescence of his parents.

Alou reported to Lake Charles (Louisiana) in the Evangeline League in 1956. After five games, Alou and his roommate were banished from the league for improper skin pigmentation. Reassigned to Cocoa of the Florida State League, the lonely, homesick Alou enrolled in a correspondence course to study English, and took along an English-Spanish dictionary on road trips. He also hit .380, hit 21 homers and scored almost one run per game. By 1958 he had become a born-again Christian, and worked his way up to the Giants, where he hit well until pitchers realized that he could time their curveballs. A period of struggle followed that culminated in the club's decision to send him to Phoenix. Alou refused to accept the demotion, citing concerns for his wife's pregnancy, and the Giants relented.

It took him several years to get estab-lished as a regular; the Giants had lots of outfielders. Jackie Brandt came back from the army in '59; Bill Rigney wanted to take a long look at him. He wasn't impressive, and Brandt and several other Giant outfielders were traded away in the winter of 1959–60, but two things happened:

a) Willie McCovey emerged as a first base-man, forcing Orlando Cepeda to the out-field, and

b) Candlestick Park opened. Candlestick was thought to—and did, in the early days—favor a left-handed hitter. With Alou, Mays, and Cepeda the Giants would have had an all–right-handed hitting outfield, and McCovey would have been their only left-handed power threat.

So Willie Kirkland got a shot. Alou fi-nally became a regular in mid-1961, but at the end of that season he realized that his wide open stance was allowing pitchers to jam him with fastballs and sliders. He re-sponded by closing his stance, and made the National League All-Star team for the first time in 1962, hitting .316 with 25 homers and 98 RBI. The Giants missed the World Championship by one run.

Alou made $18,000 that summer. The Giants offered him a $2,000 raise. "Where are you going to make any money in your country?" they asked him in a letter. "Cut-ting sugar cane in the fields?" He kept the letter.

That same winter a Dominican Republic team was to play a Cuban club in Santo Domingo. Cuba was at that time the United States' mortal enemy, and Commissioner Ford Frick warned major league Dominicans not to participate. Alou ignored him, and played in the series. When he arrived at the Giants training camp in '63 he found he had been fined $250. Felipe felt strongly that the fine was unjust, but the Giants would not let him practice until he paid, and after three days of recalcitrance he threw in the towel. Later in the summer he spoke out against what he considered neglectful treatment of brother Matty Alou's injured knee. The last straw for the Giants was probably an article ghosted by Arnold Hano in which he voiced his dissatisfaction with life in the major leagues. One month after the story appeared, Felipe was traded to the Braves.

Alou injured his knee early in his first season with the Braves, and had a poor first season with the team. The Braves moved to Atlanta, and to Fulton County Stadium, in 1966, with a team up to the rafters in power.

Bobby Bragan years earlier had advocated the idea that a team should lead off with their best hitters, claiming that the extra at bats were worth more than any other advantage. In 1965 this had meant leading off Henry Aaron for a good part of the season. In 1966, with Aaron, Joe Torre, Rico Carty, and Eddie Mathews to sop up the middle of the batting order, Bragan decided to lead off Alou. Alou was not a classic leadoff man, in that he had very good power and rarely walked; nonetheless, Bragan left him there all summer. With Alou having a brilliant sea-son, the result was one of the stranger bat-ting lines of all time. Alou hit .327 (second in the league behind his brother, Matty) with 31 home runs; he led the league in at bats (666, an unfortunate number for a born-again Christian), runs (122), and hits (218)—yet he drove in only 74 runs. He became the first leadoff man in baseball history to have more home runs than walks drawn. It was, of course, the first time in baseball history that brothers had finished first and second in the league in batting. Felipe finished fifth in the MVP voting. The Braves didn't have a great year, and Bragan was fired in August.

Alou had had such a good year that he continued to bat leadoff for several years, although it didn't make a lot of sense. He had a fine year again in '68, leading the NL again in at bats (662) and hits (210, tied with Pete Rose.)

In 1969 Felipe didn't have a good year, and another Dominican, Rico Carty, made a remarkable comeback from tuberculosis. The Braves eased the crowd in the outfield by trading Alou to Oakland, where Charlie Fin-ley was looking for veteran leadership to show his young players how to win. Alou filled the role perfectly.

"He's one of the greatest men I've ever met in baseball," said Sal Bando.

"He hustles more than we do," said Chuck Dobson. "He plays better than we do."

Alou never had another great year, and played for the Yankees, Montreal, and Mil-waukee on the way out. In the spring of '74, out of a job, he charged that he was being blackballed because he was a Dominican and outspoken, which was a pretty stupid thing to say, but baseball people understand how difficult it is to accept that you can't trigger on a fastball anymore, and no one held it against him. Alou has become a fixture in the Montreal Expos organization, coaching with the parent club in 1979–80 and 1984, and managing the triple-A affiliates in Wichita and Indianapolis. He is presently manager of the West Palm Beach Expos. His son Moises is a top prospect in the Pittsburgh Pirates organization.

(—M.K. and B.J. Alou's biography, *Felipe Alou . . . My Life and Baseball*, was helpful in preparing this article, and will be of particular interest to those of you who talk about Christ as if he was renting the next apartment.)

Jesus Alou, outfielder for the Giants and Astros, and younger brother of Felipe and Matty.

Alou signed with the Giants in 1958, and hit an aggregate .338 at Hastings, Artestia, Eugene, El Paso, and Tacoma. (When you begin to recognize the names of the cities you're getting closer to the majors.) His lowest minor league average was .324. He had an exceptional throwing arm and some speed, and arrived in the majors in late 1963. On September 10, 1963, the three Alous all appeared in the box score, the first time in baseball history that three brothers had appeared in the same major league lineup; five days later, at Pittsburgh, they formed the San Francisco outfield for one inning.

The three Alous would have loved to be functioning outfield, but there was a little problem named Willie Mays. Felipe was traded that winter, and Jesus took his right-field job.

Expectations for Jesus were extremely high, much higher than for his brothers before him. Manager Alvin Dark predicted in March a .310 season for Jesus, and this tended to make his actual performance—.274 in 1964, .298 in 1965—look shabby. The Giants came up with young outfielders by the carload. Jesus withstood the challenge of Jose Cardenal, Ken Henderson, and a few others, but eventually gave way to Downtown Ollie Brown and Bobby Bonds.

Alou was selected by Montreal in the 1968 expansion draft. On January 22, 1969, Jesus and Donn Clendenon were traded to Houston for Rusty Staub. Clendenon refused to report to Houston, announcing his retirement to accept an executive position with an Atlanta fountain pen company. According to the *1970 Baseball Guide:*

By clear baseball rule and precedent, the deal was off when Clendenon refused to report to Houston.

But Commissioner Bowie Kuhn did not want to hand a stunning blow to the new Montreal team which had centered its promotions

around Staub. Houston spent the entire spring trying to get the trade reversed as the "Blue Book" specified. Clendenon at last made a deal to play for Montreal and Kuhn ordered the trade to stand, with Houston to get substitute players for the first baseman.

This hung in the air for three and a half months. Alou became the forgotten man in the controversy. He trained with the Astros, but had no idea of his status. Was he an Astro? Was he an Expo? He never complained, but frequently expressed his desire to play in Houston, which quickly earned him the regard of his new, if possibly temporary, teammates. The fans were not oblivious to his plight, and when the Astros played their first home exhibition game, Alou received the most generous applause. However, 1969 was not destined to be his year. He started slowly, and was struggling around the .200 mark when he collided with shortstop Hector Torres while pursuing a fly ball. They were both knocked unconscious, and Alou suffered a severe concussion and a broken jaw. He missed six weeks.

Alou hit .300 for Houston in '70, the only time he would hit .300 as a regular, but even at .300 he was a marginal player—no power, no walks, no speed. His secondary average that year was .131, and that was better than his norm. He joined Oakland late in '73, hit .306 in the closing weeks and, when Bill North was injured and unable to play, played in all seven games of the '73 World Series.

After a year with the Mets, Jesus was released, and it appeared his major league career was over. He saw limited action with Cordoba of the Mexican League in 1976 before returning home to play in the Dominican Republic. To everyone's surprise, he resurfaced in Houston in 1978, playing two more years, and (in 1978) posting his best major league average, .324 in 77 games. He is now a scout for the Montreal Expos.

When Jesus (pronounced "Hey, Zeus") first came to the majors, some announcers wanted to call him Jay, because in our culture we are a little uncomfortable calling someone "Jesus." Alou put a stop to that. "My name is 'Jesus,' not 'Jay,' " he told one announcer. "There is nothing sacrilegious about it. It is a very common name in my country." Indeed it is, and it reminds me of one of the best strings of graffiti I've ever seen.

First handwriting, somebody has written "Jesus is the answer."

Second handwriting, next guy has added "What is the question?"

Third handwriting, "Who is Matty and Felipe's brother . . ."

(—M.K. and B.J.)

Matty Alou, the Dom DiMaggio of the Alou brothers, and National League batting champion in 1966.

Alou signed with the San Francisco Giants in 1957 for a two hundred-dollar bonus, the same amount his older brother had gotten. In '61 and '62 he was the Giants fifth outfielder, hitting a little over .300. In the ninth inning of the seventh game of the '62 Series, Alou beat out a bunt to lead off, and was on third base when McCovey lined out to Bobby Richardson, ending the Series.

This was followed by three years of frustration. In spring training of 1963, Mateo suffered a knee injury in camp and, hobbled, made a trip back to Tacoma. With the Giants great farm system producing so many hitters that they were always forcing them in the lineup by doing things like putting Jim Ray Hart at third base, Matty couldn't get enough at bats to stay sharp, completely lost his rhythm and demanded to be traded. On December 1, 1965, Alou was traded to the Pirates.

The Bucs were then managed by Harry "the Hat" Walker, who would today be described as a "hitting guru." Harry worked long hours with Alou, getting him to use a heavy bat and chop down on the ball, rather than using a light bat and uppercutting as do most modern hitters. Alou, who had hit .231 in 1965, won the National League batting title at .342—perhaps the most unexpected NL batting championship since the one claimed by Harry the Hat in 1947. Walker was one of those guys who had a good idea and rode it into the ground, and his idea was to get his players to stop using these damned little bats and trying to pull everything. Matty was his dream come true, his perfect pupil, and he gave interviews about how he had turned Matty's career around until everybody was pretty much sick of hearing about it.

This is a digression, but I can't resist. You hear all the time about somebody who is being "taught to hit"; John Shelby is always going to learn to hit the curveball sooner or later. Well, it's bull. Nobody learns to hit after the age of twenty-five—nobody. Some players do improve dramatically in a brief period at a young age, and a few hitters do make substantial incremental changes after twenty-five, like Dwight Evans and Brian Downing. But no hitter ever made a quantum forward leap after the age of twenty-five, period. *It doesn't happen.*

But there are a handful of cases, like Pete Runnels, Harry Heilmann, and Matty Alou, where people don't really understand what happened, and they *think* a player made a great leap forward in mid-career because somebody "taught him" how to hit. Because Harry spent so much time talking about it, Alou is the most famous of those cases. And people use those cases, day-in and day-out, to delude themselves that next year Juan Samuel or Gary Pettis or Henry Cotto or whoever is going to cut down his swing and develop into a much better hitter, or if he doesn't then it's just because he doesn't want to do it like Matty Alou did. And it's *not going to happen,* because it didn't even *really* happen to Matty Alou, who was a .300 hitter when he came to the major leagues, and just got messed up for a couple of years before Walker gave him a chance to play and get his swing straightened out.

Anyway, for three years after that Alou was amazingly consistent, hitting .338, .332, and .331. Harry only lasted half a season after Alou's batting title; by the middle of '67 his infield was about ready to arrange a necktie party for him. In 1969 Matty set an major league record, since broken, with 698 at bats, and led the league in hits (231) and doubles (41). At that time the 231 hits were the most by any major league player in thirty-two years.

Alou had two pluses besides hitting .330: He was fast, and he had a pretty good arm. In 1970, however, his average slipped below three hundred, and after the season he was traded to the Cardinals, thereby missing out on the Pirates' World Championship in '71. Alou kept his average over three hundred as he spent the next two years with the Cards and, briefly, the Oakland A's. When Reggie Jackson was injured, Matty played in all seven games of the '72 series, just as his brother would a year later filling the spot left by Bill North. He dropped out of the majors a couple of years later, but played two-plus seasons in Japan before hanging up his spikes.

(—R.N. and B.J.)

Charles "Whitey" Alperman, a second baseman with the Brooklyn Dodgers in the first decade of this century.

Sportswriter William F. Kirk described Alperman's style in the Aug. 14, 1908 New York *American:*

> The last of the fifth had plenty of action and brought victory to the Giants. Donlin started

it off with a stiff three-bagger to left. Alperman had just taken Hummell's place at second base and celebrated his arrival by laying for Captain Mike as he rounded second, giving him the shoulder in such a manner that Mike whirled several times and fell heavily on his back. It was as deliberate a piece of foul work as was ever seen on a baseball diamond, and when O'Day told Mike to go to third base, the crowd cheered the umpire and hissed Alperman roundly.

> Alperman deserved all the roasting he got . . . when a professional baseball player tries a trick that may result in broken bones and perhaps ruin a man's earning capacity, he is not thoroughbred.

Dell Alston, a marginal outfielder in the late seventies.

Alston had a degree in elementary education from Concordia Teacher's College in River Forest, Illinois. "I love to work with kids," he told *The Sporting News* in 1975, "and I want to teach kindergarten." Let us hope that that is what he is now doing.

Tom Alston, who broke the color line for the St. Louis Cardinals.

Playing in what was then the most southern and probably the most racist city in the major leagues, the Cardinals were one of the last teams to integrate their roster. When the team began to slip out of contention in the early fifties, the Cardinals decided that they had to start drawing new cards from a full deck, and so tried to choose carefully who would be their Jackie Robinson. They selected Alston, a rangy six-foot-five-inch first baseman with a bachelor of science degree from North Carolina Agricultural and Technical College, and the Cardinals paid a high price to acquire him from San Diego, an independent team in the Pacific Coast League—four players, three of whom had played in the majors in 1953, and $135,000.

At the age of twenty-two in 1953, Alston in the PCL had 207 hits and 101 RBI in a 180-game season. Although he also led the PCL in errors at first, he had a reputation as a top glove man. Alston didn't play all that badly for the Cardinals, but lost his job in June, 1954.

Why he didn't receive a better shot at a major league job, after all that had been invested in him, is a tough question to answer. Reportedly, St. Louis hero Enos Slaughter had loudly expressed his displeasure at playing with blacks, which had forced Slaughter's trade to the Yankees, but which also gave St. Louis fans an additional reason to

make Alston a target of abuse. As if that wasn't trouble enough, Alston was being managed by Eddie Stanky, a redneck hardass who screamed at his *good* players. Stanky gave up on Alston when he didn't play real well, and Alston's career was brief and unmemorable.

Walter "Smokey" Alston, who managed the Brooklyn and Los Angeles Dodgers for twenty-three years on twenty-three consecutive one-year contracts, and won seven National League pennants with the team.

Walter Emmons Alston was born December 1, 1911 in Venice, Ohio. His father, Emmons, was a farmer and automobile worker, and a pretty fair athlete himself; he played baseball on the local town team until he was nearly sixty. Walter in grade school was given the nickname "Smokey" because he was the pitcher; this was just a few years after the prime of Smokey Joe Wood.

Smokey started at Miami University in 1929, Miami of Ohio, but quit after his freshman year to get married. The early marriage is probably an overlooked key to his personality; a lot of times when a man marries young he has to grow up early, and he'll wind up as a solid, steady gentleman who is not too exciting, which is exactly what Walter became. As soon as he got married the depression hit, and good jobs were hard to find. The local Methodist church offered to help a little financially if he'd go back to college, and he could pick up odd jobs there to help work his way through. Alston talked it over with his wife Lela and his father, and decided that was maybe the best option he had, so in 1932 he went back to Miami to try it again.

It took better the second time, and Alston not only earned a degree, but wound up as the captain of both the college basketball team and the baseball team; he was a third baseman and shortstop.

The day after he graduated in 1935, Alston was standing on a ladder helping his dad paint the house when a man drove up asking for him. The man was Frank Rickey, Branch Rickey's brother, and he offered Walter no bonus but a chance to play in the Cardinal farm system for $125 a month.

He was in the majors in less than two years. Alston hit .326 in the "East Dixie" league in 1935, fielding well enough at third base to earn a transfer across the infield to first, and hit exactly the same (.326) with a league-leading 35 homers in the Middle Atlantic League in 1936. The Cardinals had a rookie Hall of Famer at first base, Johnny Mize, but they decided to call Alston in for a look, anyway. He had a good arm, so he pitched a lot of batting practice for the last couple of weeks of the season. On the last day of the 1936 season Mize was thrown out of the game after the other first baseman had already been used as a pinch hitter, so Alston got to play a few innings and bat once. Lon Warneke, one of the best pitchers in the league, struck him out. It was to be his only major league at bat.

Apart from being locked behind Mize, Alston had a couple of other problems. One was the Cardinals farm system, which was huge and booming with players like Enos Slaughter and Stan Musial. The other was that he never went to spring training. To supplement his income, Alston taught school in the off-season, taught biology and mechanical drawing and coached the basketball teams in small towns around his Darrtown home. Even in 1937, when he was invited to the big league camp for the only time, he had to report late to finish his teaching obligations. Alston jumped to the high minors for the full season in 1937, and seemed to be over his head. He began to have trouble with his knees. Although he went back to the Middle Atlantic League and had some big years there, by 1939 he was twenty-seven years old, and finished as a prospect.

In the spring of 1940 the Portsmouth team, for which Alston was laboring, started slowly under manager Dutch Dorman. Alston, one of the team's older players, one of their best players and one of their only college-educated players, seemed like a natural choice to replace him. Mel Jones, Dodger road secretary under Rickey, asked Alston if he had ever considered managing.

Alston jumped at the chance; he knew very well, he said later, that managing was his only chance to stay in the game more than another year or two. He almost played himself out of his destiny. He managed in the Middle Atlantic League from 1940 to 1942 without much success, but as a hitter he led the league all three times in home runs and twice in RBI. When the war began to create shortages of talent at the higher levels, Alston was sent back to the International League—as a player. The war wasn't creating any shortages of *managers.* Early in the season Alston hurt his back sliding into a base. He didn't hit a lick in the International League, and before the 1944 season was very

old had drawn his release, bringing his baseball career to an apparent end.

Depressed, Alston went back to Ohio and tried to reconcile himself to life as a small-town school teacher. Alston's release, however, came to the attention of Branch Rickey, which probably tells us something about Branch Rickey. Rickey, now with Brooklyn, was by 1944 building up the Dodgers farm system. Rickey tried to call Alston, but the Alston farm had no phone. Rickey left messages with people all around town; finally a grocer from Darrtown drove out to his farm to tell him, "Wait, there's this fellow named Rickey that's been trying to get in touch with you for about a week."

Rickey offered Alston a job with the Dodger chain. In 1946, when Rickey was ready for his great experiment, Alston was one of two managers chosen to lead the teams with black players.

Trying to anticipate everything, Rickey called Alston and Clay Hopper of Montreal to Brooklyn to instruct them on how to deal with possible problems on the team. Managing in the New England League, Alston had Roy Campanella and Don Newcombe, and that pretty well took care of any problems he might have had. "There was one guy, a manager, who used to ride me from the bench," recalled Alston in *The Man in the Dugout,* "asking me if I'm sleeping with Campanella. One day I met him outside the clubhouse between games of a doubleheader and I stopped him.

" 'Listen,' I said, 'You've been wondering if I sleep with Campanella. Well, the answer is no. The Dodgers go first class, we all get to sleep in separate rooms. But if you gave me my choice of sleeping with Campanella or with you, I'd sure as hell take Campanella.' " The team won the playoffs—his first championship as a manager—and Alston in 1947 moved up to the Western League. He won the playoffs there, too, and in 1948—Rickey was so damned methodical—reached the AAA level, managing St. Paul.

The Dodgers by 1950 were simply an incredible organization, with an impact—even today—almost beyond anyone's understanding. In the forties and early fifties the Dodgers had three AAA teams—Montreal in the International League, St. Paul in the American Association, and Hollywood in the Pacific Coast League. Fort Worth in the Texas League, although technically AA, was used almost in the same way as the other three teams. There were sixteen major league

teams then and twenty-four AAA teams, so that could happen, plus the Senators didn't have their farm system organized yet, and didn't have a AAA team. They were all good teams; if the Dodgers team plane had crashed, the Dodgers could easily have put together a contending team from the players trapped at AAA. Alston managed at St. Paul and Montreal for six years with great success, his poorest record being 86–68; his teams made the playoffs every year.

But what very few people understand is how many of the people who have shaped baseball in the last thirty years came out of that system—not "some" or "many", but *most* of the dominant field managers in baseball since 1960 were a product of that extraordinary St. Paul-Montreal-Brooklyn-Fort Worth axis. *Tommy Lasorda,* of course, played for Alston at Montreal and in Brooklyn, and coached for him for years. *Don Zimmer* played for St. Paul in '53 and '54, and came to the majors under Walt Alston in 1954. *Dick Williams* played years for Fort Worth, and played for St. Paul and Montreal, although he missed Alston in the minors (he played for him in the majors.) *Sparky Anderson* came from the Dodger farms in the fifties; Alston had him in spring training. *Gene Mauch,* though he never played for Alston, played for Brooklyn, Montreal, and St. Paul in the forties. *Preston Gomez,* who managed three teams in the National League, was an Alston lieutenant. *Clyde King* (Giants, Braves, Yankees) spent almost his entire playing career in the Dodgers system, and played for Alston at Montreal. *Danny Ozark,* who managed the Phillies' first divisional champion, played for Alston at St. Paul, and coached for him for years. *Roger Craig* came out of the Dodgers farm system in 1955. *Gil Hodges,* of course, the master of the Miracle Mets. *Frank Howard* managed a couple of teams; Dodger system, '59. *Roy Hartsfield,* first manager of Toronto, had been Alston's coach. *Larry Shepard,* in the majors forever as a pitching coach and manager of the Pirates for two seasons, pitched for Alston in the low minors in 1946 and 1947. *Bobby Bragan* and *Cookie Lavagetto* were Dodgers of the 1940s, long-term Dodgers. And of course all of those guys brought their coaches with them, so Dodger-system instruction has pervaded the major leagues.

Branch Rickey took instruction seriously. He had a strong belief in education, in keeping with his generation, which was a generation which built a marvelous educational system. He thought there was a right way and a wrong way to do everything. He wanted intelligent people in his system, top to bottom. The minor leagues were baseball education.

This is *one of* the reasons for the changes which have taken place in baseball in the last thirty years, in the shift away from power and toward speed, in the use of more switch hitters and some other changes. There are a lot of other factors, but *part* of what has happened has been the Dodgerization of the major leagues. When you see a major league ball game today, Branch Rickey is sitting in the seat beside you.

So anyway, being a AAA manager in the Dodgers system at that particular time is not exactly like managing Lynchburg today. Alston's salary grew to $12,000 a year by 1953, more than many major league players made, and Alston in the early fifties was able to quit teaching school in the off-season, although he would always insist that the years of teaching school had been a tremendous asset to him as a manager.

The Dodgers won the pennant in 1952 and 1953 under Charlie Dressen, while Alston, with Montreal, won the AAA World Series in 1953. In mid-October, 1953, a news conference was scheduled at Ebbets Field, assumed to be a routine announcement of Dressen's rehiring for the 1954 season. Instead, Walter O'Malley dropped a bomb shell: Dressen would not be back.

Despite the announcement, many people thought that something would be worked out to keep Dressen in Brooklyn. Within a week, however, Dressen announced that he had signed to manage the Oakland team in the Pacific Coast League. The exact reasons for Dressen's departure have been written and speculated about for thirty-five years, and I guess we'll get to that when we do Dressen. The short version: In a brief period of time, several major league managers were given multi-year contracts. Dressen asked for a multi-year contract, too. O'Malley explained that team policy prohibited multi-year contracts. Dressen's wife, Ruthie, wrote a letter to O'Malley outlining Dressen's reasons for wanting a multi-year contract and hinting that he might consider his options if he didn't get it, and O'Malley axed him.

A wild month of media speculation followed about who would get the job. Alston did not apply for the vacant position. "I figured," Alston told Tom Meany in *The Artful Dodgers*, "that I had been in the organiza-

tion long enough for them to know all about me and that if they felt I was qualified, they could get in touch with me." To the absolute astonishment of the New York press, they did. On November 23, 1953, Alston went quail and pheasant hunting near his home in Ohio. When he got back home, there was a message from Buzzie Bavasi instructing him to come to New York right away, and to buy his ticket and register at the hotel under an alias (Matt Burns). The next day a New York paper had a front-page picture of a hand-lettered sign in a store window. The sign said WALT WHO?

Alston was given a one-year contract, wrote Tom Meany, with no time off for good behavior. If it was surprising that Alston got the job, it was incredible that he kept it. Dressen was a media favorite, an outgoing, bubbly guy who had a quote for every reporter. He was a gourmet cook, and would cook things for the reporters after the game. "Charley," wrote Meany, "had an opinion on everything, from the merits of the hit and run to the hydrogen bomb. And expressed them freely." With Casey Stengel managing the Yankees and Leo Durocher the Giants, both good for two stories every day, the re-

TRACERS

In 1916, Burleigh Grimes was called up from Birmingham to finish the season in the big leagues. In his very first game as a major leaguer, he was facing the Dodgers at Ebbets Field, the score tied 1–1 in the seventh, a man on first. Wagner, who was closing down his career at shortstop, came to the mound to calm down the young Grimes. "Make him hit it to me, kid," he intoned.
In fact, the next batter did hit a grounder to short, a perfect double-play ball.
Wagner kicked it into center, the runner scored, and the batter went to third.
Wagner returned to the mound and told Grimes, "Those damn big feet have always been in my way."

—Okrent and Wulf
Baseball Anecdotes (Page 68)

This incident actually happened not in Grimes's first major league *appearance*, which was in relief on September 10, 1916, but in his first *start*, which was September 14. The game was at Ebbets Field, and it was not a 1–1 tie but a scoreless tie until the bottom of the sixth. We'll let Charles J. Doyle of the *Pittsburgh Post-Gazette* pick up the account:

> The Dodgers scored twice in the sixth when they should have been blanked. Four hits were charged against Grimes in this inning, but in one instance when Wagner kicked a ball, credited as a hit, the play turned out be exceptionally costly. Daubert singled with one out and Stengel smashed a hard grounder straight at Honus. The ball was rather hard to handle, but Honus generally gets such. He might have had a double play in front of him had he picked up the ball. As it was, the horsehide rolled into center and Daubert pulled up at third. Wheat's single scored Jake, and Stengel scored later when Cutshaw's drive to left went for three bases.

The Bucs scored two runs in the eighth to tie, but Grimes later lost the game in the bottom of the ninth when he grooved a three-two fastball to pitcher Larry Cheney, who hit a game-winning double into left field.

A few details are mixed up, but the story basically is credible. We can't confirm that Wagner visited the mound, but Wagner's supposed attempt to calm the green Grimes's nerves is consistent with the Dutchman's reputation for making life easier for his rookie teammates. And you know, he did have damn big feet.

—Rob Neyer

porters thought that a personality like that was a necessity in New York, that they had a right to expect a colorful personality as manager.

O'Malley's thinking was exactly the opposite: that it was time for a *professional* manager, a man who had learned all of the elements of managing through long years of experience. "It's the greatest thing that has happened to minor league managers in years," gushed Carl Hubbell, farm director of the Giants. "Consider what it means to every minor league manager in every one of the sixteen major league farm organizations. It means that each of them knows now, thanks to the confidence Mr. O'Malley showed in Alston, that he, too, has a chance of someday managing the 'big team'." While Dressen had dropped out of high school, Alston had finished college. While Dressen could name every restaurant in Manhattan, Alston could tell you about crop rotation and soil conservation. The papers treated him with barely disguised contempt. "If Alston doesn't win the pennant and beat the Yankees in the World Series," wrote John Lardner, "there's a clause in his contract which requires him to refund his entire salary and report immediately to the nearest Federal penitentiary."

While seventeen of the twenty-five Dodgers had played for Alston in the minor leagues, Alston had serious conflicts with the leader of the team, Jackie Robinson. Early in the season Duke Snider hit a ball into the left field stands and back out, umpire Bill Stewart ruling the ball a double. Jackie raced out of the dugout to argue, certain that a fan had grabbed the ball and thrown it back on the field—but Alston, coaching at third base, didn't join the discussion. Talking about the incident after the game, Alston referred to it as "Jackie's temper tantrum."

"The team might be moving somewhere," Robinson replied, "if Alston had not been standing on third base like a wooden Indian. That run meant something in a close game like that, so whether or not I was right or wrong, it paid to protest to an umpire . . . but not according to Alston. What kind of a manager is that?"

Alston and Robinson had words several times. Alston's strategy came under fire. On May 1, 1954, Alston ordered Ted Kluszewski intentionally walked with the bases empty and the score tied in the bottom of the ninth. It didn't cost them the game, but it led to predictable second-guessing. Alston in the

early years served as his own third-base coach, exposing himself to more criticism not only in that being a third base coach is a tough job, but simply in a physical sense; he was *there* for the fans when they wanted to object to his strategy.

But what is worse than arguing with your superstar is not winning, and the Dodgers didn't win, either. The Dodgers, winners of 105 games in 1953, came out in 1954 in a mass batting slump. Roy Campanella, MVP in two of the previous three seasons, had a hand injury which ruined his season; he wound up the year hitting .207. The Dodgers won ninety-two games in 1954 and finished five games behind the Giants, their poorest season in six years.

Alston, astonishingly, was given another chance. In the spring of 1955, Jackie Robinson found himself without a position to play; Alston's plans for him were vague. Robinson talked to the reporters, asking if any of them knew what Alston had in mind for him. Alston flew into a rage, thinking that Robinson was using the media to show him up. There was a team meeting; Alston denounced "players who went to the press with questions about the team." He claimed that those players were cowards and detrimental to the club's spirit. Robinson erupted, saying that if Alston would talk to the players they wouldn't need to try to ask the reporters those things. The two headed for each other; Gil Hodges stepped between them.

On May 5, 1955, Don Newcombe refused to pitch batting practice. Alston told him to turn in his uniform. The two met the next day and made peace. Newcombe went 20–5.

Jackie Robinson came around. "Maybe it wasn't fair to keep comparing Walt to Dressen," he told a reporter. "My feelings toward him have changed considerably. He had certain faults in my eyes. Of course, it could have been my eyesight."

Dressen, like most managers of his generation, would light into a player in public. If a player pulled a rock on the bases, for example, Dressen would scream at him across the field in full view of the fans and the press. Alston never did that, and in time his players came to appreciate the courtesy. Dressen had once told the post-game gathering that his pitcher was "gutless," and Durocher had said in the same situation that a pitcher "should be taken out behind the barn and shot." Alston, more than anyone else, changed baseball in that respect, that you would never today see a major league man-

ager showing up his player in front of the fans.

The Dodgers won 98 games in 1955, and with the collapse of the Giants it was more or less a one-horse race; the Dodgers won by thirteen and a half games. Once more, the Dodgers and Yankees met in the World Series. They had met five other times in the previous fifteen years, and the Yankees had won every time. The Yankees won the first game. The Yankees won the second game.

You could probably have gotten bets down, at that moment, at a billion to one. The Dodgers swept the three games in Ebbets Field, however, and so the series went to the seventh game. Alston selected as his starter Johnny Podres. Eleven pitchers started games for the Dodgers that summer, and Podres was the only one with a losing record, but he had pitched well late in the season, and he was a left-hander, and this was Yankee Stadium, and he had beaten the Yankees once in the series. The Dodgers scored a run in the fourth and one in the sixth, holding a 2–0 lead going to the bottom of the sixth. Alston made a defensive switch, putting Sandy Amoros into left field. With two on and nobody out in the bottom of the sixth—just moments after Amoros had been inserted into the game—Yogi Berra lined the ball into the left-field corner; the ball seemed certain to tie the score and put the lead run on second with no one out. Amoros, racing to the line, made a fantastic catch on the drive, and easily doubled the runner off first base. Podres held on for a 2–0 win, and the Dodgers, for the first time ever, were champions of the world.

Amoros's catch was regarded by some as the outstanding defensive play in the history of the World Series, and for making the move, Alston came in for his share of the credit. For the first time in his life, Walter was a star. The Dodgers won the National again in 1956, but lost the series. They had an off season in 1957, as the team grew old and was disrupted by the controversy over the move to LA. By 1958 the need to build a new team was critical, but the Dodgers, perhaps influenced by the desire to have marquee names in their new park, stayed with the veterans. Roy Campanella was critically injured in a car wreck before the season, permanently paralyzed.

Charlie Dressen returned to the Dodgers as a coach, leading to speculation that he would soon be back in the manager's chair. The Dodgers endured their worst year in memory, finishing seventh. The pressure on Alston grew more intense; Alston signed another one-year contract.

The Dodgers of 1959 were one of the strangest World Championship teams ever. Several of the old Dodgers were still around—Gil Hodges, Duke Snider, Clem Labine—but none of those was comparable to the player he had been in Brooklyn. Some of the young players who would be the stars of the sixties were on hand—Maury Wills, Sandy Koufax, Don Drysdale, Ron Fairly, John Roseboro—but of those, only Drysdale was a fair approximation of the player he would become. Only a few Dodgers (Wally Moon, Charlie Neal, Johnny Podres) were in their prime, and they were good enough ballplayers but when you stack them up against Eddie Mathews, Hank Aaron, Warren Spahn, and Lew Burdette of the Braves they look quite a bit like pond scum.

The Braves blew it, of course, and the Dodgers backed into the World Series. A rookie reliever named Larry Sherry came up in July to pitch outstanding baseball for two months. In the World Series Sherry won two games and saved two, Charley Neal played great and a journeyman outfielder named Chuck Essegian hit two pinch-hit home runs, and the Dodgers won the series. They were, in my opinion, the poorest world champion team of all time.

Managing in the largest city in the nation and then in the glitziest, Alston at length began to earn respect. He met problems directly, never backing away from an unhappy player. On the field, he pulled every lever frequently. His teams regularly led the league in stolen bases, although the numbers were not what they are today. They also led in sacrifice bunts; he bunted more often than Gene Mauch. He normally platooned at one outfield position, and sometimes at one infield spot as well. He used an above-average number of pinch hitters. He made frequent defensive changes in the late innings. He went to his bullpen early, often leading the league in saves and being comparatively low in complete games, even with Koufax and Drysdale on the team. He ordered many, many intentional walks, probably more than anybody managing today. He ordered the hit and run very often, probably as often as anyone in the league at that time. He loved switch hitters, giving him the platoon advantage, at least in theory, a huge percentage of the time. Some of the strategy may have been useless, excessive or even counter-produc-

tive—I certainly wouldn't want a manager doing all of these things—but it accomplished two things:

1) It got the entire roster involved in the game, and

2) It gave the Dodgers, and particularly Alston, control of the flow of the action.

He acted deliberately; John Roseboro described him as "slow-witted," and Roseboro thought the world of him, so you can imagine what his critics said. To the end of his career, he built up his list of noncommittal responses . . . "It could be," "It's too early to tell," "Let's wait until we have a few more workouts"; he was criticized for that, as George Bush is today, by people who wanted quick, easy answers. He never gushed about a rookie, or even a superstar; to Alston, hyping a player and criticizing him in public were two sides of the same coin, and could only cause a manager problems. He never took credit for a win. He never blamed a player or an umpire for a defeat.

Alston didn't drink or play cards. He was, however, a big, powerful man, and he was as tough as he needed to be. Once, managing St. Paul, he offered to take on a group of players who were cutting up on a train one at a time. In the spring of '61 he caught Sandy Koufax and Larry Sherry out past curfew, and followed them to their room. When they locked him out, he splintered the door with his fist, knocking the stone out of his World Series ring. In 1963, confronted by a team of players complaining about the bus reserved by the traveling secretary, Alston stopped the bus and told the entire team to stop bitching or step outside.

He was an amazing pool player, a better pool player than Leo Durocher, who had spent about a third of his life in pool halls. In college, Alston had a job racking balls and doing odd jobs at a pool hall, and he loved the game; a carpenter, he built a pool room onto his house, and had his own table. He had a quiet wit that people eventually came to appreciate, and was a notorious practical joker. Pee Wee Reese was a clubhouse agitator. When Frank Howard came up, biggest guy anybody had ever seen in a baseball uniform, Alston told Reese, according to *The Man in the Dugout*, "Hey, I'd sure like to try some more of those kids out. Why don't you get on that Howard and agitate him a little bit and see if I can't get him back into the lineup." Howard had been nursing a minor injury. Then Alston told Howard, "Frank, goddamn, you don't have to take that from

them. They're getting a little too rough, don't you think?" Next thing you know, Howard had Reese in the air like a rag doll, shaking him up a little and instructing him on how to treat a 250-pound rookie. "Fun?" asked Reese. "I think you're trying to get me killed."

Earl Lawson, Cincinnati reporter, recalled visiting Alston at his Ohio farm during the winter. "Walt insisted I have a piece of apple pie made by his wife, Lela, before I left," Lawson reported. "Then as I left he told me, 'When you write your story say the pie was lousy and send me a clipping.' "

In the off-seasons he went back to Darrtown, and spent about three months with his many hobbies. Working with wood was number one; he made furniture, cabinets, beautiful stuff. He was a quality photographer, and had a darkroom built in his house. He kept horses, loved horses, and of course hunted and fished. He was, in short, awfully sane, able to deal with pressure better than almost anybody who ever managed.

And it was a good thing, because he had to.

Leo Durocher was a Los Angeles resident, a celebrity, and it was widely expected that when the Los Angeles Angels began in 1961 Leo would be their manager. He wasn't, and in December, 1960, Durocher called reporters and charged that he had been blackballed from baseball. Walter O'Malley offered Durocher a job as Alston's coach. Alston, to create at least the illusion of control, was flown to LA from Darrtown to make the announcement.

Alston and Durocher were diametric opposites:

ALSTON	DUROCHER
Honest	Devious
Soft-spoken	Brash
Conservative	Flashy
Straightforward	Manipulative
Modest	Arrogant
Quiet	Boisterous

Walter bought his suits off the rack; Durocher patronized one of Hollywood's most exclusive tailors, and reportedly owned six tuxedoes. The two men didn't care for one another, hadn't years earlier when they had been opposing managers. Durocher, even more than Dressen had been, was a superstar coach, and was seen by the public as a manager-in-waiting.

"We have to face facts," said Alston. "Leo is a colorful figure and a bold and amusing talker. I would be a damn fool if I tried to outdo him. We must live our own way and respect each other."

"Walt's idea is to carry over a beef until the next day, when heads are clear," said Durocher. "As a manager, I never did this. When something went wrong, I preferred to sound off on the bench or in the clubhouse, while the beef was still fresh. I must admit the players respect Alston. Whether they respected me didn't matter, just as long as they played for me."

The Dodgers in 1962 had the look of a great team; no, let's say they *were* a great team. With Tommy Davis hitting .346 with 153 RBI, Maury Wills breaking a record almost a half-century old for stolen bases, Frank Howard having a great season, Willie Davis having a fine season, the '62 Dodgers scored more runs than the famous '61 Yankees. Their pitching was a whole lot better than the '61 Yankees, with, through late July, the number one and two candidates for the Cy Young Award, Sandy Koufax and Don Drysdale.

Koufax left the team in July with a mysterious circulatory problem; he would not win another game. In mid-August, during a long winning streak, an explosion hit the Dodger dugout. In a game at Pittsburgh, one Dodger player missed a sign, and another ran into his own bunt for an automatic out. Durocher, in the dugout, snapped that fines should be levied. Alston turned on Durocher angrily, and informed him that levying fines was the manager's job, and he didn't believe in it. A heated exchange followed between the two.

A newspaper criticized Alston, claiming that he should not have berated his coach in front of the players. Alston talked to a reporter from the paper. "You're pretty sensitive about Durocher's feeling," said Alston, "but you don't seem to care much about mine. What about the times he has shown *me* up in front of the players? How much of this do I have to take?"

The Dodgers were four games ahead with seven to play, but 1962 was the revenge of 1959; by 1962 the Dodgers had a great team, but this time everything broke wrong at the end, and they didn't win. As described by John Leonard in *The Ultimate Baseball Book*, "the Giants caught the Dodgers on the last day of the season and beat them, of course, in a three game play-off, because Alston wouldn't use Drysdale and Stan Williams couldn't get my grandmother out." Leonard described Alston as a "dour ex-farm boy."

The loss was devastating to the organiza-

tion. The players locked themselves in the dressing room; Alston said that he doubted that any team in history was ever so shaken by a defeat. O'Malley and GM Buzzie Bavasi vanished; they were nowhere to be found. Only Alston stood up to the shock, walking to the San Francisco clubhouse to congratulate Al Dark, and then answering questions politely for an hour after the final game, and offering not a single excuse or criticism for his players.

Dining that night in a Sunset Strip restaurant, Durocher was heard to say that if he had been managing the Dodgers, they wouldn't have lost the race. Bavasi came out of hiding. "If Durocher really said that," Bavasi told a news camera, "he's fired." A New York paper printed an exclusive story that Durocher had been hired to manage the Dodgers. Del Webb, co-owner of the Yankees, told a reporter that, "I hear the Dodgers will be making an announcement tomorrow. Pete Reiser is the new manager." Reiser was the batting coach.

Well now, that *was* a wild winter. Charlie Dressen, now sixty-four years old, was hired back as a special assistant to the general manager; he let it be known that he wasn't too old to manage if the need arose. The only thing certain was that Alston and Durocher couldn't *both* return—and yet, they did.

Even when he came in as a new manager, Alston had never been allowed to pick his own coaches. "We don't want bridge partners or cronies for assistants," explained O'Malley. "It is our job to get the most knowledgeable men, and it is the manager's place to solicit their advice and accept it or reject it. I admit that, in Durocher's case, he sometimes gives advice that isn't solicited, but that's Leo. We knew the nature of the man when we hired him."

On May 6, 1963, there occurred the famous "bus incident," when Alston stopped the bus and challenged any man on the team to a fight if he wanted to earn the right to complain. ("I have always wondered," he said later, "what I would have done if Frank Howard had stood up.") A month later, with the team in Chicago, a newspaper reported that several players on the team had complained to the front office about Alston's management. Buzzie Bavasi flew to Chicago to speak to the players in a closed locker room. "If the Dodgers lose today," said Cubs head coach Bob Kennedy, "Durocher will be manager tomorrow."

And do you know what happened? The

Dodgers won the World Championship once again.

Three times in his career, in 1955, 1959, and 1963, Walt Alston's managerial tenure had been put in extreme jeopardy—and three times, his team had responded with a World Championship.

Alston was solid after that. He had survived it all, survived an incredible round of speculation and second-guessing. After the third championship, O'Malley was committed to Alston, one year at a time forever if Walter chose. He signed a blank contract every fall, and O'Malley would fill in the figure he felt was appropriate; Alston never knew how much he was making until he showed up in the spring.

Baseball in 1963 entered a pitchers' era, and that was perfect for Alston. In a big-hitting era, with a slugging team, Alston's strategy tended to get in the way of his team; he would wind up ordering Duke Snider to bunt. In a pitching-dominated game, Walter's bunting, base stealing, and hitting and running helped the Dodgers scratch out a run or two to win games 3–2. Koufax came into his own; he was half a pennant by himself. The Dodgers won the World Championship again in '65, making Alston the first NL manager since John McGraw to win four World Championships. They won the National League in '66.

Koufax retired after the '66 season. Maury Wills was traded to Pittsburgh. There was a long coda to Alston's career; he managed another ten years after that, years during which astonishingly little of any interest occurred which directly involved Alston. He won one more National League championship, in 1974, and finished second in the division a lot. On September 29, 1976, Alston announced his resignation as Dodger manager—forty years to the day after his one major league at bat, against Lon Warneke in 1936. Altogether he won 2,040 games, more than any major league managers except Connie Mack, John McGraw, Bucky Harris, and Joe McCarthy. He finished first or second in his race fifteen times in twenty-three seasons.

Alston returned to Darrtown. In theory he remained with the Dodgers as an adviser, went to the winter meetings with the group at least. He pursued all of his hobbies and added a new one, riding trail bikes. He built a lot of furniture. In April, 1983, he suffered a heart attack, and on October 1, 1984, died at the age of seventy-two.

(There are two Alston autobiographies,

A Year at a Time, by Alston with Jack Tobin, and *Alston and the Dodgers,* by Alston and Si Burick. There are also innumerable articles about Alston in collections on managers and collections about the Dodgers.)

Porfirio Altamirano, Nicaraguan pitcher for the Phillies in the early eighties. Altamirano had nine syllables in his two names—is that a record? Anybody know? While playing winter ball in Venezuela, Altamirano hurt his shoulder in a free-for-all, and never regained his effectiveness.

Dave Altizer, a longtime minor leaguer and a utility player with a number of teams from 1906 through 1911.

In late May of 1906, the American League Washington Nationals, desperate for infield help, found the twenty-nine-year-old Altizer playing for Lancaster, Pennsylvania, an "outlaw" team, which means that the league wasn't a part of organized baseball. Signed and given the starting shortstop job, Altizer hit well over .500 his first week, making *The Washington Post* ecstatic over his "vim, snap, and aggressiveness," and their effect on the whole team.

His hitting leveled off, and Altizer finished the season at .256, with 37 stolen bases. He remained with Washington for the next season and a half, eventually moving on for brief stints with the Indians, the White Sox, and the Reds. After his major league career he played nine years with Minneapolis in the American Association, and gave them some wonderful seasons—65 stolen bases in 1910, 68 stolen bases in 1912, a .331 average in 1914. Teaming with Gavvy Cravath, Rube Waddell, and others, the Minneapolis Millers were the strongest minor league team of their generation. Altizer led the American Association in runs scored several times, scoring as many as 141 runs in a season (1913). In 1910 he set an American Association record, which still stands, with 61 sacrifice hits. A story in the Apr. 21, 1915 *Kansas City Times* referred to the thirty-eight-year-old as "the 'dare devil' Altizer."

On October 12, 1918, while Altizer was still playing with Minneapolis, his son Oren was killed in action in France. He continued to play minor league ball until 1921, when he was forty-four years old.

(—R.N. Altizer's complete record is included in Volume II of *Minor League Baseball Stars.*)

George Altman, who had one of the greatest careers in Japan of any American ballplayer.

A 1955 graduate of Tennessee A & I, ltman played for the Kansas City Monarchs in the last days of the Negro American League. Altman and Lou Johnson, also a future major leaguer, were sold to the Chicago Cubs early in 1956. He played a year in the minors, got drafted, spent another year in the minors; by the time he reached the majors, after four years of college, a year in the Negro League, two years in the minors and a year in the army, he was twenty-six years old.

Altman was a great big guy, six four and kind of gangly (he had also played basketball in college). Altman gave the Cubs a couple of excellent seasons with the bat, 1961 and 1962, before being traded to St. Louis as a part of the Larry Jackson trade. He stopped hitting, had some minor injuries, wound up back with the Cubs. Leo Durocher liked him, but he just didn't hit enough to keep a job, and was cut loose early in the 1967 season.

He began a second career in Japan. Unlike some of the *gaijin* stars, Altman made an effort to adjust to Japanese ways, to listen to his manager and coaches, and he became a popular and respected player. He hit .320 in Japan in 1969, with 34 homers and 100 RBI, hit .319 with 30 homers in 1970, hit 39 homers and drove in 103 runs in 1971, when he was also in a race for the batting title.

In 1974, as related by Robert Whiting in *The Chrysanthemum and the Bat,* Altman, at age forty-one, was having the finest season of his career, and his team, the Lotte Orions, was battling for the pennant. Altman was diagnosed as having cancer. Surgery was performed, and minus their star, the Orions surged to the pennant and a Japan Series victory.

Altman returned from the U.S. in time for the team victory celebration. The surgery was successful; he was completely cured. He would be ready for the 1975 season. But when contract negotiations for '75 began, Lotte suggested a salary cut of 15 percent. Negotiations stalled, and while Altman was back in the U.S., Lotte manager Masaichi Kaneda found a doctor who stated that Altman would be jeopardizing his life if he continued to play baseball. Altman was released, and advised to retire for the sake of his health.

Taking the advice for what it was worth, Altman returned to Japan, and was offered a position with another team, the Hanshin Tigers. In a remarkable display of pique, his

old manager Kaneda accused Hanshin of risking Altman's life in a desperate attempt to win the pennant. The accusation sent shock waves through Japanese baseball. Tigers officials began to backpedal, and only a formal statement by Altman absolving all other parties of responsibility enabled him to continue his career. It was Altman's contention that Kaneda only feared being proven wrong by the still *gaijin* Altman, proof Altman was only too happy to supply before retiring at the conclusion of the 1975 season. He had hit 205 home runs in eight seasons of Japanese baseball.

While in Japan, Altman had enrolled in a correspondence course offered by the New York School of Finance, had obtained a stockbroker's license and begun working as a broker in the off-season. This led to a career as a commodities trader, and the purchase (at a cost of $135,000) of a seat on the Chicago Board of Trade, where Altman is employed today. Maybe he wouldn't have been interested in staying in the game, but it does seem a shame that baseball did not find a place for a man of such obvious intelligence, perseverance, initiative, work habits, and integrity.

(—M.K.)

W. B. Altman, a semipro player who was killed by a pitch in a game at Morehead, Kentucky, August 9, 1908.

Joe Altobelli, manager of the 1983 World Champion Baltimore Orioles.

As a player, Altobelli spent three undistinguished seasons in the majors. He began his managerial career with Bluefield of the Appalachian League in 1966. In 1971 he took over the Rochester Red Wings, Baltimore's triple-A affiliate, and led them to four International League pennants in six years. In 1974 *The Sporting News* named him Minor League Manager of the Year.

Blocked by Earl Weaver from advancing within the organization, Altobelli was hired to manage the San Francisco Giants in 1977. After a fourth place finish the first year, the Giants in 1978 traded for Vida Blue, which, when Bob Knepper came on to win seventeen games, gave the Giants the best starting rotation in the division. Jack Clark announced his presence with a .306 average, 46 doubles and 98 RBI, and the Giants were in contention until the last weeks.

In 1979 dissension ruled. Vida Blue and John Montefusco, in their cups, ripped Altobelli on a team flight, resulting in an inflight ban on alcohol. This rule, when disobeyed, led to further confrontation. Altobelli himself, infuriated by journalistic second guessing, launched an obscene tirade which, when transcribed from tape, proved to contain more vulgarisms than a Tommy Lasorda harangue. Altobelli was replaced by coach Dave Bristol in September.

After managing Columbus in the International League for a year, Altobelli coached for the New York Yankees for two years before taking the reins of the Orioles upon the retirement of Earl Weaver. The Birds were thought by many to be on the decline, but Altobelli, getting maximum mileage from a veteran lineup (plus unexpectedly brilliant pitching from rookie Mike Boddicker), led them to a World Championship. In 1984, the decline did set in, and by June of 1985 it was apparent that Altobelli was not the man to turn it around. Peter Gammons wrote that Altobelli's "tendency to shyness and withdrawal—some players called him Foggy behind his back—had created a deadened atmosphere." Weaver was summoned from retirement in a messier-than-usual transition, which saw Altobelli wander through the Orioles offices asking "Does anyone know if I've been fired?" Jim Henneman, in The Sporting News, probably summed it up best:

> When Weaver left after the '82 season, in which the Orioles lost the A.L. East championship on the last day of the season, it was felt that his feisty style had worn thin. The easygoing Altobelli seemed perfect, and the players responded with a world championship.
>
> Now, however, the same players who were glad to see Weaver go seem glad to see him back.

In 1986, Altobelli returned to coaching for the Yankees, and later became their coordinator of minor league operations. At present he serves as hitting instructor for the Chicago Cubs.

(—M.K.)

Nick Altrock, baseball's first sideline clown.

Born in Cincinnati in 1876, Altrock began in baseball as a pitcher, and a good one. Beginning in the Inter-State League in 1898, Altrock went 17–3, starting him up the ladder; after winning twenty-eight games for Milwaukee in 1902, he reached the majors late in the year. Pitching for the White Sox beginning in 1904, Altrock posted records of 19–14, 22–12, and 20–13, with earned run averages around 2.00. He set a number of fielding records:

- On August 6, 1904, Altrock set a major league record for chances accepted in a game: 13 (three putouts, ten assists.)
- For the 1904 season he recorded 49 putouts, an American League record which still stands (tied by Mike Boddicker in 1984).
- On June 7, 1908, Altrock had 12 assists in a ten-inning game, tying the record for assists in an extra-inning game. The two other pitchers who had 12 assists in a game did it in many more innings.

Apparently some of the assists came from a phenomenal pickoff move. There is a story told that he once walked seven straight men and picked them all off first base, which of course is probably not exactly true.

In the 1906 World Series, the series between the two Chicago teams, Altrock started the first and fourth games, both times against Mordecai Brown. He beat the Hall of Famer in the first game, 2–1, and lost to him the second time, 1–0, but his team, the Hitless Wonders, upset the mighty Cubs in six games. In 1926 the Hitless Wonders held a reunion; Altrock by then was a famous clown. Ring Lardner wrote a poem for Altrock to read on the occasion. The last two stanzas read:

> Now they say I'm a clown and a funny
>   bloke
>   They laugh at my stunts and tricks,
> But the Cubs didn't think I was such a
>   joke,
>   In the Autumn of nineteen-ought-six.
>
> My speed is all gone, my arm is all in,
>   But I still have a lot of pride,
> In the thought that Nick once helped
>   to win
>   The flag for the good old South
>   Side.

Altrock came up with a sore arm in '07, and was out of the league soon enough—in fact, he was a teammate of Dave Altizer (see Altizer) on Joe Cantillon's great Minneapolis team in 1910, where he also went 19–13.

Somehow Altrock got to be friendly with Clark Griffith, and so in 1912 Altrock returned to the major leagues as a coach for the Washington Senators. Before a game in Cleveland late in the season, a local hero was introduced to the crowd: boxer Johnny Kilbane, the featherweight champion of the world. As a gag, Altrock, on the sideline, struck a boxer's pose; when the crowd laughed, he began to shadowbox, imitating Kilbane's style. Warming to the task, he threw a tremendous roundhouse punch, hit himself on the end of the nose and fell down cold. The crowd went wild; they absolutely loved it.

Well, Altrock was no dummy, and he figured he had something here. He started to do pantomime bits on the sidelines before the games. Sometimes he would wrestle himself, sometimes box. Altrock was a funny-looking guy anyway; Shirley Povich wrote that "to look at him was to laugh." He had a long face, a bulbous nose, huge, flappy ears, and a crooked smile. He began wearing his cap off to one side. If a line drive was hit near him he would very slowly topple over, stiff as a board, his foot sticking up in the air. He would mimic the batting styles, the gestures, of all of the league's top hitters, as John Morris occasionally will today, and would "shadow" the umpires. Before the game he would pretend to help the umpire sweep off the plate, all the while piling more dirt on top of it. At first base in the pre-game drills he would take throws behind his back, between his legs; sometimes he would juggle the throw as if it were a hot potato. Over the next several years he became the Senators' number two gate attraction, behind only Walter Johnson. He began appearing at other ball parks with his act, picking up a little side money. He also continued to pitch a few games, maybe one game a year, often as a last-day-of-the-season stunt, or appear as a pinch hitter.

In 1919 a 142-pound pitcher named Al Schacht joined the Senators. Schact was a funny guy, too; he'd been doing silly stuff in the minors for years. One time in 1915, or so he claimed, Schacht was ordered in from the bullpen, and rode to the mound wearing a dress over his uniform and riding on an old broken-down horse led by a little black kid. At the urging of their teammates, Altrock and Schacht began doing some stuff together, planned stuff. On July 4, 1920, as Schacht would tell it, Schacht saved Clark Griffith from a great embarrassment by taking the mound before a big crowd which had been promised Walter Johnson. Griffith told him that if he beat the Yankees that day he could have a job with the organization as long as he wanted it, and Schacht did beat them, and Griffith was as good as his word. Schacht's career as a pitcher faded after a couple of years, and so his career as a clown took off.

Altrock and Schacht never liked each other, from the very beginning, but in those days a comic always had a partner; vaudeville comedy was almost all two-man shows, not solo acts as we have today. Schacht became a coach with the team, and Altrock and Schacht were assigned to room together, just because coaches were always assigned to room together. Despite their mutual distrust, as performers they complemented one another well. While Altrock had played a lot of things by ear, doing mostly "mugging" for the seats and spontaneous humor, saving and embellishing the bits that worked, Schacht liked prepared material, really involved stuff with props and rehearsals. Altrock didn't like doing it at first, but when he saw that Schacht's stuff got a good reaction, he became a little more willing.

Altrock and Schacht were hired by the Yankees to perform before the games of the 1921 World Series. The fans loved them and the press wrote them up, and a career was launched. Altrock and Schacht began doing the vaudeville tour, spending the winters traveling around doing baseball humor. Their inventory of props grew; Schacht would appear on the field with a top hat and tails, a catcher's glove about four feet across and a large plastic shield; you've probably seen the pictures. Their most famous act was the "Dempsey-Tunney" long count skit, a slow-motion boxing patomime carried out with oversized gloves. They did takeoffs on everything in the world of sports, the Suzanne Lenglen–Helen Wills tennis match or the Gertrude Ederle swim across the English Channel. They became regulars at the World Series, invited back every year.

At the same time, Altrock and Schacht remained legitimate coaches—both, in fact, well respected in the profession; Altrock was the Senators pitching coach, Schacht the third-base coach. Altrock continued to make his occasional appearances in the ball game; in 1933, at the age of fifty-seven, he appeared as a pinch hitter, making him for many years the oldest man to appear in a major league ball game. Altrock and Schacht made good money—three incomes. They had their coach's income, the money they made going to other ball parks, and the money they made in the winter doing vaudeville. They worked every World Series through the early thirties. But while their professional relationship kept them together, their personal rela-

tionship went from sour to bitter. What the fans didn't know, but the sportswriters did, was that during the Dempsey-Tunney skit, Altrock and Schacht were actually beating the hell out of each other.

The differences between them had started, apparently, as professional jealousy, and then too we have to remember that they spent an unhealthy amount of time together—rooming together, traveling together, and working together twelve months of the year. Altrock was a real friendly guy, and he wasn't the most reliable person in the world. While they were traveling around on the vaudeville circuit Altrock had friends in every city, whom he always had to have a few beers with, and sometimes he wouldn't show up for an appearance or would show up not in the best of condition to work. In the train station in Boston, Schacht yelled at Altrock about Altrock's drinking and unreliability. Altrock swung his suitcase, hitting Schacht in the side of the head; Joe Engel, another old Senators pitcher who traveled with them as a coach, had to separate them. The act was broken.

The two of them never spoke again; when one was invited somewhere, the other wasn't. Joe Cronin, Senators player-manager, went to Boston in 1935 in the same role, and Schacht went with him, while Altrock remained in Washington.

Altrock went back to working on his own, as he had twenty years earlier; he'd still do a few vaudeville appearances. Schacht, who was the organized one, did much better out on his own, earning a reported fifty thousand dollars a year within a few years, mostly doing what Max Patkin has done in the last few decades. Clark Griffith tried for the rest of his life to patch things up between them. "I don't know which I am the most fond of, Nick or Al," he told Shirley Povich. "I count them both among my top friends. Both of them are fine men, loyal and generous. It grieves me that for nearly twenty years I have not been able to arrange the handshake that would make all of us feel better."

Altrock continued to coach with the Senators until 1953, when he was seventy-seven years old, and lived another twelve years after that. He died in Washington in 1965. (The best article about Altrock appears to be a feature in the 1954 *Baseball Register*, by Shirley Povich.)

George Alusik, a longtime minor league outfielder who had a couple of years with the Kansas City A's in the early sixties. Alusik

was a big, strong guy and a good minor league hitter (.312 average for eight years, with good power). In 1961, when the expansion created a demand for new players, Alusik was coming off a big season at Denver, but for some odd reason he held out rather than reporting to camp that year, and wound up back in the minor leagues for another season.

Luis Alvarado, utility infielder of the 1970s, and the MVP of the International League in 1969.

Alvarado was a fine runner and an excellent fielder; a White Sox press guide said that, "the ball seems to bounce from his glove to his throwing hand as if on a string." Called "Pimba," he played with six major league teams, but never hit.

Joe Alvarez, manager of the Vero Beach Dodgers (1989).

Jose Alvarez, thirty-two-year-old rookie pitcher for the 1988 Atlanta Braves.

"I was nine years old and my family was called to Atlanta because my father had to go to prison here," Alvarez told Roy Johnson of the Atlanta *Constitution*. "We drove by this place and I asked my mother what it was. She said it's where the Milwaukee Braves were going to play when they moved to Atlanta. I looked up and told her, 'I'm gonna play in that stadium someday.'"

It seemed unlikely. As a sophomore at Tampa's Hillsborough High School, proving ground for Dwight Gooden and Floyd Youmans, Alvarez was sliced from the baseball team. But after attending Hillsborough Junior College and the University of Southwestern Louisiana he became an eighth round draft choice of the Atlanta Braves, and signed with them. He had brief looks with the Braves in 1981 and 1982, and then drifted through eleven minor league teams with four organizations.

In May, 1988, desperate for pitching, the Braves summoned the thirty-two-year-old Alvarez from Richmond. He became one of the oldest rookies of modern times, and this time he stuck, his assortment of off-speed breaking pitches proving effective. In June of 1989, he was placed on the disabled list with tendinitis in his right knee, and was sidelined for the remainder of the season.

(—M.K.)

Ossie Alvarez, Washington Senators utility infielder in 1958. Alvarez made the leap from Class B Midland, Texas to the Senators in 1958, and took over the shortstop job after the All-Star break when

Rocky Bridges broke his jaw. He didn't stick.

Raul Alvarez, pitcher with the Cuban Stars, 1924–33.

Jay Alves, director of baseball information for the Oakland Athletics.

Max Alvis, a brilliant young third baseman whose career was undermined by a battle with spinal meningitis in 1964.

A native of Jasper, Texas, Alvis signed with the Indians for a reported forty thousand dollars in 1958. He moved through the Indians farms systematically, being one of the best players in the Pacific Coast League in 1962 (25, 91, .319), and one of the best rookies in the American League in 1963. He was named by Cleveland sportswriters that year as the Man of the Year. He had a fine arm—the Indians had toyed with the idea of making him a pitcher—and led the American League in putouts in four of his first five seasons.

Alvis crowded the plate, and with strong forearms could pull the ball; the Indians projected him as a player who could hit thirty homers a year. On June 26, 1964, Alvis was diagnosed as having spinal meningitis. He returned to the lineup in early August, but the illness had taken some of the snap out of his bat, and may have done so permanently; although he was a quality player, he never quite matched his rookie highs in either homers (22) or batting average (.274).

Dave Alworth, director of data processing and special projects for the commissioner's office.

Brant Alyea, outfielder in the late sixties and early seventies.

Alyea attended Hofstra College on a basketball scholarship, where he was a second team Little All-American in roundball. He also played baseball at Hofstra, just because he liked the game. He signed with Cincinnati for twelve thousand dollars, and was drafted the next year by the Washington Senators. He had a cup of coffee with the Senators in 1965, and became the first pinch hitter in AL history to hit a home run on the first major league pitch thrown to him. A minor league power hitter and a legend in the winter leagues, Alyea returned to the big leagues in 1968.

According to Shelby Whitfield in *Kiss It Goodbye,* Alyea made the Senators in 1969 after he (Whitfield) pointed out to Ted Williams that Alyea had hit over fifty home runs the previous year in Triple A ball, the American Association and the winter league, and

also that Cap Peterson, who was having a better spring, had only one kidney. Alyea was used by Williams as a platoon player, which he complained about. (According to Whitfield, "Alyea was a chronic complainer and was quick to bitch about anything.")

Alyea, who was a big strong guy, was apparently kind of a strange one. He rode a motorcycle, read books in the locker room, listened to jazz, and spent more time and energy than was desirable out carousing and chasing women. He wore mod clothes and grew long sideburns. A Senators press guide once described him as a "Jekyll and Hyde player." He quarreled with Williams in '69, and was traded to Minnesota in spring training, 1970.

On opening day in 1970, his first game with the Twins, Alyea drove in seven runs. He continued red-hot; after 12 games he had 21 RBI, earning him a *Sporting News* cover story (May 9, 1970). The first four times that Jim Perry started that year, Alyea drove in 19 runs, launching Perry to the Cy Young Award. He stopped hitting as soon as they stopped platooning him, and dropped out of the majors after tearing a groin muscle running out a double off of Jim Palmer on August 14, 1971.

Alyea today oversees the crap tables at the Tropicana in Atlantic City.

Brant Alyea, Jr., son of Brant Alyea, brought to the United States by the Toronto Blue Jays, and now with the Texas system.

While playing winter ball in Managua, Nicaragua in February, 1966, Brant Alyea met a young woman by the name of Auda Medina. The two spent a weekend together, and when Alyea returned to Nicaragua the next winter he found himself the father of a one-week old baby. On the advice of Pancho Herrara, who became the child's godfather, Alyea signed the baptismal certificate, thereby giving the child his name, and continued to play some role in raising the baby through that winter and the next two.

After that, however, Alyea was unable to get clearance to return to Nicaragua, and so never saw the boy after he was fifteen months old. At first he corresponded with the mother and sent her some support for the child, but his second wife began throwing away her letters, and after a massive earthquake hit Nicaragua in 1972 they completely lost touch. She married and had a family of her own. Alyea junior grew up with his father's name and love of baseball, but knowing nothing else about him.

In the early 1980s the Sandinistas moved Nicaragua from an American ally under the control of a harsh dictator, Somoza, to a Marxist state and America's sworn enemy. His mother left the country, but it became impossible for Alyea, or any man or boy who might have military value, to depart Nicaragua except under official escort. "If I hadn't been a ballplayer," Alyea told Peter Gammons in 1986, "I'd have had to go right into the army. Most of my friends weren't players, so they went, and a lot of them have been killed. But I always knew that my father was a ballplayer and that I'd be a ballplayer, and ballplayers in Nicaragua get treated very well."

In July, 1984, a Toronto scout (Wayne Morgan), attending the World Youth Baseball Tournament in Saskatchewan noticed a seventeen-year-old player named Brant Alyea playing for Nicaragua. He was naturally interested, and when he saw Alyea swing the bat, his interest increased. Pat Gillick, Toronto general manager, arranged to get a message to Alyea, through a teammate, that the Blue Jays were interested in him. Alyea sent a message back that he, too, was interested. Epy Guerrero, the famous Dominican scout, managed to get into Nicaragua through an old friend, disguised himself as a Sandinista and met with Alyea, offering him six thousand dollars if he could get out of the country to play baseball. Bribing an official to get a passport and dodging the police at the airport, Alyea flew to Mexico City, where he was met by Guerrero, who hid him for two days awaiting a Canadian visa. When the Canadian visa arrived, Alyea flew to Vancouver to join the Medicine Hat Blue Jays of the Pioneer League.

Reunited with his father after eighteen years, Alyea senior and junior spent time together in the spring of 1986, eventually becoming rather close. As a ballplayer he has not thrived. Once thought to be a definite major league prospect, Alyea has bogged down as a hitter, and in 1989 moved from the Jackson Mets to the Charlotte Rangers of the Florida State League.

(An excellent article about the Alyeas by Peter Gammons appears in the June 30, 1986 edition of *Sports Illustrated.*)

Joey Amalfitano, manager of the Chicago Cubs for portions of three seasons, and major league infielder in the sixties.

Amalfitano was signed by the New York Giants as a bonus baby in 1954. Under the rules of the time a player who received a bonus of four thousand dollars or more had to spend the next two seasons on the big league roster. The Giants, of course, won the World Championship in 1954, but Amalfitano didn't have much to do with it, appearing in only nine games. The series program did note that he "made himself useful and highly popular with the team with his earnest willingness to perform all the handyman chores . . ."

Amalfitano saw more bench time in 1955; then, having fulfilled his major league obligation, he headed off for four years in the minors.

Resuming his big league career in 1960, Amalfitano was a San Francisco Giant for three of the next four seasons (he was with the expansion Astros in '62), a part-timer at both second and third base, then bouncing to the Cubs, where he was managed by his first major league manager, Leo Durocher. Durocher wrote in *Nice Guys Finish Last* that Amalfitano "hustled all the time, was very bright and . . . got 120 percent out of his talent," but he gave Joey his release slightly into the '67 season—and promptly hired him as a coach. Amalfitano left the Cubs after 1971, and spent the seventies coaching for the Giants, the Padres, and the Cubs again.

With the resignation of Cubs manager Herman Franks late in 1979, Amalfitano was named interim manager for the final week of the season. Preston Gomez was the Cubs opening day manager in 1980, but was fired in July, and this time Amalfitano was given the job on a non-interim basis. The Cubs didn't improve under his direction, and after guiding the Cubs to the second-worst record in baseball in 1981, he was fired.

Amalfitano spent 1982 as a coach with Cincinnati, before joining Los Angeles in '83, where he has been the third base coach ever since.

(—R.N.)

Ruben Amaro, slick-fielding shortstop for the Philadelphia Phillies in the early 1960s.

In 1964 Amaro won the National League Gold Glove award at shortstop, despite playing only seventy-nine games at the position. The Phillies that year had four outstanding defensive middle infielders (Amaro, Wine, Tony Taylor, and Cookie Rojas) but no first baseman, so Amaro played almost as many games at first base (fifty-eight) as at shortstop—certainly a unique thing for a Gold Glove shortstop.

Amaro was basically a journeyman player, played for St. Louis, the Phillies, Yankees, and Angels. Jim Bouton wrote about Amaro that "We were good friends in New York. He's the kind of guy, well, there's a dignity to him and everybody likes and respects him. He's outspoken and has very strong opinions but he never antagonizes people with his positions the way I sometimes do. I wish I could be more like him."

Amaro was coaching for the Phillies when Pete Rose broke the record for most base hits by a National Leaguer, and was the first man to offer his congratulations. Today he scouts for the Detroit Tigers and manages the Bristol team in the Detroit farm system. A son, Ruben Amaro, Jr., is an outfielder in the California system, and is a definite major league prospect, a leadoff-type hitter.

Wayne Ambler, middle infielder for the Philadelphia Athletics in the late thirties.

The 1939 *Who's Who in the Major Leagues* said about the young Wayne Ambler that "Connie [Mack] has visions of another Eddie Collins in this youngster, now playing his second full major league year. He improved a bit in his hitting last semester, spending a lot of his mornings experimenting with various battling stances and swings. That's the spirit that wins. Although he played shortstop most of last season, you can sell him at third. He's aiming at second this year." Ambler retired with a career batting average of .224 in 271 games, significantly short of Eddie Collins's marks.

Red Ames, a pitcher who was a member of John McGraw's great New York Giants teams from 1903 through 1912.

Ames threw very hard, and his career had many highlights. He won 183 games. He threw two no-hitters, both of which are marked with an asterisk. He won 22 games in 1905. He pitched in three World Series. Although he never led the league in strikeouts, he did lead the league in strikeouts per inning in 1904, and again in 1905, and again in 1906, and again in 1907. He pitched brilliantly down the stretch of baseball's greatest pennant race, the 1908 NL race, starting and winning five times between September 26 and October 7.

In spite of these accomplishments, Ames throughout his career was known for three things, two of them negative:

1) he had poor control,

2) he always pitched well in cold weather, and

3) he was an awful hitter.

He was born Leon Kessling Ames in Warren, Ohio on Aug. 2, 1882, and grew to be a stocky (five feet ten and a half, 185 pounds) righthander. He first attracted attention while pitching for the Zanesville, Ohio club in 1901, and worked his way up to the New York Giants by late 1903, John McGraw's first full season with the Giants. In his first major league game, on September 14, 1903, he threw a five inning no-hitter. The game, the second game of a doubleheader, was stopped by darkness.

Ames pitched extremely well in 1904—very well, but not very much. The Giants had two thirty-game winners on the staff, Joe McGinnity and Christy Mathewson, and when one of them wasn't pitching Luther Taylor usually was. The Giants won the pennant, but there was no World Series that year, owing to McGraw's and owner John T. Brush's enmity toward the upstart American League, so Ames was bereft of extra cash when, on January 17, 1905, he married Rena Brainard. In the '05 season, against the same impossible competition, Ames wormed his way into regular work, winning 22, second on the club to Matty's 31, as the Giants again seized the flag.

On a less upbeat note, Ames also threw 30 wild pitches that year, which is the "modern" record for wild pitches in a season. Eventually, Ames would also become the career leader in wild pitches, with 156 (actually, Walter Johnson threw the same number, but in almost twice as many innings).

In the finally firmly established World Series of '05, Ames was relegated to a token relief appearance as Mathewson and McGinnity divided the starts in dispatching the Athletics in five games. In 1906, according to the *Reach Guide*

> Ames was pitching admirably, and seemed likely to make almost as good a record as Mathewson had the year preceding, when he injured his leg in Philadelphia, fell fainting on the floor of the hotel that night, and he did not play again for six weeks. When he did resume his place in the box he was all out of training and his effectiveness for the year had gone."

After that, Ames pitched in mostly hard luck. Compare his 10–12 record, 2.16 ERA for the '07 season with Matty's 24–13 record with a 1.99 ERA, although admittedly Ames was his own worst enemy, walking 108 men. Everyone agreed that his blazing fast ball and "wide" curve were among the league's best, but already many despaired of his ever controlling them consistently. There may have been an additional problem: in a February 1908 issue of *The Sporting News* Joe Vila wrote that Ames "cannot be depended upon because of his erratic work and his temperament." G. H. Fleming, in his excellent compilation of reportage on the 1908 race, *The Unforgettable Season,* gives us another sample: "Bresnahan signaled for one kind of curve and Ames refused to throw it . . . Ames persisted and started to throw what he wished, and Bresnahan deliberately stood to one side, refusing to catch the ball."

In 1908 Ames went on the shelf early with a kidney ailment, and when he returned in August it was the same old story: control trouble. An exasperated McGraw pulled him from his August 22 start after he walked the first two batters. But the Little Napoleon dared not bury him; McGinnity and Taylor, once mainstays, had faded badly (both would be sold to the minor leagues in the off-season), and Rube Marquard was on the scene but not yet ready.

With an overworked Matty unable to shoulder the entire burden as the Giants desperately battled the Cubs and Pirates down the stretch in the greatest pennant race ever, Red Ames stepped into the breach. On September 26 he beat the Reds, 3–1. On September 30 he beat Philadelphia 2–1; on October 2 he beat them again, 7–2. On October 5, with the pennant still up for grabs, Ames beat Boston, 8–1. On October 7, with a victory needed to force a replay of the famous "Merkle Boner" game and Matty available for duty, McGraw handed the ball to Ames one more time: He produced a 7–2 win and the fateful confrontation with the Cubs—his fifth win, as a starter, in twelve days.

Had the Giants not been beaten in that final game, Ames would certainly have played a major role in the 1908 World Series. As it was, the five late-season triumphs became the basis for his reputation as a cold weather pitcher; indeed, on three subsequent occasions he would get the call for the Giants on opening day.

On April 15, 1909 Ames pitched no-hit baseball for nine innings against the Brooklyn Superbas; but for one base on balls would have become the precursor of Harvey Haddix, as the Giants could not score and the game moved into extra innings. His no-hitter was broken up in the tenth, and in the thirteenth he was raked for three runs to lose the game. The story that appeared the next day

in *The New York Times* barely mentioned that Ames had hurled nine innings of hitless ball, there being no concept of a no-hitter at that time.

Ames's curtain-raiser in 1911 (a 2–0 loss to Philadelphia) has been mistakenly referred to as the last game played at the old Polo Grounds, destroyed by fire on the night of April 13. (In fact, a rare clobbering of Matty by the Phils that afternoon marked the end of the era.) Minus their old home, the Giants reemerged as pennant winners in 1911. Ames was quietly effective that year, with better control, and played an important role in the 1911 World Series. With the Giants down three games to one against the Athletics, Philadelphia took a 3–0 early lead in Game Five. Ames was summoned to pitch, and held Philadelphia scoreless for four innings; the Giants eventually rallied to win, keeping the series alive. In Game Six the very next day Mathewson, who had turned in a subpar performance in Game Four, was held back; Ames was given the start. This was a strange idea by modern standards—starting a pitcher who had pitched four innings of scoreless relief the day before—and Ames, after pitching scoreless ball for three innings, was battered in the fourth, ending the series.

For the 1912 season, another star pitcher arrived in New York, Jeff Tesreau, joining Mathewson and Rube Marquard. Ames, though pitching his best ball in years, was shoved to the back end of the staff. He played no significant role in one of the all-time great World Series, 1912. Early in 1913 Ames was dealt to Cincinnati along with Josh DeVore and Heinie Groh for pitcher Art Fromme and third baseman Eddie Grant. It was a terrible trade for McGraw: Fromme and Grant were washed up by '15, and Groh eventually won his battle with the bottle to star for the Reds. The trade didn't do much for Ames, either. The 1913 and 1914 Reds were horrible teams, and Ames's control, so carefully nurtured in his last years in New York, deserted him. His ERA remained good but he racked up loss after loss, leading the league with twenty-three in 1914.

Ames struggled through the National League from 1913 to 1919, not pitching badly but generally posting losing records with bad teams. Released by Philadelphia in 1920, he pitched a couple of years in the American Association, one year in the Florida State League. When he died on Oct. 8, 1936, he was residing in Warren, Ohio,

the town of his birth; he was only fifty-four years old. Kevin Kerrane, in *The Hurlers,* offered the appropriate epitaph when he wrote: "Red Ames probably deserved a better fate than pitching in the shadow of Mathewson, McGinnity, Rube Marquard and Jeff Tesreau."

(—M.K.)

Sandy Amoros, outfielder whose "miracle" catch in the seventh game of the '55 Series helped seal the Brooklyn Dodgers' only World Championship.

Born Edmundo Isasi Amoros in Havana, Cuba in 1930, Amoros picked up the nickname "Sandy" as a child, according to Tom Meany in *The Artful Dodgers,* because his hero was a boxer named Sandy Saddler. A baseball star in his native country, Amoros in 1950 played with the New York Cubans of the Negro American League. Al Campanis saw him in Cuba in 1952, and convinced Amoros to sign with the Dodgers.

Amoros was a wonderful minor league player, playing for St. Paul in '52 and Walt Alston's Montreal team in 1953, where he led the International League in runs, hits, doubles, and batting average. This enabled him to overpower the daunting math of the Dodgers farm system, and arrive in Brooklyn with Alston in 1954. With the Dodgers for all of 1954, Amoros was impressive in part-time duty. At five feet seven and a half and 170 pounds, Sandy was a compact man, and though he never hit for a high average in the majors, he was fast, got on base a lot, and hit for surprisingly good power. He was regarded at first as another Willie Mays, and while he wasn't that in fact he was a damned effective player from 1954 to 1957, although you don't notice that if you just glance at his stats. His career secondary average was .350.

In Game Seven of the 1955 World Series the Dodgers owned a 2–0 lead over the Yankees. In the top of the sixth, Walt Alston sent in a pinch hitter for second baseman Don Zimmer, which necessitated shifting left fielder Junior Gilliam in to second in the bottom of the inning; Amoros was sent to left. With no outs, the Yanks put two men on, as Billy Martin walked and Gil McDougald bunted safely. To the plate strode Yogi Berra, a left-handed hitter. With Dodgers starter Johnny Podres apparently tiring and Berra a pull hitter, Alston waved the entire outfield around toward right. But Berra crossed them up, lifting a high, slicing fly down the left field line. It looked like either a double or a long foul, but as Fried Lieb describes the play in *The Story of the World Series,* "Sandy ran full tilt at the stands, and by twisting his body and extending his gloved right hand, managed to squeeze the ball a few inches inside fair territory. It is unlikely that Gilliam, a right-hander, could have caught the ball in his gloved left hand."

Meanwhile, McDougald, sure that the ball would be a double, had advanced into no-man's land; a perfect relay, Amoros to Reese to Hodges, and he was doubled off first. When Hank Bauer grounded out, the rally was ended. The Dodgers had to quell another uprising in the eighth, but Amoros's catch was the pivotal play in the game. The Dodgers' agony had finally ended.

Asked after the game if he thought he had a chance for the catch, Amoros, whose English was never very good, replied, "I dunno. I just run like hell." Gilliam himself said that he could never have caught the ball.

"The jury to decide the greatest and most important World Series catch of all time has finally come in with a verdict," wrote Michael Gaven in the *New York Journal-American.* "Although admitting their decision was not unanimous, the jurors have ruled in favor of Sandy Amoros . . ."

In the last week of the 1956 season, with Brooklyn battling Milwaukee tooth and nail, Amoros homered in three consecutive games. In a little-remembered episode, Amoros again almost changed Series lore in 1956. In the top of the fifth of what would eventually become Don Larsen's perfect fifth game, Sandy cracked a long fly into the lower deck in right field, but it curved foul at the last instant.

Despite a productive season in 1957, Amoros was optioned to Montreal in 1958, and saw little action with the Dodgers thereafter. It would be interesting to know why this move was made; certainly Amoros was a more effective player than the men who took his place on the roster, Elmer Valo and Norm Larker. In any case Amoros was traded to Detroit in 1960, and finished his major league career that season.

Amoros returned to his native Havana, where he was a hero, and lived well for several years. He owned a ranch, bought a new car every year and had money in the bank. He continued to play baseball, in the Mexican League and in Cuba. According to Nicholas Dawidoff in *Sports Illustrated* (July 10, 1989), little boys followed him through the Havana streets. In 1959 Fidel Castro had come to power in Cuba. It's a small country,

and the dictator and the star inevitably got to know each other.

Castro decided to organize a self-contained league in Cuba, and in the spring of 1962 he asked Amoros not to go play in Mexico that summer, but to stay home and manage one of his teams. "I told Castro I didn't know how to manage," Amoros told Dawidoff. "I could play, why would I want to manage?" Castro seized all of Amoros's property, even his car, and refused to allow him out of the country to go play in Mexico. For five years Amoros was virtually a prisoner in his own home, living on standard rations—two pounds of rice a month, a pound of meat, two pounds of beans.

In 1967 Castro finally permitted Amoros, his wife, and daughter to flee the country, along with 64,000 other people. Life in the United States has hardly been any easier for him. The Amoros family settled in the South Bronx, living on welfare. Amoros was a week or so short of qualifying for a major league pension, so the Dodgers put him on their roster for a while to make him eligible. His wife divorced him in 1967, and Amoros was left alone. He worked for the New York department of parks and recreation for a couple of years, drifted south to Tampa and worked at odd jobs until eligible to receive his major league pension in 1977. The money wasn't much.

He developed leg trouble, a circulatory problem in his legs. When the pain became

TRACERS

George Earnshaw . . . was pitching for Connie Mack's Athletics against the New York Yankees on a day when the famed Bronx Bombers of old were in a deadly slugging mood. . . . Among his chief torments was the late Lou Gehrig, who in his first two times at bat had socked two home runs into the right-field stands.

After the second homer, manager Connie Mack lost his patience and faith and yanked the faltering pitcher out of the game. . . . "You sit right here next to me for the rest of this game," [Mack said] "I want you to watch how Mahaffey is going to pitch to that Gehrig fellow."

Presently, up to bat again came Lou Gehrig, and this time he pickled the first pitch into the left-field stands for another home run. There was a long and awkward silence finally broken by Earnshaw who turned to his manager and said:

"I see perfectly what you mean, Mr. Mack. He sure made Gehrig change direction."

—Mac Davis
Great American Sports Humor (Pages 75–76)

Jerry Koosman also tells this story, with Tug McGraw replacing Mahaffey, Gil Hodges subbing for Connie Mack and Willie McCovey pinch hitting for Lou Gehrig. Since three-homer days are not exactly a dime a dozen even for Lou Gehrig, the origins of the story shouldn't be too hard to track down if it really happened. . . .

On May 22, 1930, the Athletics and Yanks met at Shibe Park for a doubleheader. The Yankees scored thirty runs in the doubleheader, winning 10–1 and 20–13, which fulfills the criterion of "a deadly slugging mood." Altogether there were ten home runs in the second game, which at the time was a record. Gehrig had seven hits on the day, including three homers in the second game. Mahaffey and Earnshaw did pitch in the doubleheader.

Apart from that, the details don't match. Gehrig didn't hit any home runs off of Earnshaw *or* Mahaffey, and hit his three homers off three different pitchers (Bill Shores, Ed Rommell, and Glenn Liebhardt.)

It's a good story. It was probably an old one when George Earnshaw first heard it.

intolerable, he was taken to Memorial Hospital in Tampa. Gangrene had infected the leg, and the left leg was amputated just below the knee. Unable to pay his hospital bill, he was treated as an indigent. His pension in recent years has been supplemented by regular payments from the Baseball Alumni Team (BAT), but Amoros remains alone in his apartment in Tampa, basically unable to do very much other than sit around his apartment. "It was the biggest thing in my life to see all those fine players like Stan Musial, Ted Kluszewski, and Willie Mays," Amoros told Dawidoff. "It still makes me feel good. It's my memories of baseball that keep me alive."

(—B.J. and R.N. The Baseball Alumni Team, which assists Sandy Amoros and hundreds of other old-time ballplayers through the difficult times in their lives, has changed its name to the Baseball Assistance Team. At this point, 25 of the 26 major league teams have chosen not to help, George Steinbrenner being the exception. If you have the ability to help a little bit, the address of the Baseball Assistance Team is the same as the address of the Commissioner's Office: 350 Park Avenue, New York, N.Y., 10022.)

Rick Amos, manager of promotions for the Toronto Blue Jays.

Tom Ananicz, apparently baseball's only conscientious objector in World War II. A pitcher with the Kansas City Blues, Ananicz applied for and received deferment from the draft as a conscientious objector.

Ronald Anastasio, a minor league pitcher in the Cleveland Indians system who was killed in a car accident while reporting from one team to another in 1958.

Lee Anders, radio announcer for the Everett Giants.

Larry Andersen, contemporary relief pitcher known primarily for his off-beat sense of humor.

Andersen pitched briefly with the Indians for three seasons, but his career didn't really get started until 1981, when he appeared in forty-one games for the Seattle Mariners, mostly in middle relief. Andersen has continued to play that role with both Philadelphia and Houston.

With the latter team in 1986, he pitched three scoreless extra frames in one of the greatest games ever played, the sixth game of the NL playoffs, which the Mets eventually won in sixteen innings.

Though middle relievers don't usually get much glory, Andersen has attained a small degree of fame by coming up with lines like, "You're only young once, but you can be immature forever," and (my personal favorite), "Why do we drive on a parkway and park on a driveway?" He has also been known to entertain teammates with sustained belches of a minute or more.

At the age of thirty-six in 1989, Andersen had the finest season of his career.

(—R.N.)

Richard Andersen, vice-president, administration and stadium operations for the Pittsburgh Pirates.

Dr. Al Anderson, a San Diego dentist who was a leader in the movement to bring major league baseball to the San Diego area.

Alf Anderson, sometime shortstop for the Pittsburgh Pirates in the early forties. From *The Washington Post*, March 23, 1941:

> Just why Rookie Shortstop Alf Anderson, of Atlanta, made such a determined holdout against the Pirates was a mystery until someone pointed out he married a lovely Southern gal two weeks before he departed for camp.

Allan Anderson, contemporary pitcher with the Minnesota Twins.

After brief trials with the Twins in '86 and '87 and failing to make the opening day roster in '88, Anderson was called up in late April. He broke into the starting rotation, and with excellent control and a changeup learned from Frank Viola, won the American League ERA title. He had another big year in 1989, and now ranks among the best young pitchers in baseball.

Andy Anderson, middle infielder in the late forties with the St. Louis Browns.

Bill Anderson, pitcher with the Cuban Stars and New York Cubans, 1940–47.

Bob Anderson, pitcher for the Chicago Cubs who was on the mound in the famous two-balls-in-play episode in 1959.

In 1956, with the Los Angeles Angels, Anderson made a Pacific Coast League Record 70 appearances. In the starting rotation for the Chicago Cubs in 1959, Anderson was on the mound on June 30. Stan Musial was batting for the Cardinals, and had worked the count to three and one when Anderson threw wildly for ball four. As the ball headed for the backstop, catcher Sammy Taylor argued with plate umpire Vic Delmore that the pitch had hit Musial's bat. Manager Bob Scheffing emerged from the dugout to support this contention. No one had called time,

and as third baseman Alvin Dark pounced on the live ball near the screen, the absent-minded umpire deposited a *new* ball in catcher Taylor's mitt.

Meanwhile, Cardinals first-base coach Harry Walker, exploiting the confusion, sent Musial digging for second. Anderson, spotting this, grabbed the new ball and fired in the direction of second base. At the same time, Dark pegged the original ball to shortstop Ernie Banks. As Musial arrived at second, he saw Anderson's throw carry on into center field. The Man lit out for third, only, to his astonishment, to be met by Banks, holding the original ball, who tagged him out. You can imagine the ensuing rhubarb, which was eventually resolved in the Cubs' favor, and rendered moot by the eventual Cardinals victory.

The hard-throwing Anderson continued to start for the Cubs until 1961, when he was used mostly in relief, and produced the odd line of 57 appearances and 152 innings pitched. After the 1962 season he was traded to Detroit, where he pitched his final year of major league ball.

(—M.K.)

Bobby Anderson, Negro League shortstop and second baseman, 1915–25.

Bud Anderson, pitched a couple of years of middle relief for Cleveland in the early eighties.

Craig Anderson, a pitcher in the early sixties with the Cardinals and the expansion Mets, for whom he lost seventeen games in their first season. After a decent rookie campaign as a middle reliever for the '61 Cards, he had the misfortune of being selected by the Mets in the expansion draft.

George Vecsey writes, in *Joy in Mudville*:

> Craig Anderson . . . was another college man (Lehigh) with a pretty wife, and was another favorite of [Manager Casey Stengel's wife] Edna . . . A tall, burly man . . . His gentle, educated manner drove Stengel up the nearest clubhouse wall, particularly after Stengel learned that Anderson had a generous annuity plan.
>
> "He's got an-noo-i-tees," Casey would enunciate, "but he won't knock a batter on his butt."

Anderson pitched a few games in '63 and '64, but he never recovered from going three and seventeen. Good thing he had those annuities, I guess.

(—R.N.)

Dave Anderson

. . . managed by Del Crandall, the [1982 Albuquerque] Dukes were in the process of winning their fifth straight division championship [and] were loaded with exciting prospects like Mike Marshall, Greg Brock, Candy Maldonado, Orel Hershiser and Sid Fernandez. But the most glittering prospect of all, I was sure, was Dave Anderson. Only 22, Anderson had been the Dodgers' number one draft choice out of Memphis State University a year earlier. After a half season in A ball, he'd been promoted to the Dukes for '82. And he performed brilliantly, hitting .343 with 100 runs scored. Best of all, he was a shortstop, and reputed to be an excellent fielder. Anderson was the logical successor to Bill Russell, possibly as soon as 1983. Anderson did make the big club in '83, as Russell's caddie . . .

The Dodgers bounced back in '85, making the playoffs again, but without much help from Anderson. A back injury put him on the disabled list twice, and when he played, he hit .199. . . . In '86 he was hurt again, with a broken finger, but it didn't matter; a .245 average with no power convinced the Dodgers once and for all that Dave was a utility man. So in '87 he filled in, getting into 108 games at second, short and third, and no one was surprised when he only hit .234. His role now seems clear—a fill-in with good speed and a decent glove. . . .

—Don Zminda, *1988 Great American Baseball Stat Book*

Anderson, who turns thirty this August, has apparently lost a bit of his speed, and went to the plate fewer times in '89 than any season since his rookie year. His career appears to be winding down, though his versatility may keep him in the league for a few more years. At this writing, Anderson has just signed as a free agent with the Giants.

Theodore "Bubbles" Anderson, second baseman with several teams in the Negro Leagues, 1922–25.

Dwain Anderson, part-time shortstop with four teams in the early seventies.

Anderson was not a power hitter. In 1970, however, with Iowa of the American Association, he hit fifteen homers and led the league with three grand slams. Not coincidentally, he also led the league in strikeouts, which apparently ended that experiment.

Ferrell Anderson, who caught for the Dodgers in 1946, and also managed a few years in the minors.

Anderson appears to have been a pretty decent offensive and defensive catcher, but he missed some critical years to World War II, and then got buried in the Dodger system behind Campanella, Bruce Edwards, Gil Hodges (a converted catcher) and others. He was in his mid-thirties before he could get out of the system, and wound up giving the best years of his life to St. Paul.

Fred Anderson, pitcher and dentist.

Anderson pitched for Davidson College and the University of Maryland prior to stints in various minor leagues. He made one start for the Boston Red Sox in 1909 and pitched well, allowing just one run in eight innings.

Despite that success, Anderson retired from baseball, and spent the next two years practicing dentistry. He "unretired" in 1912, and was back with the Sox in 1913.

In 1914 Anderson, primarily a spitball pitcher (is that appropriate for a dentist?), jumped to the Federal League, and in 1915 won nineteen games for Buffalo. With the breakup of the Federal League that year, Anderson was sold to the New York Giants, where he became a spot starter and reliever. He went just eight and eight in 1917, despite a 1.44 ERA, and was raked in his one World Series appearance.

Anderson was the second Giant to enter the army in 1918, and never pitched in the big leagues again.

(—R.N.)

Harley Anderson, regional scouting supervisor (eastern region) for the Chicago Cubs.

Harold "Andy" Anderson, a quality outfielder in the American Association in the 1920s and 1930s, also known as (and listed in the encyclopedias as) "Hal" Anderson.

A player of truly extraordinary consistency, Anderson in his first seven years in the minor leagues (mostly with St. Paul) never hit lower than .295 or higher than .305. In 1931 Anderson jumped his batting average up to .314 and showed power for the first time (36 doubles, 23 homers). Combined with his usual attributes of speed (24 stolen bases, 126 runs scored, fine range in center field), this earned him a brief trial with the White Sox in 1932, after which he resumed his career in the American Association.

George Anderson, Federal League outfielder.

Goat Anderson, outfielder with the 1907 Pittsburgh Pirates.

Anderson played just one year in the major leagues, and the encyclopedias do not list whether he was a right-handed or left-handed hitter. In researching this book, Rob Neyer learned that he hit left-handed. From the March 24, 1907, *Pittsburgh Post-Gazette:*

. . . Anderson has shown marked ability in this respect [baserunning]. His favorite method of batting is bunting. He allows the ball to merely hit the bat, and he is off to the first station in a rush. There are few players in any league who get away quicker, and he has a decided advantage over many because he is a left-handed sticker.

This explains why, playing 127 games in 1907, Anderson had only five extra base hits (three doubles, one triple, one homer.) Anyway, get out your *Encyclopedia* or *Total Baseball* or whatever you use, and print in a little BL next to Goat Anderson. You're welcome.

Hank Anderson, administrative assistant with the Las Vegas Stars.

Harry Anderson, outfielder-first baseman with the Phillies and Reds from 1957–61, who showed early promise only to see his career go quickly down the toilet.

After a poor 1956 season at Schenectady, Anderson must have impressed someone at the 1957 Phillies spring training, because on opening day he was with the big club. A college graduate, Anderson put together two consecutive fine seasons, hitting 17 homers in 400 at bats in 1957, and being one of the National League's top-hitting outfielders in 1958 (23, 97, .301).

With a prospective starting outfield consisting of Anderson, Wally Post, and batting champ Richie Ashburn, the '59 Phillies looked to improve on their last-place finish of the year before. It didn't work out; in 1959 Anderson's batting totals fell precipitously, to the extent that the Phils felt it necessary to cut his salary for 1960. Anderson accepted the pay cut graciously, attributing his woes to the lack of a team hitting coach in 1959, a situation which would be remedied in '60. A February 17, 1960, article in *The Sporting News* opined that "if Anderson does respond with an outstanding season in 1960, General Manager John Quinn may be depended upon to remember Anderson's honesty and reward him commensurately a year from now."

Sure. Quinn wasn't put to the test; Anderson continued to struggle, and was out of the league in '61.

(—R.N.)

Jim Anderson, shortstop-utility man in the late seventies and early eighties.

Anderson played for three American League teams between 1978 and 1984. He wasn't much of a hitter, he was slow, and a 1981 article in the *Baseball Digest* rated his arm as the weakest of any American League shortstop. He was a good defensive player and a smart defensive player, but never could quite get over the hump.

John Anderson, assistant general manager of the Martinsville Phillies.

John Anderson, head baseball coach at University of Minnesota.

Honest John Anderson, a fine hitting outfielder from 1894 through 1908, most famous for once trying to steal second with the bases loaded.

A native of Norway, the switch-hitting Anderson starred in the New England League before making his big league debut with the Brooklyn Dodgers in 1894. He was more or less a regular with Brooklyn from 1895 on, sold to the Washington club on May 19, 1898. *The Washington Post* said that:

> Anderson is one of the most reliable batsmen in the major League, a consistent outfielder, and steady-going, conscientious ball player.
>
> . . . Anderson is one of the most stalwart figures in the major League outfield, standing six feet one, and scaling at 190 pounds.

He had a fine season with Washington, and ended up leading the league in both triples (22) and slugging average (.494). Despite quality hitting stats he moved from team to team.

In 1899 he was with Brooklyn; they won the pennant.

In 1900 he jumped to Milwaukee in the American League. At that time the American League was a minor league.

In 1901 it became a major league; Anderson stayed with Milwaukee.

In 1902 the Milwaukee team moved to St. Louis, becoming the St. Louis Browns.

In 1902 and 1903 Anderson had two amazingly similar seasons, hitting .284 and slugging .385 in both campaigns.

In 1904 he was with the New York Highlanders. They lost the pennant on the final day of the season. (The trade register in Mac-Millan has him being both traded *and* sold to New York in the space of a few months. After poring over two New York newspapers of the time, we found no evidence of either transaction.)

In May, 1905, the Highlanders sold him to Washington. *The Washington Post* noted that "John Anderson is called the 'Human Chattel' because he is shipped from pillar to post."

Anderson played well in 1907, but the Senators were a truly bad team, finishing last by a healthy margin. On August 1, while playing first base, he was booed roundly after dropping a throw from an infielder. Two days later, the *Post* reported that "John Anderson has jumped the local ball club." A number of theories were offered, but for whatever reason Anderson had gone home to Worcester, Massachusetts, where he spent the remainder of the season.

There was talk of blacklisting Anderson, but it didn't happen, and he was sold that winter to the Chicago White Sox, for whom he played one season before ending his big league career.

Now, the incident. John Anderson was not forgotten after his retirement. On April 29, 1914, *The New York Times* reported that:

> Stovall's ball club [the Kansas City Packers] had a chance to score in the second inning, but [Pep] Goodwin pulled a "John Anderson" trying to steal third with the bases loaded. . . .

A John Kieran article in the March, 1932, *New York Times* placed the incident specifically in a 1907 Senators-Tigers contest.

The 1939 Pamphlet *A Century of Baseball* wrote that "Someone other than John Anderson may have been the first to steal an occupied base, but baseball records show that that doubtful distinction is his." Anderson was with the Washingtons when he perpetrated that faux pas, and it happened in the early 1900's.

Baseball by the Rules (1987) also places the origin of the "John Anderson" as being when Anderson was with the Senators; the authors wrote that "for decades after, a stupid play was described as 'a John Anderson.' "

The Dickson Baseball Dictionary, published a year ago, defines "John Anderson" or "john anderson" as:

> Term for the particular boner committed when a runner attempts to steal an occupied base. It has been passed down from John Anderson who, while playing for the New York Highlanders in 1904, pulled a John Anderson with the bases loaded.

Dickson's source appears to be *The New York Yankees: an Informal History,* Frank Graham's 1943 entry in the Putnam team history series, which describes the play.

Facing this mass of contradictory references, we decided to do a tracer on the event. So far, no luck. Rob Neyer has become ob-sessed with tracking down the occurrence, so it's something we talk about here in the office every day. Taking Frank Graham's history of the Yankees to be a reliable source, Rob went through the game accounts of every Highlanders game for the 1904 season. He found no mention of any such incident.

If you know what actually happened, we want you to know that we hate you, but please tell us anyway. If you don't know and can hold off a year, I figure Rob will eventually find it.

Mike Anderson, strong-armed outfielder in the seventies who spent most of his career with the Phillies.

Anderson went through the Philadelphia minor leagues one year ahead of Mike Schmidt, and went through them like a bullet. At Eugene (PCL) in 1971 he hit .334 with 36 homers and 100 RBI. Mike Schmidt, in the same park the next year, had an impressive year, but nowhere near *that* impressive, and Schmidt was twenty-two years old; Anderson was twenty. His hitting in the majors was so-so, but his defense drew raves; teammate Willie Montanez said Mike was the closest he'd seen to Clemente.

Anderson never did hit consistently in the major leagues, and had a nine-year career as a reserve.

Red Anderson, Washington pitcher just before World War II. In his brief career Anderson was more successful as a hitter, hitting .282, than as a pitcher.

Rick "Arlen" Anderson, briefly a pitcher with the Mets and Royals in the late eighties, and part of a one-sided trade which sent David Cone to New York.

Anderson threw a no-hitter in high school, one in junior college, one with the University of Washington, and in 1979 he tossed one for the triple-A Jackson Mets. He didn't make his major league debut until 1986, however, at the age of twenty-nine. Shortly thereafter, in a deal infamous to Kansas City baseball fans, Anderson was a throw-in in the deal that brought catcher Ed Hearn to the Royals in exchange for pitching prospect Cone. Anderson saw little action in KC, and was out of the majors by 1989.

Rick "Lee" Anderson, marginal relief pitcher in the early eighties who died of a heart attack brought on by obesity.

Anderson spent six seasons in the Yankees minor league system before being converted to relief pitching, leading the Florida State League and the Eastern League in strikeouts. As Columbus's closer in 1979 he was the International League's pitcher of the year, earning him a late-season call to the parent club. The Yankees still had Gossage, though, and they traded Anderson to Seattle the next spring. He got a brief trial with the Mariners, but developed serious arm trouble and was released early in 1982, retiring with no won-lost record in the major leagues.

On June 23, 1989, Anderson was found dead at the age of thirty-five in the converted truck trailer he was using as a home in Wilmington, California. His death was caused by arteriosclerosis, the result of obesity. The six-foot-two-inch Anderson, who weighed about two hundred and ten pounds during his playing days, was over four hundred pounds at the time of his death. *The Sporting News* reported that "when his body was discovered, Anderson was clutching a letter from a fan requesting an autographed baseball card."

(—R.N.)

Sparky Anderson, the only man to manage world championship teams in both leagues.

George Lee Anderson was born in Bridgewater, South Dakota in 1934. His family moved to California during World War II, and at the age of nine George became the batboy for the University of Southern California team. As a teen-aged middle infielder he caught the eye of scout (and later Angels manager) Lefty Phillips. "Nothing you do in baseball will come easy," Phillips told him. "Your only chance is to become an Eddie Stanky type." After high school graduation Phillips signed him to a minor league contract with the Dodgers.

Anderson began his professional career with Santa Barbara of the California League, and commenced the long crawl through the Dodgers farm system. He was a *good* minor league player, a consistent singles hitter and a fine second baseman. At Fort Worth in 1955 he was a teammate of Dick Williams, against whom he would later manage in a World Series, and several other future major league managers—Danny Ozark, Norm Sherry, Maury Wills. That summer the radio announcer gave him his nickname, "Sarky," by which he would soon be almost universally known. After a very solid year with Montreal in 1958, where he finished second in the voting for the International League MVP Award, Anderson was traded to Philadelphia for three players (two marginal major leaguers and a pitching prospect).

It didn't work out, of course; he hit just

.218, and lasted only one year as a major league player. He played four more years for Toronto in the International League before becoming the team's manager. It was not an auspicious debut. Umpire Bill Kinnamon in *The Men in Blue* observed:

> At that time [Sparky] was not in control of himself, and he did a very poor job of handling men. He was disliked by just about everybody concerned.

Sparky, in his autobiography *The Main Spark,* concedes that

> Impatience, my inability to tolerate defeat, or to tolerate a losing mentality, remained with me until I got fired after my first year of managing at Toronto in 1964. I didn't have any feeling for people. I wasn't nice. But losing that job made me think, especially when I didn't get another job right away.

The last minute resignation of the manager of the Rocky Hill (South Carolina) team created an opening for Sparky in 1965. Bob Howsam, the St. Louis Cardinals general manager, who hired him, was soon to move on to the Cincinnati Reds. Sparky managed in St. Petersburg, Modesto, and Asheville, becoming a coach with the San Diego Padres in 1969 (coaching, of course, for another old Dodger.) In 1970 he was tapped by Howsam to manage the Cincinnati Reds. He was thirty-five years old.

The '69 Reds had been contenders under Dave Bristol, but had fallen short due to an injury-plagued pitching staff. On offense they were loaded: Pete Rose, Johnny Bench, Tony Perez, Bobby Tolan, and Lee May, all in their prime. Anderson added six rookies to the team:

- For a starting pitcher (Jim McGlothlin), outfielder Alex Johnson was traded to California, where he became a batting champion and pain in the butt for Lefty Phillips, the very man who had signed Sparky to his first contract. Johnson's place was taken by a platoon combination of rookies Bernie Carbo and Hal McRae.
- Rookie Dave Concepcion took over as a half-time shortstop.
- Rookie Wayne Simpson went into the starting rotation.
- Rookie Don Gullett, just nineteen years old, became the top left-hander out of the bullpen.
- Rookie Angel Bravo was a pinch hitter and fifth outfielder.

The young players and the rookie manager lit a fire under the ball club, while the additions of McGlothlin, Gullett, and Simpson gave the pitching staff the depth to withstand injuries. Wayne Simpson started out 13–1. Johnny Bench won the MVP Award. They became The Big Red Machine, a name applied to them early in the 1970 season. They took first place on April 12—and kept it the rest of the year.

There were complaints during the spring that Sparky ran a "slave camp," but the winning solved that rather quickly. Howsam had already established the Reds as a bastion of conservatism in a tumultuous era with his insistence on black shoes, high socks, and clean shaves, and Sparky added a fourth dictum: short hair. Ray Knight, who played for him in both Cincinnati and Detroit, recalled the Sparky of the early seventies: "He always had a scowl on his face. . . . He used to argue with umpires strongly, fingers in the face, very feisty."

After a slide backward in 1971, the Reds traded for Joe Morgan, and became perennial powers. In 1972 Sparky make what he later admitted was one of the biggest mistakes of his managerial career. Never noted for being at a loss for words (Thomas Boswell has written that during the 1975–76 World Series Sparky would yell to reporters: "Hey, guys, where ya goin'? I'm not finished talkin' yet."), he went on record as saying that the National League playoffs between Cincinnati and Pittsburgh had brought together the two best teams in baseball, and would make the World Series an anticlimax. Cincinnati won the playoff with Pittsburgh, but the words exploded on him, as Sparky was introduced at World Series time to the 1972 Oakland A's.

Sparky, in his autobiography, is remarkably candid about that and other misjudgments he has made. In a chapter titled "My Biggest Mistake" he writes regarding the suspension and eventual trade of center fielder Bobby Tolan:

> I consider this my greatest failure as a manager because I sensed what was happening to him, saw it develop, and did not take the time to do something about it early in the crisis. When I finally did, it was too late.

His crusade against long hair carried over into his own family when son Lee began wearing his hair in a ponytail.

> It was a terrible shock to me. And if ever a man handled a family crisis poorly, it was me.

. . . Me, the guy who was getting credit everywhere for running the happiest baseball family in the country . . . I failed with my own son.

Overall, he was obviously not a failure. After winning the league in 1972 (but losing the World Series) and winning the division in 1973 (but losing the playoffs), the Reds had an "off year" in 1974. They won ninety-eight games that year, but Los Angeles, giving Walt Alston his last title, won even more. The Reds opened 1975 knowing that they still had something to prove. Early in the 1975 season Sparky shifted Pete Rose to third base, giving him the outfield of Ken Griffey, George Foster, and Cesar Geronimo. (When Foster began to pile up big numbers, Anderson cheerfully added that that had been another one of his mistakes, not giving Foster a chance to play earlier.) In one of the most exciting World Series ever played, the 1975 Reds won the World Championship.

The Big Red Machine was, first of all, an incredible collection of talent. Three automatic Hall of Famers formed the nucleus—second baseman Joe Morgan, catcher Johnny Bench, and Pete Rose—but the talent was so deep that, in thinking about it, you find yourself saying, "Oh, I forgot about Tony Perez," who used to drive in a hundred runs a year, or "Oh, I forgot about Dave Concepcion," probably the best shortstop of his generation. But they were, in fact, more than a collection of talent; they were a team. Led by Pete Rose, who treated rookies as if he had been waiting all his life to meet them, they worked together, played together, and pushed each other to be as good as they could be. Like the Yankees of McCarthy's era, they considered it a sin to take a single on a ball that could have been a double. They didn't tolerate it; they corrected one another's faults before those faults became losses. And they won a hundred games a year.

Yet it would be wrong to deny Anderson his share of the credit for that team. The team did have a perennial weakness: starting pitching. They had no number one starting pitcher. Anderson compensated by going to the bullpen early and often; that became the thing that he was most known for, as a field manager, earning him a subsidiary nickname, "Captain Hook." As he told *The Sporting News*, "It just isn't practical to allow a man who has thrown a certain number of pitches to stay in there when a guy with a fresh arm can finish."

The Reds won their second World Championship in a row in 1976, winning 102 games, sweeping the League Championship series in 3 games, sweeping the World Series in 4 games; that, of course, is the only time a team has swept both series.

After second place finishes in 1977–78, however, Sparky was unexpectedly fired. There had always been an undercurrent of doubt about his managerial ability, which he acknowledged when he told Boswell years later that "I felt that when I was fired in Cincinnati, it took all those accomplishments away from me. All I heard was how I had inherited a team of superstars and was just a 'push-button' manager."

Quickly hired in 1979 to rejuvenate the Detroit Tigers, Sparky began instilling (in slightly milder form) the type of discipline made famous in Cincinnati. It did not, initially, go over well. When some players anonymously complained about Sparky to reporters, he called them "yellowbellies," and pledged to clean house. But gradually, as the team improved and moved into pennant contention, Sparky seemed to mellow. Poorly-groomed free spirits such as Kirk Gibson were no longer anathema to him.

His image changed. He allowed his hair, which had been white since he came to the majors, to show its true color. He spent many hours visiting children's hospitals around the league. He began to be a bit of a media clown, developing a mock-ignorant interview style of double negatives, pithy quotes, exaggerated humility, and mysterious gerunds. He developed a reputation for hyping his young players, not that he hadn't always done that. Kirk Gibson was "the next Mickey Mantle." Chris Pittaro was going to move Lou Whitaker off second base.

There were some frustrating years for the Tigers in the early eighties, and Anderson began to come under fire. The 1984 Tigers won thirty-five of their first forty games, won the division easily, and won the League Championship and the World Series easily. Anderson, the first man to win World Championships for both leagues, passed into myth. He began to talk about beating John McGraw's record for career wins as a manager, making him second on the all-time list to Connie Mack.

The Tigers were no factor in the 1985–86 races. By 1987 they had been widely written off as too long in the tooth, but Sparky responded with perhaps his finest managerial job, platooning extensively and overhauling the Blue Jays in the last week of the season. After a near-miss in 1988, everyone realized that the Tigers had to rebuild. Sparky went far out on a limb in 1989, trading for malingering third baseman Chris Brown and handing first base on a platter to unproven Torey Lovullo. When these moves blew up in his face and the Tigers sank to the cellar early, Sparky collapsed. The team physician diagnosed exhaustion and sent him home for a complete rest. After three weeks he returned, explaining "I don't believe there's ever been an individual, except perhaps Gene Mauch, who takes losses harder and keeps them inside longer than I do. At this stage in my career, I don't believe I can hold every loss inside. The chemicals of the body won't allow it, and when the body fires back at you, it fires hard."

By the end of the '89 season, Sparky seemed to have learned how to deal with the losses, and professed himself to be looking forward to the challenge of rebuilding the last-place Tigers. It doesn't figure to be an easy task, but Sparky is only fifty-five years old. With or without adding another championship, his place in the Hall of Fame is secure.

(—M.K. and B.J.)

Varney Anderson, pitcher with Washington in 1895, later a manager in the Three I League (Rockford).

Wayne Anderson, longtime Dodger trainer.

In *Cincinnati Seasons*, Earl Lawson recalled that Reds players had arranged for Anderson to be ejected from the bench during his first major league spring training. Herm Wehmeier sat next to Anderson on the bench, screaming at home plate umpire John Stevens. Stevens, in on the joke, feigned anger; suddenly he spun around, stalked over to the Reds bench and ordered Anderson out of the game.

While Anderson was still trying to figure out what had hit him, Bob Addie talked a Western Union operator into sending him a phony telegram from the commissioner, fining him fifty dollars for his misconduct and warning him to watch his step in the future. The rookie trainer was sure this affair was going to cost him his job.

Wingo Anderson. Pitched briefly with Cincinnati in 1910. That was his real name—Wingo Charlie Anderson.

W. T. Anderson, president of the Georgia-Florida League, 1941–58.

Bruce Andrew, a scout with the major league scouting bureau.

Allen Andrews, a scout for the Giants, 1962–73; also a minor umpire.

Brent Andrews, assistant trainer for the Toronto Blue Jays.

Doc Andrews, a minor league infielder of the late 1890's and early part of this century, whose misfortune it was to love baseball and be not loved in return. Andrews' obituary in the 1926 *Reach Guide* reads:

> Surrounded by a book of base ball clippings and pictures of old-time major league stars, the body of Jay A. (Doc) Andrews, 68, former infielder with various teams in the old Western League, was found in his home at St. Paul, Minn., on November 2 [1925]. Death was pronounced due to the accidental turning on of a gas jet. Andrews left a medical course in the late 90's to play third base for Baltimore. Later he played with Minneapolis, of the American Association, and Joplin, Denver, Topeka, Oklahoma City and Des Moines, managing the latter team at one time."
>
> [*Age given is obviously wrong.*]

Ed Andrews, the center fielder and captain of Harry Wright's Philadelphia team in the mid-1880s.

In front of a huge crowd (reported over thirty thousand) in the last days of the 1886 season, Andrews made a spectacular game-ending catch of a bases-loaded drive hit by Detroit's Dan Brouthers. The game knocked Detroit out of the race. Chicago manager Cap Anson was so delighted with the effort given by the Philadelphia players, who had already been eliminated, that he bought a suit of clothes for each Philly player.

Ivy Andrews, pitcher of the thirties.

Andrews pitched briefly with the Yankees in 1931 and '32. After he was hobbled by lumbago and upstaged by Johnny Allen early in the 1932 season, the Yanks traded him to the Red Sox. The high point of his career may have occurred that season with Boston; he struck out Mickey Cochrane, Al Simmons, and Jimmie Foxx in succession.

Andrews pitched well for Boston after the trade, but fell off in '33; he was "handicapped early . . . after his pitching hand was bitten by a dog," according to an article in the December 14, 1933 *St. Louis Globe-Democrat,* describing a trade which sent Andrews to the St. Louis Browns. Andrews was traded to Cleveland in 1937, matching him up with Johnny Allen again, and then the Yankees, desperate for pitching help, paid the waiver price ($7,500) for the curve-balling Andrews, who found himself with the best team in baseball. He pitched well for the Bombers the remainder of the year, and saw limited action in the Yanks' World Series victory that fall. Ivy (that was his real name, so of course his nickname was "Poison") stayed with New York in '38, but didn't see action in that year's classic, and he didn't pitch in the majors again.

Herman "Jabo" Andrews, outfielder, pitcher, and manager with many teams in the Negro Leagues, 1930–42.

Mike Andrews, the central figure in the scandal which tainted the 1973 World Series and eventually contributed to the breakup of the powerful A's.

Andrews broke in with the Red Sox in 1967, their miracle season. The Red Sox had finished ninth in 1966 with a second baseman named George Smith, who hit .213, while Andrews had played second base at Toronto for Dick Williams. Despite some misgivings about Andrews' defense, Williams brought Andrews with him to Boston in 1967 (at one point he had announced that his plan was to make outfielder Reggie Smith, also a member of the Toronto team, his regular second baseman). As one of the greatest pennant races in history heated up, Andrews (along with second basemen Rod Carew of Minnesota and Dick McAuliffe of Detroit) became the subject of a death threat, apparently from a demented White Sox fan. The Red Sox brass, with Andrews's agreement, kept the story under wraps, and he received a few days of FBI protection. No one on the team, other than Dick Williams, was even aware of the threat. He was apparently unfazed, raising his batting average during the September stretch run, and in the subsequent World Series batted .308 and played errorless ball.

Andrews played second base for Boston for four years, making the All-Star team in 1969. He was one of the best-hitting second basemen in the league, and his defense was considered solid until a degenerating shoulder and a back injury which had troubled him since the winter before his rookie season left him rather rigid in the field and with no arm. (He had hurt the back working out with weights.) He was traded to the White Sox in exchange for Luis Aparicio after the 1970 season, but his defensive problems made him a part-time first baseman, and by 1973 his career was choking along as a DH, spare infielder, and pinch hitter. He was released by the White Sox in July, 1973, and rejoined Dick Williams in Oakland.

In Game Two of the 1973 World Series against the Mets, Williams used a pinch hitter for Dick Green, his starting second baseman, in the sixth inning. Ted Kubiak went in for defense, and in the eighth inning Andrews batted for Kubiak, becoming the A's second baseman.

A 6–6 tie, the game headed into extra innings. In the top of the twelfth inning the Mets had a one-run lead with the bases loaded and two out. The reason they had a one-run lead, not to forget any marginalia, was an RBI single by Willie Mays which scooted just out of Andrews's reach; it was to be Mays' last hit in a major league uniform. John Milner grounded the ball to second base, which should have ended the inning, but the ball went through Andrews' legs for an error, allowing two runs to score. As luck would have it, the next batter also grounded the ball to Andrews, and Andrews' throw to first pulled the first baseman off the bag, allowing another run to score.

Well, Charles O. Finley was furious at Andrews, and wanted him removed from the World Series roster. A player can only be taken off the World Series roster if he is injured, and so Finley forced the humiliated Andrews to sign an affidavit attesting that he was unable to play because of an injury to his shoulder and pressured the team physician to do the same. Andrews flew home to Massachusetts, but the statement was a sham and everybody knew it. His teammates, the press and the fans all rallied to Andrews' defense; the mistreatment of a player who had committed a couple of simple errors became an immense *cause célèbre.* Commissioner Bowie Kuhn ordered Andrews reinstated, fined Finley and issued a statement condemning Finley's action.

Now Finley was humiliated. He ordered Dick Williams not to play Andrews. With tears in his eyes, Williams told his players that he could not manage for a man who would do something like this, that he would leave the A's at the end of the series. Defying Finley, he put the somewhat embarrassed Andrews into another game as a pinch hitter. It was surely the only time in history that 54,000 fans at a World Series game have given a standing ovation to a utility infielder from the visiting team, pinch hitting with his team down 6–1. It was to be his last major league at bat; he was released a few days after the season ended.

The Andrews incident tore apart the A's. At least as the members of that team remember it now, there had always been individual hard feelings between Finley and members of the team, but until the Andrews affair there was no real hatred in it. After that the players regarded Finley with contempt, and Finley returned fire with ever more mean-spirited behavior. When free agency arrived a few years later, there was no way for Finley to keep the team together.

Andrews played a couple of years in Japan (1975–76), hoping the back would come around, but of course it didn't. He returned to New England, where he now serves as president of the Boston Jimmy Fund, and runs a baseball camp with an old Bosox teammate, catcher Gerry Moses.

(—M.K.)

Nate Andrews, pitcher in the forties, and briefly the "prize exhibit of the Boston Alcoholics Anonymous group."

Andrews made his debut with the St. Louis Cardinals in 1937, and saw limited action over the next few years with the Redbirds and, later, the Indians.

From Cleveland he went to the Boston Braves, and in 1943, with Uncle Sam having laid claim to a good portion of the major league talent, Andrews found himself one of the best pitchers in the league. He pitched in terrible luck; despite the fifth best ERA in the league, Andrews lost twenty games while winning just fourteen.

Prior to spring training in '44, Andrews went to an Alcoholics Anonymous meeting in search of help, and was "rescued," according to the February, 1945, *Baseball Digest*. He reported to camp in 1944, however, and his first day he "was pale, weak, unsteady. He lobbed a ball to a catcher so wildly that it hit Shorty Young, the clubhouse boy, who was standing nearby, on the noggin, and sent him to the hospital." Andrews eventually regained his strength to go sixteen and fifteen in '44, and he often spoke at AA meetings; leaders of that group said that the publicity given his fall and rise helped them save 150 men during the summer.

With the return of the ballplayer-veterans in 1945 and '46, Andrews lost his effectiveness, and the latter year was his last as a major league pitcher.

(—R.N.)

Pop Andrews, pitcher with the Brooklyn Royal Giants and Pittsburgh Stars of Buffalo, 1910 to 1919.

Rob Andrews, second baseman in the late seventies with the Astros and Giants, and brother of Mike Andrews.

Starting out in the Baltimore system, Andrews in 1974 finished third in the International League batting race, making the IL All-Star team. His path to the majors was blocked by Bobby Grich, and in 1974 Andrews and Enos Cabell were sent to Houston.

Andrews's two years in Houston saw him shuffled in and out of the lineup; at the start of the '76 season he was sent to Memphis so Larry Milbourne could play second base. Eventually he got back, and spent most of the 1976 season as the Astros' regular second baseman. In 1977 he was traded to San Francisco, where he played regularly until Altobelli decided to use Bill Madlock at second. The Giants cut him loose after the '79 season.

Stan "Polo" Andrews, born Stanley Joseph Andruskewicz, Andrews was personally scouted and signed out of high school by Bob Quinn, president of the Boston Bees in the mid-thirties. Polo had two things going for him—he was a native Bostonian (actually from Lynn), and the club president always liked him—but he had four trials in the major leagues and failed to hit.

Bill Andrus. A native of Georgia although actually born in Texas, Andrus's father, Claude, was a career minor leaguer. Bill was a well-regarded minor league infielder, a consistent .300 hitter who could play any infield position, but failed two trials in the major leagues.

Joaquin Andujar, temperamental star pitcher for the St. Louis Cardinals in the mid-eighties.

Andujar—one tough Dominican, as he likes to be known—was born in that cradle of baseball stars, San Pedro de Macoris, in 1952. Because of the poverty of his parents he was raised by his grandparents; at the age of sixteen he dropped out of high school and signed with the Cincinnati Reds. After a six-year gestation in the Reds system, where he never won more than eight games in a year, Houston traded for him on the advice of pitching coach Hub Kittle, who had managed Andujar in Dominican winter ball.

Andujar came to the Astros in 1976, and entered the rotation. He earned his first major league win on June 1, 1976 with two-hit, 2–1 win over Sparky Anderson's Big Red Machine, the organization which had never given him a chance. "Every dog has his day," commented Sparky Anderson; Andujar,

thinking Sparky had called him a dog, had to be restrained from going to the Cincinnati clubhouse to tangle with Anderson. Andujar's second win, four days later, was a two-hit shutout.

In 1977 Joaquin started fast and made the All-Star team, but was hampered by a pulled hamstring the second half and finished 11–8. In 1978 he began the season as the Astros' number two starter, but after a period in which he had to leave four out of five games with assorted physical problems (in one case jock itch) he was relegated to the bullpen, where he was a conspicuous failure as a late reliever. In 1979 he both relieved and started, made the All-Star team again, and once again faded in the second half of the season.

I worked Joaquin's arbitration case after the 1979 season. At that time his career record, despite two All-Star selections, was 37–37. Analyzing his record in excruciating detail as you do for an arbitration case, we noticed a clear pattern: Andujar almost always pitched well as long as he was getting regular work, but never pitched well when he was off-rotation or in an irregular work period. "Joaquin's really a nice guy," his agent told me a year later. "He just goes crazy when he's not pitching." Bill Virdon, who regarded Andujar as a head case, wouldn't leave him in the rotation and let him pitch, and Andujar responded by agitating. In 1980, the Astros' division-winning year, Andujar was still unable to crack the rotation and demanded a trade.

Andujar was dealt to the Cardinals in 1981. Awaiting him in St. Louis was the coach he respected most, Hub Kittle. Kittle asked him to discard his old windup, and Whitey Herzog put him in the rotation. The result was a remarkable improvement in his control, which had plagued him throughout his career. With the Cardinals he went 6–1 in 1981, 15–10 in 1982 including six wins in September. He started twice in the 1982 World Series, and won both games, including the seventh game. He also established his reputation as a hot dog, particularly infuriating the Brewers' Jim Gantner with his delayed throw to first on a comebacker, and contributed a memorable Yogiism: "There's one word that says it all about baseball—you never know."

"You never know" is Joaquin's favorite English saying, and at times it also says a lot *about* the tough Dominican. He turned in a miserable 1983 season, falling to 6–16, but rebounded to 20–14 in 1984, adding a changeup to his fastball/slider repertoire, and winning the Comeback Player of the Year Award. In 1985, off to a 15–4 start, he refused to participate in the All-Star game due to pique over Dick Williams's selection of LaMarr Hoyt as the starter. He struggled in the second half, posting six more wins to get to 21–12, and was ineffective in both the NLCS and the World Series. The most notorious incident in his career occurred in the seventh game of the 1985 Series when, with the game already out of control, he entered in relief, issued a walk, and charged plate umpire Don Denkinger in an ugly confrontation that led to his suspension and a trade to Oakland.

Dominican players justifiably resent the fact that they are portrayed as hot dogs, and in fact there is a good deal of respect for Andujar among the Dominican players. Andujar, according to Steve Wulf, is "charming, evasive, humble, egotistical, intelligent, suspicious, and generous."

"You want to know about Joaquin, I tell you about Joaquin," George Bell once told me. "When I was in the minor leagues I got hit in the face with the ball, and I couldn't stay in the box. I couldn't hit, because I didn't know I was bailing out. So Joaquin, he drilled me, right in the shoulder. Fastball. I say, 'Joaquin, you crazy, man? Why you hit me?' But he say, 'You didn't die, did you? I hit you with the pitch, and you didn't die. Next time you stay in there and hit.' And I did, and he turned my career around, because he showed me what I was doing."

But Joaquin *does* act crazy at times. With the Astros he once was observed taking a shower with his uniform on. He got in a fight with his best friend, Cesar Cedeño. He stepped out of the batter's box because a butterfly distracted him. In the Dominican he was suspended by the league for jumping his team. When he would strike out a hitter he used to blow the smoke off the end of his fingers, like it was a six-gun, and make a motion of sticking his fingers back in an imaginary holster; the hitters really appreciated that one. Fancying himself an architect, Joaquin drew up plans for a house, which he had built in the Dominican. He had drums put into the ceilings of one room so he could listen to the rain beat against them, over his head. Unfortunately, he didn't have the plans cleared by a *real* architect, and the concrete cracked almost as soon as it was poured, so the house was never

habitable; when he showed it to a *Sports Illustrated* reporter in 1983 there were pigs living in the basement.

In the American League Andujar could not stay healthy, going on the disabled list four times in 1987. He was accused of having a "contract arm," of being able to pitch but refusing to because he was unhappy with his contract. He developed an increasing sense of persecution. He implied that umpires were conspiring against him. "I have to throw the ball right down the middle," he complained. In his frustration, he raved that "The whole world is against me. . . . Some big men want

me out of baseball—I don't know who." He signed another contract or three but never regained his effectiveness; at this writing he is playing with the Gold Coast team in the Seniors League, and has signed a contract to attempt a comeback with the Montreal Expos.

(—M.K. and B.J.)

Joe Angel, radio broadcaster with the Baltimore Orioles.

Angel was born in Colombia, but his family came to Chicago when he was ten. They moved to the Bay Area five years later, where Angel quarterbacked on the same

TRACERS

Cy Morgan, also of the Red Sox . . . tried to skull me regularly. Eventually, at Boston, I was the runner at second base when he made a wild pitch . . . I rounded third with the throttle tied down. Morgan was at the plate, reaching for the catcher's recovery throw. I guess I hadn't taken more than three or four strides past third going home when Morgan had the ball in his hands, waiting for me.
I thought, Well, here's where we settle this. As I came down the line and went whipping at him with my steel showing, Morgan shocked everyone in the park. He turned and actually ran away from the plate.
I scored and Morgan was released by Boston that night. The Athletics picked him up.

—Ty Cobb
My Life in Baseball: The True Record (Pages 125–126)

It has the ring of a tall tale, don't it? As best we can tell, something very much like this did happen. On June 4, 1909, the Tigers played the Red Sox in Boston, Cy Morgan pitching for the Red Sox. The account of the game published the next day in the *Detroit News* gives complete details of all of the other Detroit runs, but only this sketchy account of the run scored in the fourth inning: ". . . in the fourth Cobb was passed and took second on another wild throw. That is how the Tigers came to have five [runs]." I suspect that the *News* writer was working from a summary of the game sent him by telegraph, and didn't understand what had happened in the fourth inning. He didn't explain how the run scored, but there are reasons to think that this may have been the play Cobb recalled:

1) Morgan, who had allowed only one hit and one run through four innings, was removed for a pinch hitter in the bottom of the fourth, his team trailing 1–0.

2) Morgan was not released that night, but he was traded the next day for somebody named Biff Schlitzer, who was exactly as good a pitcher as he sounds like he would be. It's an obviously inequitable trade—suggesting that the team had developed a sudden distaste for Morgan.

In a perfect world we would have checked the Boston papers, but we couldn't get ahold of the microfilm we needed. But this is definitely the incident in question, and for all we can learn it was accurately recalled.

(Almost all of the tracers were basically researched by Rob Neyer.)

high school football team with O. J. Simpson (incidentally, their team lost twenty-one consecutive games at one point). He attended City College of San Francisco.

Angel got his first major league baseball broadcasting job with the San Francisco Giants (1976–78), and later worked in Oakland (1980–81) and Minnesota (1984–86). In 1989 he teamed with Jon Miller to carry the Orioles games on WBAL radio. Curt Smith has described Angel as "duller than grease-pocked pans."

Roger Angell, senior fiction editor of *The New Yorker.*

Roger Angell is the son of Ernest Angell, a New York attorney, and Katherine White. From early in his life his step-father was E. B. White, one of the great men of American letters. Mr. and Mrs. White were top staff at *The New Yorker,* generally recognized as one of the world's best-written magazines.

Angell worked as an editor at *Holiday* in the fifties, writing a couple of baseball articles. About 1960 he moved to *The New Yorker* as a fiction editor. In addition to writing pieces of short fiction through the sixties, Angell in 1962, with the coming of the New York Mets, began writing about baseball for *The New Yorker.* His early baseball articles were written from a fan's standpoint, from the view of someone sitting in the bleachers, observing the game, the fans, the park. In 1972 Viking Press published *The Summer Game,* the first collection of his baseball pieces; that was followed by *Five Seasons* (1977), *Late Innings* (1982), and *Season Ticket* (1988). Over the years he has moved closer to the role of the traditional sports journalists, interviewing the participants and recording their thoughts, but never reporting events in the sense of writing to pass a record of what had happened. From 1962 to the present, he has written with a grace, wit, and attention to detail which the rest of us can only envy, and that has been the basis of his reputation.

A collection of satires and parodies, *A Day in the Life of Roger Angell,* was also published in 1970; not much baseball.

In *Here At the New Yorker,* Brendan Gill wrote that:

Unlike his colleagues, [Angell] is intensely competitive. Any challenge, mental or physical, exhilarates him, and the odder the nature of the challenge the better he likes it. Given the lack of athletic prowess that distinguishes most members of the staff of *The New Yorker,* Angell's mastery of certain unexpected feats—

for example, his ability to leap straight up onto a table from a standing start—fills the rest of us with awe.

Gill tells about accidentally getting into a "small-printing" contest with Roger, and about a war between Angell and Alastair Reid to see who could construct the longest palindrome, ending when Angell built one of 144 letters, perhaps the longest palindrome every written.

Angell is near retirement age and has talked of retiring. It is much to be hoped that in retirement he will continue to feel the tidal gravity of the ball park, and continue to bring a notepad.

Louis Angemeier.
From the 1912 *Reach Guide:*

September 23, (1911)—At Louisville, Ky., Louis Angemeier, noted minor league player, aged 25, died of swamp fever, contracted while playing with the Huntsville, Ala., Club, of he Southeastern League.

Jim Anglea, field superintendent for the Texas Rangers.

Sam Angus, owner of the Detroit Tigers in 1902 and 1903.

Angus, who had made a fortune from insurance and the railroad business, bought the Tigers after the 1901 season from George Stallings and James D. Burns. He brought Frank Navin, a bookkeeper in his insurance office, to the Tigers as a part of his management team, and gave or sold him a small interest in the team. In the winter of 1903–04 he sold the rest of his interest in the Tigers to William Yawkey (Tom's uncle) for sixty thousand dollars.

Fred Ankenman, Sr., president of the Houston Buffaloes (Texas League) from 1926 through 1943.

In 1930 the nineteen-year-old Dizzy Dean was sent from St. Joe to Houston. A few days after an impressive debut, Dean supposedly strolled into the team hotel at two in the morning and found his employer in the lobby. "Well, I guess you and me will get the devil for this, Mr. Ankenman," Dizzy said. "But I won't say nothing about it if you don't."

Though Dean threw a three-hit complete game in his only big-league appearance that year, he spent the entire 1931 season in Houston, where Ankenman was able to enjoy him for a whole year.

Pat Ankenman, Jr. As the tiny (five feet four inches, 125 pounds) son of a well-off

baseball executive, Pat Ankenman, Jr., had a lot to prove in baseball, and came mighty close to getting it all done. At the University of Texas in 1934 he hit .408, leading the Southwest Conference, and was selected to *College Humor* magazine's all-America team. Texas coach "Uncle Billy" Disch named Ankenman the best shortstop in the history of the Longhorns.

After a brief, unhappy trial with his father's team that same fall (1934), Ankenman joined Columbus in the American Association, where he had a sensational season in 1935, playing every game of the schedule (157 games), collecting 219 hits and leading the league's shortstops in putouts, assists and double plays. That established him a legitimate major league prospect despite his size, and he briefly played major league ball during the war. After World War II he was a minor league player-manager and manager for several years.

Adrian Constantine "Cap" Anson, the greatest hitter of the nineteenth century, and the man often held responsible for banning blacks from professional baseball.

Adrian Anson was born in Marshall, Iowa, on April 17, 1852, the son of Henry and Jeannette (Rice) Anson; he was the first white child born in that town, laid out and developed only the previous year by Anson's father. Anson was named for two towns in Michigan—Adrian and Constantine. The Ansons, who traced their family line back several centuries to an admiral of the English navy, had lived for three generations in Dutchess County, New York, before Henry Anson moved on first to Michigan and then to Iowa. Henry settled in 1851 among the Pottawotamie Indians, which gives Cap and I something in common; I also grew up in a small town among the Pottawotami (we spelled it without the "e.") Henry named the settlement "Marshall," also after a town in Michigan; this was changed to "Marshalltown" when they applied for a post office and learned there was already a Marshall, Iowa. According to Anson's autobiography, Henry later wished he had chosen the name "Ansonia," although we might keep in mind just the possibility that Anson's father was exaggerating his role in the founding of the town and the selection of the name.

Anson's mother, also according to Anson's autobiography, stood five foot ten and a half and weighed over two hundred pounds. She died when Adrian was seven years old (extending the parallel to the author; my own mother was a big, heavy woman, who died when I was a small child). Anson was a poor student, and was sent to State College in Iowa City as a teen-ager in an attempt to instill some discipline. That failing, he moved on to the University of Notre Dame, a fact which confuses many people; Notre Dame at that time ran a kind of boarding school more equivalent to a modern high school than to a modern university. At Notre Dame Anson excelled in baseball, football, and "fancy skating," particularly the latter. The Notre Dame baseball team was called the Notre Dame Juanitas (they should have kept the name), and their best player was Sturgis Anson, Adrian's older brother.

Marshalltown, Iowa, became the county seat, and sometime probably in the summer of 1866 baseball fever broke out there; the whole town seems to have been playing or watching baseball games every evening. The Marshalltown Stars developed a reputation as the best team in the state while Adrian was still young; his father and brother Sturgis were members of the Stars, while Adrian was on the second team. Adrian worked very hard as a baseball player, then, in 1866 and 1867:

> I was practicing early and late, and if I had any great ambition it was to play in the first nine, and with this end in view I neglected even my meals in order that I might become worthy of the honor.

The quote is from *A Ballplayer's Career*, Anson's 1900 autobiography. Adrian eventually made the team as a second baseman, and the Marshalltown Stars with the three Ansons claimed the Iowa state championship for several years.

One of the first professional teams to be organized west of the Mississippi was the Forest City Club of Rockford, Illinois, starring Albert Spalding. It isn't a long distance from Forest City to Marshalltown, and in 1870 a match was arranged between the Marshalltown Stars and the Forest City Club. "They had been winning all along the line by scores that mounted up all the way from 30 to 100 to 1," wrote Anson, "and while we did not expect to beat them, yet we did expect to give them a better run than they had yet had." Forest City won 18–3 and then won a rematch 35–5, scores close enough that those wagering on Marshalltown apparently collected most of the money.

After that game two members of the Marshalltown team, outfielder Sam "Pony" Sager and shortstop Pete Hoskins, joined the Forest City team and played some exhibitions with them. During the second game a fight had nearly broken out between Spalding and the senior Anson, but at the urging of Sager and Hoskins, the three Ansons were invited to try out for the Forest City team in 1872. Henry Anson had a business to run—several businesses, actually—and he kept Sturgis Anson to help him, but allowed Adrian to sign with Forest City. Adrian was paid $66 a month.

Anson's autobiography, which is well written, is full of stories which have the scent of being told a number of times before, and having perhaps acquired some character from the repetition. One story which I will repeat because it gives a sense of the time is that Clinton and Des Moines, Iowa, had a fierce rivalry over which had the better baseball team. They arranged a big match, and Clinton offered Anson $50—almost a month's salary—to play the game for them. Dying his hair and staining his skin so he would not be recognized, Anson set off to play the game, but was intercepted at the railroad station by his father, who asked him what the devil he thought he was doing. Anson explained that there was fifty dollars at stake, but his father would not permit him to take part in the deception.

You know why I believe the story? Because Anson loved to dress up. We will see him many times in the future putting on a costume or a disguise, putting on a show.

In any case the National Association, forerunner of the National League, was organized in 1871, with the Forest City team as one of the nine original members. Spalding and several other stars had jumped the team, and the Rockford group was left as the association's weakest. The nineteen-year-old Anson played third base and hit very well. (*The Baseball Encyclopedia* says that he hit .352, but due to the nature of the record-keeping in the National Association, that is basically a guess.) They called him "Baby" Anson, or "The Marshalltown Infant."

The Forest City team wanted Anson back in 1872 at the same salary, but the Philadelphia Athletics offered him $1,250 for the season. Anson took the offer to Forest City, and told them he would have to have at least $100 a month to stay with them. Losing money, they couldn't do it, and Anson left for Philadelphia. Forest City disbanded, and

Anson would not see his hometown again for several years.

The Philadelphia team was a strong one, Anson their best hitter. The Boston Red Stockings, with Spalding and Harry Wright, won the National Association every year from 1872 to 1875; the Athletics were the league's second-strongest team. Anson's salary grew slowly, up to $1,800 a year.

Anson loved Philadelphia, an exciting place for a boy from the Wild West; he spent long hours in the billiard parlors and took boxing lessons from a championship boxer. In the summer of 1874 the Athletics and Red Stockings made an exhibition tour to England. The trip was a great success from every standpoint except making money for its promoters; huge, adoring crowds, a warm press, and a genial relationship with British cricket players made the Americans reluctant to come home.

Anson loved London, too—in fact, for a while there he became quite fond of the night life. In a bar one night in 1875, back in Philadelphia, Anson was giving all hands the benefit of his knowledge about Philadelphia pugilists, which led to a fight between Anson and a city cop. Anson, covered with cuts and bruises, was eventually hauled to the police station. The president of the Athletics at that time was also the police commissioner, which hastened Anson's release from custody. Anson was brought before a magistrate the next morning and set free with a few stern words.

Retiring to a bar to celebrate his release, he had several rounds of beer and stumbled out the door, at which point he chanced upon a young woman whom he hoped to make Mrs. Anson. She expressed her opinion about men who drank to excess and got arrested in barroom brawls, and Anson's life was altered by that moment of humiliation. He stopped going to bars, never again drank excessively, and was involved in only one fistfight in the rest of his life, that coming when Anson punched out a man on a street car who had insisted that ballplayers would win or lose as suited their pockets.

The woman in question was Virginia M. Fiegal, the daughter of a Philadelphia hotel and restaurant owner. Anson had met her when she was quite young (twelve or thirteen), and began to court her some months after that; this apparently was not considered remarkable at the time. Another Philadelphia player, Charles "Pop" Snyder, was also intent upon winning Miss Fiegal's attentions. But as this courtship was progressing, in the summer of 1875, the National Association was being torn about by internal politics.

One of the causes of the association's dispute (or one of the consequences, depending on who you believe) was that four key players from Boston, including Albert Spalding, and one key player from Philadelphia, Adrian Anson, jumped their teams and agreed to play in Chicago. Anson had originally wanted to play in Chicago, which was nearer his home; he often said later in life how lucky he was that he didn't get to play for the Chicago team when he wanted to, because the first Chicago team was wiped out by the Chicago Fire in 1871, which might have aborted his career. In any case, in the winter of 1875–76 he agreed to join Spalding, Ross Barnes, Bob Addy, Paul Hines, Deacon White, Cal McVey, and others in Chicago; he was to be paid a reported $2,000.

When he told Virginia that he had signed to play in Chicago there was a bit of a scene. Anson assured her that he could purchase his release from his new contract, and traveled to Chicago to meet with Hulbert. He offered to purchase his release; Hulbert refused. Later in the winter he made another trip to Chicago for the same purpose, offering Hulbert $1,000; Hulbert still refused. Reports say that the Philadelphia team offered to pay him $2,500 to stay with the Athletics. No deal could be arranged. In protest, Anson showed up at the park one day in a Prince Albert coat and striped trousers—the dress of an eastern gentleman—and played the entire game in that garb.

The biggest reason he wanted to go back to Philadelphia, according to his autobiography, was Virginia. Concluding that he was stuck in Chicago and had better make the best of it, Anson wrote to Virginia's father requesting his daughter's hand. Mr. Fiegal agreed, and after the team's first game in Philadelphia that year Adrian and Virginia were married in a Philadelphia church.

The White Stockings won the National League in the league's first season, 1876. Two things of note happened at the end of the 1877 season: (1) the Ansons had their first child, a baby girl, and (2) Albert Spalding resigned as manager of the White Stockings to devote full time to his burgeoning sporting goods business, though he remained as part owner and was often visible at the ball park. Bob Ferguson managed the team in 1878; that didn't work out too well. By 1879

Anson was a veteran, a mature player at twenty-seven and a star, his hellraising days behind him.

He was named to manage the White Stockings in 1879. It was the role he was born to play. He became "Cap" Anson, the captain. The son of a large, loud, blustery small-town mayor, Anson grew to be larger and louder, even more intimidating, instinctively taking charge of whatever was around him. He scheduled daily workouts for his players, hard ones. When, in his first year as manager, Spalding came onto the field to express his opinion in a dispute between Anson and the umpires, Anson lit into Spalding with a string of obscenities. When Spalding refused to leave the field, Anson reminded the umpire that he could declare the game forfeit if Spalding didn't get off the field. Spalding retreated.

Six foot tall, maybe six one, Anson weighed over two hundred pounds and was always in perfect shape. He had a bullhorn voice which he used to berate and intimidate umpires, a major strategy of nineteenth century ball clubs. (The umpires, attempting to work games solo, were subject at this time to considerable abuse—tripping, bumping, shoving. It got worse before it got better.) He spoke his mind quickly and plainly, absolutely without fear; everybody knew where they stood with Anson. He worked very hard himself, harder as a player-manager than he had before, giving him the moral authority to insist on the same from his players. He was intelligent, strategically sound, and innovative in a game which was still evolving rapidly and therefore had fluid strategy. He was a good judge of ballplayers.

The team showed improvement in 1879, and in 1880 added the services of a young player named Mike "King" Kelly, who was to become the most popular player of the early 1880s, and Anson's only real rival in terms of marquee value. In 1880 the White Sox returned to the top of the National League, posting a 67–17 record. Backed by Spalding's pocketbook, the White Stockings prospered throughout the early eighties. They won the National League again in 1881, and won a third time in 1882 before falling out of the championship for a couple of years. In 1882 the White Stockings played a post-season series against the Cincinnati team of the American Association, a series sometimes listed as the first World Series. They played two games and split.

In September of 1882 the Ansons had a

son, Adrian Hulbert Anson; he was given the middle name of the Chicago team president and founder of the National League, William Hulbert, who had died in April of that year. The little boy died just four days after his birth. A second daughter, Adele, was born to the Ansons in 1884.

At a baseball clinic in his hometown of Marshalltown in 1883, Anson saw a young man named Billy Sunday, and signed him to play with the White Stockings; Sunday was a decent player, a good base stealer, and later became the most famous evangelist of the early twentieth century.

We come then to the ugly events which, as time passes, grow ever larger in the image of Anson. In the early 1880s there were a few black players playing professional baseball, not too many. Cap Anson was outspoken in his opposition to allowing black players to play major league baseball. He didn't exactly hate blacks; he just didn't consider them quite civilized.

Anson's autobiography does not discuss his role in drawing the color line, but does discuss at considerable length his relationship with a black minstrel named Clarence Duval, who the Colts kept as a mascot. He refers to Duval casually as a "little darkie," a "coon," and a "no account nigger." He quotes Duval as saying things like, "Spec's you's a' right, Cap'n," and tells that on joining the team "Duval was taken out, given a bath, against which he fought with tooth and nail." They treated him, in short, exactly as one would treat a dog.

The Toledo team of the American Association—a major league team—had a catcher named Moses Fleetwood Walker, a black gentleman, a college graduate, well spoken and well liked. On July 20, 1884, in Toledo, the White Stockings were scheduled to play an exhibition game against Toledo. The White Stockings secretary wrote a letter to Charlie Morton, Toledo manager, reminding him of Anson's feelings about black ballplayers, and thought that they had an agreement that Walker would not play. When the Chicago team got to the ball park, however, Walker was in uniform. Anson refused to play the game unless "that nigger" was removed from the field. The Toledo management told Anson that he could play against Walker or go home. Anson played the game—but spoke out loudly against it, insisting that gentlemen did not play baseball with niggers.

The incident is frequently cited as the

beginning of baseball's color line—in fact, the version of it usually printed until a few years ago was that Toledo had knuckled under, and Anson had successfully driven Walker from the field. The irony of the incident is that Walker was injured at the time, and would not have played in the game had not Anson attempted to dictate the conditions to Charlie Morton, who then put Walker in the game despite the injury.

But the engine of discrimination was in motion. Several leagues in the following months passed covenants banning "colored" players from participation. The Toledo team dropped out of the reorganized American Association in 1885.

The situation was unresolved. Black players were banned from some leagues, but continued to play in other leagues. In some leagues no one knew whether they were banned or not. There were no blacks in the National League or the American Association, the "major" leagues, but no one knew for sure whether or not he could sign a black player if he chose. Anson resumed his career.

In the spring of 1885 Anson brought his Sox to Sulphur Dell, Tennessee, for three weeks of spring training. Although teams had gone south for training for many years, even before the beginning of the National League, Anson apparently pushed spring training to new levels of organization, or something, and so is often credited (or miscredited) with having invented spring training.

Teams in the mid-1880s still relied heavily on one starting pitcher, and the decline of the Chicago team in 1883–85 can be traced in considerable measure to the decline of their number one pitcher, Larry Corcoran, although one must caution, too, that it would be many years before anyone would suggest that baseball was 75 percent pitching. In late 1884 Corcoran was supplanted by a hard-throwing sensation named John Clarkson, who won fifty-three games in 1885. The White Sox returned to the top of the league with a sensational 87–25 record.

Let us deal with Anson as a player. He stood with his heels together, very erect at the plate, and swung perhaps the heaviest bat in history. Most of the time he allowed the first pitch to go by; some accounts insist that he almost never swung until there were two called strikes on him, although the advantage in this would be hard even for Ted Williams to explain. He had huge, powerful hands.

Anson as described by Robert Smith: "Anson was six feet two, an erect, square-shouldered, lop-eared man, tightly muscled, of a slightly dour countenance. His eyes were deep and his gaze level and clear. His mouth was firm, his nose curved and badly proportioned, like something a child might draw. There was a fierceness in his nature which took the form of a stubborn honesty and independence, a grim clinging to prejudice, a tendency to express his mind loudly and directly, and a desire to go his own way—and have his own way."

Though Anson was a fanatic about conditioning and never drank to excess after his marriage, he was in his own way a rough character. When he thought that the umpire had done him wrong, or failing that, when he thought an umpire could be intimidated, he roared at the umpires with his remarkable bullhorn voice. In the 1880s this was not uncommon, but Anson and Comiskey were the leaders in making it more common. He bullied anybody he could bully, starting with the opposition; he would stand on the sidelines as a coach, and berate the opposition pitcher in a loud and offensive voice. He was "an acknowledged rough," said Henry Chadwick, and his influence on the conduct of the game was not a healthy one—but he had put together the best team in the National League, and that as he saw it was his job.

A great champion had also emerged in the rival league, the American Association; that champion was the St. Louis team of Charles Comiskey. The Browns played baseball in the same rough manner as the White Sox, with one distinction: The Browns were even rougher. The two teams arranged to play a series to determine the World Championship, as had been done the previous season. They had the devil's own time reaching a conclusion to the series. The first two games were played in Chicago. The first was stopped by darkness with the teams tied. The second game was stopped in the sixth inning by a fight, fan melee and general confusion; the St. Louis team had led through five innings, but Chicago had scored in the sixth to take the lead before the situation deteriorated.

Moving on to St. Louis, the Browns won two games cleanly; well, not cleanly, but without dispute. Moving on to Pittsburgh and Cincinnati, the White Sox won both games by 9–2 scores. I will pick up the story from the 1886 *Reach Guide*:

When the two teams met for the sixth game on the Cincinnati grounds on October 24, it was announced by Umpire John Kelly, in the hearing of over one thousand spectators just preceding the beginning of the game, that it had been agreed between the St. Louis and Chicago clubs that the game of that day would end their series, and as each club had won two games, the result of that contest would decide the series and the question of championship. Captains Anson and Comiskey stood close by while this announcement was being proclaimed, and neither, by word or gesture, affirmed or denied it.

St. Louis walloped them, 13–4, and thus claimed the championship. The Chicago papers, however, claimed that the Chicago team had won the uncompleted second match, and thus that the series had ended in a tie.

The argument over the disputed championship roared for a year, and grew hotter when both Chicago and St. Louis repeated as champions in 1886. Anson had a great year, driving in 147 runs and hitting .371—but then, Anson always had a great year; the only higher average belonged to his utility superstar, King Kelly, who hit .388. Chris Von der Ahe, owner of the St. Louis team, challenged the White Stockings, by now also called the Colts, to settle the question of championship once and for all. "We'll play your team," Anson told Von der Ahe, "on one condition—that the winner take every penny of the gate."

Anson looked upon the American Association champions as upstarts. It is impossible, at this late date, to sort out what was really said and done from the press notices sent forward to hype the gate, but in any case a best-of-seven series was arranged, and the public was told that it was winner-take-all. For the first time, the champions of two leagues would meet in a format resembling the modern World Series—seven games, four at one park and three at the other, no games on another field somewhere, no matches tapering off in indecision or indifference.

The first three games were played in Chicago, with Chicago winning two of the three. Traveling to St. Louis to play in front of the rowdy, beer-guzzling, insult-belching fans that Comiskey and Von der Ahe had cultivated, the Colts lost games four and five to fall one game short of defeat—for Anson, one game short of humiliation.

Clarkson started the sixth game for Chicago against Bob Caruthers. Heading into the bottom of the eighth the Colts held a 3–0 lead. The Browns scored; it was 3–1. With runners on first and second and more than ten thousand fans crowding around the field and screaming like maniacs, littering the field with debris, Arlie Latham ripped a triple to left field, tying the game at three. In the tenth inning Chris Welch raced home, sliding in with the winning run—the famous $15,000 slide. The St. Louis Browns were the champions of the world.

Cap Anson would remain a proud and imposing figure until the day he died thirty-five years later, but in a very real sense Anson's life passed its peak at that moment, and was lived forever after on a downward spiral. King Kelly, beloved by the fans but never a favorite of Anson's due to his heavy drinking, was sold to Boston for $10,000, an unprecedented figure at the time. George Gore, the star center fielder, had fought with the Colts constantly for more money. Anson's response was to sell Gore to the New York Giants. "I'll go," said Gore, "But if I do, you'll never win another pennant."

And he was right. Gore and Kelly would play for championship teams again. Anson never would.

The Colts slipped to third in 1887, but rallied to second in 1888. The Ansons lost another baby boy in January of 1888; he had lived four months. In early 1888 Anson signed a ten-year contract as manager of the Chicago Colts; he was also to receive 130 shares of club stock.

The hooves of racism were heard again in the background. In September, 1887, the Cuban Giants were scheduled to play a game against the champion St. Louis Browns. Comiskey's men refused to play the game.

In July, 1888, the Colts were scheduled to go to Newark to play an exhibition game. The Newark team of the International League had a star pitcher named George Stovey, a black man. John Montgomery Ward, shortstop and captain of the New York Giants, wanted the Giants to purchase Stovey, but the owners and manager of the team were reluctant.

Some white players in the International League began to grumble about playing against blacks. After a meeting of the International League's board of directors on July 14 it was announced that they would "approve no more contracts with colored men." On that same day, oddly enough, the *Newark Evening News,* unaware of what was happening at the league meeting in Buffalo, an-

nounced that George Stovey would pitch for Newark in an exhibition game against the White Stockings on July 19 at Newark.

But when the day came, Anson refused to play against Stovey; "Get him off the field," Anson reportedly said, "or I get off." Stovey, wishing to avoid an embarrassing incident, volunteered to withdraw.

Pressing his case in full voice and the full light of day, Anson argued that the National League must not permit itself to be infiltrated by darkies. The management of the Giants backed off on the purchase of Stovey.

By opening day of the 1888 season, the International League had no black players.

The color line had effectively been drawn. Black players were in effect banned from baseball.

When these incidents are written about today, Cap Anson usually bears the full weight of the responsibility for banning blacks. On a literal level, the portrayal of the color line as being a consequence of Cap Anson's racism is extremely naïve.

Anson had no authority by which to impose a decree of racial exclusivity.

The notion that Anson "intimidated" the National League into banning blacks is silly. Certainly, Anson was a great and imposing figure, but the National League at that time was full of great and imposing figures—Spalding, Chadwick, Ward, Harry Wright—many of whom had far more impact on the decisions of the league than did Anson.

One must remember that at this time Jim Crow laws were being enacted all over the country. According to C. Vann Woodward in *The Strange Career of Jim Crow,* "it was quite common in the 'eighties and 'nineties to find in the *Nation, Harper's Weekly,* the *North American Review,* or the *Atlantic Monthly* Northern liberals and former abolitionists mouthing the shibboleths of white supremacy regarding the Negro's innate inferiority, shiftlessness, and hopeless unfitness for full participation in the white man's civilization." A series of Supreme Court decisions between 1873 and 1898 reigned in the concept of unbridled equality, and cleared the way for the institution of separate facilities for blacks and whites. In 1877, in the case of *Hall v. de Cuir,* the Supreme Court decided that a state could not prohibit segregation on a common carrier (a coach, a boat, a train). If the company wished to segregate, they had that right. In 1890, in the case of *Louisville, New Orleans, and Texas Railroad*

versus *Mississippi,* the Supreme Court ruled that the state of Mississippi could *require* the railroad to practice segregation.

In the very year, even the month, when blacks were banned from baseball, they were also banned from countless streetcars, theaters, drinking fountains, trains, and restaurants by this little city and that great state and the other private business.

It is often remarked by baseball writers that it is strange that Anson, the leader of the segregationist forces, was not a southerner, and had suffered no injury at the hands of the race he opposed. But, again according to Woodward, "One of the strangest things about the career of Jim Crow is that the system was born in the North and reached an advanced age before moving South in force." In the South, slavery created its own conditions, conditions of ultimate inequality, but conditions in which the unhappy mingling of the lives of the blacks and whites was a daily necessity of work and custom. In the North, where blacks were "free," it was therefore "necessary" to develop a code of tradition and law to define what their limits were, what their place was, what they could and could not do. The result was that there was—and probably is to this day—far less regular, daily interactivity between the races in the North than in the South.

When slavery was abolished, the relationships among the races in the South took place in a kind of ethical vacuum; for twenty years no one knew what the rules were. Blacks could and did run for office, win elections, hold office, go to schools, own property, own businesses, sit on juries, and go to public places and public events alongside whites—but not to romanticize the moment, it was also in this ethical vacuum that the Ku Klux Klan was born.

The system of Jim Crow practices probably would have come south immediately after the war, except that at first the hatred of the South for the North was much greater than the dislike for the former slaves. After a generation, the anger of the South toward the North began to cool, while the anger of white southerners toward black southerners grew greatly—and then the South adopted with great vigor the segregation practices which had grown up in the North. It was in this period—twenty years after the war—that Jim Crow laws swept the nation.

In this climate, it is enormously likely that Jim Crow would have come to baseball even had Cap Anson never been born. And the portrayal of the banning of blacks as originating in the mind of Cap Anson—which is the most common portrayal of the events in baseball histories—is bizarre.

In books written now Anson is often described as an "overt" racist—but in the context of the late nineteenth century, this is a meaningless description. There were no "covert" racists in the 1880s; if you didn't like blacks or didn't think whites should associate with them, you said so.

This is not written to mitigate Cap Anson's moral responsibility. When one makes oneself a spokesman for racial intolerance, one becomes morally responsible for the pain that racism inflicts upon its victims. But the weight of Anson's voice was derived entirely from one thing: that he was a spokesman for the *majority* position. For the sake of historical accuracy, it is important to understand that what happened in baseball was simply what was happening throughout America at the time.

Attempting to promote baseball worldwide, Spalding organized a famous world tour in the winter of 1888–89; Anson of course was a part of the tour—as, for that matter, was Clarence Duval, the black man who served as mascot. The trip went through Chinatown in San Francisco. Anson's views of "Chinamen" were as enlightened as his views of blacks. Anson's experiences in Australia, France, Egypt, etc., occupy a huge portion of his autobiography.

In August of 1889, the Ansons had their third baby girl, Dorothy.

In 1890 the National League was split in a great rift (see article in section two on the 1890 season). While most of the great stars of the game switched to the Players' League, Anson, a part owner of the Colts, stayed in the National. Naturally, Anson was outspoken in his criticism of those who departed, talking about how greedy they were.

The Colts were forced to put together a mostly new team, with young and inexperienced players. This resulted in a change of name for both Anson and the team. The Colts, because of their youth, were called the Cubs; formerly the Chicago White Stockings and the Chicago Colts, they became forever after the Chicago Cubs. Anson himself, once known as the "Marshalltown Infant," reached his final stage as "Pop" Anson.

With the aid of Spalding's pocketbook, the assembly of the 1890 team was accomplished fairly well. The Cubs, for one thing,

kept more of their key players than most of the other teams in the league. When the defectors returned in 1891, Spalding, like the other managers around the league, was forced to piece the two teams together into one, and again he accomplished this fairly well. But when the American Association folded into the National League in 1892, there was a further compression of the talent; players who had been in the AA were either retained in the National League on existing teams, cut loose to lower leagues or sold to the other National League teams.

The short-run effect was that the quality of play moved up a notch, and the Chicago team did not meet the challenge. Hugh Duffy, a rookie with the Colts in 1888, defected to the Chicago Players' League team in 1890, signed with the Boston team in the American Association in 1891, and was sold to Boston in the National League for 1892—improving a Boston team which was already the best in the league. The Chicago team also added some players, but Spalding was gone by then, and without his aid Anson didn't choose right, or didn't put out enough money, and the Cubs began to drift out of contention.

Anson himself, thirty-eight years old by 1890, was no longer a dominant player, although remarkably enough he was still a good one. On September 4, 1891, after some newspaper men had commented on Anson's age, he had an answer for them. From the September 5, 1891, *Chicago Tribune:*

> When the Chicago players straggled on the field at the West Side Park yesterday afternoon the crowd was electrified to see in their midst a figure strangely familiar except as to its facial adornment and the snowy whiteness of its flowing locks. It was a commanding figure, with a beard of fulsome quantity that concealed even the lettering on the flannel shirt that covered an expansive chest. Hoary age clad in a baseball suit is an unknown quantity, and the crowd marveled in consequence. It recalled to the bleachers youthful visions of the revered Santa Claus, except that Santa Claus in white flannel knickerbockers and spiked shoes was rather contrary to the tradition. As the figure slowly approached the diamond some one with better powers of discernment than the others cried out: "Oh! it's only Anson." And so it was. The grand old man of baseball was hurling defiance into the teeth of age by aping its appearance.

When this story is told today it is usually added that Anson, playing the game in the beard and whiskers, had three hits. Actually

he did not; he went hitless, but the Cubs did win the game.

Anson was in a creative period. On August 6 of the same season, Anson batted against Kid Nichols. Just as Nichols would get set to pitch, Anson would jump to the other side of the plate, switch around as if to bat left-handed, then right-handed, etc. Nichols looked at him as if he was half-crazy, which wasn't necessarily false, and waited for him to stand in and hit. Anson kept jumping from side to side.

At last Billy Nash, the Boston coach, asked the umpire to tell Anson to cut it out, to stand on one side of the plate or the other. The umpire, named McQuaid, said there was no rule that Anson couldn't do that if he wanted. Nichols refused to pitch, Anson continued to jump around, and the umpire, perhaps intimidated by Anson, refused to order him to stop. At last the umpire sent Anson to first base, ruling that he was entitled to first base since Nichols had refused to pitch to him. Nichols said he couldn't pitch because Anson's body was in the way.

So they made a rule about that, that if a hitter switches positions in the batter's box after the pitcher is set he is called out. The rule is still in the books; you may remember it was the subject of a beer commercial a few years ago.

Anson loved to play games like this; there are several other incidents on record in which Anson tried to exploit a hole in the rules or something similar. On July 13, 1887, Anson pulled up at third after hitting a home run. His team was down 3–0 in the ninth inning. At that time catchers played up close behind the batter with a man on base, but back away from the catcher when there was no one on. For that reason, they were more reluctant to call for fast balls with a man on base, when they had to stand "under the bat" and catch it. Anson figured if he stopped at third the other team wouldn't throw fastballs, and his team's chance of coming back would be better. It didn't work; the catcher (Connie Mach, by the way) played back away from the plate as if there was no one on base.

In the off season, Anson cashed in on his popularity by working in vaudeville. He had a slapstick routine in which he would wear green whiskers, was squirted in the face with soapy water, had buckets emptied on him, and sang silly songs.

Eventually, in December, 1895, Cap's acting career took him to Broadway. Charles

TRACERS

There were betrayals, too. Like Comiskey's promise to give Cicotte a $10,000 bonus in 1917 if he won 30 games. When the great pitcher threatened to reach that figure, it was said that Comiskey had him benched. The excuse, of course, was to rest him for the World Series.

Eliot Asinof
—Eight Men Out (Page 21–22)

Asinof's source for this is unclear, and one begins by wondering how a story of this nature surfaces forty years after the fact. Obviously there is a paper trail somewhere, in accounts of the trials or something. In John Sayles's 1988 movie, this incident was turned into a tense dialogue between Cicotte and Comiskey, occurring not in 1917 but shortly before the 1919 Series. I had assumed in watching the movie that the incident was moved for dramatic convenience, but actually, Sayles's version of the story may have a stronger foundation than Asinof's.

I made a list of every game the Sox played in August and September of 1917. In those two months Cicotte started thirteen times, just missing the team lead, and never went more than five days between starts. He pitched several times with just two days rest, and also made four lengthy relief appearances.

Cicotte *was* trying to win thirty games that year. On September 20, after a Cicotte loss, the *Chicago Tribune* reported that "Eddie Cicotte was after his twenty-seventh victory and felt the defeat keenly. He wants to win thirty games, but will hardly have a chance now unless lucky." He may well have had a bonus agreement in 1917, but the *Tribune* does not mention it, and Cicotte was *not* deprived of the opportunity to win thirty by being held out. He led the league in innings pitched by a wide margin.

But looking at the final two months of the 1919 season, I found something quite different. Cicotte started six games in August, of which he won four; he also picked up two wins in relief. His steady work enabled the Chisox to open September with a seven-game lead over Cleveland. The first of the month saw Cicotte allow just one run in beating the Tigers, and he won his eighth straight decision four days later, again allowing just one run, this time to Cleveland.

It was two weeks before Cicotte would again take the mound.

Here are the three references to Eddie Cicotte that I found over those two weeks, all from the *Chicago Tribune*.

9/13 Boss Gleason figured that Wilkinson would know just as much about how to pitch to the string of rookies Mack used as Eddie Cicotte

would, so accepted the chance to rest up his star and give his own recruit a chance, for which Wilkinson had been begging.

9/14 By giving his two pitching aces a rest, Manager Gleason figures he may be able to clinch the championship in New York by using them there.

9/19 The White Sox still have their ace pitchers in reserve and well rested up in case nobody can beat Cleveland a game. Cicotte and Williams probably will get only enough work to insure their control for the rest of the season.

While resting Cicotte in the heat of the pennant race, Gleason gave starts to Lefty Williams, Dickie Kerr, Big Bill James, Kerr again, Williams again, Roy Wilkinson, Grover Lowdermilk, Red Faber, Kerr again, James again, and Erskine Mayer, before getting back to Cicotte on September 19. After the action on the fifth, the Sox led by seven games; after the nineteenth, by six and a half.

Cicotte finally started on the nineteenth and beat the Bosox, 3–2. The following appeared in next day's *Tribune*, under a subheadline reading GLEASON SLAB ACE SHOWS RECOVERY FROM SLUMP; DESERVES SHUTOUT:

Eddie Cicotte demonstrated that he is back in form by pitching a near shut-out game against Boston's Red Sox today . . . The last previous time Cicotte pitched, as you remember, was in Chicago early in the month, and he gave six bases on balls, indicating that the strenuous pace was beginning to tell on him.

Control has always been the chief factor in Eddie's success. Frankly, [illegible] Gleason and others of the White Sox clan admitted today they were worrying about Eddie for fear he might not be right for the series. They kept their fears to themselves, however, until Cicotte showed them that all he needed was the rest he has had, for he did not give a base on balls and seldom was in the hole to the [illegible].

Obvious Question: When the heck was he *out of form?* As of September 6, Cicotte had won his previous seven decisions, including five starts and two relief appearances. In the five starts, opponents scored a total of only nine runs.

After his "comeback," Cicotte made two more regular-season starts. On the twenty-fourth he started against the Brownies, but didn't pick up the pennant-clinching win. That honor went to Dickie Kerr in relief. And on the twenty-eighth Ed picked up another no-decision when he hurled only two innings against the Tigers in what was presumably just a pre-Series tuneup.

It seems to me that there are two things we need to know here: First, was Cicotte promised a $10,000 bonus if he could win thirty games, and second, in late 1919 was he handled in a way that was designed to prevent him from reaching that plateau?

To the first question, I don't have a definitive answer.

We have more evidence regarding the second question, but we may have just as much difficulty arriving at a definitive conclusion. There are at least three factors which would seem to justify resting Cicotte for a couple weeks: 1) He gave up six walks in his start on September 5, an extremely high number for him; 2) the Sox seemed to have the pennant race well in hand; 3) Cicotte turned thirty-five years old in June of 1919. The Sox' second best pitcher, Lefty Williams, was also rested during those two weeks, though not to the same extent as Cicotte. And Cicotte, with twenty-nine wins in 1919, *was* allowed to start twice and go for his thirtieth win, though in the second of those games he was lifted after two innings.

At least by modern standards, it was an extremely strange way to run a pitching staff during the pennant race. If Cicotte *did* have a thirty-win agreement with Comiskey, he obviously would have resented being held out of the action for two weeks in September, no matter who made the decision. Cicotte almost certainly would have won thirty if he hadn't been out of the rotation (such as it was) for two weeks in September of 1919, but it is not clear whether or not this was done to prevent him from earning a bonus.

—Rob Neyer

H. Hoyt, a popular playwright, wrote a play for Anson to star in; it was called *A Runaway Colt*; it premiered in Chicago before moving on to the American Theatre on Broadway. According to James Mote's wonderful book *Everything Baseball*, the play involved a minister's son named Manley Manners who was recruited by Anson, as himself, to play for the Colts. It was a melodrama, involving a bad guy's attempts to force Manley Manners's fiancee into an unwelcome marriage. The *New York Dramatic Mirror* reported that Anson's performance was "quite as good as most of the people on the stage with him," but added that "He speaks his lines with the directness of an artillery officer, no matter whether he is accepting an invitation to dinner or defending the good cause of professional baseball." A few weeks was the extent of his Broadway career, but that was one of Anson's descriptions of himself: a better actor than any ballplayer, a better ballplayer than any actor.

Another story from this era, since we're having fun here, involved a swaybacked white horse which the groundskeeper for the Chicago park kept to pull his equipment. The horse's name was Sam, and when he wasn't working he browsed in a field behind the clubhouse down the right-field line.

Sam, for some reason, didn't like Pop Anson, and he would lay back his ears and snort whenever he saw him. Well, one day a Louisville player grounded the ball to Bill Dahlen, and Dahlen threw wildly to first base. The throw hit the stands and bounced out toward right field. Anson was chasing the ball up the right field line, when he looked up and saw a horse. Somebody had left a gate open, and Sam had gotten onto the field.

Now, Anson was not afraid of any man on earth, but a horse is another matter altogether. Anson and the horse looked at each other for a second. Anson glanced at his glove, as if maybe he would throw that at the horse, and decided that wouldn't help much, so he took out running. The horse took out after him. And the batter scored, because there just wasn't any rule that said how many bases you could advance while the first baseman was being chased by a horse.

I don't know exactly when that happened, to be honest. The other two stories, about the beard and the jumping from side to side of the plate, are true and accurately reported, but we didn't get a chance to trace this one down.

Anyway, that was 1891, which was maybe the last good year of Cap Anson's life. In May, 1892, the Ansons had their third baby boy, and for the third time the child died in infancy, at the age of four days. Though the Ansons had four daughters of whom Cap was enormously proud (the fourth was born in 1899), he idolized his own father, and no doubt very much wanted a son. He was a family man. The *Chicago Post* reported that on one occasion

"Adrian Constantine Anson has given the New York Sun a few reflections concerning the duties of womankind . . . Mr. Anson thinks that the average woman cannot attend to her regular knitting and to clubs at the same time, and he fecilitates himself that the ladies of his immediate family have been restrained by his influence and his arguments from wasting time in society work that should belong to the needs of the small and sympathetic domestic circle."

Fun guy, Cap was.

Anson began to have trouble with the team's owners. On the round-the-world trip several years earlier, one of the part-owners of the team, James A. Hart, had accompanied the team to act as financial manager. Spalding had organized an effort to get everybody together to buy a nice gift for Hart, a set of diamond cuff links. Everyone on the trip had contributed—except Anson. "Why should Hart get a gift like this?" Anson wanted to know. "I'm doing the biggest work around here. He's being well paid for what he does. I'm not going to give him a nickel."

The relationship between Anson and Hart was cool ever after that, and probably had been cool before. In 1891 Spalding resigned as president of the Colts; Hart was elected to replace him.

Hart was foolish enough to second-guess Anson on such things as Anson's choice of players and Anson's dislike of the bunt, but the most serious problem between the two of them centered on the training habits of the players. Always a strong disciplinarian, Anson attempted to deal with the decline of his team by becoming stricter. He did not allow his players to drink or smoke. He was a strict taskmaster, demanding precise performance of team drills. Anson would fine his players for drinking, misconduct, or insubordination—but Hart would not levy the fines. As the team slipped away—they finished under .500 in 1892, '93 and '94, rallied somewhat in '95 and '96, and slipped again in '97—Anson began increasingly to quarrel with everyone around him. He fought with his players, the management, the league, the opposition, the press, the umpires. "That ain't no shadow," one of his players remarked about the dark image on the ground behind Anson. "That's an argument. Everywhere Cap goes, the argument goes."

A newspaper reporter in the mid-nineties asked Anson to name his all-time team. He did, naming himself the first baseman. He was criticized, of course, for his arrogance.

"They wanted my opinion and I gave it to them," said Anson. "I did not permit a false modesty to keep me from giving him an honest answer."

Jokes about Anson's age became common. A letter to *The Sporting News* in 1897 contained the following bit of verse, from a fan named Hyder Ali:

How old is Anson? No one knows.
I saw him playing when a kid,
When I was wearing still short clothes,
And so my father's father did;
The oldest veterans of them all
As kids, saw Anson play baseball.

In 1897 the ten-year contract Anson had signed in 1888 drew finally to a close. After Chicago had lost a close game in 1897, Anson approached sportswriter Hugh Fullerton of the Chicago *Inter-Ocean* in the Pittsburgh railroad station, and accused Fullerton of being a coward. Why, Fullerton wanted to know, was he a coward? "Because," Anson said, "you won't print what I tell you. You're protecting them," Anson said.

"Protecting who?" Fullerton asked.

"These ballplayers," Anson said, gesturing toward his players. "You're afraid to write the truth."

"And just what is the truth?"

"The truth," said Anson, "is that they're a bunch of drunkards and loafers who are throwing me down."

Fullerton said that if he wrote that he'd get sued.

"Well then," replied Anson, "say that I said it."

"But what if you deny it," Fullerton asked?

Anson shook his fist under Fullerton's nose. "Do you think I'd deny it?"

"No. You're bullheaded enough to stick to it, and make it worse."

"All right," Anson insisted. "Put it in blackface type at the head of your column."

The next day Fullerton wrote:

CAPTAIN A.C. ANSON DESIRES ME TO ANNOUNCE, IN BLACK TYPE AT THE HEAD OF THIS COLUMN, THAT THE CHICAGO BASEBALL CLUB IS COMPOSED OF A BUNCH OF DRUNKARDS AND LOAFERS WHO ARE THROWING HIM DOWN.

That, of course, was the end for Anson; there was no way then that his contract would be renewed. Remarkably, Anson had survived the ten years not only as a manager, but as a player. Forty-five years old in 1897, he still hit .302—a poor average for a first baseman in that era, but not the worst in the league.

There followed a period of intense politicking, as Anson attempted to find a way to save his job. I don't really understand the ownership group of the Cubs at this time—apparently several men owned parts of the team and ran it among themselves, almost with a country-club type arrangement. Spalding remained as part-owner, and as the richest and most powerful voice in the group, although not the most active in club politics. Anson approached Spalding and asked about the possibility of his (Anson's) buying some additional stock, buying out some people who might oppose him, so that he could remain in control of the team. Spalding, who had to know that Anson's departure was in the best interests of the team, gave Anson a polite response . . . sure, he'd talk to some people, see what he could arrange. When Spalding didn't come through, Anson accused Spalding of stabbing him in the back, forcing him out after the two of them had worked together for more than twenty years. Anson was given a price on some additional stock, but couldn't raise the money. He accused Spalding of visiting the sources from

which he had tried to borrow the money, and persuading them not to make the loans.

Spalding, by 1898 a financial giant, was certainly capable of dropping a word or two with a banker, but whether he actually did will probably never be known. The public was very much on Anson's side in this dispute. His tirades against his lazy players, however much they might damage the team, sat well with the public. "Baseball as at present conducted is a gigantic monopoly intolerant of opposition," Anson said, "and run on a grab-all-that-there-is-in-sight basis that is alienating its friends and disgusting the very public that has so long and cheerfully given to it the support that it has withheld from other forms of amusement. . . ."

Trying to patch things over, Spalding sponsored a fund which was to be collected and given to Anson as a token of esteem. The goal was to raise $50,000. Anson hotly rejected the offer. "If I need help," Anson said, "I'll go to the county welfare office. Baseball owes me nothing." Spalding contacted the league office, and offered Anson a position as National League umpire-in-chief. Anson refused that, too. He accused Spalding of using his name, without his permission, to promote a "Baseball School," which in reality was a scheme to sell some of Spalding's real estate. It was a parting, in other words, to give a bad name to ugly partings.

The Cubs, without their "Pop," were for a time known as the Chicago Orphans, or

A FRIEND WISHES TO COMMENT

With respect to the burning issue of Joe Jackson's performance in the 1919 World Series, Lloyd Johnson wishes to point to the following facts:

1. During the series, *three* triples were hit to left field where Jackson was playing. (Triples normally are rarely hit to left field; almost all triples go to right field or right-center.)

2. In Game Two, Jackson held third base on a ground ball to short with less than two out.

3. In the fourth game, Jackson made a throw on which Eddie Cicotte was charged with an error, leading to a damaging run.

4. In the games which were lost by the Sox, Jackson hit poorly with men in scoring position.

5. Jackson signed a confession.

6. Jackson also told a sportswriter, Westbrook Pegler, that he had "only poked at the ball" in the key games.

7. Jackson accepted $5,000, with the knowledge that the series was being fixed.

"Anson's Orphans." The name was dropped after a while; the newspapers went back to "Cubs."

Bill Joyce was fired as manager of the Giants early in 1898. As a favor to friends in New York, Anson accepted the job as manager of the Giants, a team whose ownership group would make the Chicago arrangement look like a Boy Scout troop. He lasted only a month in that job, departing after a round of bickering with Andrew Freedman. Joyce returned for the rest of the year.

Anson tried to buy a Chicago franchise for the Western League, but Spalding, who had franchise rights to the Chicago area, refused his consent. "Twenty-two years with that man," Anson said, "and look how he treats me now."

In the spring of 1899 something called the "New American Base-Ball Association" met in Detroit, and planned to revive the old American Association. Anson was president of the League's board; they announced plans to launch the league that summer, and when that failed, retrenched and aimed for 1900. This was a different organization from that which did launch the American League in 1901, although many of the same people were involved, including John McGraw, Francis Richter, and Frank Navin. Anson was offered a chance to be involved with the "second effort" which did result in the American League, but scorned the effort, ostensibly because he did not want to dishonor his twenty-plus years in the major leagues by being involved with a minor league team, but more probably because he was not offered what he considered an appropriate position.

It is apparent that by 1900 Anson's financial position was none too strong. He had made a good deal of money over the years, but appears to have lost most of it in bad investments. His father had been a businessman, and Anson, like most athletes, idolized his father, and then too there was the longtime rivalry with Spalding, who parlayed his baseball career into a multi-million-dollar fortune. Anson figured he was just as smart as Spalding and if Spalding could do it he could, too. He invested in billiard parlors, ice rinks, toboggan slides. At one point he owned several bowling alleys. He invested in a golf course and a handball court. He invested in a company which bottled ginger beer, but the bottles kept exploding.

Some reports say that Anson did become chief of umpires in the National League for a while, although I'm not certain of this. He was elected city clerk of Chicago in 1905, and served in that capacity from 1905 to 1907.

He continued to try to find ways to market his fame. In 1909–10, Anson formed and managed a semipro team which toured the country, playing spring exhibitions against major league teams and barnstorming through smaller towns in the summer. Nearing sixty, Anson played with the team.

The venture made no money, and Anson resumed his career on the stage. He formed an act with his two daughters, "Cap Anson and Daughters." Years later, his daughter Dorothy recalled the performances:

> We had two pretty fair writers, Ring Lardner and George M. Cohan. Papa wore tails while he delivered a monologue. My sister Adele and I were dressed in fur-trimmed evening gowns for the first part of the act. The finale was all baseball. We changed to sport clothes and carried a huge bag filled with paper-mâché baseballs made for us by A. G. Spalding. As we threw the balls into the audience, we sang "We're going to take you to the game/Where dear old Dad won his fame." That was a cue for Pop to appear wearing his old Chicago uniform and carrying a silver bat which had been given to him by Notre Dame alumni.

Anson would set up in his stance, as if at bat, while members of the audience would toss the papier-mâché baseballs at him, and he would hit them back.

This didn't bring in as much money as managing the Cubs, and Anson was forced into bankruptcy. He lost his house. Once again, an effort was launched to raise money for him, and once again he refused it. The National League attempted to establish a pension fund for him. The National League president at this time was John K. Tener, who had once pitched for Anson. Anson said more emphatically than ever that he could take care of himself, and wanted no charity.

In 1921, in the wreckage of the Black Sox scandal, baseball was looking for its first commissioner. Anson let it be known that he thought himself well qualified for the post.

In early April, 1922, Anson was appointed to manage a new golf club, the Dixmoor Club in Chicago. He died suddenly a week later, April 14, the victim of an apparent heart attack. He left no estate, and a request that his gravestone read "Here lies a man who batted .300."

The league paid the funeral expenses, and established a fund to create a "fitting memorial" for Anson. The body of Anson's wife was removed from its resting place in Philadelphia, and brought to lie in Chicago with that of the man who batted three hundred. "It has been meanly stated that this was a 'belated appreciation of Captain Anson,'" wrote Francis Richter in the 1923 *Reach Guide*. "In justice to the National League let it be stated that the body for many years stood ready to come to Anson's assistance when necessary. That it was not necessary was due to the fact that the independent old man would not accept a pension, in default of which no position could be created that he could fill satisfactorily owing to his disposition which was self-opinionated and brooked neither advice or order."

Now *that* should have been on his tombstone.

He was elected to the Hall of Fame in 1939.

(Sources for this article, in addition to Anson's autobiography, include Anson's obituaries in the 1923 *Reach* and *Spalding* Guides, Robert Smith's books *Baseball* and *The Hall of Fame*, Ira Smith's *Baseball's Famous First Basemen*, *The Strange Career of Jim Crow*, by C. Vann Woodward, and *They Gave Us Baseball*, by John M. Rosenberg, as well as many other articles, histories, and newspaper articles.

Of all of the biographies here, Anson's was the hardest to write. There are many contradictory and overlapping stories, and I am not an expert in nineteenth-century baseball. In particular, there are several double images which come up in reading about Anson, and sometimes it is difficult to be certain that this is not one original event which has shattered somewhere in the century, with the shards by now so embedded in the literature that each has its own roots. Often in writing this I felt like I didn't know where to put my foot. I am sure that I have chosen badly from time to time. The only way to truly know is to double-check everything with original sources, but to be frank, in the case of Cap Anson that would have taken three months. I hope that you will at least give me credit for having honestly tried to sort through the contradictions and find the essential facts, and if you find mistakes let me know.)

THREE

•

PLAYERS

———

DON AASE
Mets

Missing and presumed released.

JIM ABBOTT
Angels

Abbott last year was the American League's most-average pitcher. He finished 12–12, .500, with a 3.92 ERA (the league average was 3.88). The league average was 5.5 strikeouts per game; Abbott struck out 5.7. The league strikeout/walk ratio was 100–59; Abbott was 100–64. He was a little better than average in home runs allowed, a little worse than average in hits allowed.

The short-term future for Abbott obviously is very bright. He throws hard, knows what he is doing on the mound. He's a learner; once he picks up a few more tricks of the trade he's going to be real good for a year or two.

I'm not optimistic about his long-term future.

1) He has worked too hard too early in his career. Most great pitchers don't throw a lot of innings before they are twenty-five, and most pitchers who throw a lot of innings before they are twenty-five have arm trouble the rest of their careers.

2) Most great pitchers start out significantly above the league norm in strikeouts per game. Abbott was barely above the league strikeout norm last year. He'll probably move up a notch this year, but I doubt that he'll reach the range where most great pitchers start out.

3) There is a slight awkwardness in the conclusion of his delivery, not particularly related to his disability (a lot of young pitchers don't follow through smoothly.) It's not severe and it won't cause an injury for several years, but in the long run it's not a positive factor.

SHAWN ABNER
Padres

Absolutely no prospect at this point. There is very little chance that Abner will ever be a major league regular.

JIM ACKER
Toronto

He's coming off his best season, and unless you add together his National League and American League stats you don't realize what kind of a year it was—73 games, 126 innings, 2.43 ERA, 92-21 strikeout/walk ratio (not including intentional walks). A middle reliever or set-up reliever isn't of much use in most rotisserie leagues and fantasy leagues, but he could produce some good RE-PLAY or Strat-O-Matic cards in the next few years.

JIM ADDUCI
Philadelphia

Still trying to find a spot in the majors at thirty, he may have extended his career by going seven-for-nineteen with the Phillies (.368). His only possible future in baseball would be as a left-handed pinch hitter, and the odds are against his being able to hold the job.

STEVE ADKINS
Yankees

A six-six left-hander who blew away the Eastern League last year, Adkins has all the obvious elements of a dominating young pitcher. He's a late bloomer, didn't pitch all that well in his first years in the Yankee system, but that's all right; a good many great pitchers have been late bloomers. The only reason I haven't marked him with asterisks is the Yankees' poor record of developing their young talent, but he's definitely got a chance to be outstanding if they'll let him work through his adjustments.

JUAN AGOSTO
Astros

Has now been effective with Houston for two and a half years, which you have to respect. His odd motion makes him an injury candidate.

LUIS AGUAYO
Indians

Probably through after hitting .175. I don't expect to see him on a major league roster this year.

RICK AGUILERA
Twins

I haven't studied his motion, but you've got to figure that a guy who has had three different elbow problems in his career is probably doing something that puts pressure on his elbow, and may well continue to have the problem. If he doesn't get hurt, he's a fine pitcher. The Twins would prefer to keep him in the starting rotation, but the departure of Reardon may move him into the role of relief ace, which if it happens would probably make his value in 1990 higher than it has ever been; he was *extremely* effective with the Mets in relief last year, but not as the closer. Pay close attention to how he is used during spring training, and if he is in the bullpen then try to acquire him. Even as a starter, he's a good third or fourth man, and is capable of going 16–10 or thereabouts.

DARREL AKERFELDS
Texas

He pitched well enough with Oklahoma City (3.33 ERA) and with Texas late in the year (3.27 ERA in six games) that he has a reasonable chance to make the Rangers as a long man out of the bullpen. He has no star potential, and he isn't anybody I'd be looking to draft.

MIKE ALDRETE
Montreal

One would have to think that his career is due for an upturn, and thus that he might be an OK late-round draft pick. Hubie Brooks is gone, opening up a little playing time for him, but then Marquis Grissom and Larry Walker are going to be around, so playing time is still going to be scarce. I never believed he was a .325 hitter, which is what he hit in 1987, but then I don't believe he's any .221 hitter, either.

Aldrete could be hurt by the possible strike/lockout in spring training. He needs the spring games to reestablish himself, and could find himself without a job if he doesn't have a good spring.

JAY ALDRICH
Atlanta

A marginal pitching prospect who will be fighting for playing time behind the *real* pitching prospects. No star potential/not a good draft risk despite 2.19 ERA with the Braves.

DOYLE ALEXANDER
Detroit (?)

Despite his ugly won-lost log, the God's truth is that Doyle didn't pitch all that badly for Detroit. If you compare him to Storm Davis, you'll note that Doyle pitched a lot more innings (223–169), and their performance rates were almost the same—4.44 ERA versus 4.36, 9.89 hits/game (Alexander) versus 9.94, and with Alexander having a little better control. That Storm Davis got a $2 million a year contract out of this and Alexander got released was based on two things, and two things only:

1) Doyle is eleven years older than Davis, and

2) The A's scored six-plus runs a game for Davis, giving him a gaudy 19–7 record, while the Tigers scored just three runs a game for Alexander, sticking him with a losing record.

There were absolutely no performance variables which contributed to Davis's having a 19–7 record, while Alexander finished 6–18. The differences between them which contributed to this disparity were luck, pure luck, sheer luck, and dumb luck.

Despite his release, Alexander can be expected to be in camp with Detroit or somebody, and shouldn't be taken too lightly. He is still very capable of going 14–11.

ANDY ALLANSON
Cleveland

The most-similar player to Andy Allanson is Junior Ortiz . . . out of a job with the acquisition of Alomar. He'll probably get another chance somewhere, in that he's hit around .250 lifetime, has some speed, and throws OK. Look for a trade.

NEIL ALLEN
released.

BEAU ALLRED
Cleveland

Decent left-handed line drive hitter, probably pretty comparable to Paul O'-Neill of the Reds. It's hard to guess who the Indians will play in the outfield, and it is unlikely Allred will get a regular job out of spring training, but he's got a chance to be a pretty good player in a year or two. I like Allred better than Joey Belle, but the Indians probably won't agree with me.

★ ★ ★
ROBERTO ALOMAR
Padres
★ ★ ★

This is my number one tip for this guide: GET ROBERTO ALOMAR. No matter who you are—rotisserie, card collector, whatever; get Alomar.

There are three truly great second basemen in history—Morgan, Eddie Collins, and Hornsby, and then some guys who are almost in the same class, like Gehringer, Frisch, and (at this point) Ryne Sandberg. I think by the time he is through, Roberto Alomar is going to be talked about along with those guys.

There are four reasons I say that. Number one, the quality of his play. Alomar has been in the league two years; he *should* have been the National League Rookie of the Year in 1988, and he stepped forward a big step from that level in 1989.

Number two, the diversity of his skills. Alomar has speed and good defensive skills at second base, but he also has some pop in his bat, and he knows the strike zone. A player with one skill has to develop in one specific direction. A player with multiple skills has a broader foundation on which to develop. Alomar *could* develop his power, and be a twenty-five-homer man like Morgan and Sandberg. But he also could develop into a singles hitter, and be a batting champion. That gives him a better chance of developing in one direction or another.

Number three, his youth. Alomar was only twenty years old in his rookie year, twenty-two this season. A player who comes up at that age has a growth expectation many times greater than a player who has an equally good rookie year at age twenty-four.

Number four, he's a switch hitter.

Now, he's a second baseman. Second basemen, as a rule, are not a good gamble to develop, because they get hurt so much; they take a step forward and two steps back. But I believe that Alomar will be an exception to that rule, for several reasons.

a. his father was a second baseman in the major leagues,

b. his father was a *durable* second baseman. That means that his father knew how to avoid getting hurt at second base, which very few second basemen ever learn.

c. his father is a coach, with his team. That means that he is perfectly positioned to work with Roberto on this critical phase of the game.

d. Roberto has been durable to this point of his career, playing an average of 147 games a year over the last three seasons.

I think that Alomar's "support network"—his father and brother being in the game—is a very positive factor for his development, also; I think that as he develops into a star, his family will be able to help him deal with the problems of growth better than might be the case otherwise.

So I think Alomar's going to be a great player, one of the best players of the 1990's.

SANDY ALOMAR, JR.
Cleveland

I am *not* excited about him. I see him as a .240–.250 hitter, moderate power, poor K/W, no speed, outstanding defense. Sure, it is possible that he will outperform that as a rookie, as Benito Santiago did, but basically he's similar to Santiago as a hitter, but without the speed. Playing for Cleveland is not a positive factor; they don't have the greatest record for developing their young players. With the buildup he's had he'll be an expensive pickup in any field—rotisserie, fantasy ball, APBA, or card collecting. Stay away from him; Todd Zeile and Joe Oliver are better investments.

JOSE ALVAREZ
Atlanta

Now that he has finally made the majors, he is probably going to hang around for several years. Obviously, at age thirty-four he is not going to develop into a star.

WILSON ALVAREZ
Chisox

Acquired from the Rangers in the Harold Baines trade, Alvarez is considered the number-one prospect in the White Sox system. Now twenty years old, he became the first player born in the 1970's to reach the major leagues when he pitched a game for the Rangers last July, leaving for someone else the distinction of becoming the first player born in the 1970's to actually record an out. A Venezuelan left-hander, Alvarez is still awfully young to be starting in the major leagues, which won't stop the White Sox from giving him a long look in spring training. The odds are he will start the season in AAA, but he has a great arm and good control, and will be in Chicago before very long.

Decent draft pick, but how well will the White Sox support him? How well will they handle him? Will they rush him along too soon, and destroy his confidence? Will their defense undermine him, as it has Melido Perez? Will they give him too many innings too soon, and hurt his arm? You have to worry about those things.

LARRY ANDERSEN
Astros

Coming off his best season at the age of thirty-seven. Given the stability of his performance in recent years (he's had four straight good seasons) and given that the Astrodome protects him to some degree, he's an OK draft pick in a late round if you're in a game that somehow rewards a middle reliever.

ALLAN ANDERSON
Twins

Despite his outstanding performance over his two major league seasons, I would *not* recommend that you draft him. His extremely low ratio of strikeouts/nine innings concerns me. There are a lot of pitchers who have a good

year or a couple of good years without striking anybody out, but there are very few pitchers who have a good *career* that way. Although he was 17–10 last season, I'm not sure he pitched as well as that record reflects; a 3.80 ERA in 197 innings isn't an impressive combination. The departure of Jeff Reardon isn't a positive for him; the Twins could find themselves giving up leads in the late innings. The park in which he pitches doesn't work to his advantage, although there is another side to that, of course (that his 3.80 ERA may be better than it looks). I know he's 33–19 over the last two years, but for me, there is still something missing.

BRADY ANDERSON
Orioles

He's been a disappointment, but I'm going to stand by him. In uniform and on the field, Anderson looks astonishingly like one of my favorite players, Brett Butler. Last year he hit .207, but if you project him up to 600 at bats you still get 99 runs scored, 97 walks, 27 doubles, 36 stolen bases—some positive contributions. With his defense in center field, Anderson can help a team if he hits .260, and I just have to believe that sooner or later he's going to hit .260. Stay with him.

DAVE ANDERSON
Giants

Role player. I don't foresee any dramatic changes for him.

KENT ANDERSON
California

Utility man. Will never be a regular in the major leagues.

JOAQUIN ANDUJAR
Montreal

You think he'll make the Expos? It's not as improbable as it seems. He's only thirty-seven, still threw hard at last notice. Here's my advice: If he starts out 4–0 with a 1.84 ERA, *don't draft him.* You'll thank me in October.

ERIC ANTHONY
Astros

Highly-rated outfielder with awesome power, only twenty-two years old. He's left-handed, but a Bo Jackson-type hitter, going to strike out every day and hope to hit a home run or two a week. He could spend part of the year in AAA, but in the long run I rate him about 80 percent sure to make it as a major league hitter, but probably peaking early. To be a star he'll have to cut his strikeout rate from nearly 40 percent, where it will start out, to no more than 25 percent, and that's not going to be easy.

KEVIN APPIER
Royals

The top-rated pitching prospect of an organization which has produced pitchers by the bushelful in the last ten years, Appier was brought along perhaps a little too fast, jumping from Baseball City to Kansas City in one year, and was over his head. The signing of Storm Davis and Richard Dotson was intended to release the pressure on Appier, and will probably have that effect, giving him a full season at Omaha to get going again. Decent long-term pitching prospect but not in the Andy Benes-Steve Avery class.

LUIS AQUINO
Royals

His record looks deceptively good (3.50 ERA in 141 innings, strikeout/walk ratio almost two to one). I don't really think he pitched quite that well, but in any case what we are more interested in here is his future. Aquino will sail along unscathed for several innings at a time, but what he hasn't shown to this point is the ability to pitch out of trouble. He doesn't have the "stuff" to be a relief

closer, and didn't pitch very well as a starter. I doubt that he will pitch as *much* for the Royals in 1990 as he did in 1989, the team having added three free-agent pitchers, and to be honest, I also don't expect him to pitch as well.

JOHNNY ARD
Minnesota

First-round draft pick of the Twins a couple of years ago, he's still highly thought of but not ready to come to the majors.

TONY ARMAS
Angels

In his career he has the lowest run element ratio of any active player, 1–3.72. . . . The bottom ten are Armas, Cory Snyder, George Bell, Jim Presley, Steve Balboni, Harold Baines, Don Mattingly, Carmen Castillo, Ruben Sierra, and Jim Rice. . . . At age thirty-six, obviously not likely to have another big year.

JACK ARMSTRONG
Reds

B–/C+ prospect—some good things about him, some bad. A big guy who has conquered his control in the minor leagues, but not yet in the majors. He was the Reds' number-one draft pick in 1987, and is well thought of in the organization. He has a chance to be a star, but then a lot of guys do.

LARRY ARNDT
Oakland

Young third baseman/no prospect as far as I'm concerned. .230-range hitter with no power, power K/W.

BRAD ARNSBERG
Texas

Once a hot prospect with the Yankees, trying to reestablish himself after an injury wiped out his 1988 season. I'm not going to be shocked if he comes on strong this year, but obviously you're

not going to pick him up until he shows something.

ALAN ASHBY
retired.

PAUL ASSENMACHER
Cubs

At the worst, he figures to be around for years as a left-handed short man, and he seems to be getting stronger. Last year he had 79 strikeouts in 77 innings, walked only twenty-eight men. Assuming that there is a good chance that Williams will fall apart as a relief ace, there must be some chance—maybe a 15 to 20 percent chance—that Assenmacher will *emerge* as a relief ace. A decent late-round draft pick.

KEITH ATHERTON
Cleveland

Inches away from professional extermination.

DON AUGUST
Brewers

Very effective in 1988, completely ineffective in 1989. I give him little chance of returning to form in 1990. A record of 51 strikeouts in 142 innings doesn't indicate to me a pitcher who is close to being on the good side of the ledger.

★★★
STEVE AVERY
Atlanta
★★★

Avery will be twenty years old on April 14. He is regarded as perhaps the best pitching prospect in the minor leagues, one of the few young pitchers who seems to have everything that is required to rank in the Roger Clemens, Jim Palmer, Tom Seaver class. Of course, there are many more young pitchers who seem to have the potential to move into that class than there are who will actually get there, but having said that, there still are not an awful lot of pitchers who even have a chance. Avery is a left-hander with a 90+ fastball, a good breaking ball, a good change, and fairly decent control. He is handsome and is regarded as very bright. He is generally described as "mature" and as possessing "incredible poise and composure." I haven't seen him pitch personally, but his mechanics are reported as "nearly perfect."

He was the third player taken in the 1988 June draft, and has been ahead of the league, posting a 7–1 record with a 1.50 ERA in the Appalachian League in 1988, a 6–4 record with a 1.45 ERA in the Carolina League, and a 6–3 record with a 2.77 ERA in the Southern League. Unless he hits a crisis of confidence or an arm problem, he seems headed for the top.

WALLY BACKMAN
Minnesota

He's only thirty, so there's no compelling reason that he couldn't return to form in 1990. Actually, he's had an on year-off year pattern, hitting .323, .272, .280, .320, and .303 in 1980, 82, 84, 86, 88, but .278, .167, .273, .250, and .231 in 1981, 83, 85, 87, 89. His career batting average is .296 in "even" years, but .254 in "odd" years. I don't imagine that has any predictive significance (see Bret Saberhagen), but the Twins don't have anybody pushing Backman, no AAA second baseman; all he has to do to get his job back is beat out Al Newman.

SCOTT BAILES
Cleveland

He's consistent. You've got to give him that. His ERAs in his four years in the majors have ranged from 4.28 to 4.95. He has never had a winning record. Here's my recommendation: If for some reason you want to have a pitcher on your team going 7–11 with a 4.59 ERA, then by all means draft Scott Bailes. Otherwise, don't.

HAROLD BAINES
Texas

Texas designated hitters last year were last in the American League in home runs (6) and RBI (53), and first in grounding into double plays (27). Baines obviously will change the first two. . . . Baines last year had the best strikeout/walk ratio of his career, by far, drawing almost as many walks as his strikeouts. . . . Card collectors may be wondering about Baines's chance of making the Hall of Fame. Because he came up early, and also because he has hit .300 several times, Baines has a realistic chance (21 percent) of getting 3,000 hits in his career. He'll have to hold up well and keep going until he's at least forty, but he could do it. If he does, obviously he'll be a Hall of Famer. Short of 3,000 hits, he has really done very little which would be characteristic of a Hall of Fame player, and basically has very little chance. . . .

DOUG BAIR
Pittsburgh

Did you realize that Bair had a 2.27 ERA in forty-four games last year? It seems hard to believe. He's never had two good years back to back, and doesn't seem likely to start at age forty. . . .

DOUG BAKER
Minnesota

Excellent defensive player; will never hit enough to play regularly.

STEVE BALBONI
Yanks

Although the Yankees didn't have a regular DH their DHs were probably the best in the league last year, hitting 27 homers and driving in 106 runs. Balboni as a DH had 14 homers and 52 RBI in just 235 at bats. . . . I don't know that it makes a lot of difference, but Balboni has really curtailed his strikeouts over the years. In Balboni's first full year in

the majors (1984) he struck out 32 percent of his at bats, which was about the same as he had done in his trials with the Yankees. In 1985–86 he struck out in 28 percent of his at bats. In 1987 it was 25 percent. Over the last two years he has struck out in only 22 percent of his at bats. . . .

JEFF BALLARD
Baltimore

His record in 1989 (18–8) is a more realistic representation of his ability than his record before that (10–20), but not a whole lot. He gave up 240 hits last year in 215 innings, an ugly ratio for a top pitcher. His strikeout/walk ratio wouldn't impress anybody. I can see Ballard going 14–12 to 17–12 as a regular thing, but I think the 1989 season was a little over his head.

CHRIS BANDO
Oakland

Playing career probably over; expect to see him around as a coach and manager. . . .

SCOTT BANKHEAD
Seattle

The Mariners announced in November that they were going to move their fences, in stages, over the next two years; the park is going to be more of a pitcher's park, and it is going to be asymmetrical, favoring a left-hander. The left-field fence is going to move from 314 feet in 1989 to 326 in 1990, then got 349 in 1991—a long poke indeed. The left-field line will drop from 316 to 313.

That being the case, it is probably good general advice to stay away from Seattle *hitters*, particularly right-handed hitters, but to consider seriously picking up Seattle *pitchers*, particularly left-handers. Bankhead, still only twenty-six years old, has pitched great over the last two seasons, and his best years are probably just ahead of him. I would regard him as a very good draft selection, a potential eighteen- to twenty-game winner, and a safe pick in any case unless he has back or elbow trouble.

FLOYD BANNISTER
Kansas City

Has signed to play in Japan.

JESSE BARFIELD
Yankees

With 20 outfield assists last year (the third time in his career he has had 20 or more) Barfield now has 133 outfield assists and 42 outfield double plays. Per game played, no one since World War II approaches those figures. . . . Didn't play as badly as his .234 batting average indicates. His batting average represents only 39 percent of his offense, a low proportion, and with his defense in right field, he can still help a team . . . a good bet to snap back this year. His typical year: 28 homers, 81 RBI, .263 average. . . .

JOHN BARFIELD
Texas

Very marginal pitching prospect. There is no reason to think he will be a successful major league pitcher.

SKEETER BARNES
Cincinnati

Minor league veteran, now thirty-three years old. A few years ago he could have helped a major league team, and he wasn't any worse than some guys who had major league careers—say, Ken Oberkfell. But he never got the chance, and he's not likely to now.

MARTY BARRETT
Boston

I'd be a little worried about him. He'll be thirty-two in June; that's a dangerous age for a ballplayer, an age when a lot of players fade. On the other hand, some people might forget about him after his injury season, and you might pick him up cheap . . . struck out only twelve times last year.

TOM BARRETT
Philadelphia

Marty's brother. He's really not a bad player—.260-range hitter, walks a lot, can steal bases and a good second baseman. But he's thirty, so he's not going to get a chance.

KEVIN BASS
San Francisco

An excellent 1989 draft pick. First, he's moving from the Astrodome, a tough park for a hitter, to Candlestick, which is not a good park for a hitter but somewhat better. Second, he's moving to a spot where he is needed, hitting fifth or sixth behind Mitchell or Williams, so he should have a decent RBI year, perhaps the best of his career. Third, he is coming off an injury year, so some people are going to forget about him, so he'll go cheap in some leagues. Against that, you've got his age (thirty-one) and the chance that there will be lingering effects of the injury (which the doctors say there won't). On balance, a good player to choose for 1990.

BILLY BATES
Milwaukee

A five-seven spark plug kind of player, was a well-regarded second-base prospect a couple of years ago, but seems to have missed his moment. His stock has fallen to almost nothing over the last two seasons.

BILL BATHE
Giants

Now twenty-nine years old, seems to have developed rather remarkably as a hitter in the last three years. No star potential; might catch on as a twenty-fourth man.

KEVIN BATISTE
Toronto

Twenty-three-year-old outfielder. Batiste was going to SMU on a football scholarship, going to be their quarterback, when the SMU football program got the death penalty from the NCAA. He converted to switch hitting in the minor leagues a couple of years ago, and you know how I hate that; it doesn't do anything but screw up a player's career, which is exactly what it has done for Batiste. Despite awesome physical skills it is extremely unlikely that he will ever develop into a major league hitter, and certainly at this point he is miles away.

JOSE BAUTISTA
Baltimore

Will start the season in the minor leagues. I expect him to get another chance somewhere sometime, and wouldn't be shocked if he were more effective then.

BILLY BEAN
Los Angeles

He's a singles-hitting outfielder with no other positives—no power, not much speed, won't walk much. If I was running a team I would have no interest in him, but I wouldn't completely dismiss the possibility of his earning a job as a fifth outfielder, hitting .280 or so and staying in the majors for a few years.

BILLY BEANE
Oakland

Big strong guy, career undermined by failure to learn the strike zone. He's about out of chances; as a major league player would have a K/W ratio of 10–1, without the other stats you have to have if you're going to do that.

DAVE BEARD
Detroit

After four straight seasons with an ERA over 5.00, I would assume we had seen the last of him.

BLAINE BEATTY
Mets

Sooner or later, I think you'll see Beatty in the major leagues. He came into baseball in 1986 as a relatively "finished" pitcher, with very good control and some ability to change speeds, and as a consequence of that overmatched the low minor leagues in the Orioles system, going 11–3 at Newark (2.11 ERA) and 11–1 at Hagerstown (2.52 ERA). As often happens when you have a young pitcher that far ahead of his leagues, his managers let him pitch too far into the game too often, and he developed arm trouble, after which he was traded to the Mets as partial payment for Doug Sisk. But he's continued to pitch effectively, going 16–8 with a 2.46 ERA in the Texas League in 1988, and 12–10 with a 3.31 ERA at Tidewater last year.

Beatty *doesn't* have outstanding stuff, and many scouts don't think he can pitch effectively in the major leagues. He does have exceptional control and a very good understanding of how to pitch, however, and sooner or later he has to get an opportunity. If by some fluke he is on the Mets roster coming out of spring training, I recommend that you consider adding him. If not, he'll be a minor league free agent in a year. His chance of being an effective long man out of the bullpen is very good.

STEVE BEDROSIAN
Giants

I wouldn't particularly recommend drafting him. He's been up and down some, he doesn't throw nearly as hard as he did a few years ago, and the departure of Craig Lefferts may increase the pressure on him. That's not to deny that he is one of the top relievers around, and probably will continue to be.

TIM BELCHER
Dodgers

Eight shutouts? *Eight* shutouts?

A very solid, safe draft investment. He will remain a dominant pitcher for several years, and will have better won-lost records than he had last season.

STAN BELINDA
Pittsburgh

Excellent, excellent draft pick. A tenth-round draft pick in 1986, he's been used in relief in the minor leagues, and has been dominant at every stage. In the majors last year he had a 6.10 ERA but in ten innings struck out ten men, and walked only two. With Jim Gott gone and Bill Landrum suspect as a relief closer, Belinda sooner or later is going to get a shot as the Pirates relief ace, and could emerge as an extremely valuable property. He's a late-round draft pick who could be pivotal in some leagues.

GEORGE BELL
Blue Jays

That George Bell will play, and hit, is as close as you can get to a sure thing. In the last six years he has batted over 600 times every year and driven in an average of 104 runs . . . has about a 17 percent chance of getting 3,000 career hits, 4 percent chance of hitting 500 home runs.

JAY BELL
Pittsburgh

At best, he'll hold his job. I do *not* believe he will develop into one of the better players at his position.

TITO BELL
Baltimore

George Bell's younger brother. He's a defensive wizard at shortstop (who would believe it?), still very young (twenty-two), and developing as a hitter. With the Orioles needing help at second base, he could be shifted to second,

where he would contribute more at bat than Billy Ripken, but not a whole lot more. I would expect him to hit around .250, little power, poor K/W ratio but not terrible, and steal 20–40 bases a year. His best chance to have a good career is to wait a year or two and get a shortstop job somewhere.

JOEY BELLE
Tribe

Don't care too much for him. He's a good enough hitter—.250 range hitter with power to hit 25–30 home runs, but his strikeout to walk ratio is going to be bad, his speed isn't a big positive now and won't be any more positive in a few years, he's a fair outfielder and has a history of behavioral problems. (He was suspended twice in 1988.) Will strike out 150 times.

RAFAEL BELLIARD
Pittsburgh

Day-to-day major leaguer. No regular; not really even a very strong bench player.

BRUCE BENEDICT
Atlanta

Retired, finally.

★ ★ ★
ANDY BENES
Padres
★ ★ ★

Super young pitcher. Benes won six out of ten starts in the majors last year and struck out a man an inning when he was struggling with tendinitis in the shoulder. The tendinitis is the *only* thing he has to worry about. If he's healthy, he's Dwight Gooden.

MIKE BENJAMIN
San Francisco

Shortstop candidate; won't hit enough to stay in the majors.

TODD BENZINGER
Reds

Don't like anything about him. Bad hitter, bad base runner, no idea what the strike zone is, glove OK but that's all. 1990 should be a better year for him than 1989, but then that's like saying Manuel Noriega's luck has got to turn sometime. If I was running the Reds I'd get rid of Benzinger in about ten minutes. . . .

JUAN BERENGUER
Twins

Valuable pitcher. Kelly uses him awfully well; if Kelly loses his job look for Berenguer to struggle. Otherwise he figures to roll right along, winning about three fourths of his decisions. . . .

DAVE BERGMAN
Detroit

Due to the departure of Darrell Evans established major league highs last year in games played (137), at bats (385), hits (103), total bases (139), and walks (44). Good reserve first baseman, but at thirty-seven really shouldn't be playing that much.

GERONIMO BERROA
Atlanta

His strikeout to walk ratio is awful and always will be, but despite that Berroa is a productive hitter. The signing of Esasky cuts off one opportunity for him to increase his playing time. If he should back into a regular job (let's say Dale Murphy retires) he will hit around .260 with uncertain power, but he could lead the National League in doubles. There is also the possibility of his hitting some home runs in Atlanta, maybe 20–25 a year.

DAMON BERRYHILL
Cubs

Solid player. I would expect his 1990 season to be the best of his career thus far.

DANTE BICHETTE
California

A big guy and a good outfielder, but won't hit enough to be a major league regular (.200–.230 range hitter with 10–12 HR power, poor K/W, no speed). Playing time could benefit if Armas is released or retires.

MIKE BIELECKI
Cubs

What a surprise, huh? I see no reason that he shouldn't remain an effective pitcher.

CRAIG BIGGIO
Houston

The Astros are talking about moving him to another position, and much as I dislike position shifts, I see the logic. He *doesn't* throw very well, so as a catcher that's always going to be a problem. If he continues to catch the strain and the collisions will probably destroy his speed within two or three years. He is a very solid offensive player, with some speed, some power and a decent on-base percentage. Why not send him to left field, clear up the problem created by the departure of Kevin Bass or insure against a wipeout of Eric Anthony?

DANN BILLARDELLO
Pittsburgh

Marginal player. Don't draft him.

MIKE BIRKBECK
Brewers

My momma always told me never to take a chance on a sore-armed pitcher.

TIM BIRTSAS
Cincinnati

A big ugly guy, he appears to have finally gained a corner on his control, and may continue to pitch well (as he did last year). The key factor in a draft here would appear to be whether the Reds trade a reliever during spring training. With the Reds bullpen being so deep, there is little likelihood of Birtsas moving into a more key role *unless* someone like Dibble is traded away.

JEFF BITTIGER
Chisox

Long odds for big league success at this point. If, by some chance, he starts pitching well, I would consider adding him, as I think in that situation he could continue to pitch well. It probably isn't going to happen.

BUD BLACK
Cleveland

Poor draft pick. He lives on the edge; even when he pitches well, as he did last year, he's an inch away from getting hammered. Working for the Indians is a major handicap. He'll be thirty-three in June. I wouldn't draft him.

KEVIN BLANKENSHIP
Chicago Cubs

Grade D prospect. No reason to think he *can't* pitch in the majors, but no reason to think he will.

LANCE BLANKENSHIP
A's

One of the A's many second basemen, he has an opportunity to increase his playing time in view of the release of Glenn Hubbard and the free-agent defection of Tony Phillips. Last year he had 8 walks and 31 strikeouts, and that ratio will improve dramatically when he gains a little more confidence in the major leagues. He can steal bases, and he's a good defensive second baseman—but he is *not* a hitter. An average in the .220s or .230s will probably prevent him from establishing himself as a major league regular.

★★★
JEFF BLAUSER
Braves
★★★

The Braves were using him primarily at third base last year, but Blauser has the ability to become one of the top short-stops in the National League. He has the arm and the quickness to be a shortstop, a *good* shortstop. As a hitter, he can improve on what he did last year, and what he did last year wasn't shabby (.270 with 12 homers.) I don't know who you'd compare him to as a shortstop—maybe Granny Hamner, if you can go back that far. If things go right for Jeff Blauser, you are going to be seeing him in the All-Star game.

TERRY BLOCKER
Atlanta

No prospect. Doesn't do anything at a major league level.

MIKE BLOWERS
Yankees

Third base candidate for the Yankees, obtained from the Montreal system. Little if any star potential. Decent hitter, .250-range with power to hit 12–15 home runs, but no speed and poor strikeout to walk ratio. That being the case, the burden will be on his defense, which doesn't come with a grade A reputation, although he does have a strong arm. Randy Velarde will presumably get the first chance to be the Yankee third baseman, with Blowers as the backup plan.

BERT BLYLEVEN
California

His cards are a good investment, in that he is a probable Hall of Famer. He needs 29 more wins to get 300, which would make him that certain, but even without it . . . well, after all, he has more strike-outs than Walter Johnson.

I sort of expect the Angels offense to go into a free fall this year, which will be reflected in Blyleven's won-lost record.

RANDY BOCKUS
Tigers

Boy, there are a lot of these guys. No real prospect; can always surprise you.

MIKE BODDICKER
Boston

A relatively safe draft investment—always pitches his 200 innings, isn't likely to wipe out on you. When you're drafting twenty-five players, of course you don't want to gamble at twenty-five spots. A good idea is to try to acquire fifteen to seventeen "safe" players, like Boddicker, and then to try to identify eight to ten players that you want to gamble on. If six of your eight "risks" come through, you'll be in good shape—but if you gamble at twenty-five spots, you'll have to be a genius to win anything.

JOE BOEVER
Atlanta

Probably has lost the role of bullpen closer to Mike Stanton. Will probably be more effective as a setup man than he was as a closer.

WADE BOGGS
Bosox

Has created far more runs per game (per 27 outs) than any other major league player. The top ten are Boggs (8.09), Mattingly (7.20), Eric Davis, Will Clark, Pedro Guerrero, George Brett, Mike Schmidt, Tim Raines, Alvin Davis, and Eddie Murray (6.54). The difference between Boggs and the number two man is greater than the difference between number two and number ten. . . . The best strikeout to walk ratios of 1989: 1. Wade Boggs (51 strikeouts, 107 walks), 2. Alvin Davis, 3. Carney Lansford, 4. Tim Raines, 5. Mark Grace, 6. Tony Gwynn, 7. Rickey Henderson, 8. Mike Scioscia, 9. John Cangelosi, 10. Pete O'-Brien. . . . He also has the best *career* strikeout to walk ratio of any active

player, 100–222; he is followed on that list by Greg Gross, Mike Scioscia, Willie Randolph, Ozzie Smith, and Tony Gwynn. . . . Most similar major league player: Paul Molitor. . . .

TOM BOLTON
Boston

Extremely marginal prospect. He's trying to fit into a role as a left-handed one-out guy in the bullpen, but the odds are against him.

BARRY BONDS
Pittsburgh

I'm sure you have heard the rumors that the Pirates are trying to trade him, and I'm sure that, like me, you wonder what the hell they are thinking of. There is always the possibility that the Pirates, despite their two-year string of bad decisions, know something that we don't—that Bonds has a life-style problem of some kind which is inhibiting his development. What is more likely than that is that they are just focusing on his batting average (.248), and losing track of all the positives—19 homers, 93 walks, 32 stolen bases, 34 doubles, excellent defense in left field. I don't know that Bonds is ever going to have an MVP season, but I'll say this. If you want to trade him, I'll take him.

★ ★ ★
BOBBY BONILLA
Pittsburgh
★ ★ ★

I went through the majors looking for the "Kevin Mitchell of 1990," the player with the best chance to explode on the league. I concluded that Bonilla was probably the best bet. His age is right—he'll be twenty-seven this year, the most common age for an MVP. He's had three straight solid years, but at a particular level; his slugging percentages and on-base percentages have been steady over that period. I think that by now, he may be a better hitter than that; he may be capable of hitting .300 with 35 homers. He is probably moving to first base this year, ending a three-year bad idea (third base) which has probably been a drain on him as a hitter; even if he has to return to third base, which is fairly likely, he should be more comfortable there now, after three years.

GREG BOOKER
Minnesota

No prospect. Don't know why he is in the major leagues.

ROD BOOKER
Cards

Not a major league hitter—no job waiting for him.

BOB BOONE
Kansas City

The most-similar player to Bob Boone is Jim Sundberg. . . .

The surprise about watching Bob Boone, as a Royals fan, is the degree to which he is a "pivotal" player. Looking at him from other teams, I thought of him as being a steady, unspectacular player who didn't make many mistakes but also didn't do a lot to beat the other team. But watching him regularly, I find that I very often go home thinking either that Bob Boone cost us the game, or that Bob Boone won the game for us. He takes a lot of defensive chances—loves to throw to the bases, will try to make the play at second or third base on a bunt in front of the plate. And he's not that quiet offensively; he finds a way to make his presence felt. He's an interesting player, and on the whole better than I thought he was before I saw him every day.

A probable Hall of Famer.

PAT BORDERS
Toronto

A good to excellent draft pick. The departure of Ernie Whitt by free agency leaves him more or less in possession of the Toronto catching job. He can do the job defensively, he's not a bad hitter and he's capable of getting better. His value this season is *very* likely to be greater than it was last year, and that's the fundamental definition of a good draft pick.

CHRIS BOSIO
Brewers

Love him. Always have, I'm proud to say. A guy who strikes out three times as many people as he walks—well, sooner or later he's going to start winning. Bosio is just the latest example of that.

THAD BOSLEY
Rangers

Career probably over.

DARYL BOSTON
White Sox

By all logic, his job should have vanished. With the additions of Sammy Sosa and Lance Johnson, there shouldn't be any place for Boston in the White Sox outfield. The White Sox have this nerdy habit of stringing players along, avoiding making a decision on who they want to go with by playing a bunch of guys half-time, and there is always the possibility that they will continue to do that with Boston. He's not the worst player in the league, but I'd have to say that my patience with him as a prospect has about run out.

OIL CAN BOYD
Montreal

There can't be anybody reading this book who doesn't already have his mind made up about the Can, can there?

PHIL BRADLEY
Orioles

The most-comparable major league player to Phil Bradley is Kevin McReynolds . . . a good player, and a "safe"

draft pick. Even his bad year at Philadelphia wasn't really all that bad.

SCOTT BRADLEY
Seattle

Another "safe" draft pick. He's not going to win an MVP award, but he does what he does every year—hits around .270, plays half-time at catcher. A decent enough player.

BRIAN BRADY
California

Twenty-seven-year-old outfielder. No prospect—absolutely cannot play major league baseball.

GLENN BRAGGS
Milwaukee

The most-similar player to Glenn Braggs is Chris James. . . .

I argue a lot about Glenn Braggs. Basically, what I argue is, "Who needs him?" He's been around for years, he's got 1,500 at bats in the major leagues, and he hasn't done anything. He's an awful outfielder, he strikes out too much, and he doesn't hit for power or average. Despite the fact that he's a wonderful athlete, as far as I'm concerned he has very little if any star potential. I will say, though, that I think he may have the best season of his career in 1990.

JEFF BRANTLEY
San Francisco

Nothing special. Extra guy in the bullpen, not likely to move up.

MICKEY BRANTLEY
Seattle

The Mariners have populated the American League with their cast-off outfielders—Dave Henderson of Oakland, Danny Tartabull of Kansas City, Ivan Calderon of Chicago, Phil Bradley of Baltimore. None of them are superstars, but all of them are solid, productive players. The problem that the Mariners have had is that they decide that a young player is going to be a superstar, and then when he isn't they decide they have to get rid of him. Mickey Brantley is probably the next one to be added to the list. In 1987 he hit .302, slugged .499, and stole 13 bases despite missing a good part of the year with an injury, so of course at that time he was a coming superstar. In 1988 he hit .263 with 25 doubles, 15 homers, 18 stolen bases, a somewhat disappointing season. So what did they do? Of course—they took his job away, and gave it to Jeffrey Leonard. Smart. And now they'll trade Brantley or give him away, and he'll go back to being a good, solid ballplayer.

SID BREAM
Bucs

The Pirates are real excited about having Bream back this year. From *The Sporting News*, January 8, 1990:

> "He was an under-rated casualty," Manager Jim Leyland said, citing the loss of Bream's defensive talents. General Manager Larry Doughty estimated that third baseman Bobby Bonilla would have been spared at least ten throwing errors had Bream been at first. . . .

Can you believe that? First of all, Bonilla fielded .935 at third base in '88, when Bream was on first, and .929 last year, when Bream wasn't on first, so I don't see a lot of hard evidence to support the idea that Bream can prevent all that many errors. But even assuming that he does, who wants a .260-hitting first baseman with 12–15 home run power? That's like hanging out a flag, says "We don't know what we're doing here. We don't know a ballplayer from a xylophone."

BOB BRENLY
Blue Jays

Career probably over.

GEORGE BRETT
Kansas City

With the retirement of Schmidt he becomes the leader among active players in career runs created. The top ten (active 1989) are Mike Schmidt (1625), Brett (1508), Dwight Evans, Jim Rice, Darrell Evans, Robin Yount, Dave Parker, Eddie Murray, Bill Buckner, and Buddy Bell. Two of those are officially retired, and two or three others (Buckner, Rice, and Darrell Evans) probably won't make a roster in 1990, so all of the lists of active leaders will be dramatically different next year. . . . A certain Hall of Famer. Estimated 58 percent chance of getting 3,000 career hits.

GREG BRILEY
M's

The most-similar player to Greg Briley is Ken Griffey, Jr. . . . Obviously, Griffey is the *better* prospect of the two, but I do expect Briley to show some development from his rookie year. A good guess is that he'll hit .280 with 18 homers and 80 RBI.

GREG BROCK
Milwaukee

A dangerous player to bank on—thirty-two years old (thirty-three in June) with a history of inconsistency. I wouldn't want him on my team.

TOM BROOKENS
Yankees

Had a big platoon differential last year, as he often has. Against left-handers he was respectable, hitting .267 with 4 homers, .422 slugging percentage. Against right-handers he was 7-for-52, a .135 average, and all singles. . . .

HUBIE BROOKS
Los Angeles

The most-similar player to Hubie Brooks is Jeffrey Leonard. . . . He's thirty-three, he's coming off an off year, he's going into probably the toughest park in baseball for a hitter, and basically I never liked him anyway. If that wasn't enough, Lasorda is for some unfathomable reason talking about moving him back to third base. Basically, I wouldn't touch him with a ten-foot pole.

BOB BROWER
Yankees

An OK player, nothing special. The Rangers hurt themselves by giving him up and putting Cecil Espy in center field. Espy is a better center fielder than Brower, but not as good a leadoff man.

CHRIS BROWN
Pittsburgh

Released this winter. Brown hit great for Buffalo last year, but continued to build on his reputation as the game's number one malingerer and malcontent, and earned his release.

KEVIN BROWN
Rangers

Brown pitched very well as a rookie, but he finished the season on September 8 due to a "strained rotator cuff." The House-Valentine combination has an absolutely awful record for keeping young pitchers healthy. Brown is a good pitcher, but I would want to make certain he was 100 percent before I invested in him.

MARTY BROWN
Cincinnati

Twenty-seven-year-old third baseman. Won't hit enough to be a regular.

JERRY BROWNE
Cleveland

The most-similar player to Jerry Browne is Roberto Alomar. . . . Browne had a quietly sensational year, and his future looks extremely bright. He is only twenty-four years old, and among his accomplishments:

- a .299 average,
- 31 doubles,
- more walks (68) than strikeouts,
- 14 stolen bases.

He's an awfully good young player, comparable to Willie Randolph ten years ago. One of the half dozen best second basemen in baseball. . . .

TOM BROWNING
Cincinnati

In retrospect, I've been slow to give Browning the respect he deserves. He's a workhorse, led the National League in starts last year with thirty-seven and tied for the lead in 1988 and 1986. In five years in the majors he's had a winning record four times, including 20–9 and 18–5. Basically, what he is is a modern Johnny Podres, a left-hander with good stuff, not great, who doesn't beat himself. At thirty, he should remain effective for at least two more seasons.

MIKE BRUMLEY
Detroit

One more player who is not going to take the shortstop job away from Alan Trammell.

TOM BRUNANSKY
St. Louis

Busch Stadium is killing him. Since he joined the Cardinals two years ago he's hit 42 home runs—11 in St. Louis, and 31 on the road. He's not like Guerrero, an all-around great hitter who can adjust the emphasis of his game from power to hitting for average.

Basically I wouldn't regard him as a great draft pick. I expressed the thought a few years ago that he was a young player with old players' skills, and that players of that type tend to peak early and fade early. I think there is every reason to believe that is what is happening to him.

BOB BUCHANAN
Kansas City

Minor league veteran/fourth line pitching prospect. Don't draft him.

BILL BUCKNER
Kansas City (released)

In his career he had six times as many hits as strikeouts, the best ratio of any active player. . . . Had more hits than any other active player of 1989. He also had made more *outs* in his career than any other active player, 7,108. Darrell Evans was second, Buddy Bell third. . . .

STEVE BUECHELE
Rangers

Uncannily consistent, but not very good. The Rangers have two young third basemen, Coolbaugh and Palmer, so Buechele's job is, to say the least, in danger. Because he can play second, play short in an emergency and hit a little, he'll stay around for several years, but probably not as a regular. Probably would hit better in a platoon role. . . .

JAY BUHNER
Seattle

There's a tendency to think that his time has finally come, he's going to have a big year so go get him. Caution might be advised. His poor plate discipline will prevent him from developing into a truly outstanding hitter. His .275 batting average/.490 slugging last year may have been a little over his head. The Mariners are moving out their left-field fence this season. Buhner is capable of having a decent season as a regular right fielder, but I don't advise going too high for him.

DEWAYNE BUICE
Toronto

If he pitches well, it will be an upset.

ERIC BULLOCK
Philadelphia

Veteran minor league outfielder—no prospect. Could probably help some teams as a pinch runner/defensive sub in outfield.

TIM BURKE
Montreal

Fine, consistent reliever. Safe pick.

ELLIS BURKS
Boston

MVP candidate if healthy.

TODD BURNS
Oakland

The best number-six starter in baseball. Burns doesn't have exceptional stuff, but he changes speeds extremely well, has a deceptive motion and throws strikes.

Burns would be an excellent player to have on your staff. The departure of Storm Davis was covered by the signing of Scott Sanderson, but Sanderson has recurring back trouble, and hasn't pitched more than 170 innings since 1982. He's the A's number-four starter, and Curt Young, also a perennial on the DL, is number five. If Burns has to step into a starting role, he's capable of doing so and making a BIG splash. I can easily see Burns winding up the year 16–5, something like that. Sure, he's a gamble, but I'd rather have Burns on my team than Sanderson or Young.

RANDY BUSH
Minnesota

Consistent to the point of being boring. Decent platoon player—no star potential.

BRETT BUTLER
Giants

I made an off-the-cuff remark on the radio last year that Butler was one of the ten greatest leadoff men in baseball history. What I was thinking when I said that was that there are remarkably few leadoff men in history who have done all three things that a leadoff man should do—hit for average, draw a walk, and steal bases. Butler does, and because of that he has scored a hundred runs in a season four times now, which very few leadoff men can match. Luis Aparicio, for example, never scored a hundred runs in a season, Maury Wills only did it twice, Richie Ashburn twice, and Eddie Stanky twice. There are whole eras in baseball history, such as the 1930s, which are devoid of great leadoff men.

After I said that, several people challenged me on it, so I had to really come up with a list of the game's ten greatest leadoff men. Number one is obvious—Rickey Henderson. There are about five players who are in the top group—Henderson, Tim Raines, Lou Brock, Pete Rose, and Billy Hamilton. Those are really the only guys who *have* to be on the list, everybody else is a "but".

• Earle Combs was great but his career was short.
• Dom DiMaggio was great but his career was short, too.
• Maury Wills was real good, but he could have been more selective at the plate.
• Richie Ashburn was real good, but he was in and out as a base stealer.
• Bobby Bonds was dominating, and would be a sure member of the list if people could have left him in the leadoff spot, but they couldn't resist the impulse to try to get his power in the middle of the lineup.
• Eddie Collins would be one of the top two or three, except that he didn't bat leadoff. He batted second.
• Ed Yost was real effective, but he was slow for a leadoff man and didn't hit for a high average.
• Eddie Stanky was like Yost, but he didn't have as many good years.

• Stan Hack should probably be on the list, but he never led the league in runs scored, and it's hard to guess how good a base stealer he really was. He led the league in stolen bases twice—with totals of 16 and 17.
• Lloyd Waner was fast and a .300 hitter, but he didn't walk.
• Matty Alou was about the same.
• If there is an "automatic sixth" to the list, it might be another active player—Paul Molitor. Molitor, like Raines, Henderson, and Butler, stacks up extremely well against the leadoff men of history. This is the era of the great leadoff men.

Then you get a whole bunch of guys who, in seasonal notation, look for all the world like Brett Butler—Jimmy Sheckard, Harry Hooper, George Burns. You can mention guys like Max Bishop, Lu Blue, Dick McAuliffe. Johnny Mostil and Ron LeFlore were great, but for very short periods of time.

In the end, I guess I am more comfortable saying that Butler is one of the *twenty* greatest leadoff men of all time, rather than one of the top ten. But you can defend him as being in the top ten. You can't put up ten guys who were *clearly* better leadoff men than Butler.

Once again last year, Butler almost led the National League in total chances, and was left off the Gold Glove team. His defensive stats are the best of any outfielder of the last ten years except maybe Jesse Barfield, and the people who have seen him play say he is a fantastic outfielder—but he's never won the Gold Glove.

FRANCISCO CABRERA
Atlanta
Cabrera is an excellent hitting prospect; I think he could hit for power *and* average in the majors. He is a catcher, unfortunately, and although he has a strong arm it doesn't appear that his defensive skills will enable him to stay in the lineup, unless the Braves want to do with him like they did with Earl Williams, and just say "Screw the glove work." He may be too big to be a catcher (six four, 200 pounds). The signing of Esasky seems to close off first base, which was his best chance of playing regularly this year, and the signing of Whitt closes off the catcher's spot. A good player to keep around in case he gets a chance, and a potential star because of his bat, but not a good player to be counting too heavily on in 1990.

GREG CADARET
Yankees
One of the Yankees forty-seven candidates for a starting job. His career has been interrupted by sustained battles with wildness. There is no reason to think that he's over that.

IVAN CALDERON
Chisox
A good offensive player/poor outfielder. May move to first base or full-time DH with the departure of Baines. Don't forget about him; he's a hitter.

ERNIE CAMACHO
San Francisco
A poor gamble, but you never know.

KEN CAMINITI
Houston
The new Ray Knight.

MIKE CAMPBELL
Seattle
Onetime super prospect, career now in danger. I'm inclined to think that he could pitch a little with a good team behind him.

GEORGE CANALE
Milwaukee
First base prospect, regarded as superior glove man but strikes out almost as much as Rob Deer. Not a major league

hitter at this point, at least in terms of hitting enough to play first base.

JOHN CANDELERIA
Montreal

He *can* still pitch when he is healthy. If the Expos can put up with him he'll help them make it through the year.

TOM CANDIOTTI
Cleveland

Knuckle-ballers are usually consistent from year to year. Candiotti hasn't been consistent in the past, but his last two seasons are very similar, and very good (14–8, 3.28 ERA and 13–10, 3.10 ERA.) He probably rates as a safe pick, or at least as close to safe as you can get with the Cleveland Indians.

JOHN CANGELOSI
Pittsburgh

Excellent spare outfielder due to career secondary average of .364. He can go in as a defensive sub at any spot, pinch run, or be used as an early-inning pinch hitter.

JOSE CANO
Houston

Caught on with Houston after being released by the Yankees and Braves, and has pitched brilliantly in the Houston system. Astros pitchers will fool you sometimes because the park helps build their confidence. Cano has a realistic chance of being the next guy like Larry Andersen or Juan Agosto to surprise the league by having several consecutive outstanding APBA cards.

JOSE CANSECO
A's

There are two active players who theoretically have a chance, based on their age and productivity, to break Henry Aaron's career home run record. The two are Canseco (3 percent) and Darryl Strawberry (.4 percent.) Unfortu-nately, we both know that neither of them has what it would take to last that long. . . . One other player has a chance to hit 700 home runs, that being Mark McGwire.

DON CARMAN
Philadelphia

Led National League in losses, with 15. Carman held left-handers last year to a .222 batting average, which suggests that he could be effective as a left-handed short reliever. Probably won't get another chance as a starter.

CHRIS CARPENTER
Cards

Part of Whitey's bullpen by committee; may move up to starting role this season. Little star potential, but reasonably good chance of moderate success as a starter.

MARK CARREON
Mets

Probably had the best year as a pinch hitter of any major league player, hitting .370 in the role (10/27) with 4 home runs. It's a tough way to make a living. I think he's likely to have another good year as a part-time player, Merv Rettenmund-like, and then fool somebody into making him a regular, but I'm pretty skeptical about him in the long run.

GARY CARTER
Giants

Released by Mets. Signed by Giants. Career in jeopardy.

JOE CARTER
San Diego

To be honest, Joe Carter *isn't* a great player. He isn't as effective as most people think he is. He plays center field, but that's a real stretch for him, in that he has large legs and doesn't accelerate quickly. As a hitter he makes a huge number of outs, without putting a huge number of runs on the scoreboard. But obviously, he's not Marvelle Wynne, either, and he's got to help the Padres. With a lineup of Bip Roberts, Alomar, Gwynn, Carter, Clark, and Santiago, they should score enough runs to make a very serious run at the National League West.

STEVE CARTER
Pittsburgh

Left-handed hitting outfield prospect, and there are some things to like about him. He's a big guy (six four, two hundred) and runs well, and I believe he could hit .280. Unfortunately, he's never shown any power. Would be surprised if he made the team this season.

CHUCK CARY
Yankees

He's thirty years old with a checkered history, but I like him all the same. He pitched damn well for the Yankees last season, and I don't really see any reason to think that he couldn't do the same in a larger role this year. Will have to fight his way through fifteen other candidates to get a full shot.

CARMEN CASTILLO
Minnesota

Effective platoon player. Will never move out of that role.

JUAN CASTILLO
Milwaukee

Spare infielder—no prospect. Trying to come back from a major injury.

TONY CASTILLO
Atlanta

I've seen him at times look devastating, and I'm not sure why he hasn't been more consistent in the major leagues. Odds are against his making the roster, but could probably do the job as a left-handed short man.

RICK CERONE
Yankees

Cerone had 48 RBI last year with just 102 total bases. That was the highest ratio of RBI to total bases of any major league player (100 or more games). . . . He was followed on that list by three pretty good hitters: Jack Clark, Kent Hrbek, and Pedro Guerrero. . . .

JOHN CERUTTI
Toronto

Seems to have established himself as a serviceable third-fourth starter. I don't see him moving up or down much in 1990.

★ ★ ★
WES CHAMBERLAIN
Pittsburgh
★ ★ ★

The MVP in the Eastern League in 1989, Chamberlain has power, some speed, and a strong arm. The major league equivalencies of his performance at Harrisburg are eye-popping: .294 with 19 homers, 80 RBI, .482 slugging percentage. He has hit well over the years. The one weakness is a poor K/W ratio, but if the long-rumored Barry Bonds trade actually occurs, Chamberlain could make the jump from AA to the majors.

NORM CHARLTON
Cincinnati

Another guy who is always going somewhere in a trade. Throws hard, and I like his chances of eventually succeeding either as a starter or a reliever.

JIM CLANCY
Houston

No reason to take a chance on him.

DAVE CLARK
Chicago Cubs

I used to like him quite a bit as a hitting prospect, and to some degree I still do. Moving from Cleveland to Wrigley Field will probably improve his batting totals. Could emerge as an effective platoon player.

JACK CLARK
Padres

Jack Clark was the freak-stat superstar of 1989. To begin with, he had 110 hits and 132 walks. This is the second time he has had more walks than hits in a season, 1987 being the other time, and I believe it has been done twenty-four times in major league history by players with at least 100 hits. The other twenty-two are Max Bishop (five times), Jimmie Wynn (twice), Eddie Joost (twice), Mickey Mantle (twice), Gene Tenace (twice), Eddie Stanky (twice), and Willie McCovey, Ted Williams, Ed Yost, Jack Crooks, Roy Cullenbine, Hank Greenberg, and Toby Harrah, once each. . . .

I did a computer run to identify the *most effective offensive players* in the major leagues *with batting averages below .250.* Both of the leaders are now Padres. In terms of runs created per out, the most effective offensive player with a batting average below .250 was Jack Clark, followed by Mark McGwire, Barry Bonds, Darryl Strawberry, Eddie Murray, Steve Balboni, Jesse Barfield, Joe Carter, Pete Incaviglia, and Craig Worthington. The list of the players creating the most runs with a batting average below .250 was basically the same players in a different order. Joe Carter created the most runs (90), and Clark was third. . . . Clark also had the highest secondary average of any player in 1989, at .521, edging out Kevin Mitchell (.510) and Rickey Henderson (.501). . . .

With just 110 hits Clark had 76 runs scored and 94 RBI, which was the highest ratio of runs scored and RBI to hits in the major leagues. Mark McGwire was also second on that list, followed by Bo Jackson, Kevin Mitchell, and Kent Hrbek.

JERALD CLARK
San Diego

He was rated the number-four prospect in the Pacific Coast League by *Baseball America,* which said that he "could be a Dawson-type player." I don't know who wrote that, but whoever he is I've got to say that he's out of his goddamn skull. Clark's a picture athlete—six four, 189 pounds, black guy with a throwing arm, and he has hit .300 at every stop in the San Diego system. But he's twenty-six years old, to begin with, and at twenty-six Andre Dawson was a long-established major league star. Dawson would steal 30–40 bases a year; Clark probably won't steal 5. And a .313 batting average at Las Vegas *doesn't* translate as .300 in the majors; it translates as roughly .250. I'll grant that he does have some power potential, but a .250-hitting outfielder (at best), who will strike out four times as often as he walks (at least) without much speed? Who needs him? If he has a good start he can hold a job in the majors for one season, but that's about as far as he's going to go.

TERRY CLARK
California

Right-handed starting pitcher—no prospect.

WILL CLARK
Giants

Clark was second on his team, and also second in the majors, in runs created (125) and runs created per game (8.2). . . . Clark hit .404 in 1989 when not striking out. He was the only major leaguer over .400. . . .

STAN CLARKE
Kansas City

Minor league veteran, pitched extremely well at Omaha but was shelled when called up by Kansas City (two outings). Actually, I was hoping they would give him more of a chance. With Leibrandt pitching so badly, I was hoping that Clarke would turn into the next Leibrandt, as Leibrandt had turned into the next Gura. It didn't work out, and Clarke will have to pitch awfully well to earn another look.

MARTY CLARY
Atlanta

He pitched very well, despite which one would have to describe him as a marginal prospect. He's twenty-eight years old, has a very unimpressive minor league record, and doesn't strike anybody out. You can draft him if you want to, but I'm not going to.

ROGER CLEMENS
Bosox

During the Cy Young "controversy," what one heard constantly was that there was no question that Dave Stewart had been the best pitcher in the league *over the last three years,* but that there was also no doubt that Saberhagen was the best in 1989. But actually, if you really look at them, the best pitcher in the league over the last three years has been Roger Clemens, with Saberhagen second, Viola probably third, and Stewart fourth:

	G	IP	W–L	Pct	H	R	ER	SO	BB	ERA
Clemens	106	799	55–32	.632	680	294	267	777	238	3.01
Saberhagen	104	780	55–32	.632	726	295	269	527	155	3.10
Viola	95	683	49–29	.628	637	251	230	528	167	3.03
Stewart	110	795	62–34	.646	724	337	301	552	284	3.41

Viola's numbers don't include his time with the Mets, or his raw totals would be up with the other three guys. Clemens over the three years has pitched more innings than Stewart, given up 44 fewer hits and 46 fewer walks leading to 43 fewer runs, and has struck out 225 more batters. The biggest difference between Saberhagen and Stewart over the three years is that Saberhagen has walked 129 fewer batters, leading to 42 fewer runs being scored against him. Stewart does have a slightly better won-lost record than Clemens and Saberhagen, but not

much, and that advantage completely disappears when you consider the performance of their teams:

	W–L	Pct.	OTHER PITCHERS W–L	Pct.
Oakland	284–202	.584	222–168	.569
Kansas City	259–226	.534	204–194	.513
Minnesota	256–230	.527	207–201	.507
Boston	250–236	.514	195–204	.489

Stewart has played for a formidable team, winning an average of 95 games a season, while Clemens' team has been under .500 without Clemens on the mound. Clemens' winning percentage over the three years is 143 points better than the rest of his team (.632–.489), while Stewart's is 77 points better (.646–.569). Saberhagen and Viola are also far better than Stewart in this respect. And then when you remember that Stewart is working in the best pitcher's park of any of these four men, and Clemens has worked in Fenway . . . well, it's a mismatch. Clemens, not Stewart, has been the best pitcher in the league over the last three years, and *all three of the men who won Cy Young Awards in the three-year period also out-pitched Stewart over the three years as a whole.*

PAT CLEMENTS
San Diego

Trying to catch on—no real prospect.

BRYAN CLUTTERBUCK
Milwaukee

Minor league veteran—excellent control. Probably could survive with good team behind him.

DAVE COCHRANE
Seattle

What he did for the Mariners last year is about what he's capable of. Two-forty-range hitter with a little power, not nearly enough to be a major league regular.

VINCE COLEMAN
Cards

The funny thing about Vince Coleman is that he has done what he has done for years, and gotten nothing but high praise for it. People have talked about how his speed disrupts the opposition, etc. Then last year he did exactly what he has always done, and got nothing but criticism for it. His career on-base percentage is .323; last year it was .316. His career stolen base percentage is 83 percent; last year it was 87 percent.

I was never wild about Coleman to begin with; to me, he was always a one-dimensional offensive player, and I've no use for one-dimensional players. But I also don't see the point in hammering on him now. I think he's the latest victim of the manager's delusion that a major league player can be taught to hit (see Matty Alou entry, "Biographic Encyclopedia.") If Herzog would accept that he is what he is, he might work with him with the goal in mind of making him one percent better. But instead, there's this idea that if he would just learn to shorten up and punch at the ball he could become a .300 hitter, and that just puts pressure on the player to do something that he really can't do, and sets up a cycle of failure and frustration. Thus, the belief that a player can improve dramatically as a hitter is ultimately a destructive belief.

Coleman's career ratio of RBI to total bases (178 RBI, 1,001 total bases) is the lowest of any active player. It's a "leadoff man's" category, of course—the lowest are Coleman, Harold Reynolds, Bob Dernier, Willie Wilson, Brett Butler. . . .

"In the history of baseball," said Whitey Herzog in the October 30, 1989, *Sporting News,* "you tell me a left fielder who batted 565 times and knocked in 28 runs. Tell me who it is. I'm interested in Vince hitting .290 and driving in 50 runs . . . when you're a leadoff man in the National League with so many guys bunting runners over, you've got to get 50 RBIs."

Actually, 28 RBI in 563 at bats is *not* a particularly unusual ratio for a leadoff man; many leadoff men, including many players regarded as stars, have done worse. Richie Ashburn in 1961 batted 564 times and drove in 20 runs. Larry Bowa in 1971 batted 650 times, and drove in 25 runs. But for a left fielder, the ratio is more unusual. The last regular left fielder who had a worse ratio than Coleman in 1989 was Vince Coleman in 1986, when he batted 600 times and drove in 29 runs. Before that, the last was Alan Wiggins in 1983, when he batted 503 times and drove in 22 runs. Ralph Garr, a left fielder and leadoff man, batted 625 times in 1975 and drove in 31 runs, a ratio slightly worse than Coleman in 1989.

In the half century before 1970, there were very, very few left fielders who were leadoff men, and thus few candidates for a worse ratio. Prior to 1920, I could find a good many.

DARNELL COLES
Seattle

Remember, *avoid* Seattle's right-handed hitters.

DAVE COLLINS
Cincinnati

Released.

★ ★ ★
PAT COMBS
Philadelphia
★ ★ ★

A hard-throwing left-hander who was the Phillies' number one pick in 1988, Combs reached the majors in 1989 and was spectacular, posting a 4–0 record, 2.09 ERA with 30 strikeouts and only 6 walks in 39 innings. You have to be impressed by that. I will point out, in caution, that he hadn't pitched *that* well in the minors, and the Phillies aren't likely to help him win too many close games in 1990. Still, he's got to be somebody you'd be happy to take a chance on in 1990.

KEITH COMSTOCK
Seattle

Back from Japan. No prospect—pitched well as left-handed short man.

DAVID CONE
Mets

The conclusion of Cone's delivery is not smooth or pretty. He brings his arm almost into his body, and then kind of "hops" as if he was trying to avoid falling down. It's not a Kelly Downs delivery, but it isn't a low-impact delivery, either. I think Cone's elbow problems will recur at some point in his career, and will probably prevent him from having a great career.

DENNIS COOK
Philadelphia

To those of you who think that Cook is a great young prospect, let me first point out that he is the same age as his fellow Texan, Roger Clemens, a year and a half older than Bret Saberhagen and two years older than Dwight Gooden. That being said, there is more to like about him than to worry about, and I think he can pitch .500 ball or a little better in the National League.

MIKE COOK
Minnesota

Twenty-six-year-old pitcher with a horrible minor league record. Grade D prospect.

SCOTT COOLBAUGH
Texas

Appears to have the inside track on Buechele for the Rangers' third base job. I like him OK. I see him starting out as a .240–.260 hitter with some power, no speed (about like Blowers of New York), but with a little more possibility of improving over the season. Fifty-fifty to hold Rangers' third base job through 1990, a longshot for Rookie of the Year. Faces long-range competition from Dean Palmer.

SCOTT COOPER
Boston

Cooper is a third baseman and well-regarded defensively, which isn't going to move Wade Boggs. His hitting stats at New Britain are poor but deceptive; most of the Red Sox hitters have hit better in the majors than they did at New Britain. He's young, and if the rumored Wade Boggs deal were actually to happen he could move up. I don't know who I'd compare him to—maybe Brook Jacoby.

JOEY CORA
San Diego

He has made progress since the 1987 debacle, when he was brought prematurely to the major leagues. There are worse second basemen around, but Roberto Alomar isn't one of them.

SHERMAN CORBETT
California

A big left-hander. There is absolutely no reason to believe that he is a major league pitcher.

JIM CORSI
Oakland

Odd delivery makes him hard to read. I think he'll remain effective in his present role (good for APBA/Strat-O-Matic players), but I doubt that he will move up to a more key role.

JOHN COSTELLO
Cardinals

Another part of Whitey's bullpen committee. Not likely to succeed in any more demanding role.

HENRY COTTO
Seattle

The most-similar player to Henry Cotto is Dave Martinez. . . . Cotto is perhaps my least-favorite major league player. He is a good base stealer and a good defensive center fielder, but he's not very good to begin with, and with the Mariners moving the left field fence out, he's not going to be getting any better. Stay away from him.

STEVE CRAWFORD
Kansas City

Pitched well in long relief. Obviously, has no star potential at this point of his career . . . just trying to hang in the game.

TIM CREWS
Los Angeles

Has pitched well for the Dodgers, and probably will continue to do so.

CHUCK CRIM
Milwaukee

Has now led the American League in game appearances for two straight seasons—70 in 1988, 76 last year. Trebelhorn uses him very well.

STEVE CUMMINGS
Toronto

Toronto's second-round draft pick in 1986, Cummings has been brought through the system slowly despite pitching consistently well. His won-lost records since signing have been 9–5, 18–8, 14–11, and 7–5, and his *worst* ERA was 3.14. He doesn't appear to have overpowering stuff, but he's been taking it one step at a time, and the next step is the American League. He may need a transition year, and I hope the Blue Jays have the self-discipline to keep him in long relief for a year, but he does look like a pitcher.

PETE DALENA
Cleveland

Twenty-nine-year-old minor league veteran, first baseman; capable of hitting .280 in the majors but secondary offensive skills not impressive enough to earn him regular work.

KAL DANIELS
Los Angeles

I've always loved Daniels, a lifetime .302 hitter with a *career* secondary average of .435, one of the best in baseball. At this point you've got to have a little caution about him. He's a poor defensive player, he's had some knee operations now, and he's not likely to hit in Dodger Stadium the way he could have in Cincinnati. He can still play for me anytime.

RON DARLING
Mets

Darling was the National League's most-average pitcher in 1989. He finished 14–14, .500. His ERA was 3.52; the league average was 3.49. He struck out 6.3 men per nine innings; the league average was 5.8. He walked 2.9 men per nine innings; the league average was 3.2.

DANNY DARWIN
Houston

Coming off the best season of his career at age thirty-four; should have another good year.

DOUG DASCENZO
Cubs

His major league average is .182, and he's a better hitter than that, a .250-range hitter with enough walks and stolen bases to be OK in center. He's comparable to Cecil Espy. He's not comparable to Jerome Walton.

JEFF DATZ
Detroit

Thirty-year-old minor league catcher— not an awful player but no prospect.

JACK DAUGHERTY
Texas

Twenty-nine-year-old first baseman, hit .302 in 52 games last year. He is *not* a .302 a hitter; he's more like a .260 hitter, with good K/W and more speed than most first basemen, but not much power. I don't recommend him.

DARREN DAULTON
Philadelphia

He's not as bad a player as his .206 lifetime batting average. His career secondary average is .292, so he'll put more runs on the scoreboard than a lot of catchers who hit .250. There is still no reason to particularly desire him on your team.

BOBBY DAVIDSON
Yankees

Twenty-seven-year-old reliever. Would like his chances in an organization that knew how to bring along a young player. Limited if any star potential.

MARK DAVIDSON
Houston

Excellent defensive outfielder. I wouldn't have figured him to hit as poorly as he has, but obviously doesn't project as a regular.

ALVIN DAVIS
Seattle

Per at bat, he was the most effective offensive player in the American League last year, creating 100 runs, or 7.51 runs/offensive game. He drew 101 walks, struck out only 49 times, one of the best ratios in the majors. He's a lifetime .290 hitter, and with his power and walks, the batting average represents only 46 percent of his offensive value. Presumably will become full-time DH with the signing of Pete O'Brien.

WARM FRONT DAVIS
Baltimore
Released.

CHILI DAVIS
California
One of the league's most consistent players—safe draft. Speed has basically evaporated at age thirty, but a very solid outfielder.

ERIC DAVIS
Cincinnati
I did a computer run to identify the most effective offensive player in the majors with a career average *below .275*. The answer was Eric Davis, by far, followed by his old buddy Darryl Strawberry, with Jack Clark third, Kevin Mitchell fourth, and Dwight Evans fifth. That's based on career stats . . . Davis has a career secondary average of .504, which is also the highest of any major league player; he is followed by Rickey Henderson (.477), Ken Phelps, Darryl Strawberry, Mike Schmidt, Gary Redus, Tim Raines, Jack Clark, Barry Bonds, and Howard Johnson. What that is, if you don't understand the concept of secondary average, is a list of ten guys who will put runs on the scoreboard even if they hit .240 . . . Davis's batting average represents only 37 percent of his offensive contribution.

GLENN DAVIS
Houston
Wonderful offensive player. A typical season is .264 with 30 doubles, 32 homers, 100 RBI. He's never had an off season . . . 16 percent chance of hitting 500 career home runs, 2 percent chance of hitting 600 . . . safe draft.

JODY DAVIS
Atlanta
No value.

JOHN DAVIS
Chisox
Big reliever. Excellent stuff but perennial control problems. No evidence he has overcome it.

MARK DAVIS
Kansas City
No one quite seems to know exactly how Wathan will use his two relief aces, Davis and Montgomery, who was really more effective last year than Davis. The odds are that he will make Davis the stopper, period, and Montgomery the setup man, but I'm not sure that's the best possible thing. Remember, it is only in the last ten years that a relief ace's job has been so tightly defined—use him *only* to preserve a lead in the late innings—and the major reason for that definition was to eliminate the excessive workloads which were destroying relievers' arms after a couple of good years. But with Davis being a left-hander and Montgomery a right-hander, I wonder if it might not be smarter to go back to the way that relief aces were used prior to 1978 (in the late innings of any close game, whether the team is ahead, tied, or behind) and then divide that larger workload between the two based on the righty-lefty advantage and the recent workload.

But I'll say this: I'm not worried. Early last year Wathan had *four* right-handed relievers pitching extremely well—Aquino, Gordon, Montgomery, and Farr. Intuitively, it would seem that you wouldn't be able to use four right-handed relievers effectively and keep them all sharp, but Wathan did. Aquino came into the game if the starter was knocked out in the first five innings and started occasionally, Gordon came into the game in the sixth and seventh, Montgomery came in in the seventh and eighth, and Farr came in to start the ninth. As of June 15 Aquino was 3–1 with a 2.83 ERA, Gordon 8–2 with a 2.54, Montgomery 6–1 with a 1.77 and Farr had 15 saves and a 2.03 ERA. Then Farr had a shoulder/rib cage injury and Gordon had to be moved out of the bullpen to patch the starting rotation, and the arrangement broke down, but if Wathan was able to use four right-handed relievers effectively and keep them all sharp, I'd think two relief aces, one right-handed and one left-handed, would be no big challenge.

MIKE DAVIS
Los Angeles
Streak hitter, has been in a slump for two years. He could come back, but obviously you wouldn't want to bet on it.

STEVE DAVIS
Cleveland
Left-hander with no prospect label, but pitched wonderfully at Colorado Springs (12–2, 2.45 ERA.) You have to respect the chance that he could be the next Doug Jones.

STORM DAVIS
Kansas City
Oakland didn't lose anything in this guy. His won-lost record is a joke, as he had the best offensive support of any major league starting pitcher.

Look at the A's staff, not as they look now but as they looked when the A's picked them up:

- Dave Stewart had been traded by Texas after going 0–6 with a 5.42 ERA, and released by Philadelphia after positing ERAs of 6.23 and 6.57.
- Storm Davis was pitching for Reno in the California League after posting a 2–7 record, 6.18 ERA for San Diego.
- Dennis Eckersley was acquired for three non-prospects after going 6–11 with a 4.37 ERA for the Cubs.
- Rick Honeycutt was picked up cheap after posting a 2–12 record, 4.59 ERA for the Dodgers.

The fact that these guys are *now* perceived as making up an outstanding pitching staff is a tribute to LaRussa, Dave Duncan, and the rest of the A's organization. But does it make more sense for the A's to pay $2 million a year to keep Storm Davis marginally happy and complaining about not starting a World Series game, or does it make more sense for them to go back into that pool of guys with good arms but six-plus ERAs, and find somebody else that they can turn around?

It seems obvious to me. Knowing what you are doing is a tremendous advantage in a pennant race.

BILL DAWLEY
Oakland
Released.

ANDRE DAWSON
Cubs
The major league leaders in career power/speed number: Andre Dawson (300.5), Mike Schmidt, Rickey Henderson, Robin Yount, Claudell Washington, Dale Murphy, George Brett, Dave Parker, Kirk Gibson, and Darryl Strawberry (193.6). Dawson has 319 home runs and 284 stolen bases, which are the two elements of the power/speed number, but has no chance to overtake the number one man on the all-time list, Willie Mays, at 447.1. Despite the abundance of power/speed players in the game in the last few years, no one on the list is likely to displace Mays as the top power/speed player in history, although Rickey Henderson could if he emphasizes his power as he ages. . . . Eric Davis will join the top ten next season.

KEN DAYLEY
St. Louis
Remarkable consistency, five straight seasons with ERAs between 2.66 and 3.26. Not likely to outgrow his role as a left-handed short man.

ROB DEER
Brewers
Both in 1989 and for his career as a whole, Deer had the worst ratio of hits to strikeouts of any major league player, striking out 61 percent more often than he got a hit. His career ratio is 1–1.59. No one else was close, either in 1989 or career. . . . The most-similar player to Rob Deer is Cory Snyder. . . .

JOSE DEJESUS
Kansas City
Awesome arm, no control. Eventually will probably get his act together, but with the Royals having more pitching than most teams he's not a good bet to surface this year, or to succeed if he does. My own guess is that he'll eventually be a bullpen closer, but whatever his role is to be, he hasn't found it yet.

JOSE DELEON
Cardinals
One of the best pitchers in baseball, with 200-plus strikeouts and a winning record each of the last two seasons. Very capable of winning a Cy Young Award.

LUIS DELEON
Seattle
Once an effective reliever, still trying to come back. Posted a 5.15 ERA at Calgary last year.

LUIS DE LOS SANTOS
Royals
Luis was the MVP in the American Association in '88, has had a tough time finding a spot in the major leagues. Physically and as a player, he is uncannily similar to Enos Cabell—a .280-range hitter with some line drive power, no real home run power, a poor third baseman but a good enough first baseman. There isn't a place for him with the Royals—wouldn't be even if Brett weren't there—but he's only twenty-three, so time is on his side. The key

thing for him probably is that he's got to develop some power, but he's probably as good a player now as Cabell was for most of his career. Hits almost exclusively to the opposite field.

RICK DEMPSEY
Dodgers
Will become a four-decade player if he can get an at bat this year . . . what a dumb idea that is. Hit .179 last year, but with a secondary average of .331.

DREW DENSON
Atlanta
Six five, switch-hitting first baseman, a first-round draft pick back in the days when the Braves were drafting turkeys. He's a .250-range hitter with 10–12 home run power (so far; may develop more), poor K/W ratio (about 3–1), no speed. The signing of Nick Esasky closes the door for him, and he's not a good enough hitter to battle for playing time (in the future) with Francisco Cabrera, Tommie Gregg, Geronimo Berroa, and Dave Justice. Pass.

BOB DERNIER
Phils
The *worst* hitters of 1989, playing 100 or more games: 1. Bob Dernier, 2. John Shelby, 3. Omar Vizquel, 4. Craig Reynolds, 5. Andres Thomas, 6. Brad Wellman, 7. Jose Uribe, 8. Felix Fermin, 9. Mike Pagliarulo, 10. Lenny Harris. . . . Even in those at bats when he *didn't* strike out—when he did put the ball in play—Dernier hit only .201, the lowest of any major league player. Closest to him was Craig Reynolds at .222. . . .

JIM DESHAIES
Houston
Big left-hander, comparable to Tom Browning but throws harder. Actually pitched better than Mike Scott did last year, but didn't get the offensive support. With two straight seasons over 200

innings and with ERAs of 3.00 and 2.91, he's a solid to outstanding draft pick.

DELINO DESHIELDS
Montreal
A young shortstop; DeShields and Marquis Grissom are regarded as the top prospects in the Montreal system.

The odds are that DeShields will wait another year before becoming the Montreal shortstop. If he doesn't, I don't think he'll be a disaster; I'd pencil him in as a .240–.250 hitter with excellent base stealing ability, with the tools of a shortstop but not the polish. In the low minors he's drawn a huge number of walks, but his K/W ratio deteriorated last year when he moved up to AAA the second half of the season. I think he will be a major league shortstop and could be one of the best in the league, but I don't expect his future to arrive in 1990.

MIKE DEVEREAUX
Orioles
Statistically the most-comparable major league player to Mike Devereaux is Junior Felix. This shows the limitations of the formula. Devereaux and Felix were both rookies last year, both playing mostly right field, and they did in fact have quite comparable years, Devereaux hitting .266 with 8 home runs, 46 RBI, and Felix hitting .258 with 9 and 46. They had almost the same numbers of games and at bats, and both stole around 20 bases (Devereaux 22, Felix 18). But Felix, because he is four-and-a-half years younger than Devereaux, has a vastly greater growth potential. . . . Don't interpret that as a knock against Devereaux. I like Devereaux, I've thought he should be in the majors for several years, and he's capable of hitting better than the .266 he hit as a rookie. But Felix could be a star, if enough things break right for him, a big star. Devereaux's not going to be an MVP candidate. . . .

BO DIAZ
Cincinnati
Thirty-seven years old, coming off consecutive seasons of .219 and .205, and Joe Oliver has the catching job. I know there's a shortage of catchers, but I think you could find somebody better to take a chance on.

MARIO DIAZ
Seattle
Very good hitter for a shortstop, but probably doesn't have a shortstop's arm. Comparable to Felix Fermin.

ROB DIBBLE
Cincinnati
Awesome fastball; figures to share late relief work with Randy Myers. Hell, you guys know all this. . . .

GORDON DILLARD
Philadelphia
Candidate for left-handed short man position; probably can do the job.

FRANK DIPINO
St. Louis
Nine-and-oh record ended a string of eight major league seasons without a winning record. . . .

GARY DISARCINA
California
Twenty-two-year-old shortstop prospect, probably a year away. I don't see him as anything to get excited about. He has no offensive positives that I can see—a .230 hitter with no power or speed—so his defense would have to be something else for him to play.

BENNY DISTEFANO
Pittsburgh
Perennial prospect, now twenty-eight years old. He's not going to run Andy Van Slyke out of the league, but he's not a bad player—about a .250 hitter with enough homers, walks, and defense to

make him somewhat valuable. The Pirates had him at first base, where he had no experience and was pretty bad, but I'd rather his bat in the lineup than Sid Bream's.

JOHN DOPSON
Boston
Has now committed the same number of balks in his career as Tommy John . . . not a great pitcher but a serviceable number-three starter. Expect him to be a steady 14–11 over the next few years. . . .

BILL DORAN
Astros
Even though he had a miserable year with the bat, Doran did have the best stolen base percentage in the major leagues last year, stealing 22 bases in 25 attempts. That was a problem early in his career . . . will bounce back, of course.

BRIAN DORSETT
Yankees
Right-handed power hitter, no real prospect. Has power, but .250-range hitter with no speed, poor K/W. Not a lot worse than Rob Deer.

RICHARD DOTSON
Kansas City
Every time John Schuerholz mentioned him he would say "he's only thirty-one, so we feel he's got several good years left." What an asinine comment. He's only thirty-one, but *he can't pitch*. His fastball died years ago, and his ERAs over the last five years are 4.47, 5.48, 4.17, 5.00, and 4.46. Sure, he might do a little better with the Royals, but who needs a pitcher like that? Not that he's any worse than Storm Davis. . . .

BRIAN DOWNING
California
One of my favorite players. Sure, he's old, but he did hit .283 last year and slug over .400, his eighth consecutive solid

season. Sure, he's slow, but he grounded into only six double plays last year. The Angels don't have any hot young hitting prospects, so Downing may make it through another season as a DH. Obviously, he's a risk.

KELLY DOWNS
Giants

On the plane down to Arizona last spring, I read a preview of the season in *Sport* magazine, picking the award winners (they didn't get any right). *Sport*'s candidate for the NL Cy Young Award was Kelly Downs, so I was anxious to see him pitch.

The first time he pitched, I talked to a beat writer about him, asking him if he thought Downs was really that good. He can definitely have a big season, replied the writer.

Well, I said, why hasn't he? Why didn't he have a big year last year?

"Shoulder trouble," replied the beat writer.

"Was he over-used?" I asked.

"No. It just happened."

"Well," I asked, "if he had shoulder trouble last year, and he *wasn't* over-used, then don't you figure he's going to have shoulder trouble again this year?"

"He's been working out with weights," explained the reporter, "strengthening the shoulder. I don't think it will come back."

So after a couple of innings, I walked down the right field line to watch Downs from a different angle. I couldn't believe it. I couldn't believe that *anybody* could watch this guy pitch for more than ten minutes and *not* realize that he was going to have shoulder and elbow trouble all his life. He finishes his motion with his arm extended straight out, and, being very thin, brings his arm across his body. Nothing slows his arm down until it slams into his body. It's unfathomable how he got to the major leagues without anybody telling him that that was going

to destroy his shoulder. That he continued to do it, even after the shoulder injury, is . . . well, what's beyond unfathomable?

Physically, Downs is very similar to Mark Gubicza, Kansas City—tall, thin, the body hanging off of broad shoulders like a shirt on a hanger. His stuff is very good—throws hard, mixes his pitches well. There's just one big difference between Downs and Gubicza. Gubicza, like virtually all Royals pitchers, is mechanically sound, and therefore able to learn his craft without the distraction of constant injuries.

When I got back to Kansas, I found out that I had Kelly Downs on my fantasy league team. I decided I'd let him have a good April, and then trade him before the arm trouble came back. I wasn't able to do it; the problem came back before I could unload him.

Can he adjust? Sure, he'll adjust—after he loses his fast ball. It's sad, but that's the world.

DOUG DRABEK
Pittsburgh

Very solid and still young. One of the top ten pitchers in the National League.

DAVE DRAVECKY
San Francisco

Retired.

TOM DREES
Chisox

This is the guy who threw three no-hitters in the minors last year, including two straight. He doesn't have an impressive fastball, doesn't strike out many people, and isn't regarded as a hot prospect, but he has pitched very well both in the PCL (1989) and at Birmingham in 1988, where he had a 2.79 ERA.

CAMERON DREW
Houston

Six five left-handed hitting outfielder, excellent minor league hitter. A year ago

he was rated the number-one prospect in the Astros system, which is kind of strange anyway because he's twenty-six years old, but anyway knee trouble wiped out his 1989 season, and changes him from prospect to suspect. He *is* a major league hitter, possibly a .300 hitter with line drive power.

TIM DRUMMOND
Minnesota

Right-handed pitcher, has been in Pirates and Mets systems. Very marginal prospect.

BRIAN DUBOIS
Detroit

1.75 ERA in 36 innings as late-season Tiger. I'm not sure who the hell he is, to be frank. He's not in the Tigers media guide last year. He's not in any list of top prospects. He pitched very well in seven games of AAA ball, but where did he come from before that? The Tigers draft list from last summer includes a *first baseman* name Brian *Dubose*—is that him? Damned if I know. . . .

ROB DUCEY
Toronto

Only twenty-four years old; career seems to have stalled a little bit but he remains a prospect. The departure of Moseby could clear playing time for him, except that Glenallen Hill has probably passed him. I see Ducey as .250–.270 range hitter with some power, excellent speed.

MARIANO DUNCAN
Cincinnati

As usual, hit very well right-handed (.283 with .465 slugging percentage), but nothing as a left-handed hitter (.226 with no power.) When are they ever going to learn that this switch-hitting-to-take-advantage-of-your-speed stuff *just doesn't work* . . . strikeout to walk ratio last year was the worst of his career, and it's always been bad.

MIKE DUNNE
Seattle

Wiped out, of course. I wouldn't anticipate a comeback.

SHAWON DUNSTON
Cubs

Played great last year, improved his plate discipline. Fine shortstop with great arm. Solid risk for 1990.

LEON DURHAM
St. Louis

Has he retired? I wouldn't mind having him on my team as a pinch hitter . . . could hit .250–.270 and occasionally pop one out.

JIM DWYER
Montreal

Turned forty this winter. Can still hit.

MIKE DYER
Minnesota

Unimpressive young pitcher. Will be surprised if he is ever an effective starter.

LENNY DYKSTRA
Philadelphia

The most-similar player to Len Dykstra is Mitch Webster. . . . Batting averages over last four years: .295, .285, .270, and .237.

Stolen base percentages: .816, .794, .789, .714.

RBI: 45, 43, 33, 32.

Hmm. It's hard to see the progress here.

LOGAN EASLEY
Pittsburgh

Twenty-eight-year-old right-hander. Has pitched well at times, but no particular prospect.

GARY EAVE
Atlanta

Six-foot-four inch, twenty-six-year-old right-hander, spent years as a marginal prospect before pitching great last year (13–3 at Columbus, three impressive starts with the Braves.) He's not a prospect comparable to Avery or Smoltz, but I kind of like him. When he went 5–9 with a 3.56 ERA in 1988 he still had 81 strikeouts and only 31 walks. I'd give him a 25–30 percent chance of being a solid rotation starter.

DENNIS ECKERSLEY
Oakland

He had 55 strikeouts and 3 walks in 58 innings. Is that the best strikeout to walk ratio in history? I wish I had time to check. . . .

WAYNE EDWARDS
Chisox

Up-and-down pitching prospect, nothing special.

MARK EICHHORN
Atlanta

He's trying to hold on, and I think he probably will. Despite generally poor performance he had 49 strikeouts and only 11 unintentional walks last year, and I'd have to think a guy who can do that can pitch.

DAVE EILAND
Yankees

Decent pitching prospect, finesse-type right-hander. Opportunity to pitch lost with acquisitions of Pascual Perez and Tim Leary.

JIM EISENREICH
Kansas City

He was the Royals' MVP last year, almost by acclamation. My, what a great player he would have been if it wasn't for the illness. Physically, he's similar to what DiMaggio must have been—strong, but also fast and remarkably graceful. He has no weaknesses. Superb outfielder, gets a great jump on the ball and has above-average arm. Gap hitter.

Expect him to have several successful seasons, some better than 1989, but that could be the Royals fan in me talking.

KEVIN ELSTER
Mets

Don't see his career taking any sudden left or right turns.

DAVE ENGLE
Milwaukee

Probably won't be on a roster.

JIM EPPARD
Angels

First baseman with no power, now thirty years old (in April). No prospect.

NICK ESASKY
Atlanta

Another guy with an on year-off year pattern; has hit well in 1983 (.265), 1985 (.262), 1987 (.272), and 1989 (.277), but poorly in all the even years, never higher than .243. His 1989 season in Boston was obviously his best, but I don't see it as being out of his league. I think he could hit 35 homers and drive in 100 runs for Atlanta.

ALVARO ESPINOZA
Yankees

Espinoza was the only major league regular last year with a secondary average below .100, at .085. What that means is that *other than what is reflected in his batting average,* he did exceptionally little to help his team score runs, as is reflected in his totals of runs scored and driven in. He drew only 14 walks, stole only 3 bases and hit zero home runs . . . the bottom ten in secondary average: Espinoza, Omar Vizquel, Felix Fermin, Brad Wellman, Andres Thomas, Dave Gallagher, Rafael Ramirez, Alfredo Griffin, Billy Ripken, and Bob Dernier . . .

CECIL ESPY
Rangers

Has lost his job to Gary Pettis. Basically a good AAA player.

DARRELL EVANS
Atlanta

While I was running the Jack Clark list (see Clark), I also did a run to find the most effective major league hitter *in his career* with a career average below .250. The answer was Darrell Evans, followed by Tom Brunansky, Rob Deer, Carmelo Martinez, and Steve Balboni. . . .

DWIGHT EVANS
Boston

Most-similar active player: Dave Parker. . . .

A Boston area talk show host was doing a show about Dwight Evans last summer when Dwight moved past some milestone, and called me to ask for my input. I spent a couple of hours looking carefully at his career, and decided that I should advocate his selection to the Hall of Fame. First, I did a computer search to find the most-similar players in baseball history. The most-similar by far was Ron Santo, and since I have always advocated Santo's elevation to Cooperstown, it seemed logically consistent to also do so for Evans. Evans, like Santo, is a durable, consistent player, an exceptional defensive player with 366 career home runs and a good average.

As much as that, what struck me was the comparison to Jim Rice. Jim Rice will walk into the Hall of Fame without anybody even checking his passport—but has he really been a better player than Evans? Rice's career average is 25 points higher, and that's important, but look at Evans's edges:

- Evans has drawn 600 more walks. Despite Rice's edge in batting average, Evans has been on base more often than Rice and scored more runs, and that's what really counts.
- Speed. Evans has a few more stolen bases, although this isn't a running team. The big difference is double plays—Rice has grounded into 113 more double plays, in virtually the same number of at bats.
- Defense. A great defensive outfielder against a marginal one.

They're even in terms of power, 382 career homers for Rice and 366 for Evans, but Evans has 83 more doubles, so their career isolated power is exactly the same, .204.

I rate Evans, over his career, essentially even to Rice as an offensive player, superior defensively and on the base paths. If I could put one of them in the Hall of Fame, I'd go with Evans.

HOWARD FARMER
Montreal

Right-handed starting pitcher; because of the departure of three starting pitchers to free agency, Farmer probably will get a shot at a major league job sometime during the summer. He's not Steve Avery, but he definitely has some things going for him, a 90 MPH fastball and a good slider. He's pitched well at Jamestown, 1987 (9–6, 3.27 ERA), Rockford, 1988 (15–7, 2.51 ERA) and Jacksonville, 1989 (12–9, 2.20) with very good K/W ratios at every stop, and he might pitch well for Montreal.

STEVE FARR
Royals

Will be scrambling for a job with the late-season emergence of Jeff Montgomery and the signing of Mark Davis. Not a good risk.

JOHN FARRELL
Cleveland

Solid pitcher, could win for a good team. Altered the grip on his fastball last year, and was throwing harder than before; got more strikeouts. If your league uses wins and losses, stay away from him because he's not going to win consistently with Cleveland. If not, he's as good a pitcher as Jeff Ballard or Ron Darling or Mike Boddicker.

MIKE FELDER
Brewers

Sensational base stealer, doesn't do anything else well enough to hold a job. I like him as much as I do your average Milwaukee Brewer.

★ ★ ★
JUNIOR FELIX
Jays
★ ★ ★

In view of his age (twenty-two), speed, throwing arm, and solid performance with the bat, Felix has more star potential than any other 1989 rookie except Ken Griffey, Jr. He can be expected to steal 35–60 bases this year, although his stolen base percentage isn't going to be outstanding, hit 12–20 homers and improve his batting average a few points. Needs to improve plate discipline to reach highest levels.

FELIX FERMIN
Cleveland

Last year 91 percent of his hits were singles, easily the highest percentage of any major league player.

SID FERNANDEZ
Mets

Does he have a couple more years before the weight catches up with him? I would guess that he does. He's not an absolutely safe pick, but he's had four straight winning seasons, with a composite winning percentage of .651. His strikeout rate remains very high. You have to respect that.

TONY FERNANDEZ
Toronto
In a strange way, a safe pick. His performance varies from category to category, but he's always in the lineup, he's a Gold Glove shortstop and he always contributes *something* with the bat. I would guess that his batting average will recover this year.

MIKE FETTERS
Angels
He's a starting pitcher, so the signing of Mark Langston would seem to close off any chance he had of starting the season in the major leagues. He's not a bad prospect, a big right-hander with five pitches; a year ago he was rated ahead of Jim Abbott as the top prospect in the organization. Basically, he has proven everything he could prove in the minors and is ready for a shot at the majors, but he may have to wait a year, anyway.

CECIL FIELDER
Detroit
Back from Japan. I have no idea what to expect of him, but if he starts hitting home runs in April you might snarf him up. He was always about that far away from being a good major league power hitter.

BRUCE FIELDS
Seattle
Minor league veteran, superb singles hitter who made land a job as a pinch hitter. He would if it was my team, anyway.

TOM FILER
Milwaukee
Now thirty-three years old and with a fastball that wouldn't put a dent in the side of a cereal box, Filer is a long-odds candidate to continue his superb pitching of late 1989 (7–3 in 13 starts.) I don't recommend that you draft him, but still, he is in possession of a job, and that's an edge.

CHUCK FINLEY
California
If he's healthy, he's going to be one of the best pitchers in the league. A pitcher with a history of getting hurt is going to continue to get hurt most of the time.

STEVE FINLEY
Baltimore
I like Brady Anderson better than Finley, but I don't think Frank Robinson agrees with me. Finley could hit .280–.300 and steal 50 bases, but with no power and not many walks. OK draft pick; expect him to play.

JEFF FISCHER
Los Angeles
Twenty-six-year-old right-handed pitcher. I'm tempted to dismiss him as no prospect, but the Dodgers will fool you once in awhile. I don't see anything to like about him.

BRIAN FISHER
Pittsburgh
In the same class with Mike Dunne. I don't expect to see him back.

CARLTON FISK
Chicago
Carlton now has more career stolen bases than any other *two* active catchers. Fisk has 117; the next two men are Tony Pena (59) and Mike Heath and Benito Santiago (each 47). . . .

MIKE FITZGERALD
Expos
The key question about Mike Fitzgerald is not Mike Fitzgerald, but Nelson Santovenia. If Santovenia develops, Fitzgerald can't keep pace with him, and will lose playing time. If not, he'll just keep rolling along.

MIKE FLANAGAN
Toronto
Is he going to be back? My memory is that he announced his retirement, but I can't find a source for that. Despite pitching for good teams, he hasn't had a winning record since 1983, and that's a long time to keep losing.

TIM FLANNERY
San Diego
Retired.

DARRIN FLETCHER
Los Angeles
A young catcher, was the Big Ten Player of the Year and is well regarded defensively, but as of now he's a .200–.225 hitter with no offensive pluses. Don't draft him.

SCOTT FLETCHER
Chisox
The most-similar player to Scott Fletcher is Marty Barrett. . . . A solid player and a reasonably solid draft, with some risk that his bat will continue to droop.

TOM FOLEY
Montreal
The most-similar player to Tom Foley is Steve Lyons. . . . Job endangered by the development of Jeff Huson and Delino DeShields. Not a bad player, but more likely to go backward than forward.

CURT FORD
Philadelphia
I've seen enough, how about you? Two years of hitting below .220 with no power . . . I mean, I know he is *capable* of playing better, but is that enough? No star potential—may lose his job.

BOB FORSCH
Astros
Bye-bye.

TONY FOSSAS
Milwaukee

Minor league veteran, caught on with Brewers as a left-handed short man and pitched well. No prospect.

JOHN FRANCO
Cincinnati

I don't understand the trade, and I wouldn't have made it. Myers is two years younger, throws harder, and pitched better last season. Franco has carried a worrisome workload, and had the highest ERA of his career last year at 3.12. I mean, I know he's a quality reliever, but what's the point? I'd take Myers any day.

JULIO FRANCO
Rangers

Since he came to the majors, Franco has shown remarkably sustained, broad-based improvement. Originally a .270 hitter, he has hit over .300 the last four years. Originally a guy who would strike out twice as often as he walked, he's been basically even over the last three years. Originally a player who would hit 3 to 8 home runs a year, he hit 13 last season. Originally a 60 percent base stealer, he was 21 for 24 as a base stealer last year, the best percentage of any American League player (20 or more attempts.) He never gets any credit for making himself better, but he sure has done it.

Valentine had him hitting fifth most of the year, which was an interesting idea. The traditional number-five hitter is a low-average power hitter who doesn't run well, like Danny Tartabull, Gary Carter, or Jeffrey Leonard, while Franco is a high-average hitter who runs very well. The man on the Rangers who fits the image of the number-five hitter is Incaviglia. But, as I have pointed out before, the traditional image doesn't necessarily make any sense. The number-five hitter often leads off the second

inning, and a guy like Incaviglia is an awful leadoff man. As far as "protecting" Sierra—well, you know I don't believe in that stuff anyway, but assuming the number-five hitter has to protect Sierra, a .300 hitter with a little power is probably best equipped to do that, rather than an Incaviglia. With a runner on second and first base empty, which is the basic "protection" setup, a single scores the run most of the time, so you're going to be more afraid of Franco's .320 batting average than Incaviglia's 25 home runs. Still, if you're desperate for a leadoff hitter like the Rangers were, and you've got a guy who hits .320 and walks and steals bases, as Franco does, I've got to say lead him off.

Franco turned twenty-eight this winter, and already has 1,232 major league hits, so he's headed for a total way over 2,000.

TERRY FRANCONA
Brewers

What a worthless player. Francona, whose father was one of my favorite players, has the lowest career secondary average of any active player (500 or more games.) What makes this especially striking is that almost everybody else in the bottom ten is a shortstop, and not really *expected* to contribute much offensively—the bottom ten are Francona, Ed Romero, Ozzie Guillen, Curt Wilkerson, Mickey Hatcher, Craig Reynolds, Rafael Ramirez, Glenn Hoffman, Alfredo Griffin, and Jim Gantner. Francona also has the fewest runs scored and driven per hit of any major league player over his career; he is followed on that list by Bruce Benedict, Harold Reynolds, Greg Gross, Curtis Wilkerson, Mike Scioscia, Jose Oquendo, Ron Oester, Jose Uribe, and Damaso Garcia. Those middle infielders, if they can chip in a single here and there you're happy with it, but what is it exactly that Francona *does?* . . .

WILLIE FRASER
California

So-so pitcher, no star potential; will scramble for innings behind Angels' big five.

LAVEL FREEMAN
Brewers

A six-year minor league free agent; presume he has fled the Brewers, but I haven't heard if or where he has signed. He *can* hit, not great but enough to help an American League team as a DH.

MARVIN FREEMAN
Philadelphia

Six foot six and with no idea of the strike zone; very marginal prospect.

STEVE FREY
Montreal

Left-handed reliever; don't know much about him. Didn't pitch well last year, but will receive another chance because of Expos' shortage of pitching.

TODD FROHWIRTH
Philadelphia

Pitched fairly well last year as mop-up man (3.59 ERA in 45 games.) I think he can continue to pitch at that level and have some years a little better, but he's not star material.

TRAVIS FRYMAN
Detroit

A shortstop in the Tigers system, often described as "another Trammell." My own opinion about him is that the Tigers are damned lucky that they still have the original. . . .

GARY GAETTI
Minnesota

The most-similar player to Gary Gaetti is Tim Wallach . . . not a Hall of Famer, but one of the three or four best in the league. . . .

GREG GAGNE
Twins

The following players in 1989 had run element ratios *lower* than .7 (see Otis Nixon), but scored more runs than they drove in: Greg Gagne, Claudell Washington, Carlos Martinez, Rob Deer, Alvaro Espinoza, Henry Cotto, Jeff Kunkel, Kelly Gruber, Jeff Treadway, Jeff Blauser, Ryne Sandberg, Bobby Bonilla, and Terry Pendleton. . . . The most-similar player to Greg Gagne is Shawon Dunston. . . .

ANDRES GALARRAGA
Montreal

Crowds the plate, led the National League in being hit with the pitch (13 times, actually tied with Robby Thompson). . . . He's been in double figures in that category three straight years, only major league player who has. . . .

DAVE GALLAGHER
Chisox

The most-similar player to Dave Gallagher is Cecil Espy. . . . The White Sox continued to play him every day last year, even after putting Lance Johnson and Sammy Sosa in the lineup. This doesn't make any sense. Gallagher isn't a very good center fielder, but he's OK—a .270 range hitter with no power, not enough speed to steal bases and not a lot of walks. But as a *right* fielder? Give me a break—he doesn't hit anywhere near enough to be a major league right fielder. If the White Sox knew what they were doing, Gallagher would hit the bench in about ten seconds, but as we're all aware, the White Sox do some strange things.

MIKE GALLEGO
Oakland

Assuming Weiss is healthy, Gallego is probably now in possession of a regular job, at second base. He's a wonderful defensive player, but marginal as a regular because of weak bat (.240 range hitter with no power). . . . One of two A's regulars born on a holiday. Rickey Henderson was born on Christmas, Gallego on Halloween. . . .

RON GANT
Atlanta

Why do the Braves do things like this? You have a young second baseman going great, hitting .259 with 19 homers, 19 stolen bases, and 85 runs scored, why can't you leave him alone? Why do you have to move him to third base? . . . Will probably have to save his career now as an outfielder, and the Braves are thick in young outfielders who can hit. He's only twenty-five, and I think he'll be back sooner or later.

JIM GANTNER
Milwaukee

The most-similar player to Jim Gantner is Tommie Herr. . . .

DAMASCO GARCIA
Yankees

Why?

MIGUEL GARCIA
Pittsburgh

Twenty-three-year-old left-handed reliever, has pitched well in the minors. Grade C prospect.

★ ★
MARK GARDNER
Montreal
★ ★

After several years of struggling, has pitched brilliantly in the Expos system the last two seasons. He's a little old for a prospect (twenty-eight), but still one of the better pitching prospects of 1990. Obviously, the opportunity for a young pitcher in Montreal is outstanding. Gardner throws hard, has control. The Expos haven't firmly decided whether to use him as a starter or in the bullpen.

WES GARDNER
Boston

Career ERA of 4.83; obviously has shed the prospect label, and will have to scramble to stay in the league. Better suited to relief than starting. May not make the team.

SCOTT GARRELTS
Giants

Garrelts led the National League in the two most-positive categories, ERA and winning percentage (actually tied in winning percentage with Sid Fernandez).

Garrelts's mechanics aren't as bad as Kelly Downs's, quite. Unlike Downs, he finishes his motion with his right shoulder in front of his body, leaning forward, so that the arm has a much longer "free swing" before it strikes his body. Still, he stops his arm with his stomach, and pitchers who do that are going to hurt themselves sooner or later. He's a fine, fine pitcher (best pitch is a hard forkball), but I think he'll have chronic arm trouble.

Tony Gwynn said during the playoffs that Garrelts gave *right-handed* hitters a lot of trouble. I checked, and sure enough, left-handed hitters hit .235 against Garrelts last year; right-handers hit just .184.

RICHARD GEDMAN
Boston

Has he been released by the Red Sox? I think so. I wish I knew what had happened to him, but I'm as puzzled as everybody else. No reason to think he'll be back in 1990—but then, I just confessed that I don't know what the problem was, so who knows?

BOB GEREN
Yankees

Big, free-swinging catcher, will get more playing time with the departure of Don Slaught. The Yankees are in for a disappointment. He was over his head last year; he's not a .288 hitter with the kind of power he flashed in 65 games. The question isn't *whether* he will fall off in 1990, but just *how far.*

KIRK GIBSON
Los Angeles

Talking about retiring after a miserable year. The biggest joke of the winter was the Dodgers thinking they had four regular outfielders—Gibson, Daniels, Samuel, and Hubie Brooks. Gibson was perhaps the most consistent player in the majors from 1984 through 1988, and he's super if he is healthy. Incidentally, I agree with his selection as NL MVP in 1988.

PAUL GIBSON
Tigers

Left-hander with no fastball. No prospect.

BRETT GIDEON
Montreal

Twenty-six-year-old right-handed middle reliever—grade D prospect.

JOE GIRARDI
Cubs

Looked solid as an emergency call-up. There are worse catchers in the majors; could platoon with Berryhill. No star potential.

DAN GLADDEN
Minnesota

Coming off his best major league season at thirty-two, and you know what that means. Don't be drafting him. He is extremely likely, at the least, to relapse to his normal level of play, which isn't all that bad, but there is at thirty-two the distinct possibility of sudden aging or injury.

TOM GLAVINE
Braves

Among the Braves' young pitchers, I would rate him comfortably behind Smoltz, Stanton, and Avery, in a group with Greene, Eave, and Pete Smith, and ahead of Clary, Lilliquist, and Mercker. He pitched well last year (14–8, 3.68 ERA), but then he pitched pretty awful the year before, and I'm always a little suspicious of control-type pitchers. They just don't last like power pitchers, and they're not as consistent. If he pitches 250 innings, he'll lead the National League in home runs allowed, granting most of them will be solo shots. His short-term future is bright, his long-term future not as bright.

JERRY GLEATON
Kansas City

Onetime prospect, struggling to stay around. Talks a lot about Jesus.

RENE GONZALES
Orioles

A better second baseman than third baseman; hasn't and won't hit enough to hold a job in the majors, probably even as a utility man.

DENNY GONZALEZ
Cleveland

Longtime Pirate prospect, now trying to stick with the Indians. He's not a bad hitter, actually, a .240–.280 hitter with some home run power, but would strike out about one at bat in four. I'd consider trying to find a major league role for him, but the Indians have a lot of hitters of this type.

GERMAN GONZALEZ
Minnesota

Right-handed reliever only twenty-four years old, pitched sensationally in the Southern League in 1988 (1.02 ERA in 62 innings.) Major league K/W data is good, 44 strikeouts and 17 (unintentional) walks in 50 innings. With the departure of Reardon and the Twins inability to deal for a closer (so far), he would have some chance to move into that role.

JOSE GONZALEZ
Los Angeles

Assuming that Samuel and Brooks stay in the outfield, Gonzalez opens the season as the Dodgers' number-five outfielder, but behind some people who get hurt a lot. He's a .250-range hitter, little power and terrible K/W, but very fast and regarded as an outstanding outfielder. He'll probably bat 400–450 times; the Dodgers think he has star potential, but I don't.

JUAN GONZALEZ
Texas

The Sammy Sosa trade came about when the Rangers apparently decided that Gonzalez was a better center-field prospect than Sosa. Gonzalez had an exceptional season in 1989 at Tulsa (21 homers, 85 RBI, .293), and that isn't traditionally a great hitter's park. He's very young (twenty), and is regarded as being comparable to Ruben Sierra about four years ago. He isn't exceptionally fast—slow for a center fielder—but has a great arm, and many people think he will hit 30 homers in the major leagues within a few years. He struggled with the bat when called up late last year, and my instinct is that he will continue to struggle for a while this year, but he's a very good pickup if you can hold him for a couple of years. The signing of Gary Pettis probably gives him a year in AAA, and that may be the best thing for him.

DWIGHT GOODEN
Mets

The outstanding major league pitcher of the 1980s.

TOM GORDON
Royals

Gordon had the Rookie Of the Year Award locked up last year; on August 24 he was 16–4 with a 2.57 ERA, averaging more than a strikeout an inning. At that point, he was still a candidate for the Cy Young Award; Bret Saberhagen on the same date was 15–5 with a 2.70 ERA, almost the same strikeout total as Gordon. Then he (Gordon) didn't win a game until his last start, and let even the rookie award get away.

Almost everybody thinks that Gordon was tired down the stretch, made the transition from relief to starter too quickly, but that really wasn't it. It was mechanical. Gordon's natural motion is to come from about ten-thirty, pivoting to the right on his hips. I saw him pitch on September 10, and I couldn't believe how messed up he was. He was trying to throw the ball straight overhand, twisting his upper body to allow his arm to go straight in the air. He had limited control of his fast ball, and his curve was hanging out over the plate like a balloon. He looked nothing at all like he had looked all year.

There would seem to be two possibilities as to how he got so incredibly messed up in a short period of time. When a pitcher is tired ordinarily he'll drop down to the side, let his arm get lazy. What Gordon was doing was hard work, harder than the way he is supposed to throw. One possibility is that he had a rough outing where his curve ball didn't bite, and some half-asleep pitching coach told him that he needed to get up on top of the ball, which is something that pitching coaches often tell young pitchers when their curve ball flattens out. That's possible, but I just can't believe that the Royals, who ordinarily handle pitchers extremely well, would have somebody incompetent enough not to know that Gordon's motion is to swing on his hips, not to drive off his thighs.

The other possibility is Gordon himself has a distorted idea of how he is supposed to throw the ball, that some-body told him when he was in high school to throw the curve ball straight overhand, and although he doesn't do it, he still thinks he ought to.

I'm not sure what difference it makes; tired or mechanically messed up, he's still a little bit of a gamble this year. As a starting pitcher, Gordon was 7–7, struck out 75 in 97 innings and had a 3.99 ERA, which isn't that great—but on the other hand, the dividing line between when he was effective and when he wasn't *isn't* the point at which he became a starter, but a month later. I'd make him about the number-fifteen American League starter on my draft list, behind the Clemenses, Saberhagens, and Bosios, but one of the first guys you gamble on.

GOOSE GOSSAGE
Yankees?
Stats aren't that bad, but apparently are deceptive. Needs spring training to see whether or not he can still fill a role.

JIM GOTT
Dodgers
He's not a particularly good gamble in my opinion. He's coming off an injury, he's been inconsistent his whole career, and he has never had a full-season ERA below 3.41, even when he saved 34 games for the Pirates a couple of years ago. The only thing that makes him interesting is that he does have a great arm, and the Dodgers do have the ability to turn around a pitcher with a great arm. So the possibility is there for him to have a big year—but just myself, I'd rather gamble on somebody else.

MARK GRACE
Cubs
The new Keith Hernandez. He's awfully good, and he's probably going to get better. He's a .300 hitter, a good percentage base stealer, has one of the best strike-out to walk ratios in baseball, he's a ter-rific glove at first base, and he's still young. Got to be one of the fifteen to twenty most valuable properties in the game.

MARK GRANT
San Diego
Pitched very well last year in long relief—8–2, 3.33 ERA. I don't see him as being effective if he gets out of that role.

GARY GREEN
San Diego
Twenty-eight-year-old shortstop—no prospect. There's a great opportunity for him, because Garry Templeton needs help, but Green isn't anywhere near a major league hitter.

TOMMY GREENE
Atlanta
Right-handed pitching prospect with the Braves. Greene was the Braves' first round draft in 1985, and seemed to be lost in the system until pitching fairly well with Richmond last season.

Basically, what I wrote about Kent Mercker also applies here—the Braves have lots of pitching prospects, and Atlanta-Fulton County Stadium isn't going to help. He could break through this year, but I don't really anticipate it.

MIKE GREENWELL
Boston
Great young player, even in an off year. See "Mark Grace." They have a lot in common besides their initials.

TOMMY GREGG
Atlanta
A broken leg destroyed what would have been one of the surprise success stories of 1989.

Gregg is one of those guys who doesn't get any respect as a prospect, but as a hitting prospect I like him a great deal. I am convinced that Gregg can hit over .300 in the major leagues, and can hit .300 with some power and a good strikeout to walk ratio. Until his injury, he seemed last year to be on the way to justifying my faith in him, but his hitting slipped badly on his return.

He faces a major career challenge. The signing of Esasky occupies first base, which was his primary spot last year, and throws him into the pool of Braves outfield candidates. It is a crowded pool—Dave Justice, Ron Gant, Geronimo Berroa, and a couple of other guys now, more coming along through the system, and no jobs open with an outfield of Lonnie Smith, Oddibe McDowell, and Dale Murphy. Gregg isn't an impressive defensive player, so despite my confidence in him as a hitter, I'd have to be cautious in recommending him at this point. Whether or not he will ever play regularly is just not known.

KEN GRIFFEY
Cincinnati

Didn't play all that badly last year, despite his age. His home run and RBI rates were about the same as Dale Murphy's, and his batting average was a lot better. Fifty-fifty chance of being on a roster this year if he chooses to come back.

★ ★ ★
KEN GRIFFEY, JR.
Seattle
★ ★ ★

OK, here's my rule. I don't like to try to project a player more than two steps ahead of himself. I have this spectrum in my mind, stacked up something like this:

Superstar
Star
Quality Regular
Regular
Major League Fringe
AAA player
AA player

A Ball and Rookie Leagues
College Player

I think it is fair to try to project a player one stage ahead of where he is, and you can try to look two steps ahead. I'm often asked to try to look further ahead than that, and I just don't think it's productive, which is not to say that I won't ever do it (see Steve Avery.) But people ask me fairly often who there is in the minor league today who I think will be a superstar, and I just don't think you can answer that question very successfully. I think an organization just causes trouble for itself when it starts talking or even *thinking* about a AA player becoming a superstar.

But if there is any young player in 1989 who has the ability to be a superstar, Ken Griffey has to be the man. He was nineteen years old last year, which gives him enormous growth potential. He already *is* a quality major league player. He has power and speed, and he hit for a decent average. He can throw. He is not a wild swinger, so he doesn't have to overcome that. Basically, Ken Griffey at age nineteen is what Mickey Mantle was at age nineteen and Henry Aaron and Willie Mays were at age twenty. Cesar Cedeño was there, too, and Tony Conigliaro; they don't *always* make it past that point. I'm not saying that he is going to be Mickey Mantle, but he has a *chance* to be Mickey Mantle, and there aren't that many players who do. He is the first rookie outfielder to come along in three years who has a chance to be that good, the last two being Ruben Sierra and Jose Canseco in 1986. There will be a lot of people who want him, but if you can get him, get him.

ALFREDO GRIFFIN
Dodgers

The Dodgers' shortstop of the future, Jose Offerman, was in the California

League last year, so Griffin appears to have a couple of years left. I've never been crazy about him, but he is what he is.

MIKE GRIFFIN
Cincinnati

Veteran pitcher, still trying to catch on somewhere. His chances are slim and none.

TY GRIFFIN
Cubs

The Cubs number-one draft pick in 1988, and a star of the 1988 Olympic team. A switch-hitting second baseman, he broke in in the Midwest League last year and played very well, playing part of the time at third base. In half a season there (287 at bats) he had 64 RBI, 49 walks and 16 stolen bases. Moving up to AA late in the year, he didn't play as well, but still had a secondary average well over .300.

With the departure of Vance Law to Japan, the third base path ahead of Griffin is wide open. There is every reason to think that he will be in the major leagues by 1991, possibly even sooner, and he's somebody you want to try to acquire when he does surface.

JASON GRIMSLEY
Philadelphia

A young right-handed pitcher with the Phillies. He had the best fast ball in the Eastern League last year, but myself, I don't see very much to like about him, and if there was anything to like the team should be able to hide it. One manager in the Eastern League told *Baseball America* that "the higher up he goes, the better he'll get." I don't believe it.

MARQUIS GRISSOM
Montreal

Highly touted outfielder in the Expos system, called up September of 1989. Grissom is more or less in possession of the center field job in Montreal, having played well in September. He was described by *Baseball America* as "an Andre Dawson clone." You will see some people listing him as the NL's most-likely Rookie of the Year.

I think he is a major league player, but I'm not that high on him. He's five eleven, 192 pounds, which is rather small to be described as Andre Dawson. I see him at this point as a .260–.275 hitter with 30–50 stolen bases and a decent K/W ratio, but with limited power. His defense in center has been reported as outstanding. I think he'll hold a job and be a Rookie of the Year candidate if he plays at the top of his range and nobody else has a monster season, but I don't see him as tearing the league apart. He's not as far along as a hitter as guys like Hal Morris, Francisco Cabrera, and Rob Richie.

GREG GROSS
Astros

Probably retired.

KEVIN GROSS
Montreal

One of these years, he's going to surprise some people. He pitches 200 innings every year, which is a rare skill in itself, and he keeps his strikeout rate up there—in fact, it keeps getting higher (7.1 strikeouts/nine innings in 1989, his major league best). Sooner or later the control will come around, and he'll have a big year.

KELLY GRUBER
Toronto

The most-similar player to Kelly Gruber is Jack Howell. . . . A "safe draft," a solid, consistent, and quality player.

CECILIO GUANTE
Texas

Not a bad pitcher, really; no star potential and, with Jeff Russell around, no chance of moving into the closer role.

MARK GUBICZA
Kansas City

The official major league position rankings, the ones designed to determine who is a Class A and who is a Class B free agent, made Gubicza the highest-valued player in all of baseball. I don't know that I'd go that far, but he is one of the half dozen best starting pitchers in the game . . . allowed fewer home runs per nine innings than any other American League pitcher in 1989, and has done that before.

PEDRO GUERRERO
Cards

Guerrero last year had 117 RBI but only 60 runs scored, the highest ratio of RBI to runs scored of any major league player. . . . Behind him on that list were Terry Kennedy, Steve Balboni, Scott Bradley, Dave Parker, Rick Cerone, Carmelo Martinez, Pete Incaviglia, Darren Daulton, and Paul O'Neill . . .

LEE GUETTERMAN
Yankees

Coming off his best season, by about three miles. The odds are tremendously against his pitching as well again, of course.

OZZIE GUILLEN
Chicago

One of the two best defensive shortstops in the American League, with Fernandez being the other. Basically doesn't contribute anything offensively; should hit ninth. A safe draft.

BILL GULLICKSON
Houston

He was a good pitcher before he left. The Japanese are famous for their conditioning programs. The Astrodome will help him. The Astros need starting pitchers. Basically, he seems like a reasonably good draft pick, although obviously a bit risky.

MARK GUTHRIE
Minnesota

Don't know very much about him. None of what I know is positive.

CHRIS GWYNN
Dodgers

A joke. He has no chance of being a major league player, but the Dodgers just keep stringing him along. He doesn't hit for average or power or run well.

TONY GWYNN
San Diego

A wonderful player, of course. A lifetime .332 hitter, creates 106 runs a year, plays good defense. Consistent. A safe draft, but an expensive one.

JERRY HAIRSTON
White Sox

Well, he did play.

CHIP HALE
Twins

Is that a name for a baseball player, or what? Chip Hale, all-American.

Chip Hale, all-American, has a chance to be an everyday player in 1990. He's a twenty-five-year-old second baseman, and the Twins need help at second base. He's the top second-base prospect in the organization. I believe that as a regular, he would hit around .250, drive 7–12 home runs and be a defensive improvement over Wally Backman. That's better than Al Newman, but not much. Limited if any star potential.

ALBERT HALL
Pittsburgh

Sort of a poor man's Otis Nixon.

DREW HALL
Rangers

Hard-throwing left-handed reliever, once projected as the successor to Lee

Smith in Chicago. Left-handed short man now; very little chance of moving into a key role.

MEL HALL
Yankees

He hit .159 last year against left-handed pitching; I think that must be his career high. He's probably got the biggest platoon differential in baseball—a formidable power hitter against a right-hander, but hopeless against a lefty. A consistent player, seems to hit 17 or 18 homers every year.

BOB HAMELIN
Kansas City

Think "Kent Hrbek." Hamelin is a big left-handed first baseman with reportedly tremendous power, a quick bat, and he knows the strike zone. He appears to be heir apparent to George Brett as the Royals first baseman, and is probably rated by the organization ahead of Luis de los Santos. I think he is a very solid major league hitter, and could probably help the Royals now as a designated hitter, but the odds are he will start the season at Omaha.

JEFF HAMILTON
Dodgers

The most-similar player to Jeff Hamilton is Ken Caminiti. . . . The Dodgers are talking about using Hubie Brooks at third. Why do they do stuff like that? Hamilton isn't great, but he's as good a hitter as Brooks, and a much better third baseman, and six years younger. Why mess with his head?

Hamilton has his negatives. He strikes out more than four times as often as he walks. He has never stolen a base in the major leagues. His career on-base percentage is a pathetic .267. But he has some power (35 doubles, 12 homers), has probably the best arm of any National League third baseman and is still

developing. I say, leave him alone until you come up with somebody *better*.

ATLEE HAMMAKER
Giants

Has pitched exactly .500 ball for three straight seasons—10–10 in 1987, 9–9 in 1988, 6–6 in 1989. I wonder if that's a record? . . . His ERAs in that period have ranged all the way from 3.58 to 3.76. . . . He's just another pitcher, absorbs some innings without doing much damage.

★★★
ERIK HANSON
Seattle
★★★

Outstanding young pitcher. If he's healthy, and apparently he is, he should win 15 games or more, with very strong peripheral stats. Hanson has an excellent chance to be a Cy Young candidate once the Mariners develop to where they are able to support him.

JACK "PARTY" HARDY
Chicago

No relation to Chip Hale.

MIKE HARKEY
Cubs

The disappointment of the season. A right-handed starting pitcher who some compare to a young Bob Gibson, he was expected to be in the Cubs' starting rotation, but pitched poorly and was sent out. He pitched poorly again at Iowa, finishing 2–7 with a 4.43 ERA; arthroscopic surgery on his left knee ended his season in late July.

It was a lost season, but I sure wouldn't write him off. He's only twenty-three; Bob Gibson stunk up the league until he was twenty-six. Harkey is bigger than Gibson (six five, 220) and almost as scary on the mound.

PETE HARNISCH
Baltimore

Didn't pitch well; remains an outstanding prospect in my book. He's only twenty-three, two years out of college. These guys, you don't want to pick them up until they do something right in the majors—but once he turns the corner, I think he'll be good.

BRIAN HARPER
Minnesota

Harper in 1989 had 125 hits and struck out only 16 times, the best ratio of hits to strikeouts of any major league player. His ratio was almost 8 to 1; the only other player over 7 to 1 was Carney Lansford. . . . The most-similar player to Brian Harper is Geno Petralli. . . .

GENE HARRIS
Seattle

Came to Seattle as a part of the Langston trade. Harris, who was a defensive back at Tulane, is considered an exceptional all-around athlete. He throws very hard, and is supposed to be one of the best fielding pitchers around. Grade B prospect.

GREG A. HARRIS
Boston

The guy who used to be with the Rangers. A serviceable pitcher, nothing special.

GREG W. HARRIS
Padres

A young right-hander, and well-regarded. He's pitched well since entering baseball, and may get a shot as a starter this season. A *strong* grade B prospect; I like his chances.

LENNY HARRIS
Dodgers

With Randolph, Samuel, and Harris on the roster, all basically second basemen, it's unclear what the Dodgers' plans are. Harris, a .250-range hitter with speed but no power and not many walks, doesn't approach the other two as an offensive player and doesn't figure to be helped by the crowd.

MIKE HARTLEY
Los Angeles

Another Dodger pitching prospect; has been in the minors since 1982. Grade D prospect.

BRYAN HARVEY
California

Phenomenal strikeout rate went largely unnoticed—78 strikeouts in 55 innings (12.8 strikeouts per nine innings). He did that regularly in the minor leagues. He was the American League's Rookie Pitcher of the Year in 1988, and I think he'll be back. He may need a little more regular work than he was getting from Rader to stay sharp.

RON HASSEY
Oakland

Released.

BILLY HATCHER
Pittsburgh

Not my kind of player. He's twenty-nine now; I wouldn't take him.

MICKEY HATCHER
Los Angeles

Now thirty-five years old. A guy who bats 200–300 times a year ordinarily will have an off year and drop out of the league, even if he is still as good a player as he's ever been (see article on John Morris, Section II). Hatcher's been able to stay around to age thirty-five because he's been able to avoid that off year, hitting .278 to .317 in each of the last six seasons. He hit .295 last year, .293 the year before. He's not my kind of player,

either, but you have to respect his effort and his consistency.

BRAD HAVENS
Detroit

Finally out of chances, I would presume. Too bad; if he'd just lasted five more years he could have gone straight from being a prospect to pitching in the Seniors' League.

ANDY HAWKINS
Yankees

A poor draft in my opinion. He was the Yankees' biggest winner last year at 15–15, but he's never been consistent, he doesn't strike out anybody, and with an ERA of 4.80, how well did he *really* pitch? With the Yankees dramatically improved starting pitching, I wonder if he'll make it through the year in the rotation.

CHARLIE HAYES
Philadelphia

No outstanding asset. A .240–.260 hitter with 10–15 home runs power, no speed, terrible strikeout to walk ratio, defense at third very suspect. Odds are he'll be out of the majors in a year or two. . . .

VON HAYES
Philadelphia

The most-similar player to Von Hayes is Chili Davis. . . .

I like Hayes. Von has his critics, but a player who plays for losing teams always gets branded a loser, even if it's completely unfair. There are a lot of positives here—four outstanding seasons in the last six years, 20-homer power, 20-plus stolen bases a year, 100 walks a year, as many as 46 doubles in a season. As the cleanup hitter on a bad team he doesn't scare you, but put him in the middle of the Oakland A's lineup, and you'd be a hell of lot more afraid of him than you would of Dave Parker.

MIKE HEATH
Detroit

Now thirty-five years old. A solid player; with the shortage of catchers you could do worse.

NEAL HEATON
Pittsburgh

Anybody who would draft Neal Heaton is probably too dumb to be helped by a book like this anyway.

DANNY HEEP
Boston

Most similar major league player: Rick Leach. . . . Hit .211 in two seasons with the Dodgers, went to Fenway and hit .300. If you ask him about it, it's ten to one he'll say Fenway Park didn't help him. . . .

DAN HEINKEL
St. Louis

Thirty-year-old lefthander; has a degree from Wichita State in Biology and won 19 games for Birmingham in 1983. Signed with the Cardinals as a six-year minor league free agent, and got to pitch a little when they had all the injuries. No prospect.

SCOTT HEMOND
Oakland

Heir apparent to Carney Lansford at third base; probably won't surface this season. He has a cannon for an arm and is a base stealer, but I'm not convinced that he'll be a major league hitter.

DAVE HENDERSON
Oakland

Somebody should give him a calendar watch that's stuck on October. Give him a bank calendar, where all the days are right but all the months say "October." See if it'll help.

RICKEY HENDERSON
A's
One of the ironies of the Cy Young controversy last year was that the effect was to create a sympathy vote for Dave Stewart in the World Series MVP voting, and thus to transfer that award away from Rickey Henderson, who has been shafted in award voting time after time, and to Dave Stewart, who has never had anything to complain about in *any* vote. . . . The most-similar player to Rickey Henderson is Tim Raines. . . .

When *Sports Illustrated* wrote an article about my work in 1981, there was a photo of me sitting near second base at Royals Stadium with the message on the board reading "There is a 97% chance that some active player will break Lou Brock's career stolen base record." This may be the year that that prediction comes true; Henderson needs 68 steals to break the record, and generally steals more than that in a year. To break Brock's record by the same percentage margin that Nolan Ryan has broken the old strikeout record (so far), Henderson would need to steal 1,357 career bases. That's a pretty good guess as to how many he will steal; with good luck he could steal 1,500–1,600.

DAVE HENGEL
Cleveland
Outfield prospect from the Seattle system; doesn't run, terrible K/W ratio and is now twenty-eight years old. He does have real power, though.

TOM HENKE
Blue Jays
Career average is now 10.6 strikeouts per nine innings, better than Nolan Ryan (9.55) but less than Rob Dibble (11.4). After a rough start, Henke had the best ERA of his career last year, 1.92. Safe draft; perhaps the most consistent top reliever in baseball other than Reardon.

MIKE HENNEMAN
Detroit
His control went bad last year, and Sparky took him out of the closer role. He might have been better off to leave him there; Henneman's 3.70 ERA isn't impressive, unless you compare it to the rest of the Detroit staff. With the departure of Hernandez, likely to regain the role of bullpen closer.

DWAYNE HENRY
Atlanta
Perennial prospect, looks awfully good at times. With the Braves' abundance of pitching prospects will have to work his way back by pitching well at Richmond.

KEITH HERNANDEZ
Cleveland
Perfect. Who else would sign Keith Hernandez? Do the Indians *really* think that Keith has a big year left in him? Do they think it would make any difference if he did? So Keith Hernandez hits .300 with 15 homers, so now what?

MANNY HERNANDEZ
Mets
Twenty-nine-year-old right-hander; no prospect.

WILLIE HERNANDEZ
Tigers
Released.

XAVIER HERNANDEZ
Toronto Blue Jays
Decent prospect; twenty-four-year-old left-hander with excellent control. He's like most of the pitchers on the Syracuse staff: he's not a great prospect, but at least *he is a prospect,* as opposed to being a thirty-year-old major league washout. While most of the league is overrun with the latter, the Chiefs have almost entirely the former—Willie Blair, Tony Castillo, Steve Cummings, Warren Giles, Mauro Gozzo, Juan Guzman, Jose Nunez, Alex Sanchez, and Bob Wish-

nevski. Hernandez ranks in the middle or toward the top of the group.

TOM HERR
Philadelphia
The most-similar player to Tom Herr is Johnny Ray. . . . The 1989 season was his best since his famous 110-RBI season of 1985. Not a safe draft pick in view of his age (thirty-four) and the Phillies' need to rebuild.

OREL HERSHISER
Los Angeles
Has now pitched exactly .500 ball in three of the last four seasons: 14–14, 16–16 and 15–15. . . . His ERA *away* from Dodger Stadium last year was 1.93. . . . Hitters who got behind him 0–2 last year hit .145. Those who got ahead of him 2–0 hit .304. . . .

JOE HESKETH
Montreal
After a 5.77 ERA last season, he may be one more pitcher that the Expos have to replace. . . . Now thirty-one; probably will keep his job as the left-handed short man. . . .

ERIC HETZEL
Boston
Twenty-six-year-old right-handed pitcher—grade D prospect. Name rhymes with "Pretzel."

GREG HIBBARD
Chicago White Sox
Twenty-five-year-old lefthander, and pitched extremely well for the White Sox last year, posting a 3.21 ERA in 23 starts. You have to respect that kind of performance, but keep in mind two things:

1) There is nothing in his background prior to last season which would suggest that kind of ability, and

2) The White Sox have an amazing ability to screw up young players.

KEVIN HICKEY
Baltimore
Fun player/dumb draft pick.

MARK HIGGINS
Cleveland
Big right-handed hitting first baseman, now twenty-six years old. Higgins is a player who could move into the first base job if Hernandez falters badly, and could be all right. It's hard to say; has up and down hitting record in the minor leagues. Little if any star potential.

TED HIGUERA
Brewers
He had an ankle injury in May of last year, couldn't push off like he normally would, altered his delivery, and hurt his shoulder. The Brewers must pray that it isn't serious, but as of this writing nobody knows.

★ ★ ★
GLENALLEN HILL
Jays
★ ★ ★
Once in awhile they fool you. We've been reading about this guy as a prospect for years, but he was hitting .235 at Syracuse with awful strikeout to walk ratios, and I had completely written him off as a prospect. He's a great athlete (six three, 210, runs like hell), and I just had him figured as a guy who was going to be a perennial prospect but never a hitter. The Blue Jays almost had written him off, too; he started the year as the number-five outfielder at Syracuse—and darned if he didn't turn it around. He hit .321 at Syracuse last year, with 36 doubles, 15 triples, and 21 homers—and Syracuse is such a tough park that you read stats there almost as if they were major league stats; if a guy hits .320 at Syracuse, he's capable of hitting .310 in the major leagues. At the end of the year he was rated the number-one prospect in the International League. His strikeout to walk ratio in the majors is going

to be awful, but with Toronto having a dark hole at DH, Lloyd Moseby leaving and Barfield traded, there's going to be a spot for him, and he's got a chance to be the American League Rookie of the Year this year.

KEN HILL
Cards
Long odds against his making it big. He was 7–15 last year, and that's kind of a bad rap because he pitched a lot better than that; Herzog used to jerk him out of the game early, which often will leave the bullpen with the win and the starter with the loss. Still, he walks a lot of people, doesn't strike out many, doesn't have overpowering stuff. I think the best he's capable of is about 14–10, and I doubt that he'll do that. . . . Hill led the National League in two categories: walks and losses.

SHAWN HILLEGAS
White Sox
More negatives than positives. He's been in the majors for three years, and he hasn't done anything impressive yet. I'd say pass.

TOMMY HINZO
Cleveland
Fun player to watch, a little second baseman who hustles. No real prospect anyway, and, being behind Jerry Browne, no chance to win the job. No draft.

GLENN HOFFMAN
California
Thirty-one years old, .212 hitter, drew three walks, slow, no power, not quick enough to play shortstop. Tell me again . . . why was this guy in the major leagues?

CHRIS HOILES
Baltimore
Twenty-five-year-old catcher, may have a future as a backup. Extremely unlikely to be a major league regular.

BRIAN HOLMAN
Seattle
I kind of like him. He had a 3.44 ERA with the Mariners last season, and they are moving their fences out, which gives him an edge. He's a pitcher, rather than a thrower, and he has a history of establishing a level and then moving forward. He could give the Mariners a solid third starter, behind Bankhead and Randy Johnson.

SHAWN HOLMAN
Detroit
Twenty-five-year-old right-hander; very poor risk in my opinion. Hasn't been consistently effective even in the minors, despite spurts of brilliance, walked 11 men in 10 innings in the majors last year, doesn't throw real hard, and working with the Tigers is a major detriment. I wouldn't draft him.

BRIAN HOLTON
Baltimore
Lives by changing speeds; it often takes a pitcher like that a little while to adjust to the league. Has little if any star potential, but could improve on 4.02 ERA of last season. He'll be in the majors, anyway.

RICK HONEYCUTT
Oakland
Thirty-five years old, coming off his best season in years, coming off a poor performance in post-season play, with no possibility of moving into a more key role. You get my drift?

SAM HORN
Boston
Released.

RICKY HORTON
St. Louis
Probably will start the season in the minors.

CHARLIE HOUGH
Texas

Had his first off season after seven strong years as a Ranger starter. I don't know how to calculate the odds on him. . . . What do forty-two-year-old knuckleballers do? Do they ever come back, once they lose their effectiveness at this age? Niekro didn't. Dutch Leonard did, but as a reliever. Hoyt Wilhelm had five straight seasons with ERAs in the ones, beginning at age forty—but when he did begin to slip, he wasn't able to turn it around. My gut reaction is that Hough won't come back, but I wouldn't want to put any money on that.

JACK HOWELL
California

The most-similar player to Jack Howell is Steve Buechele. . . . Underrated defensive player at third base, but has to get consistent with the bat.

JAY HOWELL
Los Angeles

One more reason to respect the Dodgers pitching coaches. Despite the ugly 5.89 ERA in 1987, Howell has five straight seasons with 16 to 29 saves, and, by the standards of relievers, he has to be rated a "safe draft."

KEN HOWELL
Philadelphia

Threw 21 wild pitches last year, most in the major leagues. Despite that, I think that having finally gotten his career on track, he is a good bet to stay on track, and could get better. He had more strikeouts last season than hits allowed, and there aren't very many starting pitchers who can say that. . . . Even if he pitches well, the Phillies may stick him with a losing record.

DANN HOWITT
Oakland

No relation to Dann Bilardello. . . . One fun thing about the A's system is that, because they believe in the importance of on-base percentage, you can go through their minor league records in the media guide and find a whole bunch of guys who walk 70–100 times. This is unusual; in most organizations all the marginal prospects will have K/W ratios about 4–1. Anyway, Howitt is one of those, drew 81 walks in the California League in 1988. He's a six five outfielder-first baseman with some power and a little bit of mobility, if not actual speed. He had a big year last year at Huntsville (AA), hitting .281 with 26 homers, 111 RBI (the major league equivalent would be .248 with 19 homers, 85 RBI). He's the same age as McGwire (twenty-six), so you can see that he faces a challenge in earning a job in the major leagues, but the departure of Dave Parker may enable him to slide into the designated hitter role if he has a good first half at Tacoma.

KENT HRBEK
Minnesota

Had one of the most effective seasons in the major leagues, at bat for at bat; if you projected his 109 games out to 162 you'd have 37 homers, 125 RBI. Did you know there is no word in the English language which rhymes with "Hrbek"?

GLENN HUBBARD
Oakland

Released; probably will be in spring training with somebody, maybe Baltimore. Always one of my favorite players.

REX HUDLER
Montreal

I did a nationwide radio show last summer, on every Sunday evening (5–7 eastern time, 8–10 pacific coast); it was called *Baseball Sunday*. Joe Garagiola is joining us this summer, so it will be called *Baseball Sunday with Joe Garagiola*. Anyway, we had a regular "Rex Hudler" caller, always wanted to know why Rex Hudler wasn't playing more. I never was able to come up with an answer for him. Hudler is a second baseman, a terrific base stealer and has some pop in his bat—10 homers in 371 at bats over the last two seasons. He would contribute a lot more offense to the lineup than Tom Foley, but for whatever reason—and I'm not second-guessing him—Rodgers chose to stay with Foley. With Jeff Huson coming along, Hudler this year may be pushed to number three.

CHARLES HUDSON
Detroit

Ouch. I detest pitchers like this. Hudson is one of those guys who looks great— five times a year. The rest of the time he loses. Basically, I'd rather have a cocklebur in my underwear than Charles Hudson on my pitching staff.

MIKE HUFF
Los Angeles

Singles-hitting outfielder, could hit around .265 in the majors and steal some bases. There are worse players around, but he's not likely to claim a job. Could probably hit .280–.290 in another park.

MARK HUISMANN
Baltimore

Released. There are very few pitchers who have good strikeout to walk ratios, but can't win. Huisman was one of them. In eleven innings with the Orioles last year he struck out eleven men and walked nobody—yet he had a 6.35 ERA. I defended him for years, but eventually you have to give up.

TIM HULETT
Baltimore

With Baltimore as desperate as they are for a second baseman, Hulett actually might not be a bad option, maybe a platoon combination of Hulett and somebody. He's not a long-term solution to the problem, but at least he would put a few runs on the scoreboard, and not embarass you at second base.

BRUCE HURST
San Diego

Terrific pitcher. Which is more impressive: a 2.69 ERA in San Diego (Hurst, 1989) or a 3.66 ERA in Fenway (Hurst, 1988)? It's about the same, I'd say . . . a safe pick.

JEFF HUSON
Expos

A good, not a great, player to pick up in 1990. He can play second base or center field, which gives him two chances to break into the lineup for Montreal, which isn't strong at either position. He's capable of hitting .280 in the majors, with little power but a very good strikeout to walk ratio and excellent speed. He's twenty-five, so he's essentially mature as a player, not likely to improve beyond where he is. He could win a Rookie of the Year Award, as Sabo did in 1988 (a similar player), but has little if any chance of achieving stardom. Rated by *Baseball America* as the number-four prospect in the American Association.

RODNEY IMES
Cincinnati

Imes had a big year at Albany (17–6, 2.73 ERA) and was included in the Tim Leary trade with the Reds. He doesn't have a grade A fast ball, and for that reason may face a difficult transition to the major leagues. He's six five but has very good control, which is an odd combination, and a combination you've got to like. I'm inclined to think that he will be a successful major league pitcher, although probably not a Cy Young winner, and probably not (successful) as a rookie.

PETE INCAVIGLIA
Rangers

The most-similar player to Pete Incaviglia is Rob Deer. . . . Home run totals have gone down every season (30, 27, 22, 21), and strikeout to walk ratio has gotten *worse* every season, going from 3.36–1 as a rookie to 4.25–1 last season. He's an awful outfielder, even though the Rangers insist that he isn't, and will have to play the outfield in '90 because of the acquisition of Baines.

Is he capable of having a better year? Sure.

Is he going to? I don't see any evidence of that.

ALEX INFANTE
Toronto

What a wonderful name. Infante has been at Syracuse since 1984, which must be some sort of a record. He's a Luis Aparicio, a Venezuelan base-stealing shortstop, apparently well liked. No prospect, although he could get hot and look good for three months or so. . . . Assume he will eventually leave the organization as a six-year free agent.

JEFF INNIS
Mets

Twenty-seven-year-old right-hander, no real prospect but throws enough strikes to stay on a major league roster in long relief. . . . We were making up an "Enos Envy" All-Star team the other day— Enos Slaughter, Enos Cabell, Del Ennis. What do you think, can we use him?

BO JACKSON
Kansas City

The funny thing about Bo as a baseball player is how seldom you see him run. His speed is really not of a lot of use to him. His on-base percentage is low and a good many of his hits are home runs, so that eliminates most of his opportunities to run the bases. He strikes out and hits home runs, rarely hits ground balls

to the infield, so his speed doesn't come into play too often there. He plays left field rather than center, so that somewhat reduces his opportunity to use his speed on defense. You watch him during a game, and you just don't see him run.

Now that Bo finally is the player he is going to be, there is a good deal of sentiment in Kansas City to trade him—a columnist wrote a column urging the Royals to "cash him in." It makes no sense, of course. Bo isn't a great player, and he is frustrating at times, but

a) it destroys a team to treat players as if they were stocks and bonds,

b) when you trade a player, you always get a player that somebody else wants to trade,

c) you could trade him for two *worse* players, but you couldn't trade him for one better player, and if you can't trade him for a better player then a trade isn't going to help you, and

d) a successful trading strategy always focuses not on what you want to give up, but on what you want to acquire. If you listen to most general managers at the winter meeting and virtually all talk-show hosts, you realize that their trading strategy is based upon who they want to give up, and that's why few trades actually help their teams, because most teams don't really understand what they are getting until the next season arrives.

Look at the championship teams— who built their team by trading away a player like Bo? Did Oakland get where they are by trading away good young players because they weren't great? Did Toronto? Did the Mets or the Cubs? It's just not how championship teams are built.

DANNY JACKSON
Cincinnati

He'll be back, of course, but as streaky as he has been I'd want to wait until he wins a game or two before I added him to my team. Doubt that he'll ever go 23–8 again.

DARRIN JACKSON
San Diego

Decent enough spare outfielder—no real prospect.

MIKE JACKSON
Seattle

I still like him quite a bit. His ERAs in his two years in Seattle have been 2.63 and 3.17, which ain't shabby. He strikes out almost a batter an inning. His control still isn't what it ought to be, but he still has that 92 MPH heater, and I think he is gaining command of it.

BROOK JACOBY
Cleveland

Has stolen exactly two bases in each of the last five seasons. Not a championship quality player, I suppose, but there are worse third basemen around.

CHRIS JAMES
Cleveland

Your basic Cleveland Indians player, a .240 hitter whose strike zone runs from his shoe tops halfway up the light standard. Wouldn't be a bad platoon player, actually; he can eat a left-hander alive. Maybe they'll platoon him with Dion James, make an all-James platoon. Platoon stats last year: Chris hit .292 against lefties, .217 against right-handers, and Dion hit .298 against right-handers, .212 against lefties. I'm not sure if McNamara understands the concept of platooning, though. OK, forget the whole thing. . . .

DION JAMES
Cleveland

Anybody who would trade Oddibe McDowell for Dion James has no business being a baseball executive. Sometimes people ask me if I think I could be a general manager. My answer, and this an absolutely honest one, is that there are a lot of things associated with being a General Manager that I wouldn't be good at. I don't particularly like to negotiate. I'm not the world's best at drawing up a budget. I don't have a whole lot of experience at hiring and firing people. I'm not very good at wearing a suit and meeting with bankers, if you know what I mean. But I'll say this: I WOULD SURE AS HELL KNOW BETTER THAN TO TRADE ODDIBE MCDOWELL FOR DION JAMES.

STAN JAVIER
A's

The most-similar player to Stan Javier is Mike Felder. . . . Javier is now 43 for 48 in his career as a base stealer. Time is running out of him as far as being a regular. . . .

MIKE JEFFCOAT
Texas

He throws strikes, which is a novelty for a Texas pitcher; I'm not sure why Tom House would permit him to do this. Maybe he just needs a course in remedial nibbling or something. At thirty, he's hardly a hot prospect, but he ain't a bad pitcher.

GREGG JEFFERIES
Mets

The most-similar player to Gregg Jefferies is Jeff Blauser. . . . Jefferies is a good example of why I don't like to project a AA player up to a superstar (see Ken Griffey comment). There are just too many unknowns across that great a distance, too many "course corrections" that have to be made along the way. The result of having projected Jefferies from AA player to superstar is that he had a pretty decent rookie season at the age of twenty-one, and got catcalls. Now, he's a major league regular, and you can project him up to the level of a quality player, which I think he will be. If you take what Jefferies was last year and improve it just a little, you've got a .280-hitting second baseman with 15 homers and 30 stolen bases, and that's a hell of player. He could be better than that; he could be Ryne Sandberg. But he could also get hurt, and his defense at second needs a *lot* of work.

STAN JEFFERSON
Baltimore

Now with his fourth major league team. He played the best ball of his career after joining the Orioles, slugging over .400 through 35 games, but I still have no use for him.

STEVE JELTZ
Philadelphia

Had a decent year with the bat, drawing 45 walks in half-time play, giving him a .356 on-base percentage. His on-base percentage was the second-best among National League shortstops (behind Barry Larkin), and on-base percentage is the most important offensive category. . . . Good glove, of course. Would be outstanding utility man; the recovery of Thon may free him to do that job.

DOUG JENNINGS
Oakland

A little guy (five ten, 165 pounds) who can hit a baseball a long way, his career has kind of been torn up by being bounced around. After he had a monster year in the Texas League in 1987 (.338, 30 homers, 104 RBI) the Angels left him off their forty-man roster, and the A's drafted him, so he had to spend a year in the majors or the Angels could buy him back. That was premature and there wasn't any place for him to play, and the year of not playing much seems to have thrown him off his game. He hit just .274 in the PCL last year with 11 homers, and that's not a very impressive season even with 93 walks thrown in.

He's twenty-five, and still has some time to recover.

DAVE JOHNSON
Baltimore
See "Kevin Hickey." It's fun to read about him and root for him, but you don't want him on your team.

HOWARD JOHNSON
Mets
Created more runs (120) than any major league player who didn't play for the San Francisco Giants. . . . As I'm sure you know, Johnson last year had 36 homers and 41 stolen bases, a power/speed number of 38.3. That's the seventh best power/speed season of all time:

	HR	SB	PSN
Eric Davis, 1987	37	50	42.5
R. Henderson, 1986	28	87	42.4
Jose Canseco, 1988	42	40	41.0
Bobby Bonds, 1973	39	43	40.9
Eric Davis, 1986	27	80	40.4
Bobby Bonds, 1977	37	41	38.9
HoJo, 1989	36	41	38.3

The 36/41 combination almost matches Willie Mays's best, in 1956, which was 36/40. The top ten of 1989: Johnson, Bo Jackson (28.7), Von Hayes, Eric Davis, Barry Bonds, Lonnie Smith, Rickey Henderson, Ryne Sandberg, Robin Yount, and Joe Carter.

LANCE JOHNSON
Chisox
Assuming that the White Sox have finally finished their determined efforts to screw up his career, Johnson should be their left fielder and leadoff man this year. He'll hit around .300, steal more than 50 bases, score 85–90 runs—be a very valuable player to a rotisserie team, although not as valuable in real life. And then, there's always the possibility that he'll hit .220 in April and the Sox will

decide to go with an outfield of Daryl Boston, Sammy Sosa, and Dave Gallagher.

★★★
RANDY JOHNSON
M's
★★★
A great draft pick, albeit a little bit risky. Johnson is a big, strong left-hander who has shown signs, with Montreal late in '89 and with Seattle last year, of being just a foot away from being outstanding. A lot of what shows up in the statistics of a pitcher, of course, is actually the performance of the team behind him. With a developing team, a team which *should* be better, and with the Mariners moving their fences out, that loads the odds in favor of Johnson's making a big stride forward. Of course there is a chance that his control could undermine him and he could be back in Calgary, but he *could* be a Bob Veale-, Sam McDowell-type pitcher—now.

WALLACE JOHNSON
Expos
Valuable pinch hitter, a switch hitter and you don't have to run for him. Not much use to a rotisserie team.

BARRY JONES
White Sox
A 225-pound right-hander, has an ERA below 3.00 in three of four major league seasons. It's a little hard to see him as a relief ace, but I don't know who the White Sox have who is any better qualified.

DOUG JONES
Cleveland
When you read the comments in this section for pitchers, you'll find an awful lot of hedged bets, and lot of "probablys" and "most likelys". There is one reason for that: Doug Jones. Hitters are a relatively predictable commodity; if a

guy can't hit at twenty-five, you can write him off because he ain't going to hit. He might get 10 percent better, but that's about it. But pitchers . . . well, there's always that chance. There are about 400 pitchers in this section who look for all the world like Doug Jones looked five years ago, and in five years 390 of them will be out of baseball, but one of them will be Bob Walk and one of them will be Tom Candiotti and one of them will be Dave Stewart and one of them will be Doug Jones. With a pitcher, you just can't quite be sure.

Doug Jones has almost progressed now to the point at which you'd label him a safe draft, hasn't he? He's had three-plus years now of pitching well. There aren't too many pitchers who have been consistent for any longer than that.

JIMMY JONES
Yankees
Don't see anything to recommend him. Doubt that he will be in the majors most of the season.

RON JONES
Philadelphia
Five ten and 200 pounds, he has a history of bad knees, which got worse when he tore the tendon in his right knee last April 18, crashing into the fence at Shea Stadium. He's had two brief trials in the major leagues and has hit the hell out of the ball both times, hitting .290 with a .535 slugging percentage. In all likelihood, he isn't *that* good a hitter. I don't particularly recommend him, but he could surprise.

TRACY JONES
Last Seen with Detroit
Jones is a little bit of a strange player. He loves to hit. Last spring I stood around the batting cage one day and watched him hit for about an hour. To watch him hit you'd never think he was a good

hitter, at least at that time. He's got a lot of nervous motion in his stroke, dives at outside pitches, doesn't look like he's in control. He shuffles his feet in mid-stroke. When I looked him up in the media guide I couldn't believe it was the same player I had been watching. At that time he had a lifetime .299 major league average with good power, but what was more unbelievable than that was that he had stolen 31 bases in 1987 as a half-time player, and 18 more in 1988 in very limited playing time. He's a great big guy, 225 pounds, with something of a gut.

He had a miserable year, of course, playing for San Francisco and Detroit and not hitting for either team. If he stays in the majors and doesn't go to Japan or something, I'd bet on him to make a comeback, and establish himself as an effective platoon player. What the Tigers need to do (if they still own him) is to get rid of the Chet Lemons and the Fred Lynns, and Gary Wards, and give Jones and Rob Richie and a couple of others enough playing time to get their careers established.

RICKY JORDAN
Philadelphia
The possibility exists that he could develop into an All-Star. Even assuming he doesn't, he's a twenty-four-year-old kid who hits close to .300 with some power and good defense at first base, and that makes him one of the Phillies' most valuable properties . . . hit .333 against left-handed pitchers last year, just .255 against right-handers.

TERRY JORGENSEN
Minnesota
Heir apparent to Gary Gaetti as the Twins third baseman. A second-round draft pick in 1987, he drove in 101 runs at Orlando last year. He looks awfully good to me; I would project him right now as a .250-range hitter with a slug-

ging percentage close to .400 and an on-base percentage about the league average. I think by the end of 1991 we may see him in the majors.

FELIX JOSE
A's
Felix proves that even the Oakland A's don't *always* know what they're doing. Jose is a switch hitter with a little size and decent speed, rated by *Baseball America* as the number-five prospect in the Pacific Coast League last year. The A's talk a lot about his developing into a Reggie Smith-type; according to their media guide, Felix is "considered by many to be the next Oakland A's rookie sensation, showing the ability to hit for both power and average." Fat chance. He could develop a little, but at this point he's a .250 hitter with limited power and an awful K/W ratio. I think he's a real long shot to ever do anything interesting in the major leagues, and I strongly recommend that you *not* draft him.

WALLY JOYNER
California
Most-similar player: Andres Galarraga. . . . If you forget about the 30 home runs he hit one year, Joyner's a "safe draft." In four years in the majors, the lowest he has hit is .282; the highest is .295. He's young, durable, and an excellent fielder.

ED JURAK
San Francisco
I'm glad to see him back in the majors, but obviously he's no draft.

DAVE JUSTICE
Atlanta
The Braves have been talking quite a bit about finding an outfield spot for him. He has power, speed, and a strong arm. I doubt that he can hit much more than .260, if that, although his secondary offensive skills are very good. He's the heir

apparent to Dale Murphy as the Braves right fielder, but I doubt that he's going to make a big splash right away.

JEFF KAISER
Cleveland
Cleveland has a million of these guys, don't they? How many people pitched for Cleveland last year, about forty? (It was twenty, actually.) No prospect.

RON KARKOVICE
White Sox
Fundamentally, he has always been a decent hitter, but the White Sox brought him along too fast and induced a crisis of confidence, setting him back a couple of years. His strikeout to walk ratio last year was 56–10, so I don't know that he's on the verge of superstardom, but he *can* do the job defensively, and I think he can hit. Comparable to Mike Macfarlane. . . . Is this guy an albino? I swear I've never seen anybody in the major leagues with so little skin pigment. . . . What's his batting average in day games?

PAT KEEDY
Cleveland
Third baseman—no prospect.

ROBERTO KELLY
Yankees
The most-similar player to Roberto Kelly is Jerome Walton. . . . I think his .302 batting average was probably a little over his head, but if it's not he's a hell of a ballplayer. . . . I probably won't draft him, but I can see a good argument for him.

TERRY KENNEDY
Giants
Kennedy was on base by hit or walk 115 times last year (not counting home runs), and scored only 14 runs. That was the lowest percentage of any major league player. . . . The impact of that

could easily be distorted. Probably players pinch running for Kennedy scored almost as many runs as Kennedy himself, and most of those runs Kennedy would also have scored if he had remained on base. . . .

JIMMY KEY
Blue Jays

Did you notice that Jimmie Key and Tom Henke had almost identical strikeout and walk totals last year, with Key pitching 216 innings and Henke 89? Key had 118 strikeouts and 27 walks; Henke had 116 and 25. For 216 innings, that's phenomenal control. For 89 innings, it's phenomenal power. Either way, it's a heck of a ratio. . . . Key will be back this year. He's a safe draft—safer than Stieb.

STEVE KIEFER
Yankees

Third baseman—no prospect.

★ ★ ★
DARRYL KILE
Houston
★ ★ ★

Twenty-one-year-old right-handed pitcher in the Houston system, regarded as having the tools to be outstanding. Would be surprised if he starts the year in the major leagues, but ranks with Steve Avery and Andy Benes as the best pitching prospects in the minors in 1989.

PAUL KILGUS
Toronto

Long odds prospect. Three straight losing records. ERAs over 4.00. Poor K/W ratios. Poor hits/inning ratios. Might make the Blue Jays as a left-handed short man, but seemed over-taxed as a starting pitcher.

ERIC KING
White Sox

A lot of baseball people talk very favorably about him, and he did post a 3.39 ERA in 25 starts, but I'm not recommending him. He's a decent risk, but I just think there are other pitchers who are better risks.

JEFF KING
Pittsburgh

He was the first player selected (by anybody) in the 1986 draft, and hasn't done much yet to justify the confidence. He was drafted as a third baseman, shifted to first; now the Pirates are talking about moving him back to third. What seems to be at issue is who is a worse third baseman, King or Bonilla, and the competition is stiff. King's minor league records suggest that he should hit in the .240s with some power, which is OK for a third baseman if the defense is good. I can't recommend him at this point.

MIKE KINGERY
Seattle

One of my favorite players; may have a better chance of sticking with the Mariners if they do expand their outfield area, putting more of a premium on defense. I like him, but in my heart I know he's a fringe player.

MATT KINZER
St. Louis

Another pitcher who got a few innings because the Cardinals were desperate. Could work in as a part of the bullpen committee—no real prospect.

BOB KIPPER
Pittsburgh

A decent pitcher and still only twenty-five years old, posted a 2.93 ERA in 52 games last year. No recommendation, positive or negative . . . another nominee for the Steve Trout All-Star team.

RON KITTLE
White Sox

Over the last three years he has batted 553 times—essentially one season's worth. He has hit 41 home runs in that time, driven in 108, and averaged .277.

BOB KNEPPER
San Francisco

Released.

MARK KNUDSON
Milwaukee

Six five right-hander from the Houston system, throws strikes. Pitched well in long relief, and could hang around in that role. No star potential.

BRAD KOMMINSK
Cleveland

Hit just .237 last year, but with a secondary average of .343. I think that's a reasonable representation of his skills; I think he's about a .237 hitter, but with enough power, speed, and walks to justify a part-time role.

RANDY KRAMER
Pittsburgh

Twenty-nine-year-old right-hander—no prospect.

RAY KRAWCZYK
Milwaukee

At the age of thirty he has an 0–4 record in 39 games with a career ERA of 7.05. I would hope you could find someone better to take a chance on.

CHAD KREUTER
Texas

Well regarded defensive catcher, hit just .152 but did have more walks (27) than hits (24). He's a better hitter than that, probably a .240-range hitter. He appears to have a future as a major league player, probably a fringe player.

BILL KRUEGER
Milwaukee

A thirty-one-year-old left-hander making a comeback from numerous injuries, he pitched well for Milwaukee, and appeared to be throwing harder than he did when he was with Oakland several years ago. He'll be in the majors this year.

JOHN KRUK
Philadelphia
Good hitter—reasonably safe draft. Has now hit .300 three out of four years in the majors, and seven of the last eight years in professional baseball.

MIKE KRUKOW
San Francisco
Released or retired.

JEFF KUNKEL
Texas
A former number one draft pick, he looked like a major league hitter for the first time last year, hitting .270 with 21 doubles and 8 homers in half-time play. Some caution might be in order; he still had 75 strikeouts and 20 walks, but then too, that was the *best* strikeout to walk ratio of his six-year career. His career ratio before last season was 85–6. . . .

RANDY KUTCHER
Red Sox
No draft.

MIKE LACOSS
San Francisco
Remember my Atlee Hammaker comment, that Hammaker has pitched exactly .500 ball for three consecutive seasons? Well, LaCoss has been with the Giants for four years now, and he's 40–40 over the four years. His first year there he was 10–13; the second year he turned that around, and went 13–10. The last two years, 7–7 and 10–10 . . . his ERAs in that period range from 3.17 to 3.68. A safe draft . . .

MIKE LAGA
San Francisco
Power-hitting first baseman, ceased to be a prospect several years ago . . . as a

major leaguer can be expected to hit about .220, but hasn't been up to that yet. . . .

STEVE LAKE
Philadelphia
He has a reputation as a defensive specialist, but over the last four years he's hit .261. How many regular catchers have done better? . . . Backup catchers aren't in general of much use to fantasy teams. . . .

DENNIS LAMP
Boston
Had a remarkable year, posting a 2.32 ERA in Fenway. In view of age (thirty-seven) and inconsistency, I don't recommend him. He is arguable the easiest pitcher in the league to run on, and if there were official counts of inherited runners who scored, I suspect a good bit of his perceived value would vanish.

LES LANCASTER
Cubs
One of the rarely mentioned reasons for the Cubs' success was Lancaster's 1.36 ERA in middle relief. Why is it I don't think he can do this again? . . .

BILL LANDRUM
Pittsburgh
Came into the season with a career ERA of 5.16 and posted an ERA of 1.67. I'd say that's a little incongruous, wouldn't you? Thirty-two years old with no history of consistent success, he would definitely have to be considered a risky investment. But then, he could be the new Doug Jones. . . .

BRIAN LANE
Cincinnati
Third baseman in Cincinnati system, very young and very highly regarded, but not ready yet. Keep him in mind for next season. . . .

★★★
RAY LANKFORD
St. Louis
★★★
If this guy comes up, snap him up in a hurry; he's going to be the Cardinals center fielder, and he should be good. He was the Texas League MVP, and also picked by *Baseball America* the number-one prospect in the Texas League, and I love him. His MLEs show a .284 batting average (.317 in Texas League), but he hits doubles, triples, and homers, steals bases and walks more than he strikes out, making a .376 secondary average. According to *Baseball America*, Lankford "is regraded as superior defensively because of his speed and strong arm."

MARK LANGSTON
California
Perhaps the most consistent starting pitcher in baseball over the last four years, among the good ones I mean. His strikeout totals over those four years: 245, 262, 235, and 235. His walks: 123, 114, 110, 112. His winning percentage the last three seasons has been between .533 and .594. The only thing that has changed has been his ERAs, which (going back to 1985) have been getting steadily better: 5.47, 4.85, 3.84, 3.34, and 2.74. He's a "safe draft"—but an expensive one.

CARNEY LANSFORD
Oakland
The way in which he has adapted his style to the needs of his team is rather remarkable, don't you think? For four straight seasons he was a single-digit base stealer—but moved into the number two spot, he has increased his stolen bases, in his thirties, from 2 to 16 to 27 to 29 to 37. He used to hit 19 homers a year, but, asked to hit second, he switched instead to being Wade Boggs, hitting .336 with 2 homers. In 1979 he

struck out 115 times; last year he struck out 25 times. You'd be hard pressed to find a parallel for that in all baseball history, I think.

I still don't care for him as a *defensive* player, and I still have the same problem with him that I had ten years ago: he dives for everything. He still does it, though; when the ball is hit anywhere near him, he leaves his feet, which looks good but severely limits his range. Because of the large foul territory outside third, Oakland third basemen traditionally have high range factors. Even Wayne Gross, who was hardly regarded as Brooks Robinson, had very high range factors when he played here. But not Lansford—he made 2.11 plays per game, the lowest range factor of any major league third baseman who doesn't have the name of a large hotel chain. (Actually, Gross was an underrated third baseman, who was very good at chasing down pop fouls.)

DAVE LAPOINT
Yankees
Doubt that he will make the team.

BARRY LARKIN
Cincinnati
The best offensive shortstop in the National League, and above average defensively. Only question is his health, so find out about that before you draft him.

GENE LARKIN
Minnesota
Not recommended. Outfielder/DH with secondary average barely over .200. I can do without those.

TIM LAUDNER
Minnesota
Signed a big contract and immediately lost his job to Brian Harper. Not a good gamble.

MIKE LAVALLIERE
Pittsburgh
As a player, uncannily similar to Mike Scioscia. Both are catchers, left-handed hitters, .260–.270 hitters. Both walk some and very rarely strike out. Both are strong, squat men but never pull the ball and so have no power. Both are slower than a stadium beer vendor with a full load. LaValliere was hurt most of last year; Scioscia lost most of one season with an injury. Both are regarded as good defensive catchers with good arms. I don't think there are two more-similar players in the major leagues.

VANCE LAW
Cubs
Now playing in Japan.

TOM LAWLESS
Toronto
No relation to John Kruk.

MARCUS LAWTON
Yankees
Not a major league hitter at this point.

RICK LEACH
Texas
The most-similar player to Rick Leach is John Morris. . . . Leach, who has been known to forget what he does for a living, has nonetheless been a consistent player over the last four seasons, hitting between .309 and .272 every year.

TERRY LEACH
Kansas City
Marginal pitcher. With the signing of Mark Davis, Storm Davis, and Richard Dotson as free agents, Leach probably won't make the Royals out of camp.

TIM LEARY
Yankees
Career record in odd-numbered years: 13–30, .302.

Career record in even-numbered years: 32–26, .552.

That makes this year a good one, for those of you who believe in that kind of thing.

MANNY LEE
Toronto
Good ballplayer. Above-average shortstop and second baseman, decent hitter. Excellent utility infielder, could play regularly for many teams. Very comparable to Manny Trillo when Trillo was young.

CRAIG LEFFERTS
San Diego
A good draft. Many people assume he will fail as the San Diego stopper, but I don't see why. He's never had a bad year in the majors (worst ERA was 3.83). He's only thirty-two, coming off an exceptional year for San Francisco. I'd put it this way: His credentials are a hell of a lot better than Mark Davis's were two years ago. He just got tagged as a left-handed spot reliever, and he's never had a chance to be the closer.

CHARLIE LEIBRANDT
Atlanta
Charlie's first thought on being traded to Atlanta: Oh God, that's the launching pad; there goes my ERA.

Second thought on being traded to Atlanta: Oh Lord, the Braves are a terrible team; there goes my won-lost record.

Third thought on being traded to Atlanta: What the hell, the Braves have forty-seven young pitchers; I might not even make the team.

I'm interpreting, you understand; this is what would have gone through *my* mind if *I* were Charlie Leibrandt. He must have thought he had died and gone to hell. There couldn't have been a worse place to get traded to at a moment when you're trying to get your career back together. Charlie went 5–11 with a 5.14 ERA last year; that's with a *good* team in a neutral park. You translate that to Atlanta, and it's got to be about 2–16 with an ERA of 7.00.

I wouldn't be drafting him.

DAVE LEIPER
San Diego

No prospect.

AL LEITER
Toronto

Pitched in only one game after being traded to Toronto and then suffered an injury. He's young enough and talented enough to come back, and in the long run being traded out of New York might be the best thing for him. The Blue Jays might give him three months at AAA to get his career back together, and he might do it. No draft out of spring training.

SCOTT LEIUS
Minnesota

At some point he will battle Greg Gagne for the Minnesota shortstop job. He's a better average hitter than Gagne, doesn't match him in power, comparable to him in K/W ratio (poor) and speed (limited). He led the Southern League (AA) in hitting last year; the confrontation between Gagne and Leius is still probably a year away.

★ ★ ★
MARK LEMKE
Braves
★ ★ ★

By all logic, Lemke should be Atlanta's second baseman this year. He's small (five nine, 167), quick and strong. He's a switch hitter, and has a reputation as a scrapper. With Atlanta having as many prospects as they do, nobody is going to hand him a job, but if he does get a job I like his chances of staying for eight or ten years. I see him as a .260–.270 hitter, decent K/W ratio, a little

power, good defense at second. Don't release Ryne Sandberg to pick him up, but I think he's a major league player.

CHET LEMON
Detroit

With the retirement of Buddy Bell, Chet has the worst career stolen base percentage of any active player (100 or more tries); he has stolen 55 bases and has been caught 74 times. The bottom ten (active 1989) were Bell, Lemon, Manny Trillo, Joel Youngblood, Hubie Brooks, Tom Brunansky, Tony Pena, Fred Lynn, Jack Clark, and Ken Oberkfell . . . actually, Bob Boone's stolen base percentage is almost the same as Lemon's, but he has only 86 attempts . . . the most-similar player to Chet Lemon is Claudell Washington. . . .

JEFFREY LEONARD
Seattle

Jeffrey Leonard may be the worst draft pick of the 1990 season. First of all, he wasn't that good, even the way he played in 1989. He hit 24 home runs and drove in 93 runs, but batting cleanup in a hitter's park, how good is that really? His other accomplishments include:

- he had more than three times as many strikeouts as walks (125–38) . . .
- he hit just .254, which makes an on-base percentage of .301 . . .
- he had only 20 doubles and 1 triple.

But his two "good" numbers of 1989, 24 homers and 93 RBI, were both career highs, and were dramatically up from the previous four seasons, when his best RBI total had been 64.

He is thirty-four years old, will be thirty-five in September. At that age, a sudden decline is always a present possibility.

So the odds of his having a sharp decline in productivity, even if every-

thing was constant, would be quite high. But then, when you figure that the Mariners have moved their fences out, what are the odds? The odds against his having as "good" a season in 1990 have got to be ten to one.

MARK LEONARD
San Francisco

Leonard is a left-handed hitting outfield in the San Francisco system, who doesn't have anything going for him except that he can hit. He was a twenty-sixth round draft pick of the Giants in 1986, and first caught my eye after a big year at San Jose in 1988, where he hit .345 with 50 doubles, 15 homers, 118 RBI and 118 walks. Those are some numbers, but I kind of wrote them off, figuring here's a twenty-three-year-old in the California League with not a lot of speed or defense. But last year Leonard went to Shreveport in the Texas League, which is a tough place to hit. He hit .311 in 219 at bats (had an injury), with even better power and RBI rates than he had had in the California League.

Leonard is twenty-five, will be twenty-six in August. He isn't fast. The two positions that he would have to play in the majors are occupied by Kevin Mitchell and Will Clark. There is no evidence that anybody in the Giants system believes in him or is going to give him anything he doesn't earn the hard way. Still, I think Leonard is probably the best hitter in the Giants minor league system, and sooner or later that has a good chance of surfacing. He could be a guy, like Wade Boggs or Ken Singleton, who just keeps coming and keeps coming, and sooner or later things fall in place for him.

DEREK LILLIQUIST
Atlanta

Exceptional control; suspect that he will pitch better in 1990 than he did in 1989. The development of his team around him could give him a couple of extra wins, too, so we should pencil him in for something like 15–11, maybe?

In the long run, I'm skeptical about him. I think he'll be as good in 1990 and 1991 as he's going to get.

JOSE LIND
Pittsburgh

He's a good base stealer and a marvelous second baseman. If he hits the way he did in 1989, that's not enough.

JIM LINDEMAN
St. Louis

Not a major league hitter—no prospect.

★ ★ ★
NELSON LIRIANO
Toronto
★ ★ ★

Liriano is emerging as one of the league's better second basemen, offensively and defensively. He hits in the .260s. He hit 26 doubles last year in just over 400 at bats. His strikeout to walk ratio is above average. He can steal some bases. He makes the double play well. His fielding percentage was good. Who is better, at this moment? Franco, Sax, Jerry Browne, probably Harold Reynolds and Lou Whitaker.

That makes him about the number-six man in the league—and he's just twenty-five years old. I think that's somebody you have to consider drafting.

SCOTT LITTLE
Pittsburgh

There is no evidence that he *will*, but this guy *could* emerge from the first base-third base mess in Pittsburgh with a regular job. He's twenty-seven years old, which would stamp him as a marginal prospect, but he's a third baseman, and he's capable of hitting .280 in the major leagues. If Leyland decides that Bonilla *has* to be moved off of third base and that King *can't* do the job, then where

do they turn? It's a longshot, but they could turn to Scott Little.

GREG LITTON
San Francisco

Played surprisingly well after being more or less an emergency roster move. His major league batting average (.252) and slugging percentage (.413) were almost precisely the major league equivalents of his performance at Shreveport in 1988. His K/W ratio will improve over time.

PHIL LOMBARDI
Mets

He may come in for some major league playing time due to the release of Gary Carter. I gather that he is suspect defensively, but he is a *much better hitter* than most people believe. If he gets to play some, he will hit *from .240 to .285,* but with moderate power and pretty good K/W ratio. He is a better hitter right now than Gary Carter. If he gets 150 at bats, he is *going* to surprise some people.

STEVE LOMBARDOZZI
Houston

No prospect/no player/no draft.

BILL LONG
White Sox

Trying to stick around as a sixth starter/long man, no pun intended. He'll be in the majors/no star potential.

VANCE LOVELACE
California

A 235-pound left-hander, wilder than a truckload of starving kangaroos. Former number-one draft pick, nine years ago; still hasn't found the strike zone.

TOREY LOVULLO
Detroit

He hit .115 last year, but he's not a legitimate .115 hitter. He's a .225 hitter. Basically, he has no business in the major leagues.

RICK LUECKEN
Atlanta

Didn't pitch badly with Kansas City. Veteran minor leaguer, not likely to make the Atlanta team out of spring training. If there is any spring training. If there is any team.

URBANO LUGO
Montreal

The Van Lingle Mungo of our generation. Believe it or not, Urbano is only twenty-seven, so he could keep showing up in the reference books for another ten years or so. That's all he does; he doesn't really pitch. He just makes a token appearance to keep his name in the reference books, like *Who's Who in Baseball* and the *Baseball Register.*

SCOTT LUSADER
Detroit

A .250 range hitter with speed, no power. Could make the team, but the Tigers have better options and so do you.

FRED LYNN
San Diego

His RBI total has now gone down every year since 1984 (79, 68, 67, 60, 56, 46). I'd say he's got a . . . what, 80 percent chance of extending that string? San Diego doesn't think so; they've penciled him in in left field. He is, of course, moving to a much tougher hitter's park than he is leaving, particularly for a left-hander (9 of his 11 homers last year were hit at home).

Lynn has taken a lot of bad raps in his career, and I shouldn't contribute to that. He's been a fine player, a great player in 1975. John Belushi was a great comedian in 1975, and Fred Lynn has a better chance of making a comeback than John Belushi, but not much.

BARRY LYONS
Mets

Not as good a hitter as Lombardi. His role in the future of the team is uncertain; the Mets may yet trade a pitcher to get a catcher.

STEVE LYONS
White Sox

One more player that the White Sox have absolutely no idea what to do with. He played well at third in '88, so the White Sox, of course, moved him to second. The White Sox theory of life is that its cheaper to put wings on a school bus than it is to buy a 747.

MIKE MACFARLANE
Kansas City

In 1988, when Macfarlane got a shot as the regular, a couple of Royals pitchers (notably Charlie Leibrandt) were unhappy with his pitch selection and work behind the plate, and although he was hitting well he was dispatched to Omaha to study the finer points of his craft. This was a big controversy in KC at the time, and last year Wathan went out of his way to bury that story and talk about how much Macfarlane had improved in a year. Leibrandt is gone now, so the story is probably gone with him.

But it isn't going to be that easy for Macfarlane to get back to regular status. Boone is forty-two, but he played awfully well last year, and doesn't figure to have his playing time reduced unless there is a breakdown. Macfarlane's a .250-range hitter with some power, throwing arm adequate. He's slow as hell—I swear he was almost as slow at twenty-five as Bob Boone was at forty-one. He's not star material, but there are worse catchers playing regularly.

KEVIN MAAS
Yankees

Twenty-five-year-old outfielder-first baseman. He's a little unpredictable because he's been up and down as a hitter, but Maas *appears* to be at least a good major league hitter, and possibly an outstanding one. Poor defensive reputa-tion; playing for Yankees is a major negative. It appears likely that it will be another year before Mass gets a long look in the majors.

MORRIS MADDEN
Pittsburgh

Twenty-nine-year-old left-hander; no prospect.

GREG MADDUX
Cubs

He's been one of the best pitchers in baseball the last two seasons. As a rotis-serie player, you'd have to worry about his ability to keep his ERA around 3.00 in Wrigley Field and without either awesome stuff or great control, but he's done it so far. Relatively safe draft . . . his lifetime batting average, .195, is the sixth-best among active pitchers.

MIKE MADDUX
Philadelphia

Released.

SCOTTI MADISON
Cincinnati

I root for him, like Matt Winters. After hitting .171 and .173, his major league career is in jeopardy.

ALEX MADRID
Philadelphia

Right-handed pitcher—no prospect. A member of the Darryl Boston All-Star team.

DAVE MAGADAN
Mets

A good draft, in that he is young and his playing time is still expanding, particularly with the release of Hernandez. Apparently is making progress as a defensive first baseman, from what I understand?

JOE MAGRANE
St. Louis

Allowed only 5 home runs in 235 innings, or .19 homers per game, by far the lowest rate in the majors. . . .

I've pointed this out before, but never with such a good example. *ERA predicts winning percentage much better than winning percentage predicts itself.* This is statistically unique; ordinarily nothing predicts success in any category like the category itself. The players who lead the league in stolen bases next year will be about the same as the players who led this year—Rickey Henderson, Vince Coleman if he is playing, Roberto Alomar, etc. The players who lead the league in batting next year will be by and large the same group who led last year—Wade Boggs, Kirby Puckett, Tony Gwynn, Will Clark, Carney Lansford, etc.

On the other hand, this year's ERAs will predict next year's winning percentages better than this year's winning percentages. A pitcher like Joe Magrane in 1988, who led the league in ERA but won only five games, is extremely likely in 1989 to have not only a low ERA but also a high winning percentage, as in fact he did. A pitcher like Richard Dotson in 1988, who had a 5.00 ERA but a 12–9 record, is very likely in 1989 to have not only a high ERA but a losing record, as in fact he did.

And that demonstrates that winning and losing games is not truly a skill in itself, but simply a function of two things: luck and preventing runs.

And that means that pitchers' won-lost records, if you're dealing with less than fifty games, are basically meaningless.

TOM MAGRANN
Cleveland

Twenty-six-year-old catcher, no opportunity behind Alomar and probably wouldn't hit, anyway.

RICK MAHLER
Cincinnati

Has exactly 100 decisions over the last four years: 40 wins, 60 losses . . . no draft in my book.

CANDY MALDONADO
Cleveland

On *Baseball Sunday* last year we had more calls about Candy Maldonado than any other player. None of the callers, that I can recall, were on his side, except that there was some feeling expressed that he wasn't as bad as Pat Sheridan. Playing for Cleveland, he is certain to recover to some extent, but then what? He is, like the acquisitions of Keith Hernandez, Dion James, Chris James, and John McNamara, utterly irrelevant to any eventual success that the team might have. He is, if he plays *well*, a holding action, a nothing occupying time and space. I mean, I know that there is a lot of respect for Hank Peters throughout baseball, but Jesus, what a pathetic operation he is running. . . . Cleveland, with Maldonado, Cory Snyder, Chris and Dion, Brad Komminsk, Mitch Webster, and Joey Belle, will have surely the largest and most useless collection of outfielders in the major leagues.

KELLY MANN
Atlanta

Bobby Cox, on the other hand, is sharp. Realizing he had no catching in the system, he just began collecting catchers, picking up Francisco Cabrera in one trade (a hitter, but no defensive catcher), Kelly Mann in another one (a decent prospect, but regarded as the number four catching prospect in the Cub system), signing Ernie Whitt as a free agent. Without pulling off any big trade—without giving up John Smoltz for Sandy Alomar—he has quietly reduced the scale of the problem, and thus reduced the pressure on himself to do something about it.

Mann is so young (twenty-two) that it will be years before we know what kind of a player he is going to be.

FRED MANRIQUE
Texas

The most-similar player to Fred Manrique is Nelson Liriano. . . . When the Rangers acquired Manrique in the Baines trade, there were a lot of people saying that of course he was just a stopgap at short, but they're dead wrong. I saw him play shortstop in the minors years ago, and I've never forgotten it.

KIRT (WHAT IS THAT) MANWARING
San Francisco

He may, in time, grow into a regular catcher. I'm not going to draft him this spring.

MIKE MARSHALL
Mets

This trade obviously seems to indicate that another will follow. The Mets at the moment have two right fielders, in Strawberry and Marshall, and I don't reckon they're going to platoon them. They wouldn't move McReynolds back to center, would they?

CARLOS MARTINEZ
White Sox

A weird-looking player, all bones; he's six five and his waist is six three. Here's another one—anybody in baseball could see in three-and-a-half seconds that Martinez isn't a third baseman, but the White Sox haven't figured it out yet . . . .300 batting average as a rookie was over his head, but he's a decent hitter.

CARMELO MARTINEZ
Philadelphia

Should probably be a platoon player. He hit .271 last year against left-handers but .181 against right-handers—but had over half his at bats against righties. Veterans Stadium is a better hitter's park

than Jack Murphy, and the 1989 season was subpar for him anyway, so he is enormously likely to have a *better* year this year than last year. I still wouldn't recommend him to anybody I liked.

DAVE MARTINEZ
Montreal

Marquis Grissom takes over one outfield job, but Hubie Brooks is gone. The upshot will be that Martinez, rather than platooning in center, will platoon in right.

DENNIS MARTINEZ
Montreal

Over the last three years has almost the same winning percentage as Dave Stewart (.636) and has had a lower ERA every year . . . of course, if you adjust for the DH it's really about the same. . . . Despite his age (thirty-five) and history, I'd have to say that he's a relatively safe draft. He is truly a better pitcher now than he has ever been.

EDGAR MARTINEZ
Seattle

What a sad story this one is. This guy is a *good* hitter, quite capable of hitting .300 in a park like Seattle, with more walks than strikeouts. Jim Presley, after hitting very well in 1985–86, has become an offensive nightmare—slow as hell, striking out about five times as often as he walks, and showing constantly diminishing batting averages (.275, .265, .247, .230, .236) and power figures. But the Mariners have just insisted on staying with Presley, and Martinez has wasted about three years of his career, when he could have been helping the team.

★★★
RAMON MARTINEZ
Los Angeles
★★★

There is every reason to believe that Martinez will be one of the top starting pitchers in the National League this season. He was tremendously successful at Albuquerque early last year (10–2, 2.79 ERA in the hitting-dominated Pacific Coast League.) He was very successful with the Dodgers after he moved up (6–4, 3.19). He has an outstanding fastball, and his control is not a big problem. Dodger Stadium will work in his favor. The Dodgers coaching staff for working with pitchers, Ron Perranoski, Joe Ferguson, and Red Adams (as well as Lasorda) is superb. My guess is Martinez goes 17–11 with a 2.82 ERA.

TINO MARTINEZ
Seattle

A number-one draft pick of the Mariners, Martinez is a left-handed hitting first baseman who is now blocked behind not one, but two good left-handed hitting first basemen at the major league level, Pete O'Brien and Alvin Davis. Martinez is regarded as very strong defensively, and will hit for some power. I don't look for him to be in the majors this season.

JOHN MARZANO
Red Sox

I don't know why he hasn't been playing rather than Gedman; I gather the Red Sox don't like his mouth. It's past, anyway; Pena has the job now.

ROGER MASON
Houston

Once a prospect. No longer.

DON MATTINGLY
Yankees

The most-similar player to Don Mattingly is Pedro Guerrero. At least, that's what the computer says; I don't know that I believe it. . . . In the last six years he has hit .300 all six times, driven in 100 runs five times, had 300 total bases five times, hit 37 or more doubles all six times. I'd say he's a safe investment, wouldn't you? . . .

LEE MAZZILLI
Toronto

Released.

RANDY MCCAMENT
San Francisco

No control/don't draft him. . . .

TOM MCCARTHY
White Sox

Like a good many pitchers, it took McCarthy years in the minors before he found his control, which undermined his career and gradually reduced him from a starting prospect to a guy trying to hang onto a major league job. He walked only 20 men in 67 innings last year, though, so he can probably now stay in the majors. He doesn't figure to post many wins, saves or strikeouts, so he doesn't have too much to recommend him to rotisserie or fantasy players. . . .

KIRK MCCASKILL
California

I don't think he was throwing as hard last year as he was before the injury, but he's a superb pitcher, and the second year back he might be throwing harder than he was the first year back. He's definitely a pitcher I wouldn't mind having on my team . . . should win 14–18 games . . .

LLOYD MCCLENDON
Cubs

Don't count on him to continue to hit the way he did last year, of course. He's thirty-one now, and he's not a *bad* hitter, but he's not as good a hitter as he was last year. I'd say probably no draft, with an option to pick him up very late if he's the type of player you need. . . .

BOB MCCLURE
California

Is this one of the most improbable careers of our time? This guy has been in the majors for fifteen years now, winning an average of four games a season, saving another three. The 1989 season, when he went 6–1 with a 1.55 ERA, was probably the best of his career. . . . If you were doing a really strict all-time All-star team, where for your left-handed short reliever you couldn't pick Steve Carlton, but had to pick somebody who was actually a left-handed short reliever all his life, who would you pick? You'd have to think about McClure, Steve Mingori, Joe Hoerner, Darold Knowles, Paul Lindblad. Who am I missing?

LANCE MCCULLERS
New York Yankees

Still young, could surprise with a comeback. No draft.

BEN MCDONALD
Baltimore

The number-one selection in the 1989 draft, held out most of the summer and wasn't impressive late when he did sign.

The obvious comparison is between McDonald and Andy Benes, the Padres pitcher who was among the first players taken in the 1988 draft, who like McDonald is a huge right-hander (Benes 6–6, McDonald 6–7). I saw both of them pitch last summer, Benes in the minors and McDonald in the College World Series; both were nursing injuries at the time that I saw them. McDonald, I think, may be a more impressive athlete. He gives the appearance of enormous strength, even more than Benes does, and seems a little lighter on his feet. Benes is much further along, in my opinion, as a pitcher. McDonald when I saw him was having trouble gripping his curveball, so maybe it isn't a fair comparison, but Benes changes speeds, moves the ball up and down and doesn't try to make impossible pitches. McDonald has as good a fastball, but when I saw him the curveball wasn't breaking, and he didn't seem to have any idea how to compensate for that. He began trying to make impossible pitches, and he beat himself. I suspect that McDonald can pitch in the majors—if Benes and Abbott and Gregg Olson could, why couldn't he?—but I doubt that he'll be as effective as Benes will over the next two or three years.

ODDIBE MCDOWELL
Atlanta

The most-similar player to Oddibe McDowell is Juan Samuel. . . . Oddibe, who has always been one of my favorite players, had become a media whipping boy in Texas, but finally seemed to come into his own after the trade to Atlanta, scoring 56 runs in 76 games and hitting over .300. He doesn't have to hit .300 to be an effective leadoff man. In 1986, hitting just .266 for a not-very-good team, he scored 105 runs. He is capable of doing better than that. I don't know about you, but I always like to have Oddibe on my team.

ROGER MCDOWELL
Philadelphia

His 1.96 ERA last year is deceptive because he gave up 16 unearned runs, almost leading the National League, in 92 innings. An unearned run is a funny concept, that if an error *contributes* to a run, the pitcher shouldn't be held responsible. But what if the error contributes 20 percent to the run, and the pitcher contributes 80 percent? If you counted half of his unearned runs against him (rather than the defense) and half of his inherited runs against him (rather than charging them all to the starting pitchers) his ERA would have been over the league norm. . . . With 16 to 25 saves in each of the last five years and with no real competition as Philadelphia relief ace, he would have to be considered a safe pick.

CHUCK MCELROY
Philadelphia

Struggling in the minors as a starter, became effective last year after converting to relief. Still young. Probably will make the team this year. Don't see a lot to recommend him; Grade C prospect.

ANDY MCGAFFIGAN
Montreal

Had an off year after three straight good years, but the Expos' need for pitching probably will protect his position on the staff. Chances of regaining effectiveness about fifty-fifty; no chance of moving into a key role on the staff.

WILLIE MCGEE
St. Louis

I sure wouldn't draft him. He's thirty-one, coming off an injury. He's a singles hitter whose batting average over the last four seasons is just .274. He has no power. He strikes out three times as often as he walks. His central skill is his speed—and at thirty-one, how dependable is that? The Cardinals have a crowd in the outfield; the guy who took his job while he was injured, Milt Thompson, did a fine job. The Cardinals have an exceptional center field prospect, in Ray Lankford.

FRED MCGRIFF
Toronto

The major league players creating the most runs with a batting average below .275: Fred McGriff (111), Bo Jackson, Glenn Davis, Von Hayes, Joe Carter, Barry Bonds, Jack Clark, Chili Davis, Lou Whitaker, and Cal Ripken. McGriff was the only one over a hundred, and he also led the group in runs created per out. . . .

BILL MCGUIRE
Seattle

No prospect/sub-.200 hitting catcher who filled in while Valle was injured.

MARK MCGWIRE
Oakland

The most-similar player to Mark McGwire is Fred McGriff. . . . Devastating offensive player even if he hits .230. You remember I commented in the opening essay on McGwire in spring training, saying to himself as he got in the batter's box "Runner on third, one out," and then driving the ball for a sacrifice fly. Remembering that, I checked his sacrifice fly total last year. It increased from just 4 in 1988 to 11 last year, fourth-best in the American League.

MARK MCLEMORE
California

Offense is OK for a second baseman, but defense hasn't helped his career. He could play for somebody like Baltimore or Minnesota, but he isn't going to take the job away from Johnny Ray.

CRAIG MCMURTRY
Texas

A year ago, preparing an arbitration case for Paul Mirabella, we decided that the most-comparable player was Craig McMurtry. This was a positive thing at the time; Mirabella had an ERA of 1.65 in 60 innings, McMurtry 2.25 in the same. It also proved to be prophetic. Mirabella in thirteen games last year had no wins, no saves and an ERA of 7.63. McMurtry in nineteen games had no wins, no saves and an ERA of 7.43 . . . career probably over.

KEVIN MCREYNOLDS
Mets

Extremely safe draft; durable, consistent, multi-talented. The Mets' madness whirls around him as if he wasn't there. In the last four years he has hit 22 to 29 homers every year, driven in 85 to 99 runs, hit .272 to .287 every year. He steals some bases, plays good defense in left. I hope he doesn't have to go back to center, though. . . .

LARRY MCWILLIAMS
Kansas City
He's still on the roster at this writing, but he has no realistic chance of making the Royals after the signing of Mark Davis. In the last five years he has had five losing records (aggregate 20–43) with five high ERAs (aggregate 4.48). The constant search for a left-hander was basically all he had going for him.

LUIS MEDINA
Cleveland
The signing of Candy Maldonado and the acquisition of Chris James seem to rule out any chance he had of playing regularly. He's not any worse than Chris James as a player, but he's not any better. I always root for him, but I can't recommend you draft him.

FRANCISCO MELENDEZ
Baltimore
A first baseman, could hit anywhere from .260 to .300 in the majors and good defense at first, but no power or speed. Not a useful player—not a prospect.

BOB MELVIN
Baltimore
Still in the majors. Playing time constant over the last four years (84–92 games every year, 246–278 at bats), but may drop this year unless Tettleton is hurt again. A .225 hitter/no power/no draft.

ORLANDO MERCADO
Minnesota
His best chance to stay in the game would appear to be as a traveling secretary.

KENT MERCKER
Atlanta
Highly regarded pitching prospect in Braves system; rated by *Baseball America*

the number two prospect in the International League, and the number two prospect in the Braves system. I don't recommend that you pick him up:

1) He hasn't found his control yet.
2) He is still very young.
3) The Braves have lots of candidates for starting jobs, so Mercker faces stiff competition.
4) Fulton County Stadium is a pitcher's worst enemy.

There are some Braves pitching prospects I like anyway, but I recommend you wait on Mercker.

MATT MERULLO
White Sox
A left-handed hitting catcher, probably a .240-range hitter, not a lot of power. Grade C prospect.

HENSLEY "BAM BAM" MEULENS
Yankees
He's one of those players who, for some reason, people started talking about years before he was ready to move to the majors, and he may never live that down. If he was brought to the majors now, he would probably hit .240–.250, and would strike out in about one third of his at bats. He does have power, 20-homer power, he will draw some walks, and he does have a strong arm, but fundamentally he is not ready to be a major league star. He is still very young, and in two years he may. If the Yankees behave prudently (hah!), they'll give the first look at third base to Randy Velarde, and turn to Mike Blowers as a backup, giving Meulens at least one full year in AAA. Not everybody needs a full year in AAA. Bam Bam does.

BRIAN MEYER
Houston
Grade C prospect. Right-hander, fastball in the mid-eighties but a nice slider, control record could be a lot better than

it is. Astros pitchers are always nice to have on your team, but he's got maybe a 20 percent chance to make the roster.

JOEY MEYER
Milwaukee
Joey is now playing, believe it or not, for the Taiyo Whales. Funny guys, those Japanese.

GARY MIELKE
Texas
Twenty-seven-year-old right-handed reliever with nothing much going for him/ Grade D prospect.

BOB MILACKI
Baltimore
A pitcher's second full season in the major leagues is, of course, a critical time, and a moment at which many young pitchers fall apart. Like many rookie pitchers, Milacki has been exposed in the last two years to a workload that goes far beyond anything he had experienced before 1988, and it is very much an open question how that workload will effect him. Many, many young pitchers simply can't handle it.

Apart from that, he doesn't have the basic characteristics of a future star. He doesn't have a blazing fastball. He doesn't strike out a lot of people, or have terrific control either. He hasn't been consistently successful over a period of years. The team for which he works, the Orioles, may have been over their heads in 1989.

Milacki pitched very well last year; 14–12, 3.74 ERA. He tied for the American League lead in starts, 36, and was among the leaders in innings pitched. You can, if you want, project moderate improvement for him from experience, and see an impressive pitcher—say, 17–12 with a 3.40 ERA. And you might very well be right. I'm just cautioning you that I would regard him as a high-risk draft pick. You can gamble maybe eight to ten times on a twenty-five-man roster; if he's somebody you *want* to gamble on, go ahead. But don't mark him down as a safe pick.

KEITH MILLER
Mets

Useful utility infielder—will steal a few bases. No star potential.

KEITH MILLER
Philadelphia

Also a utility player; wouldn't expect him to make the team. Would hit .250–.265 with an occasional homer, a stolen base now and then and decent K/W ratio.

RANDY MILLIGAN
Baltimore

One of the real stars of the Orioles season, he hit a respectable .268 with a secondary average of .416. He has power, walks an enormous amount and can even steal a base now and then. If you projected his 365 at bats out to 600, you'd have 38 doubles, 8 triples, 20 homers, 15 stolen bases and 122 walks. How many players make those kind of contributions to an offense?

This was a simple case of taking advantage of the available talent. What Milligan did last year in the majors was exactly what his minor league records showed that he was capable of doing. He's not a potential superstar—he was trapped in the minors too long for that—but he's not a fluke, either.

GREG MINTON
California

Now thirty-eight years old, he hasn't had an ERA higher than 3.93 for eleven consecutive years, since 1978. I don't see any reason to think that he will in 1990.

PAUL MIRABELLA
Milwaukee

Released.

JOHN MITCHELL
Mets

If you diagram the elements of a potential star pitcher, Mitchell has none. He's only twenty-four, but he entered professional baseball young and has thrown a jillion innings with an immature arm. At Tidewater in 1988 he was very effective but struck out only 60 men in 190 innings. I would have *no* interest in him.

KEVIN MITCHELL
San Francisco

Did you know Kevin had 32 intentional walks last year. That's a record for a right-handed hitter; the other people who have had 30, like Ted Williams, Willie McCovey and Brett, are all left-handers. A left-hander gets more intentional walks than a right-hander because avoiding the platoon edge is a major reason for giving an intentional walk, and the left-hander has that edge more often than a right-hander.

So anyway, Mitchell was having a great year last year, with nobody hitting behind him; Candy Maldonado was just having a terrible time. I heard this all the first half: Mitchell had to collapse in the second half, because the pitchers would pitch around him because there was nobody having a good year behind him. A conundrum, or one of them things; If Mitchell was bound to collapse because you can't have a good year with nobody hitting behind you, then how did Mitchell have such a great *first half* with nobody coming up behind him? Williams got hot behind him in August and Mitchell had a solid, unspectacular second half, and the issue kind of melted away.

What kind of a year do we expect from Mitchell? Obviously we don't expect him to hit 50 homers every year. In general, I don't believe in fluke seasons. A player who hits 47 home runs in a season has the ability to hit 47 home runs the next year, even though he

probably won't. I look for Mitchell to hit 35–38 homers this year, drive in 110 runs or so.

I drew up a list of the 1989 "overachievers of the year," based on 1989 runs created compared to career performance. The top ten were Kevin Mitchell (+34, meaning he created 34 runs more than he would have had he performed at his career level), Howard Johnson (+31), Lonnie Smith (+29), Robin Yount (+28), Ruben Sierra (+27), Julio Franco (+24), Mickey Tettleton and Will Clark (+19), Nick Esasky (+17), and Steve Sax (+15). Probably none of those is a particularly good draft risk for 1989; as a group, at least eight of the ten will probably relapse in 1990.

Mitchell in 1989:

- Led the majors in runs created, with 127.
- Led the majors in runs created per 27 outs, 8.46.
- Had the highest ratio of runs created *per hit* of any major league player.
- Had 55 percent of his hits going for extra bases, the highest percentage of any major league player.

JOHN MIZEROCK
Atlanta

Left-handed hitting catcher; no prospect.

KEVIN MMAHAT
Yankees

A member of the Winston Llenas All-Star team . . . a long-odds player; maybe a 10–15 percent chance of being a good pitcher.

DALE MOHORCIC
Yankees

Coming off of two bad years and an injury at the age of thirty-four; you'd have to be goofy to draft him. He's fooled people before.

PAUL MOLITOR
Milwaukee

The most-similar player to Paul Molitor is Carney Lansford. . . . On the list of current players who have a chance to get 3,000 hits in their careers, Molitor's name is the big surprise. The top ten are Robin Yount (94 percent), George Brett (58 percent), Eddie Murray (46 percent), Kirby Puckett (44 percent), Wade Boggs (39 percent), Don Mattingly (33 percent), Paul Molitor (33 percent), Tony Gwynn (32 percent), Carney Lansford (29 percent) and Steve Sax (28 percent). It is likely that about seven active players will get to the 3,000 hit standard; other players with a ten percent chance or better include Cal Ripken, Mike Greenwell, Dwight Evans, Rickey Henderson, Julio Franco, Harold Baines, Ruben Sierra, George Bell, Tony Fernandez, Ryne Sandberg, Andre Dawson, Tim Raines, and Will Clark. (The formula for estimating these things has been revised slightly in the two years since the last *Abstract,* for those of you who want to figure things on your own.)

Anyway, Paul Molitor? When you think of Paul Molitor you think of all the injuries he has had, and it seems impossible for him to get to 3,000 hits. Still, over the last four years he has played 83 percent of his team's games, over the last two years 95 percent. After 194 hits last year and 190 the year before, Molitor has 1,751 career hits; he needs 1,249 more. At 190 hits a year, he's six-and-a-half years away from getting to 3,000. He turned thirty-three in August, so six-and-a-half more years is not out of the question. . . . See also the Brett Butler comment.

RICH MONTELEONE
California

In the minors as a starter he posted consecutive ERAs of 5.08, 5.31, 5.54, 12.54, and 5.08 (1985–88, two stops in some years). Switched to relief, he was more effective last year, and pitched well for the Angels. Grade D prospect.

JEFF MONTGOMERY
Kansas City

Several people asked me last year whether Jeff Montgomery was as good as his stats. The answer, of course, is that *nobody* is as good as Jeff Montgomery's stats, but Montgomery is still pretty good.

If you do a close comparison of Montgomery and Mark Davis, you'll wonder why the Royals felt they needed Mark Davis. They pitched almost exactly the same number of innings—92 for Montgomery, 92.2 for Davis. They allowed exactly the same number of hits, 66 each, although for some reason the batting average against Montgomery was two points lower (.198–.200). Montgomery had more strikeouts (94–92) and fewer walks (25–31). Montgomery gave up fewer home runs (3–6). Montgomery gave up fewer sacrifice hits (1–3) and sacrifice flies (1–4), a telling point since many of those score runners charged to another pitcher. Montgomery threw fewer wild pitches, although both threw more than they ought to have, and Montgomery gave up fewer runs and earned runs.

Davis of course is more "established" as a reliever, but Montgomery was in that role the second half of the season, and virtually perfect in it, while Davis two years ago had a career total of 13 saves in seven seasons. So why the Royals payed $13 million plus for Davis is not ours to answer, other than that managers love pitchers with 90+ fastballs.

Montgomery became effective last year when he learned to challenge the hitters on the first pitch; he went from being behind in the count as often as not to pitching almost entirely ahead in the count. Jeff is an odd pitcher for a relief ace, in that he doesn't have either a 95-MPH heater or a "specialty pitch", as almost all top relievers do. He's a guy who mixes up four pitches—fastball, curve, slider, and change. Ordinarily a pitcher like that will be more effective as a starter than in relief, and for that reason I'm optimistic about Montgomery's ability to adapt to whatever role he is thrust into by the acquisition of Davis.

MIKE MOORE
Oakland

Mike is only thirty, but is blessed with the face of a much older man. I was skeptical of how well he would pitch for the A's, and in retrospect I don't know what the hell I was thinking about. He had a 3.78 ERA in 1988 in Seattle; you move that to Oakland, and you've got to be down to 3.20 at worst. At Seattle he didn't have a relief ace to back him up, and so tended to stay in the game sometimes when he should have come out; here he has a five-man bullpen if he needs it. In Seattle in 1988 he had 182 strikeouts and 63 walks, which surely indicates a quality pitcher. In spite of that, and knowing that won-lost records aren't a reliable gauge of how a man is pitching, I was focusing on his won-lost record, and I figured a guy who goes 9–15 in Seattle is going to go about 12–12 in Oakland. Why do we all do this? Why do we all forget the things we know, and make silly mistakes like that?

Despite his career record of 85–107, I would have to consider Moore a safe draft—not certain to be a Cy Young candidate as he was last year, but safe in the sense of here's a guy who is going to pitch 225 quality innings and probably go 15–12 or better.

KEITH MORELAND
Orioles (retired)

The most-comparable major league player to Keith Moreland was Hubie Brooks. . . .

MIKE MORGAN
Los Angeles

Extended his string of non-winning records to nine consecutive (he's never been a winner, but he did go 1–1 in 1985.) If the Dodgers stay with him another year, the chances are good that he will end that streak in 1990; the 2.53 ERA and 33 walks in 153 innings of 1989 are surely not the marks of a pitcher who deserves to lose. The Dodgers have many pitching prospects, and if Fernando is healthy Morgan probably won't pitch much. Hershiser, Belcher, and Martinez are certain starters, with Fernando, Morgan, and Wetteland as candidates for the other spots. Morgan, despite pitching well last year, would be the easiest candidate to push aside.

RUSS MORMAN
Kansas City

Glove man—no prospect at twenty-eight.

★ ★ ★
HAL MORRIS
Cincinnati
★ ★ ★

Good hitter, left-handed line-drive hitter who should hit .300 or thereabouts with Cincinnati. With the Reds reserves of 1989 being Ken Griffey, Herm Winningham, Dave Collins, Joel Youngblood, and Scotti Madison, you'd have to think that a new manager will be looking around for some additional help, and once Morris gets on the roster, the manager has to notice that he's a better hitter than Benzinger. He's twenty-five in April, and he doesn't have the peripheral skills (speed, defense, extra power) which would mark him as a star, but I'll be very surprised if he doesn't impress some people with his bat.

JACK MORRIS
Detroit

I usually figure that as long as a pitcher has a good strikeout to walk ratio, he has

a good chance of regaining his effectiveness. Morris's K/W wasn't great (115–59), but it wasn't bad, either. We *know* that he knows how to pitch. The Tigers can't have as bad a year in 1990 as they did in 1989. Morris is a risk and he's not a great risk, but I would expect him to be more effective than he was last year.

JOHN MORRIS
St. Louis

Perhaps the odd thing about him is that such a good defensive outfielder is used primarily as a pinch hitter. Ordinarily, you figure a pinch hitter is a guy who can hit but can't play the field, but Morris is fast and has a decent arm. Playing time could increase marginally.

LLOYD MOSEBY
Detroit

It is interesting to note that in the last two seasons, when Moseby has struggled, he has struck out *less* often than he did in his best years. I wonder if, trying to adjust to the leadoff role, he didn't perhaps try to shorten his stroke and mess up his swing? He's not a classic leadoff hitter by any means; he was forced into that role by the Blue Jays lack of a legitimate leadoff hitter.

The Tigers don't have a leadoff man, either, but if I was the Tiger manager, I'd get him out of that leadoff role, and try to get him back to his natural style. He's never been consistent, but he still has the basic skills that he has always had. Some recovery is definitely possible; a season comparable to his best is not out of the realm of possibility. He may play better in Tiger Stadium than he did in Toronto.

JOHN MOSES
Minnesota

A member of the Jesus Alou All-Star team. . . . Very fine reserve outfielder; no chance to move up in the world.

JAMIE MOYER
Texas

One more tribute to that great Ranger pitching coach, Tom House, and his sure-to-keep-you-healthy regimen. This guy's never been hurt in his life, posts a 3.48 ERA in Wrigley Field, goes to Texas and blows out a tricep throwing a curveball in late May. . . . It is hard to guess with injuries, but I'd give him maybe a 40 percent chance of making a full recovery. He's a better pitcher if healthy than his career record (32–43) and ERA (4.48) would indicate. . . .

TERRY MULHOLLAND
Philadelphia

He's a perennial prospect, which is a subtle distinction from being no prospect at all. I've seen very little about him that I like.

RANCE MULLINIKS
Toronto

Toronto designated hitters last year hit .216 with 8 homers and 55 RBI, probably the worst performance in the league. That's one of the big reasons I think the team will be better this year: the designated hitters have to have a better year than that. Mulliniks was the man most-used in the spot, and he's a good hitter if he can find his stroke. . . . The major league leaders in career doubles per at bat: 1. Wade Boggs, 2. Don Mattingly, 3. Rance Mulliniks. . . .

DALE MURPHY
Atlanta

The 1989 disappointments of the year (based on runs created compared to career performance norms): Dale Murphy (−38), Eddie Murray (−31), John Shelby (−26), Cory Snyder (−24), Cal Ripken (−23), Chet Lemon (−23), Andy Van Slyke (−22), Alan Trammell (−22), Fred Lynn (−21), and Dave Parker (−21). The remarkable name on the list is Cal Ripken. Here's a guy who was *23 runs* behind his normal performance for a season, and he still finished third in the American League MVP voting. . . . A lot of people have asked me whether I think Dale Murphy can come back, but I don't really have an opinion about it. I won't be drafting him this year, and if he gets traded out of Atlanta his numbers could quickly slide to where he earns his release. My understanding is that his salary has been one of the things preventing a trade, but with the mid-winter salary explosion his salary may not look so big anymore. . . .

DWAYNE MURPHY
Philadelphia

As he always has been, he's a better hitter than people think he is. He averaged just .218 last year, but when you remember that a fourth of his hits were home runs and that he had almost as many walks as hits, you can see that he was still causing runs to appear on the scoreboard. Once a great defensive outfielder, value is largely lost now. . . .

ROB MURPHY
Boston

Extremely effective left-hander with a good fastball, he is now thirty but I wouldn't dismiss his chance of emerging as a closer sometime. The Red Sox, of course, have two closers on their roster at the moment, but a trade will be forthcoming. Let's say the Red Sox trade Lee Smith, making Reardon the closer, and Reardon gets shelled the first three times he pitches in Fenway Park, which is very possible. Then what happens? Murphy becomes the closer. He's a good pitcher to have around if you have the roster space for him.

EDDIE MURRAY
Los Angeles

Dodger Stadium ruined his stats, as it often does; he hit 16 home runs on the road, but only 4 in Los Angeles. In re-

cent years he has turned from a legend into somebody who gets blamed for everything, but he can still hit basically as well as he ever could. He is still durable and consistent. He is still, in my opinion, a fine defensive player. He still runs the bases well. I don't put Dodger Stadium hitters on my fantasy league teams, but on a *real* team I would still be thrilled to have Eddie Murray around.

JEFF MUSSELMAN
Mets

Finished as a prospect; scrambling with three hundred other guys for a job as a left-handed short man. Don't be drafting him unless you know something that I don't.

GREG MYERS
Toronto

A year ago he was the heir apparent to Ernie Whitt as the Blue Jays left-handed hitting catcher. Now Whitt is gone, but how much good news is in store for Myers is murky. He's had a rotator cuff injury which has hampered his throwing, and through 53 major league at bats he has hit just .113. Pat Borders has emerged as a stronger-than-expected right-hander, and may take over the bulk of the job.

Despite his slow start, I think Myers is a pretty decent hitter—actually, very similar to Borders, a .260–.275 hitter with a pathetic K/W ratio but some power. My first guess is that Myers *will* get into a platoon role with Borders, and will play fairly well.

RANDY MYERS
Cincinnati

Probably won't strike out quite as many people in Cincinnati as he did in Shea Stadium (the visibility for the hitters is better). He remains a reasonably safe draft; he'll share the relief duties with Dibble and others, and should save around 20 games as he has in recent years.

JAIME NAVARRO
Milwaukee

Solid pitcher with potential to get even better. If he doesn't go too early or too high, he's an excellent number-three pickup to fill out a staff. He could also be the Brewers' ace this year, but even though he could I don't know that you'd want to be banking on that.

GENE NELSON
Oakland

Extremely consistent, ERAs in the threes for four straight seasons. He's a safe pick, but he doesn't really do much to help a rotisserie team.

ROB NELSON
San Diego

In the spring of 1987 Nelson and Mark McGwire battled for the Oakland A's first base job. Nelson won the battle, and was the A's opening-day first baseman. He got hurt, of course, and McGwire took it away.

At this point Nelson is no prospect. He never was, really; he's a sub-.200 hitter with walks and homers, but not enough to justify a .190 batting average. He may get a few more looks, but I don't ever expect him to be a major league regular.

AL NEWMAN
Minnesota

Became a regular due to the failures of Backman; has some competition in his organization, but will stay on the roster. A smart player, useful to have around; 59 walks, 25 stolen bases and good defense make him acceptable despite low batting average and no power. I don't recommend him as a draft.

WARREN NEWSON
San Diego

An outfielder in the Padres system with exceptional secondary offensive skills. He's a short, stocky guy (five seven, 190 pounds) who looks like Walt "No Neck" Williams. His career got off to a little bit of a slow start, but in 1987 at Charleston and Reno he hit a combined .329 with a secondary average of .510. In 1988, with Riverside (A ball) he hit .297 with a secondary average of .562 (22 homers, 107 walks, 36 stolen bases.) In 1988, with Wichita, he hit .304 with a secondary average of .489 (18 homers, 103 walks, 20 stolen bases.) He's old for a prospect (26) and doesn't strike you as a great athlete, but he could emerge as a John Kruk-type player, but with better speed and defense.

CARL NICHOLS
Houston

Catcher—no prospect.

ROD NICHOLS
Cleveland

Here's the Indians for you, again; Nichols was called to Cleveland in 1988 after going 2–6 with a 5.74 ERA at Colorado Springs. They have him projected as of now as their fifth starter, behind Swindell, Candiotti, Farrell and Black. Don't draft him unless you value losses.

TOM NIEDENFUER
Seattle

Believe it or not, Tom Niedenfuer, after going 0–3 with a 6.69 ERA, was still on the Mariners' forty-man roster at midwinter. I guess we can use that as a test of when the Mariners get serious; when they give up on Tom Niedenfuer, we'll give them another look.

SCOTT NIELSEN
Yankees

No prospect.

TOM NIETO
Philadelphia

Hasn't hit higher than .200 since 1985. Wouldn't expect him to be on a roster this year.

DONELL NIXON
San Francisco

Apparently a better hitter than his brother (.277 lifetime), he has the speed and batting average to bat leadoff, but probably won't. The Giants have Brett Butler to lead off and play center. Donell doesn't have the arm to play right field, and Kevin Mitchell is in left. Kevin Bass has been signed to play right. Roger Craig doesn't use a lot of pinch runners, and the Giants only have one player (the catcher) who needs to be run for. Nixon's ability to increase his playing time, and thus to increase his stolen base total, appears limited.

OTIS NIXON
Montreal

I drew up a list of the *worst* hitters in the major leagues, career stats, 500 or more games played, based on the fewest runs created per 27 outs. The list is eight shortstops, a catcher, and Otis Nixon, but Nixon, an outfielder, earned the number-one spot—the worst hitter in the major leagues. The bottom ten were Nixon, Steve Jeltz, Ed Romero, Curt Wilkerson, Wayne Tolleson, Alfredo Griffin, Glenn Hoffman, Dave Anderson, Bruce Benedict, and Jose Uribe. It's not just that Nixon has a career batting average of .223. What hurts is that 85 percent of his hits have been singles. Only one player, Tolleson, has a lower percentage of extra base hits, and that by a margin of .0002. . . .

Let me explain the concept of "run element ratio." I have always advocated the idea that to evaluate a hitter, one has to look at the whole picture—the "secondary bases" as well as the base hits. There is a vast difference between a player like Dwight Evans, who has only 2,262 hits but more than 3,000 secondary bases, and a player like Bill Buckner, who has 2,707 hits but only 1,745 secondary bases. That difference is reflected in the runs scored and RBI; although

Buckner has collected more hits, Evans has driven in more runs and scored more runs.

When a player hits a single, that is of roughly the same value no matter when it occurs in an inning—leading off, or hitting with a man on second and two out; a single is a part of a run. Of the *other* elements of an offense, however, some are more valuable *early* in the inning—specifically, walks and stolen bases—and some are more valuable *late* in the inning—specifically, extra bases on hits. Thus it is the "secondary bases" which determine what role a player plays in an offense. If a player has lots of walks and stolen bases, he is much more valuable *early* in the inning than late in an inning; if he has few walks and stolen bases but lots of power, he is more valuable *late* in the inning. I state the relationship as a run element ratio. The higher the run element ratio, the more imbalance there is between a player's value early in the inning and late in the inning.

The highest run element ratio of any major league player, both in 1989 and for his career as a whole, is Otis Nixon's. Nixon last year had 33 walks in less than half-time play, and 37 stolen bases, thus he is a reasonably effective early-in-the-inning offensive player, as much as a player can be with a .217 batting average. But he had only 7 doubles, 2 triples, and no homers, so that he has no ability to drive in a run. The highest 1989 run element ratios: Nixon, Bob Dernier, Gary Pettis, Gerald Young, and Felix Fermin. The highest career ratios: Nixon, Vince Coleman, Pettis, Ozzie Smith, and Wayne Tolleson.

A player who has a high run element ratio will also, virtually without fail, have a very high ratio of runs scored to RBI. This would be true anyway because these players have a much greater ability to score runs than drive in runs, but it is particularly emphasized because managers almost always use players of this type as leadoff men, eighth or ninth place hitters or early-inning pinch hitters.

Occasionally you will see a player miscast by his manager, a player with a low run element ratio being used as a leadoff man or a player with a high run element ratio being used in a power spot. A player who hits .300 and has some speed will sometimes be used as a leadoff man even if he never draws a walk, and a player like Gene Tenace, who has a billion walks but a low average and some power, will sometimes be used in a power spot. When you see that, you always suspect that a manager isn't really paying attention to what he is doing, but is just assigning offensive roles based on images (little fast guy, lead him off; big slow guy, hit him fifth).

Most players who are used as pinch hitters have *low* run element ratios; they are used to try to get the RBI when a man is on base. I have always believed that both elements are equally important, that for a run to be driven in it must also be scored, and for that reason I think a good manager needs to have both types on his bench—an early-inning pinch hitter like Greg Gross to start trouble, and a late-inning pinch hitter to finish it. Let's say it's the eighth inning, you're two runs behind and you have your number eight hitter at the plate. If you don't have an early-inning pinch hitter, what do you do? You *wait* for something to happen, wait to get somebody on "so you can use your pinch hitters." Did you ever hear that? Listen to post-game shows this year and you will; you'll hear Don Zimmer or somebody say that he never got a chance to use his pinch hitters because his team could never get anything going on offense. But a good manager won't have to wait; a good manager will have an option on his bench.

JUNIOR NOBOA
Montreal

One of the ongoing strange stories of major league baseball. Junior Noboa is an excellent hitter. He has been for years. At Indianapolis last year he hit .340; in a major league uniform as a regular, he would hit anywhere from .280 to .315, and even though it is mostly singles and he doesn't walk a lot, you would think that a second baseman who can hit .300 would get your attention.

Nobody will give him a job. He's only twenty-five years old, but he reached AAA ball in 1985, and has just been hanging there for five years, waiting for somebody to let him play. Reports on him as a defensive player vary, but clearly his range and arm are above average for the position.

He's got over 800 minor league games behind him now, and he may never get a major league job. There may be something to the story that I don't know. Maybe he sulks in the clubhouse; maybe he falls asleep on the bases. Maybe he couldn't handle the major league lifestyle. More probably he is, like Wade Boggs was and Mike Easler and Ken Phelps, a victim of the idiotic delusion that major league baseball and minor league baseball are different games, and that therefore a player can be a good hitter in the minors but not in the majors. Sooner or later, Junior Noboa will probably get 200 at bats in a season—and when he does, he will hit.

MATT NOKES
Detroit

Not a bad draft risk in view of having the ability to perform better than he did in 1989. He isn't a good defensive catcher, so he has to hit to hold his job. He's not a great hitter, but he will have better years than 1989.

RANDY NOSEK
Detroit

Young right-hander; long-term prospect rushed to the majors ahead of his time.

ED NUNEZ
Detroit

Career seems stuck in reverse; after eight years in the majors he is nowhere near the pitcher he was five years ago. No draft pick at this time; could still surprise, I suppose.

JOSE NUNEZ
Chicago Cubs

I love his arm; fastball seems to have very good movement. You wouldn't want to draft him, obviously, until you know that he is on the roster and getting a chance to pitch occasionally, but I wouldn't be surprised if he could be quite effective.

CHARLIE O'BRIEN
Milwaukee

A backup catcher, and in every respect typical of the genre. No draft.

PETE O'BRIEN
Seattle

A curious signing for Seattle, apparently will share the first base and DH duties with Alvin Davis. A safe draft, has had six straight seasons of relatively the same quality. Being a left-handed, his power probably will increase somewhat in Seattle (in his career he has lost about 14 home runs to the parks he has played in). I would expect him to hit about .290 this year with 18 homers, 90 RBI—a very solid season.

TOM O'MALLEY
Mets

Perennial third base prospect, and truly not a bad player. The Mets wouldn't be hurting themselves any if they would keep him around in 1990 to pinch hit and play third in the late innings of a close game. No star potential.

RANDY O'NEAL
Philadelphia
Right-handed pitcher; no prospect.

PAUL O'NEILL
Cincinnati
Probably an excellent draft pick for 1990. He's reaching the point at which his salary can explode if he has a big year, so his incentive should be very high. He is twenty-seven years old, an age at which many players have their best seasons. He has never batted 500 times in a season, because of platooning and injuries, but he probably will this season, maybe close to 600 times. He contributes across the board—power, speed, decent batting average, good K/W ratio, good defense. By all logic, if you pick Paul O'Neill for 1990, he ought to do very well for you.

KEN OBERKFELL
Houston
Never draft a hitter going into the Astrodome.

RON OESTER
Cincinnati
Had the lowest ratio of runs scored and RBI per hit of any major league regular in 1989, by far. With 75 hits he had only 23 runs scored and 14 RBI. A teammate, Jeff Reed, was second on that list, but he was way ahead of Oester. . . .

JOSE OFFERMAN
Los Angeles
The Dodgers regard him as their shortstop of the future. He's very fast, has a strong arm, and hit .288 at San Antonio in 1989. He looks pretty good to me, too, but he won't start in 1990.

BOBBY OJEDA
Mets
Not a bad draft pick—a lot of people think he will snap back in 1990—but not a recommended draft pick in view of

a) his age (thirty-two),

b) the sudden degeneration of his strikeout to walk ratio in 1989 (from 133–33 to 95–78), and

c) the overcrowding of the Mets' starting staff, which now has six pitchers.

If Ojeda gets traded away from the Mets, then by all means *unload him*, particularly if he winds up like in Minnesota or Detroit or something. He isn't going to win without a good team behind him.

JOHN OLERUD
Blue Jays
The college player of the year in 1988, and then a news story when his father, a doctor, spotted a potentially life-threatened aneurysm near his brain.

Olerud, a big left-hander, is regarded as having major league potential *both* as a hitter and a pitcher. The Blue Jays, who usually know what they are doing in evaluating talent, paid him the largest bonus that they had ever paid to an amateur player.

At this point, I honestly have no idea what to think of him as a player. I've seen him play a few games on ESPN; I thought he looked curiously unimpressive as an athlete. But at this point, I simply have nothing on which to base an opinion of his future.

STEVE OLIN
Cleveland
I definitely like him, although I haven't marked him with the asterisks. He throws low sidearm, almost underhanded, which I like, and he has "a nasty sinker, a good slider." Basically I can't recommend him too highly because he's a relief ace, and with Doug Jones around he'll be working in a support role, and under most rules it is hard for a setup reliever to help a team in rotisserie ball or fantasy leagues. Also, pitching for Cleveland is a big minus,

since the Indians don't know how to handle a young pitcher, and pitching for John McNamara isn't a plus, since McNamara doesn't like to make changes; if Doug Jones starts to struggle McNamara will stay with him longer than almost any other manager probably would. In the long run I rate Olin a good to excellent chance of developing into a relief ace.

JOE OLIVER
Cincinnati
Good Grade B prospect. A great big guy (six three, 215), with a good defensive reputation. Major league performance in 1989 (.272, .384 slugging percentage) is almost identical to major league equivalent of his performance at Nashville. Strikeout to walk ratio poor, no speed, but for a catcher, you can live with that. I don't see him as a star, but I think he'll be a good player.

FRANCISCO OLIVERAS
Minnesota
Apparently no prospect. The Twins appear to have been pitching him out of desperation.

GREGG OLSON
Baltimore
If you need a relief ace, you probably should carefully consider investing heavily in Olson. Obviously, he can pitch, a good fastball and one of the best curveballs in the game. Remember, this year he didn't get the job as the Orioles' closer until three other people had failed, and he still wound up with 27 saves, so in 1990 he could be in the thirties or even forties. He is very young, so his control record and K ratio could still improve substantially. I don't see his workload or age as being a risk factor. Maybe he's not going to have a 1.69 ERA every year, but he doesn't have to; he should be solid.

STEVE ONTIVEROS
Philadelphia

Left-handed starting pitcher; candidate for role as number four starter. Don't draft him unless you know that he has a job, but he probably can go 12–14 for the Phillies with a 3.90 ERA. Limited if any star potential.

JOSE OQUENDO
St. Louis

Set an NL record for fielding percentage at second base.

Did he win the Gold Glove last year? I guess they gave it to Sandberg. This guy is a lot better second baseman than Sandberg—a lot better range, quicker on the DP. He's more remarkable at his position now, I think, than Ozzie is as a shortstop—not quite as flashy, maybe, but better.

Oquendo is a wonderful player; I can't believe Whitey doesn't use him in the one-two spot. He was ninth in the league in batting last year (.291) and eighth in walks (79), so he's on base a great deal. It was his fourth straight good year with the bat, and the years just keep getting better. He's not very fast, but he's not Tim Wallach, either. There's no way he wouldn't score quite a few more runs than Coleman or Thompson, just by being on base so much more.

JESSE OROSCO
Cleveland

Has now had an ERA of 2.73 or lower in eight of the last nine seasons. Last year, although nobody noticed, he pitched brilliantly, allowing only 54 hits in 78 innings, striking out 79 men and with good control, resulting in a 2.08 ERA in 69 outings. He had to be the most effective left-handed spot reliever of the season, holding left-handed batters to a .138 batting average, mostly singles. In that role he won't pile up saves or wins—but he is a safe draft, and an *outstanding* pitcher in his role.

JOE ORSULAK
Baltimore

The most-comparable major league player to Joe Orsulak is Dion James . . . isn't stealing bases the way he did when he first came up, but a solid hitter (.278 lifetime) with good defense. Another example of the Orioles simply taking advantage of the available talent.

JUNIOR ORTIZ
Pittsburgh

Good backup catcher; had to play more than was desirable last year due to the injury to LaValliere. No draft.

JOHN ORTON
California

Baseball America regards him as the number-one prospect in the California system, and raves about his defensive skills. He is miles and miles from being a major league hitter—a .180 hitter at this point—and I would be surprised if he ever develops, as a hitter, to the point at which his glove can carry him to regular work. Grade C prospect in my opinion.

DAVE OTTO
Oakland

A six seven left-handed pitching prospect, has had injuries to both knees. Has pitched well at times; with the free-agent losses in Oakland and the quality of the A's coaching staff working in his favor, he has a chance to surprise. Don't draft him unless you see his name in a box score, but if you do he is worthy of consideration.

SPIKE OWEN
Montreal

An underrated player, a solid shortstop, and makes an offensive contribution by getting on base and avoiding making outs. Doesn't run as well as he used to; may lose his job in a year or so to Delino DeShields.

Spike Owen was second in the National League last year in intentional walks, with 25. Is that unbelievable? Obviously, most of those were probably cases where Owen got ahead of the pitcher with a runner on scoring position and the manager just decided, "oh, what the heck, let's pitch to the pitcher," but that in general is a strategy that I just *violently* disagree with. Managers think about that one run—the man on second—but what they don't think about is, what happens if you *don't* get the pitcher out? If the pitcher (or a pinch hitter) hits a single, you're looking at a big inning before you can say Porfirio Altimarano. If you bear down on Owen, then you've got *two* chances to get out of the inning with a fairly weak hitter, Owen or the pitcher; if you give up one of them and don't get the other you have painted yourself into a corner. I wish I had a list of those 25 intentional walks to Spike Owen. I would bet that if you studied it, you'd find five times that it just blew up all over the other manager.

MIKE PAGLIARULO
San Diego

The most-similar player to Mike Pagliarulo is Jim Presley. . . . Pagliarulo's career batting averages: .239, .239, .238, .234, .216, .197. . . . Presume Bip Roberts will play third for San Diego, making Pagliarulo no draft.

TOM PAGNOZZI
St. Louis

Backup catcher—no prospect.

REY PALACIOS
Kansas City

Number-three catcher, most used as a pinch runner for Bob Boone. (No prospect.)

If you look at the Royals team batting stats in *USA Today* or *The Sporting News*, these are the bottom three men:

	G	AB	R	H
Pecota	65	83	21	17
Thurman	72	87	24	17
Palacios	55	47	12	8

You see what is odd? Pecota, Thurman, and Palacios all have very low ratios of at bats to games, and all had more runs scored than hits.

Why is that? Obviously, all three were used extensively as pinch runners.

What's that tell you? John Wathan uses more pinch runners than any other major league manager, constantly putting his spare infielder (Pecota), his spare outfielder (Thurman), or his spare catcher (Palacios) in the game to run for Boone or Brett or Tartabull or White, and then leaving the substitute in for an inning of defense.

You have to like the fact that Wathan is aware of that little edge, that he doesn't forget to ask himself whether the man he has on base is the fastest man he *could* have on base. You have to like the fact that it gets the whole roster involved—in fact, all three of these guys played 55–72 games although they all spent a good part of the year at Omaha.

I might be happier, as a Royals fan, to have a little more punch on the bench rather than a track team. I'd like to have a Ken Phelps or a Steve Balboni, to give us a chance for a quick home run. I'd like to have a Denny Walling over there. But I do appreciate the fact that he has an idea of what he is doing, that he has an idea in his own mind of what these players can do and how he can use them. I've seen a lot of managers who didn't.

DONN PALL
White Sox

Had the best strikeout to walk ratio and (until late in the year) the best ERA among White Sox pitchers. Could move into the closer role, but not likely. Has a job, anyway.

RAFAEL PALMEIRO
Texas

The most-similar player to Rafael Palmeiro is Rickey Jordan. . . . Faded badly in the Texas heat. His strikeout to walk ratio is improvingly steadily, as is his defense; he's not exactly my kind of player, but if he hits .310 this year with 15 homers I'll change my mind, and he is clearly capable of that.

DEAN PALMER
Texas

Rivals Scott Coolbaugh for the Rangers third baseman of the future. He's two-and-a-half years younger than Coolbaugh, which makes him twenty-one, and he's bigger and stronger than Coolbaugh. He could probably hit 20 homers in the majors this season, but with an average in the .230s and 170 strikeouts. If the Rangers use their common sense, they'll try Coolbaugh at third this year, and then if he doesn't impress they can try Palmer in 1991 or 1992.

MARK PARENT
San Diego

Backup catcher; fielded 1.000. This is John Orton's future.

CLAY PARKER
Yankees

With several other pitchers—Cary, Perez, Leary—he gives the Yankees a chance to have a solid starting rotation in 1990 for the first time since 1983. You've got to like Parker quite a bit, in that he has never failed; he's pitched well wherever he has been. He has a history of groin pulls which may continue to plague him, and so he may wind up going 12–7 rather than 17–10; that will cost him a lot of money. His strikeout rate was low last year, but will probably move up in 1990. Definitely has a chance to be an outstanding pitcher.

DAVE PARKER
Milwaukee

Why does Milwaukee want Dave Parker? I know, I know—they wanted to sign Dave Parker to show that they were serious about winning, so they wouldn't lose Robin Yount. But if they're serious about winning, why do they keep playing Glenn Braggs and Rob Deer?

Obviously, Parker is a better DH than Terry Francona. But he adds to a serious problem that this team has: age. I've been writing this for years, but it's still true. Every year, you look at the Brewers' leading hitters, and who do you see? Robin Yount—magnificent, but now thirty-four. Paul Molitor—a wonderful player, but now thirty-three. Jim Gantner—a decent player, but now thirty-six. Nobody else on the team hit over .265. They have young players, but the young players don't hit. And Dave Parker just draws a line under that.

JEFF PARRETT
Philadelphia

Extremely effective long reliever for the last two years; may move into another role this year. Not a bad draft, but I'd regard him as a little risky in view of not knowing what his role on the team will be.

LANCE PARRISH
California

As Gary Carter demonstrates, *most* catchers decline sharply as hitters after having caught about 1200–1300 games. Lance Parrish has passed that mark, and rates as an extremely risky draft pick for 1990. . . . 50 RBI in 1989 was his lowest total since the strike year 1981.

DAN PASQUA
Chicago White Sox

One more player that the White Sox don't know quite what to do with. I like him, because of his power—he could hit 30 homers and drive in 100 runs if he could stay healthy and stay in the lineup. I'd find playing time for him, rather than

Dave Gallagher. But with Pasqua having back trouble and the White Sox adding Sammy Sosa and Lance Johnson, Pasqua obviously is not a good risk.

BOB PATTERSON
Pittsburgh

Another marginal pitcher trying to find work as a left-handed short man. He has a chance, but the supply is considerably greater than the demand.

KEN PATTERSON
White Sox

A young Bob Patterson type. Actually, although Patterson is a left-hander, lefties hit .297 against him last year with a .516 slugging percentage. With that in mind and his 4.52 ERA . . . no draft.

BILL PECOTA
Kansas City

Shuttles between the Royals and Omaha; doesn't hurt the team but isn't going to move up in the world. His three home runs last year were all hit against the Yankees in one doubleheader. He isn't all that fast, but in the last three years he has stolen 17 bases in 19 attempts, which is the kind of thing that keeps him in the majors roughly 60 percent of the time.

AL PEDRIQUE
Detroit

Trying to find work as a utility infielder. No prospect.

ALEJANDRO PENA
Mets

In all likelihood, Alejandro Pena's shoulder surgery in 1985 kept him out of the Hall of Fame. Alejandro in 1984 led the league in ERA; at that time he threw hard, had good control and knew exactly what he was doing on the mound. In the last two seasons, after years of struggle, he has been equally devastating in relief: 2.01 ERA, strikeout to walk ratio (not counting intentional walks) of 158–35.

He'll help the Mets. If Franco falters at all, he can step into the bullpen closer role and save 25 games. He may not be a great draft because of the way he will probably be used—but this guy can flat pitch.

GERONIMO PENA
St. Louis

Outstanding second base prospect, but not likely to move Oquendo in 1990. He strikes out too much, but I'll say this: I sure would like to see him in a Royals uniform.

TONY PENA
Boston

It will be interesting to see how the switch to the American League and Fenway Park effect him. Although he is, like Parrish, into the danger zone for a catcher, I would be inclined to describe him as a good risk; my guess is that he'll hit .270–.285 with 12–15 homers, and not many catchers will do better . . . still runs better than your average catcher.

TERRY PENDLETON
St. Louis

Led National League third basemen in fielding percentage (.971), assists (392), and total chances (520). If your league rewards defense, he's a good pick. Otherwise, he doesn't contribute a lot on offense, and he hasn't been consistent with what he does do . . . has stolen only two bases over the last two seasons.

MELIDO PEREZ
White Sox

A much better pitcher than his stats show. This guy will benefit more from having Sammy Sosa in center field than anyone else, and is quite capable of winning 15–17 games . . . probably will have arm trouble in two to three years from having pitched too many innings with an immature arm.

PACUAL PEREZ
Yankees

There have been a lot of snide comments since Perez joined the Yankees about Perez being a pitcher who once got lost on the Interstate around Atlanta, and how is he going to deal with the pressures of New York, etc. Well, I don't dismiss the pressures of pitching in New York or the possibility that Perez could wind up as the next Ed Whitson or Doyle Alexander, but I think he is entitled to more respect then he has gotten as a pitcher. In his three years in Montreal he was 28–21, posted a 2.80 ERA and struck out four times as many people as he walked. That's a pretty damn good pitcher, and it has been a long time since the I-285 incident; I think we can bury that one now. It seems to me that there is a very real chance that the Yankees in 1990 will have the best pitching staff they have had in several years.

GERALD PERRY
Kansas City

As a Royals fan, I'm happy to have him. I'm happy to have him first of all because he takes Bill Buckner's spot on the roster, which means there is almost no chance Buckner will return. But Perry is a lifetime .270 hitter, still in his prime, and in all probability much better suited to Royals Stadium than he was to Atlanta. He can steal some bases, fill in at first and take some of the DH work away from Pat Tabler, another player we could do without. He gives us a legitimate left-handed bat on the bench—and for Charlie Leibrandt, a pitcher who really had no value. A fine trade for the Royals.

PAT PERRY
Cubs

Another guy who contributed quietly to the Cubs upset, posting a 1.77 ERA in 19 games. He'll be trying to stick as a left-handed short man, and probably will but probably shouldn't be drafted.

JEFF PETEREK
Brewers

Right-handed pitcher; may start for the Brewers because they need pitching. Grade C prospect, and I may be a little kind.

ADAM PETERSON
White Sox

Peterson has pitched *extremely* well in triple-A for two straight years (14–7, 14–6 with good ERAs). Common sense tells you that when you are badly in need of starting pitching and you have a pitcher who is winning 70 percent of his games at AAA, you should bring him up. The White Sox operate on a more subtle level than that; they talk a lot about Peterson's needing to learn an off-speed pitch. What seems obvious to me is that Peterson has learned everything he needs to dominate AAA, and therefore isn't going to learn any more by that experience; the only place he is going to learn how to get major league hitters out is in the major leagues.

Peterson isn't a Grade A prospect. He doesn't have a 90+ fastball, and his K/W ratios aren't real impressive. Pitching for the White Sox may not help him. But he is young (twenty-four), and he has been consistently successful. I wouldn't mind having him around; I make him a Grade B prospect.

GENO PETRALLI
Texas

No defense, but one of the few backup catchers who will help you with the bat. A safe pick.

DAN PETRY
California

I give him very little chance of a successful comeback. No draft.

GARY PETTIS
Texas

Pettis last year had the highest run element ratio (see Otis Nixon) of any true regular in the major leagues. Not coincidentally, he also had 77 runs scored and only 18 RBI, the highest ratio of runs scored to RBI of any major league player . . . he had 18 RBI with 114 total bases. That was also the lowest ratio of RBI to bases of any major league player. . . . He will help Texas. . . .

MARTY PEVEY
Montreal

Wants to stick as a backup catcher—apparently no hitter. Grade D prospect.

KEN PHELPS
Oakland

Phelps last year drove in 13 runs as a pinch hitter, the most of any major league player, despite having a subpar season. Actually, Phelps leads the majors in all kinds of things, some of them important. He has hit more home runs per at bat in his career than any other major league player. The top ten: 1. Ken Phelps, 2. Ron Kittle, 3. Eric Davis, 4. Mike Schmidt, 5. Darryl Strawberry, 6. Jose Canseco, 7. Rob Deer, 8. Steve Balboni, 9. Kevin Mitchell, 10. Glenn Davis. . . .

The major league leaders in *walks* per plate appearance: 1. Ken Phelps, 2. Mike Schmidt, 3. Rickey Henderson, 4. Darrell Evans, 5. Jack Clark. . . .

I ran separate lists of the major league career leaders in *runs created* per hit, which is an estimate using my own method, and *runs scored and driven in* per hit, which of course is a precise fact. The lists are almost identical. The major league player who has *created* the most runs per hit is Phelps, followed by Eric Davis, Mike Schmidt, Darryl Strawberry, and Jack Clark. The major league player who has *scored and driven in* the most runs per hit is Eric Davis, followed

by Phelps, Schmidt, Rob Deer, and Strawberry. . . .

I suppose I should comment on his chances of bouncing back. I don't see why he wouldn't. Sure, he wasn't very productive last year by his own standards, but 194 at bats doesn't mean very much. He still drove in more runs last year in 194 at bats than Vince Coleman did in 563.

With the departure of Dave Parker, their *only* left-handed hitter who can make an impact, the A's will be needing left-handed help. Felix Jose isn't the answer. I don't see any reason to think that Phelps in 1990 won't do the things he has always done so well—bat 300 times, hit 25 homers and draw 80 walks.

TONY PHILLIPS
Detroit

The most-similar player to Tony Phillips is Spike Owen. . . . Phillips is a fine player, much better than he has been given credit for being over the years. He's an outstanding second baseman, was a decent shortstop, and he could always get on base and hit left-handed pitching. He is the one free agent whose departure could hurt the A's. . . . I don't know that he will hit enough to be highly regarded as a third baseman, and so don't recommend that you draft him in 1990.

JEFF PICO
Cubs

Apart from one's general leeriness of pitchers in Wrigley Field, there is also the problem of the limited value of middle relievers in fantasy games, and then too, Pico struck out only 38 men in 91 innings. Pass.

DAN PLESAC
Milwaukee

Despite some concerns about his health, you have to regard the stupefying consistency of his performance over the last four years, and mark him a safe pick, and a valuable one. His major league high in games pitched is 57; his *low* is 50. His four major league ERAs: 2.97, 2.61, 2.41, and 2.35. His save totals: 14, 23, 30, 33. What more could you want? If you need a reliever, go after him.

ERIC PLUNK
Yankees

No draft in my book. K/W ratios are poor and aren't improving. As I see it, if you can't succeed as a pitcher for the Oakland A's, your chances of doing so somewhere else are pretty slim.

GUS POLIDOR
Milwaukee

Utility infielder. No hitter/no prospect.

LUIS POLONIA
New York Yankees

Obviously, a risky draft. No one can predict how he will react to his arrest and imprisonment, and he could well emerge from it as a *better* player, more determined and more consistent. The other direction is perhaps a little more likely. At his best, what is he capable of? A .320 hitter, maybe, with 60 stolen bases. You can use a player like that, obviously, but with no power, no walks, no throwing arm, even then you don't have Kirby Puckett. I'd take a wait-and-see attitude toward him.

MARK PORTUGAL
Houston

The Astros have worked wonders with some pitchers in the past, and you have to think this may be another one. His record in Minnesota is pretty awful, but it's hard to develop any confidence in a park like that. Certainly, he's not a safe pick—but in view of his tremendous second-half performance, I would have to rate Portugal an excellent risk.

DENNIS POWELL
Seattle

Left-handed reliever; may be helped by the Mariners' fence move. Probably no prospect.

TED POWER
Pittsburgh

Solid journeyman, can help the Pirates by soaking up some innings when other pitchers are hurt. Most effective when not used too much.

JIM PRESLEY
Seattle

Seattle is reportedly trying to trade him. Sure, you can't absolutely rule out the possibility of a comeback, but how long can you wait. Presley wasn't *that* good when he was good; there were a lot of negatives hidden underneath the power stats. I don't want him on my team, anyway, which seems to be the general attitude of the people the Mariners have tried to trade him to.

JOE PRICE
Boston

Left-handed spot reliever; not very effective in the role, and no chance of moving up now.

TOM PRINCE
Pittsburgh

Another catcher who doesn't hit. No draft.

KIRBY PUCKETT
Minnesota

The most-similar player to Kirby Puckett is Tony Gwynn. . . . There are six active players who have now established a chance to get 4,000 hits in their careers. The best shot by far is Robin Yount's (19 percent), followed by Kirby (10 percent), Don Mattingly, Ruben Sierra, and Wade Boggs (each 2 percent), and Tony Gwynn (1 percent). The chance that

some active player will be the third to get 4,000 career hits is 32 percent. . . .

TERRY PUHL
Houston

Moved back to semi-regular status after years of declining play. The loss of Kevin Bass is offset, from his standpoint, by Eric Anthony and Cameron Drew, and he is unlikely to play regularly unless both struggle.

CHARLIE PULEO
Atlanta

Hanging in there at thirty-five. Almost no chance of making the team in '90.

LUIS QUINONES
Cincinnati

Got considerable playing time due to injuries of Sabo and Larkin, and established clearly that he doesn't hit enough to be a major league third baseman. Will stay around, but doubt that he will ever again play as much as he did last year.

REY QUINONES
Pittsburgh

Released. What a strange story he was.

CARLOS QUINTANA
Boston

A good hitter, about a .290 hitter in the majors with a slugging percentage over .450. Supposed to be a good outfielder, too. The release of Rice and Sam Horn may open up some playing time for him, but with Greenwell, Burks, and Evans he still may not get a chance to play. Knock 15–20 points off that batting average if he's in another park.

JAMIE QUIRK
Oakland

Turned down an offer to manage in the Baltimore system to take a shot with Oakland. He's not all *that* old—thirty-five—and a useful player to have (to a *real* team) if he can hit at all.

DAN QUISENBERRY
St. Louis
May go to spring training, may not. In 78 innings last year he walked only 5 men unintentionally. Now has a career average of 0.79 unintentional walks per nine innings.

ROCK RAINES
Montreal
Still holds the major league record for career stolen base percentage, .867; last year it was .820. Actually, Eric Davis's career stolen base percentage is a hair better than Raines (.869), but the record requires 300 attempts. . . . At one time Raines had an excellent shot to break Lou Brock's National League career stolen base record, with 938, but he hasn't stolen as many in recent years, and the odds are now that he will not. He still has about a 30 percent chance to catch Brock, though. . . .

Raines is third on a lot of lists, usually behind Rickey Henderson and somebody else. The major league leaders in career runs scored per at bat: 1. Rickey Henderson, 2. Eric Davis, 3. Rock Raines, 4. Wade Boggs, 5. Mike Schmidt. . . . The leaders in stolen bases per game: 1. Vince Coleman, 2. Rickey Henderson, 3. Rock Raines. . . . The leaders in stolen bases, total: 1. Rickey Henderson, 2. Willie Wilson, 3. Raines (Raines will pass Wilson early in the season; he trailes 588–585). . . .

RAFAEL RAMIREZ
Houston
Played better for Houston than ever had for Atlanta. I still wouldn't say, really, that he was a championship quality shortstop.

DOMINGO RAMOS
Chicago Cubs
Utility man. He used to be a joke at bat, but his batting average over the last three years is .271, and that's with four different teams. But is he a *safe* pick? Obviously not. If you buy the theory

that you only want to gamble with maybe eight roster spots, then obviously he isn't somebody you would want to gamble on.

WILLIE RANDOLPH
Los Angeles
Very quietly had another Willie Randolph season, playing almost every day and leading the Dodgers in hitting. The major league leaders in career runs created, among middle infielders: 1. Willie Randolph (936), 2. Lou Whitaker, 3. Alan Trammell, 4. Frank White, 5. Garry Templeton, 6. Chris Speier, 7. Cal Ripken, 8. Ryne Sandberg, 9. Ozzie Smith, 10. Manny Trillo. . . . The acquisition of Samuel throws his future into doubt, as the acquisition of Steve Sax did a year ago, but he landed on his feet then, and there's no reason to think he won't do it again.

DENNIS RASMUSSEN
San Diego
Four straight years of 30 or more starts, double figures in wins every time. His record over the four years is 57–34, a .626 percentage . . . projects as the Padres' number-four starter, behind Whitson, Hurst, and Benes. Who else has a number-four starter with a .626 winning percentage?

SHANE RAWLEY
Minnesota
Chances of a comeback? I'd say 20, 25 percent. No draft.

JOHNNY RAY
California
A safe draft. Has hit .289 to .306 in each of the last four seasons.

RANDY READY
Philadelphia
One of my favorites. Over the last two seasons he has batted 585 times—one normal season. Neither has been a particularly good year for him; 1987 was

much better. But over those 585 at bats he has 29 doubles, 15 homers, 81 walks, 10 stolen bases, 80 runs scored. How many regular third basemen contribute more than that?

JEFF REARDON
Boston
Has progressed from hard thrower to extreme finesse-type pitcher, never walks anybody by doesn't strike out many either.

I have to wonder, to be honest, how effective he really is. His ERA has been 3.94 or worse in three of the last four years—for a relief ace. The league batting average against him last year was .246, not terrible but not all that good. Although he had 31 saves, I saw a list of the league leaders in saves as a percentage of save opportunities (see Jeff Russell). He wasn't on the list. He is in possession of the job as the closer, and Kelly kept using him that way because before Reardon came he didn't have *anybody,* but I wonder how much value he really has.

GARY REDUS
Pittsburgh
Had perhaps the best season of his career, hitting .283. Project him out to 600 at bats, and you get 39 doubles, 15 triples, 13 homers, 54 stolen bases, 86 walks, 90 runs scored, and 71 RBI. And you're telling me that guy can't play regularly? Maybe he can't play for you, but I think I'd find a place for him.

JEFF REED
Cincinnati
The most-similar player to Jeff Reed is Andy Allanson . . . not a quality regular; Joe Oliver probably will take the job. . . .

JERRY REED
Seattle
Consistent middle reliever, keeps his ERA in the threes. No star potential but a safe draft.

JODY REED
Boston

One of the best hitting shortstops in baseball; accomplishments last year included .288 average, 42 doubles, and excellent K/W ratio . . . teams with Barrett to give Boston outstanding offense in the middle of the field . . . in fact, if you look carefully at Boston up the middle . . . Pena, Barrett, Reed and Burks. Two of them are up in years (Barrett and Pena) and two of them were hurt last year, but if they're healthy and don't age suddenly, that's about as strong a team up the middle as you could find, ain't it?

RICK REUSCHEL
San Francisco

The interesting question here is whether he has a shot at the Hall of Fame. Not too much, I would think; he's pitched for some poor teams, and he's only 28 games over .500 in his career. Unless he just defines the odds by pitching well for at least three more seasons, I'd say his chances are slim. . . .

JERRY REUSS
Milwaukee

Reuss, actually, has a little better career record (220–191) than Reuschel (211–183). . . . I see no reason to believe that Reuss is capable of another comeback as a starting pitcher, but he could probably move into the role of left-handed spot reliever if he chose to do that. . . .

CRAIG REYNOLDS
Houston

Released or retired. Not on the mid-winter roster, anyway.

HAROLD REYNOLDS
Seattle

I did a computer run to identify the *least* effective offensive players in the majors who hit .300. Reynolds, who hit .300 on the nose with zero home runs and negative baserunning stats, was number one on that list, followed by Luis Polonia, Carlos Martinez, Danny Heep, and Steve Sax. . . .

R. J. REYNOLDS
Pittsburgh

Is he the most *consistent* platoon player in baseball? Platoon guys, because of the limited number of at bats, normally swing from good years to bad, but Reynolds has driven in 48–51 runs in each of the last four years, 42 the year before that. Over the last three seasons is 51 for 59 as a base stealer, 86 percent. . . .

RICK RHODEN
Houston

Who has had more comebacks: Reuss, Rhoden, or Reuschel. . . . Maybe Rhoden will make his next comeback as an outfielder . . . no draft.

JIM RICE
Boston

When Johnny Bench and Carl Yastrzemski were taken into the Hall of Fame last August, it seemed like every sportscaster in the country had to comment that they were "the last of a dying breed," meaning players who had spent their entire careers in one city and with one team. Now, with free agency and the death of loyalty, it's all big bucks and go wherever the money is, and you don't have any players like that any more.

What is strange about this is that *there are more of those guys than there have ever been.* Look around you—Schmidt just retired in Philadelphia, Brett is still in Kansas City, Rice is apparently retired after a career in Boston, Yount has gotten 2,600 hits for Milwaukee, Dwight Evans has had fifteen years in Boston, Dale Murphy is still in Atlanta, Trammell *and* Whitaker are the first Hall of Fame duo to spend their entire careers together as a double-play combination, Frank White has been in Kansas City forever. I can't believe that there have ever been so many outstanding players who had long careers in one city. Look back to thirty years ago, 1959, and make a list of the veteran superstars, twelve years in the majors, who were still with their first major league team and city. I think your list would be about three (Musial, Williams, Berra.) Go back to 1929 or 1939, and I think your list might be even shorter.

It has never been common for a superstar to spend his career with one team. Babe Ruth, Ty Cobb, Honus Wagner, Cy Young, Tris Speaker, Willie Mays, Henry Aaron, Harmon Killebrew, Frank Robinson, Rogers Hornsby—none of those guys spent his career in one city. It's just in recent years that that idea has developed.

What a lot of people don't see, because of their preconception, is that *free agency creates the possibility of loyalty.* When a player had no choice in where he played, there wasn't any such thing as "loyalty" to the city; the player went where he was told. When his value was higher one place than another, they sold him. But with free agency, a player like Robin Yount or Dale Murphy has *some* choice in the matter; he can still be traded, but he can influence the decision. So Yount *chooses* to remain in Milwaukee, and Brett *chooses* to remain in Kansas City. Players, for the first time in baseball history, are allowed to express their loyalty to their teams—and quite often, they do.

JEFF RICHARDSON
Cincinnati

Shortstop candidate, not as bad a hitter as his .168 batting average last year would suggest. Return of Larkin probably sends him back to the minors, but he'll get another shot, and hit better.

★★★
ROB RICHIE
Detroit
★★★

Good hitter, .280 hitter or better with a little power, runs the bases well. He was the Eastern League MVP in 1988, and hit well last year in the International League, although he wasn't listed by *Baseball America* as one of the top prospects in the league. Could be a surprise American League Rookie of the Year candidate.

DAVE RIGHETTI
Yankees

Rumor has it that he will return to the starting rotation in 1990; I guess by the time you will read this you will know more about that than I do. He hasn't started a game since 1983, and he's a completely different pitcher now from what he was in 1983. He's a quality pitcher, but a relief ace needs to have an ERA below 3.00, and he hasn't for three years.

JOSE RIJO
Cincinnati

Another one of the 112 injuries which derailed the Reds last year was an inflammation of the muscles in Rijo's back; probably won't effect him this year. Not an absolutely safe pick, but a first-class pitcher if he is healthy.

ERNEST RILES
San Francisco

Excellent platoon player. The development of Matt Williams would appear to crowd his playing time, and makes him less than a desirable pickup if he remains with the Giants. The ideal situation for him would be to go somewhere like the White Sox or Tigers where he could play third base against right handers.

BILLY RIPKEN
Baltimore

Not a major league player. Good glove, good bunter, but his bat is just too weak

. . . most comparable player: Brad Wellman. . . .

CAL RIPKEN
Baltimore

In the 1983 *Abstract* I commented about Tim Wallach that his offensive states for 1982 were "about as close to Ripken's as they could get—28, 97, .268 against 28, 93, .264"—the parallel extended to doubles, triples, strikeouts, walks, runs scored, and GIDP, all of which were very close. Seven years later, I did a search for the most-comparable major league player to Cal Ripken, and the answer is: Tim Wallach. . . . Since his MVP year in 1983, Ripken's slugging percentage has declined every season, six straight years. His slugging percentages, 1983–89: .517, .510, .469, .461, .436, .431, and .401.

KEVIN RITZ
Detroit

Projects as a rotation starter for Detroit after 12 solid starts in the second half. I'm not down on him—in fact, I kind of like his stuff—but with his control record (44 walks in 74 innings, basically the same in the minor leagues) and with the Detroit team behind him (or against him, however you look at it), I wouldn't think you would place him too high on your draft list.

LUIS RIVERA
Boston

Middle infielder; played short for Reed while Barrett was injured and Reed was at second. OK defensive player but even hitting .257, as he did last year, contributes so little on offense that he doesn't project as a regular. . . .

BIP ROBERTS
San Diego

Got a second chance and made the most of it, hitting .301 and scoring 81 runs in 117 games. I've always liked him, even when he flailed around in his first major

league opportunity in 1986. He should be the Padres third baseman this season, and I've no reason to think that he won't do a good job.

DON ROBINSON
San Francisco

His career batting average, .243, is the best of any active pitcher (200 or more at bats). That list: 1. Don Robinson, 2. Dan Schatzeder, 3. Rick Rhoden, 4. Bob Forsch, 5. Sid Fernandez, 6. Greg Maddux, 7. Fernando Valenzuela, 8. Orel Hershiser, 9. Rick Sutcliffe, 10. Mike Krukow.

JEFF D. ROBINSON
Pittsburgh

Outstanding relief pitcher in 1987–88, didn't handle the starting role last year. I would assume that he would regain his effectiveness with a full season of relief work. . . .

JEFF M. ROBINSON
Detroit

Extremely effective starting pitcher in 1988, but missed most of the *first* half of last season with assorted nagging injuries. I don't like to take a chance on a pitcher who can't stay healthy, and his very low strikeout rate (40 in 78 innings) is another negative indicator to me. A third is the Detroit team, which even if he pitches well might stick him with a 9–15 record and a 4.11 ERA. I'd say approach with caution, recognizing that he has pitched very well at times.

RON ROBINSON
Cincinnati

Robinson last year had elbow surgery in March, missed the first three months, came back and pitched well in August and September, finishing 5–3 with a 3.35 ERA. He is not a bad risk for 1990, a slightly better risk than Jeff Robinson (because Jeff Robinson didn't pitch that well upon his return). But again, this

Robinson had 36 strikeouts in 83 innings, and he's been hurt two straight seasons. If you're looking for a half-time pitcher from 1989 who might be an effective full-time pitcher in 1990, I'd much rather you took a chance on Jose Rijo or Mark Portugal rather than Ron Robinson, because there just aren't very many effective starting pitchers who don't strike out at least five men per nine innings. And must pitchers who have elbow trouble once will have it again within a couple of years.

VIC RODRIGUEZ
Minnesota

Has a lifetime major league batting average of .429 after hitting .412 for Baltimore in 1984 (7 for 17) and .455 for Minnesota in 1989 (5 for 11). His minor league records show him to be a good hitter, hitting somewhere between .270 and .300 in the majors, but he's not going to displace Gary Gaetti, and he wasn't on the Twins roster at mid-winter.

MIKE ROESLER
Cincinnati

Twenty-six-year-old, six foot five inch right hander; no history of consistent success anywhere. Grade D prospect.

KEN ROGERS
Texas

Left-handed spot reliever, pitched 74 innings in 73 games. Valentine does that a lot—uses three or four relievers in a game. Rogers held left-handed hitters to a .173 batting average, and posted a 2.93 ERA. He will have his job back next year.

ED ROMERO
Last spotted with Atlanta

Romero's career ratio of runs created per hit is the lowest of any major league player (35 runs created per 100 hits); he is followed by Curtis Wilkerson, Ozzie

Guillen, Alfredo Griffin, Glenn Hoffman, Wayne Tolleson, Terry Francona, Bruce Benedict, Otis Nixon, and Rafael Ramirez . . . not listed on anybody's roster at mid-winter. . . .

KEVIN ROMINE
Boston

Spare outfielder-pinch hitter, reportedly has outstanding arm. Extremely unlikely ever to be a regular.

ROLANDO ROOMES
Cincinnati

Roomes last year struck out 100 times while drawing only 13 walks, the worst strikeout to walk ratio of any major league player. The bottom ten: Roomes, Mookie Wilson, Cory Snyder, Andrew Thomas, Brad Wellman, Jim Presley, Greg Gagne, Bo Jackson, Pete Incaviglia, and Alvaro Espinoza. . . . Roomes is a legitimate hitter. His 1989 performance is consistent with his minor league performance translated into major league equivalencies. Actually, he is capable of having a somewhat better season . . . departure of Kal Daniels opens up some playing time, and the Reds are not deep in outfielders, but I think Hal Morris is a somewhat better hitter than Roomes. . . .

BOBBY ROSE
California

Good prospect, probably capable of hitting .280 in the majors with 10–15 homers, as many stolen bases and 60–80 walks, good defense. Not likely to be a superstar, and probably a year or two away from getting a full shot at a major league job. . . . I like Howell, but I think Rose might be a better player.

STEVE ROSENBERG
White Sox

Very marginal. Last year went 4–13 with 4.94 ERA; I see no reason to think he will turn it around.

BRUCE RUFFIN
Philadelphia

Consistency has a down side, too. Ruffin has the same record each of the last two seasons: 6 wins, 10 losses. His earned run averages over the last three years: 4.35, 4.43, and 4.44. . . . Ruffin has a good sinking fastball, and could probably pitch well for a team like Los Angeles or Oakland, but he was brought to the majors too quickly by the Phillies, and has never been properly schooled in how to use what he has.

JEFF RUSSELL
Texas

I wonder how many pitchers have made the All-Star team in consecutive seasons as a starter and a reliever? Not many, I'd think . . . (Rob Neyer checked, and found one other: Ewell Blackwell) . . . had 71 games and 73 innings pitched, almost the same ratio as Ken Rogers. . . . The American League leaders in saves as a percentage of save opportunities: Russell (38 of 44), Dennis Eckersley, Lee Smith, Tom Henke, Mike Schooler, Dan Plesac, Greg Olson, Steve Farr, Bobby Thigpen, and Bryan Harvey (25 of 32).

JOHN RUSSELL
Atlanta

One of Atlanta's non-catchers. Russell is a converted outfielder who has to hit to stay around, because he has very limited defensive skills as a catcher. Last year he hit .182, had 53 strikeouts and 8 walks and showed little power. No draft.

MARK RYAL
Philadelphia

Now with his fourth team, still trying to catch on as a pinch hitter-extra outfielder. No prospect.

NOLAN RYAN
Texas

There were 36 stolen bases against him last year, the most against any American

League pitcher. The top ten in stolen bases allowed: Ryan (by far), Bobby Witt, Jim Abbott, John Dopson, Charlie Hough, Jack Morris, John Candiotti, Randy Johnson, Dennis Lamp, Bob Welch, Frank Tanana.

On the good side, the batting average against him was .187, by far the lowest in the league (Tom Gordon was second at .210). How many times has he led in that, I wonder? About fifteen times, maybe? . . . I think at his age, Ryan can't possibly last more than another ten years or so. . . .

BRET SABERHAGEN
Royals

A lot of people are convinced that Saberhagen will have an off year this year because he's had an on-year, off-year pattern throughout his career. I doubt that that pattern has any predictive significance. I've seen many players over the years have an on-year, off-year pattern (Vada Pinson, Willie Davis, Vida Blue), but the pattern always breaks down sooner or later, generally at the moment when it is recognized. I guess Blue is the best parallel:

	BLUE	BRET
Age 21	24–8	20–6
Age 22	6–10	7–12
Age 23	20–9	18–10
Age 24	17–15	14–16
Age 25	22–11	23–6

At the age of twenty-six Blue went 18–13 with a 2.36 ERA. Anyway, with exactly the same pitching but just different luck, Saberhagen could have gone 18–13 in 1988 and 20–9 last year, and then nobody would be talking about it. I'll still hold with Clemens as the best pitcher in the league and the most likely man to win the Cy Young Award, but Saberhagen's got to be number two on the list.

CHRIS SABO
Reds

I was critical of the Rookie of the Year Award to Sabo, which I thought was a joke, and I'm sure some people thought I was knocking Sabo. I wasn't; Sabo is an OK third baseman, although he has no star potential. He's a middle-of-the-pack third baseman.

MARK SALAS
Cleveland

He's got a lot of chances because he's a type of player that managers like to have around—a left-handed DH who can catch a couple of times a week. He hasn't hit in four years, and may be out of chances.

LUIS SALAZAR
Cubs

One of my least-favorite players. He has aged well, having two straight good years with the bat in his mid-thirties. I'm still not going to recommend.

JUAN SAMUEL
Dodgers

The thing about Samuel is, *what do you do with him?* He's a great player, but what do you do with him? With a career on-base percentage of .309, he is sure as hell not a leadoff man. Striking out 140 to 160 times a season, it is hard to see him as a second-place hitter; besides, he's right-handed and doesn't get on base, assuming that the ideal number two hitter is a left-hander who puts the ball in play and gets on base. With a slugging percentage in the low .400s, he's hardly qualified to hit third or fourth. So he's a great player, but he obviously can't play any of the key offensive roles.

The same thing defensively: What do you do with him? He may be the worst center fielder I've even seen, and I saw Ed Kirkpatrick out there a few games. He doesn't pivot very well on the

double play at second base, and if you leave him at second you have to worry about an injury.

The conclusion, of course, is that he is not a great ballplayer at all; a great *talent,* but a very ordinary ballplayer. By talking about him as if he was a great player, the Phillies created a monster; it became impossible to just put him in the sixth or seventh spot where he belonged, and see if he would *develop* into a player who could play a key offensive role.

ALEX SANCHEZ
Blue Jays

Right-handed pitcher, twenty-four years old, throws hard. He was a first-round draft pick in 1987, and was listed by *Baseball America* the number-three prospect in the International League in 1989. I make him about a C+ prospect. His control record at Syracuse wasn't great; in the majors he walked 14 in 12 innings. There are reports that his fastball is rather straight. Toronto isn't wide open as far as starting pitching goes; with Key, Cerutti, Stieb, and Stottlemyre and a pennant race, Sanchez probably won't get more than a few starts to show what he can do. My guess is he'll spend most of the season at Syracuse.

RYNE SANDBERG
Cubs

The only middle infielder to create 100 runs in 1989 (106); the top ten were Sandberg, Julio Franco, Steve Sax, Jerry Browne, Lou Whitaker, Roberto Alomar, Cal Ripken, Harold Reynolds, Jose Oquendo, Jody Reed.

It's surprising to me that he didn't receive more support in MVP voting (he finished fourth). What do you expect an MVP to do? Hit for average? Sandberg did that (.290). Hit for power? Sandberg did that (30 homers). Play defense? Sandberg did that in spades, playing a key defensive position and establishing a major league record for consecutive errorless games. Run the bases? Sandberg does that. Contribute to a championship? The Cubs were the surprise champions of the season. I mean, I know Pedro Guerrero had a great season, but do you *really* think Guerrero is more valuable to the Cardinals than Sandberg is to the Cubs?

It is too early to answer this question, but perhaps not too early to ask it. Where does Sandberg fit in among the greatest second basemen of all time? Among the great ones he is probably more like Charlie Gehringer than anyone else—smooth, graceful, multi-talented offense without any one exceptional performance area. I usually rate Gehringer the number-four second baseman of all time; it is clearly too early to put Sandberg even with him.

DEION SANDERS
Yanks

He gives the appearance of being a pretty decent player, based both on his two weeks in the major leagues and on his stats at AA. Apparently he would hit for a decent average, have a reasonable K/W ratio, and of course he has speed. No draft, but I'm interested.

SCOTT SANDERSON
Oakland

Gives you about 150 good innings a year. If you have rotation anchors, like Stewart, Welch, and Moore, a guy who gives you 150 innings a year is a help. If you're basing your staff around guys who pitch 150 good innings a year, like the Yankees have tried to do, you're just waiting for a disaster.

BENITO SANTIAGO
San Diego

I probably like him less than almost anybody else. For one thing, I've always thought he was a .260 hitter, even when

he hit .300. His K/W ratios, though *improving substantially*, are still very poor. He cuts off the opposition's running game, but I've always thought that was an overrated part of the defense. Santiago will have better seasons than he had in 1989, but I'm not going to go too high to get him.

NELSON SANTOVENIA
Expos

Above-average young catcher, excellent defense. Cut his strikeouts in *half* last season, from 77 to 37 in the same number of at bats.

MACKEY SASSER
Mets

The third of the group, with LaValliere and Scioscia, except that he doesn't walk as often as they do and probably is not as strong defensively. Playing time will increase in '90, making him a reasonably good draft.

STEVE SAX
Yankees

I did a computer run to find the *least effective* offensive player in the majors with a career average over .280. The answer, somewhat surprisingly, was Steve Sax, followed by Johnny Ray, Terry Puhl, and Willie Wilson. . . . Has almost a 30 percent chance of getting 3,000 career hits, which would make him just the third second baseman to do that. . . . Has never scored 100 runs in a season, despite twice getting over 200 hits. . . . an extremely safe draft; has had only one off season with the bat in eight years. . . .

DAN SCHATZEDER
Houston Astros

Shaky pitcher but excellent hitter. Only Don Robinson has a higher career batting average among pitchers. . . . No draft, but could fool you.

CURT SCHILLING
Baltimore

Very highly regarded pitching prospect, but has pitched so badly in the majors that it has been difficult even to ease him into a job. Sixty percent chance of being a major league starting pitcher within two years. . . .

CALVIN SCHIRALDI
San Diego

The Padres may move him back to a starting role, although they are not needing a lot of help there. He gives the appearance of fading toward mediocrity, but I wouldn't be too quick to give up on him. He still has a great arm. He has pitched in two of the toughest parks in baseball for a pitcher, Wrigley Field and Fenway Park. He has been shuttled between starting and pitching in relief. I wouldn't be surprised if he turned out to be an effective pitcher yet.

DAVE SCHMIDT
Orioles

No draft.

MIKE SCHMIDT
Philadelphia

Retired, of course. To me his only real competition as the greatest third baseman of all time is his contemporary, George Brett. . . . There were three active players in 1989 who had 3,000 career secondary bases: Mike Schmidt (3,851), Darrell Evans (3,346), and Dwight Evans (3,035). . . .

DICK SCHOFIELD
Angels

Love him. Not a good hitter, but a smart player, excellent shortstop, underrated shortstop. Excellent base stealer. A better player in real life than in fantasy leagues.

MIKE SCHOOLER
Seattle

His 33 saves and 2.81 ERA mark him as a top draft, and are generally supported by his peripheral stats—69 strikeouts and 16 walks in 77 innings, allowed only *two* home runs in the Kingdome. Moving out the fences can't hurt him. A solid draft.

BILL SCHROEDER
California

Last year he struck out 44 times, walked only three. Has had some good years with the bat, but lack of plate discipline ultimately has to undermine him.

RICK SCHU
Detroit

Acquisition of Tony Phillips probably eliminates his job. I like some things about him—charges the bunt awfully well—but he just hasn't *quite* been able to get over the hump.

MIKE SCHWABE
Tigers

In the minors he has had sensational K/W ratios, but last year, in the majors, he struck out 13 and walked 16, leading to a 6.04 ERA. A lot of young pitchers, when they come up, think that every hitter is Don Mattingly, and try to make perfect pitches. We won't get a fair reading on whether Schwabe can be successful until he gets past that stage, and begins to challenge major league hitters as he has minor league hitters.

MIKE SCIOSCIA
Dodgers

When he gets on base, he is less likely to score a run than any other major league player. He has been on base (not counting home runs) 1,251 times in his career, and has scored only 249 runs. . . .

MIKE SCOTT
Astros

The National League leaders in stolen bases allowed: 1. Mike Scott (39), 2. Kevin Gross, 3. Dwight Gooden, 4. John Smiley, 5. Bob Ojeda, 6. Jim Deshaies, 7.

David Cone, 8. Ken Howell and Ron Darling, 10. Rick Sutcliffe and Jeff Robinson. . . . Would rate Scott over Hershiser as the number-one starting pitcher in the National League, the first man I would draft. He's had five straight winning seasons, aggregate record of 86–49, and while his strikeout totals have bounced around, his strikeout to walk ratio the last two seasons has been superb. A great pitcher, who probably started too late to make the Hall of Fame. . . .

SCOTT SCUDDER
Cincinnati

Walked 61 men in 100 innings, posted 4.49 ERA. To me, he looks like he needs to spend about three years in the minor leagues, and figure out what he's doing.

RAY SEARAGE
Los Angeles

I can't figure out why the Dodgers wanted him. I mean, there's a jillion candidates for left-handed short reliever. Why Ray Searage? Why the guy with all the losing records and the high ERAs.

The Dodgers are super with pitchers, but sometimes the arrogance of the organization overpowers them. They think they can turn *anybody* into an effective pitcher, Ray Searage, Mike Morgan, anybody. Anybody with a good arm. It doesn't always work, and sometimes they wind up forcing a quality pitcher out of the nest to make room for one of their reclamation projects.

STEVE SEARCY
Detroit

Rated the top pitching prospect in the Tigers organization a year ago, Searcy came down with soreness in his left shoulder in spring training last year, and suffered a lost season. He pitched 9 games at Toledo, where he had been highly effective in 1988, and posted a

7.54 ERA, and 8 games in Detroit, where it was 6.04. Obviously, no draft pick until he shows evidence of turning it around.

BOB SEBRA
Cincinnati

Onetime top prospect, now busily pitching his way out of the game.

KEVIN SEITZER
Kansas City

A good player even in an off season. Seitzer wasn't driving the ball last season, and wound up hitting below .300 for the first time in his professional career, but with 102 walks he moved into the leadoff spot, where he will probably remain. Late in the year he began wearing glasses for the first time, then switched to contacts, and after an adjustment period was hitting the ball in the gaps, for the first time all year, beginning about September 10. . . . Had his best year as a base stealer, stealing 17. He worries people as a third baseman because he has an odd throwing motion, but he also does some things well at the position, chases down fouls well and moves to his left extremely well. He's an outstanding player, but somehow I suspect the question will always be "Who succeeded George Brett as the Royals third baseman?", rather than "Who preceded Kevin Seitzer as . . ."

MIKE SHARPERSON
Los Angeles

I like Sharperson, as a player, very much. His big chance at Toronto came at a moment when the Blue Jays were under enormous pressure, and when he failed to hit they dumped him very quickly, in part because they had two other players of the same quality, Manny Lee and Nelson Liriano. He was in a slump, the team was in a slump, he was the only unproven regular, and he became the scapegoat. He went back to the minor leagues, where he remains today at age twenty-nine; with the Dodgers adding Juan Samuel to Willie Randolph, he is in deep water.

But if he ever gets another chance, he *can* play; in fact, I think he is one of the fifteen to eighteen best second basemen in the game. As a major league hitter, I think he could hit .260–.290, draw 60–80 walks, and steal 20–30 bases a year. Defensively, he may be a little inconsistent, but he is *strong* on the double play and appears to have good range. Time is rapidly running out on him, but he is a major league player.

LARRY SHEETS
Baltimore

He's a mystery. He's been a mystery all his life—why he went home and quit baseball, was it his religion, wasn't it his religion, would he come back, wouldn't he come back? His family are Mennonites, you know; I guess he is, too. But if he doesn't start hitting more than 7 home runs a year, we're going to lose interest in how the mystery turns out pretty quick.

GARY SHEFFIELD
Milwaukee

He has *some* potential as a major league hitter, probably enough that he can make the majors and stick as a third baseman or right fielder. I do not believe that he is ever going to be a major league shortstop, and I have an open mind on the question of how good a hitter he will be.

In my opinion, Sheffield needs to spend about two years more in the minor leagues. He needs to understand that the baseball world doesn't revolve around Gary Sheffield, that if he wants to have a place in that world he will have to adjust to it, not it to him. It is a good sign for the Brewers that they did send him down, but they've got to stay the course. If the Brewers don't stand up to him now, I predict a rocky career.

JOHN SHELBY
Los Angeles

Not a major league hitter. Outstanding outfielder, but little chance of ever playing regularly again.

PAT SHERIDAN
San Francisco

Pat has now played for four championship teams in seven years in the majors—Kansas City in 1983 and 1984, Detroit in 1987, and San Francisco in 1989.

I did his arbitration case a year ago. Sometimes, when you are doing an arbitration case, you come away secretly convinced that the player you are analyzing is not as good as he appears on paper. In Sheridan's case, I came away convinced that he was substantially better. With Detroit in 1988, Sheridan played left field, center field, and right field. He batted first, second, third, and fourth. He was used as a defensive replacement several times. He was used as a pinch hitter several times. He was used as a pinch runner several times.

Overall, his stats weren't that impressive—but when you looked at each assignment he had been given and how he had handled it, it appeared in almost every case that he had done the job. He had had to hit third for about a month of the season due to an injury, and had driven in 27 runs in that month. When he was asked to hit leadoff, he drew walks and stole bases. I mean, I know he's not a great player, but if a guy hits well enough to pinch hit, runs well enough to pinch run, gets on base often enough to be a leadoff hitter, throws well enough to play right field, fields well enough to play center, and pops an occasional home run . . . well, I think he's a valuable man to have around.

ERIC SHOW
San Diego

Had back surgery in early August, which opened up the slot for Andy Benes, who pitched so well that he will have the devil's own time getting his job back. Show has a winning record in seven of the last eight seasons, so something will probably happen to get him some work. Rasmussen or Whitson will flame out, and Show will get another chance.

RUBEN SIERRA
Rangers

Led the American League in runs created, 119. . . . The most-similar player to Ruben Sierra is Jose Canseco. . . . A very good bet to continue his outstanding play, in the long run probably a better bet than Canseco. Perhaps the most valuable *property* in the American League—but not the most valuable player.

ROY SILVER
St. Louis

No defensive position, but a good singles hitter in the Cardinal system. Capable of hitting .300 in the major leagues.

JOEL SKINNER
Cleveland

Down to number three on the depth chart with the acquisition of Alomar. He is sure to be in the majors somewhere, because he is a better player than many of the number two catchers around. . . . No reason to draft him.

DON SLAUGHT
Pittsburgh

Decent hitter, decent defense; will share job with LaValliere. . . .

JOHN SMILEY
Pittsburgh

A safe draft after two almost identical seasons, records of 13–11, 12–8 and good ERAs. I don't see him as a great pitcher, but I suspect he may remain strong for several years.

★ ★ ★
BRYN SMITH
St. Louis
★ ★ ★

Fine pitcher; he could be the new John Tudor. Smith is very capable of leading the league in ERA with the help of Busch Stadium, the exceptional Cardinal defense and Herzog, who won't leave a starter out there to get hammered (not that Rodgers did). If he stays healthy, he'll be more effective with the Cardinals than he was with Montreal, and he was a consistent winner with Montreal with excellent ERAs.

DAVE SMITH
Houston

Basically, I have *never* understood why this guy is effective, but he is. He has 24 to 33 saves in each of the last five years, and his highest ERA in the last six years is 2.73. He has given up 2 home runs in the last three years. Despite his age and weight, a relatively safe draft.

DWIGHT SMITH
Cubs

A better hitter than Walton, probably a better hitter than Mark Grace. When he and Grace were teammates in the minors, Smith was the better hitter, as he was last year with the Cubs. If his defense doesn't undermine his career and he gets out of the platoon role, he is *very* capable of leading the National League in hitting. . . . His platoon partner, Lloyd McClendon, is likely to drop off sharply, so Smith could take the job. Also has more speed than he showed last year (9 stolen bases); could easily steal 30, and maybe 60. A devastating offensive player.

LEE SMITH
Boston

I selected him the outstanding reliever of the 1980s. I know that selection will cause a lot of people to yelp, but I concluded that it was the *only* nomination which was justified by the player's performance. Three players were at the head of the list in saves—Jeff Reardon, Dan Quisenberry, and Lee Smith, with Smith in third, Reardon well in front. In the other performance categories, though, Smith was far superior to Reardon and somewhat superior to Quiz. He had done this despite pitching all of his career in hitters' parks, Wrigley Field and Fenway. He was extremely consistent from 1982 to the end of the decade, far more so than Quisenberry or Reardon; even last year, when the perception was that he was off his game, he struck out 96 men in 71 innings, went 6–1 and saved 25 games in 30 opportunities, a ratio exceeded by only two pitchers in the league (Jeff Russell and Dennis Eckersley). . . . A safe pick, and a great reliever.

LONNIE SMITH
Braves

Per at bat and without park adjustments, Lonnie last year was the third most-effective offensive player in the majors, behind Clark and Mitchell. Lonnie created an estimated 7.7 runs per 27 outs. . . . He did this despite striking out 95 times in 134 games. When not striking out he hit .393, second-highest in the major leagues (behind Will Clark) . . . hit .418 with runners in scoring position, the best in the National League. . . .

MICHAEL ANTHONY SMITH
Baltimore

Twenty-six years old, and hasn't yet mastered his control. If and when the control comes around, he may be an effective pitcher.

MICHAEL ANTHONY SMITH
Pittsburgh

Veteran minor league reliever, throws strikes but has indifferent stuff. Good chance to make the majors in 1990, but certainly not in a key role. . . .

OZZIE SMITH
St. Louis

Ozzie is now fifth among active players in career stolen bases, with 432. . . . He certainly is not the defensive player that he once was, but considering offense, defense, and durability, there still isn't a better shortstop in the National League. . . . Hit .361 in the late innings of close games, best in the National League. . . .

PETE SMITH
Atlanta

I probably like him better than anybody else does. It's a tough situation for a pitcher—a hitter's park, a bad team—and a pitcher who is just a millimeter off his game can get stuck with an ugly record. If I were a general manager, I wouldn't mind trading for Pete Smith. As long as he is in Atlanta, I don't want him on my fantasy team.

ROY SMITH
Minnesota

Was one of the surprise successes of 1990. There is no reason he can't continue to pitch winning baseball—16–12, that kind of thing. He has no star potential, and we'll have to see whether his arm will withstand a major league workload.

ZANE SMITH
Montreal

The best 1–13 pitcher in the major leagues.

MIKE SMITHSON
Boston

He has four straight seasons with an ERA of 4.77 or higher—and yet he is still pitching a lot of innings, 144 last year. How far can you stretch this? Wouldn't you think the demand for your services would diminish after a while if you kept giving up 5 runs a game?

JOHN SMOLTZ
Braves

One of the *really* good ones, obviously. I don't see any element of an outstanding young pitcher that Smoltz doesn't have, except possibly that the park will work against him. There is every likelihood that Smoltz will win 200 games in the major leagues.

CORY SNYDER
Cleveland

For his career he has the worst strikeout to walk ratio of any active player (500 or more games), 100–21. The only man close to him is Tony Armas (100–22), followed by Shawon Dunston (100–23) . . . Bill Schroeder actually is worse (100–17), but hasn't played 500 games. . . . Snyder had back trouble, as big strong guys often do. He will have better years, but back trouble doesn't go away. In my opinion Snyder's chances of having a Hall of Fame career have gone from slim to none.

LUIS SOJO
Toronto

Young shortstop, rated by *Baseball America* the number-four prospect in the International League. My view of him is that he very probably is a major league player, but with Tony Fernandez around, who's going to know? He'll be battling not only Fernandez but Liriano and Manny Lee for a job, and I doubt that he's any better than they are or enough better than they are to take a job away from anybody.

PAUL SORRENTO
Twins

Slugging left-handed first baseman, blocked by Kent Hrbek. He was acquired by the Twins in the Bert Blyleven trade, and drove in 112 runs in the Southern League last year, but probably won't surface for another year at least. Appears to have major league power.

SAMMY SOSA
Chicago White Sox

He doesn't know the strike zone from the Swahili alphabet, but with that he is some prospect. He's twenty-one years old, fast, strong, and a major league center fielder. There is always the possibility of a relapse (he hit .229 for Charlotte in 1988), but the odds are he'll hit around .270 with 12–15 home runs and 25 or more stolen bases for the Sox. His throwing arm may be his best asset. He's the best center field prospect that the White Sox have had since Chet Lemon. Except possibly for Darryl Boston. And we all know what happened to Darryl Boston.

CHRIS SPEIER
San Francisco

Will Chris Speier
Ever retire?
Can the Giants fire
Christopher Speier?
Will the totals of Speier
Go higher and higher?
How do I
get out of this?
Give me a closing line,
And I'll try'er.

BILL SPIERS
Brewers

Played exactly as well as Gary Sheffield, whom he replaced at short, but didn't get the whole team pissed off at him in the process. Actually, he played a little better than Sheffield at short, but about the same on offense.

Spiers appears to have all of the elements of a major league career. He can hit major league pitching all right, which is to say about as well as Chris Speier. He has a shortstop's arm, and appears comfortable at the position. He can steal some bases—ten last year in twelve tries. He looks to me like a major league player.

HARRY SPILMAN
Houston

Spilman in his career has the highest ratio of RBI per total base of any major league player (500 or more games). The reason for that, of course, is that he has been a career pinch hitter, and thus has hit most of the time with men on base, but that's not to deny him credit for what he has done. Second on the list is Jose Canseco. . . .

RANDY ST. CLAIRE
Minnesota

Twenty-nine-year-old right-hander—no prospect.

BOB STANLEY
Boston

Retired.

MIKE STANLEY
Rangers

He's a good player to consider, for the simple reason that he is probably a far better hitter than he has yet been able to show us. The Rangers have been trying to make him a catcher, and the defensive strain (he's not a catcher) has interfered with his offensive performance, which even so hasn't been awful (in 617 major league at bats, he has 11 homers, 76 RBI, a .253 average, and 83 walks). He may not have a defensive position, and with Baines around and Incaviglia, he may not be able to get many at bats as a DH. But . . . well, keep him in mind.

★★★
MIKE STANTON
Braves
★★★

A great pickup in a draft—a guy who could be the next Bruce Sutter or Goose Gossage. Stanton is a left-handed pitcher, was a thirteenth-round draft pick in 1987, pitched extremely well in the low minors in '88, pitched sensationally at three levels last year, the top one being the major leagues. He's probably the best bet to be National League Rookie of the Year this year.

JIM STEELS
Giants

Oh, does he? Well, he should cut it out before he gets caught. Steels goes on an All-Obnoxious team with Glenn Braggs, Greg Swindell, Harry Chiti, Harry "Stinky" Davis, and Pat Meaney. That's in the winter; in the summer he's going to stay in AAA. Steels must be one of the great March hitters of all time; it seems like every time I see him in Arizona he is hitting .438. Him and Luis Polonia. That's gotten him on the major league roster several times, but he's really not a major league hitter.

TERRY STEINBACH
Oakland

Very fine catcher; could develop to a yet higher level. But a lifetime average of .275, for a catcher . . . nobody's complaining. . . .

PHIL STEPHENSON
Padres

He's the brother of Gene Stephenson, coach of the NCAA champion Wichita Shockers. He'll be thirty in September, so he is rapidly running out of time to establish himself in the majors. Despite that, I think he *is* a major league hitter, pretty comparable to Pete O'Brien as a hitter (that is .260–.280 average, 12–17 home runs, 60–100 walks, a few stolen bases). If I was running a team like Boston (losing Esasky), Cleveland (losing O'Brien) or Pittsburgh (gaining Sid Bream), I'd love to pick up Stephenson as a platoon first baseman, and there are several other teams that could use him as a pinch hitter-designated hitter-backup first baseman. I doubt that he'll stick with the Padres.

LEE STEVENS
California

Stevens is a big, strong, left-handed hitting outfielder, rated the number-two prospect in the Angels system a year ago, and one of the top ten in the PCL in 1989. He's from Lawrence, Kansas, which is sort of my hometown, so I'm supposed to be high on him. Unfortunately, I'm not. Although he is still young enough to develop, at this point he would hit in the low .200s (as a major leaguer) with 12–20 home run power, very poor K/W ratio, no speed and marginal defense. He's got a long, long way to go to make it as a major league player.

DAVE STEWART
Oakland

A great pitcher, of course. A safe draft.

DAVE STIEB
Toronto

Stieb has been in double figures in wins in eight of the last nine years, and has had winning records all eight of those seasons. In spite of that, he may *not* be an especially safe draft; he may be near the end of his run. His age isn't a problem, but his strikeout frequency has gradually decreased, from 6.7 per game in 1984 to 4.4 last season. That is a worrisome sign. He was 17–8 last year, but I doubt frankly that he pitched that well. He's a *fine* pitcher, but *not* a safe draft.

KURT STILLWELL
Kansas City

Still young, making slow progress. He's only played 130 games a year, and we hear a lot about that in KC, but how many middle infielders play 150 games a year, anyway? Not many. Stillwell's a solid player, potentially one of the three or four best in the league but not there yet . . . a couple of years ago was selected as having the best infield arm in the league by a poll. . . .

TODD STOTTLEMYRE
Toronto

Still moving into the job, it's hard to evaluate him—too late to evaluate him as a prospect, too early to evaluate him as a pitcher. Would appear to be a decent selection as a fifth starter, and could emerge as a Stieb-like pitcher.

DOUG STRANGE
Detroit

Infielder. Probably won't hit quite enough to be a regular third baseman, or field quite well enough to be a regular shortstop. Signing of Phillips means that he'll be depending on injuries to Trammell and Whitaker to get him at bats. He'll probably get some . . . no draft.

DARRYL STRAWBERRY
Mets

The major league leaders in career RBI per at bat: 1. Jose Canseco, 2. Eric Davis, 3. Mike Schmidt, 4. Darryl Strawberry, 5. Don Mattingly, 6. Ken Phelps, 7. Danny Tartabull, 8. Jim Rice, 9. Ron Kittle, 10. Kent Hrbek. . . .

In his career, 47 percent of Strawberry's hits have gone for extra bases. That's the highest percentage of any major league player. Second on the list was Mike Schmidt. . . . In 1989, although he had an off year, he was the only major league player other than Kevin Mitchell to have over half of his hits going for extra bases. . . . The most-similar player to Darryl Strawberry is Jesse Barfield.

Among active players, Strawberry

has the best chance to 600 career home runs (21 percent). There are nine active players who have established a chance to hit 600 home runs; those are Strawberry, Canseco (20 percent), Mark McGwire (16 percent), Fred McGriff (8 percent), Kevin Mitchell (6 percent), Eric Davis (6 percent), Ruben Sierra (4 percent), Glenn Davis (2 percent), and Howard Johnson (2 percent). There is a 60 percent chance that some active player will become the fourth man to hit 600 career homers.

I like Darryl, as a player. Am I concerned about him? Sure. But it seems to me that his off season is within the range of his ability, and thus that there is no particular reason to think that his abilities have changed. He doesn't have to hit 39 homers *every* year; once in awhile let him hit 29.

FRANKLIN STUBBS
Los Angeles
Lifetime .227 hitter, coming off a .291 season. What does that tell us?

JIM SUNDBERG
Texas
Retired.

B. J. SURHOFF
Brewers
Surhoff was the worst percentage base stealer of 1989 (20 or more attempts); he was 14 for 26 . . . the bottom five were Surhoff, Gerald Young, Junior Felix, and Rolando Roomes . . . the most-similar player to B. J. Surhoff is Scott Bradley . . .

RICK SUTCLIFFE
Cubs
Finally seems to be gaining some consistency. His last three seasons, despite a losing record in 1988, are really about the same. His K/W ratio last year was his best in five seasons. A safe draft.

BILLY SWIFT
Seattle
May be helped by the fences moving out; may not warrant a draft pick anyway. He throws a hard sinking fastball, which is a pitch that I love, and he has good control. I've always believed he could win with the right team—but sooner or later, you've got to produce. After four years his best ERA has been 4.43, and even if you knock .20 off for the park, that don't get it.

GREG SWINDELL
Cleveland
I think he'll be better off with Edwards gone. I think Doc Edwards *intended* to protect Swindell's arm, but I don't think he knew *how* to protect his arm. I think Doc Edwards *forgot* things, like checking to see whether his starting pitcher was tired after the seventh inning. McNamara is a veteran manager and doesn't abuse his pitchers' arms, and Swindell should be free to have his best season. He carries a little extra weight, and he could pitch great for Cleveland and still finish 14–17, but I recommend you consider him. He's a fine pitcher.

PAT TABLER
Royals
The following major league players had run element ratios of 1.2 or higher, but still had more RBI than runs scored: Pat Tabler, Bob Boone, Rance Mulliniks, Jeff Reed, Darren Daulton, Jack Clark, and Terry Kennedy. . . . The surprise about Tabler, in watching him, is that he has a terrific arm. He doesn't make long distance throws, but if he has a throw of less than two hundred feet, he'll nail it. . . . Regarded by KC media as a good apple.

FRANK TANANA
Detroit
His 10–14 record doesn't reflect how he pitched. He's very strong, throws harder now than he did five years ago. If he can

get with a good team, he can still have a big year.

KEVIN TAPANI
Minnesota
A part of the package for Viola. He's young, has a great arm, and throws strikes. He also has history of shoulder trouble. . . . Grade B prospect.

DANNY TARTABULL
Royals
Did you know Tartabull has a brother in the Seattle system? His brother got his daddy's power, unfortunately, and so doesn't appear headed for the major leagues. . . . The most-similar player to Danny Tartabull is Jose Canseco. Canseco's career slugging percentage is .503; Tartabull's is .502. . . .

Tartabull's *career* batting average, when not striking out, is .383, the best of any major league player; he is followed by Wade Boggs, at .381. Bo Jackson, although he hasn't played 500 games and doesn't qualify for the list, would be third at .380, and in that there is a point to be made.

Tartabull is not what anybody would think of as an "artificial turf" type player. He has tremendous power, but he doesn't run very well. He doesn't throw particularly well, for a right fielder. He strikes out a lot. His average isn't high.

The Royals, as a team, also have those characteristics. As a team, they strike out quite a bit. They're not a fast team, with Boone, Brett, Frank White, and Tartabull in the lineup. They aren't a team of "contact" hitters or "gap" hitters, as a team playing in a large park with artificial turf is supposed to be. When the Royals were the dominant team in the division in the late seventies, they hit more doubles than any team in the majors (at that time) in forty years. Last year the Royals hit only 227 doubles, tenth in the league. The Royals have only one player in the lineup who hits the ball in the gap and runs well, that being Jim Eisenreich. They don't hit for a high average. They *do* have very good team power, enough to out-homer their opponents by a substantial margin, although the total was low because of the park. They don't have great throwing arms in the outfield, with Tartabull in right and Willie Wilson, who has the weakest arm of any major league outfielder, in center.

So the Royals shouldn't do well on artificial turf, right? Wrong. The Royals on artificial turf last year were 67–33, by far the best record of any team in baseball. On grass fields they were 25–37, just barely missing the *worst* grass record in the league. Why?

We don't know why, but the point I am making is this: that *nobody really knows what goes into playing well on artificial turf.* There is an idea that is in circulation about what type of team should play well on artificial turf, but if you look at the teams which have those characteristics—speed, contact hitters, good arms in the outfield—you'll find that they don't *really* play any better on artificial turf than they do on grass. And, conversely, if you look at the teams which *really* play well on artificial turf, you'll find that they *don't* match the profile of a team which is supposed to. And the 1989 Royals are just the latest example of that.

The whole area is one that we *really* know very little about. What kind of pitcher does best in Fenway Park: a "nibbler" like Chuck Finley, who walks people but avoids the home run, or a pitcher like Bert Blyleven, who will risk the home run to avoid getting behind in the count? We don't really know, do we? We're just guessing. Who is more valuable in Atlanta, where home runs fly out: a power-hitting third baseman, who might get an extra 5–8 homers a year because of the park, or a defensive wiz-

ard, who might keep the opposition's big gun from coming to the plate? We simply don't know.

Eventually, sabermetrics will be able to answer these questions objectively. The answers will come from "modelling" the problems, models of a subtlety and complexity that will enable us to determine, finally, what the advantage of speed on artificial turf is really worth. Those models don't exist as of yet, but the information to construct them *does* exist, trapped inside of countless scoresheets, and that is a major step forward from ten years ago. Eventually, somebody will get around to studying the problem with the patience, determination and intelligence required, and then we will really know something about what kind of team does well on artificial turf. But as of now, we don't know nothing about it.

Tartabull hit .403 in the late innings of close games last year, the best of any major league player. . . .

WIL TEJADA
San Francisco
Minor league catcher; supposed to have the best throwing arm in baseball. No hitter; won't help you in most rotisserie or fantasy leagues. . . .

KENT TEKULVE
Cincinnati
Retired.

GARRY TEMPLETON
San Diego
Extremely consistent over the last eight years. He hasn't been *good,* but he's been *consistent.* In the last two years he has had an on-base percentage of .286, both years. In the last two years he has had a slugging percentage of .354, both years. That's terrible, but it is consistent.

WALT TERRELL
Pittsburgh
No draft. A 18–34 record over the last two years, doesn't strike anybody out and gives up lots of homers.

SCOTT TERRY
St. Louis
Assuming that the Cardinals don't have fourteen injuries in their pitching staff, the signing of Bryn Smith probably sends Scott Terry back to the bullpen, where he is a part of the committee. You put this guy on a bad team, and he'd have a record that would curl your toes. But in St. Louis, carefully handled by Herzog, he looks like he's doing fine.

MICKEY TETTLETON
Orioles
I know nobody will believe it, but Tettleton really has been a good player for several years. His average has been low, but he's a better than average hitter for a catcher if he hits .220, because of a career secondary average of .331. Also, ever since he came to the majors, the ERA of his team when he was catching has been dramatically better than the ERA of his team when he wasn't catching. He's like Kevin Mitchell—I wouldn't necessarily bet on him to be 100 percent as good in 1990 as he was in 1989, but I would bet on him to be 85 percent as good, and that's still a player that you want to have on your team. . . . The most-comparable major league player: Benito Santiago. I didn't say he was comparable, mind you; I said he was the closest. . . .

TIM TEUFEL
Mets
Solid enough backup infielder. Don't anticipate any sudden career moves for him.

BOBBY THIGPEN
White Sox
Not really a very good pitcher, but has an apparent value because he is used as

the bullpen closer, and piles up lots of one-inning saves. He's about as good a pitcher as Jerry Reed, I suppose. Maybe not quite.

ANDRES THOMAS
Braves

Had the lowest run element ratio of any major league hitter in 1989 (see Otis Nixon). The bottom three were Thomas, Jeff Hamilton, and Brian Harper.

MILT THOMPSON
St. Louis

What he did in St. Louis, as much as it was a surprise, was to exactly duplicate his career norms. His career batting average is .289; he hit .290. His career on-base percentage is .343; last year it was .340. His career slugging percentage is .383; last year it was .393. His career stolen base percentage is 78 percent; last year it was 77 percent. He did exactly what he could have been expected do across the board—but for some reason people were surprised. A safe draft.

ROBBIE THOMPSON
San Francisco

Boy, the National League has got some second baseman, don't it? If I had to rank them Thompson would probably rank about sixth, and I know the Giant fans would be outraged by that, but then they don't see the other five guys every day. Sandberg is number one, obviously, but two other guys are tremendous players, Alomar and Oquendo. Billy Doran stunk last year with the bat, but he's really a good hitter and a great defensive player. Willie Randolph is a fine player. The Pirate fans rave about Jose Lind's defense.

Thompson . . . well, he's a fine defensive player and a number-two hitter of sorts. For a number-two hitter he strikes out a lot and doesn't get on base very much, but this is more miscasting than incompetence; he does have some power, and he can steal some bases. He was in double figures in doubles, triples, homers, and stolen bases. He's consistent. A safe draft.

DICKIE THON
Philadelphia

He'll never get back to where he was *going,* but at least he is back where he *was,* or somewhere near there. He probably had the best year with the bat of any National League shortstop, although Ozzie and Dunston could argue. An interesting risk, as a draft pick.

GARY THURMAN
Kansas City

He was 16 for 16 as a base stealer last season, which tied an American League record for most stolen bases with no caught stealing. Extremely fast, good arm, .250-range hitter with some walks. I would like to see Willie Wilson released and his playing time given to Thurman, but he isn't a potential star.

MARK THURMOND
Baltimore

He had his best season in six years, and American League hitters hit .288 against him. Left-handers, the people he is brought in to get out, hit .283. He has good control and gets ground balls, but still . . . no draft.

JAY TIBBS
Orioles

Was pitching the best ball of his career last season (5–0, 2.82 ERA) when season was destroyed by arm trouble. He underwent surgery for a partially torn rotator cuff in September, and is not expected to pitch again until at least the middle of the 1990 season.

WAYNE TOLLESON
Yanks

In his career, 85 percent of his hits have been singles, the highest percentage of any major league player (500 or more games). . . .

JIM TRABER
Baltimore

No prospect—no player. Had one of the most worthless seasons of 1989, a first baseman hitting .209 with no power.

ALAN TRAMMELL
Detroit

Will surely bounce back. You know how you can tell who is going to have a better year, Trammell or Whitaker? Whichever one is behind in the career totals. Their career totals track precisely, so whenever one of them gets ahead in some category, the other one has to beat him to even out. At the moment they are almost even—721 career RBI each—so it's a little hard to tell.

BRIAN TRAXLER
Los Angeles

A hitting prospect in the Dodgers system who is absolutely square—five nine, 220 pounds. He didn't hit all that well once he got to AAA last year, but he can hit, and could have a big year at Albuquerque this year. I don't know how good he'll be at the major league level, but he's fun to watch.

JEFF TREADWAY
Braves

The most-similar player to Jeff Treadway is Nelson Liriano. . . . I may have shorted Treadway a bit when raving about Mark Lemke. Lemke deserves to play; that doesn't mean that Treadway deserves to lose his job. He hit .277 last year with no obvious weaknesses, had some power. He's a little slow for a second baseman, but a quality player with the potential to improve.

ALEX TREVINO
Houston

Hit .290 last year, exceptionally high for a backup catcher. In fact, he has a unique distinction for a backup catcher: He's been in the majors for twelve years, and has *never* posted a batting average in the ones. His worst was .216 in 1983. Think about it . . . what other backup catcher can match that?

STEVE TROUT
Seattle
Retired, I hope.

JOHN TUDOR
St. Louis
Back with the Cardinals. A longshot, but if he pitches he will pitch well.

JOSE URIBE
San Francisco
Grade A shortstop, no hitter. No draft unless your league is somehow able to give credit for being a flashy shortstop.

FERNANDO VALENZUELA
Los Angeles
Appears to be almost back. I don't know if the Dodgers can carry him another year pitching the way he has the last three. Sooner or later, they've got to start treating him like a normal person: Start pitching or get out.

JULIO VALERA
Mets
Probably the top pitching prospect in the Mets system, but with the Mets having six starters he'll have at least a half-season wait before he gets a look. I like him; I'd rate him among the ten-top pitching prospects in the minor leagues.

DAVE VALLE
Seattle
I've never been able to understand why he doesn't hit more homers. To watch him hit, you'd think he was a 30-homer guy. He isn't, and with the fence being moved, he isn't going to be.

ANDY VAN SLYKE
Pittsburgh
One of the season's top underachievers. Began hitting in August; likely to bounce back 100 percent, and he was one of the best players in the league in 1987–88.

GARY VARSHO
Cubs
Not a prospect in view of his age (twenty-eight), and .184 batting average may pull him out of the majors.

GREG VAUGHN
Brewers
A lot of people are going to be telling you this spring that Vaughn is going to be a star. Well I'm telling you he's not. As I read him, Vaughn's a .240-range hitter who is going to strike out at least twice as often as he walks, and although he does have real good power and will steal some bases, that makes him a sort of a poor man's Joe Carter, and Joe Carter isn't any superstar. I think he's not going to be worth what he costs.

RANDY VELARDE
Yankees
Probably will get a long look after hitting .340 late in the season. Here's another guy I have advocated for years, as I do Junior Noboa and Mike Sharperson. I think he can hit—not .340, but a lot better than Mike Pagliarulo.

ROBIN VENTURA
Chicago
The White Sox number-one draft pick of 1988, may be rushed to the majors in 1990 although he hasn't done anything much in the minors. Suspect if he does come up he will hit around .250–.260 with little power, but lead the team in walks. Apart from the general point that I don't like to project a minor leaguer up to the level of a star, there isn't anything about him as of now that says "STAR."

FRANK VIOLA
Mets
He pitched great, despite his 13–17 won-lost record. He struck out 211 men, walked 74. A safe pick; one of the game's top-ten pitchers.

JOSE VIZCAINO
Dodgers
A six one, 150 pound shortstop, switch hitter, rated by *Baseball America* the number-seven prospect in the Pacific Coast League. The Dodgers plan to convert him to second base, and he is projected as their second baseman of the future. He has almost no chance of playing regularly in 1990, and basically I'm not optimistic about his long-term future. At present he's about a .235 hitter in terms of major league ability, with no power and extremely few walks. He's very young and may develop, but a 150-pound second baseman, converting from shortstop at the AAA level, is an injury looking for a place to happen. I don't recommend him.

OMAR VIZQUEL
Seattle
Glove man, no hit. Don't draft him; the Mariners will find somebody else to look at within a year or so.

BOB WALK
Pittsburgh
I don't like him nearly as much as I did two or three years ago, although his 1989 won-lost record was the best of his career. His strikeout rate has declined, his hits allowed have increased. I think he's working on a dangerously thin margin; not a safe pick in my mind.

GREG WALKER
Chicago
Of course it is possible for him to come back. But with all of the young hitters around waiting for their *first* chance, why does he get another one? The White

Sox are overloaded with players who can play first base or DH (Walker, Kittle, Pasqua, Calderon, Carlos Martinez), but can't really contribute to the team defensively. Why keep around another one when he hits .210?

LARRY WALKER
Expos

Rated by *Baseball America* the number-three prospect in the American Association. To be honest, I don't know exactly what to make of him. He's an odd prospect—six two and weighing close to 200, but very fast. His batting stats at Indianapolis don't suggest a particularly good hitter, but he was recovering from a year out of baseball after suffering a knee injury in Mexico the previous winter, and could be a much better hitter than his '89 stats show (he stole 36 bases last year with a big brace on his leg.) I think in time he *will* be a good player, but, based on his high strikeout rate at Indianapolis (he struck out 87 times in 385 at bats), and also at Jacksonville before the injury (struck out 120 times), I can't quite recommend him as a 1990 draft. However, there is a definite possibility that Walker will develop into a quality player.

TIM WALLACH
Montreal

Forget about 1987, when a lot of people had atypical years (Wallach hit .298 with 26 homers, 123 RBI), and he's been consistent. A durable player, hits some doubles and drives in runs. A safe draft.

DENNY WALLING
St. Louis

One of the leading pinch hitters of all time, hit .344 in the role last year (11 for 32). In his career he has 93 pinch hits, which places him thirteenth all-time, and a .278 average, which places him twenty-first.

JEROME WALTON
Cubs

If you look carefully enough at his rookie numbers, you'll see a lot of things you don't like. He had 27 walks and 77 strikeouts, not a healthy ratio. He had two outfield assists in 115 games. He showed no power. In spite of those things, I like him quite a bit. His .293 average as a rookie is not the top; he's probably going to be well over .300 this year, with a big improvement in the strikeout to walk ratio. A batting championship is very possibly in his future.

DUANE WARD
Toronto

Fifteen saves in each of the last two years, strikeout rate has *increased* dramatically to 122 in 115 innings. You don't want him to be your closer, but he can definitely help out in the bullpen.

CLAUDELL WASHINGTON
California

An incongruous career, started out so well and has lasted so long. Still runs well and still has power (13 homers, 13 stolen bases last year.) A safe pick, and there's no particular reason not to make use of what he can do.

GARY WAYNE
Minnesota

The Twins left-handed spot reliever, pitched well in the role. There is an outside chance that the loss of Reardon could force him into the role of closer, but it isn't likely.

MITCH WEBSTER
Cleveland

A good defensive outfielder, had a big year with Montreal in 1987, and if 1987 ever comes back will probably have a big year again.

BILL WEGMAN
Milwaukee

One more reason that I have no use for finesse-type pitchers. Wegman in his career has allowed more home runs per nine innings (1.25) than any other active pitcher (500 innings). The bottom ten: Wegman, Curt Young, John Cerutti, Keith Atherton, Brad Havens, Oil Can Boyd, Mike Smithson, Scott Bankhead, Tom Browning, and Floyd Bannister. . . . His season, and quite possibly his career, was ended by arthroscopic surgery on his shoulder in July.

WALT WEISS
Oakland

Despite the Rookie of the Year Award, he has no star potential. Assuming he is healthy, will play better than he did last year.

BOB WELCH
Oakland

A hell of a number-three starter, wins 17 games a year. He hasn't *really* had a bad year since 1979, when he was drinking. His only losing record since then was in 1986, which was a fluke due to abysmal run support.

BRAD WELLMAN
Kansas City

Good defensive player—no prospect.

DAVID WELLS
Toronto

Excellent left-handed spot reliever. With Henke and Ward, can't move up.

DAVID WEST
Twins

We've all heard about his ability. Just on form, you know, I would want to make him start pitching well before I drafted him. I'm sure he'll get started eventually, but it might be a year. Do you want to carry him for a year, waiting for his confidence to turn a corner? Great potential, or so they say.

MICKEY WESTON
Orioles

Real interesting pitcher. He's moved through the minors at a snail's pace, being used almost entirely as a mop-up man in six years in the Mets system, but never being released because he never had an off season. He's an *extreme* finesse-type pitcher, doesn't throw hard but never walks anybody. In 1988 he was 10–6 with Jackson and Tidewater in the Mets system, pitching 155 innings with only 25 walks and a 2.09 ERA. He jumped to the Orioles as a six-year free agent, and at Rochester was 8–3 with the same 2.09 ERA, walking 19 men in 112 innings. When he got to the majors he got hurt almost immediately.

He's got maybe a 30 percent chance of establishing himself in the majors, but if he does he'll be very effective for a couple of years. Finesse-type pitchers have to face a prejudice—a manager, given his druthers, would always prefer to take a chance on a hard thrower—and they also take a little longer to settle into a major league job. They don't last as long once they get established. But I do like Weston's chances of sneaking up on the league, as Dan Quisenberry did a few years ago, and having some big years.

JEFF WETHERBY
Atlanta

Pinch hitter. A much better hitter than his .208 average, but among Atlanta's prospects, not the one you would want to be banking on.

★ ★ ★
JOHN WETTELAND
Dodgers
★ ★ ★

This guy is a *great* middle-round draft pickup. He's had control troubles, but last year in 102.2 innings he struck out 96 men and walked only 30 (plus 4 intentionally). Strikeout to walk ratio is the best leading indicator of a pitcher's development; a guy with a good strikeout to walk ratio is probably going to win sooner or later. He's young, and best of all he's got Dodger Stadium going for him; that'll knock a half run a game off his ERA right there. With Fernando struggling and Leary traded, the opportunity is there for a starting pitcher to step forward, and this is the guy who's going to do it. I look for him possibly to be one of the top pitchers in the National League within two years.

LOU WHITAKER
Tigers

The most-similar player to Lou Whitaker is Alan Trammell. . . . In double figures in home runs for eight straight seasons. A safe draft, more so right now than Trammell.

DEVON WHITE
Angels

The major league players making the most *outs* on offense last year: 1. Devon White (516), 2. Joe Carter, 3. Cal Ripken, 4. Todd Benzinger, 5. Steve Sax, 6. Roberto Alomar, 7. Ozzie Guillen, 8. Terry Pendleton, 9. Eddie Murray, 10. Bobby Bonilla (466). . . . the most-similar player to Devon White is Glenn Braggs. . . .

FRANK WHITE
Kansas City

The most-similar player to Frank White is Lou Whitaker. . . . Kansas City fans are very curious about his chances of making the Hall of Fame. I think they have become pretty good. Among defensive players who don't hit, career length is a critical indicator of Hall of Fame chances. White, with 2,072 games played at second base, is now in seventh place on the all-time list at the position, ahead of him being three Hall of Famers and two people who will probably get in sooner or later (Nellie Fox and Bill Mazeroski.) Mazeroski is the most-comparable player to him in history, and has drawn solid Hall of Fame support, growing until the last couple of seasons, but White has now gone ahead of Mazeroski in most career categories. . . . He has a hundred more doubles, for example, and twenty more homers. His Hall of Fame case is becoming more and more credible.

ED WHITED
Braves

Big, strong third baseman, has some power and drew 97 walks in the minors in '88. Basically hasn't done anything to make anybody think he's a major league player, and he got a shot out of the Braves' desperation.

ED WHITSON
San Diego

Appears to have achieved some stability for the first time in his career. I don't know; I can't quite brink myself to call Ed Whitson a "safe draft."

ERNIE WHITT
Atlanta

The most consistent hitter among major league catchers, but he, too, cannot be labeled a safe draft at this moment. Sure, Atlanta could help his numbers, but he is moving to a new league at the age of thirty-eight. What if his manager isn't religious about platooning him, but lets him play against some left-handers? There's more running in this league; how will he handle the increased defensive pressure? A good player and a much underrated player—but I'd be a little bit cautious in 1990.

CURT WILKERSON
Chicago

May get some of the playing time abandoned by Vance Law. No draft.

BERNIE WILLIAMS
Yankees
Think "Reggie Smith". Williams is a switch-hitting center fielder with speed and power from both sides of the plate. At this point he'd hit about .240 in the major leagues, but he is very young (20), and he also drew 60 walks in 314 at bats in the Eastern League. Being with the Yankees obviously hurts his chances.

EDDIE WILLIAMS
White Sox
Hit .274, but was judged a failure by the White Sox because of his defense. I'd have gone with him a little longer, but I wouldn't bet on him to get another trial.

FRANK WILLIAMS
Detroit
Veteran right-handed reliever; doesn't play a key role. If I collected pitchers like this, which I don't, his 1989 K/W (33–46) would surely deter me.

KEN WILLIAMS
Tigers
His major league batting average has shrunk to .224, and he's probably going to have to earn his next shot at a job with some time in the minors. Excellent defense in left field with a history of hitting . . . very similar to Darryl Boston in Chicago.

MATT WILLIAMS
Giants
One thing that you hear about Williams is that he had a year like Mike Schmidt's first season. The comparison is valid up to a point:

	G	AB	HR	RBI	Avg
Williams, 1989	84	292	18	50	.202
Schmidt, 1973	132	367	18	52	.196

Both players are twenty-three years old at the season in question, and both were regarded as an outstanding defensive third baseman.

There are a few differences. Schmidt had an additional asset at that time, speed, which Williams does not have. Schmidt at this age had hit .197 through 401 major league at bats; Williams has hit .198 but through 693 at bats. Schmidt as a young hitter was striking out even more than Williams has (Schmidt 38 percent, Williams 26 percent), but Schmidt was both striking out and drawing walks (K/W ratio 100–44), while Williams is striking out without drawing walks (ratio 100–21). Schmidt's development from that plateau was extraordinary, not "normal," so you can't assume another player in the same position will develop in the same way. Still, there are more valid parallels between them than valid differences, and I do think Williams has a realistic chance to be the top third baseman of the 1990s.

MITCH WILLIAMS
Cubs
I remain *extremely* skeptical about him. His motion is awful, and his control is terrible. He may continue to rack up some saves, but I sure wouldn't want him saving *my* ball games.

MARK WILLIAMSON
Baltimore
After struggling for two years, pitched very well in right-handed middle relief. No prospect.

FRANK WILLS
Blue Jays
He still has that wicked slider, and he still has nothing to go with it. Time has run out on him as far as being a prospect.

GLENN WILSON
Houston
Has hit .256 to .275 for five straight seasons, although his other stats have been up and down. Doesn't have the speed you look for in an Astros outfielder, but

maybe it will work out. Safe draft, but little interest.

MOOKIE WILSON
Blue Jays
Thirty-four years old now, and facing stiff competition from young outfielders like Glenallen Hill and Junior Felix. A safe draft if he plays—but if he has a minor injury, it could get away from him in a hurry.

STEVE WILSON
Cubs
Had 4.20 ERA as left-handed middle reliever. There's a lot of candidates for a job like that, but suspect he will hold it. He is seen as a pitcher whose role could expand.

TREVOR WILSON
San Francisco
Well regarded prospect; best pitch is a cut fastball. He walked 76 men in 115 innings at Phoenix, which is enough to discourage me. . . .

WILLIE WILSON
Kansas City
The most-similar player to Willie Wilson is Garry Templeton. . . . The major league leaders in career triples: 1. Willie Wilson (130), 2. George Brett, 3. Robin Yount, 4. Garry Templeton, 5. Andre Dawson. . . . The major league leaders in career triples *per at bat:* 1. Willie Wilson, 2. Juan Samuel, 3. Andy Van Slyke, 4. Willie McGee, 5. Brett Butler. . . .

HERM WINNINGHAM
Reds
No prospect—no player. All right as a reserve, can play center, pinch run and hit a little, but not likely to move up.

MATT WINTERS
Kansas City
Signed in January to play in Japan.

BOBBY WITT
Rangers

As frustrating as he has been, Witt is probably a good *calculated* gamble, particularly in an APBA or Strat-O-Matic League where you can keep your players forever. Despite his struggles, Witt has pitched about .500 ball, so he doesn't kill you while you are waiting on him. He is only twenty-six years old, so he still has time to develop into a superior pitcher. He's an *extreme* power-type pitcher, and most great pitchers start out as extreme power-type pitchers. Like a lot of young pitchers, Witt tends to make pitching harder than it needs to be, but I still believe there is a chance he will suddenly turn a corner, and be one of the top pitchers in the league.

MIKE WITT
California

He will be back. The signing of Langston leaves Witt, at least for the moment, without a job; the Angels' front four will be Langston, Finley, Blyleven, and Abbott. Witt is a lot like Blyleven was a couple of years ago, making an adjustment to having lost a foot off his fastball, but I think he will be back where he was in a couple of years.

ED WOJNA
Cleveland

No chance with the Indians; would be acceptable fill-in starter with a good defense behind him. Consistent winner in the minor leagues.

TODD WORRELL
Cardinals

Elbow surgery in December clouds his future; won't be back this year before June, and may not return until 1991. *Do not draft.* Wake up; do not draft.

CRAIG WORTHINGTON
Orioles

Although you won't hear anybody say it, Worthington may have been the one player most responsible for the Orioles' dramatic improvement last season. The Orioles at third in 1988 had neither offense nor defense, with Rick Schu and Rene Gonzalez. Worthington gave them outstanding defense, which would show up mostly in the staff ERA, and solid offense.

Most-comparable major league player: Ken Caminiti of Houston. . . . Worthington is the heir apparent to Gary Gaetti as the American League's Gold Glove third baseman, and will develop into a solid offensive player, possibly comparable to Sal Bando.

RICK WRONA
Cubs

Hit real well as a third catcher, .283. He's basically the same age as Berryhill and Girardi, so time isn't going to work in his favor. His minor league batting records, not to mention a K/W ratio worse than 10–1, suggest that his .283 average may have been over his head. He is mentioned often in trade talks, so could be leaving Wrigley Field. Grade D prospect.

MARVELL WYNNE
Cubs

The most-similar player to Marvelle Wynne is John Shelby. . . . The accumulation on their roster of players like Wynne and Salazar, acquired to help in the stretch run in 1989, is the biggest obstacle the Cubs have to face in 1990. The Cubs have terrific young talent, in Grace, Walton, Dwight Smith, and Berryhill. They have fine veteran talent, in Dunston, Dawson, and Sandberg. They have the best big three in the league, in Sutcliffe, Bielecki, and Maddux. But they've also got a lot of dead weight on the roster, and they won't win unless Zimmer is brutal enough to cut some veterans. . . .

ERIC YELDING
Houston

At this point, a pinch runner and defensive sub. Will be tried in more challenging roles later on.

(ARE WE) RICH YETT
Cleveland

In five major league seasons, he has had an ERA below 5.00 once; then it was 4.62. He walks as many as he strikes out. (See Scott Bailes and double it.)

FLOYD YOUMANS
Philadelphia

Injuries have ruined his career. No prospect; extremely unlikely to come back.

CURT YOUNG
Oakland

Very much like John Tudor, except that the injuries started early in his career. He doesn't take the mound and get hammered; he fights injuries all year, but pitches fairly well when he is on the mound. If the A's can get 125 innings out of him and 125 out of Sanderson, that makes one good starter.

GERALD YOUNG
Houston

Didn't hit the first half of the season, and didn't steal any bases the second half. (He was on my team the whole year, and I was a week away from cutting him all year, but I never did.) Walks a lot, should steal bases more successfully if he is healthy . . . defensively, he led National League outfielders in almost everything—fielding percentage, putouts, assists, total chances, and double plays. A defensive "triple crown"—putouts, assists, and fielding percentage. I don't know if I've ever seen an outfielder do that before. Have you?

MATT YOUNG
Oakland

Unsigned at this writing; that 6.75 ERA is costing him about $3 million a year.

MIKE YOUNG
Cleveland

Not on the Indians' mid-winter roster, but otherwise indistinguishable from five people who are.

JOEL YOUNGBLOOD
Cincinnati

A free agent. He might return to Cincinnati, but more likely his career has ended.

ROBIN YOUNT
Brewers

I had a little bit of egg on my face when the American League MVP Award was announced last November, in that I had told everybody who would listen that Ruben Sierra was going to win it. I have spent a lot of time studying who wins MVP Awards and why, and as often happens I thought I knew more about it than I did; I was certain that leading the league in RBI would be enough to give Sierra the award.

I was happy to be wrong; Yount did more to help his team, and deserved the award. Attacking the selection in the December 25 edition of *Baseball America*, Tracy Ringolsby established new standards for simple-minded sophistry. "Yount had an edge on Sierra in only three statistical categories," wrote Ringolsby, blithely ignoring the other ten or twenty categories in which Yount was also superior to Sierra. The three which Ringolsby acknowledged were batting average (Yount led .316–.308), hits (195–194), and doubles (38–35), but without getting into the small stuff like sacrifice hits and hit batsmen, Yount also led Sierra in stolen bases (19–8), stolen base percentage (86 percent–80 percent), walks (63–43), and strikeouts (Sierra struck out 82 times, Yount 71.) Yount led by a wide margin in the most important statistical category of individual offense; on base percentage. Yount, at .384, was among the league leaders;

Sierra, at .347, was near the league average.

According to Ringolsby, "Sierra, meanwhile, ranked among AL leaders in 13 categories, and was the only player to reach double figures in doubles, triples (a major league-leading 14) and home runs (29)." A remarkable sentence. First of all, Sierra was *not* the only player to reach double figures in doubles, triples, and home runs; Phil Bradley and Devon White both accomplished this. Second, Yount had nearly as many doubles and homers as Sierra did, but had only *nine* triples, so what kind of an idiot basis is that for determining an MVP Award? And third, Ringolsby doesn't tell us what the thirteen categories are in which Sierra was among the league leaders, but the American League official stats list league leaders in sixteen offensive categories. Sierra is listed in ten categories. Yount is listed in eleven. So what the hell does that mean?

"Yount couldn't match Sierra in either area—playing for a contender or personal accomplishment," wrote Ringolsby. Say wha'? Yount's team finished 81–81, and 8 games out of first. Sierra's team finished 83–79, and 16 games out of first. Both teams finished fourth. I have a hard time understanding why that arrow points to Sierra.

Ringolsby covers the Rangers (and very well, I might add), and so of course he believes Sierra was better than Yount. Believing that, he uses the statistics, as the saying goes, as a drunk uses a lamp post—for support, not illumination. But if one approaches the statistics not intent upon making them support one position or the other, but intent only upon seeing what they have to show us, you get a different picture: Yount and Sierra are essentially even. There simply isn't any big difference between them. Yount went to the plate 690 times, Sierra 689, so their context is almost the same. They are statistically

close in every category, with three moderate exceptions:

- Sierra had 8 more home runs, which is worth about 11 runs.
- Yount had 20 more walks, which is worth about 7 runs.
- Yount had 11 more stolen bases, which is worth about 3 runs.

Using the runs created method that I prefer at the moment (which has evolved a couple of steps from the last one I introduced in an *Abstract*), I estimate that Yount created 118 runs, and Sierra 119—but Yount did that while using only 422 outs, while Sierra used 442. Since 1 run is not worth as much as 20 outs, Yount rates a very narrow edge as a complete offensive player.

Which means almost nothing.

The difference between the two of them, as offensive players, is not enough to carry any particular weight in the MVP discussion.

So then we have to look carefully at other factors:

1) The performance of their teams. A virtual wash—two fourth-place teams, one winning 83 games and the other 81, one finishing 8 games out and the other 16.

2) Defense. Again, not much to separate them, although there is some edge to Yount. Yount plays center field, Sierra right field. Sierra has a better arm, but makes more mistakes.

3) Outside illusions on the statistics. Sierra plays in a slightly better hitter's park than Yount, so his statistical accomplishments need to be taken with just a little bit more salt. In Texas Sierra hit .317 with 21 homers, 73 RBI, and a .621 slugging percentage—but on the road he hit .295 with only 8 homers, 46 RBI, and a .468 slugging percentage. In Milwaukee Yount hit .307 with 14 homers, 49 RBI, and a .533 slugging percentage—but on the road he hit .328 with 7 homers, 44 RBI, and a .490 slugging per-

centage. In neutral parks, Yount was an unmistakably better hitter.

4) Leadership. Yount, a respected veteran, has to rate the advantage on Sierra, a young player with a reputation for some moodiness.

5) Clutch performance. With runners in scoring position, Yount hit .355; Sierra hit .335. Sierra had a few more RBI, but Sierra hit cleanup virtually all season, while Yount hit second, third and fourth. Should we penalize Yount because, being a better base runner and a better contact hitter, he is more versatile within the lineup? Sierra hit .248 in August, when the Rangers fell out of contention. Yount hit .265 in April, better than .300 in every other month.

6) Areas of play not well measured in the statistics, such as baserunning and hitting behind the runner. Yount is a better base runner and handles the bat better. Who would you rather hit and run with? It's obvious, isn't it?

It's not a mismatch; Sierra had a great year. It's a tough choice. But considering all factors honestly, it seems quite clear to me that Yount was the better player. I was very pleased that the MVP voting structure was able to sift through all the factors and come to a just conclusion. . . .

In the last two years, Yount has developed into the first player with a serious chance to break Pete Rose's career record for hits (4,256). He is still very much of a longshot, of course, but his chance of breaking Rose's record is now about 9 percent, or 10–1 against him. A couple of years ago it was 2 percent . . . the only other player with any chance to break the record is Kirby Puckett (about 5 percent). . . .

CLINT ZAVARAS
Seattle

Zavaras has a good chance of *eventually* being a successful major league pitcher. He has a real good arm, and is regarded as a bright young man with good work habits (his father, incidentally, is the chief of police in Denver). There is little reason to think that that success is going to arrive in 1990, despite the improved park-team situation in Seattle. At Cal-gary last year he was 6–9 with a 6.04 ERA; in the majors, 1–6 with a 5.19. If he was with a good team, he might possibly be successful right away, but his control seems to me to be a pretty big obstacle for him to get over in one year.

TODD ZEILE
Cards

I like him a little better than Alomar, the other top young catcher. He's probably my number-two candidate to be NL Rookie of the Year, behind Stanton; I see him as hitting about .265 in the majors with 15 homers, 70 RBI. That's pretty good for a player with his defensive skills.

PAUL ZUVELLA
Tribe

Thirty-one-year-old shortstop; time has run out on him as far as being a regular. I think he'd be alright as a utility infielder, but basically I wouldn't be taking a chance on him unless it was a very unusual league, where *everybody* has to be used.

NOTE TO THE READERS

(SHAMELESS SELF-PROMOTION, DISGUISED AS PUBLIC INFORMATION.)

In addition to writing this book, I am involved in a number of other projects which might be of interest to the reader:

The Radio Show.

I do a Sunday night radio show, called *Baseball Sunday*, which can be heard almost anywhere in the country. It's a call-in show, and I don't know if I'll do it *every* week this year, but I did it every week last summer, and I'll be there pretty regularly. We're on from 5:00 to 7:00 P.M. every Sunday from April through October, Joe Garagiola and myself and probably Hal Bodley of *USA Today* and maybe Jason Dorfman. Call in, please; we value callers who read books. Maybe it isn't too appropriate to call in and tell me on the air that you liked this book (or didn't), but the biggest thing in making a talk show work is to get informed, intelligent people to call. So call, please.

Bill James Fantasy Baseball.

A year ago, I designed a set of rules for a fantasy baseball game, in which you "own" players and follow them. It's somewhat like rotisserie, except that I tried to design a set of rules which more carefully mimics the real game, a set of rules under which every player's value would be, as nearly as possible, what it is to a real team. In other words, I didn't want Vince Coleman to be a hot property because of all those stolen bases; I wanted Vince Coleman to be worth what Vince Coleman is really worth. I wanted the person playing the game to be obliged to develop a *real* team, with a leadoff man, a power hitter, a number one starter, a relief ace, a shortstop, etc.

Inevitably, the rules are a little more complicated than rotisserie rules, but they aren't complex. You get one point for each run scored by a member of your team, four points for a home run, that sort of thing. It's not a perfect game, but it is fun; if you pick enough players who have good years, you win your league.

Bill James Fantasy Baseball is run by STATS, Inc., of Lincolnwood, Illinois; if you're interested in playing you can reach them at 1–800–63–STATS; that is, 1–800–637–8287. STATS does weekly mailings to everybody in the game, giving you your complete team stats, the league standings and leaders and whatever other information you need to have. It isn't cheap; STATS has to do many mailings during the summer, and an incredible amount of bookkeeping. It cost several times what this book costs to do that. But I enjoy it, and I think that most of the people in the league enjoy it.

Hardcover copies of this book.

This year there is a limited hardcover edition of *The Baseball Book 1990* available only from me. I don't know how much it will cost yet, but obviously it will be a little more expensive than this paperback. If you want to own one or you want to put in an order for a hardcover edition of next year's book, write to me, Bill James, P.O. Box 327, Oskaloosa, Kansas 66066. Be sure to include your address and phone number so I can get you the price information.

Thanks, and I hope you enjoy the book.